here that Roberts's study makes its central contribution. His systematic exploration of fascist perceptions and purposes enables us to understand, for the first time, how fascism could be at once populist and elitist, modernizing and traditionalist, procapitalist and anticapitalist, nationalist and anti-Italian, totalitarian and anticollectivist. The author traces the emergence of the fascist perspective in terms of the crisis of classical Marxism and sheds new light on the role of Italian fascism in the greater drama of European history.

David D. Roberts is associate professor of history at the Eastman School of Music, The University of Rochester.

D1462182

The Syndicalist Tradition and Italian Fascism

The Syndicalist Tradition
and Italian Fascism

by
David D. Roberts

The University of North Carolina Press   Chapel Hill

© 1979 The University of North Carolina Press
All rights reserved
Manufactured in the United States of America
Library of Congress Catalog Card Number 78-23347
ISBN 0-8078-1351-6

Library of Congress Cataloging in Publication Data

Roberts, David D., 1943–
  The syndicalist tradition and Italian fascism.

  Bibliography: p.
  Includes index.
  1. Syndicalism–Italy.   2. Fascism–Italy.
  3. Corporate state–Italy.   I. Title.
HD6709.R58   335'.82'0945   78-23347
ISBN 0-8078-1351-6

To Merrill J. Roberts
and the memory of Janet Dion Roberts

Contents

Acknowledgments

I wish first to acknowledge an old debt—to the Overseas Campus Program at Stanford University, which made possible my first serious experience in Italy, in 1962–63. A traveling fellowship from the University of California at Berkeley and a grant from the University of Virginia enabled me to return to Italy for extended periods of research during 1969–70 and 1973, and I would like to thank each of these institutions for their support.

This study has grown out of my doctoral dissertation, which I completed at Berkeley in 1971. The present work is quite different in scope and argument, and this is due in no small measure to the recommendations and encouragement of the dissertation's readers, Richard Webster, Nicholas Riasanovsky, Neil Smelser, and Randolph Starn. More recently, Stanley Payne, Charles Delzell, Thomas Sykes, Michael Holt, Joseph Kett, Charles Maier, and Enno Kraehe have read various versions of the manuscript, and their suggestions have benefited the book considerably. My particular thanks to Professor Kraehe, whose confidence in this project has meant a great deal to me. I am also grateful to three former teachers—Lorie Tarshis, Robert Middlekauff, and Richard Kuisel—and a former colleague—Alexander Sedgwick—for providing inspiration, guidance, and friendship, always in the right proportions.

A number of Italian scholars shared ideas with me and helped me locate materials; I especially wish to thank Gaetano Arfé, Alceo Riosa, Renzo De Felice, Giovanna Procacci, and Francesco Perfetti. In addition, several relatives and friends of this book's major figures discussed their remembrances with me. Vito Panunzio, Renato Melis, Neos Dinale, Ugo Barni, and G. N. Serventi were particularly generous in this regard, and I am especially grateful to Livia Olivetti for the many courtesies she extended to me.

It is one of the pleasures of scholarly work in Italy that the scholar has to move about, encountering fresh challenges and making new friends among librarians and archivists. I did most of my work in Rome—at the libraries of the Senate and the Chamber of Deputies, at the Biblioteca Nazionale, at the Istituto Gramsci, at the Biblioteca Universitaria Alessandrina, at the Biblioteca di Storia Moderna e Contemporanea, and at the Archivio Centrale dello Stato—although my research also took me to the Biblioteca Nazionale Centrale in Florence, to the Istituto Giangiacomo Feltrinelli and the Biblioteca Nazionale Braidense in Milan, and to the Biblioteca Comunale Ariostea in Ferrara. The staffs of these institutions were almost invariably courteous and helpful, and I thank them all.

A few paragraphs in chapters 1, 8, and 12 have been published previously, in somewhat different form, as part of my essay "Petty Bourgeois Fascism in Italy: Form and Content," in *Who Were the Fascists? Social Roots of European Fascism*, edited by Stein Ugelvik Larsen et al. I am grateful to the Norwegian Universities Press for permission to use this material in the present volume.

Finally, my thanks to Beth, who shared this experience with me, never losing confidence that the result would be worth the effort.

The Syndicalist Tradition and Italian Fascism

1 / Ideas, Ideologies, and the Problem of Italian Fascism

"Fascism" and "totalitarianism" have become part of our everyday political language, yet it is not clear what disaffected Italians had in mind when they devised these terms in a context of political crisis after World War I. From one perspective, Italian fascism appears to have been an elitist reaction; from another, some sort of populist revolt. In some respects fascism seems to have been an attempt to modernize a relatively backward country, and yet it is often portrayed as an attempt to check or channel modernization, thereby preserving the socioeconomic position of the established elites. On the other hand, fascism seems, in part at least, to have been symptomatic of a more general "modern crisis," and not merely a product of Italian backwardness. Perhaps fascism was primarily a response to essentially modern problems —problems in liberalism and capitalism afflicting societies that have already modernized. We know that fascism moved toward a corporative state, but the relationship between economics and politics in the corporativist conception remains obscure. There is disagreement over whether Italian fascism and German Nazism can be understood as species of the same genus. And even though the Italian fascists invented the term, it is not clear whether "totalitarianism" can accurately be applied to the regime they created or not.

It is possible to make sense of these contradictory patterns, but only if we ask some new questions and develop more complex and imaginative interpretive categories. In seeking to do so in the ensuing chapters, we will take advantage of a neglected and disprized body of evidence—fascist ideas. Our major focus will be on the political and intellectual tradition that began as revolutionary syndicalism and turned into one form of fascist corporativism, but our inquiry will suggest new ways of thinking about the overall problem of Italian fascism.

3

Sensitive Italian observers from Benedetto Croce and Costanzo Casucci to Delio Cantimori and Reno De Felice have warned against the facile moralism and schematism that make it difficult to place fascism in genuinely historical perspective.[1] But our memories are long, contemporary political concerns intrude, and so we still have trouble approaching the problem with an open mind. The very thought of fascism brings forth forbidding images: the squat figure of Mussolini, jaw protruding, fists on hips, leading his country to humiliation and disaster as Hitler's very junior partner; the ghosts of Giacomo Matteotti, the Rosselli brothers, and other noble victims of fascism, refusing to let us forget the needless suffering that fascism caused. Any approach to fascism that does not begin with contemptuous ridicule or outrage seems to smack of moral insensitivity, and thus the detachment— and even sympathy—necessary for historical understanding has been difficult to achieve. At the same time, two canons of interpretation consistent with our initial contempt seem to provide a ready-made explanation: fascism as reaction, and fascism as a petty bourgeois revolt against modernization. These schematic categories seem plausible because of the nature of Italy's postwar crisis and the characteristics of the fascist response.

With Italy readjusting to a peacetime economy, important sectors of heavy industry faced a difficult situation, particularly because the government no longer afforded an easy market for their expanded output. During 1919 and 1920, moreover, Italy experienced the most extensive and militant strike wave in her history, culminating in the factory occupations of September 1920. Italian Socialists, infatuated with the Bolshevik example, fanned expectations and fears by proclaiming that the dictatorship of the proletariat was imminent, and fascism began to gather momentum late in 1920, in violent reaction against the Socialist labor movement. In their precarious postwar situation, some Italian businessmen sought new political arrangements that would enable them to tame the unions and to absorb public power for their own ends. The Fascist regime was apparently serving their purposes when it outlawed strikes and forced the workers out of their traditional labor organizations and into new ones controlled by fascists, when it emphasized national solidarity and the further viability of Italian capitalism, when it brought economic and political power together through corporativism. Ultimately fascism mobilized society in order to instill the discipline necessary to keep the workers in their place, to enhance production, and to wage imperialist war.

A major source of fascism's reactionary content is easily identified. The Italian Nationalist Association, formed in 1910, merged with the Fascist party early in 1923 and gave the regime some of its leading functionaries, as well as a relatively sophisticated doctrine and program. Italian Nationalism was explicitly elitist and imperialist and was bitterly opposed both to socialism and to the liberal parliamentary system. The most substantial Nationalist ideologue, Alfredo Rocco (1875–1935), served as the regime's Minister of Justice between 1925 and 1932 and played a major part in replacing the liberal parliamentary system. It is often suggested that, through a kind of symbiosis, fascism provided Nationalism with the popular support it lacked and got in return the measure of doctrinal consistency and direction it needed to endure.[2]

There is general agreement that the mass base for fascism came from the lower middle class, which suffered especially in the difficult postwar economic situation.[3] High rates of inflation, stemming from government financial policies during the war, meant a redistribution of wealth in favor of the industrial classes, including the workers, who managed to hold their own or even to improve their position not only during the war, but also during the readjustment to peacetime. The postwar economic dislocations, including unemployment, reached their peak early in 1921, just as discontented petty bourgeois elements were making fascism a mass movement. Political observers had quickly recognized that disaffected lower-middle-class sectors constituted a new and volatile political force after the war.[4] Once fascism began its rapid rise late in 1920, discussion began to focus on the thesis of Luigi Salvatorelli, who collected his articles on the subject in his classic *Nazionalfascismo* in 1923.

Salvatorelli emphasized the autonomy and internal consistency of petty bourgeois fascism; since it opposed industrial capitalism as well as the working class, fascism could not be explained in simple, dualistic terms as bourgeois capitalist counterrevolution. On the contrary, Salvatorelli argued, fascism "represents the class struggle of the petty bourgeoisie, squeezed between capitalism and proletariat, as the third between the two conflicting sides."[5] But he found it necessary to distinguish between the "technical" petty bourgeoisie—those with a place in modern industrial society—and the "humanistic" petty bourgeoisie—preindustrial groups like school teachers, lower government officials, and marginal lawyers, who were often university-educated, but who lacked the solid economic roles of their "technical" counterparts. It was this humanistic petty bourgeoisie, threatened economically, socially, and psychologically, which created fascism. Since they lacked modern productive roles, Salvatorelli contended, these groups were too weak to struggle openly with the industrial classes and to develop a genuine "ideology," or political program, of their own.[6] They relied instead on hollow rhetorical ideals, especially the myth of the nation, as a way of denying the modern world of class and class struggle; but such ideals, derived from their superficial humanistic education, were ever more irrelevant as modern industrial civilization developed. It was only because Italy was relatively weak economically that these marginal, preindustrial sectors of the lower middle class could attempt through fascism "to play the primary role on the political scene."[7]

It is testimony to the force of Salvatorelli's argument that it has a central part in the major interpretations of Italian fascism even today. Renzo De Felice strongly endorses Salvatorelli in insisting that fascism emerged as an autonomous petty bourgeois expression, that it was not simply a counterrevolution.[8] It has been argued, however, that De Felice accepts Salvatorelli's categories so completely that he underplays the essentially reactionary content of fascism and fails to emphasize sufficiently the role which petty bourgeois fascists played as a mass base in the interests of big business.[9] And indeed most historians employ Salvatorelli's categories to show how the petty bourgeoisie could be manipulated by irrational and rhetorical nationalism into doing the dirty work for the restricted groups that were in fact behind the fascist reaction.[10] For Roberto Vivarelli, who delineates this interpretation with exceptional force and clarity, Mussolini served essentially as a mediator, giving Nationalist ideas a populist veneer and thereby making them attractive to petty bourgeois sectors who would have found the language of Alfredo Rocco unacceptable.[11]

But whether autonomy or subservience is emphasized, current interpretations almost invariably explain the petty bourgeois role in fascism in terms of socioeconomic crisis and the traumas which industrial modernization causes the lower middle class. This class was indeed overrepresented in fascism, and the "petty bourgeois" quality of fascism, with its rhetoric and gestures and uniforms, is unmistakable. Since it is possible to characterize so many fascists in terms of socioeconomic grouping, it is easy to assume that socioeconomic concerns lay at the root of their common response. These lower-middle-class elements were discontented and turned to fascism, it would seem, because the universal process of modernization was either leaving them behind or threatening to drag them along, undermining their traditions, their status, and their self-esteem. In the words of a major American historian: "What makes a revolution specifically fascist is its slogans and its appeal to certain kinds of people who see themselves as losers in modern technological civilization."[12] By implication these people, since they were losers, could have played no progressive role in history; they could not seriously have hoped to lead the way in solving genuine modern problems. Even De Felice, while emphasizing the autonomy of the lower-middle-class elements in fascism, judges their aims as too absurd for practical implementation; the "confused and contradictory amalgam" of aspirations in early petty bourgeois fascism stemmed from a psychosocial crisis comprehensible in terms of Salvatorelli's categories, and not from genuine political awareness.[13]

At first glance, this socioeconomic interpretation seems plausible enough. In their vicious assault on the labor movement, resentful fascist *squadristi* apparently were seeking to undermine the source of the workers' relative economic advantage. After destroying the existing unions, the fascists tried to force the workers into new fascist organizations which also included nonmanual "intellectual labor" from the middle class—an attempt, it would seem, by threatened middle-class groups to defend themselves against the two-sided squeeze from capitalists and workers. In calling for a corporative state, these groups sought to overcome their disadvantageous position and to become the arbiters of conflicts between labor and capital.[14]

Fascist slogans and myths seem to indicate a backward-looking orientation, an attempt to defend the traditional values of the culture in the face of modernization. In glorifying the romantic preindustrial nationalist Giuseppe Mazzini, and in proclaiming his superiority to Marx, petty bourgeois fascists were apparently seeking to deny the modern world of class conflict represented by Marxism and repudiated by Mazzini. It is certainly true that these fascists called for class solidarity—and had misgivings about Italian capitalism. At the same time, Fascism stressed nationalism and the value of Italy's war experience, thereby offering a kind of psychological compensation to those whose place in society was eroding.[15]

Early fascism bitterly opposed the liberal parliamentary system—because, says a leading Italian scholar, its nucleus of declining petty bourgeois sectors could not get its interests represented through the existing parties and factions in parliament.[16] Fascism thus became an antiparty, denying the legitimacy of political parties and the whole parliamentary system. In the same way, Renzo De Felice invokes Salvatorelli's categories to account for the peculiar antipolitical thrust of early fascism, its "reactionary anarchism." Early fascism did propose some positive political alternatives, but De Felice also finds it possible to explain Dino Grandi's call for a national syndicalist "democracy," to bring the masses of "producers" into political life, in terms of Salvatorelli's thesis.[17]

So the elements of the standard interpretation converge in a neat synthesis. Even though petty bourgeois fascism emerged independently, and even though these fascists did not see themselves as the tools of big business, they were apparently incapable of developing a coherent program of their own. Confused and alienated, they were easily exploited; ultimately they constituted the mass base for the reaction which the Nationalists spearheaded through fascism. The standard explanatory principles thus complement each other nicely: the forms of fascism were plebeian and petty bourgeois, but the content was Nationalist and reactionary.

Yet there is an anomaly in this approach. These interpretations rest on assumptions about the meaning of fascist ideas, about the intention behind fascist departures, but historians have been unwilling to take the fascists seriously enough to analyze their ideas systematically. Interpretive categories have been adopted a priori—based on hindsight, on the Nazi experience, or on schematic views of history—and have then been imposed on the evidence. The oppressive outcome of the Fascist regime is not in question, but the frustrations and intentions that gave rise to fascism are not so obvious.

Italy was, to be sure, a modernizing country, experiencing the kinds of socioeconomic strains that present accounts assume to be fundamental. However, she also had political and sociocultural problems that were not merely manifestations of her economic difficulties. Some of these problems were peculiarly Italian, having to do with the way Italy was put together as a nation, with the way she experienced World War I, with long-standing patterns of political alienation, social fragmentation, and cultural self-doubt. But Italy was also subject to more universal problems; though relatively inexperienced politically, she was modern and experienced enough to have encountered some perplexing, still-unanswered questions about the liberal parliamentary system. Given the nature of Italy's postwar crisis, moreover, plausible questions could be raised about the priorities of the Italian Socialist party—and even about the relevance of Marxist categories in general. For those seeking solutions to Italy's long-term national and political problems, it was reasonable to doubt the value of liberalism and Socialism and to begin casting about for alternatives.

Since the Italian crisis cannot be understood solely in terms of the standard socioeconomic categories, and since there were plausible reasons to reject both liberalism and Socialism, it is at least conceivable that some of the themes and actions which at first seem to confirm the prevailing interpretation might have had more than one meaning. Thus we have to approach the assault on Socialism, for example, and the antiparliamentarianism, and the revival of Mazzini, and the glorification of the war and the nation, more flexibly and imaginatively. Under the circumstances, even individuals from preindustrial middle-class backgrounds could have been more concerned about autonomous political and cultural problems than about problems stemming from socioeconomic change. In fact, a variety of concerns contributed to the petty bourgeois revolt, and responses to different problems inevitably got mixed up together—even in the same individual. We need a pluralistic interpretive framework to account for this variety of motives and purposes. It is necessary to penetrate the minds of those involved, but misconceptions about the role of ideas in history, and especially in Italian fascism, have precluded that kind of analysis. By pinpointing certain inadequacies in three of the best accounts of Italian fascism, we can begin to see what is required for a more convincing interpretation. This will not, of course, do justice to the three authorities, all of whom have made major contributions to our understanding of fascism; my own considerable debt to each of them will be obvious in the ensuing chapters.

Adrian Lyttelton finds a contradiction between the corporativist ideology and the desire for a command economy in fascism. Corporativism, he says, was hostile to politics, while a command economy seemingly would have entailed an expansion of the political sphere.[18] In fact, however, the corporativist idea was sophisticated enough to transcend this apparent contradiction; Lyttelton's assertion manifests the widespread uncertainty about the intention behind fascist corporativism. In the same way, Lyttelton contends that the state syndicalism of the young fascist Piero Marsich strongly resembled that of the Nationalist Alfredo Rocco.[19] But Marsich's syndicalism resembled Rocco's only superficially; it was virtually identical, instead, to that of the former revolutionary syndicalist Sergio Panunzio, from which it was no doubt largely derived. Lyttelton's failure to grasp this crucial difference skews his interpretation of what was at stake for Marsich and others during the important disputes within fascism in 1921 and 1922. Although the meaning of national syndicalist and corporativist ideas is central at a number of points in his account, he misinterprets them again and again. These are, it must be emphasized, honest mistakes; Lyttelton simply did not devote much attention to the fascist corporativists who defined the concepts and goals in question. Like so many others, he takes it for granted that the "ideology" of fascism "can easily be written off as a tissue of inconsistencies if one analyzes it for formal doctrinal content."[20] At best, that ideology merits attention because of its instrumental and tactical import, its function as window dressing, its appeal to wider social groups.

Roberto Vivarelli, on the other hand, takes seriously the doctrinal core of fascism, but he assumes that its meaning is self-evident. To emphasize class collaboration and the further progressive role of the capitalist bourgeoisie, to oppose both Socialism and parliamentary government, to glorify the "mythical" nation, and to propose a national syndicalist or rudimentary corporative order—all this could only have served to defend the restricted interests in Italian society that found ideological expression in Nationalism.[21] Vivarelli's interpretation of fascism depends on the meaning of these ideas and themes, but he has considered only one of their sources—the Nationalist tradition—and neglected others. Neither the intentions behind these ideas, nor their implications for practice, are as obvious as he supposes.

Renzo De Felice strives for greater flexibility and for a more genuinely historical perspective, and thus he has run afoul of those who insist on fervent moralistic denunciations. But even he views fascism in terms of schematic conceptions of political possibilities and purposes. Neither the antipolitical thrust of early fascism nor Dino Grandi's national syndicalism requires sustained analysis, since the petty bourgeoisie can play no progressive role and since those who oppose Socialism and the immediate pretensions of the proletariat by definition occupy a position on the right.[22] Having neglected the systematic study of these ideas, however, De Felice cannot explain the origins and meaning of the antipolitical, national syndicalist thrust of early fascism, nor can he grasp the practical political implications—what an attempt to implement the national syndicalist idea would involve.[23] Indeed, confusion about the intention behind fascist ideas inevitably impairs our understanding of the interplay of components that gave the regime its internal dynamics and overall shape.

These examples indicate that, despite the widespread denigration of fascist ideas, present interpretations of fascism rest on implicit assumptions about the meaning of ideas—especially national syndicalist and corporativist ideas and the themes that appealed to the petty bourgeois component in fascism. At issue, it must be remembered, is not social composition; fascism really was a kind of petty bourgeois revolt. But it is not obvious what those involved were trying to do, nor is it clear how their purposes fit into the long-term processes of European history.

It is well known that many one-time revolutionary syndicalists found their way into fascism, but the relationship between Italian syndicalism and fascism has never been studied systematically. Since Mussolini, with his interest in myth and activism, is widely considered to have been a syndicalist himself, it is often assumed that the others simply followed him as they moved from the heterodox Italian left to fascism.[24] On the other hand, since revolutionary syndicalism, emphasizing class struggle, and fascist corporativism, emphasizing class harmony, were apparently so dissimilar, many assume the syndicalists must have lost their intellectual bearings—and their autonomy—on their way from one to the other. The syndicalists seem to have fallen under the hegemony of the Italian Nationalist movement when they became interested in nationalism and war between 1910 and 1915.[25] Systematic study reveals, however, that the syndicalists were never Mussolinians or Nationalists, that they had something of their own to offer fascism.

The petty bourgeois component in fascism drew considerable inspiration from the political and intellectual tradition that began as revolutionary syndicalism and ended up a populist, nationalist corporativism, intended as a political alternative to liberalism. This neosyndicalism was the synthesis of a variety of ideas, perceptions, concerns, and experiences shared in more rudimentary form by wider sectors. In the postwar period, the ideologues and labor organizers working within the syndicalist tradition sought to give direction to the vague aspirations of younger fascists and ultimately converged with the populist, petty bourgeois component in fascism. Syndicalism was the other source, besides Nationalism, of the antipolitical, totalitarian corporativism which was in many ways the major thrust of fascism.[26] By subjecting the syndicalists' ideas to serious historical analysis, we can develop the framework we need to explain the range of motives that led discontented young lower-middle-class Italians to fascism. Not all of these fascists embraced the neosyndicalist program, but our study will enable us to place such diverse young fascists as Dino Grandi, Roberto Farinacci, Augusto Turati, and Giuseppe Bottai in clearer perspective.

There is considerable testimony, both from contemporaries and from recent historians, that such syndicalists as Sergio Panunzio, A. O. Olivetti, Paolo Orano, and Agostino Lanzillo were among the most influential fascist ideologues. Giovanni Spadolini, for example, cites these four figures in emphasizing that some of fascism's "most authoritative and influential theorists" came from syndicalism.[27] Spadolini also stresses the importance of the *Carta del Carnaro*, a neosyndicalist constitution written in 1920, in shaping fascism. As fascism was rising to power, prominent liberals like Guido De Ruggiero, Vittorio Emanuele Orlando, and Umberto Ricci viewed neosyndicalism as a formidable threat, requiring a sustained counterattack, while the young fascist spokesman Curzio Suckert claimed late in 1925 that Sergio Panunzio had given fascism its content and direction.[28] Among contemporary foreign observers, Louis Rosenstock-Franck found Panunzio and Olivetti to be among the most influential theorists of corporativism; Marcel Prélot judged Panunzio to be one of the three major interpreters of the Fascist state, along with the Nationalist Rocco and the neoidealist philosopher Giovanni Gentile; and *New York Times* correspondent Herbert Matthews identified Panunzio and Gentile as the two major ideologues upon whom Mussolini could rely.[29] Even today Panunzio is frequently mentioned as one of the major theorists of fascism, yet he has not been read systematically, and he is sometimes neglected altogether.[30]

Italian syndicalism began to emerge in about 1902 as a reaction against reformism within the Italian Socialist party. Both intellectuals and labor organizers were involved, but there was always a good deal of interchange between them; the leading organizers contributed to—or even edited—syndicalist periodicals. Most, but not all, ended up active fascists. Syndicalism was based on common perceptions, values, and goals that persisted over time, despite some changes in personnel and despite considerable differences in style and emphasis among the individuals involved. It is useful to consider several early syndicalists who did not become fascists, as well as others who participated in the tradition later, after it had undergone some modification. Two figures provided a significant measure of continuity: Sergio Panunzio and A. O. Olivetti, the most important of the syndicalists who helped to shape fascism.

Sergio Panunzio (1886–1944) became active in syndicalist circles in 1903 and continued until the fall of fascism in 1943 to develop and publicize the ideas that began to take shape in his mind then.[31] He came from a prominent family in Molfetta, in the southern region of Apulia. His grandfather had been a Risorgimento patriot and the first mayor of Molfetta after Italian unification; an uncle had served in the Chamber of Deputies. In 1902, while still in high school, Panunzio became a Socialist, gravitating to the sector of the party's antireformist wing that was on its way to revolutionary syndicalism.[32] He continued his education, earning degrees from the University of Naples in jurisprudence in 1908 and in philosophy in 1911, but during the same period he established himself as one of the most original theorists of revolutionary syndicalism. He subsequently held teaching jobs in Ferrara and Bologna before winning the chair in Philosophy of Law at the University of Ferrara in 1920.

As a fascist, Panunzio served in the Chamber of Deputies beginning in 1924 and occupied a variety of other positions in the regime. He was, at various times, a member of the directorate of the Fascist party, head of the educators' union, undersecretary in the Ministry of Communications, a member of the National Council of Corporations, and a member of the commission for reform of the Italian legal codes. At the same time, Panunzio continued his academic career, moving in 1925 from Ferrara to Perguia, where he served as rector of the university. In 1927, he assumed the chair of Doctrine of the State in the Political Science Faculty at the University of Rome, and in 1928 he began serving simultaneously as head of the first specifically fascist institution of higher education, the Fascist Faculty of Political Science at the University of Perugia. Panunzio used his university positions as platforms from which to publicize his conception of fascism; for example, his inaugural lecture at the University of Rome in 1928, soon published as the title essay of a book, was one of the most widely discussed doctrinal statements of the fascist period.[33] He also contributed frequently to newspapers and periodicals, especially Mussolini's *Il popolo d'Italia* and Giuseppe Bottai's *Critica fascista*, and played major parts in such well-known gatherings as the meeting on fascist culture in Bologna in 1925 and the meeting on corporativism in Ferrara in 1932. In addition, Panunzio was frequently called upon to speak at fascist propaganda sessions. For example, at Giuseppe Bottai's invitation, he gave the lecture inaugurating the Roman Center for Fascist Studies in March of 1925. This lecture, too, was promptly published as the title essay of an influential book.[34]

Angelo Oliviero Olivetti (1874–1931) came from a well-to-do Jewish landowning family in the Romagna. His father, Emilio Olivetti, served with distinction in the wars of independence and ended up a colonel in the Italian army.[35] While a student at the University of Bologna in the early 1890s, Olivetti became active in socialist circles, speaking, arranging meetings, and eventually helping to organize the forerunner of the Italian Socialist party. The police reported that Olivetti was an especially effective apostle of socialist ideals—among both the workers and his fellow students—"because of an effective speaking style, which displayed his considerable knowledge and talent."[36] He remained active as a Socialist organizer and journalist in Bologna until 1898, when he moved to Switzerland to escape prosecution for his role in the riots of that year. There he enjoyed considerable success as a lawyer, and his house in Lugano became a center for exiled Italian Socialists—including, at one point, Benito Mussolini. By early 1905, Olivetti was calling himself a revolutionary syndicalist, and he promptly became a leading figure in the movement, founding and editing one of the most important syndicalist periodicals, *Pagine libere*. This semimonthly publication appeared from late in 1906 until the end of 1911, then again during the debate over intervention in 1914 and 1915, and yet again from early 1920 until the end of 1922. As a fascist, Olivetti was an influential member of the Commission of Eighteen, instituted to propose constitutional reforms in 1925, and served on the National Council of Corporations and on other bodies concerned with fascist corporativist development. Shortly before his death in 1931, for example, he was invited to join the technical advisory committee of the Confederation of Fascist Commercial Unions.[37] When he died, Olivetti was also a member of Panunzio's Fascist Faculty at Perugia.

Like Panunzio, Olivetti was recognized as a major authority on fascist corporativism and was frequently called upon to lecture on the subject—as he did, for example, in one of the major speeches at the Bologna meeting on fascist culture in 1925, and as guest speaker at the Center of Fascist Studies in Lausanne, Switzerland, in 1928. He contributed frequently to fascist periodicals as well, especially *Il popolo d'Italia* and the two organs of the Fascist labor movement, the newspaper *Il lavoro fascista* and the monthly magazine *La stirpe*.

Panunzio and Olivetti were the most influential of the former revolutionary syndicalists in fascism, but there were many others. Agostino Lanzillo (1886–1952), a southerner from Reggio Calabria, became active in syndicalist intellectual circles in about 1908. Among the syndicalists, he had the closest personal relationship to Georges Sorel, who took an interest in the young Lanzillo before the war, using his influence to find journalistic positions for his Italian admirer.[38] Lanzillo was involved with fascism from the outset, serving as a member of the Central Committee of the *Fasci di combattimento* in 1919–20. During the regime, he served in the Chamber of Deputies, on the Commission of Eighteen, and on the National Council of Corporations. Although trained as a lawyer, Lanzillo was especially interested in economics and held various academic positions in economics during the fascist years. By the late 1930s, he had become rector of the *Regio Istituto Superiore di Economia e Commercio* in Venice.

Paolo Orano (1875–1945) was the son of Giuseppe Orano, a distinguished criminologist and professor at the University of Rome. Before the war, he taught philosophy in various Italian lycées, becoming active in syndicalist circles in 1905. Orano was the most restless of the syndicalists, the one most willing to try out ideas and political positions in a superficial, bombastic way. He collaborated with Olivetti on *Pagine libere* off and on, and he edited his own journal, *La lupa*, in 1910 and 1911. As a fascist, Orano served in the Chamber of Deputies, edited the Roman edition of *Il popolo d'Italia* in 1924–25, participated in a variety of Fascist educational and cultural organizations, and was made a senator in 1939. He was also a member of Panunzio's Fascist Faculty at the University of Perugia and became rector of the university after Panunzio's departure.

Among the revolutionary syndicalist labor organizers who found their way into fascism, the best known is Edmondo Rossoni (1884–1965), who headed the Fascist trade union confederation from its inception in 1922 until 1928. Before World War I, Rossoni worked as a labor organizer in the province of Modena and, beginning in 1912, in New York among the Italian immigrants. He returned to Italy with the outbreak of the war and played a leading role in the postwar syndicalist trade union confederation before casting his lot with fascism. Though not a talented thinker, Rossoni was involved in various syndicalist and fascist journalistic endeavors, in addition to his activities as a labor leader.

A number of other one-time revolutionary syndicalist organizers played important roles in the Fascist labor movement, especially Luigi Razza, Livio Ciardi, and Mario Racheli. Ciardi was a leader in one of the railroad workers' unions before the war, while Razza and Racheli were disciples of Filippo Corridoni (1888–1915), the leader of the revolutionary syndicalist labor movement in Milan and the most remarkable of the syndicalist organizers. A committed and charismatic leader, Corridoni might have rivaled Mussolini during the volatile postwar period, but he was killed at the front in 1915. As fascists, Razza, Ciardi, and Racheli headed Fascist trade union confederations: Ciardi led the transport workers; Razza, the agricultural workers; and Racheli, the workers in commerce. All three served as deputies as well, and Ciardi and Racheli ended up senators. With his interest in the problems of agricultural labor, Razza was the first President of the Commission for Internal Migration and Colonization and became Minister of Public Works shortly before his death in a plane crash in 1935.

One of Rossoni's closest collaborators during the early years of the regime was Armando Casalini (1883–1924), who had originally been active in republican circles but who converged with many of the syndicalists after the war, collaborating on syndicalist publications and contributing to the clarification of syndicalist ideas. He was a deputy, and second in command in the Fascist union confederation, when he was murdered on a trolley in Rome in September of 1924, apparently in retaliation for the murder of the Socialist deputy Giacomo Matteotti by fascists a few months earlier.[39]

Among the other former syndicalists active in fascism were the intellectuals Alighiero Ciattini, Antonio Renda, Luigi Viesti, and Alfonso De Pietri-Tonelli, and the labor organizers Michele Bianchi, Amilcare De Ambris, and Tullio Masotti. Bianchi (1883–1930) is relatively well known, since he was one of Mussolini's leading collaborators during the early years of fascism. But while he had been important as a revolutionary syndicalist labor leader in the province of Ferrara before the war, Bianchi had not contributed significantly to syndicalism as an intellectual tradition. As a fascist, he was more a tactician than an ideologue; despite his ready access to Mussolini, he was not a major carrier of syndicalist ideas into fascism. Other important fascists had been on the fringes of the syndicalist movement at various times, including, for example, Massimo Rocca (prewar pseudonym: Libero Tancredi), Ottavio Dinale, Cesare Rossi, and Franco Ciarlantini.

The transition from syndicalism to fascism was by no means inevitable, however, and several important syndicalists split off from the evolving mainstream. Arturo Labriola (1873–1959) was the first leader of the syndicalist current when he served as editor of the newspaper *Avanguardia socialista*, while Enrico Leone (1878–1940) edited *Il divenire sociale*, the most substantial syndicalist theoretical review, from its inception in 1905 until its demise in 1910. Neither of these two Neapolitan syndicalists contributed directly to fascism. After years in exile, Labriola did return to Italy and rally to fascism at the time of the Ethiopian War, but he had shared little in the intellectual evolution that had made a number of his former syndicalist colleagues major fascist theorists. Leone shared in this evolution even less; in 1921, while many of the other syndicalists were turning to fascism, he reentered the Socialist party, but he ended up in a mental hospital in 1925. On the other hand, Alceste De Ambris (1874–1934) played a central role in the syndicalist doctrinal evolution toward what eventually became fascism, but he refused to take the final step and died in exile. Before the war he had been a labor organizer, first among Italian immigrants in Brazil, and then in Parma, where he became one of the two most influential revolutionary syndicalist organizers of the prewar period, along with Filippo Corridoni. Though active as an organizer, De Ambris could certainly hold his own with the intellectuals of the movement; he edited *Il rinnovamento*, one of the central periodicals in the emergence of fascism, during the pivotal years 1918–19. We will also encounter the names of a few others who played secondary roles in elaborating the original syndicalist doctrine but who did not become active fascists—Paolo Mantica, Alfredo Polledro, Franz Weiss, and Tommaso Sorricchio. Another secondary syndicalist, Giulio Barni, was killed in World War I.

Especially after 1907, when the syndicalists left the Socialist party, Italian syndicalism was in some ways only a collection of individuals, each going his own way. Free of any institutional discipline, the syndicalists were able to emphasize and develop various aspects of their doctrine until, one writer contends, there were almost as many varieties of syndicalism as there were syndicalists.[40] But while generalization about Italian syndicalism is hazardous, a core of common concerns and ideals continued to unite figures as diverse as the pompous Orano and the selfless Corridoni, the scholarly Panunzio and the modest labor organizers Ciardi, Razza, and Racheli. The syndicalist tradition persisted, evolving in light of frustrations and events. After World War I, their long experience as anti-Socialist leftists gave the syndicalists considerable prestige among the young populists who sought alternatives to the old patterns of Italian politics but who found themselves unable to follow the Socialists. Carlo Curcio has recalled, for example, the aura of legend that surrounded Olivetti when the old syndicalist joined the Fascist Faculty at Perugia in 1930.[41]

If we are to grasp the relationship between the syndicalist tradition and Italian fascism, we must consider briefly the place of ideas in such political movements and the use of ideas in historical explanation. There is widespread confusion over these matters because it is difficult to establish the relationships among such central categories as power, social composition, ideas, ideologies, purposes, and motives.[42] In considering a movement like Italian fascism, it seems somehow "soft-minded" to consider ideas and "tough-minded" to focus on social composition and power relationships—to look at who the fascists were and what they did, not at what they said. But their actions are not transparent and self-explanatory; nor does social composition provide a ready-made answer to the central question of motivation. Interpretation requires that we make judgments about how coherently the fascists grasped the problems of their society, about how well they understood the inadequacies of liberalism and Marxism, and about how realistic was their vision of an alternative to both. There is no escaping such judgments as these, and they cannot convincingly be made without analysis of ideas.

Use of the ambiguous category "ideology" especially obscures the value of ideas as evidence about purposes—and thus about the origins of political movements. As George Lichtheim noted in considering the concept of ideology: "One encounters a terminological vagueness which appears to reflect some deeper uncertainty about the status of ideas in the genesis of historical movements."[43] We often assume that ideologies are merely justifications or unconscious rationalizations, but in fact a body of ideas may reveal purposes even if it contains an element of "ideological" distortion. On the other hand, we often assume that there is no connection between ideology and the real world. Practical men who influence the course of events are concerned with concrete objectives as opposed to ideologies, which are merely fanciful castles in the air. At most, ideology has a functional role in a political system, serving as a manipulative tool, an instrument of propaganda.

Since most of the ideologues with whom we will be concerned lacked major institutional power bases in the Fascist regime, it is especially tempting to dismiss their ideas as irrelevant. Given the characteristics of Italian fascism, however, ideologues like the syndicalists could be highly influential—even powerful. In the first place, as fascists went, the syndicalists were articulate and experienced, and they offered a blueprint practical enough to give direction to the vague aspirations of younger, less experienced fascists. They provided an interpretation of Italian problems and a conception of what fascism ought to become. Because the syndicalists shared many of the frustrations, perceptions, and values of these other fascists, they could speak for and influence them. Especially in a movement like Italian fascism, which emerged in action, and quite suddenly, there was a major role for such political "educators" as these.

Moreover, ideologues can influence practice even if they lack direct personal power—if those who have power are not sure what to do with it.[44] The direction which Mussolini provided for the Fascist regime was hesitant and uncertain at best. It was only because the syndicalists and other publicists prepared the ground and continued to insist on their conception of fascism that the regime began to move toward totalitarian corporativism in the wake of the crisis of 1924.

Ultimately, the Fascist regime failed to create a meaningful new order, but many Italians continued to believe in fascism's potential for serious innovation even as the regime was nearing its collapse. This was true in part because ideologues like the syndicalists served as myth makers, giving the regime an aura of radicalism and purpose, distorting the perceptions of others about its real prospects. In playing this role, such publicists exercised another kind of power, justifying the regime's imperfections, keeping up expectations, and thus helping the largely haphazard regime to hang together. If we are to understand why the regime worked as well as it did, it is essential that we identify these myths, explaining their structure and showing why they had the force that they did. At the same time, we should remember that the difference between myth making and revolutionary education is largely a matter of hindsight. To a serious fascist, the role of ideologue and educator could appear a powerful one indeed—more powerful, in some ways, than a position in the state apparatus, where compromise and focus on immediate problems were inevitable.

Still, some political movements have more impressive intellectual pedigrees than others, and we are especially liable to relegate "intellectual" evidence to the shadows when we encounter Italian fascism. We tend to assume that an ideology, to be taken seriously, must be systematic and rigorous, so rhetoric and superficiality in a set of political ideas seem evidence of intellectual adventurism, of a lack of seriousness and commitment. The syndicalists devised a doctrine with some measure of plausibility and force, but they were not systematic thinkers operating on the frontiers of European thought. Even the most cogent of them, Sergio Panunzio, sometimes lapsed into rhetorical superficiality and failed to examine premises or resolve inconsistencies. While some of the syndicalists read and learned from more substantial thinkers like Durkheim and Pareto, they borrowed selectively, without coming to terms with the full body of thought in question. But this does not mean that they were intellectual adventurers, or that their ideas were too superficial to have affected fascism. The syndicalists began, for example, by adopting some of the simpler and more accessible—but still essential—categories of Marxism. They were not "really" Marxists, to be sure, but one need not grasp the dialectic, or Marx's concept of alienation, to embrace other Marxist categories, to see problems and solutions in terms of them, and to ask questions on the basis of them. Despite their selective and in some ways superficial use of Marx, the syndicalists were quite serious about the Marxist categories they borrowed.

There is a vast middle ground between innovative political theory and opportunistic intellectual adventurism. The syndicalists and others who learned from them tried to use their heads in order to make sense of the problems around them and to devise rational solutions. In this endeavor, they certainly managed to ask serious questions about both liberalism and Marxism. We can understand why they argued as they did, and why they proposed what they did for fascism, only by following the logic of their ideas, seeing why their attempt to think led them in the direction it did.

Italian fascism did enjoy the services of a major social philosopher, Giovanni Gentile.[45] And students of fascism with a bent toward the history of ideas have tended to focus on Gentile's ideas, since they have the philosophical rigor we expect of an authentic political doctrine. Mussolini gave Gentile's ideas a kind of official imprimatur when he incorporated material actually written by Gentile into his well-known article on fascist doctrine for the *Enciclopedia Italiana* of 1932. Some have tried to draw analogies between Mussolini's ideas and Gentile's system in an attempt to establish the existence of a genuine philosophy of fascism.[46] But it is fruitless to try to make Mussolini into a consistent ideologue, and Gentile's philosophical system was both too abstruse to be accessible to most of those who created fascism and too abstract to be helpful to them as they sought alternative political institutions. To be sure, Gentile integrated ideas from other traditions into his system as he sought to establish himself as the quasi-official philosopher of fascism, and he was no doubt serious about the populist corporativist themes he helped to publicize. But he was not the source of these ideas, nor did corporativism require "actualism," Gentile's brand of philosophical idealism, as a foundation. Mussolini, despite his power, lacked long-term purposes of his own, while Gentile's ideology, despite its rigor, served only as window dressing, displayed in Mussolini's encyclopedia article to give the regime the appearance of a philosophical basis.

The syndicalists were able to provide "middling" ideas, more coherent than Mussolini's and more relevant and accessible than Gentile's, to the alienated young Italians who spearheaded fascism. The syndicalists were perceptive and articulate enough to make explicit the concerns of other fascists and to offer convincing solutions. The non-intellectual sectors of the Fascist movement could embrace these simpler ideas about problems and solutions and act on the basis of them.

Those who recognize syndicalism as an autonomous current within fascism tend to restrict its scope by identifying it with the cause of labor and by linking it to the Fascist trade union movement. From this perspective, promotion of working class interests vis-à-vis the capitalists must have been the syndicalists' chief concern, and Edmondo Rossoni, the first head of the Fascist trade union confederation, must have been the leading syndicalist within fascism—especially since this important institutional position gave him more direct power than the other syndicalists. A leading American historian of fascism, pointing to Nationalism and syndicalism as the two principal components of fascist ideology, takes Rossoni as representative of syndicalism, pitting him against the Nationalist Alfredo Rocco.[47] This is an obvious mismatch, but the contest becomes more interesting when Rocco is set against a more plausible opposite number—and his adversary in fact—Sergio Panunzio. The syndicalists within fascism aimed at something far more sweeping than defense of the workers. Their real constituency was not the working class at all; it consisted of politically alienated young people from the lower middle class who were seeking a populist alliance with the workers in order to make sociocultural and political changes.

Even though some of the most important of them came from relatively prominent families, the syndicalists were certainly not part of the emerging industrial bourgeoisie, nor were they "establishment" intellectuals with secure places in Italian society. Rather, they were in important respects representative of Italy's "intellectual petty bourgeoisie." This category, which initially seems to non-Italians almost a contradiction in terms, has a major place in modern Italian historiography; it embraces the marginal, superfluous sectors of the educated in an overpopulated country, lacking enough productive roles to go around. We have already seen that the category is central to Luigi Salvatorelli's classic interpretation of fascism. Writing in 1925, Gaetano Salvemini indicated some of the characteristics of the intellectual petty bourgeoisie as he criticized that segment of the Italian interventionist movement in which the syndicalists were especially important:

Almost all of them came from the intellectual petty bourgeoisie. . . . They discerned in the war a good chance to foster disorder in the existing society, in which they had still not managed to assure themselves a means of livelihood. They were the ones who invented the myth of the war as revolution. But no sooner had they found themselves a secure and passably comfortable little position, in a propaganda office, in a division command, in a committee on the so-called domestic front, than they immediately became rabid patriots, arch-militarists, ultrabourgeois, bringing to these new attitudes the same noisy violence with which they used to run off at the mouth about revolution.

These elements, Salvemini went on, recognized Mussolini as their "natural condottiere"; ultimately, "they provided fascism with its general staff and cadres."[48]

Even though the "petty bourgeoisie" category is problematic, and although it has been overused in discussions of European fascism, it can be a helpful generalization or approximation if employed flexibly, without schematic reductionism, as part of a much broader interpretive framework. In this book I use the category to refer to propensities of mind and personality that reflect the traditions, forms of education, and socioeconomic insecurities of middle-class Italians lacking ties to modern industrial production.

These "superfluous" Italians tended to view politics as a vehicle for personal place-seeking, so historians of prewar Italian socialism have often assumed that the syndicalists' political evolution can be explained away in terms of narrow, self-serving aims. According to Gaetano Arfé, for example, revolutionary syndicalism in Italy was "a form of extreme protest of the most restless strata of the intellectual petty bourgeoisie, attempting to avail themselves of the labor movement in order to conquer in society that position of superiority lost in the dialectic of the modern class struggle, and for which they were unable for the moment to glimpse another means of access. The leaders of syndicalism retained of their socialist experience only a generic subversivism and an organic predilection for adventures. The Libyan War, World War I, and fascism would find them in the most turbulent and extremist positions of agitation."[49] Arfé finds in the prewar syndicalist doctrine remnants of the anarchism which the Socialist party and the labor movement had by then outgrown. And given the syndicalists' presumed interest in irrationalism and violence, he finds nothing mysterious about their turn to fascism.[50]

When we encounter the syndicalists in print, the exaggerated and rhetorical forms of their ideas may strike us first, apparently confirming the charges of adventurism and opportunism. Umberto Ricci, a noted economics professor at the University of Rome, turned to a recent book by A. O. Olivetti when he sought to understand syndicalist ideas in the uncertain political context after World War I. But he obviously found Olivetti's style and mode of argument rather appalling. Olivetti's writing was imprecise and highly rhetorical, and he sometimes indulged in extravagant metaphysical speculation, noting, as Ricci remarked sardonically, the parallel between molecules and syndicates and finding support for his conception of association in the theories of modern physics.[51] Moreover, especially after World War I, certain accents in syndicalist writings seem to betray some of the standard petty bourgeois prejudices and traumas. During the postwar crisis, for example, the syndicalists had solid theoretical reasons to oppose Italian labor, but the tone of their remarks about the workers reveals a strain of classic socioeconomic resentment.[52] The criticisms which Olivetti and Panunzio leveled at Marxism during the fascist period were often mere rhetorical exercises devoid of intellectual substance.[53] The syndicalists also worried about the family during the fascist period.[54] It would be silly to suggest that those desiring to preserve the traditional family cannot adjust to modernity, but here again, the shrill tone of the syndicalists' statements manifests a kind of petty bourgeois cultural and psychological substratum.

With their rhetoric and superficiality, the syndicalists seem to fall into the category of surplus petty bourgeois intellectuals unable to find a place in overpopulated Italy and venting their frustrations by trying out the most extreme positions, one by one, with little assimilation of serious ideas. As the syndicalists found their way into fascism, it could be argued, the petty bourgeois concerns underlying their position began to surface; now they found the personal positions they had always craved and settled down to defend traditional values.

The petty bourgeois cast to their thought, then, has reinforced the tendency to neglect the syndicalists. But it is precisely because they do fit the petty bourgeois stereotype in certain respects that the syndicalists are significant. They transcended petty bourgeois prejudices to some extent and developed a program with some progressive and modernizing features. At the same time, it was largely because they shared some of the basic concerns of the petty bourgeoisie that the syndicalists were able to reach many of the creators of fascism, offering ideas and proposals that rang true.

In the ensuing chapters, we will explore the interaction between the syndicalists, as ideologues striving to find a constituency and to develop a realistic response to Italian problems, and a petty bourgeois political revolt which was striving for sufficient coherence to be effective. The young populist malcontents in fascism were seeking to transcend a narrow, class-based perspective and to develop a progressive program responding to the genuine problems affecting Italian society as a whole. The syndicalist tradition was the major source of the blueprint for change which these alienated populists sought to impose upon Italy. These fascists certainly did not see themselves as a mass base for Nationalist reaction, and they had, thanks to syndicalism, an alternative conception of fascist purposes. As a result, a genuine struggle developed to determine what fascism was to become.

The syndicalists are worthy of attention, then, because they were intelligent and articulate enough to have left direct evidence of what they were thinking, but not so intelligent and articulate that they were completely atypical. Unlike less articulate fascists, they at least are able in principle to stand up to our a priori categories, to resist our tendency to explain them away, and to fight back, forcing us to see things from their perspective. By examining the frustrations and hopes of some concrete, living fascists, we can get a better sense of the range of frustrations and aspirations that were possible for other fascists who have not left us the same kind of direct evidence about their concerns.

At the same time, the syndicalist tradition constituted a bridge between the petty bourgeois populist current in Italian fascism and the ongoing European movement of radical opposition to the bourgeois order. The syndicalists tried at first to work with some of the basic categories of Marxism, the dominant force within the European radical tradition by the 1890s, but frustration in practice soon forced them to take a fresh look at the problems around them. They ended up involved in the reorientation of the radical tradition that was occurring on the European level, and the result, for them, was the petty bourgeois "socialism" that came to be called fascism. The suggestion that syndicalism affords a link between Italian fascism and certain problematic features of the European experience in the early twentieth century is not surprising, but we are liable to assume that the new irrationalism or the new cult of violence or the new vogue of Nietzsche was instrumental in the syndicalists' evolution from Marxism to fascism. Study of the Italian syndicalist tradition will reveal what that evolution in fact involved and ultimately will enable us better to understand the place of fascism in European history, in terms of the dilemmas confronting radical critics of the bourgeois order in Europe.

Since the syndicalists were "organic" intellectuals, speaking to and for a particular social constituency, their experience does not simply constitute another chapter in the rather overworked story of "fascism and the intellectuals," a story concerned with fascism's appeal to thinking people who should have known better. The syndicalists cannot be understood in terms of the personal and ontological malaise that we find underlying the appeal of fascism to many discontented European intellectuals between the wars.[55] They differed sharply, for example, from the romantic malcontents like Pierre Drieu La Rochelle, Robert Brasillach, and Lucien Rebatet who considered themselves fascists in France. The syndicalists had in mind something more precise than, for example, a revival of "energy" or "vitality" to overcome the decadence afflicting a "materialistic" age. Moreover, the intellectuals whom we will consider were not simply responding to the appeal of fascism—as a political phenomenon; rather, they helped to create fascism as they sought concrete solutions to the problems bothering them. We will examine their ideas, then, not to get at why fascism appealed to those who should have known better, but to get at what fascism was in the first place.

Nor is this a book about the "intellectual origins" of Italian fascism, as opposed to some other kind of origins. We will use "intellectual" evidence to determine which of the political, social, economic, and psychocultural problems in Italy were operative causes of the rise of fascism. Ideas are the links between the people who did the things we seek to explain and the problematic phenomena in reality that might have been causes; critical analysis of ideas enables us to gauge the relative weight of these problems in the responses comprising fascism. Since fascist actions are not simply transparent, with the intention behind them obvious, it is not immediately apparent what the fascists themselves found troublesome; so we have no choice but to turn to our second line of evidence—to fascist ideas, such as they are.

Of course the second-rate ideas we will be considering are by no means transparent either. We must begin by taking the syndicalists seriously, on their own terms, but we will not end up taking what they said at face value. Their ideas call for interpretation, which requires that we make judgments about how well they understood problems and about the plausibility of the solutions they proposed. This approach will not result in some sort of "rehabilitation"—the reader need have no fear. On the contrary, a deeper historical understanding of the syndicalists and fascists will make it possible to criticize them on the basis of more valid criteria and to learn more significant lessons from their experiences and mistakes.

2 | The Politics of Pessimism

An interpretation of the origins of Italian fascism depends on an evaluation of the quality of the liberal regime from which fascism emerged. Some historians emphasize the inadequacies of liberal Italy, highlighting its oligarchic and repressive features, while others insist that the liberal regime, for all its imperfections, was moving at a respectable pace toward viable democracy. If liberal Italy was basically healthy, then fascism can be seen as a mere "parenthesis," an unfortunate accident resulting largely from an exogenous shock—World War I. From this perspective, the "pathological" tendencies in Italian life had a chance to develop political force only because of the dislocations of the war. Moreover, those tendencies were symptomatic of a crisis that was by no means confined to Italy. On the other hand, those viewing liberal Italy in a less favorable light stress the continuity between fascism and what went before: fascism was the "revelation" of all the traditional Italian vices, the "autobiography" of a flawed nation.[1]

But a third relationship between liberal Italy and fascism is theoretically possible—the one that the fascists themselves claimed was operative. From this perspective, liberal Italy was indeed inadequate, and fascism was to do precisely the things that the liberal regime had proven unable to do. Even though the Fascist regime in practice never created a viable alternative to liberal Italy, this claim cannot be dismissed out of hand; it may have been a plausible attempt to create such an alternative that motivated fascists in the first place. But if we are to address this central interpretive question, we must explore the way in which Italy's situation as a fragile young nation affected the development of her liberal institutions. We must probe the complex set of problems with which our fascist spokesmen grew up and keep those problems in mind as we watch syndicalism evolve and fascism emerge. In this exploration, we will be talking about matters of degree. The questionable features of the liberal parliamentary system in Italy can be found elsewhere as well. But the difference in degree may account for the fact that the kinds of people who supported that system elsewhere turned against it in Italy. Italy was a weak link in the liberal parliamentary system of bourgeois Europe: tensions and deficiencies in the system in general were closer to the surface in Italy than elsewhere.

After the foundation of the Kingdom of Italy in 1860, a restricted class of generally able and upright men found themselves trying to consolidate a precarious new nation and to shape liberal institutions at the same time. The liberal system developed some peculiar features in Italy primarily because it was made to work in a situation of national infancy, political inexperience, and social fragmentation. As a result of these special difficulties, Italy's political elite, including those who shaped educated political opinion as well as those who governed, shared a common perspective, despite vast differences in methods and priorities. Its essential feature was a basic pessimism—a lack of confidence in their society, a lingering sense that their nation was flawed and fragile. Many liberal rulers had misgivings about the masses and about real democracy in the later nineteenth century, but in Italy doubts about the civic capacities of the Italians exacerbated the usual defensiveness. The Italian political elite viewed itself as the embodiment of liberal principles and viewed the state as the sphere through which it could nurture those principles in the face of a superstitious, illiberal society. Not only did Italian society appear to lack political experience, it seemed to have been corrupted by centuries of government at the hands of Spaniards, Bourbons, and priests.

When they looked downward into Italian society, members of the Italian political elite perceived fragmentation and atomization at all levels. The problem was most obvious in Italy's regional diversity, especially in the difference between North and South, but it also extended to narrow local *campanilismo*, and even deeper, to basic cultural values and attitudes. Social solidarity and civic virtue seemed to be rare among Italians, and this seemed to explain why national political awareness, organizational capacity, and respect for law were relatively scarce in Italian society. Sensitive Italians confronted troubling questions about the implications of Italy's unfortunate past for the task of nation building. Why had Italian culture become narrow and provincial, and why had Italy fallen prey to foreign domination in the centuries since the Renaissance? Was Italy fit to become a modern, self-governing nation? These concerns found moving expression in an influential essay by Francesco De Sanctis, "L'uomo del Guicciardini" ["The Guicciardinian Man"], written in 1869. De Sanctis was concerned with the central problem of Italian history, how the buoyant and advanced culture of the Italian Renaissance could have led, beginning with the

French invasion of 1494, to centuries of subservience to foreigners. The key, he felt, was a moral hollowness and superficiality in sixteenth-century Italian culture.[2] And he warned that, despite the achievement of formal Italian unity, "the Italian race is not yet cured of that moral weakness; we still bear the scars which our history of duplicity and simulation has inflicted on us." De Sanctis concluded that modern Italy would encounter her problem of character at every turn and would continue to find her history flawed if she proved unable to transform herself.[3]

De Sanctis's laments and exhortations were part of a long tradition of Italian self-criticism. Fifty-two years later, in the aftermath of World War I, Giustino Fortunato explicitly invoked De Sanctis's analysis in the jeremiads which made up his deeply pessimistic *Dopo la guerra sovvertitrice* [*After the Subversive War*].[4] With the liberal regime crumbling around him, Fortunato felt that all the weaknesses underlying Italy's development as a nation were emerging in stark relief: egotism and cynicism, a propensity for facile rhetoric, a lack of civic discipline stemming from a lack of moral discipline. Italy still needed "the mystical sense of duty from which derives the kind of love of country which is so lacking among us and which we never had in sufficient measure to enable us to repel—or contain—the foreign invasions."[5] The Italian masses were shortsighted and egotistical, but the Italian middle classes, grasping for parasitical bureaucratic jobs, were no better. Fortunato also blamed the liberal governing class—in fact, all Italians had in common certain characteristics impeding the development of healthy political institutions: "Every one of us, in private, makes fun of the law and, in public, pretends to be unaware of it, amid a furious, blind scramble for advantage, in which everybody seeks to prevail with whatever means available, for it is precisely a sense of the rights of others that we most lack."[6] Writing a few years later, a younger liberal, Guido De Ruggiero, found the combination of a narrow, decadent ruling class and a fluid, apolitical populace responsible for the degeneration of the liberal parliamentary system in Italy during the later years of the nineteenth century. Sensing that Italy was somehow different, he lamented the persistent lack of solidarity and national identity among his fellow Italians.[7]

These are tricky and sensitive matters, but there is no question that these pessimistic perceptions had a basis in fact. Historians of liberal Italy, as well as political scientists seeking the factors underlying modern Italian political culture, have similarly noted a lack of the civic consciousness and national awareness necessary for coherent political organization.[8] Alberto Aquarone finds healthy integration between state and society to have been especially lacking in the Italian South, "because of the old and still persistent poverty of civic life, as measured by the weakness or absence of spontaneous forms of association in the social body."[9] The American historian Edward Tannenbaum sees as modern Italy's most serious weakness "a conditioned inability to work together in a spirit of trust and cooperation"; as a result of this defect, civic culture and national identity were still seriously underdeveloped in Italy by 1914.[10]

The same cultural features can be found in other liberal parliamentary systems, but matters of degree are crucial, so it is worth considering recent comparative analyses by political scientists. To be sure, studies of Italian political attitudes since World War II are not directly applicable to the period before World War I, especially because so much that happened subsequently might well have fostered political alienation and cynicism. But, as contemporary political scientists themselves insist, their findings indicate deeply rooted propensities underlying modern Italian history. And in fact those findings only confirm what pessimistic Italians had long been saying about their society on the basis of less systematic evidence.

In *The Civic Culture*, Gabriel Almond and Sidney Verba compare political attitudes in Germany, Great Britain, Italy, Mexico, and the United States, and conclude that Italy is "an alienated political culture," especially lacking in social solidarity and in confidence in political action. The Italian political culture is

one of relatively unrelieved political alienation and of social isolation and distrust. The Italians are particularly low in national pride, in moderate and open partisanship, in the acknowledgement of the obligation to take an active part in local community affairs, in the sense of competence to join with others in situations of political stress, in their choice of social forms of leisure-time activity, and in their confidence in the social environment.

If our data are correct, most Italians view the social environment as full of threat and danger. Thus the social fabric sustains neither an allegiant political culture nor an allegiant pattern of political participation. And perhaps as sobering is the fact that the Italians are the most traditional of our five peoples in their attitudes toward family participation.[11]

After centuries of foreign domination, Italians tend to understand all governments as external, almost natural forces—to be endured or corrupted from within—and not as instruments responsive to social needs and organized involvement. Thus, Almond and Verba note, Italians have a low propensity to form groups for political action.[12]

In the same way, Luciano Gallino finds Italian society to be especially fragmented among European societies, while Joseph LaPalombara argues that Italians since unification have remained less likely than Britons or Americans to form voluntary organizations and to participate in the political process.[13] Italians tend to rely passively on the central government to solve problems. The result is an ambivalent attitude toward the state: "The Italian, despite his suspicion and mistrust of the government or the central administration, still thinks that all the problems affecting him ought somehow to be solved by some minister, or some bureaucrat, in Rome."[14]

We must be careful, needless to say, in using such broad socio-cultural categories in historical explanation; they can easily be misused or overused. Writing in 1956, the noted historian Piero Pieri remarked that Italy's history of provincialism and foreign domination had of course left its mark on the Italian character, fostering a petty individualism, but this, he said, was obvious and trite.[15] The problem for historians was to demonstrate in concrete terms that this underlying cultural syndrome had had a significant impact on historical events, and that other, more tangible kinds of explanation were not sufficient to make sense of those events. In fact, however, it is not necessary to insist on a direct relationship, explaining the transition from liberalism to fascism as a result of the cultural patterns we have discussed. We will find in operation an indirect relationship: those responsible for the events—both liberals and fascists—acted as they did because they believed such sociopolitical alienation to be especially acute in Italy and to be a major source of her problems. And we have seen that this perception was not implausible, that it did have some basis in fact. Given Italian self-doubts, moreover, contemporaries critical of their society were liable to magnify the defects in Italian political culture, exaggerating the discipline and political competence of non-Italians and the corresponding deficiencies of Italians.

Some of the fundamental characteristics of liberal Italy stemmed from the nature of the unification process and its immediate aftermath. Cavour and his followers saw Italy's situation in 1860–61 as a period of emergency to be surmounted as quickly as possible. And disintegration of the hastily constructed new nation was indeed a possibility, given the active hostility of the Church and the Bourbons and given the limited diffusion of Italian national identity. Italy seemed to lack the framework of consensus for a constituent assembly, giving the people a share in choosing basic institutions, fostering serious discussion among the various regions, and demonstrating that the Italian people had come together to create a new state. Instead, the Piedmontese monarchy, the Piedmontese constitution of 1848, and the Piedmontese administrative and legal systems were simply imposed on the rest of the country, with discussion deliberately kept at a minimum. The regions of Italy were added to Piedmont in piecemeal fashion, behind the facade of carefully engineered plebiscites. When King Victor Emanuel II of Piedmont became the first king of Italy, he did not become King Victor Emanuel I, but chose to remain Victor Emanuel II.

It seemed best to get the period of uncertainty and transition over with as quickly as possible, keeping things firmly under control. And that control apparently required centralized administration on the French model, even though Cavour and most of the Piedmontese moderates would have preferred a pluralistic system, with a greater measure of local autonomy and self-government.[16] They were confronting a cruel dilemma. Italy's great regional diversity made a federal solution especially appropriate, and if the new Italian state had taken a federal form, preserving local procedures and traditions, it would have seemed less an alien intrusion to ordinary Italians. By encouraging participation at the local level, a federal system would have fostered the political education the country so badly needed. On the other hand, the very regional heterogeneity and lack of national consciousness that made federalism theoretically desirable seemed to make centralization essential in the short term; only through centralized control and uniform procedures, it seemed, could the nation be kept from falling apart.

Cavour felt there was no time to study local conditions and procedures, to see what might be salvaged from the old order to provide a more organic basis for the new one. Consequently, a flurry of decree laws fundamentally altered the legal and administrative structures of the various regions, imposing centralization and Piedmontization—all before the first meeting of the new Italian parliament. Cavour feared that parliamentary discussion would be too lengthy and too divisive.

The cautious liberals who comprised the Destra Storica, or old Right, after their leader Cavour died in 1861, hoped that gradually the level of civic virtue in society could be raised so that the state could become more popular. Massimo D'Azeglio gave voice to the prevailing view in the ruling class when he uttered the best-known imperative in modern Italian history: "Fatta l'Italia, bisogna fare gli Italiani"— "Having made Italy, it is necessary to make the Italians." But since the political elite was defensive and pessimistic about the society, the state which it created was, for a liberal state, unusually aloof and restricted. The state was quick to respond to popular disorders in heavy military fashion, by declaring martial law or even a state of siege, and as a result ordinary people continued to experience the state as alien and unresponsive. However necessary the state's exclusiveness may have been at first, it could only breed more of the antistatism and "anarchism" which had caused the political class to lack confidence in the society in the first place. The central problem of modern Italian history was how to break out of this vicious circle: how to enable a society that apparently could not be trusted to gain enough political experience and civic consciousness so that it could be trusted.

With the state distant and aloof, and with decision making centralized, opportunity for participation on the local level was limited. Some historians maintain that the new system actually stifled political capacities in society, but others point out that centralization could have done only limited damage, since the impetus for political organization and initiative was so weak. In either case, Italy remained even decades later "a shattered society," relatively weak vis-à-vis the state and lacking in organizational capacity and confidence in political action.[17]

A major turning point was reached in 1876, when an inevitable expansion of the political base occurred. As the issues and passions of the Risorgimento receded, the Right began to splinter along regional and personal lines, and the leftist opposition changed in character. The "historic" Left, its roots deep in the Risorgimento, constituted a loyal opposition after 1860, advocating somewhat more democratic policies on the basis of a slightly different sense of the nation's priorities. But increasingly, during the Right's long period of predominance, others without much political vision or experience became frustrated with government policies and thus became politically active, naturally gravitating toward the Left. This process occurred especially in the South, which had suffered economically from unification and was restive under centralized administration. But there were also more specific sources of frustration which make clearer the nature of the sectors that were becoming politically active in the South. Local banking and financial groups resented the ties that had developed between the Destra governments and the Banca Nazionale, the oldest, most firmly established Italian financial group. These other banks were often interested in questionable kinds of financial speculation, but the policies of the upright Destra, and the dominant position of the conservative and responsible Banca Nazionale group, constituted major obstacles.[18] By 1876, the Left was becoming a coalition of local groups, seeking political access in order to pursue such narrow interests as these.

By 1876, the Right was too narrowly based and too limited regionally to be viable, despite its achievements and its high moral level. And so when Marco Minghetti's ministry fell in March of 1876, King Victor Emanuel II chose Agostino Depretis, leader of the moderate Left in parliament, to form the new government. The fall of the Destra, and the Left's sweeping victory in the parliamentary elections a few months later, seemed to constitute nothing less than a revolution. Democrats were enthusiastic, feeling that now at last there would be serious changes, including the institution of universal suffrage, to enable Italy to move quickly to genuine democracy. While the suffrage reform which Depretis finally engineered in 1882 hardly justified the buoyant hopes of 1876, it did expand the electorate from six hundred thousand to over two million, or from 2 percent to 7 percent of the total population, and established that further expansion would accompany increases in literacy.

It fell to Depretis to make the political system work in the new situation, and no one grasped the nature of the challenge better than he. Depretis fully shared the pessimism of the Italian political class, but he recognized that since the immediate emergency was over, the political system had to be expanded to encompass a broader segment of society, and the South had to be more fully integrated into Italian political life. The expansion of the political base entailed new risks, however. A high percentage of the deputies elected in 1876 had never served in the Chamber before; they lacked not only experience in national politics, but also the moral legacy of participation in the Risorgimento. Enjoying the support of local notables, they were sent to parliament to serve as brokers for restricted local interests. So the rigidly upright men of the Destra Storica were giving way to men with a different conception of the purpose of politics.[19]

As a coalition of heterogeneous local interest groups, the Left lacked common long-term commitments, and after the elections of 1876, the huge Left majority in the Chamber began to splinter.[20] As a result, Depretis found himself confronting the fundamental political problem of liberal Italy—the problem of consensus, of forging a workable majority out of a fragmented Chamber representing a fragmented society. To make the political system work under these conditions, he felt it necessary to pander to the appetites of whatever deputies were willing to offer their support. The priorities of the deputies apparently reflected the priorities of a society still prone to corruption, and there seemed no choice but to make the most of the situation. So between 1876 and his death in 1887, Depretis managed both to expand the basis of consensus for the system and to maintain a workable majority in parliament—by means of government favors for loyal deputies and the local interests they represented. The clientele involved were often interested in the kind of financial speculation we have already mentioned; Depretis thus became the link through which they gained access to the state administration.[21] If he needed it, the cooperative deputy could also count on the ministry to intervene in his behalf at election time, through the centralized administrative apparatus, which gave the Minister of the Interior close control over the local situation through the appointed prefect and, through him, the police.

Through his system of state favors and influence peddling, Depretis managed to link together the heterogeneous regional interest groups that were now being brought into the system. The essential measure of consensus could apparently be achieved only on the basis of the least common denominator, participation in the state's patronage network. Depretis feared that attempting to bind these heterogeneous interests together by means of a coherent program might lead to a dissolution of the majority, perhaps to a bitterly divisive system of regional parties, and ultimately to political chaos. Italy was not yet ready for real politics; the chief objective continued to be preserving the state itself—in its expanded form.[22]

In principle, expanding the base of the political class to include newer business sectors could have meant an injection of dynamism and vision. However, the Italian capitalist bourgeoisie lacked both entrepreneurial vigor and the confidence for political leadership. The European recession from 1873 to 1896 hardly encouraged confidence, but there was widespread doubt about Italy's long-term potential for industrial development in any case. The country seemed to lack the necessary resources, especially coal, and new Italian industries would have difficulty finding markets, given Italy's overall poverty and the competition which her more industrialized neighbors could offer. As a result, Italian businessmen during the Depretis period tended toward speculative maneuvering—in urban real estate, for example—not productive industrial enterprise.[23] They did not constitute an assertive, self-conscious class, claiming to merit political power because of their unique capacities, because they could modernize the country, because they had a new program to offer.[24] They sent deputies to the Chamber simply to win the bureaucratic favors upon which their speculative activities depended. And these deputies played into Depretis's hands by competing with each other for governmental favors, giving him their political support in return. Thus the priorities of the Italian bourgeoisie and the political tactics of Depretis combined to produce *trasformismo*, or transformism, that peculiar set of political relationships characteristic of prewar Italy.

Through the patronage network, Depretis succeeded in expanding the political consensus "vertically," pushing the lower limit of political access a bit further down into society. But transformism also had a "horizontal" axis, linking Depretis's old Left with important sectors of the old Right. Not surprisingly, Depretis's strategy of compromise with the flawed society alarmed the paternalistic liberals of the old Right, but given the potential danger from below, some felt it necessary to go along with Depretis if the state itself was to be maintained. Marco Minghetti's position epitomized the ambivalence of the old Right in the face of this dilemma. He criticized the abuses which political interference in the administration and the judiciary produced under the

Left, but he was still willing to support Depretis in practice in 1882, in the wake of the suffrage expansion. In fact, Minghetti served as a mediator between Depretis and members of the old Right who were uneasy about Depretis's methods but who desired to support the state in light of the apparent threat from below.[25] By 1882, a major part of the old political elite, from both left and right, was coalescing into a conservative bloc seeking to defend basic institutions.

The transformist system which Depretis established and Giolitti later expanded did provide the short-term consensus and stability that seemed essential to the pessimistic Italian governing class. The country stayed together; institutions endured; parliament functioned, after a fashion; and a kind of unity was forged among the heterogeneous regional elites. These were real accomplishments, which perhaps afforded the basis for a more productive and democratic future. But the stability was superficial: the consensus was a short-term stopgap, an ongoing compromise made of a multiplicity of individual deals, serving to paper over the deeper lack of consensus in the fragmented society. This was a politics of expediency that worked only by neglecting the country's deep structural problems—the impact of unification on the South; the need for economic development, agrarian reform, and regional autonomy; the need to make the state and the political process more popular and responsive, once the post-Risorgimento emergency was over. These were divisive issues which seemed best avoided or indefinitely deferred. It was necessary to endure. And so the real problem of the new order in unified Italy, as the years after 1860 turned to decades, was not instability—but stasis.

The costs of short-term stability and consensus were thus enormous; the system seriously corroded Italian parliamentary institutions and, in the last analysis, prevented the political process from becoming a vehicle through which the society could confront basic problems and make reasoned choices. On the horizontal axis of transformism, concern for order and short-term stability produced an emphasis on homogeneity not conducive to real politics; the dangers from the untrustworthy society seemed so immediate that politically conscious Italians felt they had to focus on what they shared, rather than develop competing long-term programs. To pose the basic choices confronting the country would fragment the ruling class and thereby weaken the common defense of established institutions.[26] On the other hand, the vertical axis of transformism produced a degree of heterogeneity and fragmentation equally incompatible with genuine politics. Depretis sought to prevent the deputies from grouping around substantive political issues in the Chamber, since definite choices and programs would apparently threaten his precarious coalitions. As the manager of parliament, Depretis was free to maneuver, but he dared not use his freedom to provide real political leadership, articulating choices and proposing reforms. Politics had to be restricted to the level of personal relationships between the parliamentary manager, on the one hand, and the deputy and his local clientele, on the other. Political activity involved merely the bargaining and influence-peddling necessary to keep the fragile majorities together. Here again, basic choices and problems were sidestepped; here again, the result was stagnation.[27]

Some serious decisions had to be made, of course, but the system kept parliament relatively weak within the decision-making process. In exchange for favors, the deputies in the Chamber were willing to go along passively while the ministry and the upper bureaucracy made the decisions. Procedural problems also damaged the effectiveness of parliament, so the executive invoked special powers to make laws by decree.[28] The bureaucracy became an important de facto legislative organ as a result. The monarchy and its inner circle remained powerful as well, especially in military and foreign policy. In general, parliament provided a shield for an oligarchic system of government—a system that tended to keep the society weak in political capacity vis-à-vis the restricted political elite. And since it compromised the standing of parliamentary government, Depretis's system ended up perpetuating the country's political alienation and cynicism.

These political patterns also reinforced the tendency toward parasitical and speculative forms of economic activity in Italian society. The emerging economic sectors became heavily reliant on the state, showing little taste for direct competition or for developing their own organizations to pursue their interests. Alberto Caracciolo has well summarized the consequences: "The protectionist mentality impoverished autonomous initiatives, discouraged tendencies to rely on oneself or on the spontaneous association of producers. . . . In the phase of the growth and establishment of the national state, . . . the poverty of initiative on the local level stands out. It is an indisputable phenomenon, whatever its causes, and one heavy with consequences for the maturity of the ruling class and for political participation in the country for decades to come."[29] The political system, then, undercut whatever potential society had to develop political alternatives.

The system also warped the industrial development that was no doubt essential for the nation's long-term viability. Government help enabled questionable financial interests to prosper and even to establish a stifling hegemony over the economy. Newer industrial sectors quickly manifested the same parasitical propensities as the dominant economic groups. This pattern was most obvious in the Italian steel industry, which began to develop in earnest in the 1880s. A viable steel industry could have been created in Italy, despite her lack of coal, but only by industrialists willing to engage in long-term planning, to sacrifice immediate profit in order to reinvest, and to replace capital stock frequently in order to maintain efficiency.[30] But short-term financial and speculative concerns were foremost, so there was very little long-term planning. Bankers, stock promoters, and contractors with well-established political links promoted the new Terni steel complex, for example, not entrepreneurs and investors seriously interested in industrial development. Efficiency in Italian steel remained low; it was clear from the beginning that the industry would depend indefinitely on state help, and a variety of government orders and subsidies were forthcoming to keep it on its feet.[31]

Above all, steel required tariff protection. And the culmination of the interrelated economic development and political maneuvering of the 1880s was the tariff of 1887, which protected both southern grain and northern steel, thereby cementing the alliance of regional interest groups that formed the basis of the Italian state.[32] Although it was possible for Italians to favor protection on rational economic grounds, political criteria predominated in fact, and the tariff system did more to hinder than to further economic development.[33] The high grain duties preserved outmoded techniques in the South, as well as a landowner class with little interest in modernization. Steel protection meant higher costs for steel consumers like the promising young machinery industry, which now had to devote some of its energies to the scramble for state favors, bargaining for a few more percentage points of protection.

Some sensitive Italians, troubled by the direction of Italian politics after 1876, began splitting off from the mainstream to form a current of principled conservative opposition to transformism—and even, in some cases, to parliamentary government in general. The old Right had understood the state as a bastion of civic virtue, but parliamentary government under Depretis seemed to be allowing the particular interests of the backward society to undermine the state's integrity. Rather than form a political party to work within the parliament, those who blamed the popular, elective, parliamentary side of the state for this apparent degeneration began to identify with the permanent, administrative side of the state, which they viewed as the preserve of a permanent ruling elite embodying the national interest in the context of an untrustworthy society.[34]

Although Marco Minghetti was willing to work with Depretis, and although he remained committed to the parliamentary system in principle, he was deeply troubled by the patterns being established after 1876. In an influential book published in 1881, Minghetti dissected the links in the vertical axis of transformism, showing how the political managers interfered in the administration and the judiciary for the benefit of their parliamentary supporters.[35] The resulting abuses, he complained, only discredited the state in the eyes of a populace already tending toward political cynicism and hostility. The flaws in Italian political life were partly the result of inexperience, but Minghetti thought he saw a deeper problem as well—an unusual dearth of organizational capacity in Italian society. If Italy's unhealthy political patterns were to be overcome, Italians would have to learn to join together on their own initiative, for organization, Minghetti insisted, serves to discipline individuals and to enhance their political effectiveness.

Two other critics, Gaetano Mosca and Vilfredo Pareto, worried especially about the hypertrophy of the state in its parliamentary form; it seemed to be stifling the energies of society.[36] Parliamentary government depended upon favoritism and corruption, and the bureaucracy had to expand to provide the favors which the ministers needed to maintain their majorities. Pareto, writing in 1893, described with remarkable precision the vicious circle ensnaring Italian parliamentary government: the absence of a stable party structure made patronage necessary to forge a majority, but the resulting extension of government functions kept the society weak and disorganized and thus impeded the formation of parties. "It is not easy to say," he concluded, "whether the political disorganization of Italy is the cause or the result of the existing corruption."[37] But the result was clear, as Pareto lamented a few years later: on the one hand, the people lost all respect for the state, but on the other hand, everyone looked to the state for favors and solutions.[38] Individual and societal capacities atrophied as people scrambled for the protection of some politician. Mosca shared these concerns, but he was more clearly in the tradition of the old Right than Pareto, and his accents were more conservative and traditional. While Pareto began to anticipate the emergence of a new elite, Mosca emphasized the role of the nonelective apparatus of the state as the protector of liberal values and individual rights against mass democracy.[39]

The results of the opening to the left in 1876 and of the suffrage expansion in 1882 also disillusioned principled political observers on the Left. Some, their vision skewed by the dreams of the Risorgimento, had expected government quickly to become more popular and effective after the fall of the old Right. But if the Right had been aloof and unresponsive, the Left was corrupting and ineffectual. And the suffrage expansion of 1882 hardly raised the quality of the deputies in parliament—transformist favoritism worsened.[40] At the same time, the preindustrial radical traditions of republicanism and anarchism seemed to offer no viable solutions. The laments of the great poet Giosuè Carducci gave voice to the frustration, the sense of betrayal and impotence on the left in the 1880s. In a famous speech on the death of Garibaldi in 1882, he commented with sadness about the sectarianism and the infatuation with empty formulas which he felt had become characteristic of republicanism.[41] Yet Carducci's own perspective was in some ways backward-looking, his thinking colored by the generous hopes of the Risorgimento. And now Garibaldi was dead: the Risorgimento was over. But surely Italy was not without hope of regeneration, and surely all the promise of the Risorgimento was not to be forgotten for good.

In the 1890s, crises and turning points were reached in several crucial areas simultaneously, setting the stage for the promise of the Giolittian era to follow. Confidence in Italy's potential for industrial development reached its nadir in 1893–94, when a wave of banking scandals and failures shook the Italian economy, raising new doubts about Italy's capacity for industrialization.[42] It now became clear that her industrial growth during the 1880s had been fragile and that her banking system was still underdeveloped and highly speculative. But reforms designed to overcome the immediate banking crisis established a foundation for the industrial takeoff which Italy finally began to experience after 1896.[43] Italian friendship with Germany was at its peak during these years, and Prime Minister Francesco Crispi got German help in the renewal of Italian banking. While the major banks that had crashed had been oriented toward financial speculation, new German-led banks like the Banca Commerciale of Milan immediately became involved in industrial development, providing the young companies in which they invested with entrepreneurial guidance as well as capital. In addition, these new banks were instrumental in moving the Italian economy into areas of industrial development that Italian businessmen lacked the confidence and experience to enter on their own.[44] For example, the Banca Commerciale promptly began to develop Italy's hydroelectrical industry, and electricity emerged as a leader in the rapid growth which began in 1896. Still, the surge in industrialization did not depend entirely on the initiative of banks; in the auto-machinery industry, initiatives were more decentralized, more dependent on individual entrepreneurs.[45]

Hydroelectric development had a major psychological impact, promoting confidence that Italy could hope to industrialize after all, despite her lack of coal.[46] Sectors of the Italian middle class now began to show more interest in developing the country industrially, in preparing for the new industrial world. And the revival of confidence that accompanied industrialization soon led to greater optimism about Italy's potential as a nation.

Marxist ideas became widely known in Italy beginning in 1891, when Filippo Turati began publishing *Critica sociale* in Milan. In his history of liberal Italy, Benedetto Croce recalled the stimulating effect that Marxism had had on many young, educated, middle-class Italians during the 1890s.[47] With its universal model of historical development, Marxism offered a healthy dose of cosmopolitanism to a culture that was still ingrown and provincial, a way of transcending its debilitating self-doubt. Marxist inquiry also required scientific study of concrete social and economic phenomena, a significant departure from Italian rhetorical traditions.

Marxism was particularly attractive to Italian leftists growing disillusioned with the republican and anarchist traditions. In contrast to preindustrial radicalism, Marxism viewed solutions to present problems in terms of the industrialization process; Italian society had the potential for radical change precisely because it was participating in this universal process. This meant that Italy could no longer claim either a special spiritual mission or a special revolutionary vocation, but neither was she permanently flawed by peculiarities of character and history. Confidently facing the future, Italian socialists formed a national party at Genoa in 1892, adopting a Marxist program designed to burn all bridges with the anarchist and republican past of the Italian Left. But while the new socialism of the 1890s gained strength from the apparent inadequacy of the earlier leftist currents, it also fell heir to some of their concerns and sensibilities. Certainly the Socialists of the 1890s wanted to be Marxists, but their movement was partly a populist reaction to the static transformist bloc that had been cemented in the 1880s.[48] This element of radical populism in Italian socialism mixed uneasily with Marxism.

Trade union organization began in Italy at about the same time. The first Italian Chamber of Labor, modeled on the French *bourses du travail*, was founded in Milan in 1889, and by 1893 there were fourteen of these local labor centers, linked in a national organization. The first large May Day demonstrations took place in the major cities in 1890, symbolizing the genesis of a class-conscious Italian labor movement. The advent of modern socialism and trade unionism rekindled old fears about the fragility of Italian institutions and colored ruling class perceptions of the great popular unrest of 1893–94 and 1897–98. In fact this unrest stemmed from immediate economic hardship, not socialist subversivism, but it helped to cause the most severe crisis that Italy had experienced since the 1860s. It looked for a while as if things were finally starting to come apart.

The crisis of 1893–1900 had several facets. The banking scandals produced serious financial disarray, and the complicity of Prime Minister Francesco Crispi and other leading politicians undermined the already shaky prestige of established institutions. But most important was the quasi-insurrectionary popular unrest and the inadequacy of the repressive strategy adopted to confront it. The major political leaders of the years from 1893 to 1900—Crispi, Antonio di Rudinì, and Luigi Pelloux—all began with relatively moderate approaches to the ongoing crisis, but the insecurities in the ruling class were so great, and the situation so apparently explosive, that they were soon drawn toward authoritarian reaction. Crispi blamed Socialist subversivism for the *fasci siciliani*, a movement of peasant demonstrations and land seizures in Sicily in 1893–94, so he responded with severe repression—martial law, mass arrests, large-scale deportation to penal islands without trial, dissolution of workers' organizations and cooperatives, and then, in October 1894, dissolution of the Socialist party itself and arrest of the Socialist deputies. When the bad harvest of 1897 produced a wave of demonstrations and riots throughout Italy in 1898, Antonio di Rudinì, Crispi's successor, responded in the same way, with wholesale arrests and a declaration of martial law. The culmination occurred in Milan in May, when as many as 118 people were killed, hundreds wounded, and thousands arrested in a reaction that included the suppression of newspapers and the dissolution of unions and cooperatives.

The reaction reached its climax under General Luigi Pelloux in 1899–1900, with a serious attempt to circumscribe parliamentary government. Having kept order in Apulia in 1898 without recourse to martial law, Pelloux was supposed to be a conciliatory figure, but he lacked political experience and soon fell under the influence of Sidney Sonnino, an able and upright man rooted in the tradition of right liberal opposition to Italian parliamentary government. In an article published in 1897, Sonnino had advocated a return to the letter of the constitution of 1848, with the ministry responsible to the king rather than to the chamber.[49] When Pelloux promoted a tough bill for the preservation of order, giving the executive wide powers to ban public meetings and to dissolve organizations deemed subversive, he insisted on promulgating the law by royal decree, bypassing parliament. But a complex combination of events ultimately defeated this attempt at reaction. Pelloux resigned in June 1900, and a new era in Italian politics followed. By now it had become clear that the authoritarian policies of 1893–1900 were inappropriate and counterproductive. Even Sonnino became reconciled to parliamentary government. It seemed more and more evident that Italy did not have to resort to the methods of Crispi or Pelloux to preserve order and national unity.

The man who dominated the new era was Giovanni Giolitti, Minister of the Interior and major force in Giuseppe Zanardelli's cabinet from February 1901 to October 1903, then prime minister for all but a few interludes until March 1914. Especially before 1908, this was a buoyant and prosperous period—the most promising that liberal Italy ever enjoyed. With much of the bitterness of the 1890s left behind, there was at last a chance to come to grips with the nation's congenital problems. Giolitti was honest, able, and effective, and there is increasing agreement that he seriously desired to expand the Italian political system, to bring about fuller popular participation. It was Giolitti who engineered near-universal manhood suffrage for Italy—in time for the parliamentary elections of 1913. But while some have lauded Giolitti as the architect of Italian democracy in the making, others have vilified him as an arch-corrupter who impeded democracy by cynically exploiting the most unfortunate weaknesses in Italian society.[50] It is symptomatic of the basic explosiveness of the Italian situation that a figure as hard-headed, sober, and even bland as Giolitti could become one of the most controversial figures in modern European history.

Giolitti was more optimistic than his predecessors: Italy was modernizing and maturing; the political system could safely be expanded—to include, especially, the emerging industrial proletariat of the North. The popular classes were bound to assume a greater share of political and economic power, but this change could be advantageous for the existing order—if the established political class responded wisely. The state, Giolitti insisted, must cease to view the labor movement as inherently subversive and strikes as inherently threatening to the established order. Strikes were legitimate attempts by the workers to better their condition, so the state should remain neutral when they occurred, no longer siding automatically with the employers in the name of order.

In practice, Giolitti generally followed this strategy of conciliation toward the workers. His governments sometimes pressured employers to make concessions in order to avert strikes or to agree to a relatively generous settlement in the event of a strike. Socialist cooperatives in the Po Valley were granted public works contracts on attractive terms and even a special bank of labor to provide credit. Hoping to lure the Socialists into the government, Giolitti made overtures to Filippo Turati as he was preparing his new ministry in 1903, although Turati declined. Giolitti wanted to undercut socialism as a political alternative while extending the existing system to include the organized workers of the North.[51] At the same time, his insistence on the state's neutrality in labor conflicts was part of a more general policy of elevating the state to a higher level of impartiality and universality. The situation no longer seemed precarious, so he fostered greater rectitude in the administration and the judiciary, and even defied powerful private interests by creating a state life insurance monopoly.

Giolitti believed that the divorce between people and state in Italy could be overcome, but it was necessary to be patient, avoiding rhetoric and panaceas. It was necessary above all to be realistic—about what could be expected from the existing society and especially about the political implications of Italy's regional differences. And here we penetrate the surface optimism of Giolitti's strategy and encounter deeper perceptions and values that linked him to the traditions of the post-Risorgimento Italian political class. Giolitti was pessimistic about human nature in general, but he was especially skeptical about the political maturity and moral fiber of his own people.[52] There seemed to be strict limits to what he could hope to accomplish.

Italian society was slowly growing more unified and homogeneous, but fragmentation and heterogeneity remained its essential characteristics even in Giolitti's time. So Giolitti, like Depretis, was preoccupied with the problem of political consensus, which on the immediate level was the problem of forging a majority in the Chamber.[53] He not only continued, but perfected, the old system of electoral interference and government favoritism, secure in his belief that the state remained more liberal than the society, that the state was gradually redeeming the society. Given the greater political immaturity of the South, and given the more restrictive suffrage in the South resulting from the literacy provision of the electoral law, southern electoral districts were more easily manipulated, and it was the South that provided the core of Giolitti's majority. Giolitti not only exploited the backwardness of the region, but also prevented the political education it needed.[54] At the same time, he sought to keep his majority loyal and passive through individual favors, to keep real political issues from developing, so that he could govern essentially without parliament.

Giolitti's system, which reached near-perfection during his longest ministry, from May 1906 to December 1909, involved a highly ambivalent relationship between ministry and bureaucracy because of the balancing act he was trying to perform. In order to deliver the favors necessary to maintain his majority, Giolitti exerted an unprecedented measure of direct, minute control over the bureaucracy. But in doing so he was seeking the maneuverability he needed to bypass parliament and govern through the bureaucracy, which, for him too, was supposed to stand above parliamentary politics and societal particularism, pursuing the long-term interests of the nation.[55] No wonder Giolitti drew bitter criticism from both conservative liberals and democrats. The former complained that Giolitti's interference with the administration compromised the integrity of the national state; and they argued, plausibly enough, that it was only because the ministry ultimately depended on parliamentary support that such corruption was necessary. From the democratic perspective, on the other hand, Giolitti and the permanent apparatus of the state formed a conservative bloc intended to undercut parliamentary government and genuine democracy.

The advent of near-universal manhood suffrage must be viewed in light of Giolitti's overall attempt to develop the outer shell of parliamentary democracy without the internal substance. Despite this major step toward democratic forms, Giolitti continued to interfere in the electoral process, to fragment the Chamber through petty dealing, and to enhance the role of the nonelective side of the state at the expense of parliament. Thus critics could deny that the coming of universal suffrage improved the quality of Italian democracy; thus they could argue that the Chamber elected in 1913 did not represent anything at all.

Giolitti used the breathing space afforded by relative prosperity not to change the Italian political system, but simply to expand it, especially by spreading favors to the emerging working class of the North. Rather than reform the tariff and tax structure, he opted for public works and increased government spending. He had no real sympathy for the big southern landowners, but he was unwilling to attack the grain protection which maintained not only the landowners themselves, but also, indirectly, the southern parliamentary contingent —the core of his majority.[56] Government involvement in the economy continued, with the state offering subsidies to a wide range of industries, from sulphur to sugar beets. Most important, government favors for the protected steel complex were expanded. With state help still available, the steel industry failed to confront its congenital structural defects; leaders of the industry continued to worry more about short-term dividends and stock prices than long-term productivity. By 1914 the steel industry had the capacity to produce more than the domestic market could absorb, but its efficiency remained so low, and its prices so high, that many domestic firms still bought steel abroad, despite the high tariff.[57]

So while Italy began to experience some healthier kinds of industrial development after 1896, the parasitical sectors that had emerged in the 1880s were not forced out. Consequently, as comparative studies have shown, the Italian industrial takeoff between 1896 and 1908 was relatively weak.[58] The Italian state impeded rational economic growth by reinforcing a tariff structure which protected the least deserving sectors of the Italian economy and by subsidizing certain industries for essentially noneconomic purposes. With its access to state favors, the Italian bourgeoisie remained lethargic and lacking in entrepreneurial vigor, despite the context of industrial takeoff.[59] Much of Italian industry continued to rely on the German-dominated investment banks, showing little evidence of growing independence. In general, Italian culture still placed a low premium on industrialization and business expansion.

Still, there were critics. The influential southern economist Francesco Saverio Nitti chastised the Italian bourgeoisie for its lack of productive vigor and suggested that an aggressive labor movement might prove a valuable stimulant.[60] Since the unhealthy aspects of the Italian economy depended on protection, those desiring more efficient industrial development tended to be militant free traders, often without understanding Italy's economic condition or the more fruitful uses that she could have made of protection.[61] Laissez-faire principles led some to criticize even the new investment banks for excessive concentration of economic power. These critics were generally seeking to promote economic progress, but it was difficult to sort out the contradictory patterns of the Italian economy.

Giolitti's determination to open the system to the organized workers and his reluctance to challenge the protectionist basis of much of northern industry were closely linked in his overall design.[62] He could get businesses to agree to relatively high salaries for certain groups of workers because he offered continued favors or acquiesced in the formation of cartels. These policies kept prices artificially high and ultimately produced a redistribution of wealth that reinforced Italy's regional imbalance. The South paid the price for favors to business and labor in the North.

Giolitti's opening to the left proved only partially successful. The Socialists and workers did not have to be enemies of the state, but Turati's refusal to join Giolitti's new ministry in 1903 made it clear that neither could they yet provide a reliable political base. So, increasingly, Giolitti relied on newly organized Catholic political groups for support, a strategy which reached its culmination in the elections of 1913, the first held under near-universal manhood suffrage. Since the electorate was now almost three times as large, the system could not be so easily managed by the old methods. Corruption and intimidation continued, but Giolitti's men also worked out a clandestine deal to guarantee Catholic support for Giolittian candidates in exchange for promises to respect Catholic interests in education and divorce. Like Depretis before him, Giolitti found it necessary to engineer a new conservative bloc to keep the system firmly anchored in the wake of a suffrage expansion.[63]

In working with the Catholics, Giolitti hoped to keep his system of personal domination intact. He was not trying to encourage an autonomous Catholic party and political role; indeed, his compromises with the Catholics were intended in part to prevent a cohesive Catholic political grouping from developing.[64] From the Giolittian perspective, a system of autonomous mass parties, with programs of their own, would be divisive and unstable. Giolitti's opposition to "modern" mass parties is sometimes taken as evidence that he could not adjust to twentieth-century inevitabilities. But in fact he anticipated the dangers of a more comprehensive party system and tried to prevent the party fragmentation and inflexibility that later helped to ruin, for example, the Weimar Republic in Germany. Attempts to promote a more "modern" party system in Italy after World War I led to precisely the problems that Giolitti had feared. The basic pessimism of the Italian political class—from Cavour and De Sanctis to Giolitti and Mosca—was not without foundation, but it is still not clear that Italy required a system as restrictive as Giolitti's fifty years after unification.

The Giolittian program, then, was not a qualitative departure from the established patterns of liberal Italy. Despite the greater margin for progressive action after 1900, Giolitti was too concerned with keeping the system together to attempt basic changes.[65] The rickety system of favors, compromises, and expedients continued to keep the country together—in some ways better than before—but as confidence developed within the maturing and industrializing society, more and more Italians were becoming convinced that Italy could do better.

Some of Giolitti's most influential critics were part of the tradition of critical liberalism that began to emerge after 1876. To right liberals like Gaetano Mosca and Luigi Albertini, editor of the *Corriere della sera* of Milan, Giolitti was simply furthering the process of degeneration which Depretis had begun, compromising the state's integrity by lowering it to the level of societal particularism. Mosca continued to worry about the hypertrophy of the bureaucracy, as the state sought to satisfy the interest groups represented in parliament, while Albertini especially deplored Giolitti's policy toward strikes, which seemed to indicate weakness in the face of a developing threat from below.[66] The influential laissez-faire economist Luigi Einaudi denounced the parasitical protectionism which Giolitti perpetuated, but he found reason to hope that the industrialization process was enabling a more productive middle class to emerge in society. And as it developed consciousness of itself, this new entrepreneurial bourgeoisie would give rise, in turn, to a new political class.[67]

These critics remained securely within the liberal tradition, but some of their insights could influence others less committed to liberal values. And a different kind of opposition movement began to emerge around 1903, centering at first around a series of avant-garde journals in Florence, especially Enrico Corradini's *Il regno*. Corradini (1865–1931) had been a writer cultivating his own esthetic sensibilities until Italy's defeat at Adowa in 1896, and public indifference to it, jolted him into political consciousness. He founded *Il regno* to express his disdain "for the vileness of the present moment in the national life" and to promote national pride among Italians.[68] While Corradini at first relied on rhetorical invocations of ancient Rome, his two major collaborators, Giovanni Papini and Giuseppe Prezzolini, sought to look to the future. Italy's industrial development excited them tremendously. Italy seemed finally to be developing a vigorous industrial bourgeoisie, a class that stood in sharp contrast to the parasitical middle-class sectors clustered around the parliamentary state. In a symptomatic exchange in *Il regno* in 1903, Prezzolini and Vilfredo Pareto disagreed over whether the Italian bourgeoisie could renew itself.[69] Pareto saw only continued decadence, but Prezzolini, who was thirty-four years younger, disagreed, pointing to examples of growing middle-class fortitude—in employer resistance to strikes, for example. To be sure, Prezzolini admitted, the Italian bourgeoisie was still insecure, but the very existence of *Il regno* was evidence that some middle-class sectors in Italy were beginning to assert themselves. Despite this disagreement, however, Prezzolini and his colleagues learned a great deal from Pareto and used his categories as they sought to come to grips with the problems of their society.[70] They agreed that Italian parliamentary government under Giolitti indicated a ruling class in an advanced stage of decadence, and they agreed that renewal could only come from new elements untouched by the corrupting political process.

Prezzolini and Papini remained influential cultural innovators throughout the Giolittian era. Through their review *La voce*, which appeared from 1908 to 1916, they continued their efforts to promote the political education of the nation and to speed the emergence of a new ruling class. They hoped to make Italian culture more practical and serious, but their interests were eclectic and they sometimes fell into rhetorical excesses themselves. With their calls for a more dynamic culture bound up with the modern industrial world, they had much in common with F. T. Marinetti, who launched the famous futurist movement in the arts with the clamorous manifesto of 1909. Worshipping speed, violence, energy, and the power of machines, the futurists expressed in extreme and sometimes ridiculous form the growing sense that Italy, thanks to industrialization, need not be stuck with her old provincial culture and her static transformist politics. Papini and others associated with *La voce* came together with the futurists through the review *Lacerba* from 1913 to 1915. Papini's glorification of bloodshed and war in this review hardly furthered the development of a more serious and practical culture.[71]

Prezzolini and Papini had had a major hand in shaping the new nationalist sensibility which began to crystallize with *Il regno* in 1903, but they proved to be mavericks unwilling to support Nationalism as it became a formal movement and took on a more precise political coloration.[72] Instead, Enrico Corradini constituted the major link between the new nationalism of 1903 and the concrete political movement.

The earlier, more literary nationalism began to give way to a more systematic political ideology in 1908. Austria-Hungary's annexation of Bosnia-Herzegovina that year—and Italy's passive response—raised questions about the cautious foreign policy which Italy had followed since 1896. Moreover, the relatively buoyant industrial growth experienced since 1896 began to slow down in 1908. Now there was less margin for concessions to the unions, and it began to seem that Italy needed to penetrate foreign markets, by imperialist expansion if necessary, to provide outlets for expanded Italian industries.[73] By 1909, Corradini had developed the concept of Italy as a proletarian nation, one of the cornerstones of the new Nationalist ideology.[74] In December of 1910, nationalists of various kinds met in Florence to constitute a formal movement, the Italian Nationalist Association. Considerable heterogeneity and ambiguity remained: some members of the association advocated protection, others free trade; some emphasized irredentism, at the expense of Austria-Hungary, while others emphasized imperialist expansion in the Mediterranean, at the expense of France. But all of them were concerned with foreign policy and believed that Italy was ready for a more assertive role. This preoccupation with Italy's international position stemmed in part from the troubling phenomenon of accelerating Italian emigration. From 1909 to 1913, an average of 680,000 Italians, or about 2 percent of the population, emigrated each year. The exodus reached a peak of 873,000 in 1913.

Italy's war with Turkey over Libya in 1911–12 forced the Nationalist movement to define itself more precisely and made it a serious force in Italian political life. Through a new Nationalist newspaper, *L'idea nazionale*, and through speeches delivered all over Italy, Corradini, especially, played a major role in whipping up support for the Libyan War. The Nationalists portrayed war in general as the kind of educational experience that Italians needed.[75] Willingness to wage war indicated Italian renewal; the experience of war itself would complete the process, binding the Italians together in national solidarity for the first time. But the Nationalist Association began to establish a doctrine with real coherence only at its third congress, held in Milan in May of 1914. Here the jurist Alfredo Rocco emerged as the most forceful Nationalist ideologue, and it was Rocco, above all, who oriented Nationalism clearly to the right, forcing a sharp break with liberalism.[76]

We can best discuss the substance of Nationalism when we consider the program it offered Italians during the crisis following World War I. For the moment, it is sufficient to note that Nationalism had roots in the conservative, critical liberal tradition, with its distrust of the Italian masses and its disdain for transformist expedients. But in Nationalism, that tradition lost its links to liberalism and turned into something else. At the same time, Nationalism was more confident and assertive than the tradition it was leaving behind. Italy's industrial development seemed evidence of new energy in the Italian middle class; the Nationalist movement was itself the vanguard of the new bourgeoisie that would eventually assume the leadership of the nation.

Nationalism emerged in reasonably straightforward fashion; it was aware of its intellectual and political roots and had no difficulty identifying its social constituency. By 1914, it had established itself as a major focus of opposition to the Italian political system. The development of syndicalism was much more tortured.

3 / The Origins of
an Antipolitical Vision

Italian revolutionary syndicalism developed not from within the labor movement, but from within the Socialist party, as a product of the strategic disputes which Giolitti's conciliatory policy occasioned. Socialist collaboration with progressive middle-class groups in the resistance to Luigi Pelloux in 1899 and 1900 had already indicated that, in a relatively backward country like Italy, Socialists had much to gain by working with others in parliament. But some Socialists objected to the reformist minimum program which the party adopted in 1900 and to the support for the government which Socialist deputies provided during an important vote of confidence in 1901. When matters came to a head at the party's national congress in 1902, reformism emerged the victor; the congress approved parliamentary support for the government, sanctioned tactical alliances with progressive bourgeois parties, and endorsed the pursuit of reforms. The current that became syndicalism began to develop at the same time, as the young Neapolitan Arturo Labriola denounced reformism and called for the radical structural change that the reformists seemed willing to put off indefinitely.[1] At this point, however, there was no specifically syndicalist doctrinal alternative, and those on their way to syndicalism were difficult to distinguish from other antireformist intransigents like Enrico Ferri.

By 1902 Ferri and Labriola had established themselves as the chief spokesmen for the antireformist Socialists. In February Ferri had founded a review, *Il socialismo*, to compete with Filippo Turati's *Critica sociale*, but Labriola had his doubts about Ferri and in December of 1902 founded a weekly newspaper, *Avanguardia socialista*, to serve as his own journalistic instrument in the fight against reformism.

By early 1903, the antireformists seemed to be in the ascendancy. In 1902 Giolitti had temporarily altered his tactics, becoming less congenial to the left. So after numerous successful strikes during the previous year, strikers began encountering stiffer resistance both from the employers and from the authorities, and part of the Socialist rank and file began to sense the limits of the reformist strategy. Moreover, the reformists themselves were hesitant and uncertain; the Socialist parliamentary deputies officially withdrew support from the Zanardelli-Giolitti government only in March 1903, well after their support had ceased to yield tangible benefits.[2] Consequently, increasing numbers of Socialists and workers were receptive as Labriola and the *Avanguardia socialista* group worked to publicize protosyndicalist ideas. These intellectuals developed close contacts with labor organizers, and Labriola especially developed a considerable personal following among the Socialist workers of northern Italy.[3] Despite their bitter criticism of Turati and reformism, however, Labriola and his colleagues could offer, even during most of 1904, only vague, unimaginative proposals to intensify the class struggle as a strategic alternative.[4] They vehemently opposed collaboration with the bourgeoisie, but most of them still considered the Socialist party, not the labor union, to be the key entity in creating socialism.

When the Socialist party held its biennial congress at Bologna in April 1904, the syndicalists had distinguished themselves sufficiently from the other antireformists to offer their own motion on party strategy, but when they failed to win a majority, they quickly accepted Ferri's generic intransigent motion. Together the Ferri and Labriola groups managed to defeat the reformists and win control of the party. Despite Ferri's doctrinal leadership, the success of the Labriola current in drawing rank-and-file support away from reformism was primarily responsible for this antireformist victory.[5] As syndicalism gained doctrinal coherence, friction between Ferri's intransigents and the syndicalists quickly developed, indicating the limits to the compromise between them. The syndicalists grew increasingly frustrated with the Socialist party, but syndicalism seemed to be gaining momentum within the labor movement by the end of 1904. And the doctrinal alternative they were developing emphasized the role of the unions, as opposed to the party, in creating socialism.

Italy's first national general strike, which crippled Italian economic life for four days during September 1904, helped focus attention on revolutionary syndicalism.[6] The strike began, largely spontaneously, as a protest against the repeated killings of demonstrating workers by the authorities, but it quickly assumed a syndicalist tone when Labriola and other syndicalists active in the Milanese Chamber of Labor assumed important leadership roles. When Giolitti adroitly called for parliamentary elections just after the general strike, the Socialists lost a number of seats. This defeat discredited syndicalist methods in the eyes of some proletarians, but syndicalism remained strong enough in the labor movement to be the dominant faction at the Genoa congress of the Labor Resistance Organizations in January of 1905.

The syndicalists looked to the future with confidence as 1905 began. That same January, Enrico Leone and Paolo Mantica launched *Il divenire sociale*, a bimonthly theoretical review, to provide a forum for the further discussion of syndicalism. Writing later in the year, Georges Sorel expressed his admiration for Italian syndicalism, praising the ideologues around *Il divenire sociale* and *Avanguardia socialista* as authoritative and stressing his optimism about the prospects for syndicalist development in Italy.[7] But 1905 proved the high-water mark of syndicalism as an autonomous current in Italian socialism. The ensuing decline in both the party and the labor movement raised difficult strategic questions that we will consider in the next chapter. First we must analyze the syndicalists' revolutionary blueprint, and their vision of the socialist future, as these were emerging during this period of relative promise.

The Giolittian strategy split Italian socialism partly because of the movement's heterogeneous social and regional bases. In both the party and the unions, reformism was the expression of new industrial working-class sectors, centered in Milan and the industrial North, who sought to combine material improvements within the system with the gradual development of socialism. However, Turati and the reformists were still thinking in the positivistic, quasi-deterministic terms that more imaginative socialists had begun to question in the 1890s, and they were not very clear about the relationship of their strategy either to long-term socialist goals or to the special Italian problems that were bound to obstruct the achievement of those goals sooner or later.[8] For Turati, revolution was the result of a consistently applied reformist strategy. But some reforms are more profound than others; in collaborating with Giolitti, the reformists were settling for short-term gains benefiting restricted groups in the North and neglecting structural reform concerned with the place of the South in the Giolittian system. With reformism setting the tone between 1900 and 1912, Italian socialism was becoming a kind of interest group within the system. The party collaborated with the reformist General Confederation of Labor (CGL), founded in 1906, in pressuring the government for special favors much the way business leaders did; sometimes business and union leaders combined tacitly to share government concessions.[9]

Believing that a deterministic and universalistic doctrine was applicable to Italy, the reformists could be calm and patient. From their perspective, up in Milan, Italy seemed increasingly a normal industrializing country; the Italian idiosyncracies that preoccupied others seemed less troubling to them. Italian socialism could safely be rather limited in its short-term concerns, and the northern workers could enjoy with a good socialist conscience the material benefits which Giolitti offered. They could ignore the underlying flaws in the system, secure in their belief that they were history's chosen class and that the process in which they were involved would lead to socialism in the long run.

The pitfalls of reformism did not go unremarked in the Italian socialist movement, though the bulk of the opposition, led by Enrico Ferri and Costantino Lazzari, did not propose sophisticated alternatives.[10] Ferri understood the problematic side of the reformist strategy and insisted that the Socialist party must retain greater flexibility, supporting bourgeois governments when the situation seemed promising, but always warily, and only on a case-by-case basis. This strategy was plausible, but it could lead to opportunism and inconsistency—as it did in Ferri's case. On the other hand, those like Lazzari who offered more unconditional opposition to collaboration with bourgeois governments called simply for strict class separation and rigid intransigence. They were not asking questions about the circumstances or the methods that would be appropriate to a socialist revolution.

The most effective socialist critiques of reformism came from the independent southern socialist Gaetano Salvemini, on the one hand, and from the syndicalists, on the other. The basis of their criticism was essentially the same, but the alternatives they proposed were radically different. For Salvemini, it was the Socialist party's responsibility to take the lead in overcoming Italy's long-standing structural defects; there could be no evolution toward socialism unless those defects were overcome.[11] Salvemini showed persuasively how Giolitti's system rested on exploitation of the South through the tariff structure and through electoral interference. In playing Giolitti's game, the reformists were helping to perpetuate the present pathological system. As an alternative, Salvemini called on Socialists to build an alliance between advanced northern workers and southern peasants to fight for fundamental change. Without an approach to the South and the peasants, the Socialist party would remain a regional interest group, ensnared within the corrupting patterns of the present. For Salvemini, the first crucial reform was universal suffrage; given the right to vote, the southern masses would eliminate the South's rotten borough system, thereby destroying one of the bases of transformist politics. Then it would be possible to attack the tariff system. In general, the Socialist party had to overcome its restricted, regional character and become a national populist party, confronting Italian sociopolitical problems.

A disproportionate number of the syndicalists were also southerners. Panunzio, in fact, came from the same town as Salvemini—Molfetta, in Apulia—while Labriola, Leone, Lanzillo, and Razza also had roots in the South. Among nonsouthern syndicalists, a disproportionate number—including Olivetti, Corridoni, and De Ambris—came from Emilia-Romagna and the Marches, where preindustrial radical traditions remained strong, just as they did in the South. It is not surprising, then, that historians almost invariably portray Italian syndicalism as a reversion to these southern and preindustrial radical traditions. The syndicalist current is generally seen as a partly healthy reaction against reformism on the part of dissidents from geographical areas being left out as the Socialist party became predominantly northern in orientation. Syndicalism seems to have proven unproductive, however, because its strategy embodied too much of anarchism and old-fashioned catastrophic conceptions of revolution.[12]

The most influential interpretation of syndicalism as a demand for a southern strategy in Italian socialism is Antonio Gramsci's, outlined in 1926: "In the ten years 1900–1910 there took place the most radical crises in the Socialist and workers' movement: the masses reacted spontaneously against the policy of the reformist leaders. Syndicalism was born, which is the instinctive, elementary, primitive but healthy expression of the working-class reaction against the *bloc* with the bourgeoisie and in favor of a *bloc* with the peasants, and in the *first place with the peasants of the South*. Just so: moreover, in a certain sense, syndicalism is a weak attempt by the southern peasants, represented by their most advanced intellectuals, to lead the proletariat."[13] It is plausible, if a bit sanguine, to assume that syndicalism had a modicum of success in the labor movement because certain workers sensed the limits of the reformist strategy. And certainly the syndicalists reacted against the reformist compromise with Giolitti and shared the concerns about emigration and tariff protection typical of southern intellectuals. Moreover, Gramsci perceived correctly that syndicalism lacked an organic relationship with the industrial workers, that syndicalism was the orientation of disaffected nonproletarian elements seeking an alliance with the working class. But he lapsed into dogmatic schematism when he sought to link syndicalism to the special concerns and revolutionary aspirations of the South—and especially the southern peasantry. Gramsci had been strongly influenced by Salvemini, and he too considered the reformist strategy counterproductive because it neglected the South—and thus the potential for radical structural change which he felt the South embodied. He assumed that the syndicalists, as southern antireformists, must have envisioned a similar kind of revolutionary role for the South, even if they themselves were not clear about it. From Gramsci's perspective, there were only two alternatives: reformism, favoring northern workers and neglecting the South, and a revolutionary alliance of northern workers and southern peasants to bring about structural change. The only coherent basis for rejecting the northern strategy of proletarian exclusiveness was belief in the southern strategy of worker-peasant alliance.

Such dualistic thinking, with its geographical determinism, has distorted our understanding of Italian syndicalism, producing some striking anomalies in recent interpretations. One major authority, insisting on the southern basis of Italian syndicalism, is hard put to explain why the syndicalists discerned absolutely no revolutionary or socialist capacity in the southern peasantry, finding this "one of the major deficiencies of a group that also derived from the experience of the proletarian world of the South."[14] But a disaffected southerner was not bound to believe the southern peasantry could play a central role in solving Italy's problems. Their southern experience convinced the syndicalists that the Italian problem was deeper than the reformists thought, but precisely for this reason, they felt that the solution required something radically new, which they found to be developing almost exclusively in the North.

The syndicalists were heirs to the preindustrial populism traditionally strong in the South and in Emilia-Romagna, but they sought a more modern and convincing blueprint for change. The Italian problem was especially acute in Naples, but the solutions lay in Milan—in industrialization, in the new industrial proletariat, and in modern Marxism. Many of the syndicalists were part of the generation of the 1890s that fastened on Marxism as a way of transcending apparently outmoded radical traditions. Although their radical populist underpinnings were never far beneath the surface, they began by considering themselves Marxists and by trying to work with orthodox Marxist categories.

This does not mean—obviously—that the syndicalists grasped the philosophical bases of Marxism, or shared Marx's grandiose conception of the meaning of the socialist revolution, in terms of man's alienation and potential for fulfillment in the unfolding of the historical process. Like most of those calling themselves Marxists at the time, the syndicalists simply were not operating on that level. It now seems, in retrospect, that what passed for orthodox Marxism during the first decade of the twentieth century was a bit simplistic, although interest in the Hegelian underpinnings of Marxism during the past half-century has made it easy to downplay features of Marxism which are less inspiring but at least as fundamental to Marxism as a doctrine capable of guiding active socialists. Certainly the syndicalists tried to understand reality in terms of what seemed a reasonably orthodox Marxism at the time.

Nevertheless, Marxism meant something different to them psychologically than it did to the reformists. Both the syndicalists and the reformists accepted the basic categories of the new Marxist socialism and experienced the upsurge of confidence that accompanied industrialization, but the syndicalists looked to Milan with longing, from a distance, while the reformists, we might say, had been born and raised in Milan—and were a bit complacent as a consequence.[15] They had the kind of comfortable, organic relationship with the industrial system and the working class that the syndicalists lacked. The syndicalists fastened onto Marxism since it made uniquely Italian problems less important and showed how the universal process of industrialization, and the emergence of new industrial classes, promised a better future for Italy. But as outsiders, watching from a distance as Italy industrialized, the syndicalists were subject to gnawing doubts that Italy had access to a universalistic escape route. This explains, in part, their shrill insistence upon the Marxist model, rigidly interpreted, including the need for intransigent class struggle. But this also meant that their commitment to Marxism was tenuous and contingent. The blander, more sheltered reformists could accept the universalistic categories of Marxism in a more absolute and untroubled way.

Arturo Labriola's case best illustrates the relationship between preindustrial concerns and Marxist perspectives in the development of Italian syndicalism. Born in Naples in 1873, the son of a modest artisan, Labriola became active in Neapolitan republican circles when only fifteen. But he promptly moved toward Marxist socialism as he grew frustrated with preindustrial Neapolitan radicalism. He began to contribute to *Critica sociale* in 1891, helped to organize the first truly socialist organization in Naples in 1893, and then joined the new socialist party which had been formed at Genoa the year before.[16]

In his conception of Italian problems, Labriola was deeply influenced not only by the situation in his native South, but also by conservative critics of the Italian state like Pasquale Turiello and Gaetano Mosca. As he searched for solutions to those problems, however, Marxism came to him as a revelation, since it seemed to offer a rigorous doctrine and method, in contrast to the vague, sentimental ideas of anarchism and Mazzinian republicanism.[17] At first Labriola insisted on a rigid, abstract brand of Marxist orthodoxy, even in the face of the developing revisionist challenge of the late 1890s. Writing in 1898, he strongly criticized Francesco Saverio Merlino and Georges Sorel for abandoning economic determinism and reverting to sterile, moralistic utopianism.[18] If socialism was an ethical and juridical matter, as these revisionists suggested, and not the necessary product of the unfolding of capitalism, there would simply be no socialism. But there was still a dualism underlying Labriola's radicalism at this point: clinging to what then passed for Marxist orthodoxy afforded a measure of intellectual reassurance, but this sort of Marxism was of no immediate help in dealing with the Neapolitan and Italian problems he saw around him. Thus, despite his rigid Marxism, Labriola became a leading figure in the Neapolitan radical circle around the periodical *Propaganda*, founded in May 1899. *Propaganda* was concerned with local and regional problems from within the republican and antistatist traditions of southern radicalism. The revolutionary syndicalism which Labriola developed between 1901 and 1905 was an attempt to bridge the gap between his abstract Marxism and his more immediate local concerns.

Naples only frustrated Labriola, and he decided that the hope for radical change lay elsewhere. Late in 1902 he left for Milan, where he began publishing his antireformist newspaper *Avanguardia socialista* in December. Years later, Labriola recalled how different Naples and Milan had appeared: "For me, coming as I did from an area of old-fashioned artisan production, an area, in fact, in which this system was in decline, causing widespread and abject misery as it decomposed, that class of industrial entrepreneurs—especially in Milan—with its business sense and its audacity, was tremendously attractive."[19] It was the healthy new industrial classes who could redeem Italy, not the decaying preindustrial classes of the South. In the same way Filippo Corridoni, who gravitated to Milan from his native Marches in 1905, praised the city as one of the few in Italy rich in all the conditions necessary for the triumph of syndicalism—including a rapidly developing industrial system and vigorous class conflict.[20]

At the Socialist party's national congress in 1902, Filippo Turati sought to divide his opponents by dismissing Labriola as a petty bourgeois anticollectivist and republican obsessed with southern problems, as a radical considerably removed from the socialist orthodoxy which Ferri professed.[21] Turati was both right and wrong: in his sense of the Italian problem, Labriola remained a southerner shaped by pre-industrial radical perspectives, but in his quest for solutions, Labriola looked to the emerging proletariat of the industrializing North.

The syndicalists, then, shared Salvemini's basic premise—that reformism was undermining the force of socialism as a radical antithesis to the Italian status quo. But this concern led them to argue that socialism must become more purely proletarian, not more populist in scope and not more immediately Italian in emphasis. They felt, implicitly, that the problems in Italy, including those of the South, were deeper than Salvemini realized and required more radical solutions than he proposed. They insisted on a variety of Marxist orthodoxy: only the universal Marxist blueprint offered a way out for Italy; only insofar as Italy, through industrialization, approached the Marxist model could solutions be found. They agreed with Salvemini that the proletariat must not settle for gains within the system, jeopardizing the chance for radical change, but neither must the proletariat let itself be dragged into a populist alliance with suffering preindustrial groups like the one Salvemini proposed. Southern peasants, and disaffected preindustrial groups in general, were capable merely of sterile, old-fashioned insurrection, not of genuine revolution bringing new values to society.[22] The proletariat could redeem Italy only if it remained autonomous, developing its own values and institutions, as separate as possible from the other classes.

When syndicalism proved able to penetrate only limited sectors of the labor movement, the syndicalists began to ask some new questions and eventually to recognize the national and political nature of the problems that had bothered them all along. Finally, in the aftermath of World War I, they began to encounter their natural constituency. But that constituency was not the southern peasantry; it had nothing specifically to do with the South at all. Nor did the syndicalists, as they evolved from would-be Marxists back to populists, begin to look more favorably on the innovative potential of Italy's South. It was possible for "southerners" to devise strategies for radical change in Italy quite different from those of Salvemini and Gramsci.

Italian syndicalism, then, was not merely a throwback to preindustrial populism, but neither was it a genuinely proletarian expression. Rather, it was an attempt by preindustrial radicals to find in the working class, and in the industrialization process generally, the basis for solution to problems that did not specifically afflict the workers and that did not stem from the organization of the means of production. Syndicalism in Italy was a quest for Marxist solutions to "populist" problems, and the result, inevitably, was an unstable combination of elements. But in attempting to work with Marxism, the radical populists who created syndicalism were led to consider Italian problems in new ways. And this experience, in turn, enabled them to devise the unusual synthesis which some of them suggested for fascism.

By 1902 Marxist socialism was in some disarray, and those who would become syndicalists could not, despite the attractions of orthodoxy, close their eyes to the revisionist challenge.[23] In criticizing Merlino and Sorel in 1898, Labriola had insisted that Marxist socialism must rise or fall with Marx's economic predictions. But he had changed his mind by 1902, when he published a highly significant series of articles in *Rivista popolare di politica, lettere e scienze sociali*, edited by the Sicilian republican Napoleone Colajanni. Now Labriola was willing to admit that it was futile to try to make economic facts fit Marxist theories: the betterment in the condition of the working class during the preceding forty years could no longer be ignored. Moreover, there had been limits to the concentration of capital, and economic crises had not been the fearful phenomena which Marx had foreseen, but merely periods of adjustment, restoring equilibrium *within* the capitalist system. Such crises became increasingly rare as the industrial economy matured. But while Labriola had argued in 1898 that this revisionist view of the economic facts doomed socialism altogether, he now sensed that the success of capitalism, and the betterment of the workers' economic conditions, were actually stimulating the development of European socialism. Even though capitalism was not developing according to the Marxist blueprint, socialism seemed to be emerging anyway—especially through the institutions of the labor movement.[24]

It was only logical, if capitalism was not going to collapse on its own, for socialists to focus on the other side of the equation, the emerging industrial proletariat. Socialist conceptions were bound to become less deterministic and more voluntaristic: the coming of socialism depended not on objective economic factors but on the subjective will and capacity of the proletariat to replace the bourgeois capitalist order with an order based on its own principles. There was nothing inevitable about it; as Labriola put it in 1908, "If the working class does not decide to intervene in the economic relationships created by capitalism, capitalism will not break down."[25] But the new focus on proletarian psychological development raised troublesome questions. If capitalism could remain viable indefinitely, gradually improving the economic condition of the workers, why would the proletariat develop the will and capacity for socialist revolution? And if capitalists could eventually manage the economy without periodic crises, would a proletarian regime necessarily be superior? Classical Marxism had recognized the importance of the psychological development of the proletariat, but this was to have taken place in a context of growing misery and desperation; an altogether different psychological process was required in a context of economic improvement. Indeed, the solid, objective underpinnings dropped out altogether if socialism depended on the proletariat's noneconomic motivation. What had formerly been a necessary relationship between the proletariat and the new values that redeem society now became open and contingent.

The rapid growth of the Italian labor movement during 1901 and 1902, and the numerous successful strikes of those years, offered grounds for optimism, but socialist theory required a description of the mechanism through which the organized workers were developing new, postbourgeois values and the will to implement them in the wider society. Labriola had the rudiments of a revolutionary syndicalist description in his important 1902 series; and he was borrowing from his former antagonists Sorel and Merlino, as well as from Vilfredo Pareto. These three thinkers offered the most helpful ideas as the syndicalists sought to develop a doctrine consistent with their instinctive opposition to reformism.

Arturo Labriola had come into contact with both Pareto and Sorel during the two years he spent abroad avoiding arrest for his involvement in the disturbances of 1898. In Switzerland, his former economics professor Maffeo Pantaleoni introduced him to Pareto, for whom Labriola then worked as a research assistant, compiling information on socialism and on income distribution that Pareto used in *Les Systèmes socialistes*.[26] And in this book, Pareto explored features of the emerging labor movement which the syndicalists would soon use as the basis for their new conception of socialism.

Seeking to observe social behavior from a detached, scientific perspective, Pareto perceived new moral qualities—those characteristic of new social elites—developing within the organized working class, the result of the education and discipline which the new labor organizations offered the workers. He was impressed by the self-discipline involved, for example, in the workers' willingness to pay regular dues and in their circumspect use of violence in strikes. Organizational membership and activity imposed a rigorous selection on the working class; in the event of a strike, especially, only the most committed workers remained, carrying out their duties in a selfless, disciplined manner. The energy and solidarity and self-reliance developing among the organized workers contrasted vividly with the symptoms of decadence which Pareto found in Italy's old elite, relying more and more on intrigue, corruption, and special favors like tariff protection to pursue its interests. Pareto concluded that this new elite was likely to assume the leadership of the society.[27]

It is possible to extrapolate the fundamentals of the syndicalist vision from Pareto's antithesis between an old decadent elite, surviving through its control of the political process, and an energetic new elite, emerging in society, uncontaminated by Italy's network of corruption. This conception helped the syndicalists formulate their theory, and they frequently cited Pareto's writings to buttress their own position.[28] Pareto offered direct support in 1905, when asked to contribute to one of the first issues of *Il divenire sociale*; within the "popular classes" in society, he said, a new elite, disciplined and self-confident, willing to use force, was gradually emerging.[29]

During his period in exile, between 1898 and 1900, Labriola also made contact with Georges Sorel, Hubert Lagardelle, and the circle around Augustin Hamon's *Humanité nouvelle* in Paris, although this direct encounter did not immediately affect Labriola's thinking.[30] He and Sorel still disagreed fundamentally over the best direction for Marxism, and besides, French intellectuals were too preoccupied with the Dreyfus affair to think much about the labor movement at this point. Still, Labriola and Sorel did discuss Sorel's recent essay, "Avenir socialiste des syndicats," which had appeared in *Humanité nouvelle* in March and April of 1898. A few years later, despite continued disagreement with Sorel, Labriola published a translation of this work in his *Avanguardia socialista*, in installments from 21 June to 22 November 1903. And Sorel's essay proved very helpful to the dissidents around *Avanguardia socialista* as they sought to devise an alternative to reformism; in fact, it ultimately proved more important in the development of Italian syndicalist ideas than Sorel's more famous *Reflections on Violence*. Still, Sorel's ideas were already accessible to Italian socialist intellectuals by 1903, for he was deeply involved in Italian socialist debates, through his correspondence with Francesco Saverio Merlino, Benedetto Croce, and Antonio Labriola, and through his contributions to such major Italian socialist reviews as Turati's *Critica sociale* and Merlino's *Rivista critica del socialismo*.

The idea of a link between Sorel and Italian fascism is not surprising, but it is usually assumed that Sorel taught future fascists about violence, myths, and elitism. The young Mussolini found these aspects of Sorel's mature syndicalist conception worth exploring as he sought to revitalize Italian socialism. But it was Sorel's earlier, quite different conception of socialism that attracted the Italian syndicalists and contributed to the doctrine of radical change that they later proposed as fascists. Sorel's conception of proletarian psychological development in 1898 did not depend on the categories of myth and creative violence that he developed later, under Henri Bergson's influence, in *Reflections on Violence*. In his earlier phase, Sorel was interested in the ideas of Francesco Saverio Merlino and in the practice of trade unionism both in England, the most advanced country, and in France, where Fernand Pelloutier was spearheading a kind of revolutionary syndicalism in practice.

As Sorel himself emphasized in 1910, it was Merlino's *Pro e contro il socialismo*, published in 1897, that first indicated to him how to renew the socialist doctrine, how to overcome the abstraction that was creeping into it as the inadequacy of Marx's description of capitalism became apparent.[31] Sorel wrote a thirty-five page review article on Merlino's book in 1897, then a preface to the expanded French version the next year.[32] Merlino convinced Sorel that socialism was ultimately an ethical proposition, that it depended on the moral and psychological development of those who were to create it. For the workers themselves, Sorel argued, socialism was an ethical imperative, the expression of a desire to overcome exploitation and implement justice in society.[33] And Merlino, according to Sorel, was abandoning the dogmatic letter of Marx only in order to return to the scientific spirit when he called for an examination of actual social movements to determine whether values and institutions that would make possible a radically different society were in fact developing.[34] As Sorel put it in *Avenir socialiste des syndicats*, the key question for serious socialists was "to determine whether there exists *a mechanism capable of guaranteeing the development of morality.*"[35] Despite Merlino's great contributions, however, Sorel found his conception too bland, too oblivious of the irreconcilable conflict between socialism and present society. While Merlino envisioned reform and growing solidarity within the present order, Sorel insisted that rigid class separation was necessary if the workers were to develop an alternative system of values.[36]

Merlino's emphasis on the concrete developments in the labor movement led Sorel to look there for evidence of the emergence of socialism. He turned first to Paul de Rousiers's study of the English labor movement, and this promptly led him to write *Avenir socialiste des syndicats*.[37] Sorel wanted to explore the value of labor organizations for moral development, and he concluded that the organized proletariat was in fact developing the virtues necessary for socialism. Strikes, especially, demonstrated that the old, narrow egotism was giving way to solidarity in proletarian behavior: "The workers consider that the strikers must all be taken back, and they do not hesitate to make the greatest sacrifices in order to obtain the reinstatement of their excluded comrades."[38] Gradually, a socialist society was emerging in the practice of the workers' syndicates; new values were developing, and the syndicate was assuming ever more practical functions, indicating that it could become the proletariat's institutional alternative to the bourgeois parliamentary state. In his early syndicalist works, Sorel consistently emphasized the socialist import of mundane, everyday activities, in order to make socialism a proposition for the here and now, in opposition to the utopian, catastrophic conceptions which he imputed to the orthodox.[39]

Francesco Saverio Merlino (1856–1930) influenced Italian syndicalism not only indirectly, through Sorel, but also directly.[40] A Neapolitan who grew up in the traditions of Neapolitan anarchism during the 1870s, Merlino spent many years in exile, during which he began to make a substantial contribution to the European revision of Marxism.[41]

His articles in the Belgian review *La Société nouvelle* in 1891, criticizing Marxism and German socialism from an anarchist point of view, were promptly translated into German and discussed by Eduard Bernstein in *Die Neue Zeit*. At the same time, Merlino was also questioning the basic tenets of anarchism, finally breaking with the anarchists around his old friend Errico Malatesta in 1897. The first major fruit of his questioning of both Marxism and anarchism was *Pro e contro il socialismo*, published in 1897, the book which especially attracted Sorel. Sorel and Merlino began a regular correspondence in 1897, and Merlino played a major role in the diffusion of Sorel's ideas in Italy during the years that followed.

Like Sorel, Merlino found the new syndical organizations to be instruments of the new values and juridical relationships necessary to make socialism a reality.[42] He also saw in the labor movement the basis for a form of socialism that would avoid the dangerous utopianism of both anarchism and collectivism. Against the anarchists, Merlino insisted that the moral influence and discipline which social groups exert on the individual were inevitable and beneficial. On the other hand, he warned that collectivism and centralized control of the economy would inevitably lead to authoritarianism, to proliferating bureaucracy, and to economic inefficiency. The mechanisms of price, competition, and supply and demand would be necessary even in a socialist economy. Still, Merlino's central concerns were political, juridical, and ethical. The orthodox socialist overemphasis on economic matters, he charged, led to simplistic assumptions about the political side of present problems and socialist alternatives.[43]

Although these ideas helped the syndicalists devise their doctrine, Merlino was not a revolutionary syndicalist himself; he valued the unions as instruments for decentralized decision making in society, not as instruments of revolutionary class struggle. In fact, Merlino emphasized the scope for reform within existing society, for harmonious cooperation with the progressive bourgeoisie. The syndicalists, on the other hand, would portray the union as the instrument of class separation and revolutionary struggle. Only later, while they were revising their doctrine, did they begin to realize that they had always viewed the deeper social significance of the labor movement much as Merlino had.

Though less directly influential, Emile Durkheim's ideas were also involved in the intellectual interchange which served to focus Italian syndicalism. Sorel's *Avenir socialiste des syndicats* was partly a response to the corporativist proposals which Durkheim had recently offered in *Suicide* as an antidote to anomie. In a long essay in 1895, Sorel had discussed Durkheim's sociology, claiming to find difficulties that could be resolved only if Durkheim adopted social class categories and turned to socialism.[44] Still, Durkheim's ideas helped to clarify Sorel's thinking about social problems, for Durkheim emphasized the need for a new moralizing agent in society and suggested that organizations based on economic function could play the decisive role. But Sorel insisted in *Avenir socialiste des syndicats* that Durkheim's proposed corporations would be less effective than the emerging labor syndicates, which had already demonstrated such remarkable capacities.[45]

Durkheim reviewed Merlino's *Formes et essence du socialisme* in 1899, praising its basic thrust and drawing out implications that pointed beyond traditional socialism: "It especially would be a considerable step forward, benefiting everyone, if socialism would finally quit confusing the social question with the question of the workers."[46] The social problem, Durkheim insisted, was moral and cultural at root and transcended matters of economic class and material distribution. He found Merlino's antistatism excessive, since the development of the state had made possible the liberation of individuals, but he agreed that the modern state tended to become oppressive and needed to be balanced by intermediate groupings. And of course Durkheim had already begun to emphasize the moral value which organizations based on economic function could have for the atomized individuals of modern society.[47] Organizing society into a network of occupational groupings was the key to overcoming the basic defects of the liberal and capitalist order.

Despite major differences, Durkheim, Merlino, Sorel, and Pareto converged in some significant ways as they sought solutions to present problems. And the cluster of ideas we have discussed provided a foundation for the supplement to traditional Marxism that the dissident socialists around Arturo Labriola were seeking to develop. The syndicalists borrowed selectively from these critics of orthodox Marxism as they sought to come to terms, simultaneously, with the revision of Marxism and with Italy's peculiar problems. Even those who ended up fascists continued to pay homage to these four figures and to use their ideas. In 1917, at the pivotal moment in the syndicalist evolution toward fascism, Panunzio returned to Merlino for intellectual guidance, and later, as a fascist, he frequently credited Merlino with initiating the process of socialist revision which had culminated, he insisted, in fascism.[48] We will have occasion to consider this provocative assertion, and to return to the network of intellectual relationships we have just discussed, when we seek to place Italian fascism in the perspective of European history in the concluding chapter.

By 1900, Labriola was beginning to admit that much of value could be found in the ideas of Merlino and Sorel,[49] but it was not until 1902, in his articles in Colajanni's *Rivista popolare*, that Labriola began to integrate their ideas into a coherent synthesis of his own. In this series, in fact, the conception of present problems and the vision of socialist ends that would underlie Italian syndicalism were becoming clear, even though Labriola was still far from proposing a revolutionary syndicalist strategy. He portrayed the syndicate as the crucible in which the proletariat was developing its own ethical and juridical alternative to the bourgeois order.[50] The syndicates were ideal nuclei for the future society; they would provide the institutional framework for the coordinated but decentralized economic system in the socialist order. In their concern over salaries and working conditions, the labor organizations were already preparing for the noncollectivized economic planning required for socialism. Labriola expected that manual workers and technical and managerial employers would soon come together within the syndicate, making it possible to overcome the hegemony of the capitalist within the factory.

Labriola's emphases had changed considerably since 1898; the essence of socialism had become ethical, juridical, and, in the broad sense, political. Thus the task for socialist theorists was to analyze not the flaws in capitalism, but the flaws in bourgeois values and in bourgeois legal and political relationships, in order to explain how alternatives could develop within the labor movement. This was the doctrinal task that the emerging syndicalist current would soon set for itself. Writing in *Avanguardia socialista* in November 1903, the young student Sergio Panunzio, who had been strongly influenced by the translation of Sorel's *Avenir socialiste des syndicats*, pinpointed the central tenet of syndicalism: since socialism was the unique expression and responsibility of the proletariat, then the labor syndicates, as specifically proletarian products, had to play the crucial role in achieving socialism.[51] The workers' organizations could serve both as pedagogical instruments, fostering revolutionary capacities and socialist values, and as the alternative, postbourgeois institutions necessary for the new proletarian order. The source of social redemption was to be found in the labor movement; the treacherous path of parliamentary politics led nowhere.

As we have seen, Giolitti welcomed the industrial development that produced a more sophisticated working class and sought reformist collaboration in order to bring the workers into the system. The reformists, for their part, believed that they could best promote socialism by taking advantage of the opportunity to win improvements for the most advanced sectors of the working class. Syndicalism was the radical antithesis of this relationship between the Giolittian system and reformist socialism; leave the society alone, the syndicalists were saying, so that the workers can develop their own values and institutions and gradually lead society as a whole beyond the traditional sociopolitical patterns. The workers seemed a unique and precious source of novelty.[52]

Through industrialization and syndical organization, the proletariat was emerging as an elite, distinguishing itself from the people, the great masses of Italians. Only insofar as the proletariat made itself an elite, the bearer of new values and capacities, could it make a real revolution. Conversely, only the organized industrial proletariat narrowly defined (though including the landless workers in the heavily capitalized agriculture of the Po Valley), and not the Italian masses, could constitute a revolutionary force. According to Olivetti, "The syndicalist mentality can only mature in the factory or in intensive, industrialized agriculture: it supposes, then, large industry and the intense vibration of capitalist life, and of necessity must leave behind itself all the grey zone of small industry and small agriculture: the artisans and the petty bureaucracy, the various kinds of domestic wage-earners, etc.; that is, a whole mass which is specifically proletarian, but incapable by its very structure and economic position to feel the unique revolutionary impulse that is syndicalism pulsating in its veins and stimulating its will."[53]

Because they were more pessimistic than the reformists about the depth of Italian problems, the syndicalists were less confident about the resiliency of the emerging socialist alternative. They sensed that the reformists underestimated the menace Giolitti represented. Reformism meant contact with politicians and the existing state, and this could only contaminate the labor movement, leading the proletariat to settle for favors within the system. The workers would come to understand socialism as a mere accumulation of reforms, won by the Socialist party in parliament, rather than a genuinely new form of life, which they themselves had to develop.[54] Labriola argued in a 1910 lecture that "the syndicalists are preoccupied above all with the *transformation* of society. The question of the *betterment* of the workers within the limits of the current society is very important, but it is not connected to the specific end which the syndicalists propose."[55] If that end was to be achieved, the syndicalists argued, the proletariat had to create something new on its own.

There were further implications of the reformist strategy which made reformism—and ultimately the Socialist party itself—seem dangerous to the syndicalists. The reformists' determination to pursue reforms within parliament made them excessively concerned with winning electoral support; as a result the Socialist party was becoming too heterogeneous, representing not the class interests of the proletariat, but those of any social group that offered votes.[56] Moreover, the party leaders, and especially the Socialist deputies in parliament, were developing narrow, personal interests of their own, even their own clienteles, like other Italian parliamentary groups.[57]

Despite this emphasis on the proletariat, the syndicalists lacked a serious understanding of the industrial labor experience; they based their doctrine on an abstract, unrealistic conception of proletarian behavior and never devised an effective alternative to reformism on the level of strategy.[58] Revolutionary syndicalism in France and Spain emerged more organically and spontaneously from the experiences of certain sectors of the working class.[59] There were few middle-class intellectuals involved in Spanish syndicalism, which won control of the labor movement in Catalonia, the country's leading industrial region, between 1908 and 1910. The situation in France was more complex, but Sorel and the "New School" around *Mouvement socialiste* were seeking merely to interpret the actual practice of the French labor movement, which developed a militant, revolutionary syndicalist orientation from within the Fédération des Bourses du Travail, founded in 1892 and spearheaded by Fernand Pelloutier until his death in 1901. Syndicalism seemed firmly established within the French labor movement by 1906, when the Confédération Général du Travail formally adopted the syndicalist blueprint at its national congress at Amiens. To be sure, the resolutions of labor leaders at national congresses do not necessarily reflect the priorities of the workers themselves, but syndicalism seems for a few years to have expressed the aspirations of certain sectors of the French working class. In Italy, the syndicalist doctrine was more clearly the product of a group of intellectuals, operating within the Socialist party and seeking an alternative to reformism.

Generally, the Italian syndicalists were willing to concede that syndicalism had not developed spontaneously in the Italian labor movement and that the Socialist party still had an essential, though temporary, educational role—to make the organized workers aware of their crucial revolutionary and socialist mission.[60] Although the development of the labor movement seemed cause for optimism, there remained the danger that the young unions might become mere interest groups, concerned only with their members' economic betterment. Once the party had made certain that the unions were firmly committed to syndicalism, it could still serve as the political instrument of the organized workers, representing purely proletarian interests in parliament.[61]

The syndicalists admired the proletariat as a new, productive class born of the industrialization process. But it was particularly the experience of organization which seemed to be preparing the workers for social leadership, fostering not only the capacity for revolution but also the anti-bourgeois values that would give the new proletarian regime a socialist character. The individual industrial worker had revolutionary value only after he had been transformed by organizational membership. Sergio Panunzio summarized the central proposition of Italian syndicalism when he wrote in 1906: "Thanks to today's syndical organizations, the brute and disorganized labor forces, which have exerted so many vain efforts throughout history to redeem themselves from slavery, become intelligent, aware, organic forces; the static masses are converted into dynamic, distinct, and stable combinations and associations. So the syndicate marks a high degree of perfection, or elevation, in the mental, psychological, moral, and social evolution of the proletariat."[62] Following Gabriel Tarde and the Italian social psychologist Pasquale Rossi, Panunzio explained how groups elaborate norms which the members internalize. He also borrowed selectively from Durkheim to buttress the syndicalist view that the workers' organizations were developing new ethical patterns.[63] This emphasis on the value of organizational membership recurs constantly in syndicalist writings.[64] The syndicalists, even as fascists, never abandoned their heavy emphasis on the value of organization for radical change in Italy. Organization seemed a source of both moral development and political consciousness for the atomized, egotistical Italian masses. In organizing, moreover, Italian society seemed to be developing the strength and resiliency it needed to stand up to the exploitative Italian state.

We can best understand the mechanism through which the syndicalists expected socialism to emerge if we examine Enrico Leone's position first, and then show how most of the syndicalists went beyond it. Because Leone was one of the most able and well-educated of the syndicalists, some have assumed that he spoke for the others on complex theoretical matters.[65] But Leone's conception was atypical. All of the syndicalists recognized that the workers had organized in the first place to better their economic position. Leone sought to stay on the economic level, trying to ground his theory of syndicalist revolution solidly in the economic interests of the workers. His conception of the historical mainspring that would produce socialism was already worked out in its essentials by 1900; his later revolutionary syndicalism only described the mechanism whereby his conception would be implemented in practice.[66] Although he accepted the revisionist critique of Marxist economics, Leone fashioned another strictly economic conception of the coming of socialism based on the new marginal-utility, welfare economics of Léon Walras and Vilfredo Pareto. He agreed with the other syndicalists that the making of socialism depended on proletarian will, rather than on internal contradictions within capitalism; he conceded that voluntarism and a consequent measure of indeterminacy must again be part of socialism. But he sought to minimize this indeterminacy by showing that it was economic interest, not some new subjective value system, that inspired the workers' will to create a new order.[67] Although socialism depended on the subjective motivation of the proletariat, rather than the objective unfolding of capitalism, that motivation was the utilitarian hedonism of economic man. Pursuing their own economic self-interest, the organized workers would continually strike, thereby cutting into the share of output going for profit. Ultimately, profit would be eliminated altogether, because it prevented the proletariat from maximizing its own economic well-being; parasitism would be eradicated as the producers took over the economic apparatus. Leone insisted that socialism would now become truly scientific, since it turned out to be the consequence of laws elaborated independently by scientific economists.

Because the proletariat could win this economic struggle against its capitalist adversaries only if it were stronger, Leone's conception, like the majority syndicalist position, required that the proletariat acquire the new virtues of solidarity and self-sacrifice which would give it power in the class struggle. But these virtues were merely instruments that would make victory possible; they were not viewed as the primary motivating force that had set the workers on a revolutionary course in the first place. The essence of the revolution remained the elimination of capitalism, not the implementation of the new values. Leone feared the abyss that seemed to open as soon as socialists ventured beyond the economic level; if modern socialism was "an ethical ideal, instead of the expression of a relationship of economic forces, any expectation of ours about its future chances would amount to a mere expression of confidence, not to a conviction derived from the real development of historic, social and economic facts."[68]

With his quasi-deterministic vision of the revolutionary future, Leone was able to face with greater equanimity than his colleagues the failure of syndicalist ideas in the Italian labor movement. Success required new virtues, but the motivation for socialism was merely a matter of economic interest. When the proletariat proved more interested in pursuing immediate economic gains than in developing antibourgeois values, Leone's syndicalism was not undermined to the same extent that the majority syndicalist position was. It was partly for this reason that Leone maintained his faith in the proletariat, opposed the Libyan War and Italian intervention in World War I, and did not share in the postwar redefinition of the social revolution that led so many of his former colleagues to fascism. In fact, Leone's ideas evolved very little; his postwar pamphlet for the railroad workers could almost have been written in 1905.[69]

The other syndicalists tended to follow Leone's hedonistic model whenever they argued in purely economic terms.[70] But in their view, the workers' movement would become increasingly independent of the economic concerns which provided its original impetus.[71] The hedonistic economic strike could produce merely quantitative adjustments within the present system, not a qualitative departure. But even though purely economic disputes did not have revolutionary implications, they did lead to organization and to a method of struggle that produced, as Franz Weiss put it, "a psychological transformation in the proletariat, developing within it the sentiments of brotherhood, of solidarity, of sacrifice, of personal dignity, of individual responsibility, of self-help."[72] The external bonds of interest which had originally united the workers were becoming new internal links of duty and solidarity, and the specifically proletarian morality which resulted was the key to the workers' will, and capacity, to institute a superior order.[73] Gradually, the organized worker would come to understand both the essence of the bourgeois order and his capacity to replace it with an order based on his own radically different principles. And it was this desire to implement new values, not a desire for economic betterment, that would lead the proletariat to revolution.

Two major steps beyond the deterministic version of Marxism were necessary to reach the kind of socialist voluntarism that most of the syndicalists professed. Leone took the first step, arguing that the proletariat must actively intervene in the historical process and willfully destroy capitalism if there was to be revolutionary change. He emphasized explicitly that the impetus toward socialism lay within man, not in abstract economic laws.[74] But he refused to accompany his colleagues as they made the second, far more treacherous step. The new voluntarism for the others meant not merely that the proletariat had to act to create socialism, but that its role as a universal class depended exclusively on its subjective qualities, rather than its objective place in the economy. The new values were not merely instruments enabling the workers to fulfill their revolutionary role, but the justification for that revolutionary role. With this second step, the relationship between the proletariat and the new order—whether it was called socialism or something else—became far more problematic and contingent.

Whether one emphasizes materialism or voluntarism in Marxism, the proletariat's place in the historical process is defined objectively and follows from its position in the system of production. Whatever subjective values the proletariat must develop to create socialism follow from its objective socioeconomic position. For the syndicalists, however, the proletariat could be considered the universal class only if it made itself such through a process of psychological development. It did not enjoy this unique historical status automatically, "objectively," because of its special place in the socioeconomic sphere, as it did even for the voluntaristic Marx. The implication was that the leadership role in the revolutionary process was defined subjectively, in terms of values or psychological states, and not objectively, in terms of socioeconomic situation. The proletariat was apparently in the best position to develop new values—and seemed to be doing so during the first years of the new century. But in fact the leadership role was up for grabs, since it depended exclusively on subjective states. Thus the syndicalist commitment to the proletariat was merely empirical—and depended upon the further development of new values in the labor movement.

The workers could be counted upon to lead only because, through a difficult process of psychological maturation, they were coming to embody values diametrically opposed to those underlying the liberal capitalist system. Solidarity was the most important. The workers were learning to live according to the principle of solidarity on a day-to-day basis; the revolution would extend this principle of solidarity to the whole society.[75] The foundation of the new solidarity would be common productive labor. As he reached maturity and lucidity, the industrial worker would come to understand the need for labor in society and to embrace his own productive role.[76] The syndicalists idolized the worker partly because he was the special product of the new industrial age and would come to affirm industrial labor, machine production, and the factory system. A crucial criterion of the workers' maturity was the extent to which they had overcome their nostalgic resistance to the technical forms of modern economic organization and had embraced the industrial system as their own. In attacking the existing order, the proletarian elite would be seeking to extend its principle of labor to the whole society as the foundation for the new solidarity; the workers would overcome the nonproductive elements, thereby making possible a classless society of producers.[77]

This solidarity did not imply a leveling in the production process. The syndicalists stood in awe of the complexities of modern industrial production and respected those who knew how to organize businesses and run factories. As a major part of their socialist maturation, the workers were developing the technical capacities necessary to manage society's productive apparatus effectively, but the syndicalists considered that some sort of functional hierarchy within the factory would always be necessary, for objective, technical reasons.[78] Since this differentiation would meet productivist criteria and thus serve the general interest, the syndicalists did not worry that a new kind of political privilege or domination would result.

Extraordinary training, involving a good deal of hardship and sacrifice, would be required for the workers to come to maturity. The strike was essential as an instrument for this training, not primarily as an instrument for economic improvement. The criteria that distinguished a pedagogically valuable strike emerge most clearly in syndicalist polemics against revisionist, nonrevolutionary labor union supporters like Antonio Graziadei and Leonida Bissolati. Graziadei agreed with the syndicalists that the workers' organizations, and not the Socialist party, would play the determining role in the creation of socialism. But his conception of socialism was still evolutionary and reformist: simply by struggling for the economic betterment of their members, the syndicates were pursuing socialism. The criterion of success in a strike was immediate economic gain.[79] From the syndicalist perspective, this conception of the strike was narrow and egotistical; a truly revolutionary and "syndicalist" strike, like the one in Parma in 1908, was distinguished by its explicitly political tone, by its class consciousness, transcending a narrow corporate outlook, and by the strikers' awareness that together they were creating something new, which would ultimately provide the basis for a socialist society. A valuable strike both fostered and manifested the solidarity, lucidity, idealism, and self-sacrifice of the organized workers.[80] Even a defeated strike could widen horizons and engender new capacities in the workers involved.[81] But it was this contempt for the merely utilitarian in their conception of the strike that led the syndicalists into tactical excesses in practice and soon made their doctrine unpopular in most of the working class.

The syndicalists never translated their dream of an alternative society into a practical blueprint, showing how the values they thought they saw developing in the labor movement could be generalized to the whole society. The new social order was to be a network of syndicates, but they never explained the mechanics of organizational relationships in future society. Still, the syndicalists' images of the future reveal the frustrations and aspirations that had made these particular Italians radical opponents of the present order. Through the vigorous, self-reliant economic organizations now emerging, the society would gradually become capable of governing itself, without the corrupting parliamentary state and the stifling centralized bureaucracy, without politicians as intermediaries.[82] The conventional political sphere would disappear altogether, replaced by a direct democracy of producers, in which "political" participation would be more constant and immediate than under the liberal suffrage system. Social authority in the new order would be at once stronger and more decentralized, in response to the contradictory qualities of the Italian state, which was in some ways too weak to govern an especially atomized society, and in some ways so strong that it stifled society.

The syndicate itself afforded an image of the tightly knit, highly organized society the syndicalists desired as an antidote to the disorganization and atomization of Italian society.[83] They conceived the alternatives in extreme terms: the petty egotistical individualism of the present could be overcome only by giving a strong social dimension to all aspects of the individual's experience and behavior. Within the labor organizations that would eventually make up the new society, undisciplined individuals were already learning to accept their social duty, to internalize ever more social obligations.[84]

So the syndicalists sought antidotes to the disorganization and indiscipline of their society, but their vision also responded to the stifling centralization of the Italian state. They envisioned a society composed of semiautonomous organizations with plenty of scope for grass-roots initiative and economic competition. To overcome the peculiar cluster of problems in Italy, it was necessary to elevate and socialize the individual through organizational membership and, at the same time, to diffuse political decision-making into the society, making the economically-based organizations themselves the focus for participation in public life.

The syndicalists clearly fell heir to some of the antistatism of the Italian anarchist tradition, but they were neither proindividualist nor antiauthoritarian. Again and again, in fact, they explicitly denounced anarchism and proclaimed the superiority of their own conceptions of both the revolutionary process and the socialist future. Panunzio, for example, longed for something more solid and structured than the simple, transitory groups of isolated individuals which he found in the anarchist vision: "[Syndicalism] acknowledges not *unstable*, fleeting human aggregations, but *stable* and durable ones; it acknowledges, like anarchism, 'free associations,' but those having an *organic* not an *atomistic* character, an *institutional* and not a *contractual* basis."[85] Arguing explicitly against the anarchists, Panunzio, Labriola, and Olivetti each explained that syndicalism anticipated the destruction of the state in its present bourgeois configuration, but not the disappearance of formal social authority in general.[86] The workers' organizations seemed to be developing their own forms of authority, even within the confines of present society. Manifesting the tight psychological unity characteristic of proletarian organization, this syndical authority was much stronger and more effective, not more relaxed, than the social authority of the bourgeois system.[87] The syndicates, in fact, were already beginning to evolve a system of collectivist law, ensuring the social character of individual behavior. In the socialist order, this new kind of law would govern society as a whole, giving juridical expression to the new solidarity and replacing the bourgeois legal system, with its individualistic assumptions. Indeed, revolution was required in large part because the present bourgeois ruling class was too decadent to bind society together with an effective legal system; the proletariat, in contrast, would extend the sphere of law, arresting the present trend toward generalized exploitation and social disintegration.[88]

Despite their antistatism, then, the syndicalists were hardly antiauthoritarian individualists. As they later recognized more clearly, they rejected the existing state not only because it was stifling and corrupting, but also because, paradoxically, it was too aloof and limited—and ultimately too weak—to protect the collective from exploitation and to constitute an effective source of authority in the lives of Italian individuals. The syndicates were attractive as intermediate bodies which had emerged in opposition both to the state and to the reigning individualism of bourgeois society, and which seemed to be narrowing the gap between individuals and the source of social authority. The new order would not rest, like the bourgeois order, on a mass of isolated individuals, but on the network of syndicates, with their strong bonds among individuals.[89]

Since specifically proletarian institutions were essential for socialism, the syndicalists denied that a genuine revolution could be made through traditional forms of popular insurrection. Here again, the accents of syndicalism and anarchism were radically different, although historians have usually lumped the two together. It has been argued, for example, that De Ambris and Corridoni shared the anarchists' simplistic conception of the requirements for overthrowing the Italian regime, their Bakuninist belief in a spontaneous rising of the people.[90] But the syndicalists consistently held that a viable new order could not be created suddenly, through barricades and violent insurrection, but only through a long, gradual process of industrial development and proletarian maturation.[91] Writing explicitly in critique of anarchism, Lanzillo insisted that "if the proletariat wants to make the revolution . . . a life of sacrifice, of labor, of intense technical and psychological, intellectual and moral preparation is necessary."[92] This patient preparation served, as Tommaso Sorricchio put it, "to preserve syndicalism from anarchist and insurrectionary follies and degenerations."[93] Anarchist tactics produced only pointless revolts, which appealed to peasants and declining bourgeois groups; the syndicalist general strike had nothing to do with old-fashioned popular insurrection.[94]

The syndicalists did not expect a general strike to overthrow the capitalist system in the foreseeable future. The proletariat still needed a long period of maturation before it would be fit for leadership. Syndicalism required patience.[95] The syndicalists did not consider any of the great Italian strikes of the prewar period to be definitive revolutionary episodes—not even the general strike of 1904, the Parma strike of 1908, or the Red Week agitation of 1914.[96] Alceste De Ambris, discussing the Parma strike while in progress, emphasized that "the idea of a catastrophe capable of creating a new world is not one that we advocate, since we are persuaded that the road to be traveled is still very long and that we are scarcely in the first stages."[97] Although he portrayed this strike as an especially valuable pedagogical experience, De Ambris consistently denied that it was intended to spark full-scale revolution against capitalism.[98]

The episode in which syndicalist purposes have been most seriously misunderstood is Red Week, the spontaneous, quasi-insurrectionary popular uprising which paralyzed almost all the major cities in Italy for at least two days in June of 1914. Students of the movement, failing to distinguish syndicalism from anarchism, have simply assumed that the syndicalists considered Red Week to be the great revolutionary opportunity they had been waiting for.[99] In his detailed account of Red Week, Luigi Lotti lumps the syndicalists with the anarchists and republicans, but nowhere does he show that the syndicalists saw Red Week as a genuine chance for revolution. Indeed, his account makes clear that it was real anarchists like Errico Malatesta and Armando Borghi who believed the uprising had serious revolutionary possibilities. De Ambris and Corridoni did work to intensify the strike movement, but only in order to enhance its psychological value, not because they wanted to transform it into the revolution. When, during Red Week, the movement in Parma began to get out of control with stone throwing and violence, the syndicalists called off the strike in only its second day.[100] In this episode and in general, the syndicalists simply did not share the anarchist belief in the value of spontaneous popular uprisings.

Those who misinterpret the syndicalists' intentions during Red Week also misinterpret the lessons they drew from the experience. It has been argued that the failure of Red Week finally brought the syndicalists down to reality, proving to them that the revolution they advocated was not possible in Italy, at least for now.[101] But since the syndicalists had always distinguished their revolution from spontaneous popular insurrection, Agostino Lanzillo could argue, quite plausibly, that the failure of Red Week had confirmed, not undermined, the syndicalist strategy, with its emphasis on gradual proletarian maturation.[102] Just after the end of Red Week, De Ambris reaffirmed what he and the other syndicalists had been saying for years—that the Italian proletariat was still not ripe for revolution, and that revolutionary capacity could only be developed gradually, over a long period.[103]

Just as Italian syndicalism was not a throwback to preindustrial insurrectionary traditions, neither was it an aspect of the new antipositivist, antirationalist culture that began to emerge, in Italy as elsewhere, with the dawn of the new century. At first glance, the revolutionary syndicalist reaction against reformism, in both Italy and France, seems part of the more general voluntarist reaction against positivism and deterministic socialism. It is often assumed that the Italian syndicalists can be dismissed as second-rate participants in this cultural movement because of their alleged cult of violence and elitism and their apparent interest in myth and irrational forms of mass mobilization and behavior.[104] The syndicalists were apparently Sorelians, and Sorel, though easily misunderstood, was a major figure in the European revolt against positivism. Some dialogue did develop between a few of the syndicalists and the avant-garde intellectuals around Giuseppe Prezzolini's *La voce*. Prezzolini included several syndicalist pieces in *La voce* and even published a book about syndicalism in 1909.[105] But this dialogue never amounted to much; the syndicalists continued to develop their own ideas in their own way. Indeed, they had little use for the esoteric notions of their antipositivistic contemporaries. Sergio Panunzio, writing in 1910, attacked Marinetti and the futurists for their irrationalism and exaltation of violence. Since they ignored the need for rational limits to human activity, Panunzio argued, Marinetti's ideas could only lead to "the most brutal and mechanical irrationalism."[106] During the debate over Italian intervention in World War I, when any syndicalist fascination with violence could surely be expected to have come to the fore, the fervently interventionist Panunzio went out of his way to express his contempt for what he considered the bestial morality of Stirner and Nietzsche.[107] Panunzio portrayed the war as a means of expanding the sphere of justice against the sphere of irrational force. In the same way, A. O. Olivetti repeatedly criticized the revival of "mysticism" in Italy, singling out Giovanni Papini for special scorn.[108]

The syndicalists owed only a limited intellectual debt to Sorel, as they themselves recognized when they reflected honestly on the development of their ideas. Writing in 1918, Sergio Panunzio stressed that the Italian syndicalist emphasis on the values of organization gave syndicalism "a clearer and less involved, more comprehensible and more rationally intelligible aspect than it had with Sorel."[109] The Sorelian and Italian versions of revolutionary syndicalism already differed fundamentally in 1905, when Sorel first published, in *Il divenire sociale*, the articles that would form the basis of *Reflections on Violence*. Sorel had developed new interests and concerns since he had written *Avenir socialiste des syndicats* in 1898, while the Italian syndicalists had continued to refine the ideas they had derived, in part, from Sorel's earlier work. They had more in common with Hubert Lagardelle than they did with Sorel, for Lagardelle, too, continued to stress that the workers were gradually maturing and that socialism was gradually emerging through the everyday activities of the labor organizations.[110]

In their conception of the proletariat's revolutionary motivation, the Italian syndicalists did not follow Sorel in emphasizing the role of myth. The workers, in the Italian conception, would come to embody principles and values antithetical to the present order. When they recognized that they had sufficient power for success, their will to realize the values they embodied would be sufficient to motivate them to act. The vision of future success, of course, would stimulate the proletariat in its gradual process of maturation, but the workers would be lucid, would clearly understand what they were doing. They would make a revolution because they knew they were capable of creating the society they wanted. Italian syndicalism seemed to have no need for Sorelian myth.[111]

During the prewar period, the syndicalists were reluctant to admit their differences with Sorel, no doubt because of the prestige which Sorel enjoyed in wider Italian intellectual circles. Once Sorel had made available his theory of the social myth, some of the Italian syndicalists were tempted to take advantage of it, applying it to any type of nonrational motivation. Leone's hedonistic motivation might be considered rational, but the proletariat's will to realize its own values involved sentiment and passion, so the syndicalists sometimes portrayed the revolutionary transformation in Sorelian language.[112] However, since their own syndicalism, with its stress on lucidity, was ultimately incompatible with myth, their use of the concept was invariably confused and awkward. Gradually the syndicalists came to admit that they had never really embraced the categories of Sorel's mature conception. We have seen that by 1918 Panunzio was explicitly distinguishing Italian from Sorelian syndicalism; this divergence culminated in Enrico Leone's postwar attacks first on Sorel in *Il neomarxismo: Sorel e Marx* and then on the philosophical underpinnings of Sorel's mature syndicalism in *Anti-Bergson*. Of course, Leone was especially likely to reject Sorel's ideas, since of all the Italian syndicalists he was the most concerned with economic analysis and the most determined to rely on economic motivation. Lanzillo and Orano found Sorel's approach temperamentally more congenial, yet even their ideas were ultimately incompatible with his. True to Sorel's earlier position, the Italian syndicalists continued to stress the key role for workers' organizations as both moral instruments and institutional alternatives to the bourgeois state. Sorel, however, under the influence of Bergson, began to place less emphasis on the values of organization and to seek the agency of moral regeneration elsewhere. Compared with Sorel's mature position, the Italian syndicalists' conception was a bit simplistic, but they ultimately could not accept the emphasis on myth as a motivating force and the links between myth and moral development so important in his revised theory.

Sorel found excessive rationalism to be both a source and a symptom of the contemporary decadence which the revolution was to overcome; the redemptive potential of the proletariat depended on its freedom from this excessive rationalism of the bourgeois order. Sorel admired the "primitive" qualities of mind which made the proletariat especially susceptible to myths.[113] He found the proletariat capable of the sublime and heroic sensibility which was crucial for moral renewal precisely because of these "myth-making" qualities of mind. The Italian syndicalists, on the other hand, did not find excessive rationalism at the root of bourgeois decadence, so the proletariat's ability to redeem society did not depend on nonrational qualities of mind. For Sorel, the sublime revolutionary spirit would underlie moral renewal.[114] For Italian syndicalism, the reverse would be true: the new morality would be the source of the proletariat's will to a new order. The Italians expected a new morality from group suggestion and experience, not from heroic, warlike passions, not from the revolutionary spirit itself.

We have seen that the syndicalists from the beginning had wanted to transcend anarchist conceptions of revolution; Marxism came as a revelation because it seemed a more precise, scientific kind of socialism. As participants in the revision of Marxism, of course, the syndicalists focused on the psychological development of the proletariat, rather than on the internal contradictions of capitalism. But they continued, consistently enough, to criticize anarchism and all catastrophic conceptions of revolution. Socialist voluntarism did not have to mean mysticism and non-rational motivation. Since the Italian syndicalists remained strongly positivistic, it is not surprising that Sorel's conception of socialism as a mystery, its coming as a catastrophe baffling description, ultimately proved abhorrent to them.[115] Panunzio argued that syndicalism would cure the Italian workers of their previous quasi-anarchistic socialist beliefs; with the advent of syndicalism, he said, socialism was no longer a matter of religion and faith, but a matter of lucidity and real capacity.[116] Writing in 1908, Labriola found Sorel's theory of myth ingenious but clearly subversive of Marxism's attempt to dissolve myths and illusions by getting at the material bases of truth.[117] In his memoirs of 1939, he recalled the Italian syndicalist skepticism about the Bergsonian elements in Sorel and reaffirmed a basic principle: "Myths, fables, and revelations are precisely the contrary of socialism, which proposes to teach individuals as such to fashion for themselves their own lives, and in thus constructing their lives, to see within themselves as in clear, transparent water."[118] This lucidity was a constant syndicalist ideal; if the worker was to make a revolution and create socialism, he had to understand precisely and cognitively the nature of the process and his own role in it. Since, in the Sorelian conception, a transformation motivated by myth would not necessarily produce any of the situations foreseen in the myth,[119] the Italian syndicalists wondered why a revolution based on myth could be expected to create socialism. To them, this conception seemed dangerously close to old-fashioned catastrophic conceptions of revolution, while, for Sorel, the problem dissolved, because the myth-making mind was also the morality-making mind. Morality for Sorel was incompatible with rationalism; indeed, myth and morality would grow together.

The syndicalists were no more fascinated with violence than they were with myth. The final expropriation of capitalism would probably be violent, and the proletariat would succeed only if more powerful than its adversaries. But violence was simply the moment of transition in revolution, the final test of proletarian capacities; it was not, in itself, creative. Nor did the Italian syndicalists argue that strikes had to be violent if they were to have a psychological impact. The exercise of violence had no intrinsic moral or creative value in Italian syndicalist theory.[120]

Finally, the elitism of Italian syndicalism was not so much a cult and goal as a tactic and instrument. Following Pareto, the syndicalists argued that revolutionary change in history occurs only when new elites emerge to impose their new values on the inert remainder of society. So a creative minority would have to lead; to wait for a majority could only undermine the possibility of a genuinely new order.[121] The syndicalist conception implied that some measure of mobilization and indoctrination would ultimately be required to enable the new elite to instill its values. But the syndicalists were emphasizing the essential role of elites only in periods of revolutionary transition, not in society in general. They were not advocates of permanent elitism, but socialists who believed that man as such was capable of internalizing the superior values which a new elite offers society. The elite, then, would be open; ultimately its values and attributes would become universal. Here the syndicalists departed from Pareto, as we will see in more detail in chapter seven.

It has been argued that the elitism of Olivetti and Panunzio meant the authoritarian leadership of "a minority of class conscious leaders" over the rest of the proletariat in the revolutionary process itself.[122] From this perspective, syndicalist elitism converged with the revolutionary vanguard conceptions of Mussolini and, ultimately, Lenin. But the syndicalists did not envision a manipulative relationship between elites and followers within the revolutionary movement. All the organized workers had the potential for elite status; the organized industrial proletariat would make the revolution on its own, imposing on an inert society the new values it embodied. After 1906, since the workers' organizations were not proving equally receptive to revolutionary syndicalist ideas, the syndicalists had to admit that the organized industrial workers would not all attain elite status simultaneously. For the moment, the workers of Parma, for example, formed an elite within the industrial proletariat because they were particularly syndicalist in orientation. But never did the syndicalists foresee a revolution in which the enlightened workers would lead while the much larger number of nonsyndicalist workers followed. The syndicalists did not deny the function of leadership or propose a cult of mass spontaneity, but there would be no qualitative distinction in consciousness or value between whatever leaders emerged during the revolutionary transition and their followers.

Despite its eclecticism and revisionism, then, Italian syndicalism cannot be explained either as a reversion to outmoded insurrectionary traditions or as a modern irrationalist heresy. The syndicalists genuinely desired—and tried—to work within the Marxist tradition. But theirs was bound to be an unstable variety of Marxism, since their populist underpinnings were never far from the surface, and since it was not clear that convincing diagnoses of Italian problems could be found through Marxist categories. Despite tensions and obvious inconsistencies, however, the syndicalists clung to Marxism until about 1910, because it was easier, psychologically and intellectually, than probing the troubling Italian problems on their own terms. Those problems, they told themselves, could be understood in terms of Marxism's universalistic categories. Capitalism was at the root of the divorce between individual and society in Italy, and between the public and private spheres of the individual's existence; capitalism determined the exploitative character of the Italian state, which was merely an instrument for the interests of the bourgeoisie. At the same time, the syndicalists portrayed the revolution in essentially economic terms, as the expropriation of capitalism by the workers.[123] And they believed in international proletarian solidarity. Insofar as Italy had some peculiar, "prebourgeois" problems, these could also be understood in Marxist terms—as feudal leftovers.

But some of the syndicalists' intuitions about what was wrong with Italy could not be satisfactorily explained in Marxist terms, even though Marxism was the most attractive doctrine of radical change available. In analyzing the Italian state, the syndicalists followed the standard line of criticism developed over the past several decades by both conservatives and radicals: the state promoted the protectionism, the high military spending, the electoral and bureaucratic corruption which skewed Italian economic development and degraded Italian public life.[124] In analyzing these patterns, Olivetti noted the existence of a parasitical "political class," dependent on the state and independent of the usual economic classes, yet he still found this class to be a product of the normal Marxist class struggle.[125] But if the state was the expression of a new, ill-defined political class, and not the tool of the capitalist bourgeoisie, could it really be understood in Marxist terms— and overcome through a Marxist revolution? The syndicalists were not yet ready for such questions. When they sought to explain the unhealthy features of the Italian state, they withdrew into their Marxist framework, portraying the state simply as the organ of political domination for the capitalist bourgeoisie.[126] Nevertheless, the syndicalists repeatedly strayed from the basics of Marxism, contending that the state, rather than the capitalist substructure, was the fundamental enemy, that its destruction was the basic goal of the revolution.[127]

The Italian state hardly seemed the vehicle of a vigorous productive middle class; it was rather the corrupter of Italy's bourgeoisie. The class charged in classical Marxism with the task of developing Italy economically was not fulfilling its historic function. Lacking entrepreneurial energy, its members clung to state favors for their economic well-being.[128] But Italian bourgeois decadence was, for the syndicalists, only one aspect of a deeper problem of the Italian character itself. In his introductory article to the first issue of *Pagine libere*, Olivetti expressed very clearly this gnawing syndicalist concern: " . . . the virus of all the foreign dominations still runs in our veins; our outlook is still degraded by all the humiliations we have suffered; the cunning we learned in the age of servitude takes the place of real competence in us. We are still dragging behind us the rags of our baroque and Arcadian seventeenth century; nor have we yet dusted from our backs the filthy powder of our frivolous eighteenth century; we still have in our veins the Papacy, the Saracens, the Spaniards, Aretino, Loyola, and our shoulders still ache from the Croat's club."[129] A petty anarchical individualism, a lack of organization and discipline, and a propensity for parasitical, exploitative activity seemed to the syndicalists somehow characteristic of the modern Italian. Panunzio, writing in 1905, found the Italians "accustomed to the academy and infected with the spirit of the Baroque seventeenth century," and went on to warn that "we are not an *orderly* and *organizing* people, but a disorderly and disorganizing race." Olivetti cited "the monotony of our traditional national *dolce far niente* [sweet idleness]," while Paolo Orano satirized the parasitical mentality and social uselessness of Italy's swarms of lawyers.[130]

In discussing the transition to the new order, the syndicalists emphasized change in political forms and social values, not economic revolution to change the organization of the means of production. Alighiero Ciattini, for example, contrasted the emerging syndicalist solidarity not with the ethics of capitalism, but with the narrow sectarianism underlying the behavior of political parties.[131] At first, the syndicalist divergence from Marxism appears only a matter of emphasis, for obviously Marxists too are concerned about solving the problems of political exploitation and social atomization they see in liberal bourgeois society. But in fact, the divergence was more profound, for it concerned the autonomy—and thus the sources—of those extra-economic problems. The syndicalists' emphases suggested that those problems were autonomous, problems in their own right, and not, as in Marxism, derivative of the economic substructure. But if they were autonomous, those problems could be—indeed, had to be—attacked directly. And this in turn raised questions about how much of the Marxist blueprint for solution, focusing on the role of the proletariat and on changes in economic organization, really had to be followed. It was by no means clear that a mechanism for overthrowing capitalism was required, nor was it clear that the proletariat had to play the lead role.

The syndicalists' initial doctrine was abstract and riddled with tensions, because, in their desperate search for solutions, they fastened onto a mechanism for revolution that kept them from thinking clearly about the nature of the problems to be solved. They liked the new values and institutions that emerged from the proletariat's struggle against capitalism, so it seemed necessary to insist that capitalism was the basic problem in society—and the target of revolution. In fact, however, those new values and institutions were appealing because they seemed antidotes to an altogether different set of problems. Focusing on capitalism prevented the syndicalists from explaining those problems, and thus from determining which aspects of the revolutionary process they envisioned were essential and which were secondary and contingent.

The initial syndicalist vision responded to genuine Italian and liberal problems, but in a hopelessly abstract and utopian way. Still, elements of this conception could be developed further, producing greater theoretical clarity and a more effective practical program. It was possible, for example, to devise ways of basing political life on a network of socioeconomic organizations, decentralizing decision making and strengthening social discipline, without all the excesses of revolutionary syndicalism. But the syndicalists had to be clearer about what they were trying to do if they were to offer a more realistic blueprint for solving the problems that had bothered them all along.

The failures in practice which the syndicalists encountered after 1904 revealed the inadequacies of their doctrine—both the revolutionary syndicalist emphasis on vigorous class struggle, and the Marxist interpretation of Italy's problems. Frustration and defeat soon forced the syndicalists to confront more explicitly the problems that had made them alienated radicals in the first place. By the time they became fascists, they understood both their underlying objective and the obstacles to its fulfillment more clearly than they had during the orthodox period of revolutionary syndicalism in Italy. But the syndicalists never abandoned their quest for the kind of society which found utopian expression in their vision of a syndicalist future—a disciplined, closely knit society of producers governing itself through economically based organizations, with no need for old-fashioned politics. This was the goal they proposed for fascism.

4 / The Corruption of the Proletariat

In introducing the Italian translation of Sorel's *Reflections on Violence* in 1907, Benedetto Croce gave Sorel credit for identifying the central uncertainty of modern socialism—the question of how the proletariat was to develop the capacity to institute a superior order.[1] According to socialist theory, the proletariat was to play the kind of historical role the bourgeoisie had played when it led European civilization beyond feudalism, demonstrating great courage, ability, and idealism in the process. But it was questionable whether the proletariat was developing comparable attributes. Croce reminded his readers that the socialist labor movement could be of transcendent historical interest only if it was preparing to create something new, not if it was merely a force for material improvement within the existing order. By 1911, Croce felt that further experience had closed the matter; he pronounced socialism dead in a widely discussed interview in *La voce*.[2] Socialism could have emerged only according to the syndicalist blueprint, from within the labor movement, but the labor organizations were concerned solely with immediate material advantage. If the proletariat was not interested in socialism, hopes for a socialist society had no basis. Croce noted that the Italian syndicalist intellectuals were turning away from the usual socialist concerns and were developing instead a critique of the modern parliamentary state.

Croce and Sorel had known each other since 1895, when Croce agreed to collaborate on Sorel's new review, *Devenir social*; they began a long correspondence that same year. In a letter just after the *La voce* interview was published, Sorel endorsed Croce's observations on the death of socialism, and indeed he was coming to the same conclusion himself.[3] Writing to Mario Missiroli the previous November, he lamented that "syndicalism is falling apart" and claimed to be "happy no longer to have any connection with the revolutionary movement."[4] In letters to Croce early in 1911, Sorel complained that the existing system had succeeded in absorbing the workers, and especially their leaders, by offering political and economic advantages.[5] As a result, the socialist labor movement was no longer of interest to philosophers, and Sorel resolved to write nothing further on the subject.

A series of defeats had by now forced the Italian syndicalists into a similar disillusionment, dissolving the bright hopes of 1904. During 1905 there was considerable dispute in the Italian labor movement about the validity of the syndicalist strategy, with its emphasis on militant strikes. Dissension between syndicalists, whose strength lay primarily in the locally based chambers of labor, and reformists, who were stronger in the more modern trade federations, linking workers of a particular industry, soon undermined the effectiveness of the major coordinating body in the Italian labor movement, the Central Resistance Secretariat. In April 1905, the secretariat's refusal to declare a general strike of solidarity contributed to the disastrous failure of a railroad strike which the syndicalists supported. Despite syndicalist protests that this strike, with its poor showing of worker solidarity, was not a fair test, the reformists were able to convert many organizers and workers in the aftermath by insisting that the strike's outcome proved the folly of syndicalist methods.[6]

During 1905 and 1906, the reformists defeated the syndicalists again and again in the Italian labor organizations. The syndicalists even lost control of the Milan Chamber of Labor, their major foothold in the vitally important Milanese labor movement, early in 1906. By October of 1906, when the General Confederation of Labor (CGL) was founded, the syndicalists were clearly a declining minority in Italian labor; the reformists dominated the new confederation from the beginning. Despite its formal independence, the CGL soon implicitly recognized the political suzerainty of the Socialist party and concerned itself primarily with the immediate economic well-being of its members, not with overall socialist strategy.[7] Syndicalist ideas remained influential only in a few scattered organizations, especially in the chambers of labor of Parma, Ferrara, and Piacenza, in one of the railroad unions (the Sindacato Ferrovieri), and in the Merchant Seamen's Union.

At the same time, the syndicalists were faring no better on the political level. Their tactical alliance with Enrico Ferri quickly broke down as the syndicalist doctrine became more coherent and as the party suffered electoral defeat in the wake of the general strike of September 1904. The opportunistic Ferri began moving toward the center, dissociating himself from the increasingly unpopular syndicalists and finding political allies in other sectors of the party. By October 1906, when the party held its national congress at Rome, Ferri had put together an ambiguous but still nonreformist majority which excluded the syndicalists altogether. By now syndicalism was growing isolated, numbering only about 5,000 of the 34,000 members of the party.[8]

Shaken by these defeats, the syndicalists sought to regroup and to reexamine their strategy at a congress of their own, including both organizers and intellectuals, held at Ferrara in June 1907. Over the objections of Enrico Leone, they decided to abandon the Socialist party altogether and formed a Federation of Autonomous Syndicalist Groups to coordinate syndicalist activities. The party returned the favor at its national congress of 1908: the reformists regained the majority, and revolutionary syndicalism, deemed irresponsible and insurrectionary, was officially declared heretical.[9] It was harder for the syndicalists to contemplate formal schism on the trade union level, however, so the syndicalist congress of 1907 decided not to form a new confederation of revolutionary syndicalist labor organizations to compete with the CGL. The struggle against the reformists, most felt, could best be waged from within the existing confederation, so the syndicalist organizations were to remain or become CGL members. In fact, however, revolutionary syndicalism made virtually no headway within the CGL. Determined to maintain their hegemony, the reformist leaders of the confederation refused to admit solidly syndicalist organizations like the Parma Chamber of Labor.[10] They did admit syndicalist organizations with strong reformist minorities, hoping that CGL affiliation would help the reformists to overturn the syndicalist leadership. These syndicalist organizations had little effect on CGL policy, although most managed to retain their syndicalist orientation. Given these frustrations, the question of unity or schism remained a source of uncertainty and division for the syndicalists until a rival confederation was finally formed in 1912.

A series of major syndicalist strikes took place during 1907 and 1908, but the outcome only furthered the disillusionment in Italian syndicalism. The most publicized was the strike at Parma, involving mostly agrarian workers, which Alceste De Ambris and the local chamber of labor led during May and June of 1908. The syndicalists had led a more limited strike to success in Parma in May 1907, and both employers and workers had spent months preparing for the renewal that came a year later. The strike began, in fact, when the landowners' association imposed a lockout on the organized agricultural day laborers. The ensuing strike was especially "syndicalist" in tone, because it seemed so clearly a battle in an ongoing class war. Despite almost two months of remarkable discipline and solidarity, however, the strike failed to produce the tangible gains that were its immediate objective.[11] De Ambris and syndicalists elsewhere tried to make the best of the defeat by emphasizing the strike's educational value and long-term revolutionary significance, but the workers themselves were skeptical. The unfavorable outcome produced a disastrous drop in the membership of the Parma Chamber of Labor, from 28,719 on January 1, 1908, to 7,034 on January 1, 1909.[12] De Ambris fled to Switzerland and would return to Italy only in 1913.

The pattern of events in Ferrara and Piacenza, two other major syndicalist centers, was similarly unfavorable to syndicalism from 1907 to 1910. Here, too, initial successes in achieving relatively limited goals produced confidence and expanding membership. But a second phase quickly followed, as the unions stepped up their demands and the employers prepared for more concerted resistance. In each area, the outcome was a major unsuccessful strike, producing huge membership losses, frustration, and finally stagnation by 1909 and 1910.[13] The syndicalists simply had not devised a viable tactic, one combining tangible benefits with revolutionary psychological development.

With their movement in crisis, the syndicalists sought to regroup at two consecutive meetings in Bologna in December 1910. The Second Italian Syndicalist Congress, in the tradition of the Ferrara meeting of 1907, included individual syndicalists and delegates of about sixty syndicalist intellectual and propaganda groups; the Second Congress of Direct Action, a follow-up of a similar meeting held in 1909, included the representatives of syndicalist unions and had responsibility for strategy on the economic level. The major fruit of these meetings was a Committee for Direct Action, established by the union leaders to coordinate the activities of the syndicalist organizations within the CGL. The new entity did little during its first year, but as the cracks in the Giolittian edifice widened with the Libyan War of 1911–12, the committee began to step up its activities, attacking the reformist majority in the CGL for its hesitancy in light of the wartime challenge. Friction between the syndicalists and reformists grew so intense during the spring of 1912 that the CGL finally declared adherence to the Committee for Direct Action incompatible with CGL membership.[14] Meanwhile, the committee was reestablished on firmer footing as the syndicalists finally began moving toward schism.

In a series of bitterly polemical articles, Alceste De Ambris condemned the CGL for its increasingly hard line against syndicalist organizations and for its continuing refusal to admit the Parma Chamber of Labor.[15] He sought to blame the CGL for the coming schism in the organized working class, but he had no doubt such a division was necessary. Illusions about the viability of unity had only paralyzed syndicalism, and it was time to overcome qualms about schism and organize a rival confederation. When the syndicalists were ousted from the Milanese Chamber of Labor early in 1912, Filippo Corridoni insisted, like De Ambris, that it was no longer possible to ignore the existence of two irreconcilable mentalities in the Italian proletariat—the one revolutionary and syndicalist, the other legalistic and reformist.[16]

Finally, in November 1912, the schism in the Italian labor movement became formal: a variety of antireformist organizations, including anarchists and republicans as well as syndicalists, joined together at Modena to form the Unione Sindacale Italiana (USI). After six years of hesitation and vacillation, this definitive break with the GCL provided a major boost to syndicalist confidence, but the future remained clouded, partly because it was not clear how effective such a heterogeneous confederation could be.[17] Nor had the syndicalists begun to reverse the membership losses of the previous years. The USI represented about 100,000 workers, while the syndicalists alone had represented about 200,000 as of late 1907.[18] The new USI had little more than one-fourth the numerical strength of the GCL.

In 1912 and 1913, however, syndicalism seemed to be gaining again in the industrial cities, where some of the workers were becoming more militant in response to the growing crisis of the Giolittian compromise. In Turin, for example, reformists had effectively excluded syndicalism from the labor movement after some defeated strikes in 1907, but by 1911 membership losses and financial problems were clearly weakening the reformist organizations vis-à-vis the increasingly militant employers. Some of the auto workers split off from their reformist federation and turned to syndicalism for an alternative, but the poorly conceived strike which the syndicalists led early in 1912 quickly discredited syndicalism in the eyes of the workers once again. The strike lasted an impressive sixty-five days, but a well-organized lockout finally forced the workers to settle on disastrous terms, including the loss of gains previously won. Bitter recriminations against syndicalism followed among the Turinese workers.[19]

In Milan, too, what seemed a promising revival of revolutionary syndicalism in the labor movement quickly fizzled. By early 1913, sectors of the organized industrial proletariat were growing frustrated with reformism as the employers became increasingly intransigent in wage disputes. Filippo Corridoni and his Unione Sindacale Milanese (USM), founded in March 1913, offered the militant tactical alternative which the situation seemed to require. Although Corridoni won considerable support for a series of militant strikes in Milan during the summer of 1913, effective employer lockouts and reformist opposition eventually produced defeat here as well. Corridoni himself was arrested and jailed for inciting to violence during the strike wave of 1913. On the eve of Red Week and war in 1914, Corridoni's organization in Milan was clearly in crisis.[20] As usual, the unsuccessful outcome of the 1913 strikes had caused a disastrous decline in membership and had led the USM to the verge of bankruptcy. It suspended publication of its newspaper and even applied to the Socialist city government for a subsidy and for office space. At one point, the USM sought membership in the CGL—without success.

On the national level, there was already considerable disillusionment and frustration in the USI by December 1913, when the organization held its second national congress. Writing just after this meeting, Tullio Masotti articulated explicitly syndicalist anxieties for the future, lamenting the ongoing problems of finance, membership, and regional imbalance.[21] The congress had decided to transfer the seat of the USI from Parma to more industrial Milan, but financial problems forced the organization to postpone the move indefinitely.[22] By 1914, it was clear that the vision in 1912 of a second chance for syndicalism had been only a mirage. Militant tactics continued to make syndicalism its own worst enemy. But it was not obvious that reformist tactics were more likely to produce a new order.

All the failures after early 1905 led the syndicalists to emphasize elitism and to stress that the revolution was a long way off, but not to abandon the essentials of their revolutionary strategy. For the time being, in the labor movement, they could only work harder at syndicalist organization and practice, so they stubbornly continued to exhort the working class and to promote militant strikes. The fact that syndicalism was presently confined to a conscious elite within the proletariat was a symptom of weakness, not a source of virtue.[23] All the discussion about "elitism" in syndicalist circles during these years concerned not ultimate values or goals, but merely the tactical question of working class schism or unity. Tommaso Sorricchio criticized the elitism of Olivetti and others because he favored continued unity within the CGL, while those calling for schism wanted to face up to the fact that syndicalism was presently confined to a minority.[24]

Since 1907 the syndicalists had faced tactical choices not only on the level of trade union activity, but also on the political level. Here there was apparently more scope for innovation in response to the failure of syndicalism to convert most of the working class. The situation seemed to call for some sort of supplementary, more purely political activity—beyond work in the labor movement. The nature of this supplementary activity depended on the nature of the obstacles impeding evolution according to the syndicalist blueprint. So we must consider the syndicalists' attempts to understand these obstacles before examining the political departures they were beginning to discuss at the same time.

Beginning in 1906, with the founding of the CGL, the syndicalists complained sporadically that the organized workers, despite a few inspiring exceptions, were proving depressingly reformist and un-heroic—more concerned about immediate economic gains than about the creation of socialism.[25] By 1910, such disillusionment had become the dominant note in all syndicalist discussion. The organizer Enrico Loncao, for example, complained that the solidarity and self-sacrifice so crucial for the creation of socialism were seldom evident in the Italian labor movement: "All the proletarian agitations, whether led by syndicalists or not, have found their inevitable and fatal outcome in increases in salaries and in some decrease in working hours. Whenever a question of general import for the proletarian class has arisen (a killing, a violation of the right to strike or of the right of association and so forth), the proletariat has remained indifferent or almost so."[26]

In 1904, the organized labor movement had seemed so promising, so pregnant with new energies and virtues; why had it ended up repudiating syndicalism? Through reformism, the syndicalists claimed, the present system had corrupted the most advanced elements of the Italian working class. It turned out that the proletariat, too, could win favors from the parliamentary state, thanks to its links with the Socialist party. The organized workers had succumbed to bourgeois materialism, so Italian socialism was nothing but a parliamentary sham, another narrow interest group, hardly the bearer of superior values for society.[27]

For now, the syndicalists were not willing to conclude that they had been on the wrong track in the first place. The model was sound, they assumed, but unforeseen problems, apparently of a political and cultural sort, had obstructed evolution according to the model. Still, new questions about the problems in Italian society were necessary—and so perhaps was a supplementary program to overcome those obstacles. Since individual syndicalists differed over what had gone wrong and over what should be done, dissension and even fragmenta-tion of the syndicalist current resulted, especially after 1910. There was some divergence between intellectuals and organizers, and there were contacts between syndicalists and other critics of the established order. Subsequent developments would prove, however, that the fragmenta-tion was not irrevocable and that the syndicalists, while asking new questions, were not losing their intellectual autonomy. They recon-verged in the struggle for intervention in 1914, and they subsequently sought to weave into a new synthesis the insights and proposals that had been developed during the period of fragmentation.

The one major syndicalist who diverged from the mainstream for good during this period was Arturo Labriola. He understood the rea-sons for the failure of syndicalism in different terms than his colleagues and thus called for a different form of supplementary activity. When we see how the others differed from Labriola, we will begin to grasp the basis of the revision that would lead to fascism.

Labriola was one of the first to admit that syndicalism was not working out in practice. In 1906, he ceased publishing *Avanguardia socialista* and returned to Naples, where he developed a successful law practice and taught economics at the university. He remained active in syndicalist intellectual circles, serving as coeditor of Olivetti's *Pagine libere* from its inception in December 1906 until 1909, but he was increasingly divorced from the practice of revolutionary syndicalism in the labor movement. At the syndicalist congress at Ferrara in 1907, Labriola went along with the decision to leave the Socialist party without enthusiasm or confidence in the future.[28] And now he began the reappraisal that would lead him to diverge from his colleagues and to win, first, election to the Chamber of Deputies in 1913 and, second, appointment as Minister of Labor in Giolitti's postwar government of 1920.

Labriola remained a syndicalist in theory, but Italy, he felt, was simply not ready for syndicalism, which could only be put off for the future. He insisted on syndicalist orthodoxy, refusing to tamper with the doctrine, and argued that there was nothing to be done directly to promote syndicalism at the moment. He had serious misgivings about the practice of revolutionary syndicalism under organizers like De Ambris and Corridoni. The great Parma strike of 1908, for example, gave him no comfort, since the workers involved were overwhelmingly agrarian; syndicalism could emerge only within the most advanced sectors of the industrial proletariat. Excessive use of the general strike, he feared, was discrediting syndicalism in the eyes of the working class.[29] But still much could be done at present—and had to be done if syndicalism was ever to emerge in Italy.

Labriola sought to determine what the immediate problems were, and what had gone wrong with the syndicalist blueprint, in his perceptive dissection of the Italian political system, *Storia di dieci anni*, published in 1910. In pages that can still be read with profit today, he showed how important sectors of the new industrial proletariat had emerged together with sectors of the new industrial bourgeoisie under the umbrella of the tariff of 1887, with all that it implied about the relationship between the economy and the state in Italy.[30] Virtually from birth, much of the working class was thus involved in the network linking industry to the state through protection and military orders. The advent of Giolitti, Labriola argued, meant the political triumph of these new industrial sectors after the old political class, represented by Crispi and Pelloux, had been proven bankrupt during the crisis of the

1890s. But while Giolitti was genuinely a departure, he ended up encouraging the unhealthy, speculative propensities of the Italian industrial bourgeoisie, rather than the productive potential that had recently become evident. The Giolittian system was simply a network of favors for groups with political strength, including the Socialists; and the Socialists, in working with Giolitti, had helped to maintain a system which not only impeded rational economic development, but also exploited the South.[31]

Labriola was coming to agree with Salvemini about the basis of present problems and about the strategy for radical change appropriate in the short term. In *Storia di dieci anni*, he quoted at length, and with explicit approval, Salvemini's analysis of the Giolittian system.[32] Like Salvemini, Labriola concluded that socialists should devote their efforts to structural reforms, focusing on the South. Turati's brand of reformism could not produce serious change, but there was still a place in Italy for a different kind of reformist bloc, including progressive bourgeois sectors as well as socialists and workers.[33] In Labriola's practice, socialism and radical democracy became interchangeable as he sought to galvanize broad popular support for an attack on immediate southern problems, such as illiteracy, the land tenure system, and poor communications. The obvious institutional base for this effort was not the industrial labor movement, but parliament, which Labriola entered in 1913 as a deputy representing Naples. He was leaving revolutionary syndicalism far behind. De Ambris's *L'internazionale* commented on Labriola's election campaign with a mixture of sadness and sarcasm.[34] The syndicalist newspaper proclaimed Labriola's reform proposals to be incompatible with the syndicalism he still claimed to profess; the new monopolies he advocated, for example, would only strengthen the state. And Georges Sorel, in a letter to Mario Missiroli in the aftermath of the 1913 election, expressed continued admiration for Labriola's intellectual prowess, but wondered what Labriola could possibly hope to accomplish as a member of the Italian Chamber of Deputies.[35]

Although Labriola's evolution was in part a return to his radical populist origins, he still sought to portray Italy's problems and the process of change he advocated in reasonably orthodox Marxist terms. The South was so backward because the Spaniards and the Bourbons had systematically obstructed the formation of a capitalist bourgeoisie. In Italy in general, syndicalist socialism was presently impossible because the bourgeoisie had not yet fully triumphed, creating a genuine liberal-democratic order. When Labriola sought to explain the persistence of prebourgeois elements in contemporary Italy, including the unhealthy relationship between politics and economics and the pecu-

liarities of Italian parliamentary government, he pinpointed the monarchy as the essential problem. The monarchical, not the parliamentary,
side of the Italian state was responsible for the obstacles to syndicalism.[36] Thus Labriola was willing to work within parliament, collaborating with progressive bourgeois elements, to reform the system, to
dilute the power of the monarchy, and to complete the bourgeois
revolution. Only in this way, he argued, could socialists remove the
obstacles to normal progress toward a new society.[37]

In his quest for reforms, Labriola was willing to serve in Giolitti's
postwar government as Minister of Labor, but he continued to view
events in terms of a reasonably orthodox Marxist perspective. He
found Italian fascism, for example, to be symptomatic of a general
postwar crisis of international capitalism. In relatively backward countries, the insecure capitalist bourgeoisie found it necessary to supplement its economic dictatorship with political dictatorship.[38]

By 1913, Labriola was well along the road that would lead him into
Giolitti's government in 1920 and into exile as an antifascist a few years
later. At the same time, however, many other syndicalists were making
the first tentative steps in a revision that would lead them to fascism.
They responded to the impasse of syndicalism in a more innovative—
and more treacherous—way, because they doubted that the corrupting
patterns which Labriola had identified could be understood so easily,
in traditional Marxist terms. They felt that it was not the monarchy that
lay at the root of the unhealthy features of the Italian state, but the
parliamentary system. Parliamentary government and the Italian political class seemed to be autonomous problems which eluded explanation in Marxist terms. As the expected evolution toward syndicalism
bogged down, the syndicalists' critique of the existing political system
deepened, becoming more central to their position.

Given the nature of Italy's political problems, catch-up reforms
did not seem to offer a way out, although years would pass before the
syndicalists would begin to define precisely what was necessary instead. Ultimately, however, they would not fall into Labriola's dualism,
making syndicalism a distant ideal unrelated to immediate Italian political practice. They sought to refine syndicalism, to make it the basis
for solving the problems that had impeded syndicalism in the first
place. If the problem was monarchy, as Labriola believed, then parliamentary democracy was the solution and syndicalism had to wait; but
if the problem was parliament, then perhaps a redefined syndicalism
could be the solution.

Labriola's orthodox categories were attractive, however, since they
were familiar and easy to grasp and since it was not clear how to devise an alternative. The syndicalists sometimes sounded like Labriola,

blaming the monarchy and the forces it nurtured for what seemed to be only prebourgeois lags in Italian political and economic life. In his *Sindacalismo e repubblica*, published posthumously in 1921 but circulating in syndicalist and Milanese leftist circles by 1915, Filippo Corridoni vacillated, sometimes accenting Italy's precapitalist backwardness, sometimes implying that the problems of liberal Italy were modern and autonomous. Nevertheless, Corridoni's tone differed from Labriola's; he was moving, haltingly and reluctantly, toward a new conception.

Corridoni began his diagnosis in orthodox fashion, emphasizing the power of the prebourgeois elements, especially the monarchy, which had kept both parliamentary government and the industrial bourgeoisie relatively weak in Italy.[39] But there were tensions in Corridoni's account, for the villain responsible for the unhealthy features of Italian political life seemed to be a political class that was a product neither of backwardness nor of modern capitalism:[40]

. . . the state is always controlled, as Mosca has shown convincingly, by a "political class" composed of a handful of people who make of politics an unscrupulous profession and who, while originating from bourgeois stock, are more or less the excess or dross of the productive bourgeoisie itself.

In order to maintain their own power, these elements need to keep the active bourgeoisie far from the management of the state, and they succeed in doing so by favoring not its virtues and strengths, but its vices and weaknesses.[41]

Corridoni considered monarchical states especially prone to this pattern, although he did not explain why. But in any case, the political problem for him was not merely a function of monarchy and backwardness, but something more modern and hard to explain, perhaps having to do with the parliamentary system itself. In using Mosca, in fact, Corridoni was well on his way to a postorthodox interpretation of the problem of the Italian state.

Corridoni believed that Italian society was capable of something better, but the dominant political patterns undermined its potential, draining its energies and resources for unproductive uses.[42] As a way out, he called for decentralization, for greater democracy to highlight the futility of the parliamentary system, even for a republic. But the key was to overturn protection and the whole set of corrupting relationships between the political and economic spheres in Italy. Free trade, Corridoni argued bravely, would ruin two-thirds of Italy's industry, but he found such a thorough purge essential if "that bit of vitality and health that our economic organism still has" was to be saved.[43]

Proletarian pressures, including violence, could have stimulated Italy's inert bourgeoisie, but Corridoni argued that the proletariat, too, had been corrupted by the political system. For the time being, the workers were part of the problem, so some sort of supplementary movement was needed to bring about the essential changes. Sensing that Labriola's reforms, pursued through parliament, would not be sufficient, Corridoni suggested, very tentatively, that a preliminary revolution might be necessary instead.[44] This would be a revolution in which the proletariat would have no direct role. By implication, since the problem was centered in the present political system, this revolution would make radical political changes, attacking the political class and perhaps even the parliamentary system itself.

As the syndicalists sought to determine what had gone wrong, the parliamentary state began to seem the major obstacle. But since the bourgeois groups represented in parliament were not promoting rational industrial development, the parliamentary state could hardly be portrayed in orthodox Marxist terms, as the executive committee of the capitalist bourgeoisie. And if the state's class character was not to blame, why was it that the liberal parliamentary state neither represented nor protected the collective interest? The problem of the Italian state led Corridoni to move, very hesitantly, beyond the old orthodoxy; Paolo Mantica went a bit farther in the antiparliamentary polemics he wrote between 1910 and 1914.

Mantica sought to explain the connection between parliamentary politics and the weakness of Italian society. The liberal regime was "a system of greedy and pervasive exploitation which has transformed Italy into a kind of insurance company which has the Chamber of Deputies as its general headquarters. Everyone applies there; the glances of all the greedy and all the starving are directed there, and there the deputies tower as the indispensable intermediaries, the supreme dispensers of the national manna."[45] In Italy parliamentary government "has constantly increased the monopolizing tendency of the state and has discouraged or impeded any spontaneous activity: ultimately, it has founded an anonymous, oppressive tyranny of the basest minority of politicians. . . . The parliamentary system can maintain itself only because of the situation of social disorganization and the crisis of languor that social life is going through."[46]

Writing in Orano's *La lupa* in 1911, Mantica described this spirit of parasitism as the essential characteristic of any parliamentary regime, whether monarchist or republican.[47] He sensed that he had discovered an autonomous problem, one that could not be reduced either to problems of capitalism or to prebourgeois remnants in Italy. The other syndicalists were beginning to see the situation in similar terms. According to Alfonso De Pietri-Tonelli, parliamentary government "has put the state in the hands of a class of bureaucrats and politicians . . .

who are not the direct expression of the bourgeois class."[48] It was this political class, and the political system generally, that had enervated Italian society and warped Italian economic development, undercutting the syndicalist model in the process.

It was possible to argue, of course, that parliamentary government was not very healthy in Italy because the country had not gone far enough along the road to democracy, and when Italy finally got universal manhood suffrage in 1912, some assumed that a happier era for parliamentary government was dawning. Arturo Labriola had enough faith in the prospects for parliament under the new suffrage law to stand for election to the Chamber in 1913. The advent of universal suffrage forced the other syndicalists to specify what they found inadequate about parliamentary government—and even to consider how syndicalism might provide the basis for an alternative.

Paolo Mantica discussed the matter explicitly in October 1913, in one of the most revealing syndicalist statements of the prewar period.[49] A significant combination of confidence and lack of confidence in popular political capacities informed Mantica's thinking. He wanted the popular will to determine public policy, but he denied that universal suffrage provided an adequate mechanism. The suffrage system enabled the individual to participate only in a passive and discontinuous way. In voting, the individual was subject to momentary caprice and to the most superficial and egotistical interests—and so did not really express his will. The state and the political process simply remained too distant from ordinary individuals. Consequently, Mantica concluded, universal suffrage would yield even more corruption and favoritism, as deputies pandered to the worst instincts of their constituents in order to get elected and reelected.

Although the alternative he had in mind was not at all clear, Mantica suggested, for the first time in the syndicalist literature, that syndicalism itself could provide an alternative to political participation based on universal suffrage and the parliamentary system. Rather than swallow the myths about democracy, Mantica argued, the workers should organize, should multiply the centers of life, will, and energy in society. He envisioned some sort of continuous political participation through socioeconomic organizations: "The genuine and lasting will of the individual can only be expressed in action. It is the man who acts, participating in an effective and continuous process, who is a social element, a component in the world of production, a citizen—not the man who thinks he is, simply because he exercises a vain and ephemeral right. Socially, this latter individual amounts to nothing at all."[50] Social organizations based on economic function offered the individual the continuous involvement and supraindividual framework for his activity that the liberal state was too remote to provide. Mantica found the necessary network of organizations already emerging in society. The society, in fact, was presently outgrowing the state, which could no longer "contain all the life of the people" and which thus had to be replaced—by the society itself, understood as a network of economically based organizations. Faith in universal suffrage and parliamentary democracy only prevented the full flowering of the necessary capacities in society.

Although his vision was imprecise, Mantica was sharpening the syndicalist focus on the problems in Italian society that had made syndicalism appealing in the first place. Popular political apathy and incompetence, which universal suffrage could not heal, made it possible for parliamentary corruption to go on; the existing state was too weak to order the society, including the economy. A new system of socio-economic self-government, based on economic organizations, could provide an antidote. Mantica was on his way to bridging the gap between syndicalism and immediate political problems that remained so wide in Labriola's thinking. Syndicalism was for now; it was relevant to immediate political problems and was not merely to be held in abeyance until those problems were overcome. At this point Mantica could offer only a cluster of images—social organization and energy, popular political capacity, continuous participation, productive activity —which he sensed were interrelated, even though he was not able to establish the links among them. The subsequent evolution of Italian syndicalism proved that this embryonic vision was capable of further development, both in theory and in practice.

Mantica's conception seemed to require a supplementary revolutionary force, outside the labor movement, but he remained tactically cautious, fearful of jeopardizing proletarian autonomy.[51] Some of his colleagues, however, were a bit more adventuresome.

In their meetings from 1907 on, the syndicalists had to choose a course of action not only for the trade union level, but also for the political level. As soon as they left the Socialist party in 1907, some of them began to contemplate a new political organization, something stronger than the loose and ineffective Federation of Syndicalist Groups created in 1907. By 1910, when the failure of syndicalist ideas in the unions had become obvious, there was increasing interest among the syndicalists in forming a revolutionary party to complement the labor movement. At first, the accents were orthodox: a revolutionary party was needed to educate the organized workers in the revolutionary syndicalist conception of socialism, the crucial task which the Socialist party, with its reformist orientation, could not be expected to carry out.

Such a party would have only this temporary pedagogical role; the labor syndicate was still the crucial organ of revolution.[52] As the syndicalists considered the obstacles to their original program, however, they began to contemplate a more grandiose kind of political supplement—a revolutionary bloc to clear away the obstacles as well as educate the workers. Even nonsyndicalist revolutionaries could participate. Still, such a bloc would not be intended to make the ultimate revolution, or to set itself up as a leadership cadre vis-à-vis the labor movement, but only to do whatever was necessary to make syndicalism possible.[53]

The proposals of Panunzio, Alfredo Polledro, and others for a syndicalist party grew sharp disagreement from more cautious syndicalists like Franz Weiss, Tommaso Sorricchio, and Enrico Leone, who were less willing to admit that revolutionary syndicalism in Italy was the creation of a group of intellectuals, not a spontaneous proletarian expression.[54] These syndicalists were more patient and more absolute in their commitment to the proletariat, but their inflexibility produced increasing ambiguity, since the workers showed so little interest in revolutionary syndicalism. If any organized proletarian expression is syndicalist, as Weiss argued in 1908, then disillusionment with the proletariat is impossible, and revolutionary syndicalism becomes indistinguishable from the revisionist laborism of Graziadei and Bissolati.[55] Weiss was implying that the proletariat could be syndicalist without being revolutionary, yet his own vision of the syndicalist future explicitly required certain new values which the existing Italian proletariat no longer seemed to be developing. In fact, these cautious syndicalists lamented Italian working class priorities just as bitterly as their more flexible colleagues did: Enrico Leone, for example, complained that the workers remained satisfied with the present system as long as their salaries increased.[56] Despite this disenchantment, however, Leone and his followers feared the consequences, especially for proletarian autonomy, of so uncertain an expedient as a revolutionary bloc or party.

These concerns were certainly plausible, but it was also plausible, and in some ways more consistent, to acknowledge that syndicalism did not necessarily coincide with the practice of the labor movement— and to conclude that supplementary activity might be legitimate. Still, this was a treacherous step, for those syndicalists who advocated a revolutionary party were implicitly admitting the contingency of their original commitment to the proletariat. During the first years of the century, its most advanced sectors had actually appeared to possess in embryo the qualities necessary to create a superior order. But syndicalist ideals and values were theoretically distinguishable from those of the proletariat; if the workers did not adopt the syndicalist vision as their own, they could have no claim to a special historical role—or even to the special solicitude of socialist intellectuals.

This basic difference in perspective led to much internal squabbling during the period of defeat and disillusionment. Labriola periodically accused Leone and his followers, like Weiss and Sorricchio, of an excessively conservative tactical position bordering on reformist laborism. These relatively conservative syndicalists, on the other hand, condemned their more militant colleagues for advocating outmoded Blanquist tactics and for treating the strike as a kind of mystical exercise.[57] Given the seriousness of these differences, it is not surprising that the Bologna congresses of 1910 only produced further disillusionment and dissension among the syndicalists.[58] Labriola advocated a syndicalist party, but the majority followed Leone and repudiated the proposal, invoking the sacred principle of proletarian autonomy.

Continued frustration, however, made supplementary political activity seem all the more necessary to some of the syndicalists. And in July 1912, an interesting new possibility developed. With the Giolittian system suffering severe strains, and with Italy involved in the Libyan War, the left wing of the Italian Socialist party won control from the reformists at the party's national congress at Reggio Emilia. One result was the rise to national prominence of a remarkable young Socialist journalist, Benito Mussolini, who soon was named to the influential editorship of *Avanti!*, the party's national newspaper. Only twenty-nine years old, Mussolini seemed the bright young face of the Socialist party, and some, including Gaetano Salvemini, thought he might be the leader who could revitalize Italian socialism.

Mussolini and some of the syndicalists had come into contact before. For example, Mussolini and Olivetti had met in Zurich in March 1904, at the congress of the Italian Socialist Union of Switzerland.[59] Olivetti, who was nine years Mussolini's senior, was a leading figure in Italian socialism in Switzerland and served as president of the congress, while Mussolini was merely the delegate of the Geneva section. Olivetti, Panunzio, and the other syndicalists had an important influence on Mussolini during his years of intellectual maturation, which began with his stay in Switzerland from 1902 to 1904.[60] Mussolini was enthusiastic about Sorel's *Reflections on Violence* and frequently called himself a syndicalist.[61] But as a Socialist party man, he was never part of the syndicalist current, and by 1910 he certainly did not anticipate a significant role for revolutionary syndicalism in Italian socialism. After the syndicalist congresses of December 1910, Mussolini sarcastically denounced syndicalism for its divisiveness, incoherence, and futility.[62]

While Mussolini did learn from the Italian syndicalists and from Sorel, he borrowed selectively, creating a revolutionary conception of his own which departed from syndicalism, especially the Italian variety, in crucial respects. Most important, Mussolini did not share the syndicalists' belief in the pedagogical qualities of organization. In his conception, the unions were to be clearly subordinate to an elite party which would lead the revolution; the labor movement was only to provide the mass base. Indeed, the elite would use non-rational myths in order to galvanize the necessary mass support for revolution. Mussolini's conception was considerably more elitist and manipulative than that of the syndicalists; he did not have the same confidence in the workers' potential for initiative, responsibility, and lucid self-discipline, nor did he value decentralization and autonomy for socioeconomic groups as antidotes to underlying Italian problems. He was interested in the catastrophic, activist, and irrationalist elements in Sorelian syndicalism, precisely the elements that the Italian syndicalists played down.[63]

Writing early in 1913, Alceste De Ambris delineated the differences between the Mussolinian and syndicalist concepts of direct action.[64] He found Mussolini's notion too catastrophic, too close to old-fashioned popular insurrection, and emphasized the patient quality of syndicalism, which meant by direct action simply the activities of the modern labor organizations. The syndicalists wanted to teach the workers what they could accomplish on their own, without relying on intermediaries; they did not envision some sort of miraculous transformation, giving the working class a force it lacked objectively.

When the left wing won control of the Socialist party in 1912, the syndicalists certainly did not see Mussolini as one of their own. Nevertheless, Mussolini was no reformist, and with syndicalism in trouble, reappraisal of the relationship between syndicalism and the party seemed called for. As the left wings in their respective spheres, syndicalists and Mussolinians perhaps had enough in common for a tactical alliance. And indeed each group viewed the other as potential support —and assumed that ultimately, given the logic of revolution, the other side could only accept its leadership. The syndicalists could consider alliance with Mussolini and his party because they assumed that syndicalism was so much more realistic than anything the revolutionaries in the party had to offer that it was bound to establish its hegemony in the end.

De Ambris discussed the possibilities in a long dialogue with Giuseppe De Falco, an articulate member of the party's left wing and editor of *Avvenire del lavoratore*, the organ of the Italian Socialist party in Switzerland.[65] To De Falco, the new situation suggested the kind of symbiosis between syndicates and revolutionary party that some of the syndicalists had advocated in 1910. Ultimately, De Falco admitted, only the workers, through their own autonomous organizations, could create socialism, but there was much a revolutionary socialist party could do to further the process. Rather than worry about electoral successes and parliamentary activity, such a party would work, first, to infuse revolutionary socialist ideals into the labor movement, and, second, to promote the necessary political and economic context for the unfolding of syndicalism. As far as De Falco was concerned, revolutionary socialism was now at a crossroads: as the now-dominant current in the party, it could no longer get by on doctrinal intransigence; if it did not renew itself through syndicalism, it would simply disintegrate.

At first, the symbiosis which De Falco proposed seemed at least possible to De Ambris; he felt that Mussolini's position had a certain logic, that it in some ways complemented syndicalism.[66] If Mussolini neglected the unions, it was only because of the present sorry state of the CGL and the Italian labor movement in general. As a genuine revolutionary, he would necessarily have a different attitude to the kind of labor movement the syndicalists were trying to create. The only problem, De Ambris argued, was that the majority even of the revolutionary current in the party was not as coherent as Mussolini and De Falco. Perhaps events would force the revolutionaries to clarify their thinking, but for the time being the syndicalists could only wait and see.

The events of 1913 in some ways favored and in some ways impeded a symbiosis. Mussolini solidified his position, clearly emerging as the dominant figure in the left wing of the party, thereby overcoming a major source of De Ambris's initial skepticism. Moreover, Mussolini looked with favor on the apparent revival of syndicalism in the labor movement during 1913. To be sure, he had misgivings about the schismatic USI, since he wanted the labor movement to become a unified mass base for revolution; he had opposed formation of the USI in the first place. But the syndicalists, especially Corridoni and his Unione Sindacale Milanese, could play a valuable role by winning the industrial workers away from reformism and back toward revolutionary militancy. Mussolini assumed that the party, with its elite of politically conscious revolutionaries, would ultimately assume the leadership of this militant mass base. So he was relatively supportive as Corridoni led the imposing Milanese general strike of May–June 1913. When the strike was finally defeated, Mussolini criticized revolutionary syndicalism, but only because he felt that greater unity among revolutionaries and more coherent leadership were essential if such strikes were to be productive. On the other hand, Mussolini bitterly denounced the

USM's follow-up strike of July–August 1913, which quickly fizzled. The general strike, he argued, was being used excessively—and with poor preparation; this could only alienate the workers and undermine the essential rank-and-file support for the revolutionaries.[67]

Mussolini's ambivalent attitude hardly converted the syndicalists to alliance with the Socialist party. Just after the strike of May and June, De Ambris severely scolded the party for its lack of support during the strike.[68] And a full-scale polemic developed after Mussolini's unsparing criticism of syndicalist methods in August. Many of the syndicalists, still stressing proletarian autonomy, continued to deny on principle that even a revolutionary Socialist party could be an ally of syndicalism.[69] Some of the others, however, were beginning to consider actually rejoining the party, since some political framework for present action seemed essential. One evening in November of 1913, a number of them met with Mussolini at a café in Bologna to discuss the options available. Panunzio and Leone were among those favoring a return to the party, but only if the syndicalists made the move as a group—not just as individuals.[70] Nothing came of this meeting, but frustration and restlessness were increasing among the syndicalists, many of whom were ripe for a shift in short-term alignments, despite the ongoing questions about the compatibility of Mussolinian socialism with syndicalism. The chance came in 1914, first with Red Week as a preliminary, then with the outbreak of the war and the struggle for Italian intervention.

Contrary to what some have argued, the Red Week uprising of June 1914 was not a crucial turning point in the evolution of Italian syndicalism; but it did mark a significant step in the direction in which many of the syndicalists were already moving. Alceste De Ambris, who considered the lessons of Red Week most explicitly, was not disillusioned by its outcome, for he was hardly expecting revolution in 1914; definitive syndicalist revolution was still a long way off. Instead, De Ambris was surprised at the revolutionary energies and the hostility to the status quo which had welled up spontaneously during Red Week. The situation in Italy was more volatile than he had realized. If directed by a new revolutionary coalition party, these unsuspected energies could make possible the sweeping changes necessary for the normal development of syndicalism in the future.[71] So De Ambris began to insist that syndicalists, revolutionary Socialists, anarchists, and republicans, despite their continuing differences, should strengthen the links that had developed spontaneously during Red Week and work together for a kind of preliminary revolution to create the context for syndicalist development. The spectacle of Red Week, with the people spontaneously rising up against the existing order, obviously fascinated De Ambris, but he retained a sense of the limits of such popular uprisings, along with the newer, specifically syndicalist values he had developed over the past decade.

De Ambris anticipated that some of his syndicalist colleagues were bound to object: "Yes, I know: it is not a matter of syndicalism in the rigid sense of the word. Syndicalism is carried out on the economic level, and a political struggle is at issue here. But on the other hand, is it not true that certain political conquests are indispensable to create the atmosphere necessary for syndicalism to live and develop?"[72] Agostino Lanzillo was not convinced: to drag the workers into insurrectionary experiments mobilized by a political party could only compromise proletarian self-reliance and undermine the possibility of syndicalism in the future.[73] Red Week, he insisted, had revealed not unsuspected revolutionary energies, but the futility of revolutionary blocs and popular insurrections—and the superiority of the syndicalist method. From the syndicalist perspective, both De Ambris and Lanzillo were partly correct. Syndicalism was at an impasse, and supplementary activity to make political changes was apparently necessary. At the same time, however, there really was a danger that the original content of syndicalism would be compromised by the shift in strategic emphasis that De Ambris proposed. But it would be possible to bridge the gap if syndicalism itself, instead of remaining suspended for the future, could be revised and made relevant to the solution of immediate political problems. De Ambris and Lanzillo, despite their disagreement in 1914, were both on the way to the neosyndicalist synthesis that fully emerged only after World War I. The key was to make syndicalism the basis of an alternative to liberal parliamentary politics, in the way that Mantica had already described in tentative terms.

Lanzillo opposed the revolutionary alliance which De Ambris proposed in part because he expected that it would become preoccupied with the role of the monarchy.[74] For Lanzillo, the question of the monarchy was largely irrelevant—a republic of politicians, he said, would be no improvement over a monarchy. For the syndicalist current to get involved with Italy's old antimonarchist forces, with their outmoded priorities, could only obstruct the maturation of the proletariat. De Ambris was less worried about contamination, but for him, too, the issue of monarchy versus republic increasingly seemed irrelevant. In proposing the goals for the projected revolutionary alliance, he specifically denied that the monarchy was the underlying Italian political problem.[75] He found the source of Italy's problems instead in the highly centralized, bureaucratic quality of the Italian state, which seemed to be stifling and corrupting the society. De Ambris and Lanzillo were both moving toward the new conception of Italian political problems that would eventually enable them to combine syndicalism with immediate political action.

While the syndicalists were debating the lessons of Red Week, the European war broke out, raising new questions and possibilities. During the previous decade, most of the syndicalists had maintained an orthodox antimilitarist position, although a few had occasionally expressed interest in the moral and regenerative qualities of war. Writing in 1904, Sergio Panunzio argued in a general way that wars can have a progressive impact: peace is conservative, while war creates new situations.[76] Labriola developed some of the same ideas in an article on Gustave Hervé in 1907, while Panunzio went further in 1908, in an article clearly influenced by Pareto.[77] After contrasting the pacifism typical of a declining bourgeois elite with the combativeness of an emerging proletarian elite, Panunzio argued that war can have a revolutionary impact both on its participants and on situations. By implication, participation in a war could enable a new, tightly united elite to emerge. To "Calcante," a periodic contributor to *Pagine libere*, war seemed the only possible source of regeneration for Italy, now that the socialist movement had degenerated "into a despicable organization of local clienteles."[78]

By 1911, with syndicalism in disarray, three leading syndicalists were prepared to follow the logic of these ideas in practice and take their chances on a war. Olivetti, Labriola, and Orano outraged most of their colleagues by advocating proletarian and socialist support for Italy's imperialistic war with Turkey over Libya. These mavericks supported the war primarily because of the revolutionary psychological effects they felt it might have on the Italian workers and on Italian society. Labriola framed the question dramatically: "O my comrades, do you know why the Italian proletariat is not fit to make a revolution? For precisely the same reasons that it is not fit to wage war. Let the proletariat get used to fighting seriously, and then you will see that it will learn to strike the bourgeoisie itself! Make it possible for us to break out of our customary stinking laziness! Today perhaps there is no enterprise more revolutionary than this to attempt in Italy." The decadence of the proletariat was only an aspect of the overall decadence of Italian society, and war, continued Labriola, would force the society as a whole to change: "[War] will make us more serious; it will accustom us to a deeper examination of things, to a more vital and effective way of thinking. It will give to us Italians a sense of our strength as a nation. Victorious or defeated, we will overcome all the dreadful superficiality of our customary opinions. War will impose on us new, more precise problems, having greater importance and more enduring consequences than those to which we are accustomed. It will be a tremendous and

painful experience, but under that pedagogy we will remake ourselves."[79] In the same way, Paolo Orano expected the Libyan War
to force both the bourgeoisie and the proletariat to strengthen themselves, thereby rekindling the class struggle and paving the way for
revolution.[80] Whatever the plausibility of such assumptions, these
syndicalists were not advocating war as a means to overcome class
conflict and to create national solidarity. Clinging to orthodoxy, they
envisioned the war experience as the kind of preliminary revolution
Italy required before syndicalism could fully develop.

Labriola, Olivetti, and Orano were the only leading syndicalists to
support the Libyan War. Enrico Leone wrote a book criticizing Italy's
lust for Libya, and *Pagine libere*, by now the official organ of Italian
syndicalism, was forced to cease publication because of the bitter
dispute among its editors over the issue.[81] Those like De Ambris who
attacked the three defectors opposed the war for traditional socialist
reasons. This imperialistic venture could only reinforce the reactionary
elements in Italian society—the militarism and nationalism—that were
obstacles to the coming of socialism. Proletarian support would compromise the class separation and autonomy crucial for the elaboration
of nonbourgeois values.[82] But Giulio Barni, in the most sensitive syndicalist critique of the Libyan War, admitted that his adversaries' emphasis on the educational value of war had some merit.[83] Apparently a
different war, fought for a nobler cause—one related to the fortunes of
socialism and thus more valuable pedagogically—could win more enthusiastic syndicalist support.

Well before 1914, some syndicalists had admitted that, in certain
circumstances, the proletariat could have a major stake in the outcome
of a European war. Paolo Mazzoldi, writing in 1905, insisted that
socialists had to be concerned with all the obstacles to the free and
natural emergence of socialism on the international plane, above all the
militarism, imperialism, and protectionism which Germany especially
represented.[84] A German victory in a European war would threaten
democracy and thus seriously affect the prospects of the European
proletariat. In the event of war between France and Germany, Mazzoldi
concluded, the Italian workers would have to support Italian intervention against Germany and offer their full support to the national war
effort.

When in 1914 Italian leftists sought the best response to the European war, the syndicalists began with the line of argument which
Mazzoldi had developed in 1905. Since the argument had a certain
logic, it provided the syndicalists with an orthodox veneer for their
support of intervention and war. But deeper concerns were also at
work as the syndicalists began the pivotal period of their political
evolution.

5 / Socialist Society and the Italian Nation

As Austria-Hungary prepared for a showdown in the Balkans after the assassination of the Archduke Franz Ferdinand at Sarajevo, Italy invoked the Triple Alliance in an attempt to win compensation for any Austrian territorial gains. Despite German pressures, the Austrians dragged their feet, and on August 2, 1914, five days after Austria-Hungary declared war on Serbia, Italy announced her intention to remain neutral in the developing European war. This left her in a flexible position, and she was courted by both sides as the war bogged down in a stalemate during the months that followed. After the declaration of neutrality in August, however, there was no longer a serious chance that Italy would actively intervene on the side of Austria-Hungary, Italy's hereditary enemy and present rival in the Adriatic and the Balkans. But Austria, still prodded by Germany, became increasingly generous in offering Italy compensation for staying neutral. On the other hand, Italy could win even more attractive gains, including the Italian-speaking areas still within the Habsburg Empire, if she intervened actively on the side of the Entente.

With the Russian successes in Galicia in March of 1915, Italy began negotiating in earnest with the Entente powers, fearing a separate peace between Austria-Hungary and Russia that would leave Italy empty-handed. Negotiations with Austria proceeded simultaneously, but when Austrian offers of compensation still failed to satisfy growing Italian appetites, Foreign Minister Sidney Sonnino finally came to terms with the Entente. The secret Treaty of London, signed April 26, awarded Italy generous territorial compensation at the expense of the Habsburg Empire. In exchange, Italy was to intervene on the side of the Entente within one month. She entered the war on May 24, badly divided by the intervention issue itself.

At first, there was a broad consensus in the country for neutrality, and most Italians remained opposed to war throughout the debate over intervention between August 1914 and May 1915. Catholics and socialists were generally neutralist, and so were most of the liberals, who agreed with Giolitti that Italy, since she was unprepared for a major war, should settle for the lucrative compensation she could win by remaining neutral. The majority in parliament, still loyal to Giolitti, similarly opposed intervention.

But almost immediately dissenters stepped forward: first, radicals from the old Masonic and democratic traditions, long loyal to France, then people from other parts of the political spectrum. Liberals like Luigi Albertini, democratic socialists like Salvemini and Leonida Bissolati, the Nationalists, the syndicalists, the futurists, much of the young educated elite, and ultimately Mussolini and a few revolutionary socialists joined the interventionist current. They had in common only their commitment to Italian intervention and their belief that, one way or another, the war experience would force Italy out of the stasis of the Giolittian system. Especially during the "radiant days" of May 1915, interventionists mounted impressive demonstrations, sometimes threatening to challenge the monarchy itself if intervention was not forthcoming. But those in charge of Italian foreign policy—Sonnino, Prime Minister Antonio Salandra, and the king—committed Italy to war for conventional territorial and military reasons, not because they were coerced by an interventionist minority in the piazzas. Still, it looked as if the interventionists, as a minority using direct action, had succeeded in imposing their will on the inert majority in the country, represented by the neutralist Giolittian majority in parliament.[1]

The leading syndicalists came out for intervention quickly and almost unanimously. Speaking in Milan on August 18, at a meeting called by the USI to consider the war, De Ambris made the first tentative step, suggesting that it might prove necessary for the syndicalists—and the workers—to support Italian intervention.[2] A German victory would threaten severely the bourgeois democratic order, which was a crucial prerequisite for the development of a syndicalist society. Hence the outcome of the war was by no means irrelevant for the proletariat, and if Italian intervention should prove necessary to tip the scales against Germany, the proletariat must be ready to support the national effort. De Ambris ventured only haltingly beyond this defensive and still reasonably orthodox posture in his initial interventionist speech. He claimed that a victorious war would have such beneficial economic, political, and moral consequences as to constitute nothing less than a revolution. "To be sure," he was quick to add, "this is not yet *our* revolution; but it is perhaps necessary to free the world of all the cumbersome debris that still survives from the middle ages." So even though the war could amount to the preliminary revolution that Italy needed, De Ambris retreated from the more flexible interpretation of the obstacles to real revolution he had offered after Red Week and back into the haven of orthodoxy. Here the obstacles are essentially feudal leftovers.

Despite the element of caution, De Ambris's speech made an enormous impression. It provoked much bitter hostility on the Italian Left, but it also marked the birth of revolutionary interventionism.[3] Almost all the other syndicalists quickly followed De Ambris, including organizers like Corridoni, Masotti, and Livio Ciardi, as well as intellectuals like Olivetti, Panunzio, and Lanzillo. Facing the challenge of war, the syndicalists reconverged, closing the gap between organizers and intellectuals that seemed to be developing after 1910. In October, Olivetti began publishing a new series of *Pagine libere*, which became the mouthpiece of the new group that some of the syndicalists quickly formed to promote intervention, the Fascio rivoluzionario d'azione internazionalista.[4] Although the syndicalists predominated, the Fascio brought together a variety of left interventionists; thus it not only consummated the reunification of the syndicalist current, but also pointed beyond, toward the wider regrouping of revolutionaries that some of the syndicalists had advocated before the war. On October 5, the organization issued its *Manifesto*, calling on the workers to support intervention and stressing that a German victory would seriously compromise the prospects for European socialism.[5]

The accent on orthodoxy in this manifesto was typical. De Ambris had been quick to reply to critics of his initial interventionist speech that his position violated no tenet of syndicalist doctrine, that he was still an internationalist, an antipatriot, and a socialist. The other syndicalist interventionists also defended their orthodoxy: the war concerned the proletariat as a class and did not compromise its ultimate revolutionary aims; support of intervention involved no conversion to militarism and nationalism. It was only because the Italian bourgeoisie was so weak, Lanzillo argued, that the proletariat had to assume the responsibility for spearheading the defense of the national context for socialism against German reaction. The syndicalists liked to think that the war was a kind of international duty for the proletariat—to make the world safe for socialism.[6]

But the syndicalists' interventionist position, even when only carried this far, raised troubling questions about some traditional socialist canons. Interventionism did not necessarily mean a patriotic commitment to the existing nation, but if the interests of international socialism sometimes required support for national wars, then socialists had at least to refine their conception of the relationships between the proletariat and the nation and between socialism and internationalism. The fact that socialists in Germany, France, and elsewhere rallied enthusiastically to their national war efforts raised further questions. Perhaps—in the short term, at least—the proletariats of different countries might have conflicting interests. The syndicalists were quick to note that the old assumptions about international proletarian solidarity had been too simplistic. And Olivetti argued in introducing the new series of *Pagine libere* in October of 1914: "To coordinate the social revolution with the fact of the existence of nations is the most serious problem for true and sincere revolutionaries at the present time."[7]

In fact, the evolution of events in Italy and elsewhere had led some of the syndicalists to begin this redefinition even before 1914. When Edmondo Rossoni, who had organized Italian workers in New York for several years before the war, spoke at the first congress of Fascist unions in June 1922, he recalled his own conversion to a kind of nationalism. The Italian workers in America, he maintained, had learned the hard way how much their own nationality affected their prospects—and not only because of the attitudes of the American bourgeoisie: "We have seen our workers exploited and held in low regard not only by the capitalists but also by the revolutionary *comrades* of other countries. We therefore know from experience how internationalism is nothing but fiction and hypocrisy."[8] It was especially the prewar Italian emigration experience that led the syndicalists to reject the facile categories of orthodox socialist internationalism. Italian immigrant workers often encountered ethnic discrimination by governments and employers and hostility on the part of their local proletarian comrades. De Ambris, who had worked as an organizer among the Italian workers in Brazil, bitterly denounced the treatment of Italians by business and government in Argentina in two influential *Pagine libere* articles, which were promptly reprinted in pamphlet form.[9] Paolo Orano described the hierarchy existing within the industrial proletariat in the United States. The native workers were clearly the superiors, while Italian immigrants were left to do the dirty work: "The immigrants from Italy know that the improvement of the salaries of the Italians in the United States is a chimera. There the sons of the Abruzzi and of Sicily empty the garbage and wash the dirty clothes even of the American workers. The Italians are the servants of their American 'comrades.'"[10] In a similar vein, when the Austrian socialists failed to protest their government's repression of Italian students in Vienna in 1908, Olivetti concluded that socialist internationalism was "a joke and a lie."[11]

In two perceptive books, *La guerra di Tripoli e l'opinione socialista* (1912) and *La conflagrazione europea e il socialismo* (1915), Arturo Labriola attempted to discover the underlying causes of this failure of inter-national proletarian solidarity. To begin with, he argued, socialists had to try to understand "the effects which belonging to a political unity predominant in the military and economic sphere have had on the psychology of the working classes. The way the American unions treat foreign workers; the ill-concealed disdain of German workers for Italian immigrants . . . the international dictatorship of German Social Democracy in the socialist congresses; all this demonstrates that the feelings of hegemony of the upper classes pass even into the working classes, and that it is not probable that their arrival in power would coincide with renunciation of their by-then customary hege-mony."[12] Classical Marxism, Labriola explained, had anticipated an increasingly homogeneous international capitalist order based on free trade. The growing protectionism after 1879, however, had forged links between producers and consumers in each country which Marx-ism had not foreseen: "Capitalist society . . . makes the barriers be-tween countries even higher—thanks to the import duties of every kind—and thus the proletariat very well did come to have a fatherland, so that in America the Italians—precisely because of their fatherland!—were declared undesirables, and negotiations between national states proved necessary to obtain legal protection for immigrant labor; other-wise those dear proletarians without a country would not have found even a dog that would have concerned himself with them."[13] As im-perialism followed protectionism, workers in favored countries found that they too had a stake in the imperialistic successes of their ruling classes. Through imperialism, capitalism managed to expand its sphere of exploitation, producing a transitory community of interests between bourgeoisie and proletariat within a particular nation. It was this part-nership that led the workers of favored countries to adopt a pose of superiority toward workers elsewhere—and that led socialists and workers to the support of national war in 1914. But Labriola concluded that the internal solidarity forged by imperialism was only temporary; class struggle would ultimately reemerge and determine future devel-opment.[14]

The other syndicalists by 1914 were likewise beginning to doubt that socialist internationalism could have any practical effect as long as some capitalist countries were more prosperous than others—and as long as protection and imperialism cemented the differences. Workers in a rich capitalist country were following their own economic self-interest, not merely sentimental patriotic ideals, when they supported their government's policies and enjoyed their share of their nation's prosperity. A disillusioned Agostino Lanzillo, writing during the inter-ventionist debate, noted that faith in socialism had "definitively collapsed" since it had now become clear that conflicting interests among the various national proletariats had wrecked international proletarian solidarity.[15]

As we have seen, Labriola concluded that a privileged proletariat, even in power after a revolution, would not be likely to renounce its customary hegemony and advantage. Given their skepticism about international proletarian solidarity, the syndicalists could not adopt a Leninist conception and assume that the revolution in Italy could be saved or helped along by socialist victories in more prosperous countries. If the Italians were to have a socialist society, they would have to build it themselves. But if they were to do so, they had to concern themselves directly not only with Italy's domestic problems, but also with her international situation, for problems on the international level could hinder Italian economic development, which was still the most obvious prerequisite for socialism. Italy seemed especially vulnerable to pressure by her wealthier, more powerful neighbors. Labriola had admitted in 1907 that the proletariat would have no choice but to support a war of national defense, and he viewed the Libyan War partly as an attempt by Italy to protect herself from geographical encirclement.[16] These geopolitical concerns for Italy's future were, he said, a necessary corollary to his socialism, since failure in the international sphere would doom Italy to economic decadence. Some of the syndicalists began to argue that if Italian economic development required imperialistic expansion in order to provide raw materials and population outlets, then an Italian socialist could even favor imperialism.[17] Not surprisingly, once the European war had broken out in 1914, the syndicalists began to focus on the benefits that might accrue to Italy, benefits necessary for the coming of socialism, from Italian participation in an Entente victory. For example, Filippo Corridoni anticipated that the war would not only bring about free trade, but also give Italy natural frontiers, thus enabling her to devote resources presently used for military defense to industrial development.[18]

Once the syndicalists began to see socialism as a national proposition, they found the war not only a defensive necessity, to ward off international reaction, but also a positive opportunity; the war could improve Italy's international position and even redeem the Italian nation, making it fit for socialism. Writing in *Il popolo d'Italia* in February 1915, Lanzillo portrayed the European conflict as "the war of redemption" for a nation that had emerged accidentally, without really deserving it, in the nineteenth century.[19] As his other writings during this period make clear, he was not choosing the nation and its redemption at the expense of the proletariat and socialist revolution.[20] But to Lanzillo and the other syndicalists, national redemption was an essential prerequisite for socialism, and it seemed that the war could be the essential preliminary revolution.

Once the orthodox line of argument brought them to this point, the syndicalists were bound to encounter their national populist underpinnings. But even some of the concerns originating on this populist level could be made compatible with socialist orthodoxy, since orthodoxy itself had to change to encompass the fact of nationality. During the years before the war, some European socialists had already posed the central questions about the relationship between nationality and socialism—for example, the Austrian Otto Bauer, who insisted that national and cultural attributes transcend class differences.[21] The war brought the issue sharply into focus. The syndicalists, too, had always sensed the importance of national differences and sometimes had emphasized that socialism could not—and need not—deny the nation, understood as the context of individual development, as a community of language, culture, and custom.[22] They had always viewed the socialist revolution as an antidote to particular Italian problems, as well as to the problems of capitalist society in general. There had been tensions in their doctrine, since they were concerned about Italy and proud to be Italian while, at the same time, they were seeking to build a socialist society by following an abstract internationalist model. But now the tensions seemed to disappear: objective, external phenomena had convinced the syndicalists that the orthodox socialist emphasis on international proletarian solidarity and deemphasis on nationality had been misplaced, so their underlying concern for Italy could come clearly to the surface. It seemed that socialism had to be a national proposition, that an Italian committed to socialism had to be committed to Italy. As the syndicalists adjusted to this perspective, it became easier for them to suggest solutions for Italian problems. Still, this newly explicit commitment to Italy was not the decisive step in their departure from traditional socialism. This generic form of nationalism did not undermine their belief in proletarian revolution.

Although economic differences among capitalist nations had undermined international proletarian solidarity, the syndicalists did not conclude that the pursuit of socialism had to be abandoned altogether. They had simply discovered that each proletariat had to create socialism in its own way, within its own national collective: "There are as many socialisms as there are countries."[23] Thus Agostino Lanzillo, writing early in 1915, found the war a prerequisite for a specifically Italian form of socialism, one that would embody and carry to fruition the best elements of the national tradition, but one that would, nevertheless, still be made by the proletariat using syndicalist methods—all according to the orthodox blueprint.[24]

The nationalism that was becoming increasingly important in syndicalist thinking by 1915 meant, above all, that the abstract "society" of traditional socialism could only be the nation, understood as the area in which the struggle was to be waged and solidarity achieved. With national economic differences and divergent proletarian interests no longer possible to ignore, it was necessary to recognize that the nation was the only collective possible, the concrete historical manifestation of society itself. As Panunzio put it in 1920: "Nationality is only an organic, concrete, *historical* form of sociality. The Nation is nothing but a *specific* society, an organic, concrete, historical form of society."[25] In socialist theory, class solidarity and class struggle are merely methods of achieving solidarity in a wider collective. If the nation is the only meaningful society, then the object of the revolution can only be to achieve national solidarity. Thus the syndicalists, while becoming nationalists in this special way, continued to emphasize class struggle and class solidarity—as the means to a revolution that would make national solidarity possible.

The syndicalists, then, could integrate some of their new perceptions and concerns into a reasonably orthodox framework: their nationalism, their desire for natural frontiers, their call for Italian participation in the war—none of it was logically incompatible with their continued belief in proletarian revolution against capitalism. The syndicalist revision began only as a change of emphasis, a shift in focus from long-term to short-term. But the new elements in their thinking that they first managed to integrate—albeit precariously—within an orthodox framework became ever more difficult to control as the long-term objective, proletarian revolution, receded into the distance.

The wartime situation really was surprising and confusing, of course, and the syndicalists were not the only ones who had trouble understanding what the war was to mean for the future. Sometimes they tried to make a virtue of the strangeness of things, claiming that the war would bury for good the forms and ideologies of the past and prepare the way for something radically new. Events were out of control, and the only prudent course was to evolve with them; one could hope to keep abreast only by acting, by getting involved in the epic presently transpiring. Whoever remained passive would be left behind as history accelerated and Europe entered a new era. Thus the syndicalists called on the proletariat to depart from the passive fatalism and determinism which they claimed lay at the root of the neutralism dominant in both the Socialist party and the unions.[26]

Even in De Ambris's initial interventionist speech, in August 1914, there were accents incompatible with the orthodoxy that he sought to emphasize. The war, he said, would be so vast an experience that it would transcend every present conceptual framework; it would be a kind of shot in the dark that, for better or worse, would shatter the present impasse.[27] Panunzio took the same tack in an article in Mussolini's *Avanti!* in September of 1914, arguing that socialism could emerge in Europe only as the consequence of a major war, the longer and more difficult the better.[28] The exhaustion and economic crisis that would result from such a war would affect winners and losers alike and thereby pave the way for revolution all over Europe.

In statements like these, the syndicalists were clearly falling into the kind of adventurism for which they have often been condemned. But they were not comfortable with this perspective on the war, nor with the sense of chaos and indeterminacy from which it sprang. When he wrote his article on the war for *Avanti!*, Panunzio was already involved in the intellectual reconstruction that would enable him to go beyond the imprecision in this piece and to spearhead a thoroughgoing redefinition of syndicalism.

The redefinition stemmed in part from the shifts in alliances that developed during the struggle for intervention itself. The vast majority of the organized workers failed to respond to the syndicalists' appeals and continued to oppose intervention, shunning what seemed a futile capitalist war. The syndicalists failed to convince even a majority within the USI. De Ambris and his interventionist colleagues made their pitch at a meeting of the confederation's general council in September 1914, but the majority opted for the neutralism of Armando Borghi, leader of the anarchists within the USI.[29] Schism followed as De Ambris led the interventionist minority out of the confederation. The split was complex, penetrating to the rank-and-file level and even dividing individual unions, but the result was a further loss in working class support for the syndicalists. For example, while Corridoni retained control of the Unione Sindacale Milanese, the organization lost its vitality and the majority of its members as a result of the dispute over intervention.[30] The war issue made final the divorce between the syndicalists and the bulk of the workers that had developed after 1905. From the proletarian perspective, the syndicalists' call for intervention was nothing short of treason.

If the syndicalists' arguments failed to convince Armando Borghi, they did gradually win over another leader of the Italian left, the dynamic young editor of *Avanti!*, Benito Mussolini.[31] Strongly influenced by the syndicalists, Mussolini ceased to advocate absolute neutrality in mid-October, then came out for intervention the next month. This breach of orthodoxy quickly produced Mussolini's departure from the Socialist party, for the vast majority of Socialists remained unmoved by his appeal for intervention. But Mussolini immediately became a major leader in the interventionist movement, especially through his daily newspaper, *Il popolo d'Itália*. Panunzio praised Mussolini's conversion, and the collaboration between Mussolini and the syndicalists that some had explored since 1912 now became a reality.[32] Panunzio, Lanzillo, De Ambris, Rossoni, and other syndicalists contributed frequently to *Il popolo d'Italia*, which remained the focus of revolutionary interventionism throughout the war. The development of a revolutionary interventionist bloc raised interesting new possibilities, but the syndicalists were by no means becoming Mussolinians, losing their intellectual autonomy. As they sought to develop a more viable framework for their perceptions and goals, they retained the underlying values which had separated them from Mussolini all along.

Working through the interventionist Fasci, the syndicalists succeeded in stimulating support for intervention—in Milan, for example, where the charismatic Corridoni led impressive demonstrations, especially during the "Radiant Days" of May 1915.[33] Syndicalists were also influential in the struggle for intervention in Ferrara, where syndicalism had been relatively strong in the labor movement and where syndicalist ideas had already attracted the interest of students and others alienated from Giolittian Italy. Now the interventionist movement brought together syndicalists like Sergio Panunzio, who was teaching in Ferrara, and wider sectors of idealistic, nonproletarian young people like Italo Balbo. Panunzio headed the local Fascio, which De Ambris had come from Milan to help organize in January 1915. According to the influential fascist publicist Nello Quilici, the Fascio and the interventionist syndicalists attracted the most politically sensitive young people from the university and the liberal professions in Ferrara.[34] Now at last, the syndicalists were encountering a new constituency.

As a result of their interventionism, then, the syndicalists found themselves without many working-class allies, and their redefinition had to come to terms with the proletariat's disappointing response to their appeal for intervention. This response only furthered their disillusionment with the proletariat, for the war seemed precisely the kind of issue, transcending everyday economic concerns, which a maturing proletariat should be able to grasp. In one of his interventionist speeches, De Ambris questioned with disarming candor the fitness of the proletariat for socialism: "It is not only bread that we want, but also liberty; and a proletariat that satisfies itself by filling up its stomach, refusing every time we ask it to make sacrifices for conquests having an ideal character, would not be worthy of the destinies that syndicalism assigns to it."[35] Corridoni took the same tack: "The problem of the war is too much for the proletarian mind. The worker sees in the war only massacre, misery, hunger—massacre, misery, and hunger that he, he himself, must suffer—and thus he is against the war. What does it matter to him if, within ten or twenty years, today's sacrifices yield incalculable benefits?"[36] The proletariat's neutralism seemed to indicate just how essential Italian intervention was, for participation in a war that was crucial for the future of socialism would be an invaluable educational experience for the workers.[37]

In stressing the educational value of the war, however, the syndicalists did not envision some sort of mystical purification through violence, nor were they glorifying, or even admitting, the primacy of force in human affairs. On the contrary, the war was a struggle against the rule of force and for an ideal, a more just order of things.[38] Through participation in the war, the workers would begin to understand the nature of this struggle and would come to grasp their own role in it. Not long before his death, Corridoni wrote from the front that he deeply hated war, that he was fighting this one only because he believed it would both end the era of wars in Europe and yield advantages to Italy which would speed her evolution toward syndicalist socialism.[39] In the same way, De Ambris, writing from the front in November 1915, sought to describe the brutalities he saw as realistically as possible, without romanticizing. In his view, war was by no means permanently healthy or inevitable for the human species; the present war was necessary "precisely to prevent this immense horror from recurring tomorrow."[40]

The war experience would help make the workers fit for socialist revolution in the long run, but for now the syndicalists themselves, as leading interventionists, were playing major roles in a struggle that apparently had revolutionary implications of a different sort. Speaking to a large interventionist rally in Milan in January 1915, Olivetti insisted that even without the workers, he and his fellow interventionists were creating something new, transcending ordinary politics and parties.[41] He linked the interventionist cause, with its emphasis on international justice and national liberation, to the great populist leaders of the Risorgimento—especially Giuseppe Mazzini. Speaking during that same January, De Ambris similarly invoked Mazzini as the prophet of the new revolutionary grouping. Interventionism seemed the catalyst for the leftist alliance De Ambris had advocated in the aftermath of Red Week, so he called on revolutionaries of all varieties to take advantage of the present situation to weaken the Italian state and to create the solidarity now lacking in Italian life. Mazzini had indicated the values that would inspire the preliminary revolution and bind together the new revolutionary force.[42]

Writing in *Il popolo d'Italia* in June 1915, Panunzio sought to give this new movement more precise objectives, calling on revolutionaries to work together to replace the present parliamentary system, the source of all evils. Panunzio anticipated the destruction of parliament and the emergence of new political institutions all over Europe as a result of the war experience. At some points in this confused but significant article, Panunzio seems to have found the revolutionary meaning of the war precisely in these expected political consequences, but at other points, he apparently expected the war to pave the way for the proletarian revolution itself.[43] From the latter perspective, the war amounted to the self-destruction or death throes of the old bourgeois order, but the relationship between proletarian revolution and war as revolution remained unclear in Panunzio's thinking. It was one thing to anticipate the destruction of parliament as a result of the war; it was something else altogether to see the possibility of full-fledged proletarian revolution. In fact, however, Panunzio was on his way to a kind of antiparliamentary populism. With much rhetoric and abstraction, he declared the movement which had just succeeded in imposing intervention on parliament to have been the kind of supralegal constituent assembly which Italy had never had during the Risorgimento. He recalled the "ever fresh" Italian democratic publicists of 1848 and contrasted the true democracy of this extraparliamentary mass movement with parliamentary democracy. The defeat of parliament in the intervention dispute was the first step in the process of transforming Italy from a parliamentary monarchy into a "national monarchy" that would accompany the war.

As the war dragged on, such national populist accents increasingly came to the fore in syndicalist thinking. Thanks to the war, Ottavio Dinale wrote in December of 1916, the Italian people were outgrowing the old political system and the nation was finally coming to maturity, facing up to its defects, seizing control of its destinies.[44] Still, the parliament and the bureaucracy were not participating in this renewal. By implication, a vast political change would have to follow the war, but Dinale had nothing to say about what might happen or about the relationship of such an upheaval to proletarian revolution.

The syndicalists from 1914 to 1917 were being pulled in several directions at once. In discussing the war and its potential impact, their accents were sometimes orthodox, sometimes heterodox, and the nationalist, populist, Mazzinian, and antiparliamentary themes coexisted uneasily with the conventional socialist revolutionary themes. It was only later in the war, beginning in 1917, that the syndicalists began to weave these heterodox concerns together with elements of their original syndicalism, creating a new synthesis intended to respond to the needs of the immediate postwar period.

Georges Sorel confessed that he was simply unable to fathom why the Italian syndicalists favored intervention and war. Italy, he felt, had little to gain and much to lose. Sorel even envisioned the possibility that the temporal power of the papacy might be restored; the Trentino was simply not worth such risks.[45] The Italian syndicalists had left the *maître* of the New School far behind, but where they were headed remained unclear.

It is widely assumed that the syndicalists, in embracing the nation and the war, essentially converged with the Italian Nationalists, thus laying the basis for the later collaboration of leftists and rightists within fascism.[46] Since the blueprint which the Nationalists offered fascism fully emerged only in light of Italy's postwar crisis, we are not yet ready to consider in detail the fundamental problem of the relationship between syndicalism and Nationalism. But Enrico Corradini was blocking out some of the more basic features of the Nationalist doctrine well before 1914, and there was some mutual interest between syndicalists and Nationalists as early as 1910. If we are to grasp what the syndicalists' commitment to war and the nation did and did not mean, and if we are to understand what their evolution toward fascism involved, it will be useful for us to consider here some of the initial Nationalist ideas—and what the syndicalists thought of them.

Despite some attempts at communication on both sides, the syndicalists remained hostile to the Nationalists, even well into the postwar period, for two basic reasons. First, even as nationalists, the syndicalists continued to call for proletarian revolution within the nation; it required more than a commitment to the nation and the war for them to advocate, like the Nationalists, proletarian solidarity with the other "producers" in Italian society. Second, the syndicalists in supporting the nation and the war were not accepting—and indeed they would never accept—the Nationalist vision of international relations as "an amoral struggle of isolated peoples for the breadbasket."[47]

Well before 1914, Enrico Corradini began trying to woo the syndicalists by emphasizing apparent areas of convergence between Nationalism and syndicalism. Speaking late in 1909, he praised syndicalism for its opposition to pacifism, humanitarianism, and parliamentary democracy, for its premium on will and force. Both Nationalism and syndicalism, said Corradini, were manifestations of a rebirth of stern moral values, and both stressed solidarity and elitism. He even admitted that Nationalism could learn from syndicalism: the Nationalists were willing to envision the nation in the future ordered like a giant syndicate, composed of a network of individual syndicates of producers. The aims of syndicalism could be contained within the nation, which was essentially "a corporation of classes, one big syndicate."[48]

In wooing the syndicalists, Corradini hoped not only to win further support for Nationalism among the educated middle class, but also to establish a bridge to the working class. In a speech delivered in Milan and several other cities early in 1914, he pointed to the alleged convergence between Nationalism and syndicalism as evidence that the Nationalists were not antiproletarian.[49] But Corradini also sought to reach the workers more directly, through his interpretation of Italy's international position. By 1909 he had worked out the essentials of a counterideology designed to lure workers, syndicalists, and anyone else who would listen away from Marxist ideas of domestic class struggle and toward the Nationalist doctrine of domestic solidarity and international struggle.

The class struggle, said Corradini, was real enough, but it pitted not workers against capitalists within the nation, but poor proletarian nations against rich plutocratic nations on the international plane.[50] It was here, not on the limited national level, that the revolutionary struggle over economic distribution took place. "Have" and "have-not" nations competed for economic advantage in perpetual war— sometimes cold war, sometimes hot war. Since some capitalist countries were richer than others, and since the workers of a rich country did share in their nation's wealth, international proletarian solidarity was a sham, a doctrine which served the plutocratic nations by helping to keep proletarian nations like Italy divided along class lines. Much like the syndicalists, Corradini emphasized that everywhere Italian emigrants went, they suffered discrimination in favor of native workers— in France, for example, where the pension system treated French and foreign workers unequally.[51] Thus the working class would be well advised to support the Nationalists in their quest for colonies to provide the necessary outlets for surplus Italian labor. But above all, Corradini argued, the workers should wake up to the fact that it made a real economic difference for an individual to be born in a prosperous country like Great Britain, no matter what class he belonged to. And in a poor country like Italy, the proletariat could significantly improve its lot not through domestic class struggle against the bourgeoisie, but through collaboration with the other classes. Italy's overall poverty meant that there was little margin for shifts in distribution; improvement could come only from increased production. And since the economic prospects of all Italians depended on the international well-being of their proletarian nation, they should work together to ensure success on the crucial international level.

Corradini's overtures to the syndicalists appeared not only in Nationalist publications, but also in Paolo Orano's review *La lupa* in 1910.[52] It was precisely then that classical revolutionary syndicalism was starting to break down, and it is tempting to see Corradini's appearance in *La lupa* as an indication that new alignments were already developing. Corradini's overtures did not go unheeded: communication between the Nationalists and some of the syndicalists did develop between 1910 and 1915. But the significance of these flirtations has been much overplayed; the two movements did not converge, as the ongoing syndicalist hostility to the Nationalists makes clear. Orano, responding to Corradini's *La lupa* article of 1910, agreed that there were interesting similarities between Nationalism and syndicalism, but he stressed the gulf that remained between them, especially because of the Nationalist conception of the role of war.[53] And Arturo Labriola, in his book supporting the Libyan War, emphasized that Nationalism, with its call for national solidarity, was a fraud, merely a smokescreen for bourgeois interests.[54]

Nationalism in general need not involve a commitment to solidarity within—and thus unqualified support for—the nation as constituted at some particular time. For the syndicalists, national solidarity was not merely a necessity to be accepted, but an ideal to be created. It could be created, they continued to argue, only by eradicating the parasitic element within the present nation—through socialist revolution. Thus class solidarity remained essential within the present nation, even if only as a means to make genuine national solidarity possible. Rossoni's widely repeated motto for *L'Italia nostra*, the organ of the syndicalist labor movement in 1918, effectively summarized this national-revolutionary position: "La Patria non si nega, si conquista"—"The Fatherland is not to be denied, but won."

Even as the war dragged on, even after it was over, the syndicalists contended repeatedly that their nationalism did not diminish their desire for revolution within Italy. A real nationalist had to be a revolutionary: to accept class collaboration in the present order, based on exploitation and parasitism, would be treason not only against syndicalism, but also against the nation. Thus Orano, writing in 1919, called on Italian workers to conquer a fatherland for themselves—and to redeem the Italian nation in the process.[55]

The Italian Nationalist movement seemed to the syndicalists to represent the elements in Italian society—especially the protectionist plutocracy—that had to be overcome if meaningful national solidarity was to be possible. For Panunzio, writing in July of 1917, Italian Nationalism was "the theory for the rescue of the bourgeois economy in decadence."[56] Olivetti's review *La patria del popolo* attacked Nationalism in similar terms late in 1922: "Since the majority of Italians is composed of workers and producers . . . a doctrine which claims to identify the concept of Fatherland with the defense of the parasitical classes and interests in the nation cannot really be a national doctrine."[57] The revolution the syndicalists proposed, continued Olivetti's publication, was intended to eliminate precisely the parasitical classes represented by Nationalism.

We have seen that the syndicalists did not argue consistently for orthodox proletarian revolution after their turn to war and the nation. But their growing interest in national political change did not make them allies of the Nationalists. Genuine nationalism, the syndicalists insisted, had to be popular and was tantamount to a kind of populism abhorrent to the elitist Nationalists.[58] While criticizing parliamentary democracy in April of 1918, Panunzio explicitly sought to defend the substance of the democratic ideal against the attacks of "those abstract 'doctrinaires' who are our 'Nationalists.'" He warned that those who resisted institutional change to make democracy more meaningful were playing into the Nationalists' hands; indeed, they were in danger "of provoking certain . . . baneful *revivals*. The monarchical-clerical-military-nationalist legitimism of Charles Maurras in France is indicative."[59]

The Nationalists' conception of international relations conforms to prevailing conceptions of the fascist worldview; history was a perpetual, quasi-Darwinian struggle among nations, with each nation understood as a distinct biological organism. In his "Manifesto" introducing the new Nationalist review *Politica* in December of 1918, Alfredo Rocco portrayed struggle both as the fundamental law of life for societies and as the method whereby the natural evolution of peoples takes place. Without such struggle, humanity would only sink into dissolution and decadence. To be strong was the first duty of any state "because," as Rocco put it with his customary bluntness, "the opposition which democratic ideology has seen fit to create between justice and power does not exist."[60]

The value—and inevitability—of struggle, imperialism, and war were always central themes in Nationalist thinking. Enrico Corradini and his colleagues publicized these notions as they worked to drum up support for Italy's imperialist war with Turkey over Libya in 1911 and 1912. Corradini stressed a nation's right to take whatever it could get and its duty to conquer the bases of its own prosperity. Turkey and Libya, of course, were hardly plutocratic nations, but the Nationalist doctrine had no room for international solidarity among proletarian nations. Plausibly enough, Corradini pointed out that there was nothing rational or just about the present distribution of the earth's surface among nations or population groups: "No people has an absolute, innate right to a particular territory; rather, all peoples have only a relative right, an historical right, to the territory which they occupy." This right lasts only "as long as a people is a vital and active nation."[61] In the geographical area known as Libya, the Berbers had been overrun by the Arabs centuries ago, and the Arabs had been overrun by the Turks a few centuries later. Italy could now claim title to the same territory by the same never-ending method of conquest from peoples grown too decadent to defend that territory. Of course, some countries, their perspectives skewed by self-interest, would fail to grasp Corradini's world-historical logic and would point an accusing finger at dynamic Italy, while mouthing platitudes about peace and international law. Pacifism and humanitarianism and the rule of law were fine ideals for countries that had already conquered empires and that were free of the shame of emigration. Such conservative ideals simply served to legitimize the status quo, thus enabling the rich countries to preserve a favorable situation without having to fight.[62] Corradini might have returned to his transposed Marxist framework at this point: the humanitarian and pacifist ideals characteristic of the plutocratic nations constituted a classic example of ideology.

When the World War broke out, the Nationalists promptly advocated Italian intervention, and they were not fussy about their choice of enemies. Ultimately, the Nationalists felt, Italy had to focus on the whole Mediterranean and challenge France and Great Britain, but for now, while she was still in the early stages of her national revival, she could concentrate on the Adriatic and the Balkans and take on Austria-Hungary. There would be plenty of time for the wider struggle later on. Either way, the war, for the Nationalists, was simply a matter of imperial expansion for Italy. They would have none of the humanitarian ideals which many leftist interventionists espoused. Francesco Coppola, writing in October 1914, portrayed the war as starkly as possible, as a conflict "of peoples and races for existence, for wealth, for power and superiority"; the present war was a national-imperial struggle even for Great Britain and France, whatever arguments they used to justify themselves.[63]

Coppola's thinking after the war followed the same lines. By means of the war, history finally had reimposed its eternal laws on the European peoples, after the reign of false internationalistic and democratic ideologies during the nineteenth century: "Constrained by the truth of war, the nations once again came to feel themselves what they are in fact: armies; armies in the universal struggle for selection and improvement."[64] Alfredo Rocco's accents were similar. The war, he insisted, had been the product of conflicting imperialisms, pitting aggressive, unsatisfied nations like Italy and Germany against the old, saturated empires, which had sought to head off the war through pacifistic ideologies, but which finally found themselves dragged into it nevertheless. The anomalous lineup of the conflicting sides, with Italy fighting alongside Britain and France against Germany, was merely one indication that this war could not have been definitive, despite all the rhetorical gloss about a war to end all wars. The Great War had been only "a grandiose and terrible episode—by no means novel, by no means final—in the eternal struggle of peoples for existence and dominion."[65] A new era of imperial struggle would follow, and the Nationalists' postwar program was intended to enable Italy to rise to the challenge.

Despite their nationalism and interventionism, the syndicalists never viewed history and international affairs from the perspective we have just considered. Indeed, their thinking differed from that of the Nationalists in highly symptomatic ways. Even as fascists, the syndicalists continued to believe in internationalism and in the possibility of greater justice among nations. Panunzio, writing early in 1918 and still calling himself a socialist, denied that national exclusiveness and mutual hostility followed from the fact of national cultural differences. Internationalism remained possible and desirable, but to be viable it had to involve the harmonious coexistence of different national cultures in some sort of federal system, one admitting the value of national differences. In other words, nationalism for the syndicalists was the necessary substratum for a rational, authentic internationalism, which could only be based on freely contracting nations.[66]

In the prewar international order, different nations and even different proletariats had sufficient interests in conflict to make genuine international solidarity—whether it involved classes or whole nations—difficult to attain. But harmony among nations, though not yet achieved in fact, remained for the syndicalists an ethical imperative, an ideal to be sought. Thus they bitterly criticized the Nationalists for their espousal of perpetual international struggle. Even in the aftermath of the Libyan War, which he had so vigorously supported, Arturo Labriola found the Italian Nationalists "drunk with militaristic rhetoric" and warned that if all nations were to follow their prescriptions, perpetual war and the end of civilization would inevitably result.[67] During the European war, De Ambris wrote a number of articles for *Il popolo d'Italia* in an explicit attempt to distinguish the syndicalists' conception of the war from that of the Nationalists, which some neutralists were citing to discredit intervention and the war in general.[68] He condemned Nationalism for its gloomy vision of perpetual war and insisted that the syndicalists, in contrast, understood the present war as a means to make possible a greater degree of peace and harmony among nations. De Ambris envisioned a new federal organization of the nations of Europe and ultimately the world, one capable of dealing peacefully with such sources of conflict as international trade and access to colonies and the seas. Panunzio's emphasis was similar throughout the war: the irrationalities which produced the war could only be overcome through the war itself, which would make possible a dialectical resolution, a new form of international organization, diminishing the chances of future wars.[69]

Panunzio developed these ideas most fully early in 1916, in a lecture at the University of Bologna that was published in book form the next year. This statement, entitled *Il concetto della guerra giusta* [The concept of the just war], is one of the central documents in the syndicalist transition to fascism and makes strikingly clear the deep chasm between the syndicalist and the Nationalist conceptions of history. Panunzio affirmed precisely what the Nationalists denied: the reality of the category of justice and the ability of human beings, acting in history, to order their affairs in a more just way.[70] Belief in the possibility of justice, however, did not mean for Panunzio pacifism and an acceptance of the status quo, for the present order, despite its legalistic underpinnings, was still riddled with injustices. Thus just wars were possible, and these were not merely defensive wars, preserving the status quo, but "offensive" wars, imposing a new, more just order of things. When, as at present, there was a chance for mankind to move a step closer to justice, pacifism and the present international framework could legitimately be cast aside. Nations and classes profiting from the present imperfect system could be expected to resist, calling for peace, equilibrium, and respect for the existing system of laws.[71]

We have seen that Corradini and the Nationalists portrayed doctrines of peace and international law in similar terms, as "ideologies," but the psychological mainsprings of Panunzio's position were different. For the Nationalists, wars were amoral tests of power that would continue throughout history. There could be no justice, no progression toward justice as a transcendent absolute. For Panunzio, on the other hand, wars could be genuine revolutions which "bring about the rectification of juridical experience in light of the Idea and the preparation of the final triumph of Justice, which is the implicit end of history, without which human history would be blind, like the statue of Polyphemus."[72] Panunzio obviously believed that sometimes violence, as in a war, could be creative, in the sense of carrying mankind closer to justice. But he warned explicitly that he did not celebrate war and violence for their own sake, and he heaped scorn on the "litterateurs and false poets" who did.[73] From Panunzio's perspective, then, a war could be only a blind and useless slaughter; everything depended on the quality of the peace, the new order, that developed from it.[74]

In his contributions to *Il popolo d'Italia*, Panunzio sought to establish what a just outcome of the present war would involve. The new order would include free trade, freedom of the seas, and a more equitable sharing of colonial space, especially with the anticipated dissolution of the Ottoman empire. Like other socialists from Marx to Bernstein, Panunzio said that socialism could not oppose colonial enterprises which spread civilization to backward areas and made underutilized resources available to those who could develop them. The colonial system would obviously survive the war, and it was essential that the existing disproportions in colonial holdings be overcome: "everyone ought to participate in them equitably—each state in proportion to its needs and to its forces of labor."[75] Panunzio wanted Italy to get a larger share, but this did not lead him to espouse aggressiveness and international hostility. In his important *Introduzione alla società delle nazioni*, which grew out of a lecture given at the University of Bologna in December 1918, he suggested that colonial areas, when they were unable to become viable nations in their own right, should belong collectively to the new League of Nations and not remain or become the property of individual states.[76]

Panunzio had no illusions that the Great War would produce absolute justice; it was not possible to eliminate all injustices—and thus all the roots of future wars—from within the present framework.[77] But a new era of peaceful adjustment could follow from the war, and as the war was ending, he sought to propose ways of organizing a viable society of nations. His major book on the subject won the prize of a Milanese group seeking to promote international organization after the war.[78] Panunzio's proposals offer further evidence of the commitment to international understanding and justice which made his position so different from the Nationalism of Corradini and Rocco. He called on each nation, for example, to develop more cosmopolitan varieties of education in order to foster the supranational form of sociality necessary for a new kind of international order.[79] It was essential to free education from the cultural chauvinism which Panunzio considered an even more serious source of international hostility than economic rivalry. And more generally, he called for increased cultural contact to broaden human sensibilities and thereby help to develop psychological underpinnings for a new internationalism. Just as individuals, over the centuries, had been educated to understand the state and the law on the domestic level, they could be educated gradually to accept supranational forms. Once again, Panunzio found no incompatibility between nationalism, properly understood, and internationalism; the right kind of national education, free of nationalist prejudice, could help develop the political awareness which was essential for the new international order.

Humanitarian education and cultural interchange were essential to establish lasting foundations, but Panunzio also proposed a network of international institutions with considerable power. Together constituting the new "League of Nations," these entities would provide the international coordination so lacking before. To be effective, they would have to develop their own formal patterns of obligations and guarantees. Panunzio envisioned, for example, an international body to coordinate production and economic exchange and another to regulate armaments and military inventions. Through this network of specialized international organizations, mankind would finally begin to extend the sphere of law to the international level.[80] Since he was committed to expanding international collaboration after the war, it is hardly surprising that Panunzio judged the economics of Nationalism, with its emphasis on imperialism, absurd and self-defeating.[81]

Although Panunzio considered these matters more systematically than his colleagues, the other syndicalists portrayed the war, international affairs, and their own nationalism in essentially the same terms.[82] They supported the league of nations concept, advocating a new internationalism based on free and equal nations; they portrayed the war as the instrument of greater justice in international affairs, repudiating the Nationalist conception of the war and the postwar world. De Ambris worried about the dimensions of Italy's demographic and economic problems, but he specifically rejected the Nationalist solution, because it involved the imperialism, protectionism, and periodic war which he sought to avoid.[83]

The syndicalists' proposals for a new international order were idealistic, needless to say, and they themselves were quick to point out that the new League of Nations could turn out to be a sham. Panunzio warned that some conceptions of the league manifested "the spirit of conservative reaction of the old Holy Alliance of the three Empires," and disillusionment among the syndicalists with the results of the war was not long in coming.[84] Addressing a labor congress in September 1921, De Ambris complained that the war had not brought forth the new era of international justice that he had expected, but only new forms of imperialist conflict.[85] When the syndicalists viewed the international situation in terms of socialist concerns, the flaws in international proletarian solidarity stood out more sharply than ever. De Ambris, Olivetti, and Panunzio cited the advantages which English and American workers enjoyed thanks to imperialistic exploitation.[86] Organized labor in America was currently supporting the exclusion of Italian immigrants in order to keep its own wages up. Privileged proletariats sought to preserve their positions, and it seemed that the only recourse of their less fortunate counterparts, at least for now, was to help improve the international positions of their respective nations.

By 1921 the syndicalists were beginning to adopt a more aggressive form of nationalism as a short-term expedient, while continuing to insist on the desirability and possibility of international justice in the long term. Sometimes they even portrayed Italy in Corradinian terms as a "proletarian nation"; the war had not substantially changed the basis of international relations, and Italy had to look out for her own interests, some of which resulted from her "proletarian" status in a world dominated by "plutocratic" nations.[87] Italy's gloomy economic prospects—her overpopulation and her lack of raw materials and capital—worried them considerably. However, despite some rhetoric about proletarian nations in his speech of September 1921, De Ambris could not accept the Nationalist vision of ongoing struggle and imperialism. He called instead for free trade and for a system of equal access to colonies, in order to provide each nation with the opportunity to solve its problems of raw materials and living space without resort to war. While international struggle between "have" and "have-not" nations was permanent for Corradini, De Ambris advocated solidarity among proletarian nations—and struggle with plutocratic nations—in order to create the equal economic opportunity which could provide the only basis for meaningful international harmony.[88] Whatever the feasibility of such proposals, they exemplify the continuing difference between the syndicalist and Nationalist conceptions of international relations.

Still, syndicalist disillusionment with the outcome of the war by 1921 helped make possible a measure of short-term collaboration between syndicalists and Nationalists within fascism later on. Given the present international context, it seemed, Italy would have to consider imperialism. But even those syndicalists who ultimately turned to fascism continued to believe that a more harmonious international order was possible. A. O. Olivetti, for example, posed the Italian demographic problem as a test for the international community, a challenge to work out a just and peaceful solution to a complex international problem. Writing in *Il popolo d'Italia* in 1924, he pointed to France's possession of Tunisia as an example of international disequilibrium, given the radically different demographic situations of France and Italy. A disequilibrium of this sort, he warned, could not last indefinitely, but it remained unclear whether the resolution would take the form of contractual justice or imperial conquest. Olivetti stressed his preference for the former, but the matter depended, he said, "almost exclusively on the good will of the other nations. The problem of our emigration must promptly be placed before the League of Nations as an international problem the solution to which cannot be put off. It will be the test of fire for this organization in the process of formation."[89] Under the auspices of the league, for example, Italians should be able to emigrate collectively, with the Italian state able to negotiate collective contracts for them and to help them preserve their Italian identity abroad. If fair and cooperative solutions could not be worked out, Olivetti insisted that Italy could legitimately turn to imperialism.

As the years went by, Olivetti grew more bitter, complaining that the Great War had not proven the catalyst for the emergence of a more just international order. As evidence, he cited the barriers which other nations were erecting against Italian immigration, thereby exacerbating Italy's demographic problems.[90] By the late 1920s, Olivetti was boasting that Italy, thanks to fascism, was sufficiently disciplined and unified for the imperialist solutions that increasingly seemed necessary.[91] He even began to lump Italy with Germany and Japan. But writing in 1931, only a few months before his death, Olivetti affirmed once again his preference for nonmilitary solutions and his belief in the possibility of international cooperation and justice. He insisted that Italy, in confronting her economic problems, wanted "to forget the teaching of history, according to which a dynamic people which finds it impossible to live its life necessarily attacks the wealth of someone else," and he expressed the hope of Italians that the selfishness of others "will not force us to remember that lesson."[92]

A few years later, at the time of Italy's war with Ethiopia, Panunzio bitterly lamented the frustration of all the postwar aspirations for a new kind of international order. The League of Nations had proven a "flawed masterpiece" serving to preserve an unjust status quo in the interests of the "have" nations, who were seeking to cement their hold on colonies they had acquired through force before. But Panunzio had not given up. He recalled his own insistence, as the Great War was ending, that a viable international order would have to embrace the socioeconomic sphere and called again for a supranational corporativism, with international councils to coordinate socioeconomic relationships. Despite the disillusionment and bitterness, despite the Ethiopian War, Panunzio did not advocate autarky and national exclusiveness; the way out was more international coordination, not less: "Egotism among nations is a material and moral absurdity; nations . . . cannot live closed and isolated but must interact and cooperate."[93]

Obviously then, some of the syndicalists' statements as fascists did help to rally support for the kind of aggressive foreign policy that the Nationalists had always wanted, but not because the syndicalists had adopted the Nationalist vision of international relations and human history. Nor did this measure of convergence stem from the syndicalists' belief in war and the nation beginning in 1914 or before. It was not the syndicalists' desire for war, but their disillusionment with the peace, that helped to make possible a degree of short-term collaboration with the Nationalists. But foreign policy was never primary for the syndicalists in any case. Even after they began to recognize the importance of the nation's position in the world, their central objective remained domestic change.

Domestic changes seemed to be necessary everywhere if Europe was to have an era of peace and justice in the aftermath of the Great War. While the Nationalists blamed popular government for being short-sighted and pacific, Panunzio called for changes to make the European governments more popular, as the way to overcome militarism and chauvinistic nationalism.[94] Even the parliamentary governments had to be transformed to enable the people genuinely to control foreign policy. So while the Nationalists wanted government to become less popular in order to enhance the nation's capacity to wage war, the syndicalists wanted government to become more popular in order to enhance the prospects for justice and peace.

6 / The Postwar Crisis and the Nationalist Response

The war lasted longer, and proved a more grueling test, than its advocates had anticipated in 1914–15. It had not been the buoyant interventionists who had sensed what was coming, but pessimistic neutralists like Giolitti and Giustino Fortunato, who had opposed intervention partly because they feared that Italy could not handle the challenge of a long war. Italy's disastrous defeat by Austria-Hungary at Caporetto in October 1917 seemed to confirm such gloomy presentiments, but this proved to be the nadir of her war experience— and a major turning point in modern Italian history. Although the defeat resulted from new Austro-Hungarian military tactics, contemporaries—both interventionists and neutralists—immediately became preoccupied with moral sources, since they viewed the defeat, like the whole wartime challenge, in terms of the long-standing problems of Italian national integration. And of course even if the defeat itself was comprehensible in strictly military terms, it still had to be asked whether this poorly integrated nation could hold together and recover.[1] Perhaps the neutralists had been right to doubt Italy's resiliency as a nation. Panunzio and Lanzillo were among those who were to participate in a project to rewrite Italian history in the light of Caporetto.[2] Now Italy was to have her examination of conscience.

The immediate situation looked brighter a month later when the philosopher Giovanni Gentile reflected on what this examination of conscience had meant for Italians. In discussing the terrifying self-doubts that he and his countrymen had felt just a few weeks before, he gave voice to all the crisis of national self-image that was—and would long remain—inextricably bound up with the Italian experience of World War I: "In its crudest, yet simplest and truest form, it was the

129

realization that an Italy destined to die as the result of a military defeat would not have been worthy of living. It would not have been a people created to live as a free state, precisely because, as our enemies love to depict us, it would indeed have been too much a heterogeneous crowd of people without any kind of discipline (lacking in political discipline because lacking in moral and religious discipline) and without the capacity for serious intellectual work (for this too involves method and organization)."[3] It was only because Italy had undergone this self-examination that her recovery after Caporetto and her eventual participation in the victory proved such a stimulus to her self-confidence. Caporetto transformed the war from a narrow exercise in *"sacro egoismo"* into a test of national viability and cultural worth—and Italy passed it. In the same article, Gentile stressed that Italy, in recovering from Caporetto, had proven her ability as a nation to respond to adversity and thus had earned both self-esteem and the esteem of foreigners. Writing a few days later, on Christmas Day 1917, he portrayed the ongoing wartime challenge as an opportunity for Italians to overcome their indolence and frivolous skepticism and to build "a more steadfast, compact, serious, hard-working Italy, more aware of its mission."[4]

Seeking to rally the nation after Caporetto, the government began to talk about the political renewal that would accompany victory, and the war began to seem a great popular crusade for the first time.[5] By the end of the war, the belief was widespread that the war experience had been the catalyst for the moral and civic renewal which Italy needed. The war had involved the whole people in a great collective enterprise requiring discipline and self-sacrifice. Many of the interventionists, despite their differences, had pushed for war in 1914–15 precisely because they believed that Italy could achieve national integration and political renewal only through an initiation rite like this. At last it would be possible to complete what the Risorgimento had only begun: to create a genuine national community out of the atomized mass of Italians. Clearly, the ongoing insistence on the value of the war for Italy can only be understood in terms of Italy's long tradition of cultural self-doubt, her enduring crisis of self-image.

In fact, Italy's share in the final victory was relatively modest. She did hold after Caporetto and repel the last-ditch Austrian offensive in June 1918, but the Italian high command, expecting another year of war, remained extremely cautious. As events accelerated during the fall, however, fears that Vienna might suddenly ask for peace prompted Italian military leaders hurriedly to plan and carry out the Battle of Vittorio Veneto. The Italian victory resulted above all from the retreat of an Austrian imperial army already in advanced stages of internal collapse.[6] The ambiguous nature of Italy's contribution to the victory, and the high-handed way that she was soon to be treated at the Paris peace conference, did not help Italians supporting the war to put the value of the experience in clear perspective. The myth that immediately developed portraying Vittorio Veneto as the decisive battle of World War I was symptomatic of the deep feelings of inferiority and the strong desires for national redemption underlying the Italian war experience.

The war did bring new segments of the Italian population to political consciousness, first by making it all too clear that what happened to Italy deeply affected them and their families. By the war's end, 5,750,000 Italians had served under arms, 600,000 had been killed, and over 700,000 wounded. Ultimately, the war had affected everyone; it became the first great collective experience of the Italian people, engendering a sense of community and shared destiny.[7] At the same time, ordinary Italians had become more aware of their long-standing separation from the Italian state.

The war also changed Italian society by stimulating industrial development, and this, in turn, contributed to the new buoyancy and confidence.[8] Accelerating industrialization seemed to indicate that Italian society was more dynamic than the pessimists of the political elite had suspected. Important sectors of Italian industry responded to the wartime challenge by adopting more progressive methods in management and production. Some firms—Fiat, for example—took advantage of the situation to establish themselves on a solid productive footing once and for all. But the most striking feature of the war years was the fantastic expansion of ILVA and Ansaldo, the two big conglomerates centered around the steel industry. This growth involved some solid enterprise, as these firms sought to supply the government with military supplies, but also much unproductive dealing and financial manipulation. During the most difficult years of Italy's postwar readjustment, from 1921 to 1923, the two giants suffered severe crises, which ultimately led to the bankruptcy of Ansaldo and the fall of its principal creditor, the Banca di Sconto. Fiat, on the other hand, quickly surmounted its relatively minor problems; the electricity and chemicals industries, both relatively healthy, similarly endured the postwar readjustment quite well.[9] In fact, it was possible for those desiring viable industrial growth to be quite ambivalent about the overall condition of Italian capitalism as the war came to an end, since much of the economic expansion during the war had been too chaotic to be healthy, and since traditional financial manipulation had accelerated along with productive enterprise.[10] Contemporaries sometimes had difficulty distinguishing the healthy from the unhealthy, but it was clear that the ascendant economic sectors included not only solid industrial producers, but also speculating parasites with links to the Italian state.

During the war, new relationships developed between sectors of the bureaucracy and sectors of industry and finance that were symptomatic of more basic changes in the nature of the Italian state.[11] Inevitably, given wartime pressures, the parliament became less important in the overall system, and the executive governed increasingly by means of decree laws. At the same time there was some fragmentation of the state's authority, as private sectors established more direct and permanent links with the bureaucracy and thus with the decision-making process within the state.

Those in the trenches were the most deeply affected by the war experience. At the beginning of the war, the bulk of the young Italians called to serve were indifferent to the patriotic and antimilitarist ideals through which the interventionists had sought to arouse popular support for the war. They were especially resentful of the interventionists, who seemed to have gotten them into it in the first place; in October 1915, some even welcomed the news that Corridoni had been killed. But gradually, many of them—especially among the junior officers— began to see themselves as embodying the potential for healthy change in Italy thanks to the experience they shared at the front—the solidarity, the idealism, the common sacrifice. They felt separate from those not directly involved, from the old Italy they had left behind. It was widely believed in the trenches that civilian indulgence in luxuries was at a peak and that military suppliers were using fraud to gain excessive profits. Real wages for workers, profits, and private consumption did all go up during the war.[12]

The sense of community developing in the trenches bound together junior officers and enlisted men, since they shared the same sufferings, dangers, and purposes. There was a kind of equality, or classlessness, to their whole experience, despite the necessary hierarchy of military rank. Later on, memories of this wartime classlessness transcending formal hierarchy would inspire the creators of fascism as they sought to develop a new order from the embryo that had emerged during the war. Not surprisingly, however, the young junior officers from the middle and lower middle classes developed a more positive attachment to the war than did the masses of enlisted men, mostly peasants, who served under them.[13]

While the war experience was crucial in forging the generation that created fascism, the war for these young Italians was not primarily a brutalizing experience, undermining old values and certainties. It was not so much the danger, the violence, and the adventure that defined the war experience for them as it was the new sociopolitical awareness and idealism, based on their experience of solidarity and common enterprise. The soldiers became more aware of what had previously been lacking in their fragmented society and began to glimpse the possibility of an alternative. The war experience, then, was a source of new ideals, even if it also led some to be impatient with theories and to glorify action, to link the new values with military trappings, and to be less than scrupulous about the means of implementing their new ideals. Partly because of their wartime origins, these new ideals could become hollow and rhetorical and subject to manipulation by others. But the ideals were genuine; the postwar role of the young soldiers cannot be explained without them.

Increasingly, and especially after the war was over and Italy had won, soldiers and veterans insisted on the value of the war and defended it against its detractors, despite their hatred of the war's hardships. With the domestic propaganda in 1918, the resignation of 1915–17 became impatient expectation of radical change in postwar Italy, to be based somehow on the war experience itself.[14] Thus an element with strong but confused aspirations for cultural and political change emerged from the war—a new, potentially revolutionary force defined by common wartime experience, not by social class. They constituted the spearhead of the wider hopes for renewal that the war had engendered. The outcome of Italy's postwar crisis depended in large part on what would happen to these veterans and their fragile ideals. Would the old liberal elite succeed in absorbing them into the liberal parliamentary system and, in the process, manage to revitalize both itself and the system? If not, would the Socialist party, apparently the most obvious vehicle for a change in the system itself, manage to develop a basis of understanding with them, giving their aspirations more coherent political expression? If not, could these new sectors develop sufficient intellectual coherence to constitute an autonomous challenge to the existing order and to develop a viable alternative to it?

The postwar crisis out of which fascism emerged was a political crisis, a crisis of the old restrictive transformist system which, thanks to the war, the society had simply outgrown. It was widely believed that the war had revealed an Italian people far superior to their unfavorable image in the minds of the pessimists in the political class.[15] But the political class proved inadequate to the task of self-renewal. Orlando, Nitti, and Giolitti, the prime ministers from 1917 to 1921 and the last hopes of Italian liberalism, all had important strengths, but none of them proved able to grasp what the war had meant or to bring to fruition the potential for change bound up with the Italian war experience. Vittorio Emanuele Orlando was an outstanding juridical scholar and a generous man, with qualities that made him an effective wartime leader, but he was too sentimental and rhetorical to get a firm grip on the complicated postwar situation. Like many others in the ruling class who had favored the war, Orlando understood its value for Italy in terms of her international position: the war was not the beginning of radical domestic change, but the culmination of both Italian territorial unification and the long process of Italy's affirmation as a world power.[16]

Orlando's successor as prime minister in 1919–20 was Francesco Saverio Nitti, an economist whose hard-headed practicality contrasted with Orlando's sentimentalism. But Nitti failed even more completely to grasp the import of the war experience. With much justice, he was widely perceived as the heir of *giolittismo*—and thus was bitterly opposed by interventionists of both left and right. He was essentially an opportunist lacking an overall conception of the difficult postwar situation. As a result, he tended to vacillate, to let things slide, to look for expedients, adjusting to events as they occurred. Ultimately, he failed not only to lead serious renewal, but also to respond coherently as the threat to the liberal system itself began to gather force out in society.[17]

The one major attempt at political innovation was the institution of proportional representation to replace the old system of single-member constituencies, in time for the first postwar elections in November 1919. Proportional representation favored the emergence of relatively disciplined mass parties and thus seemed to portend the eclipse of the old transformist system based on individual bargaining. But in the volatile postwar situation, the new system only produced the instability which the old political managers had sought through transformism to avoid. The elections of November 1919 gave the Socialist party 156 seats and the new Catholic Popular party (Popolari) 100. Together, these two modern mass parties had a majority of the 509 seats in the Chamber of Deputies, yet they failed to form a joint government to make the sweeping reforms which much of the country desired. Such a course—which might genuinely have revitalized the liberal parliamentary system—was never remotely a possibility. In the first place, the Popolari were seriously divided between progressive and very conservative elements. Collaboration with the Socialists was anathema to the strong conservative faction, as well as to the Vatican, which could obviously exert a strong influence despite the party's nonconfessional character. But the Popolari never had the option of collaboration with the Socialists to form a workable parliamentary majority anyway. The Socialist party was anticipating a Bolshevik-style revolution in Italy and thus was not concerned with translating its 1919 electoral success into an immediate reform program. Proportional representation made it difficult to forge an effective parliamentary majority and thus did not prove an adequate vehicle for filling the political vacuum. Since its outcome only tended further to discredit parliamentary government, the reform played into the hands of those like the Nationalists and syndicalists who had advocated a more radical change, moving beyond parliamentary government, in the first place.

Nitti's successor in 1920, and the last hope of the traditional political system, was none other than Giovanni Giolitti, now seventy-eight years old. The return of Giolitti was symptomatic; the system was nearing its bankruptcy. Giolitti did set about earnestly to bring the rapidly deteriorating situation under control, although he worked through the old manipulative methods, seeking to fragment the emerging mass parties so that he could treat with individuals or small groups. But the advent of universal suffrage and proportional representation inevitably strained the old system; and now, as a result of the elections of 1919, two modern mass parties had an absolute parliamentary majority. But Giolitti hung on. He had always sought to impede the development of a Catholic mass party, and it is not surprising that he and Don Luigi Sturzo, the Sicilian priest who led the Popolari, were constantly at loggerheads. In addition, Giolitti sought to "transform" and bend to his purposes the new Fascist movement through an electoral alliance in 1921, but like the Popolari, this new force had too much internal consistency to be fragmented by Giolittian manipulation. Ultimately, Giolitti's outlook and method had changed too little. Unable to transcend the pessimistic and rather narrow perspective that had made him a neutralist, he did not really understand the psychological impact or the potential significance of Italy's war experience.[18] To the young idealists emerging from the war, Giolitti remained the epitome of the old politics of pessimism.

The frantic backroom political maneuvering which characterized the period from 1920 to 1922 represented the death throes of the old politics based on personal clienteles and alliances. Finally, after Giolitti fell in 1921, secondary figures like Ivanoe Bonomi and Luigi Facta were elevated to power, while those with real political weight bargained behind the scenes to determine who had sufficient support to put together the next ministry. By October 1922, the old political system was bankrupt, and the old political class knew it. Thus it was willing to acquiesce in the advent of a new man, Benito Mussolini. Renewal had to come from outside the system, but it was hoped that Mussolini could be domesticated. Perhaps he could play a role analogous to those played by Depretis in 1876 and Giolitti in 1901, opening up the system but preserving the basic institutions of the state. This was a considerable gamble, but for now, at least, there seemed to be no other choice.

Thus the traditional ruling class failed to bring about the necessary renewal from within the system.[19] Sensitive contemporaries who were by no means favorable to fascism have left us much eloquent testimony that the old liberal system was simply losing its legitimacy. The noted liberal historian Adolfo Omodeo, seeking to come to grips with the Italian crisis early in 1920, saw Nitti and Giolitti as manifestations of the basic Italian problem—the lack of confidence in their country on the part of those in the political class.[20] Omodeo admitted that Giolitti's pessimism had not been without foundation. But Giolitti—and now Nitti—had made no consistent effort to overcome the defects in Italy's political culture; these leaders were satisfied to work with those defects and thus ended up reinforcing them. Omodeo believed very deeply in the potential value of the war for Italian renewal. In the resistance after Caporetto, he argued, the nation had found itself and come together at last. The contact between elites and masses that had been lacking before had finally developed in the trenches, and this contact, he felt, could be the key to bridging the long-standing gap between the people and the state. But now the bitter and frustrated Omodeo could only denounce the Italian political class, which was letting slip this precious chance for Italy to come to grips with her long-term problems. Given the bankruptcy of the existing leadership, he insisted, the young Italians who had fought the war could legitimately see themselves as the spearhead of the new Italy and claim the right to lead the national renewal.

The decline of liberal Italy had deepened considerably by December of 1921, when the astute young liberal Guido De Ruggiero analyzed the divorce between state and society at the root of the Italian crisis; Italy, he argued, was experiencing

the uneasiness of a society that feels that it is not being governed by itself, but, instead, by minorities now necessarily exhausted; of a society in which the most significant elements are outside the state, and express, each one individually, their own private authority, which strike out in conflict with their adversaries and with the marginal authority of the state. Given this situation, all the useless remedies—changing ministries, transferring ten prefects, recruiting a thousand new royal police—are ridiculous.

The crisis of authority afflicts the whole substance of our political life. This crisis thus can be resolved only by the gradual absorption into the state of those forces which now express themselves outside it. Only then will we be able to have a strong state—thus enabling us even to reduce the immense armies of police that we have today.

. . . The strength of the state is nothing but the resultant of the forces which converge in it. Give to the great masses the clear, concrete sensation that the state is not aloof from and opposed to them, and they will obey the state, because they will feel themselves to be obeying their own law. . . .

And given the situation of relative strength today, we must understand by "the masses," in large part, the socialist masses, the only ones who have up to now a clear definition and a solid organization, and who, as such, can constitute a permanent support for the state.[21]

But those who led these "socialist masses" did not view the Italian crisis in anything like De Ruggiero's terms. Indeed, the role of the Italian Socialist party during and after the war severely complicated the crisis—and severely complicates historical evaluation of its outcome. If the old politics was bankrupt and the old political class exhausted, if the society had become mature enough for a more genuinely popular political system, then surely the Socialist party was one possible vehicle for renewal. As it happened, however, the Socialist party did not seek to promote a national political revolution or to embrace the cause of the idealistic young war veterans. The Socialists had remained aloof from the war from the beginning, expressing both indifference and strategic uncertainty through Costantino Lazzari's ambiguous formula "Neither support, nor sabotage." They simply were not able to come to terms with the war, assessing its meaning for their country and its implications for their own postwar role.[22] In the aftermath of Caporetto, it is true, Turati and the reformist wing began to reexamine their position and finally, during the spring of 1918, declared their support for the war, embracing Woodrow Wilson's interpretation of its meaning and explicitly repudiating Lenin's. But as they moved toward the democratic prowar position of Leonida Bissolati, Turati and his colleagues found themselves increasingly isolated within the Socialist party. The large majority of Socialists, led by the intransigent or "maximalist" wing, continued even after the armistice to scorn the war, denying it had any special meaning for Italy and making fun of the war veterans and their aspirations.

There were, to be sure, serious obstacles to any populist alliance between the soldiers and veterans, on the one hand, and the Socialists and workers, on the other. Not only had the two groups long differed over the meaning of the war, but the veterans resented the fact that so many workers had spent the war years not in the trenches, but in the factories making what seemed to be very high wages. Industrial workers were generally exempt from military service during the war, and many of them did enjoy rising real wages as they manned the factories.[23] But whatever the obstacles, the Socialists made no effort to win over the veterans and to articulate their aspirations. Instead, they became infatuated with the Russian Revolution and talked incessantly about a Bolshevik-style revolution in Italy, although they neglected the planning and organization that were necessary if Italy was to have such a revolution.[24] Socialist leaders were simply waiting for the bourgeois state to become moribund.

Socialist propaganda gave a revolutionary cast to the remarkable wave of strikes, land seizures, and factory occupations that gripped Italy during the *biennio rosso*—the "two red years" of 1919 and 1920. Some of this popular ferment stemmed from the expectations aroused during the period after Caporetto. Often those expectations were frustrated, for the advent of peace only led to worsening economic circumstances; with the end of artificial wartime conditions, including interallied exchange controls, Italy faced a grave economic situation involving inflation and shortages. Membership in the CGL, still the largest trade union confederation, swelled from 249,000 at the end of the war to 1,258,000 in October 1919 and up to 2,150,000 when the *biennio rosso* reached its climax during the fall of 1920. The number of strikes and strikers also shot up to record levels.[25] The strike wave included several serious general strikes, including the imposing *scioperissimo* of July 1919. In some areas of the Po valley—Ferrara, for example—Socialists and unions were strong enough virtually to control local economic life. Finally, during the fall of 1920, the Socialist and labor challenge reached its culmination with a series of factory occupations which exacerbated tensions but which ultimately failed, signaling the end of the *biennio rosso*. Throughout this tumultuous period, Socialists continued to ridicule the war experience as they exalted bolshevism and exhorted the workers to revolution.[26] Soldiers and veterans who wanted to follow the Socialists were often barred from party membership.[27]

In his classic analysis of the Socialist party's postwar failure, Pietro Nenni insists that the Socialists had no irreducible conflict of interest with the veterans, who, he feels, would have accepted enthusiastically a Socialist offer to embrace their cause.[28] In the fluid situation of postwar Italy, the old divisions could have been overcome, but the party lacked the flexibility to make its revolution a national revolution, one with a place for nonproletarian war veterans. Nenni's negative assessment is not unique, for the Socialist posture has drawn criticism from a wide variety of historians.[29] Costanzo Casucci, for example, insists that the Socialist stance was neither appropriate nor realistic, given the political problem at issue in postwar Italy and given the cultural legacy of the war experience. Prone to demagoguery and abstraction, the Socialists and workers failed to acquire the "universal" consciousness worthy of a ruling class and so could not legitimately claim to replace the old liberal elite.[30]

If the Socialist alternative was insensitive and inflexible, then the discontented young war veterans did not have the option of following the Socialists after the war. In fact, they faced a political situation that seemed to offer no exit. The old politics of personalities was bankrupt; the new mass-party politics, represented by the parliamentary Socialists and the Popolari, was apparently at an impasse. And those in control of the established revolutionary channels seemed unsure of what they were doing but threatened, nevertheless, to make a revolution which was inappropriate and impractical for postwar Italy. If neither the established parliamentary system nor the normal Socialist channels for revolutionary change were viable, then some sort of third way had to be created—a vehicle for the appropriate kind of radical change.

The fundamental question was whether the vague ideals of the war could develop sufficient coherence to provide the foundation for a viable alternative to both liberalism and Socialism. By the end of the war, there were many proposals for political change more radical than proportional representation but short of Socialist revolution. Most envisioned changes in institutions as well as changes in the personnel of the nation's political elite. This renewal would have to respond not only to the long-standing problems of the Italian state, but also to the changes in the relationships between bureaucracy and parliament, and between private interests and public power, that had taken place during the war. There was widespread interest, especially, in some sort of professional representation, or system of technical councils, to replace or supplement existing parliamentary institutions.[31] The Nationalists and the syndicalists offered the most thoroughgoing proposals for postliberal and non-Socialist change to those searching for a way out of the present impasse. Each group was seeking to interpret the meaning of the war and to offer an immediately relevant program that would enable Italians to create a healthier political system. The essentials of the two programs were already beginning to crystallize before fascism emerged as a serious political force.

The Nationalists were preoccupied with Italy's international economic position in the new industrial age, and especially in the new situation emerging from the war. Because the war had spurred a sharp increase in industrial capacity throughout the modern world, the international economic struggle would inevitably take on new dimensions in the future. If Italy adjusted quickly, taking advantage of her industrial development and her tempering by war to reorder herself domestically, she might be able to compete on more favorable terms than before. The Nationalists found encouraging the greater emphasis on productivity and economic values that seemed to characterize Italy during the war. But they warned repeatedly that Italy's economic situation was precarious, given the objective limits and weaknesses of her industry.[32] The rapid industrial expansion during the war had been based on state orders that could not continue indefinitely. Italian businessmen were themselves responsible for some of the difficulties they faced; we have seen that during the war especially, growth in certain industrial sectors was chaotic and had nothing to do with long-term productivity. Things would be bad enough, the Nationalists felt, even if Italy were a well-integrated nation, but in fact her congenital defects as a nation made her particularly vulnerable. Italy, then, could not afford the luxuries of others. If she was to meet the challenge and survive as an autonomous nation, she would have to discipline herself in an especially thorough-going way. In the new era, Italy could no longer maintain her ambiguous position on the fringes of great power status: she would either become a fully viable nation, reordering herself for production and international competition—or she would become a kind of colony.

The domestic program the Nationalists proposed was designed to make this reordering possible. The fundamental premise was national solidarity and cooperation, but more specific changes were also necessary—to replace the old liberal elite, giving political power to those more aware of the needs of production, and to coordinate the society's energies from the top, making the workers, and the Italian people in general, instruments of the nation's essential economic purposes. Ultimately, as Alfredo Rocco argued explicitly in 1919, the whole nation had to organize itself for the imperialist struggle that the terms of Italy's economic and demographic situations made necessary.[33]

It is easy to see why Italian Nationalism is generally interpreted as an ideological expression of the interests of certain sectors of Italian big business.[34] During the war, close links had developed between the Nationalist movement and such firms as Ansaldo, and the Nationalist vision reflected the inherent precariousness of large-scale industry in a country that offered a limited domestic market and few raw materials. The Nationalists' postwar program, aiming to subordinate all the nation's energies to the requirements of production, responded to the needs of firms facing an uncertain future after the chaotic wartime expansion. Nationalism articulated the perceptions and convictions of certain business leaders—the belief, for example, that Italy could not afford a strong labor movement, given her relatively weak position in international competition. So to portray Nationalism as an Italian capitalist ideology is a plausible and useful beginning. It does not, however, constitute a fully convincing interpretation, and it can easily become a formula that obstructs understanding in depth.

Italian Nationalism grew out of traditional Italian right liberalism but finally split off from it, repudiating its genuinely liberal component and giving new form to the elitist, defensive component. Nationalism made more explicit the traditional right liberal identification of the state and the long-term national interest with an elite, operating beyond the reach of the untrustworthy Italian people. In many respects, however, the Nationalists' doctrine was more modern and forward-looking than the right liberalism they left behind. They were seeking changes appropriate to the modern industrial world, with all the new possibilities it offered, with all the new dangers it brought in its wake.

The old liberals had lacked confidence in Italian society, and thus they had devised a relatively restricted political system. But they had not considered Italy's flaws to be permanent. Italy could hope to become ever more like Great Britain, with its pluralistic liberal parliamentary system. In Nationalism, social sectors that had formerly supported liberal institutions were giving up on a political system that had come to seem simply inappropriate for Italy. The Italian problem was too deep; and besides, whatever the chance that Italy might ultimately develop the preconditions for a viable liberal system, her present international economic situation was so precarious that she could not wait, living from day to day by means of transformist expedients. Alfredo Rocco, like the right liberals, admired Great Britain, but he denied that it could offer a model for Italy. The liberal democratic state, he said, had done well in the Anglo-Saxon countries because there the people had qualities the Italians lacked, qualities which compensated for the serious problems inherent in liberalism. Above all, in the Anglo-Saxon countries and in France, there were great national traditions, which meant that "the idea of the state has been strengthened through centuries of struggle sustained by the state in order to affirm its supremacy."[35] But Italy had been divided and dominated by foreigners for centuries, and indiscipline and political indifference were now deeply rooted among the Italian masses. The liberal democratic state had not been able to provide the necessary political education and discipline. This sense of a special Italian weakness was basic to Nationalism. Even Francesco Coppola, who was less thoroughgoing than Rocco in supporting postliberal solutions, stressed that the centuries of foreign domination in Italy had produced a mentality that prevented the major political virtues from being consolidated among the Italians.[36]

In Nationalism, the relatively authoritarian relationship between elitist state and untrustworthy society which the liberals had seen as a temporary expedient became a brutal and permanent fact of nature. Only an elite could ever grasp the long-term interests of the nation; the masses must always be led—by the elite, securely anchored in the state. There would be no need for the expedients of transformism—to mediate between political elite and society—once this overtly elitist relationship had been cemented. In order to justify it, the Nationalists portrayed the nation as an organism having interests which transcended those of the finite, contingent individuals who happened to be alive at any particular moment. The national interest was not merely the arithmetic sum of their individual interests. And it was up to the state, understood as an enduring focus of stability, existing prior to the society, to discern and promote the nation's permanent interests. As Rocco put it, the Nationalists advocated "the concept of government of the most capable, that is, of those who through tradition, through culture, through social position, are able to raise themselves above the contingent interests of the generation to which they belong and to discern and to realize the great historic interests of the State."[37] The alternative, popular sovereignty, led only to a kind of anarchy, with each individual seeking his own well-being, unconcerned about the survival of the national species. In opposition to liberal individualism, the Nationalists insisted that existing individuals had to be understood as instruments for the nation's long-term ends, as determined by the elitist state. The individual had, for example, no natural right to liberty; the state could concede liberties to him, insofar as this was consistent with its aims.[38]

The Nationalists, however, were not simply authoritarians seeking to undo the damage that Depretis and Giolitti had done. If the state was to pursue the long-term interests of the nation, maximizing Italy's productivity and capacity for international struggle, the masses would have to be involved and would have to identify with the state and its purposes in a much more thoroughgoing way. Liberalism had to be transcended in part because of its inability to galvanize the energies of the masses for great national enterprises.

The Nationalists dared to oppose Giolitti and the established patterns of Italian politics because they were confident that through industrialization, especially, the society was developing the capacity for a more effective system. The first step in reconstructing the national state was to bring elements from the new industrial bourgeoisie into the state, to give them political power. In contrast to the lawyers of the old political class, these products of the emerging industrial world would understand the terms of the international economic challenge and thus would grasp the changes which Italy required. Such people would assume political leadership at the expense of parliament, which seemed to have little grasp of the world of production and international economic competition.[39] In fact, of course, parliament had remained relatively weak in liberal Italy, but it had been the potential power of parliament that had made transformist expedients necessary. But now Italy did not need—and could not afford—the pure politics bound up with the old parliamentary system.

The new ruling class was not to be composed solely of the new industrial bourgeoisie, but would be a kind of hybrid, reflecting the

Nationalists' hybrid origins and sensibilities. They were seeking to replenish the political elite with more productive elements, but they also wanted to restore the power of the conservative, nonparliamentary sectors of the state—especially the upper bureaucracy—vis-à-vis the political, parliamentary sector, including those like Giolitti who had been willing to compromise with parliament. The Nationalists sought to act as mediators between the newer industrial and the older bureaucratic sectors, helping them to recognize their common mission. Together they could pursue the long-term interests of the nation.

Again and again in his wartime speeches and writings, Enrico Corradini called for these two groups to overcome their long-standing separation and join together, forming the basis for the new dynamic state that would emerge from the war.[40] He spoke frequently to business groups, exhorting the new industrial bourgeoisie to organize, to become politically active, and to grasp its mission of national leadership. Corradini was seeking to promote the self-confidence and political vision which the Italian industrial bourgeoisie had traditionally lacked. The war, he recognized, was already bringing about the necessary interpenetration of the state and the productive bourgeoisie, although this phenomenon seemed to him to be less pronounced in Italy than elsewhere in Europe. So the present wartime situation offered grounds for optimism, but there was still much goading to be done.

Increasingly, as the war dragged on, Corradini envisioned not merely increased political participation by business, but an entirely new regime, based on the logic of production, structured to serve the interests of the national economy.[41] The state had to provide the more thoroughgoing economic coordination that was now becoming necessary. Luigi Federzoni, speaking in Rome in March 1917, blamed the dominant economic liberalism, the absence of coordination from the state, for the chaotic quality of Italy's recent economic growth.[42] In the new postwar situation, he warned, Italy would require a far greater measure of economic regulation and planning; new productive sectors had to assume political power precisely to make this possible. Moreover, all of Italy's social and foreign policy would have to be coordinated with the needs of the economy. Federzoni's thinking in this speech, and Nationalist thinking in general, pointed toward totalitarian coordination of the entire society to meet the requirements of production and international competition.

Corradini insisted on calling the regime the Nationalists envisioned a "national democracy," but he left no doubt that it would be something quite different: "The state will finally create a true national democracy . . . in which the bourgeoisie will occupy the leading positions of power and the lower classes will participate in a well-coordinated way, with everybody, the former and the latter, subordinated to the ends of the nation." So the masses were not to be left outside the new regime: "To them, too, belongs a part of the power that is held above. They are the base of the pyramid."[43] In this harmonious productivist order, Corradini felt, universal suffrage would simply wither away "through the force of reality" sooner or later, but in the meantime, the productive bourgeoisie would have to work to keep the system under control. In the same way, Corradini assumed that, once political parasitism had been eliminated, objective laws of production would come into play, revealing beneath the class struggle the deeper basis for the natural collaboration of classes.[44] For now, however, the productive bourgeoisie must strenuously wage the class struggle. Indeed, Corradini was seeking to exhort the bourgeoisie, to enhance its confidence, not only vis-à-vis the old political elite, but also vis-à-vis the labor union challenge.

Trade unions posed a serious danger to the nation's production, but they also afforded an opportunity. Alfredo Rocco grounded Corradini's wartime visions in more concrete proposals for institutional change by showing how the syndical phenomenon could be transformed from a threat into the basis for the new productivist order. In Rocco's thinking about the modern labor movement, we can see clearly the hybrid quality of Italian Nationalism—the juxtaposition of defense and dynamism, of desperation and confidence, of traditional and modern concerns. For Rocco was of two minds about the advent of economic organization and trade union power, and he had two converging, but distinguishable, purposes in mind when he advocated first a Nationalist system of labor organizations and ultimately a corporative state to replace the liberal state.

As early as May of 1914, Rocco proposed that the Nationalists develop a union movement of their own, for a system of national syndicates could be a valuable means to foster class collaboration and to cement a permanently hierarchical system.[45] But Rocco's proposal had to wait until after the war to be formally adopted as Nationalist policy. Consideration of the national syndicalist idea dominated the pivotal meeting which the Nationalist Association held at Rome in March of 1919, amid all the anticipation of radical sociopolitical change in Italy. Now the purpose of the proposed Nationalist unions was clarified, and a variety of syndicalism was integrated into the Nationalist program as a basis for a serious change in Italian institutions.[46]

Corradini called explicitly for the formation of Nationalist unions in the meeting's opening speech, while Rocco sharpened the argument in the discussion that followed, stressing the precariousness of Italy's economic situation and insisting that national syndicalism would enable her to survive in the new era.[47] Through a network of organizations based on economic function, the state could mobilize the society and foster, or even impose, the class collaboration in production that Italy's economic vulnerability made necessary. The new unions would make the workers understand the community of interests among all classes in the production process. But the syndicates were to be extended to the employers as well, making possible the coordination which each economic sector required: "Only through this kind of unitary organization will each industry be able to confront foreign competition in international markets, to produce more—and more cheaply—and to eliminate internal competition and create a harmonious fusion between the interests of the workers and those of the industrialists."[48] Rocco applauded the concentration of industry into large organizations like Ansaldo and Fiat which the war had brought about, but the process of economic organization had to be extended further.[49] Ultimately, the political order itself had to become the vehicle for economic coordination, and the emergence of syndical organizations provided the state with the mechanism it needed to pursue its economic ends.

Rocco proclaimed the twentieth century to be "the era of syndicates."[50] The modern industrial system had given rise to these economic groupings, which could not be encompassed, politically or juridically, within the framework of liberal individualism. By giving structure to the mass society of atomized individuals, such organizations could enable the nation to compete effectively, as long as they were properly directed from above. And so Rocco advocated that the "organic" economic groupings replace "amorphous" individuals as the basis of political life. For now, he proposed merely a corporative senate as a check to the chamber, but it was clear that his position implied a more thoroughgoing departure from parliamentary liberalism.

The Nationalists, then, were by no means nostalgic for the earlier period of mass political apathy and disorganization in Italy. In their desire to make use of the energies of the masses, especially the new industrial proletariat, they were moving beyond traditional authoritarianism, which is happy with mass indifference, and toward modern totalitarianism, requiring mass involvement and enthusiasm. But the masses could be allowed to participate only within a rigidly hierarchical system, controlled and manipulated from the top. Through the corporative state they soon proposed for fascism, the Nationalists intended to involve the masses more constantly, but to give them less potential for real political power. Modern social organization was tremendously valuable, but as a way to mobilize the society, not as a way to educate the people for fuller political participation. The Nationalists deeply desired a more dynamic, richer, healthier Italy, but the other aspects of their thinking—their deeper defensive and elitist conservatism—determined their criteria of national viability.

As the labor organizations came to seem more threatening during the *biennio rosso*, the purely conservative side of the Nationalist doctrine became more explicit. To organize the masses through national syndicates was not only a means to Italian national integration, but also an end in itself, a response to a more universal problem. The advent of labor unions was a major manifestation of the threat which the masses posed to order and value in modern society. The modern crisis, stemming from the long-term rise of the masses, was presently more threatening in Italy than elsewhere; but Italy was not unique, and the crisis by no means afflicted her alone. As we penetrate to his deepest concerns, we find not Rocco the Italian, seeking a more viable nation, but Rocco the threatened, conservative, elitist psychological type—a man who deeply needed order and who, to an extreme degree, perceived institutions as vulnerable and fragile. Still, the Nationalists' uniquely Italian concerns deepened and hardened their universal conservative sensibility. The Italian masses were especially threatening, partly because their antinational traditions made them especially susceptible to socialist demagoguery.

From the Nationalist perspective, the liberal ideas of 1789 had been doubly ruinous: the dogma of egalitarianism had led the masses to a counterproductive challenge to the natural hierarchical order; the dogma of laissez-faire had made the liberal state first too indifferent, and then too weak, vis-à-vis the society. Thus the masses had been left free to organize out in society—and ultimately to mount a dangerous challenge to the sovereignty of the state itself. The advent of syndicates enabled the society to get out of hand, for now it was no longer a mass of atomized individuals, capable of acting only sporadically, chaotically, by means of popular insurrections. Organization enabled people to pursue their special interests, even at the expense of the state and the general interest. So the same qualities which made the syndicates potentially valuable instruments of the state's purposes made them particularly threatening in the present context—because of the weaknesses inherent in the liberal political order. The trade union threat highlighted the inability of the state in its liberal form to pursue the long-term interests of the nation.

The Nationalist critique of liberalism and the liberal state became especially shrill and bitter in light of the *biennio rosso*. Left liberals like Giolitti had compromised the state's sovereignty in a foolish attempt to undercut the threat of socialism through bargaining and deals. The liberal ruling class had been so eager to avoid tough measures that

Italian society was now in danger of coming apart altogether. Speaking in Milan in 1922, just a few weeks before the March on Rome, Luigi Federzoni insisted that the wrong-headed conciliatory policy toward the socialists stemmed from a habit of mind and a method of government which had dominated the whole of Italian public life for twenty years.[51] The problem was not merely a political compromise that could be reversed by changes in tactics. Even for the relatively moderate Federzoni, the socialist threat seemed to call for a postliberal response. But it was Rocco who denounced the liberal mentality most bitterly, as, for example, when he warned early in 1920 that liberal weakness in the face of the present socialist threat was "paving the way for the collapse of the state, the disintegration of social life, and the ruin of civilization itself."[52] In an influential lecture at the University of Padua later that year, Rocco portrayed the current crisis as a return to medieval anarchy.[53] The weak liberal state found itself unable even to keep order, as organized groups in society pursued their own interests, resolving conflicts by private force. The dissolution that resulted was not only an evil in itself; it also undermined the national organism's ability to compete effectively in the international struggle.

Since, from Rocco's perspective, the syndical phenomenon had become so threatening only because liberalism allowed the unions to become "states" above the national state, a short-term restoration of order within the liberal framework would not be sufficient.[54] But neither would a greater dose of old-fashioned authoritarianism serve to restore the sovereignty of the state, for the masses had risen for good. They had learned to organize, and the organizations they had created to pursue their particular interests would not go away. The situation called for both a more aggressive ruling class and a more totalitarian form of state—one which organized the mass society. The state could use the intermediary organizations that had emerged spontaneously in society to mobilize society from the top, from the preexisting elitist state, in order to keep the masses permanently under control.

Rocco envisioned not merely juridical recognition and regulation of the existing unions, but a much more sweeping transformation. There must be new mixed syndicates in each industry, under resolute state control, with membership obligatory.[55] Moreover, given the terms of the modern crisis, restoration of the state's sovereignty required extension of its sovereignty. First in an article in *Politica* in April 1919, and repeatedly thereafter, Rocco called for a Magistracy of Labor to extend the state's sovereignty to labor relations.[56] No longer would salaries be determined "anarchically," through supply and demand or through a test of power in a strike. Instead, the state would prohibit strikes and impose through law the level of salaries which it determined to be in the nation's economic interest. This was the most obvious example of the way the Italian state would move in a postliberal, totalitarian direction, extending its sovereignty over the new areas of social life, both to keep the society under control and to coordinate the nation's activities for the long-term international struggle.

So Rocco's two basic purposes in calling for a new corporativist order converged, and thus in part the great force of his argument in the postwar Italian context. By organizing society from above, it would be possible to regiment the society for production and international expansion while simultaneously checking the dangerous threat which the masses posed through their unions. The Italian problem of insufficient national integration and the universal problem of the rise of the masses could be solved at the same time. Given the realities of the modern industrial world, solutions to both sets of problems pointed toward totalitarianism, with expanded state sovereignty and more constant mass involvement.

It was above all the menace of trade union power during the *biennio rosso*—and the apparent weakness of the liberal state in the face of it—that brought the differences between liberalism and Nationalism into sharp focus and made the Nationalists' proposals attractive to wider middle-class sectors. Even before World War I, Giolitti's strategy of state neutrality in labor conflicts had led many right liberals to worry about the implications of strikes, especially public service strikes, for the sovereignty of the state.[57] The *biennio rosso* intensified these concerns, but now the older, relatively conventional right liberals—such as Gaetano Mosca, Oreste Ranelletti, and Umberto Ricci—simply did not have very imaginative or convincing solutions to propose. In the second edition of his classic *Elementi di scienza politica*, Mosca merely called for a larger dose of patriotism—to provide the moral cohesion which he found the only antidote to the syndicalist peril.[58] The old liberals generally disapproved of proposals to make economic groupings the basis of political life, fearing that the merely "material" socioeconomic sphere would thereby contaminate the "ideal" political sphere.[59]

Perhaps the most bitter critique of the *biennio rosso* from within the liberal tradition was Giustino Fortunato's *Dopo la guerra sovvertitrice*, published in 1921. Given Italy's backwardness, Fortunato argued, the Italian masses were especially egotistical and materialistic, and particularly unable to grasp the collective interest or the liberal idea.[60] Thus they had proven easy prey for Socialist demagoguery, and the excesses of the *biennio rosso* had been the result. As far as Fortunato was concerned, all the current proposals to give the labor unions direct political power stemmed from this same illiberal, particularist mentality. The triumph of this mentality, he warned, would lead not to greater social harmony, but to a new syndicalist feudalism—an order "in which the sovereignty of the state is broken up into so many groups, with each of them obedient to its own syndicate and directed to its own particular benefit."[61] Fortunato contemptuously criticized the Italian bourgeoisie—with its smugness and cynicism—for failing to oppose socialism and the rise of the masses, but he found little hope for the future in the current crisis. All the confident pronouncements about postwar renewal, all the talk about the great potential of the latent forces of the country, seemed to him nothing but the empty rhetoric to which Italians were especially prone. This rhetoric, he felt, only obscured the real economic and demographic problems of the country, which in fact he grasped quite well.[62]

It is not surprising that Fortunato, writing in 1921, dismissed the young Fascist movement as a confused petty bourgeoisie expression. Of greater interest is his high-handed dismissal of Nationalism as "noisy" and "purely French in origin."[63] The latter charge was simply untrue. Others who shared Fortunato's concerns, but who were younger and less embittered and resigned, were beginning to find the Nationalists' responses to the same problems more convincing than his sane but bland calls for realism. Indeed, it was not such a big step from Fortunato's conception of Italian problems to Nationalist proposals for solution. For example, Fortunato felt that the Italian masses had remained backward and illiberal because Italy's capitalist bourgeoisie had been so weak. He noted that socialism, contrary to Marx's expectations, was strongest in countries that lagged economically. Moreover, he complained about the ambitious lawyers and others extraneous to the world of production who had gradually come to dominate Italian political life.[64] These were the people who had proven willing to compromise with socialism. It would be possible to develop some novel proposals for political change on the basis of these conceptions of Italy's problems, but Fortunato himself refused to follow the logic of his diagnoses in a post-liberal direction. The old liberalism seemed to have reached an impasse; Fortunato's gloom was symptomatic.

The Nationalists saw Italian problems in terms much like Fortunato's, but they proposed postliberal solutions to younger middle-class Italians who doubted that Fortunato's gloom had to be Italy's lot. The Nationalists, too, deplored the composition of the old ruling class, but they worked to change it, to give political power to more self-confident bourgeois sectors involved with the new world of industrial production. The Nationalists, too, perceived the difficulties of Italy's postwar economic situation, but they insisted that Italy could make it if all the national life were coordinated and subordinated to the needs of production. Most important, the Nationalists, too, were alarmed by the threat of labor union power to the sovereignty of the state, but they proposed a way to transform the syndical phenomenon from a threat into a useful instrument of the state's purposes. Thus it was easy for people who agreed with Fortunato's conception of problems to respond to Nationalist proposals for solution.

Rocco's proposals in light of the trade union challenge were offered partly in polemic with the traditional liberals. His influential inaugural lecture at the University of Padua in November of 1920 responded to a much-discussed lecture which Oreste Ranelletti had given earlier that year, and which Rocco himself had published in the Nationalist review *Politica*.[65] Insofar as the right liberals' suggestions had any substance at all, they seemed to point—haltingly, to be sure—to precisely the kinds of change that the Nationalists were seeking to promote. So in calling for a new ruling class, and a new form of state based on national syndicalism, the Nationalists could claim to be more consistent and systematic than the old liberals—and could erode the liberal constituency from the right.

An overall explanation of Nationalism, of why it emerged in this particular context, must begin by recognizing that the Nationalist program included a core of plausible responses to genuine problems. It was reasonable to be concerned about Italy's international economic position, about Italian emigration, and about the quality of Italy's old ruling class. It was reasonable to believe that nations are here to stay, to emphasize the rationality of collaboration in production, and to worry about the implications of strikes, especially public service strikes. It was not merely because of ideological distortion that the Nationalists believed that the richer countries enjoyed a position of international economic privilege which tended to perpetuate itself, keeping poorer countries like Italy in their place.[66] There were plausible reasons to insist that Italy required a more forceful foreign policy. Indeed, given the difficult economic and demographic situations which Italy faced, it was not anomalous to consider imperialism and to suggest that the nation must be ordered for imperialist struggle.[67]

Up to a point, then, the Nationalist doctrine need not be explained away in terms of socioeconomic ideology or psychological maladjustment. In important respects, however, the program was excessive, and its extremism indicates the admixture of "ideological," psychological, and traditional Italian elitist components. The Nationalists' preoccupation with the problems facing vulnerable sectors of Italian industry did color their thinking. Italy had to move toward totalitarianism to enable the state to coordinate all aspects of the national life for production and expansion. It is possible to recognize, without falling into a schematic reductionism, that the Nationalists were in part "ideological" spokesmen in very nearly the classic Marxist sense. However, the extremism of their doctrine also resulted from traditional Italian sensibilities and doubts, which persisted independently of the more modern problems of Italian capitalism. At the same time, a more universal psychological admixture also contributed to this extremism. Nationalism responded to the frustrations of individuals with an especially low tolerance for disorder and conflict and an especially great need for order and structure. These were individuals who, to an extreme degree, perceived social institutions—and even the cultural bases of society itself—as fragile and vulnerable. Psychologically, Rocco clearly had a good deal in common with Charles Maurras of the *Action Française*, despite the greater dynamism of the Italian Nationalist conception. It was not a common "ideological" perspective, based on common socioeconomic interests, that linked men like these, but common psychological characteristics cutting across social class lines. This psychological extremism led Rocco and his colleagues to perceive the threat to order and value as so serious that it was necessary, here again, to move toward totalitarian control of society from the top. From their perspective, totalitarianism was the only alternative to anarchy; rigid hierarchy in society was the only alternative to leveling.

The Nationalists tended to overestimate the dangers inherent in essential contemporary phenomena. Speaking in 1909, Enrico Corradini condemned the egalitarianism underlying the democratic ideas of 1789, accusing it of undermining the very reason for being of the collective life, which is the diversity of individuals.[68] Nationalism, he stressed, lauded inequality and differentiation. Similarly, Alfredo Rocco feared that what he considered to be the logical implications of democracy would soon be drawn out, producing absolute equality among individuals and the abolition of hierarchical social differentiation.[69] Only through inequality could discipline and organization in society be preserved. And despite his desire to revitalize the Italian ruling class, Rocco's accent was on the value of traditional hierarchies. His preoccupation and dread were so extreme that he ignored altogether the middle level between the total "equality" he feared and the traditional hierarchy he sought to preserve—namely, equality of opportunity to produce a legitimate hierarchy or meritocracy. Even in this overreaction, however, there is an element of plausibility that should not be overlooked. The Nationalists feared that the "leftist" demand for equality and justice, if admitted at all, would lead ultimately to the extreme, to complete leveling, because they sensed, with Maurras and others involved in the European conservative tradition, that the democratic aspiration was itself ambiguous and poorly thought through. Democrats, too, would ultimately neglect the middle level, for they were unlikely to admit that equality yields legitimate inequalities. Rocco feared, in other words, that democrats would find any differentiation and hierarchy as inherently illegitimate, as a violation of the equality imperative. So Rocco viewed traditional hierarchy as the only alternative to complete leveling because he sensed an ambiguity that can indeed be found in some expressions of the democratic imperative in the twentieth century. But since twentieth-century reality has remained so far from leveling, and even from genuine equality of opportunity, we must judge Rocco's fears on this score obsessive. We can understand his overreaction only in terms of "ideological" distortion, traditional cultural lags, and psychological extremism. It was only because of his own place in society, and because of a psychological propensity, characteristic of extreme conservatives, to assume that situations tend to be carried to their absurd extremes, that Rocco could have seen reality as he did. And in general, the Nationalists' priorities, their preoccupation with some problems facing Italy and their neglect of others, resulted from these kinds of distortions.

Because it synthesized a variety of concerns and perceptions and developed a rigorous program in response, Nationalism became a major focal point during the postwar crisis, as Italians seeking to transcend the old order looked about them for convincing diagnoses and proposals. It was not necessary to share all the fears that went into Nationalism to find the doctrine a useful indication of the direction in which Italy must begin to move. Indeed, since Nationalism was so obviously important, it is tempting to see all the national syndicalist, nationalist, prowar, procapitalist, anti-Socialist, and antiparliamentary ideas at work in Italy's postwar crisis as variations on Nationalist themes. The syndicalists, however, were developing a program which also pointed beyond parliamentary liberalism toward totalitarian corporativism, but theirs resulted from an altogether different set of needs and aspirations. Their neosyndicalism became the other main focal point for those who sought a convincing alternative to both liberalism and Marxism in the confused situation of postwar Italy.

7 / *The Neosyndicalist Program,*
   1917–1921

We have seen that the Italian revolutionary syndicalist doctrine which began to emerge in 1902 started to break down between 1910 and 1917, as tensions and ambiguities crept into it. But despite their doubts about the workers, despite their support for the war and their concern for the nation, despite their increasing preoccupation with Italian political problems, the syndicalists' stated objective continued to be proletarian revolution against bourgeois capitalism. They had not yet made a definitive theoretical step toward fascism. In 1917, however, the tensions reached the breaking point; confusion and ambiguity remained, but now the syndicalists managed to combine elements of their underlying populism with elements of their original syndicalism, creating a blueprint for change which they claimed was appropriate to immediate problems in postwar Italy. The Italian war experience after Caporetto, the Italian Socialist response to the Bolshevik revolution, and the theoretical revision which Panunzio led, all pushed the syndicalists in the same direction: away from the orthodox proletarian revolution against capitalism and toward a new populist revolution against liberalism, to be spearheaded by a new elite defined in terms of values or psychology rather than socioeconomic class. This doctrinal reconstruction took place before the syndicalists began to mix with fascism for good, and certainly it was not the result of Mussolini's influence. Ultimately, however, it did enable the syndicalists to encounter and influence a new constituency within the Fascist movement.

Italian syndicalism had been an unstable combination of Marxism and populism from the beginning, and the process of doctrinal revision involved evolution toward a new position from both directions at once. The syndicalists were not simply repudiating a tenuous Marxism in order to embrace explicitly a deeper populism. While the war experience rekindled their national populism, the syndicalists were also involved as European socialists in a theoretical revision which led them to advocate the kind of national political revolution they wanted in any case, as Italian populists. Since this revision was troubling and difficult, however, the syndicalists sometimes thought in terms of the old orthodox framework. But even on the Marxist level, their immediate focus during the postwar crisis was not on the proletarian revolution against capitalism, but on a preliminary, essentially political revolution not to be led by proletarians at all. Since this preliminary revolution largely coincided with the implementation of the potential for national redemption bound up with the war experience, populist and Marxist concerns were hard to distinguish in the syndicalists' thinking even between 1917 and 1921. They did not have to choose explicitly, since they envisioned a single process of radical change that would simultaneously sweep away the obstacles to Marxist-syndicalist development and create a viable, productive, "popular" nation. Gradually, however, the syndicalists' accents shifted, and they began to portray their neosyndicalist program not as a mere preliminary, but as an alternative to the Marxist revolution, a program relevant both to long-standing Italian problems and to the more universal problems of the European liberal order. The war experience was essential for all aspects of the process of revision since it simultaneously promised national redemption, raised questions about the relevance of Marxism, and seemed to have created new opportunities for the radical change needed to remove the obstacles to "normal" evolution according to the Marxist-syndicalist model.

Paolo Orano gave striking expression to the syndicalists' conception of the war's value for national redemption in his immediate postwar writings, collected in *L'Italia e gli altri alla conferenza della pace* (1919). In his enthusiasm over the Italian victory, he seemed to anticipate that a hard-working, productive Italy would emerge spontaneously and fully realized because of the war experience. Orano paid lip service to working-class leadership, but the transformation he envisioned required no special revolutionary role for the proletariat, which he found to be too immature to create a new society anyway. The war, he felt, had restored Italy's self-confidence by proving the country capable of serious things; now, at last, after centuries of indiscipline and disorganization, she would be able to get down to work, creating "the new miracle, that Italy of the labor aristocracy that can be the model of every other people that intends to endure." The new Italy would have an important new role in the world, not as a military-imperial power, but as the bearer of new productivist values: "The world needs the Italian; Italian is synonymous with worker; he is an organism of extraordinary energy, is resistant, adaptable, sober, thrifty; he is the poet of toil, the hero of excavations, the vanguard of the harvesters of the land, the essential raw material for the effort of continuing human progress."[1] Orano clearly wanted to believe that the war itself had been the Italian revolution, but all his exaggeration and forced optimism indicate his sense that it would not be so easy to reap the harvest of the Italian war experience.

And despite Orano's inspiring images, of course, the end of the war soon led to the *biennio rosso* and the threat of socialist revolution. In response, the syndicalists finally began cutting themselves off from the old orthodoxy for good, condemning the working class, declaring the class struggle to be counterproductive, and calling for collaboration between the workers and productive sectors of the bourgeoisie. Although some of them had begun to contemplate a nonproletarian preliminary revolution before the war, it was the *biennio rosso* which finally led the syndicalists explicitly to repudiate the orthodox revolution and to determine more precisely what an alternative revolution would have to involve. It would be a national, populist, political revolution, one with no special role for the proletariat.

We have seen that disillusionment with the Italian working class had become a common theme in syndicalist writing by 1910. World War I had seemed, in part, a chance for the Italian proletariat to redeem itself by selflessly joining the crusade to make the world safe for socialism. But since the workers, led by the neutralist Socialist party, had never grasped that the war was a crucial episode in their own struggle, syndicalist disenchantment with the proletariat had deepened. Then came the Bolshevik revolution in Russia and the threat of the wrong revolution in Italy in the aftermath of the war.

From the first news of the Bolshevik takeover, syndicalist criticism was unceasing—and sometimes quite penetrating. Russia seemed to have experienced the sort of revolution the syndicalists had always warned against: a revolution made not by a mature industrial proletariat, but by a party of nonproletarian intellectuals; a revolution in a country where capitalism had not completed its task of economic development, where the economy, seriously strained by war, was in severe crisis. This could only be a parody of the socialist revolution.[2] The syndicalists insisted repeatedly that since the Russian revolution was an arbitrary utopia imposed on a backward country by a group of intellectuals, it could only produce a new variety of class domination.[3] Moreover, the disastrous economic effects of premature revolution were already becoming evident in Russia.[4] The problem appeared to stem partly from the technical incompetence of the Russian proletariat, but even more important, Bolshevism did not seem to be based on the new productivist ethic which the syndicalists had always considered one of the crucial prerequisites for socialism.

The syndicalists' deepest fear during the immediate postwar period was that Bolshevism would intoxicate the immature Italian workers, leading them to premature revolution. And of course maximalist rhetoric and labor unrest did seem to threaten a Bolshevik-style revolution during the *biennio rosso*. In a moving statement early in 1919, De Ambris expressed the dilemma confronting the syndicalists as they faced the possibility of the wrong revolution:

For more than twenty years we have lived in the midst of the workers because of the sincere affection that we have for them, and we dare say that we know them as few others do. We would be lying to ourselves and we are convinced that we would be betraying the proletariat as well if we were to keep to ourselves our conviction, which can be summarized in this way: only a small part of the proletariat is able to understand and carry out the great duties which the revolution would require of it. The great majority, ignorant of everything, disorganized and amorphous, feels only the negative elements of the revolutionary fact. The members of this majority would understand the revolution in the Russian way and would be easy prey to all the demagogues wanting to exploit them. The revolution in progress would thus produce the exercise of power in the name of the proletariat but for the benefit of this new band of parasites, along with the destruction of everything which has been produced by the slow conquest accomplished by humanity through centuries of painful effort.[5]

All syndicalist literature during this period, but especially statements intended for the organized workers themselves, constantly stressed the same anti-Bolshevik, antirevolutionary theme: the Italian proletariat was simply not mature enough for a real socialist revolution.[6] Olivetti introduced the postwar series of *Pagine libere* in February of 1920 by reminding his readers that such a revolution could not take place until the workers had developed superior moral, political, and technical capacities—capacities that would enable them, among other things, to enhance production.[7]

But of course most of the Socialists and workers were not listening to the syndicalists' warnings, and the quasi-revolutionary agitation of the *biennio rosso* continued. Denunciations of the proletariat increasingly supplemented antirevolutionary statements in syndicalist writing. Responding to the occupation of the factories in 1920, Paolo Orano bitterly condemned the Italian proletariat for its alleged hostility to the discipline of production and stressed the importance of hierarchical differentiation in the factory.[8] Agostino Lanzillo, after some initial ambiguity, similarly condemned the occupation of the factories, judging the movement infantile and counterproductive—the result of the workers' infatuation with Bolshevism.[9] And Panunzio offered a novel proposal for one still calling himself a socialist. Writing in *Pagine libere* in 1921, when he was finding fascism more and more interesting, he advocated longer hours and lower wages for the workers. The proletariat, having proven itself incapable of revolution, must get back to work and *"contribute to the economic reconstruction of society, which is the formal premise of every social transformation."*[10]

The tone of some of these remarks indicates that the syndicalists' bitterness against the workers stemmed not only from plausible differences in perceptions and strategy. Already in March 1918, in fact, the syndicalists were denouncing the workers in terms that betray an element of classic "petty bourgeois" resentment. Agostino Lanzillo, for example, deplored the workers' "frenzy for enjoyment" and the "lack of political and moral consciousness which permits the Turinese metal worker to fail to consider putting aside some part of his earnings in order to improve the condition of his children and to make possible the reproduction of those goods which he enjoys so voluptuously." This "frigid and ignoble egotism" makes the worker "despise any sacrifice" and "forget family and country."[11] A few weeks later, Panunzio praised Lanzillo's article and added his own scathing criticism:

The workers from now on should of course think of material improvements, but also and above all of their moral and intellectual instruction and culture, and must give up the idea that society is conquered by deserting and scorning schools and culture and by passing a good part of the day in bars, in taverns, and in other such places.

The organizers of Milan know better than I do these bitter facts; they well remember the cardinal principle of Georges Sorel that *socialism is entirely in the psychological evolution of the proletariat.* . . .

If a serious, rigorous, austere moral and educational character is imposed on the movement—precisely the kind of character that was the glory of the early, heroic period of socialism and of *socialist discipline* in Italy!—we will have in our country a political and social force of the first order, one destined, perhaps, to achieve greater success than is foreseeable today.[12]

Panunzio clearly was not giving up on the workers, but new ways of raising their collective consciousness apparently had to be found if they were to realize their potential. And in the short term, the workers could not be expected to bring about whatever radical change was possible. Despite their resentments, however, the syndicalists continued to admire the workers as modern industrial producers. Even as they began to argue for a different kind of radical change, they considered working-class support essential if a viable new order was to be created. So the syndicalists' statements about the proletariat between 1917 and 1921 manifested a fundamental and symptomatic ambivalence: the egotistical, antinational proletariat could justifiably be coerced and manipulated; the productive proletariat must play a major role in the new populist order.

The consequences of the Russian revolution seemed to confirm that capitalism, despite its excesses and injustices, could not be dismissed lightly before it had completed its task of industrial development. The immaturity of the Italian workers was simply one indication that capitalism in Italy could not yet be scrapped. The war had greatly stimulated industrialization in Italy, but the adjustment to peacetime would be difficult even for the healthy side of the Italian industrial economy—and no time for revolutionary experiments. The syndicalists continually emphasized that bourgeois elements still had crucial economic roles to play in Italy after the war. De Ambris, writing in May of 1919, as the possibility of change in economic organization was being widely discussed, warned that "industry requires . . . a sum of technical and administrative capacities, a constant application of enlightened will, an intelligent audacity, and an exercise of individual initiative so remarkable that it is not presently to be found outside the industrial class."[13] Obviously, then, there were valuable, productive members of society who were not workers. De Ambris perceived "certain industrial groups, within which persons having really superior intelligences and spirits ready for all the necessary audacities are to be found, examples of the captain of industry type, who can certainly by no means be accused of representing the parasitical segment of society, and who, in a society organized on different principles, would even occupy a place among the most valued elements of leadership."[14] By implication, the task for now was to make the sociopolitical changes necessary to enable these groups to assume such positions of leadership.

The workers' task was to get down to work and to cooperate with this dynamic segment of the Italian bourgeoisie in order to maximize production and develop the country. The program of Rossoni's *Cultura sindacale*, a periodical intended for proletarian education, stressed that "If production is to be intensified, the cooperation of the proletariat with directing, intellectual labor is necessary. The proletarian and managerial forces, who today are unknown to each other or even combat each other, must come to know each other and join together."[15] The syndicalists repeatedly urged Italian revolutionaries to concentrate on pushing the Italian bourgeoisie to fulfill its economic mission and called for cooperation between industrial workers and dynamic capitalists.[16]

Stress on the continued utility of capitalism and calls for solidarity among producers did not mean passive acceptance of the Italian status quo. Indeed, Italy's producers had to join together partly in order to overcome the parasitical elements that kept the healthier, more dynamic sectors of Italian society from coming to the fore. Class collaboration to make such immediate, "preliminary" changes was possible, even though a measure of conflict over distribution was built into the capitalist order. The newspaper of the syndicalist trade union confederation, *Battaglie dell'UIL*, laid out the bases of the new program by quoting Filippo Corridoni, whose tentative proposal to shift the axis of social division had come to seem quite convincing to the syndicalists by 1919: "But has the present European war not made crystal clear to us the immaturity of the proletariat and the fact that there are still various problems for the classes to resolve in common, before they can confront each other without encumbrances? And has it not made clear how capitalist interests themselves can be dominated by other interests —dynastic or caste interests—entirely to their detriment?"[17] Thus it was essential immediately to make the productive elements in the bourgeoisie aware of themselves—and of the differences that separated them from the less productive sectors.[18]

Once the syndicalists began to distinguish healthy from unhealthy economic activity, they had no difficulty seeing that the Italian political system was the immediate problem, for it was political links that enabled the parasites to thrive. Seeking to pinpoint the enemy, Olivetti found the speculative, parasitical element to be much too powerful within Italian capitalism and called workers and "authentic capitalists" to "a common defense against super-capital, which pushes everyone together to ruin."[19] Olivetti had a reasonably accurate grasp of the financial manipulation involved in Italian heavy industry and of the role of the political system in making such activity possible. Early in 1920, he analyzed the bonds between the government, the Ansaldo steel trust, and the Banca Italiana di Sconto, and discussed the power which Ansaldo exerted within the Italian state.[20] In the same way, Lanzillo portrayed the protected steel industry, with its special access to bank credit and state support, to be at the center of a parasitical plutocracy dominating the entire Italian economy, as well as Italian politics.[21] The syndicalists were pointing to a political problem calling for a political solution. The workers could not help to solve it by taking over factories from productive industrialists, but they could participate in the necessary change in political relationships and institutions.[22]

Such polemics against "big finance capital" sound superficially like the petty bourgeois, anti-industrial protest which is often assumed to have been a major source of both fascism and revolutionary syndicalism. However, Olivetti attacked finance capital not because it threatened the little man, but because in Italy such capital had sought high short-term profits through speculation and governmental favors, not long-term industrial development. In the same way, Lanzillo's anti-protectionism cannot be understood simply as a lower-middle-class consumerist and anti-productivist ideology.[23] The syndicalists had always been free traders, because of their belief—which was partly illusory, partly "rhetorical," and partly plausible—that the rigors of international competition would undermine the unhealthy portion of the Italian economy, thereby enabling the productive portion to flourish. The interpretive categories usually applied to fascism are so ambiguous that almost any fascist statement about the economy can be taken as evidence of petty bourgeois opposition to modern industrial society. In reality, it was not necessary to be a worker or an industrialist to develop a plausible and progressive view of the contemporary capitalist economy.

As they focused on the short term, the syndicalists began to sense that Italy's political problems were more fundamental than they had realized before. The political problem was apparently deeper than the economic problem—liberalism was apparently worse than capitalism. The parliamentary system seemed to have nurtured a parasitical "political class" that had to be distinguished from the vigorous capitalist bourgeoisie.[24] Now the syndicalists began seeking to explain the sources of the Italian political problem more systematically—and to propose solutions. Olivetti, for example, sought to explain why the parasitism of Italy's swollen bureaucracy was an integral part of her parliamentary system, by no means a superficial abuse that could be eliminated by reform from within the system.[25]

As the problem of the bureaucracy made clear, Italy's political patterns had reinforced the problems of national character that were partly responsible for the condition of Italian society. For Olivetti, the corruption of the political class set an example which encouraged petty fraud at all social levels, while the stasis of Italian politics reinforced the superficiality to which Italians seemed especially prone.[26] Politics was inherently trivializing: "Everything is contingency, expediency, second-rate ability. Everyone seeks to circumvent difficulties, not to confront them. . . . All the parties have equal worth: all the groups are in communication among themselves, like the sewage system. All the men are only half-men, even masks. . . . The programs sound in the void: the words have use and exchange value and as such form the basis of the system of political bargaining."[27] Exploring the same set of problems, Alighiero Ciattini insisted on the distinction between the political and economic spheres that was by now fundamental to the neosyndicalist critique: "Although the parties promise the resolution of the universal problem, with their partisan and restricted activity they complicate the simplest problems. They constitute real 'political' —and thus artificial—classes. The economic classes are a logical and natural reality. But the political classes constitute a fraudulent and parasitical incrustation."[28]

It was possible to portray immediate political change and even short-term class collaboration in orthodox terms, as expedients necessary to remove the obstacles to "normal" social maturation. But as the syndicalists focused more sharply on the immediate situation, it seemed increasingly obvious that the present task eluded the old orthodoxy; what they had in mind was not merely an attack on feudal remnants like the monarchy in order to complete Italy's bourgeois revolution. Simultaneously, Panunzio, especially, was trying to reexamine the bases of socialism, asking about the place of Marxism in the socialist tradition. The rethinking that Panunzio spearheaded enabled the syndicalists to formulate more clearly what they were beginning to sense about the meaning of the immediate revolution.

When it had become clear—by about 1910—that syndicalism was not developing as expected, the syndicalists had tried to understand what had gone wrong in orthodox terms, focusing on feudal, prebourgeois remnants. Their thinking became confused and contradictory, however, because they sensed that the obstacles in Italy were anomalous, yet they did not question the socialist-syndicalist model itself. But finally the cumulative effect of wartime events and experiences forced the syndicalists to ask some new questions; too much was happening that seemed to escape the orthodox framework.

In his influential book *La disfatta del socialismo*, written in 1917, Agostino Lanzillo claimed that the war amounted to the definitive defeat of the old socialism—both as a doctrine and as a party with pretensions to leadership. Since they insisted on their traditional theoretical framework, the Italian Socialists could not grasp the significance of the war and thus could not hope to lead after the war was over. Lanzillo stressed that syndicalism, in contrast, could make a vital contribution to the new theoretical framework which had to be created if the European countries were to come to grips with the new reality after the war.[29] For Panunzio, too, the war raised questions and afforded opportunities which escaped the traditional socialist framework, yet the Socialists remained oblivious, refusing to participate in the essential doctrinal reconstruction.[30] As a result, the Italian Socialists would not be able to offer a credible claim to leadership after the war. The syndicalists would have to do better.

But they could hope to do so only if they faced up to the basic question about all the unforeseen obstacles and events: just how appropriate had the original model been in the first place? And how much was left—and still usable—of the original syndicalist conception? Gradually, as they considered these questions, the syndicalists began to

view the revolution they were proposing as something more fundamental than a mere preliminary; it was an end in itself, for the problems
to be overcome were neither feudal remnants nor anomalous Italian
obstacles to the universal model, but autonomous and universal problems in their own right.

In a tentative way, Panunzio had already begun the doctrinal
reconsideration before the war, in response to the apparent impasse of
socialism. After reaching a nadir of intellectual uncertainty late in 1913,
he sought to formulate the questions that seemed necessary in an
article in Mussolini's review *Utopia* in May of 1914.[31] Influenced by the
neo-Kantian thinking of the philosopher Igino Petrone, he argued that
socialism is an aspiration which ought to be realized, a matter of
idealism, not materialism; socialism's scientific pretensions were falla-
cious. Panunzio sought to develop the implications of this notion in a
series of articles which appeared in Ivanoe Bonomi's *Vie nuove* from
1917 to 1919. Socialism was currently in crisis, he argued, not only
because of the war, but above all because of its theoretical bankruptcy,
which should have been evident to socialists well before the war. If
socialism was to survive, its theoretical foundations had to be completely reconstructed. Above all, socialism had to be more pluralistic
and less reductionist; it was not the exclusive concern of the proletariat,
to be created solely through the economic class struggle.[32] In addition,
Panunzio warned, socialism must cast aside its ruinous pseudoscientific
trappings and recognize its utopian underpinnings. The essence of
socialism was an aspiration to justice; creating socialism meant eliminating exploitation and, conversely, achieving solidarity through the
universalization of productive labor. Panunzio found this instinctive
negation of injustice—this utopianism—even at the basis of Marxism,
which "is really the most powerful demand for a juridical ideal,"
despite its trappings of materialism.[33]

The source for many of Panunzio's ideas in these articles was
Francesco Saverio Merlino, the revisionist from the turn of the century
whose ideas had helped to launch Italian syndicalism in the first place.
In fact, Panunzio recommended Merlino's *Pro e control il socialismo* to
his colleagues as the basis for a socialist revision which would deny the
canonical status of Marxism, relegating it to its proper, less exalted
place in the socialist tradition.[34] For Merlino as for Panunzio, the heart
of socialism was an aspiration toward justice, which required "the
elimination of the parasitical class—the equality of men before the
necessity of labor."[35] The obstacles to justice and solidarity in modern
society were cultural patterns and social divisions that could not be
understood merely as functions of capitalism. Ultimately, the lazy class
of political parasites, not the vigorous class of capitalists, was the

enemy. The industrial workers had no special relationship to the social problem: they were not especially afflicted by it; they had no special responsibility for solving it. Socialism, in fact, had no connection with economic class at all: "Socialism is not the victory of one class over the others, but the triumph of the general interest over particular interests." The victory of socialism meant "the extension of culture and of the reciprocal sympathy among men; the spreading and intensification of public life and the multiplication of common interests and needs."[36] Merlino envisioned a greater social dimension to the individual's behavior and experience as the key to the new society.

Several implications followed from Panunzio's ideas in *Vie nuove,* including his intellectual encounter with Merlino. It seemed that reality was more complex than orthodox socialists admitted. There were many social problems, some of which were not reducible to the capitalist organization of the means of production, and they could not all be solved at once. Conversely, it was possible to go ahead and solve some of them without attacking capitalism. Even within a capitalist framework, there could be a significantly greater measure of solidarity and justice and a much greater premium on the collective interest. These goals had always been central to socialism, but they were not the responsibility of any particular socioeconomic class; the industrial proletariat had no special role in achieving them. Moreover, if there was no single blueprint, if all problems were not interrelated in a determined way, socialists would have to become more eclectic and pragmatic. They could go ahead and attack particular, immediate problems, but they would have to be willing to learn, first, from any social thinker whose insights illuminated the problem at hand and, second, from experience. Writing in 1918, Panunzio found Marxism still to be relevant, but he warned that if socialists continued to look to it for the solution to all social problems, they would undermine its ongoing value.[37]

Merlino could help the syndicalists to deepen their understanding of social problems and of socialist ends, but the problem of means remained. If the proletariat had no special role, where were the new values to come from? In their initial revolutionary conception, the syndicalists had been much concerned with the mechanism that would produce new values and capacities, because they sensed how difficult it would be to break out of the prevailing patterns in Italy. Indeed, this concern dominated their thinking, impeding systematic consideration of the problems they were seeking to overcome. The proletariat was to struggle against capitalism not so much because capitalism seemed the basic problem in society, but because something new could apparently develop through the process of struggle itself. It was this belief in the value of proletarian autonomy, organization, and struggle for developing a solution to the social problem—whatever it was—that the syndicalists had learned from Sorel.

The syndicalists, then, had originally done precisely what Merlino warned against and portrayed socialism as the special concern of the proletariat because they sensed the depth of the strategic problem. Despite his clearer analysis of social problems and socialist purposes, Merlino could not explain how social solidarity and the collective interest might eventually triumph. He insisted that the moral-psychological change in society which was crucial for socialism would not follow automatically from a change in society's material and institutional structure.[38] Indeed, he found such moral change a prerequisite for effective institutional change. So the crucial moral change could not wait until after the revolution—but how could it be brought about from within the present institutional structure? The path to socialism turned out to be a vicious circle. At least intuitively, the syndicalists grasped quite well this fundamental dilemma of radical change; their original doctrine was primarily an attempt to show how the new social virtues could be created within the present flawed society. In the labor syndicates, those virtues would have an autonomous institutional basis for their development.

Panunzio's rediscovery of Merlino was a two-edged sword. On the one hand, it helped the syndicalists to understand what they had always sensed about social problems and to articulate what had always been essential in their vision of the future. Economics, capitalism, socioeconomic class, the proletariat—the syndicalists had originally overemphasized all of them because of their preoccupation with the strategic problem. On the other hand, the problem of means now returned; if the syndicalists were to deemphasize the proletariat and class struggle in their conception of socialist revolution, their original explanation of how the new values could be created was no longer of any use.

Another long-time acquaintance, Vilfredo Pareto, offered ideas which helped the syndicalists redefine the revolutionary force—and which reinforced the change in their conception of immediate Italian problems that was already under way. As they cast off the components of their Marxist superstructure, the syndicalists found Pareto increasingly relevant and explicitly admitted their intellectual debt to him.[39] Pareto also paid attention to what the syndicalists were saying as he sought to fathom the future during the volatile wartime and postwar years. In *The Mind and Society*, published in 1916, he anticipated that syndicalism might play a major part in saving a disintegrating society.[40] After the war, he discussed and quoted Lanzillo's *La disfatta del social-*

ismo, citing with approval Lanzillo's contention that syndicalism could have a key role in creating the new "ideology" that was essential if the radically new postwar world was to be confronted effectively. Pareto also found in Olivetti's introduction to the postwar series of *Pagine libere* evidence of the pragmatism and realism that had made the syndicalists immune to abstract conceptions like Bolshevism.[41]

Marxism had been attractive to the syndicalists as a universalistic doctrine of radical change based on industrial development, but Pareto's anti-Marxist categories seemed better to illuminate what they sensed was wrong with their society. Pareto insisted, in explicit opposition to Marx, that the basic differentiation in society is according to value-psychological states, not socioeconomic class. A society ripe for revolution is one whose ruling elite has grown too egotistical and effete to promote the collective interest or even to keep society together. As the ruling elite grows decadent, elements in the society mature, developing new collectivist values; if the ruling elite fails to renew itself by absorbing these new elements from below, then only revolution can revitalize the society. The new elite throws out the old and disseminates its new solidary values. Since the crisis is one of values, it must be values or psychological states—and not socioeconomic class—that define the revolutionary force.

Viewing the situation from this perspective, the syndicalists had no trouble identifying the elements in Italian society that had the potential to constitute a new elite. The key was the war experience. The syndicalists sought at first to portray the war as a full-fledged revolution, but increasingly, they had to admit that the war had only started the process, creating a new, nonproletarian revolutionary elite.

In *La disfatta del socialismo*, Lanzillo portrayed the war as revolutionary in both senses, betraying the ambiguity in his thinking. On the one hand, the war had been a mysterious attempt to overcome the increasing decadence and moral anarchy of European society, and it had indeed turned into the cataclysm necessary to change everything. Above all, the war experience had instilled the social discipline and solidarity that the syndicalists had always considered the keys to the new order.[42] On the other hand, Lanzillo invoked Pareto and suggested that the war was producing a new revolutionary elite—a new ruling class that "must assume the leadership of the nation" after the war was over.[43] The austere mentality of those who had been involved in the war would play a fundamental role in forming a new national consciousness in Italy. Hence the war had forged a revolutionary force— one which did not coincide with any particular socioeconomic class, but which was imbued with virtues much like the ones the syndicalists had originally expected the revolutionary proletarian elite to develop.

Writing in 1919, De Ambris similarly recognized the existence of a new revolutionary force, produced by the war and distinct from the proletariat, and advocated a coalition of war veterans and workers to make the limited, non-Bolshevik revolution that Italy needed.[44] Two years later, he denounced the Socialist party for its blindness to the revolutionary potential of nonproletarian elements in Italy after the war. The self-sacrifice and solidarity engendered by the war were precisely the virtues required for revolution. The party's failure to approach the veterans, De Ambris felt, was the logical corollary of its dogmatic neutralism, its narrow indifference to the war and the war's impact on Italy.[45] By this time, as we will soon see in more detail, De Ambris himself was seeking to build a movement of renewal around the veterans and "legionnaires" who had followed Gabriele D'Annunzio to Fiume and there applauded De Ambris's own neosyndicalist constitution, the *Carta del Carnaro*. His major collaborator was A. O. Olivetti, who also called for a national revolutionary coalition—including syndicalists, legionnaires, veterans, and other interventionist leftists—to create a new producers' Italy.[46]

As fascists, the syndicalists continued to portray the revolutionary force in Paretan terms; the proletariat had failed, but a nonproletarian elite could assume the mantle of leadership.[47] Now the syndicalists could admit the contingency of their initial commitment to the proletariat. Massimo Rocca made the point in an article with the telling title "Sorel's Error," published in July 1922 in the Fascist journal *Gerarchia*. Experience had proven, he insisted, that both Sorel and the Italian syndicalists had been wrong in assigning to the workers—and to them alone—the task of moral renewal in society. The moral regeneration of Italian society initiated by the war was manifested primarily, though not exclusively, in the middle classes.[48] Under the circumstances, dogmatic emphasis on the proletariat could only contaminate the still useful parts of syndicalism. Writing a year later, in the newspaper of the Fascist trade union confederation, Panunzio subsumed the initial Sorelian conception of the role of the proletariat under Pareto's more general conception of the role of a new elite. A key role for a Paretan elite remained, even though experience had indicated that it was not to be Sorel's proletariat.[49]

But the syndicalists accepted only in part Pareto's conception of the elite's role, for their objectives had always been—and continued to be—fundamentally incompatible with his overall social theory. They never ceased to believe that there is genuine progress in history toward justice and solidarity, while Pareto viewed history as cyclical and society as permanently elitist—despite periods of postrevolutionary solidarity. Pareto insisted that the new elite, even if it happened to be the proletariat, would govern society in its own interests, preaching solidarity simply in order to maintain its position. It would not attempt to universalize the new values in an effort to establish an authentic democracy. Moreover, this elite as well would ultimately grow too egotistical and effete to hold society together, so it would have to be replaced by still another new solidary elite as history continued its cyclical course. The syndicalists were coming to understand the characteristics and purposes of revolutionary elites in terms much like Pareto's, but they continued to believe that the revolutionary elite would provide a greater measure of solidarity and justice than society had known before.

Every crack in the Marxist "superstructure" of syndicalism opened the way for elements from the populist foundations that were forcing their way to the surface at the same time, independently, thanks especially to the war experience. The whole process was obviously pointing the syndicalists toward a synthesis of the socialist-syndicalist tradition and Italian populist ideals. The ideas of Giuseppe Mazzini enabled the syndicalists to complete the synthesis, for the great populist prophet of the Risorgimento seemed to have anticipated many of the essentials of the new national syndicalist revolution. Writing in *Il popolo d'Italia* in January 1917, Panunzio called for the study of Mazzini, whom he deemed the greatest Italian since Dante; Mazzini's lofty concepts would inspire the politics of the future.[50] Panunzio anticipated a new socialism, to be derived from various systems—from Mazzini's above all. But socialists could learn from Mazzini, Panunzio warned, only if they distinguished the living elements in his thought—the ideas about association, education, and mission—from the outmoded elements—especially the romantic religious ballast. Olivetti highlighted the similarities between syndicalism and Mazzinian populism again and again, finding especially significant their common emphasis on the collective basis of the moral ties which hold society together.[51] Quotations from Mazzini were sprinkled throughout issues of postwar syndicalist periodicals, while an untitled, boldface manifesto in the first issue of Olivetti's *La patria del popolo* exhorted Italians: "Onward to the People's Italy which Giuseppe Mazzini prophesied!"[52]

Mazzini seemed relevant because he had repudiated both liberalism and Marxism, claiming to offer an alternative to both. He opposed the abstract liberty and individualism of 1789, but at the same time he rejected the primacy of class struggle and denied that the industrial proletariat had any special progressive role. On the purely national level, Mazzini remained the symbol of the unfulfilled promise of the Risorgimento, since he had envisioned a different kind of Italian unity, a genuinely popular community based on tight psychological bonds and deep social commitments. In contrast to the pessimistic, defensive political class which emerged from the Risorgimento, Mazzini was confident, even wildly optimistic, about his country's prospects. Not only could Italy put herself together along genuinely popular and communitarian lines, but she had a universal mission of moral leadership in overcoming the major problems of the present liberal era. While Mazzini was a fervent nationalist, his nationalism was not exclusivist and aggressive, but congruent with internationalism and humanitarianism.

The syndicalists' new interest in Mazzini helped make it possible for them to join forces with wider groups of disaffected Italians, including Mazzinian populists like Armando Casalini who were interested in the labor movement as the basis for bringing Mazzini's ideas up to date. Just as the syndicalists were doing, Casalini emphasized the populist elements in Sorel's thinking and portrayed Mazzini as a precursor of syndicalism, "the teacher of moral energy" who sought to inspire the worker to fulfill his mission as a producer for society. Thus syndicalism and Mazzinianism were complementary; syndicalism—modern social organization rooted in the economy—was necessary to make Mazzini's populist, communitarian vision concrete. Through syndicalism, Casalini felt, it would finally be possible to implement the Mazzinian and democratic ideal of popular government, which individualistic ideas and parliamentary institutions had only frustrated.[53]

By synthesizing what seemed to be the living elements in syndicalism and Mazzinianism, the syndicalists also helped to make their blueprint accessible to young war veterans like Dino Grandi and Italo Balbo, who would provide the core of fascism as a mass movement in 1921. A cult of Mazzini was intimately bound up with their conception of the meaning of the war experience and with their dreams of radical change.

As the syndicalists reconsidered their position, they discovered, above all, the autonomy of the political. The liberal parliamentary system was inadequate because of problems of its own, not because it was the instrument of the capitalist bourgeoisie, not because the means of production were organized in a certain way. Nor was it simply the lack of economic equality that made a mockery of political and juridical equality in the liberal system. And since the inadequacies of political liberalism did not stem from economic inequality and exploitation, it was neither necessary nor possible to focus on the economic sphere in the quest for solutions. This meant that radical leftists did not have to wait for capitalism to mature and give way before lasting solutions to some of the central problems of the liberal system could be found. The democratic aspiration that had guided leftists all along could be achieved by changing political forms, by moving beyond universal suffrage, popular sovereignty, and the parliamentary system to a more radical, concrete kind of democracy, a postliberal superdemocracy.

This conclusion seemed to result from the breakdown of the Marxist framework. But the syndicalists' populist concerns were pushing them in the same direction, for they argued increasingly that the war experience could prove the catalyst for a populist political revolution—the solution to the long-standing national political problem. The war enhanced political consciousness, and the organization of ever more economic categories during and after the war meant that the society was spontaneously overcoming the atomization that had made the old political patterns possible—and even necessary. Since the Italian people were maturing, Olivetti contended, Italy could finally do away with "this filthy political class which shamefully rots and exploits her." He anticipated "a revolution of the Nation against the State, of the producers against the politicians, of the concrete economic categories against the spurious and lying parties."[54]

So the universal leftist and the national populist levels in Italian syndicalism finally came together. Through a populist revolution against the liberal political system, it would be possible to overcome peculiarly Italian problems and general problems of the present order in Europe at the same time. As conscious leftists, seeking to participate in the most advanced European radical currents, the syndicalists could do what they had "subconsciously" most wanted to do all along—to replace the Italian liberal political system. Still, since their new synthesis stemmed in part from a reconsideration of the bases of socialism as a universal doctrine, the syndicalists could consider their conclusion about the autonomy of the liberal political problem to be valid for the radical leftist tradition in general. Socialism was in crisis everywhere, not just in Italy, but the syndicalists had found the key to the necessary revision.

Panunzio, especially, showed how Italy's potential for populist renewal could be translated into concrete sociopolitical change, solving the basic problems of liberalism. Writing in 1918, he emphasized that Italy's "classes" were finally developing solid organizations as a result of the industrial development and the social awareness which the war had fostered.[55] After the war, the "concrete and organic" economic groupings in society would become the bases of political life, replacing the parties, the electoral districts, and the suffrage system of liberal politics. So despite all the doctrinal revision, the syndicalists continued to view social organization based on economic function as the key. But now they began to realize what had been implicit in their conception:

to organize society on the basis of economic function was necessary in order to create the foundation for a new politics—not for a new economy. And the syndicate was not primarily an instrument of class struggle, but a source of new values and capacities. Thus syndicalism was a doctrine of organization for all those with productive roles, not just for the proletariat. The syndicalists pointed to the spontaneous organization of nonproletarian sectors—those they often characterized as "intellectual" labor—as evidence that the Italian nation was coming to maturity.[56] Thus the syndicalists were still insisting on the elements of their original doctrine which had enabled them to depart from preindustrial populist radicalism in the first place. In a letter to Mussolini published in *Il popolo d'Italia* in November of 1919, Panunzio stressed the superiority of his national syndicalist blueprint for political change, based on the realities of modern socioeconomic development, to the much-discussed constituent assembly idea, which reflected, he said, an abstract and outmoded form of populism.[57] Two years later, Panunzio returned to *Avenir socialiste des syndicats*, which he termed "the *fundamental* work on syndicalism by Sorel," to accent the continuity in the syndicalist tradition; he highlighted the moralizing attributes that had always attracted the syndicalists to socioeconomic organization.[58]

Before considering proposals for a neo-syndicalist political order more systematically, we will find it useful to examine Panunzio's highly significant article, "Nationality and Humanity in Education," published in *Coltura popolare* in October 1918. Although Panunzio here did not explicitly emphasize the role of economic groupings, he did consider carefully the link between the war experience and the opportunity for a new kind of populist politics. This piece reveals with unusual clarity the basic purposes that would later guide the left fascist quest for a postliberal, totalitarian superdemocracy.

Panunzio was concerned with one of the central questions about the modern European political experience—whether the liberal parliamentary system had proven to be an effective vehicle for genuine democracy. The answer could only be negative, he concluded, and the reason lay "in the fact, the irrefutable fact, of the lack of popular culture and education." Panunzio revealed what he felt had been wrong with the liberal parliamentary system when he outlined his conception of the way out of the long impasse of democracy. In participating in the war, the people learned to ask political questions—about, for example, the responsibility for this war that so deeply affected them. They became aware of the stakes of political decisions and began to sense their own potential political weight:

All those who fought and who felt the war will no longer lack interest in politics and public affairs. . . . Until yesterday, a worker, an ordinary woman, a peasant could not care less whether the radicals or the conservatives were in power, whether protection is better than free trade or not. How we had to struggle and sweat, as true friends of the people, to attract the common people and the obstinate and uncultured multitudes and interest them in politics and political problems! Politics was "abstract." The people shrugged their shoulders and let things go their own way. The few political manipulators . . . went about their business. . . . But today *the people* . . . have understood in concrete terms what politics means. They have understood . . . that politics is their business—and a very important kind of business at that. They have understood that politics means the possibility of war, of wars that are of *direct* concern to the people. They have understood that to abstain . . . from politics is to leave the way open to the latest oppressors of the people, the petty politicians and demagogues. . . . They have understood, in sum, that they have to control politics *directly* and participate actively and effectively in public affairs.[59]

First, the people would insist on control of foreign policy; for Panunzio, this would constitute mankind's greatest advance since 1789. But the people would immediately discover that mastery of foreign policy required mastery of domestic policy and that if they were to direct both, they would need the right kind of education. The problem of democracy was above all a problem of popular education, and thus Panunzio was quick to heap scorn on modern apostles of irrationalism. But it was not enough merely to defend existing forms of education, which relied too heavily on "formulas and mechanical exercises and memorization and rhetoric." The Italians, Panunzio felt, had remained politically incompetent because for generations they had been given abstractions about civic "rights and duties." Instead, they should be taught to grasp, for example, Italian economic and demographic problems, the requirements of industrial and agricultural development, and the workings of commercial relations and diplomacy.[60] In the aftermath of the war, the people would demand from education the expertise they needed to deal effectively with the complex domestic and international problems that had always eluded them before.

At the same time, however, Panunzio warned that narrow technical training was not the answer. This point merits special emphasis—first, because of the instructive contrast between Panunzio's educational proposals and those which the Nationalist Luigi Federzoni was offering during the same period, and second, because Panunzio's position could easily be misinterpreted, given the usual interpretive categories. Speaking in Rome early in 1917, Federzoni called for a more technically oriented education as a means to overcome the indiscipline and indifference in Italian labor, defects that damaged the competitive position of Italian industry.[61] He proposed to educate working-class youth directly for their economic role—for apprenticeship in the factory. Federzoni obviously had no qualms about stunting the potential political capacity of the workers through a system of education that would prepare them technically and psychologically for subordinate roles in the industrial system.

Panunzio had proposals like Federzoni's in mind when he warned: "The people, from now on . . . will demand—as I have always advocated . . . against our backward supporters of professionalism in education and in culture and of technical instruction in general—an education of general culture, a humanistic education, an education that instructs the spirit; and unlike certain people who—whether out of ignorance or out of cunning—would like to divert and prevent the development of an education appropriate for a democracy, the people will not call for education to become 'the maid-servant for the economic interests' of the bourgeoisie."[62] At first glance, we might see Federzoni as the dynamic modernizer, seeking to make education relevant to the modern industrial world, and Panunzio as the petty bourgeois intellectual, resentful of the new technical culture and seeking to preserve traditional humanistic forms of education. But Panunzio issued his warning not because he resented modern industrial civilization, but because he feared that a narrow technical education would undermine the chance of the lower classes for real political competence. This concern certainly did not keep Panunzio from seeking a more practical education—to equip ordinary Italians to make judgments about the problems of the new industrial world.

Panunzio felt that if education was to promote meaningful democracy, new techniques would have to be used as well.[63] For example, newspapers and films could be used in the classroom to make education more politically relevant. Panunzio obviously sensed the novel possibilities which the mass media offered for politicizing people. At the same time, he proposed to broaden popular political horizons by developing a system of free international and domestic travel—ultimately to include everyone, not just those in school. Experience indicated that real democracy required mobilizing people, organizing and politicizing more of their leisure time and everyday activity.

The syndicalists were beginning to envision a postliberal, totalitarian kind of politics. In a perceptive analysis of the crisis of modern liberalism published in 1921, Alighiero Ciattini concluded that the parliamentary state in Italy—and in general—was in crisis because of its illegitimacy, stemming from the divorce between the people and the political system. Bridging this gap, he insisted, "requires that the collective will be expressed not only at intervals, by means of the suffrage, since in fact it cannot be expressed in this way. It is essential instead that it continuously pulsate and overflow with regard to the most vital problems of the collective life."[64] The crisis of the liberal state could be overcome only by making the people more political, by involving them more directly and constantly in public life.

The best vehicle for more thoroughgoing political involvement seemed to be the syndical organization, since it mobilized the individual on a day-to-day basis, in terms of concrete economic functions and problems. Thus the syndicalists proposed to change the foundation of political life from automatic membership in a geographically defined electoral district to more or less obligatory membership in a grouping based on economic function. The first step was to change the basis of political representation. In an influential article published in *Il popolo d'Italia* in May of 1919, Lanzillo insisted that representation based on economic grouping would yield "the authentic representation of the legitimate interests and the organic forces of the country."[65] He proposed a bicameral system, with the lower house to be composed of representatives of the trade unions, business associations, and other productive groups in society. As a reflection of the nation's legitimate economic interests and conflicts, this corporative chamber would contrast sharply with the democratic parliament, which reflected illegitimate, merely "political," concerns. A senate elected by the lower house would deal with more general problems and defend the interests of society as a whole. Lanzillo insisted that only those producers who were politically conscious enough to join an association should be represented; the others were too weak and asocial to merit a political role. But even though some members of society presently lacked the virtues they needed for participation, political activity remained open to all those who became involved in economic organizations. Potentially, at least, full mass participation could be attained by organizing all of society and by instilling the necessary political virtues.

The other syndicalists offered similar proposals, often departing from Lanzillo's conception by advocating obligatory syndical membership for all categories of producers. Panunzio proposed obligatory membership and added some other novel proposals when he discussed Lanzillo's blueprint in an influential article in De Ambris's *Il rinnovamento* a few months later.[66] Like Lanzillo, Panunzio wanted both the chamber and senate to be based on syndical representation, but he insisted that it would not be enough merely to alter electoral procedures and the composition of parliament. Legislative capacity itself had to be transferred from the parliament and the bureaucracy into the economic groupings comprising society. At this point, Panunzio was only trying to indicate the most fruitful direction for change, not to outline a fully developed system. A plurality of economic-technical parliaments might prove superior to one single parliament, but in any case, it was necessary to move cautiously, learning from experience.

Olivetti devised a similar neosyndicalist political order in his *Manifesto dei sindacalisti* of 1921, which the syndicalist trade union confederation, the Unione Italiana del Lavoro, adopted as its official program.[67] Armando Casalini singled out Olivetti's document for special praise, arguing that the neosyndicalist politics it envisioned would at last make possible an effective form of popular sovereignty. He insisted, moreover, that populism and productivism were two sides of the same coin.[68] Casalini's conception manifests the interpenetration of the economic and political spheres that was basic to neosyndicalist thinking. The nation—the polity—was essentially an economic entity, and politics had to move toward economics in its composition and functioning. Ultimately, politics would become a kind of popular technocracy serving, in particular, to order the economy. The old forms of political grouping and political conflict were unnecessary, even illegitimate, and could be eliminated altogether.

Given the nature of the problems in liberal Italy, however, simply changing the forms of political participation would not suffice. Often the syndicalists failed to explain what was required, partly, no doubt, because they were reluctant to face up to the manipulative implications of the strategy they proposed. They overemphasized the extent to which the members of modern society, in Italy and elsewhere, were spontaneously organizing into economic groupings, and they indulged in much rhetoric about the war and the "real nation" of the producers. Thus they sometimes argued as if the Italian nation was already a vast confluence of economic organizations, a tightly knit productive entity that had only to free itself from a parasitical political encrustation to realize its full potential. In fact, however, the underlying sociocultural patterns that had given rise to Italy's old political system had not been fully overcome, so the revolution would have to penetrate to the social and psychological levels. Panunzio insisted again and again that if Italy was to develop a new political system, Italian society had to be made into a network of syndicates—"in order that they themselves can organically constitute the state."[69] And he admitted that certain new values had to inform an organization before it would be fit to serve as a unit in the society he envisioned. Contemporary Italy had lots of syndicates, "but these are bodies without a soul . . . the muscles and bones, the vertebrae and detached pieces of an organism *that has not yet been formed.*"[70]

So the new political order required not merely the continued organization of society, but also something deeper—a psychological revolution, a transformation of values.[71] As Ottavio Dinale put it in 1921: "Beyond reforming the bureaucracy, there are habits to be inverted, a new ethic to be constituted: To suppress parasitism and to erect in its place . . . the criterion of production, of labor; to substitute the interests of the collective for those of the cliques and clienteles. A rather vast program, which implies nothing less than the complete remaking of that entity which is the Italian."[72] Alighiero Ciattini linked the habits that had to be changed to liberal political forms: "if neither the governed nor the governing prove equal to the situation, because they are corroded and decayed by cheap parliamentary competitions; if particularism triumphs everywhere;—then legislative reforms . . . are [a] mockery. . . . Something else is necessary. Our ethical foundations must be completely rebuilt. Our entire intellectual patrimony must be restored. The time has come to have our examination of conscience."[73] Writing in 1921, Ciattini emphasized that solution could take place only on the level of values and minds; given the depth of the problem, political reforms and institutional changes could not in themselves be sufficient.[74]

Society had to be organized, then, not only to provide a new basis for political participation, but also to create a vehicle for instilling the perennial syndicalist values. Through the new organizations, it would be possible to politicize the Italians, to make the people fit for the ongoing participation in public life that would now be expected of them. All aspects of the individual's behavior and experience had to be given a greater social dimension—above all his labor, his key social function. The industrial economy under capitalism still required a hierarchical differentiation of function, but a kind of classless society of producers would result once common national productivist values had been instilled. The same vision of a monolithic society had guided the syndicalists from the beginning: the "real" Italian nation would be a hard-working productive unit, without parasites, without political parties—indeed, without traditional politics at all.[75] In the short term, however, a new revolutionary elite would have to further the organization of society into economic groupings and instill the requisite political values.

As the syndicalists began to propose their new program, syndicalism as a form of socialist economic organization came to seem a secondary objective. Olivetti explained in 1919 that syndicalism "can accept not only the violent conquest of the state, but also peaceful evolution within the confines of a free democracy."[76] The most important thing was to create this new context. The changes in economic organization which productivist criteria might dictate in the future would take place gradually, industry by industry. Further revolution would not be required because the real revolution, creating a new sociopolitical order and new "socialist" values, would already have been accomplished. As capitalism fulfilled its tasks of development, perhaps it could peacefully grow old and wither away. The syndicalists generally did not rule out the possibility, but this was not their chief concern for the present.

The economic sphere was no longer the focus for revolutionary change, but a major purpose of the new political system would be to order the economy. From their new, non-Marxist perspective, the syndicalists did not find it necessary to overthrow the capitalists or to change the organization of the factory in order to overcome some of the problems of the present economic system. The kind of political and cultural change they were proposing would lead property and capital to be used more productively, in the general interest. According to Olivetti, socialists did not question the potential productivity of capital, but they did find much of it presently used in a sterile, speculative way, because it remained purely private, free of political coordination.[77] In the program he proposed in 1919, Panunzio suggested ways of transforming property from an individual right into a social function.[78] Ownership of the means of production would no longer be absolute; if the present "owner" proved inept or lazy, the state could entrust the property in question to someone else. The capitalist economy's operations, then, were not determined by its own internal laws; the right kind of political coordination would make possible qualitative improvements in its functioning.

The fruit of the reappraisal which the syndicalists carried out from 1917 to 1921 was a blueprint for radical change that could have considerable appeal to the young war veterans, with their vague hopes for renewal. What Italy required was not economic revolution against capitalism, achieved by the proletariat, but political revolution against liberalism, led by a new revolutionary force defined in terms of values, not socioeconomic class. In making this revolution, Italy would be redeeming herself as a nation and leading the world beyond liberalism at the same time. And the war, which meant so much to the veterans, had indeed been vital, having made Italian society capable of the new postliberal order, and having forged a revolutionary vanguard with the will and capacity to bring it about.

By late 1920 the neosyndicalist conception was beginning to capture the imagination of many of the veterans who were becoming involved with Mussolini's *Fasci di combattimento*. But before we can understand the relationship between syndicalist ideas and early fascist aspirations, we must consider what the syndicalists were doing in practice during this pivotal period from 1917 to 1921. Despite everything—all the mutual hostility, all the theoretical revision—the syndicalists remained much concerned with labor organization and education. Even though the workers could not presently claim to lead, there remained important pedagogical tasks to be carried out in the labor movement since the new order would require proletarian support and involvement. At the same time, however, the syndicalists were looking around for the nonproletarian elite that could bring about the new revolution. This two-sided practice reflected continued ambiguity in their thinking about the role of the proletariat and about what they themselves should be seeking to accomplish in the immediate future. But generally, given their new theoretical perspective, there was room for both kinds of enterprise.

Syndicalist activity in the area of labor organization and education focused on the Unione Italiana del Lavoro (UIL), the syndicalist trade union confederation founded in June 1918. Edmondo Rossoni and Alceste De Ambris were the most influential organizers in the new confederation, while Olivetti's intellectual leadership was officially confirmed in 1921 when the UIL adopted his *Manifesto dei sindacalisti* as its program. The syndicalists hoped to win over the mass of Italian workers to the UIL and national syndicalism, but the UIL's attraction in the labor movement proved limited. This is not surprising, given the widespread enthusiasm for Bolshevism in Italian labor and the interventionist and nationalist orientation of the UIL itself.[79] And of course the UIL's neosyndicalist conception of present prospects was not flattering to the working class. While warning against premature revolution, the syndicalists continued to exhort the workers to improve themselves morally and technically. But now the emphasis shifted away from anticapitalism and the class struggle, toward love of labor and austere self-sacrifice.[80] Filippo Corridoni was held up to the workers as an exemplar, a selfless hero who had died for the nation. Olivetti praised Corridoni as "the quintessence of the new humanity that is being fashioned in the world of labor."[81]

For now, however, leadership could not come from the workers, and the syndicalists experimented with a variety of supplements to the UIL in search of a nonproletarian revolutionary force. Some, like the Unione Socialista Italiana, an organization of left interventionists founded in 1918, never really got off the ground. But another organization of left interventionists, Mussolini's *Fasci di combattimento*, formed in Milan on 23 March 1919, proved more promising.

The discussions between Mussolini and the syndicalists in 1913 and 1914 about an alliance to break out of the impasse of contemporary socialism had finally come to fruition in November 1914, because of the war. As the journalistic focus for much of the interventionist Left, Mussolini's *Il popolo d'Italia* provided a major vehicle for the ideas of Panunzio, Lanzillo, and other syndicalists during the war and the immediate postwar period. Relations between Mussolini and the syndicalists were cordial enough to make possible an ongoing exchange of ideas. When early in 1918 De Ambris and others prepared to begin publication of *Il rinnovamento*, which was to play such an important role in the syndicalists' doctrinal revision, *Il popolo d'Italia* offered its greetings and best wishes to the new publication. *Il rinnovamento* sent the proofs of the lead article of its first issue to *Il popolo d'Italia*, which eventually reprinted the article.[82]

Like the syndicalists, Mussolini reconsidered his socialism during the war, and by 1919 he had apparently embraced some of the most important neosyndicalist tenets—including productivism, national syndicalism, and corporative representation. The syndicalists significantly influenced Mussolini's thinking during this period.[83] Mussolini visited Panunzio in Ferrara for a few days in January 1916, while on leave from the front, and this contact may have been especially important in Mussolini's evolution toward a new perspective.[84] On the eve of Mussolini's departure, Panunzio was the major speaker at a dinner gathering of interventionists, given partly in Mussolini's honor.[85] Agostino Lanzillo's ideas seem to have been influential as well: Mussolini's conception of the role of the war in rendering irrelevant the old socialism clearly owed a great deal to Lanzillo's *La disfatta del socialismo*.[86]

So there was much interaction between Mussolini and the syndicalists after they came together in November 1914, and by the end of the war they had some important things in common. As part of the same interventionist sector of the Italian Left, they faced the same practical problems in the postwar context, especially the isolation from the bulk of the Italian labor movement. Like the syndicalists, Mussolini was warning against Bolshevism and premature revolution, stressing the further viability of capitalism and the need for collaboration among producers, calling on the workers to identify with the nation, and affirming the value of the war. Both sides foresaw that a new kind of political force would emerge from the war, one which might have a decisive impact in postwar Italy. But even though the syndicalists had enough in common with Mussolini to continue contributing to his newspaper after the war, the most important of them maintained their intellectual autonomy, along with certain of their prewar ideas which Mussolini had never shared. By 1919 the syndicalists certainly did not consider Mussolini to be their intellectual leader. But given his apparent interest in neosyndicalist themes, he was coming to seem a plausible political leader for the uncertain postwar period.

It was clear that Mussolini had a good deal of political talent, and his *Fasci di combattimento* immediately attracted the interest and participation of a number of syndicalists. Agostino Lanzillo was a member of the unsuccessful Fascist slate of candidates in the elections of November 1919, while Alceste De Ambris maintained close ties with the *Fasci di combattimento* in 1919 and drafted the first Fascist program.[87] But both became disillusioned with fascism in 1920, when the movement seemed to become merely an instrument of bourgeois reaction. De Ambris definitively broke with Mussolini at the end of 1920 because of Mussolini's relative indifference to the fate of Gabriele D'Annunzio's regime at Fiume, in which De Ambris, strangely enough, had become the chief adviser to the *Comandante* himself.

The city of Fiume, formerly the major port of the Croatian-Hungarian portion of the Habsburg Empire, was the subject of a complex and bitter dispute between Italy and Yugoslavia after the war. In September of 1919, with Italy's hopes for the annexation of Fiume frustrated at the Paris peace conference, the noted poet and adventurer Gabriele D'Annunzio led a band of "legionnaires," mostly soldiers and veterans, in a march on Fiume, where he established a regency to hold the city for future Italian annexation. De Ambris, seeking a force to lead the Italian revolution, traveled to Fiume late in November 1919 to meet with D'Annunzio and to assess the situation, which, he decided, offered serious revolutionary possibilities. At the same time, a number of D'Annunzio's followers were pressuring him to give the Fiume regime a more clearly leftist orientation. The most influential was Captain Giuseppe Giulietti, a colorful figure and something of a syndicalist himself, who used his position as leader of the powerful Italian maritime union to get supplies to Fiume periodically. The Nationalists, who had supported D'Annunzio from the beginning, began to fear that his movement might escape their control and pose a serious threat of leftist revolution within Italy. As the Nationalists grew cooler, D'Annunzio began to rely on De Ambris, whose ideas and personality he found most impressive. Finally, early in January 1920, De Ambris replaced the Nationalist Giovanni Giuriati as head of the Fiume cabinet; he remained one of D'Annunzio's closest collaborators until the Fiume regency was suppressed the following December.[88]

The most significant fruit of the year-long collaboration between De Ambris and D'Annunzio was the *Carta del Carnaro*, the neosyndicalist constitution which the Fiume regency promulgated in September 1920. This quickly became the most important single vehicle of syndicalist influence on the young veterans in fascism. D'Annunzio gave the document a high-blown rhetorical form, but De Ambris provided its substance, synthesizing the major elements of the neosyndicalist conception that he and his colleagues had been developing since 1917.[89] De Ambris portrayed the *Carta del Carnaro* as the basis for the political and cultural revolution which Italy presently required.[90] This revolution, he admitted, would not fully achieve syndicalism, but it would not be possible to replace capitalism with a full-fledged syndicalist economic system in the foreseeable future. And in any case, syndicalism proper was "a world in process of formation" which could not be created all at once. The immediate task was for syndicalists and other revolutionaries to complete the movement for renewal which began with interventionism, to overcome the political and sociocultural patterns which, among other things, were obstructing the evolution of syndicalism. Yet this immediate revolution would not be merely a preliminary, despite some ambiguity in De Ambris's thinking, because it would create an order based on new postliberal values and on the same solidarity of producers which the syndicalists had always considered the essence of socialism. Like Lanzillo, Panunzio, and the others, De Ambris devised a bicameral legislative system, with both houses based on economic groupings. All producers would be obligatory members in one of the ten corporations, which would organize each of the productive categories comprising society. In addition to representative and other political functions, the corporations would strive to perfect both the techniques of production and the discipline of labor. With political sway extended over the economy, property would become a social instrument, and a magistracy of labor would adjudicate labor conflicts. The new state was to be the authentic expression of a unified, homogeneous community of producers.[91]

Since the Fiume regime was by now in crisis and would last only three more months, there was little opportunity to test the constitution in practice. Still, De Ambris was hoping primarily to provide a model which would attract much wider support for a national syndicalist revolution in Italy itself. The *Carta del Carnaro* was quite influential among the heterogeneous sectors that made up the nationalist, anti-Bolshevik Italian Left, but De Ambris had hoped that the document would also attract the Socialist party's rank and file into the new revolutionary movement. In this hope he was frustrated, for his interventionism had made him a traitor in the eyes of most of the workers. Besides, D'Annunzio wanted leftist support in order to put pressure on the Italian government, not because he was seriously interested in some sort of revolutionary march on Rome.[92]

As he sought to forge a revolutionary coalition around the Fiume experience and the *Carta del Carnaro*, De Ambris assumed that he had sure allies in Mussolini and the Fascist movement. When in September and October of 1920 De Ambris was working on a program for insurrection, complete with a march on Rome, he circulated a draft within the *Fasci di combattimento*, subsequently modifying the program to meet fascist objections.[93] But Mussolini was himself in the process of a fundamental change in strategy, completed between mid-October and mid-November 1920, which required a kind of double game with the Fiume movement.[94] This new strategy soon led to a rebellion against Mussolini within the mushrooming Fascist movement, in the name of the antiparliamentary revolution of the *Carta del Carnaro*. Before we can understand Mussolini's strategic shift, which led to his definitive break with De Ambris and ultimately to a severe crisis within fascism, we must focus more sharply on the future Duce and his purposes in the fluid situation of postwar Italy.

8 / The Varieties of Italian Fascism

Because Mussolini was the founder and leader of fascism, our initial tendency is to look to Mussolini when we seek to discover fascist purposes. But Mussolini was not the source of the dynamic element in fascism, the ongoing push in a totalitarian and corporativist direction that finally did destroy the liberal parliamentary system. Unlike Hitler, who struggled to develop a consistent world view and sought to implement his vision in practice, Mussolini was not an innovator desiring power in order to implement an ideological program. Mussolini tossed off varied, sometimes contradictory ideas from one day to the next, without trying to order them according to a consistent framework.[1] This lack of long-term purposes reflected basic traits of character in the impulsive, egocentric, and theatrical Mussolini; he was essentially an opportunist, content to deal with problems one day at a time.[2] His instinct was to avoid irreversible choices and commitments, to try to keep his options open. From the beginning, Mussolini understood fascism as his personal instrument, to turn loose or restrict depending on the short-term situation, to be used to achieve power, to intimidate his adversaries, to prove his own indispensability to the old elites. In the back of his mind, Mussolini saw himself as a "supertransformist" mediator, standing above the existing political forces in the country, including fascism, and providing a focus for consensus, an overall unity of direction. And so, despite everything, the advent of Mussolini did not wholly defy Italian political traditions. Thus sectors of the pessimistic ruling class were willing to acquiesce in Mussolini's rise to power. They hoped he was the man who could do what Depretis and Giolitti had done in comparable situations before: find new expedients and defuse a potentially dangerous movement in society. To have a new man like Mussolini in power signaled the opening up of the system that was obviously necessary, but it did not have to mean fascist revolution against the system—quite the contrary.

Mussolini himself shared some of the traditional pessimism and cynicism of the Italian ruling class. However serious he was about his socialism before the war, there is no question that he was beginning to lose his intellectual bearings even before he jumped to interventionism in 1914. As events in Europe seemed increasingly to defy expectation, all the old principles and ideologies began to seem bankrupt, all of them seemed to have been shown up as phony in this era of war and revolution. Mussolini became less and less consistent, even less concerned with consistency, and began to espouse activism and relativism, to rely more and more on his own intuition, out of a sense that there was nothing left. Pessimism about principles, about other people, about life in general, determined his conception of his own role and affected his practice after he became the leader of Italy. Above all, from the outset of his regime, and perhaps increasingly as the years went by, Mussolini's outlook was colored by a profound contempt for his own people, for the Italians.[3] He was content to drift, living from day to day, because he sensed that nothing could really be changed in Italy anyway. Thus he never used the power he eventually accumulated as vigorously as he might have—to purge the old elites, to "fascistize" the country, to coordinate all elements in the national life. At his most optimistic, Mussolini felt that the most important thing was to endure, waiting for a new generation to grow up as fascists—with a greater sense of discipline and a deeper sense of the national interest. Perhaps something better could be expected of them.

Insofar as Mussolini had an intellectual framework, he viewed society in terms of the theories of crowd psychology and collective behavior that he had read in Sorel, Pareto, and, above all, Gustave Le Bon. He sensed the possibility of manipulating the masses through irrational myths—a perception that was consistent not only with his overall cynicism, but also with his low regard for the Italian people. But he did not even seek to exploit thoroughly the opportunities for galvanizing mass energies that seemed to follow from the new theories of collective behavior.

Ultimately, Mussolini ended up a mediator or balancer, standing above the heterogeneous collection of forces that composed the fascist mixture. He moved now this way, now that, giving just enough to convince each component that it was the heart of fascism—that its purposes were fascism's purposes. Mussolini's ambiguity, his ability to avoid irreversible choices, his skill at juggling groups and purposes— all were essential to maintain a regime composed of barely compatible components. At the same time, he had to work hard to create the illusion of energy and purpose necessary to give his system the appearance of an ongoing raison d'être.

Thus the regime turned out to depend on the genius of Mussolini, even though he was not a dynamic innovator responsible for the degree of radical change there was. As the regime reached an impasse in practice, he became ever more the central figure, indispensable to all the components. And obviously Mussolini could increase his own power if he juggled successfully, convincing fascist radicals that he was radical enough and the old elites that he was conservative enough. The cult of the Duce that developed during the 1930s justified Mussolini's unique role, but it also contributed to the growing stultification in the regime. Mussolini relied increasingly on his own intuition, on energy, vigor, and high-spiritedness, on improvisation and personal magnetism as opposed to careful study and patient organization.

Institutional innovations continued, however, and despite Mussolini's cynicism, there remained a measure of genuine uncertainty and dynamism in the situation. As he established himself in power, Mussolini made many compromises—precisely in his effort to avoid irrevocable choices and commitments. As a result, the more powerful he became in one sense, the more circumscribed he became in another, for it was not clear that he was free to use all the power he managed to accumulate. Mussolini's major biographer has characterized his plight with a striking metaphor: "Believing himself to be the arbiter of everything, he did not realize that, from compromise to compromise, his margin of autonomy was becoming smaller and smaller and that the logic of the situation, with the underlying problems remaining unsolved, was progressively suffocating him and reducing him to a little Laocoön who appeared strong only because he could flex his muscles, but who was irremediably caught in a tangle of coils that slowly would have suffocated him."[4] This in itself made the situation explosive, for Mussolini, feeling himself trapped, was bound to react sooner or later.

Some of the resentment of the old Italy that had helped make Mussolini a revolutionary in the first place still burned within him. So there was always a possibility that he would commit himself at last and begin forcefully to implement the program which his old friends among the syndicalists were advocating. Mussolini seemed to have embraced some national syndicalist ideas as the war was ending, and he no doubt had then—and continued to have—some genuine interest in the left corporativist program.[5] These ideas were not uppermost in his mind as he established himself in power, and he was not the source of the corporativist thrust in fascism, but corporativist themes remained among the secondary impulses in his mind. They helped to make Mussolini credible as a leader to committed fascist corporativists.

As it turned out, however, Mussolini sought to break out of the impasse not through corporativist revolution, but through foreign policy and war. By means of an unpopular war at the side of an unpopular ally, he gained vengeance against the established powers that had turned him into a Laocoön, but brought his regime down in the process.

In the uncertain situation at the end of 1918, however, Mussolini was simply trying to get his bearings and to regain a political base. At this point, he still hoped to woo the workers in the trade unions away from the political hegemony of the Socialist party, in the process reconstituting his own working-class mass base on the left.[6] The *Fasci di combattimento* were to be instruments in this struggle, helping Mussolini and his followers win support in the upcoming parliamentary elections, which were eventually held in November 1919. His mass base would have to come from the rank and file in the existing trade unions; there was no thought that the new Fascist movement might in itself provide a mass base. In his quest for renewed political prospects, Mussolini supported the UIL as an autonomous and antimaximalist labor organization and worked to separate the CGL from the Socialist party. His personal political needs were leading him toward the syndicalist position, with its emphasis on working-class autonomy vis-à-vis political parties. But Mussolini was forced into this position by circumstances; in times more promising for his personal fortunes, before the intervention crisis, he had considered the trade union rank and file as a mass to be manipulated by political leaders in the Socialist party.

Meanwhile, the problem of relations with Mussolini and his *Fasci* was damaging the cohesion of the UIL. Already in 1918, the UIL's syndicalist leaders had disagreed over what position their organization should take toward the existing state and toward political activity in general, and the founding of the *Fasci di combattimento* exacerbated this internal squabble. When De Ambris played a major part in drafting the Fascist program of 1919, he found himself in trouble with many of his union colleagues. At the UIL Congress of October 1919, Edmondo Rossoni reaffirmed the absolute incompatibility between the UIL and the political sphere and insisted that the *Fasci* were especially to be shunned, since they were guilty of reactionary activity. Protesting that the fascists were friends of the UIL, De Ambris resigned as the confederation's general secretary.[7]

Mussolini claimed not to understand the logic of Rossoni's position, but the persistent indifference or hostility of much of the UIL to fascism led Mussolini to wonder whether there was any possibility he could renew his political ties with the workers. And then the November election produced complete failure for Mussolini and his fascists; Mussolini's leftist policy had come to nought. Disoriented, Mussolini began to drift, indulging in some reckless antistatist remarks, as well as some rather vindictive statements against the working class. His hopes for support from the existing labor movement had not died altogether, but it appeared, for now at least, that his political space might lie on the right. He had to be realistic, he said, and to recognize that his failure to patch things up with the workers necessitated a change of direction. So the second national congress of the Fascist movement, held in Milan in March 1920, disavowed both the CGL and the UIL.[8]

Agostino Lanzillo sought to oppose this antilabor turn, insisting that fascism must defend the struggles of the working class, although later in 1920 he discerned some utility for fascism as a kind of bourgeois mass party, a counterpart of the Popolari and Socialists, serving to represent middle-class sectors in parliament.[9] But it was not for this that Lanzillo himself had become an important fascist in 1919; nor had this anything to do with the revolutionary conception of fascism Lanzillo held later on. Fascism by 1920 no longer looked like the political supplement that the syndicalists were looking for.

Two new sets of circumstances during the fall of 1920 fundamentally altered the situation, immeasurably improving Mussolini's uncertain prospects. First, Mussolini unexpectedly found himself with a chance to get involved in the national political maneuvering centered in Rome. At the end of the last chapter, we saw Mussolini becoming cooler toward the Fiume movement and to De Ambris's attempts to forge a new revolutionary coalition. Between mid-October and mid-November he was adopting a whole new strategy, as he began to realize how he could exploit the Fiume situation for his own political ends.[10] Giolitti, who had succeeded Nitti as Prime Minister in June, was determined to settle the Adriatic question and have done with D'Annunzio's regime, which was a direct affront to the sovereignty of the shaky liberal state. Hoping to minimize domestic reaction against his Adriatic policy, Giolitti sought the journalistic acquiescence of Mussolini, who was widely associated with support for D'Annunzio and with a hard line on the Adriatic. Mussolini, for his part, saw a chance to enter the Giolittian majority that would emerge from the forthcoming elections; from there he would be in a position to make the most of the impending Socialist split over adherence to the Third International, luring some of the Socialists back into his orbit. He had privately been wary of revolutionary ventures in any case, since he desired to keep his options open, and since the leader of any movement growing out of the Fiume experience would necessarily be D'Annunzio, not he himself. So Mussolini essentially abandoned D'Annunzio, De Ambris, and hopes for a new revolutionary coalition in exchange for a national political role within the parliamentary system. He hypocritically went along in principle with De Ambris's designs, while in fact delaying and vacillating in the expectation that, partly because of his own double game, the project would never come to fruition.

The immediate results of this understanding between Giolitti and Mussolini were satisfying to both sides. Mussolini proclaimed Giolitti's treaty with Yugoslavia to be acceptable, even though it gave Dalmatia to Yugoslavia and left Fiume, for now, an independent city-state; he offered only perfunctory protest when Giolitti dispersed D'Annunzio's regime in Fiume by force, in four days of fighting beginning Christmas Eve 1920. Five months later, in May 1921, thirty-five fascists, including Mussolini himself, were elected to parliament with Giolitti's anti-Socialist national bloc. Giolitti felt he had tamed fascism; Mussolini felt he had a foot in the door.

Mussolini could aspire to a national political role only because a second set of circumstances had also changed fascism's direction during the fall of 1920. With Mussolini taking his antilabor tack, the Fascist movement began to grow rapidly in the provinces, especially in the Po Valley, taking the form of violent reaction against the Socialists and workers. Now squads of young fascists—the *squadristi*—began their dread "punitive expeditions," setting fire to Socialist meeting halls and dispersing socialist and Catholic labor organizations by force.

As fascism moved simultaneously toward parliamentary maneuvering and violent reaction, most of the syndicalists began to doubt that it could play any long-term progressive role. Accusations that fascism had lost its initial, potentially revolutionary content and had become merely the instrument of bourgeois reaction dominated syndicalist literature on the movement from mid-1920 to mid-1921. The syndicalists generally portrayed fascism as a purely negative—though partly useful—reaction against maximalism and the *biennio rosso*, having no positive political future.[11] Ottavio Dinale, in the first extended consideration of fascism to appear in *Pagine libere*, doubted that the new movement could overcome the ambiguity and heterogeneity that had made it easy prey for the reactionary elements that seemed to be exploiting it. Nonetheless, Dinale discerned some possibility that fascism might become a coherent revolutionary force, and he challenged his old friend Mussolini to overcome the vacillation which had so far prevented this outcome.[12]

But Mussolini's deepening involvement in the parliamentary game, and the election of thirty-five fascists to parliament in May of 1921, seemed to indicate that fascism was being absorbed into the existing system. Writing in the aftermath of the elections, Lanzillo observed that fascism was becoming the bourgeoisie's mass party, acting within the traditional parliamentary framework, just as he had anticipated a few months before.[13] Meanwhile De Ambris, joined now by A. O. Olivetti, was still seeking to organize a revolutionary coalition around D'Annunzio and the Fiume legionnaires, even though the Fiume regime itself had been suppressed. Bitter over Mussolini's betrayal, and still hopeful of winning greater working-class support, De Ambris sought to give his new organization of Fiume veterans, the *Federazione nazionale dei legionari fiumani*, a clearly antifascist color.[14] Especially after fascism abandoned its special status as a "movement" and officially became a party in November of 1921, De Ambris and Olivetti scorned fascism as just another ordinary political party. And Mussolini seemed merely a run-of-the-mill politician, interested primarily in the traditional parliamentary jockeying for power, not in the revolutionary renewal of Italy.[15]

De Ambris and Olivetti continued their fruitless efforts to put together a non-Socialist and antifascist revolutionary coalition even into 1923.[16] But in 1921 it began to seem to many of the young Fiume legionnaires—and to many of the syndicalists—that, despite everything, the best hope for radical change in a national syndicalist direction lay with fascism after all. Before we can understand why, we must examine the new provincial fascism of 1920–21 and establish the interpretive framework we need to grasp the nature of the intersection between syndicalism and fascism.

Fascism finally became a force to be reckoned with during the second half of 1920 in the reaction against Socialism and the *biennio rosso*. Much of this early fascism was nothing but narrow reaction, most brutal in the countryside. It included a significant dose of criminality and violence, partly symptomatic of the brutalizing side of the war experience, and plenty of the vulgar bullying that has been associated with fascism ever since. Yet fascism developed the potential for an ongoing "positive" push to create an alternative regime at the same time. Some of those involved in the fascist reaction did not see beyond it, but others understood fascism not merely as an immediate instrument against Socialism, but also as a vehicle to destroy and replace liberalism. Participants in this antiliberal reaction had important perceptions and objectives in common, but ultimately their challenge to liberalism stemmed from different, even incompatible values and concerns, which can usefully be characterized in terms of left and right, or populist and elitist. This difference in the basis of the antiliberal reaction corresponded roughly to social differentiation within the Italian bourgeoisie—between upper- and lower-middle-class elements. Italian fascism gained the force to go beyond short-term anti-Socialist reaction to a change of regime because important sectors of the "normal" bourgeois constituency for parliamentary government were breaking off simultaneously, from the bottom and from the top, and turning against the liberal parliamentary system.

We have already discussed the appeal of Nationalism to middle-class elements who saw beneath the immediate Socialist challenge a deeper problem of liberal weakness. Their perceptions and objectives found their most coherent expression in Nationalism, even though the Nationalists did not officially merge with the Fascist party until February of 1923. This right-wing variety of fascism, like the Nationalism which gave it doctrinal expression, was by no means homogeneous. Although right fascists shared a common elitist defensiveness vis-à-vis the mass society and a common desire to replace the liberal parliamentary system, they differed along a continuum from more conservative and authoritarian perspectives to those more radical and genuinely totalitarian.

Nearer the radical end were those like Alfredo Rocco who found the present threat more menacing and who grasped more fully the necessity—and the possibility—of a new kind of elitist politics in a mass industrial age. Others, like Luigi Federzoni and Francesco Coppola among the Nationalists, were departing from right liberalism in the same postliberal direction, but less thoroughly and consistently. Since they were closer to right liberal traditions and less troubled by the present crisis, they were willing to settle for a more conventional solution, closer to a mere restoration of law and order around existing institutions. They were less convinced than Rocco that national syndicates and other mass organizations were necessary. At the Nationalists' pivotal meeting at Rome in March 1919, Federzoni expressed misgivings about Rocco's corporativist proposals and, as an alternative, simply stressed that the existing unions had to be made to acquire a sense of limits and responsibility.[17] It was necessary to convince the workers that since they were living in a proletarian nation, they should subordinate class interests to the ends of the collective. At this point, Federzoni's antidote to the present crisis had not gone much beyond the exhortations of right liberals like Mosca. Even in February 1921, Federzoni was calling not for institutional change in response to the trade union challenge, but merely for the restoration of law and order.[18] While Rocco saw the *biennio rosso* and the Italian crisis as the inevitable outcome of the individualism underlying the European liberal tradition, Federzoni was content to blame particular, short-term factors like proportional representation and the recent policies of the Socialist party.

However, Federzoni shared the basic Nationalist perceptions about the nation as an economic organism, the importance of international competition, and the need for total coordination of the nation for production and international struggle—perceptions which implied that institutional change in a totalitarian direction was necessary. Speaking in Rome during the parliamentary election campaign in May 1921, he claimed that the solution to the present crisis of indiscipline and disorder required remaking the Italian mentality and that only Nationalism, as a doctrine of authority, could overcome the defects at the root of the crisis.[19] So Nationalism, even according to Federzoni, intended to create a new order by changing psychology and values, but unlike Rocco, Federzoni did not face up to the manipulative implication of this notion and propose institutional changes to make possible the essential indoctrination. Instead, he continued to call for the defense of Italy's established institutions and for the restoration of all the prerogatives of the crown vis-à-vis parliament.[20]

Federzoni, then, was less rigorous than Rocco, but from his place near the moderate end of the right fascist continuum, he was able to provide an important bridge between genuine, active fascists and conservative monarchists who were willing to acquiesce in fascism. Obviously those near Federzoni's end of the spectrum contributed much less than those like Rocco to the ongoing push toward radical institutional change within the Fascist regime. When in 1925 the chance came to make fundamental institutional change, Francesco Coppola, as a member of the Commission of Eighteen set up to offer proposals, favored little departure from traditional right liberalism.[21] And Federzoni himself, occupying the key post of Minister of the Interior during the same period, was more concerned with "normalization" than radical innovation; he sought especially to impose the authority of the traditional, monarchical state over the unruly society, including the Fascist party. On the other hand, Alfredo Rocco was not willing to settle for the outcome of the fascist revolution even in 1925, and so, as Minister of Justice, he proved one of fascism's leading innovators.

In his memoirs, published in 1967, Federzoni contrasts his own attempt to defend order and existing institutions with the naive, apocalyptic revolutionary projects of other fascists at the same time.[22] He even groups Rocco with extremists like Roberto Farinacci, implying that the fundamental differentiation within fascism was between those who sought radical change during the pivotal period from 1924 to 1926 and those who thought fascism had gone far enough. Although it is bizarre to lump the unruly Farinacci with the jurist Rocco, the axis of division which Federzoni proposes is valid and important on one level and helps us to grasp the uniquely important function that Rocco, as a right fascist seeking radical change, was able to fulfill in the regime. He served as a bridge between, on the one hand, fascists who shared his values and perceptions but not his desire for radical institutional change and, on the other, fascists who wanted superficially similar institutional changes, but as a result of different values and goals.

In formally merging with the Fascist party in February of 1923, in the aftermath of the March on Rome, the Nationalist association did not envision an ideological compromise. The Nationalists were seeking to keep fascist radicalism in bounds, but they also had a more positive objective: they would give fascism the intellectual content and political direction it seemed to lack; fascism was the means through which the Nationalist program could be implemented. Both before and after the merger, the Nationalists continually insisted that their doctrine was the latent core of fascism; as Balbino Giuliano put it, "fascism is Nationalism not yet well understood."[23] Fascism's very confusion and immaturity, Giuliano felt, made it especially useful as a Nationalist instrument, for it was partly the empty gestures, the romantic rebelliousness, the vain phrases against the bourgeoisie that had made fascism so popular. Had fascism eschewed these non-Nationalist forms and embraced the Nationalist doctrine explicitly from the start, it could not have been such a useful instrument for Nationalist purposes in the long run. Meanwhile, Giuliano insisted, the Nationalists themselves should not compromise and move toward fascism, but rather maintain their vision in pure form, as a focal point helping the new nationalist consciousness take firm root and spread. Nationalism, then, was the intellectual vanguard of fascism, and ultimately Nationalism would determine what the Fascist regime was to become.

But not all of the anti-Socialist reaction with long-term antiliberal purposes found ideological expression in Nationalism. A heterogeneous populist current also emerged in the fascist reaction, as disaffected Italians with more modest middle-class backgrounds began turning against the liberal order for a different set of reasons. It is well known that fascism began to take on the proportions of a mass movement, losing the more limited and quasi-socialist character it had had in 1919, because of the influx of discontented lower-bourgeois elements which began late in 1920.[24] Any interpretation of the origins of fascism depends on what we make of this lower-middle-class revolt. The Nationalists were trying to exploit lower-middle-class fascism, denying that it had or could develop any force and consistency on its own. Obviously much depended on how well this current would be able to resist the Nationalists, to maintain its autonomy, to devise its own program, and to impose that program on fascism as a whole. And this meant that much of the drama was being played out on the level of ideas.

As we saw in the first chapter, it is widely assumed that these lower-middle-class fascists were subject to socioeconomic traumas that made them resentful of the industrial classes and susceptible to irrational nationalist appeals. Since these were apparently the losers in the process of modernization, they could not have developed a progressive, "universal" perspective of their own. Ultimately, it would seem, these rootless elements were merely "available" as a mass base for a reaction spearheaded by the Nationalists. At the same time, this new form of fascism is often viewed in terms of a dualistic conception of the political spectrum which identifies the left with Socialism and defense of the working class and assumes that any opposition to them must by definition be on the right. Since the Nationalists gave the most coherent expression to right-wing political anti-Socialism in this particular case, it is easy to assume that fascism was essentially a movement of right-wing reaction, with Nationalism its most lucid doctrinal expression. Moreover, when we focus sharply on the workings of fascism during the period from 1921 to 1925, we find mostly confusion, infighting, personal bickering, local power rivalries, and tactical disputes. Fascism as a mass movement seems to have been so chaotic, so splintered, that whatever consistency and continuity the regime had apparently must have come from elsewhere.

These perceptions and categories are unquestionably valid in part, but we can make better sense of what we know of fascism, especially what happened in the long term, if we recognize that the lower bourgeois revolt in postwar Italy gave rise to an autonomous, populist—even leftist—variety of fascism, with enough force and consistency to have had considerable practical impact. The thrust toward radical change that it produced was the result of a variety of pressures, which often worked at cross purposes in the short term, but which had enough in common to contribute to a single long-term movement for change. Taken as a whole, the left fascist current had an important measure of continuity and direction—not just the power rivalries, infighting, and juggling by the leadership that strike us if we focus on fascism at any one moment. Nationalism, then, was not the only component in fascism that transcended irrational activism and "availability." Petty bourgeois populists constituted another current pushing for radical change through fascism on the basis of reasonably serious purposes—and they kept pushing, even sometimes against Mussolini, despite temporary setbacks and compromises, right up until the fall of the regime in 1943. The populist current was largely responsible for the radical change that fascism did bring about—the destruction of the liberal parliamentary system and the beginnings of a totalitarian alternative based on corporativism and mass mobilization.

But the standard petty bourgeois traumas and the short-term power rivalries were important as well, so we must devise more complex and flexible ways of grouping the elements within this heterogeneous current. We need a conceptual framework that encompasses a variety of motives and purposes, a variety of ways of being a petty bourgeois fascist. Since the industrial workers did relatively well economically during and after the war, at a time when inflation and accelerating industrialization produced the classic insecurities in the Italian lower middle class, it is undeniable that the fascist assault on the socialist labor movement stemmed in part from socioeconomic resentments. Some of those involved on this basis were content merely to destroy by force the existing trade union movement, the source of labor's economic power, while others sought to pursue their interests by developing a political alternative that would, among other things, overcome the class struggle that seemed to be leaving them out.

But fascism emerged above all in response to a political crisis, one which did not stem primarily from the socioeconomic dislocations, but which had deeper roots of its own in the problematic features of the political life of liberal Italy. Some with lower-middle-class backgrounds saw fascism as a way to overcome this political crisis; their fascism was fundamentally a populist revolt against the old politics. Since political power and confidence are to some extent a function of socioeconomic position, it is not surprising that the petty bourgeoisie was overrepresented in this populist reaction. In this case the overrepresentation was especially pronounced, because most of the political discontent among the other "populist" sectors, the workers and the peasants, found an outlet in Socialism or political Catholicism. Yet this overrepresentation of the lower middle class can lead us astray. Because we find that a disproportionate number of those involved can be characterized in terms of a particular socioeconomic grouping, we are liable to infer that socioeconomic problems were the major source of the common response.

While the petty bourgeoisie was overrepresented in fascism, the fascist revolt obviously did not involve the entire class. And it was largely political perspectives and values that distinguished those who were involved from those who were not. Those who did help to create fascism constituted a kind of vanguard best characterized in terms of two substantially overlapping categories. First, they were political outsiders. Some had been politically indifferent or alienated before; others had been active in preindustrial populist and republican groupings hostile to the political establishment; many were young people just coming of age politically.[25] Second, they were war veterans, often from the ranks of the junior officers. Populist fascism was comprised especially of young, politically alienated war veterans who claimed to embody the moral legacy and promise of renewal bound up with Italy's war experience. Their enemy was not industrial capitalism but the Italian political system; they were alienated not because of declining economic prospects and social status, but because they felt excluded politically. Their resentments were directed less at the industrial classes than at the old political class, with its lack of confidence in the Italian people.

The young veterans in fascism are generally described as "military desperadoes" unable to readjust to civilian life or "dropouts" from the established order, which seemed to have no acceptable place for them.[26] But when we remember what the war experience had meant, and consider what these young veterans did not like about the established order, it becomes obvious that their reasons for revolting against the old Italy cannot be so easily explained away. To say that they could not readjust after the war is trivial and tautological: they chose not to adjust—first, because they believed, quite plausibly, that the situation called for significant political and cultural change instead; and second, because they believed, much less plausibly—but not absurdly—that they themselves could spearhead that change, because of their role in the war. Whatever their prospects of success, it was not merely petty bourgeois prejudice to insist on the value and the political implications of the war experience; and it may have been neither desirable nor possible for Italian society to return to normal, to traditional patterns. When the old liberals, the new politics of mass parties, and the "normal" Socialist alternative to the system all failed to fill the developing political vacuum, lower-middle-class outsiders and veterans set out on the perilous course of trying to develop their own political challenge— and political alternative—through the fascism of 1921. They based their claim to legitimacy on their wartime role; and it was Italy's wartime experience that gave them confidence enough—in themselves, and in the potential of the Italian people—to seek to create a new political order.

This is not to suggest that fascism fell heir to all of the moral idealism bound up with Italy's experience of World War I. Ultimately, the same ideals nourished the resistance to fascism, and in 1934 the distinguished liberal historian Adolfo Omodeo published his famous collection of letters from victims of the war—letters saturated with generous national idealism—in the hope of rekindling a moral legacy that could help his country go beyond fascism. But while Omodeo's negative assessment of fascism in 1934 was essentially correct, the cult of Mazzini, for example, which Omodeo found bound up with the idealism of the war,[27] helped to inspire the young veterans who turned to fascism. It is striking evidence of the difficulties of thinking about these relationships that Alessandro Galante Garrone, in his otherwise very fine introduction to the 1968 edition of Omodeo's volume, fails even to consider the possibility that the wartime cult of Mazzini could have contributed to the creation of fascism, even though, following Omodeo, he certainly understands the tremendous significance which Mazzini's ideas had for disaffected Italians in the context of the war and the postwar crisis.[28] On the other hand, those who have linked the postwar cult of Mazzini to fascism have failed to grasp the significance of this Mazzinianism, dismissing it as a romantic petty bourgeois remnant from the past.[29]

It is generally true, however, that those who carried the Mazzinian idealism of the war into fascism did not have the same moral and intellectual qualities that we find in Omodeo and others of his generation who perceived the war in similar terms—men like Guido De Ruggiero, Carlo Rosselli, and Piero Gobetti. Thus the radical populism in fascism tended, on the one hand, to become extreme and totalitarian and, on the other, to get bogged down in petty personal resentments and place-seeking. But there were tensions of a different sort in the positions of postwar idealists who avoided these excesses. Most, like De Ruggiero or Omodeo himself, remained firmly within the Italian liberal tradition, but their ideals were vague, lacking precise commitments for social and political change. These cultivated liberals tended to identify the educated bourgeoisie with the Italian nation and state—and so tended to fall into a continuum with those who turned against the liberal parliamentary system from the right, also in the name of the war and a revitalized middle class embodying the national interest.[30] Others like Gobetti ultimately insisted on the hegemony of the working class and portrayed social forces in ways that were hardly compatible with the fundamental assumptions of liberalism.[31] It was symptomatic of the depth of the crisis of liberalism in Italy that even people of the quality of De Ruggiero and Gobetti were in danger of falling off the liberal tightrope to the right or left, precisely in their attempt to foster liberal values in the volatile postwar context.

Insofar as the Italian political system was genuinely in crisis, and insofar as the liberal parliamentary system in general has genuine defects, young fascist war veterans could at least attempt to make their own political discontents the basis for a new political program—transcending narrow class interests and having validity for the whole society. And there was a struggle for coherence, universality, and autonomy in this populist fascism, but the current proved fragile, its program clumsy and in some ways superficial, because of the social insecurities, the deficiencies of education, and the lack of experience with the modern industrial world that resulted from the social background of those involved.

Although the fascist struggle with the Socialists and workers stemmed in part from socioeconomic resentments, it was above all a dispute over the value of the nation and the meaning of the war—and over the kind of change appropriate for Italy at that moment. The near civil war which gripped postwar Italy was partly a class struggle, but it was primarily a conflict of two different revolutions, operating on a collision course. In a sense, it was a struggle for hegemony in the process of political expansion that had to come in one form or another. In evaluating this bitter battle, we must remember that the Socialists were not yet offering the sensitive, flexible alternative which Antonio Gramsci later elaborated, partly in response to the inadequacies of the Socialists' postwar strategy. Rather, they proposed an alternative which historians have portrayed, with a rare measure of unanimity, as inflexible, insensitive, and inappropriate. Since the Socialists and workers ridiculed the veterans and the war and eschewed any national-political leadership role, the discontented young veterans did not have the option of following the Socialists. But under the circumstances, they felt, they did not have to wait for Socialist and working-class leadership anyway; they represented the new Italy of World War I, so they themselves could lead. And their alternative movement inevitably took shape first in opposition to the Socialists and workers, who seemed to be threatening the wrong revolution. In the short term, of course, this movement could be exploited for the purposes of others, especially reactionary landowners, but these fascists did not deny labor's right to full citizenship, nor were they seeking to erect a permanent apparatus of repression. It was not the workers' rising socioeconomic position that seemed appalling, but their denial of the war and the nation, their pretensions to superiority and leadership, their indifference to Italy's longstanding national and political problems at a time when solutions seemed possible.

The young fascists sensed that they would have to have labor's involvement if they were to create a viable alternative to the old order. Thus they sought to transcend a restricted class perspective and to find a basis of accommodation with the workers, a common denominator of basic goals and socioeconomic roles, to make possible a populist political challenge. By using the umbrella "producer" category, they insisted—somewhat defensively—that they too were valuable, productive members of society, just like the workers. They destroyed the existing unions not simply to undermine the advantageous economic position of some sectors of labor, but to force the workers into new unions organized for different purposes. They included petty bourgeois "intellectual labor" in these organizations not simply as a means of static socioeconomic defense, but to forge an alliance of populist "producers" as the basis for a new order. The initial conflict between petty bourgeois fascists and Socialist workers deformed the popular political challenge at the outset, but it was impossible to foresee in 1921 whether this would be fatal.

Fascists with similar political resentments and wartime experiences differed in the quality of their political vision, so we must differentiate even among those whose concerns were primarily political rather than socioeconomic. The various possibilities can be arrayed along a continuum from personal to ideal-social kinds of motivation. Nearer the first pole were those with relatively limited horizons; they understood the fascist revolution largely as a mere change in personnel, one from which they themselves would profit, and tended to focus on short-term tactical questions and power rivalries which affected their personal fortunes. Those nearer the second pole acted on the basis of a principled and reasonably forceful critique of the Italian political system; they sought to develop a program of serious institutional change as a way of realizing their political ideals in the future. Of course, the place-seekers also had some broader social purposes, and those with political ideals to implement also had careers to make. But the proportions varied greatly.

Near the first, more familiar end of the spectrum, we find people like Achille Starace and especially Roberto Farinacci (1892–1945), the local chieftain, or *Ras*, of fascism in Cremona and the national party leader from February 1925 to March 1926. Farinacci was an especially unattractive type who is often portrayed as the archetypal fascist. The son of a small-town policeman, he was identified first with violent provincial fascism and ultimately with the Fascist party in its rivalry with the traditional state apparatus. But despite his extremism, Farinacci did not have the more coherent sense of problems and long-term solutions that we can find in other fascists of the same generation.[32] Those like Farinacci lacked the intelligence, the education, the idealism, or the breadth of vision necessary to understand present problems and to propose institutional alternatives. Propelled by personal ambitions and resentments, they sought merely an "empty" social revolution, enabling energetic new elements from the people, like themselves, to assume the leadership of Italy. They assumed themselves to embody the values of the war—so it was not necessary to have a long-term vision or a coherent program. They were new men from the people; they would do more for the people.

Even for those at this end of the spectrum, then, fascism was to be the vehicle for a kind of populist revolution, but one which would merely create a new ruling class. They championed the new Fascist party vis-à-vis the old state apparatus because they were seeking to establish an institutional power base for themselves, not because they believed that new institutions could make possible a qualitatively different kind of democracy. As party leader, Farinacci sought to extend party control over the Fascist union movement, but more as an end in itself than as a means to foster ongoing revolutionary development in a corporativist direction.[33] He was simply unable to grasp the relationship between politics and economics that serious corporativists had in mind.[34] Still, personal ambitions and resentments like Farinacci's led important groups of fascists to keep pushing for a purge of the old elites and for a greater party role at the expense of the old bureaucracy, so this kind of motivation contributed to the measure of openness and dynamism there was to the regime.

The motivation involved at this end of the spectrum produced a variety of strategies in practice. While Farinacci's ambitions often led him to defy Mussolini, others satisfied their aspirations, and often found places for themselves, by identifying with Mussolini, linking their fortunes to his. It soothed their resentments to have their leader running the country, for he was a new man like themselves, and a man identified with the cause of the war. Some, like Achille Starace, were essentially Mussolinians from the start, but this identification with the Duce was operative especially in the 1930s, when it had become clear how limited even the empty social revolution, the circulation of elites, was to be.

If radical, populist, "petty bourgeois" fascism was only this, if Farinacci, say, really was the archetypal fascist, then obviously the interpretation of fascism would be much easier. But categories of interpretation which illuminate Farinacci's end of the left fascist continuum turn out not to be adequate to explain such major figures as Dino Grandi, Augusto Turati, and Giuseppe Bottai, although they too were new men of modest middle-class origin, basing their claim to leadership on their experience in the war. As we move along the continuum, leaving Farinacci behind, we begin to find a more coherent critique of the liberal parliamentary system and a more sensitive consideration of what fascism was to do with the power it sought.

The petty bourgeois current in fascism managed to offer a political program, envisioning not merely a change in personnel but a change in institutions, and it was derived—directly or indirectly—from the syndicalist tradition. Occupying the "ideal" end of the populist continuum, neosyndicalism enabled the alienated young veterans in fascism to give their vague, radical populist aspirations a measure of precision and content. They were looking for political guidance, and the syndicalists, with their interventionist and heterodox leftist past, enjoyed considerable prestige among them. Moreover, the program of concrete institutional change the syndicalists offered seemed to provide the needed alternative to both liberalism and orthodox socialism. So the syndicalists had considerable success as they worked to shape this young fascist current, to give its energies a national syndicalist direction. As they mixed with these fascists, gradually losing their separate identity, the syndicalists found their natural constituency at last. From the beginning it had not been the industrial proletariat, as they had originally sought to convince themselves, nor the southern peasantry, as Antonio Gramsci later argued, but the politically alienated lower bourgeoisie, seeking a new political order based on an alliance with the industrial proletariat.

Most of the radical young war veterans like Dino Grandi, Italo Balbo, Augusto Turati, and Curzio Suckert, who were involved at various stages in the ongoing push for institutional change, became fascists not in the first, more obviously radical phase of 1919, but in the more problematic phase of 1920–21. Their social origins were generally petty bourgeois; many had radical or leftist republican pasts, and most, like Grandi and Balbo, participated in the vogue of Mazzini's ideas that accompanied the Italian war experience. They emphasized the value of the nation, glorified the war, and insisted that the fascist revolt must culminate in a kind of revolution, not in parliamentary compromise. Their vision was antipolitical—just as the syndicalists' was—and they were attracted to syndicalism as a way of transcending the apparently corrupting politics of the liberal parliamentary system.

Some of those near this end of the populist continuum were closer in style to the educated Nationalists than to the unruly fascists operating nearer the personal end, and thus the imprecision in some attempts to define the components in fascism.[35] Style, of course, can be a genuine basis for differentiation, and thus in his memoirs the Nationalist Federzoni could praise the "humanity" even of Italo Balbo, while he had no use for Farinacci.[36] But convergence on the level of style and tactics should not lead us to infer that there was a similar convergence on the level of motivating goals. It was not necessary to embrace the Nationalist program to dislike the style and tactics of a Farinacci.

We have seen that the *Carta del Carnaro* was at first the most important vehicle of syndicalist influence among the young populist war veterans in fascism. The day it was published, and just after he himself had returned from Fiume, the influential Venetian fascist Piero Marsich wrote to Mussolini to laud the document as "a very noble, magnificent thing" in which "all the postulates of fascism find their concrete application."[37] After Giolitti's government suppressed the Fiume regency in

December 1920, many of the Fiume legionnaires began gravitating to fascism, and more and more it began to seem that it fell to fascism to implement the ideals of Fiume. For example, the first issue of *Audacia*, which Edoardo Malusardi founded in January 1921 as the fascist newspaper of Verona, proclaimed the principles of the *Carta del Carnaro* to be the keys to fascism. In its third issue the newspaper endorsed the neosyndicalist doctrine as it had recently been outlined by Marsich in an article in *Il Popolo d'Italia*.[38] And Marsich was publicizing ideas undoubtedly drawn not only from the *Carta del Carnaro*, but also directly from syndicalist writings. Fascism's essential task—to reconstruct the state on a new basis—could be achieved by organizing society along economic lines and by giving the resulting syndicates legislative capacities and public duties.

We can better grasp the role of neosyndicalist ideas in the populist current in fascism if we consider four of its most significant and influential representatives—Dino Grandi, Giuseppe Bottai, Augusto Turati, and Curzio Suckert. These figures were dissimilar in important respects, but they shared a core of common values and purposes, and each played a major role—though in different ways and at different times—in the long-term push toward a postliberal political system within fascism. Because we have generally focused on aspects of fascism which manifest the differences among figures like these, we have tended to miss the deeper common purposes which differentiated them from other fascists and led each of them to contribute to a single long-term process. In approaching these exemplars, we must avoid assuming a priori that those whose political ideas had a measure of coherence were unrepresentative, an assumption which simply forecloses the possibility that petty bourgeois fascism could have produced something other than the expected irrationalities and prejudices. Relatively articulate fascists like Grandi and Bottai were young populist veterans speaking for and to a populist middle-class constituency, but one whose members varied greatly in intelligence and commitment.

The most coherent spokesman for the new radical fascism of 1921 was Dino Grandi, a war veteran and a *squadrista* involved in the violent "punitive expeditions" in Emilia-Romagna. In the words of one observer, Grandi "is ideologically and in fact a typical petty bourgeois."[39] He indulged in the sort of rhetoric that is usually seen as typically fascist —about, for example, the primacy of will over intellect for revolutionary change.[40] Because Grandi was typical in important respects, he was able to lead, to help others with less precise goals think more clearly about problems and solutions. And Grandi was a neosyndicalist.

Grandi was born in 1895 in the province of Imola, in Emilia-Romagna, where his father was an agricultural estate manager and later an agrarian in his own right. The elder Grandi was a passionate reader of Mazzini and held progressive views about agricultural management and about the value of organizations for agricultural workers. Grandi's mother was an elementary school teacher. Grandi distinguished himself during the war, winning three medals of valor, and ended up a captain. After the war, he completed his studies at the University of Bologna, then began practicing law. He found that wearing his uniform, complete with medals, led to encounters with antiwar Socialists and workers. According to Grandi himself, it was after one such episode, in which, he says, his life was endangered, that he joined the *Fasci di combattimento*. This was in September of 1920, just when fascism was starting to gather momentum in reaction against Socialism and the *biennio rosso*.[41]

But even before turning to fascism, Grandi was active in political journalism, anticipating a revolution linked to the war experience, and publicizing the national syndicalist vision he would soon seek to have implemented through fascism. He had encountered Italian syndicalism in theory and practice even before the war; he started reading Olivetti's *Pagine libere* while a high school student, and he was active in the interventionist *Fascio* which Panunzio headed in Ferrara. In April of 1915, he and Panunzio were two of the three featured speakers at a large interventionist meeting at the University of Ferrara that accompanied a student strike favoring intervention. Explaining his intellectual development after the war, Grandi numbered Agostino Lanzillo —as well as Georges Sorel—among his mentors.[42] Before the war, he admired syndicalism for remaining immune to the petty ambitions and compromises of political socialism, but he warned that syndicalism in its present form was too much a rigid class instrument.[43] Grandi sensed however, that a refined and more general syndicalist movement could play a central role in the future, and after the war, in July 1920, he made explicit his conception of the fundamental historical significance of syndicalism:

> The European revolution of the last century was a revolution of the individual, of the *ego*, of *man*. Luther, Kant, and Rousseau.
> The revolution of the twentieth century is the revolution of *a larger individual*.
> This larger individual is the *organization*, the *group*, the *syndicate*.
> The syndicate is not, as many believe, a *method*, an instrument. The syndicate is a *person* that tends to replace the old single physical person, who is insufficient, impotent, and no longer adequate.
> . . . The syndicate as person, as will, as an autonomous, dynamic, organic nucleus, is by now such a vital and living force that to deny it means to place oneself in absurdity, outside reality, outside the revolution, outside history. . . .

In the syndicate is the *true* revolution, and in it can be found already solidly constructed *the framework of the new state* of tomorrow. . . .

The syndicate will remain. New functions will gradually be entrusted to it and new ones will continually be born.[44]

Grandi's emphasis on the revolutionary role of organization was part of a wider vision linking syndicalism to the deficiencies of the Italian Risorgimento, to the ideas of Giuseppe Mazzini, to the possibility of a new kind of democracy, and to the revolutionary meaning of the war for Italy.

Already in 1919 and 1920, Grandi denied that the Socialists could bring about the radical change that Italy required. Socialism had made a major historical contribution in developing syndicalism, but the Socialist party failed to grasp the significance that the syndicates could have in the present context. This failure was symptomatic of the Socialists' more general inability to grasp the meaning of great contemporary events—the war, the Fiume episode, even the Russian revolution. Grandi's thinking indicated that those more lucid about present possibilities had to seize hegemony over the unions from the socialists, in order to make the right kind of revolution. Even in 1919, he envisioned a new party, opposed to both liberalism and Socialism, that would combine the productive economic elements of the nation with the young war veterans in a postliberal political alliance. He also called for free trade as a way to stimulate productivism, to overcome Italian bourgeois decadence, and to force capitalism to get on with its task of developing Italy.[45] Grandi wove all these themes together in the conception of fascism and its mission that he publicized in 1921.

As a fascist, Grandi portrayed Nationalism and syndicalism as aspects of a single deep Italian spiritual revival that had begun before the war.[46] The two movements had come together during the war, and now fascism would synthesize the principles of both as the basis of its own revolutionary program. Grandi numbered Alfredo Rocco among his mentors and no doubt derived his own national syndicalist vision from Nationalism as well as syndicalism. It was certainly possible to learn from both, partly because Nationalism and syndicalism had important features in common. But Grandi sometimes glossed over the deeper differences between them, and thus there was some ambiguity in his thinking at first. These differences could be blurred temporarily, while fascism was still gathering force in opposition to both Socialism and the liberal state, but for Grandi and others, the need to implement a positive fascist alternative soon posed fundamental choices and dissolved most of the ambiguity.

Nationalist influence is especially clear in Grandi's conception of Italy's international position and in his understanding of international relations in the short term. But here again there were tensions, for his vision included elements which pointed toward the syndicalists' neo-Mazzinian conception of international relations. Writing in December 1914, Grandi portrayed the war as but the first act in an international class struggle pitting proletarian against plutocratic nations.[47] Logically, the present war should have involved Germany, Russia, and Italy on one side against Great Britain and France on the other. Largely because it did not, it was but a confused episode which could be expected to solve only limited problems facing particular nations—the problem of the Italian irredenta, for example. A more sharply defined revolutionary war would soon follow. During the immediate postwar period, Grandi continued to anticipate that the next war would be a revolutionary class struggle pitting Germany, Italy, and Russia—the three proletarian nations "that work and have children"—against France and Great Britain.[48] The Russian revolution, in fact, was the vanguard of the revolution of the proletarian nations against English capitalism, "which has emerged from the war the tyrannical and absolute master of the world."[49]

But Grandi was not calling for autarky or glorifying perpetual war. He was a vehement free trader who believed in growing economic interdependence among nations—an international division of labor. Indeed, according to Grandi, "Humanity tends, with an irresistible inclination, to transcend conflict, moving simultaneously toward cooperation."[50] And since wars stemmed from economic factors—especially the need for raw materials and markets—only international economic freedom and cooperation could provide a viable basis for a lasting peace. However, this condition did not obtain at present; Grandi saw the League of Nations both as a conservative instrument to maintain the status quo in the interests of France and Britain and as a venture too utopian to be able to prevent further war.[51] Thus there was a place in Grandi's conception for a future "just war," but such a war for Grandi, as for the syndicalists, would move humanity closer to the ideal, a rational international configuration in which wars would no longer be necessary. Even though Grandi's thinking on international problems was subject to Nationalist influence, his vision ultimately eluded Nationalist categories and coincided with the neosyndicalist conception.

The young fascist who would spearhead the drive for a populist corporative state in the practice of the Fascist regime after the crisis of 1924–25 was Giuseppe Bottai (1895–1959). He was born in 1895, the same year as Grandi, into a modest middle-class family of "longstanding republican tradition."[52] As one of the elite *arditi* troops during the war, Bottai fought at the front, was wounded and decorated. In his memoirs, published in 1949, he linked his wartime experience to the political maturation and idealism of his generation.[53] Bottai was politically active as a republican when he became a fascist in 1919, helping to organize the Rome *Fascio*. While he was not an old Mussolinian interventionist, like so many other leading fascists of 1919, neither was Bottai part of the new fascism of 1921, centered in Emilia-Romagna, with its violence and extremism. Because of his relative moderation in matters of tactics, he sometimes differed with the newer fascists, even those whose ultimate purposes for fascism were much the same as his own. In his conception of fascist ends, however, Bottai, too, was an extremist, one who gradually developed a vision of corporativism as a radical, postliberal kind of democracy.

Bottai's intellectual background was more literary and less political than Grandi's, and even in 1923 his ideas about the positive aims of fascism were not well worked out. At this point, he was bitterly hostile to parliament, and he shared the widespread notion that the war experience and the ideas of Giuseppe Mazzini were somehow important for creating an alternative.[54] But in introducing the first issue of his important review *Critica fascista*, Bottai portrayed the central task of fascism as merely to create a new fascist ruling class; he still did not have the corporativist content, the vision of concrete institutional change to create new political forms, that he would begin to develop in 1924–25, when basic decisions about the purpose of fascism could no longer be postponed.[55]

Like Grandi, Bottai learned from the Nationalists as well as the syndicalists, and sometimes there was ambiguity in his thinking over questions involving populism versus elitism and the relationship between state and syndicates.[56] But as he absorbed neosyndicalist ideas and came to view corporativism as the core of fascism, and as the regime began to implement a postliberal alternative to the parliamentary system, the ambiguity in his thinking dissolved. Fascist corporativism was to make possible the fulfillment of the democratic ideal, the immortal principles of 1789. By the end of the 1920s, Bottai had a fully developed corporativist vision and program, derived primarily from concepts the syndicalists had been publicizing for years.[57] His mature corporativism was indistinguishable in its essentials from the neosyndicalist conception, and he now became the major political leader of the left corporativist current in fascism which absorbed most of the syndicalists.

A major ally of Bottai in the struggle for a leftist corporativism was Augusto Turati (1888–1955), head of the Fascist party during the crucial period from 1926 to 1930. In background and style—and in the path which led him to fascism—Turati was typical of the new lower bourgeois fascism. The nearly insufferable froth and rhetoric that we associate with this current are much in evidence in his speeches as party secretary. Nevertheless, while not an intellectual, Turati was reasonably intelligent and managed in these speeches to articulate the aspirations of the wider groups of fascists who looked to him for leadership. His vision of fascism's purpose, while not as well developed as Grandi's during the early years or Bottai's later on, still was considerably more coherent than Farinacci's and did include a radical, totalitarian form of democracy centered on economic groupings.[58]

After participating in the interventionist movement, Turati saw frontline service during the war, which he considered the decisive experience of his life. He was decorated several times and ended up a captain in the infantry. After the war he was active as a radical democrat before joining the Brescia *Fascio* in 1921.[59] He was one of the *squadristi* specializing in violent assaults on the socialist labor movement, but at the same time he played a major role in organizing an alternative Fascist labor movement in the province of Brescia. In 1925, as head of the Fascist unions there, he led the much-publicized strike of the Fascist metalworkers' union, which spread to Milan and Turin and ultimately involved almost 80,000 strikers. As a young fascist *squadrista* and organizer, Turati was strongly attracted to the neosyndicalist conception of the *Carto del Carnaro*. In 1922, in the aftermath of the strategic dispute within fascism, which we will consider in the next chapter, Turati supported Piero Marsich and other fascists disillusioned with Mussolini and hoped that D'Annunzio could be persuaded to lead a national syndicalist revolution.[60] This particular course did not materialize, but even as party secretary later on, Turati continued to understand the purpose of fascism largely in neosyndicalist terms.

Turati's conception of the place of the party in fascist corporativist development merits special attention, since it is easy to overemphasize the antagonisms between fascists associated with the party and those associated with the economically based organizations. In his speeches as party head, Turati insisted, plausibly enough, that both kinds of organization had essential roles in the fascist revolution; indeed, they were complementary. But this did not mean simply that the party was the revolutionary instrument in the political sphere, with the corporative system the revolutionary innovation in the economic sphere. The party had the central ideological role in "fascistizing" Italian society, which involved giving the corporations that constituted society the political values necessary for them to become autonomous political entities. For now the party had an essential role of education and surveillance, but Turati looked forward to the fulfillment that would be reached once the masses had learned to involve themselves with the great problems of the nation, once the fascist mentality had become universal in the society. The party would then no longer have any special function, and Italy would be left with the kind of free corpora-tivist order that De Ambris had envisioned in the *Carta del Carnaro*.[61]

While Turati, the party man, insisted on the central role of corpora-tivism, Giuseppe Bottai, from an institutional base in the Ministry of Corporations, certainly did not deny that the party had a central role in implementing the fascist revolution.[62] Turati and Bottai did have po-tentially complementary roles, and they were allies in the ongoing struggle for serious innovation. They worked together, for example, to give the Fascist Labor Charter of 1927 a clearly leftist thrust. There was, to be sure, an important rivalry between the party and the corporativ-ist current. It stemmed in part from a plausible difference in strategic emphasis, and of course those involved had careers to make and found their fortunes bound up with the power of their particular institutions within the regime. But if we focus on the ambitions and rivalries char-acteristic of the personal end of the continuum, important as these were for some aspects of the regime, we may miss the deeper, long-term thrust provided by those operating nearer the ideal end, including both party men and corporativists.

It is easy to overemphasize the contrast between party and neo-syndicalist currents because Turati, like his predecessor as party chief, Roberto Farinacci, was hostile to the syndicalist Edmondo Rossoni, the leader of the Fascist trade union confederation from its inception in 1922. In 1928 Turati and others engineered the ouster of Rossoni, along with the breakup, or *sbloccamento*, of the confederation, which had provided Rossoni with a powerful institutional base. Those who define power in limited, immediate terms, and those who identify the syndi-calist current in fascism with trade unionism and protection of working-class interests, tend to focus on Rossoni as this current's chief repre-sentative.[63] From this perspective, the hostility of leading party men to Rossoni seems evidence of a basic cleft between party and syndicalist factions.

Rossoni sought to make the Fascist unions genuine vehicles of working-class interests, and he did not hesitate to criticize business in surprisingly outspoken terms; his position, then, was leftist and syndi-calist on a superficial level. In breadth of political vision, however, Rossoni could match neither the syndicalist intellectuals nor the most important of the other syndicalists who became major Fascist union leaders, particularly Mario Racheli, Livio Ciardi, and Luigi Razza. Although Rossoni was not devoid of ideals, and although he had played some role in the syndicalists' doctrinal revision, his conception lacked the totalitarian unity of politics and economics that we will find in the mature fascist conceptions of these other syndicalists. Partly because of these intellectual limits, he was more involved in personal ambitions and rivalries than the others and so operated nearer the personal end of the populist continuum. He was seeking especially to keep the confederation as his own fief—as free as possible from party supervision and influence—and to enhance its power within the regime. But it was possible to understand the purpose of the Fascist unions more broadly, in terms of an integral, totalitarian conception of the fascist revolution—one which required a more complementary relationship between the party and the socioeconomic organizations. It was not only the party leader Turati, but also long-time syndicalists like Olivetti and younger corporativists like Bottai, who questioned Rossoni's priorities.[64] When the party leader Turati spearheaded the opposition that led to Rossoni's ouster, this did not constitute a basic difference between party and syndicalist currents, but a difference along the personal-ideal continuum. In this case the party man Turati was more the radical idealist than the syndicalist Rossoni, just as, for example, the corporativist Bottai was more the radical idealist than the party man Farinacci. And more generally, emphasis on those like Farinacci and Rossoni, with their limited conceptions of fascism and their conflicting personal ambitions, makes it difficult to see the convergence of fascists like Turati, Bottai, Olivetti, and Panunzio around the neosyndicalist conception at the ideal end of the left fascist continuum.

The contrast between the party leaders Turati and Farinacci points to a related obstacle to clear thinking. In delineating the components of fascism, historians often distinguish "moderates" from "extremists" on the basis of tactics and focus, for example, on differences over the utility of further violence after the March on Rome. Emphasis on tactical differences, however, makes it easy to miss more fundamental axes of division over the basic purposes of fascism. Radical purposes did not necessarily correspond to extreme tactics. When Turati replaced his enemy Farinacci as party secretary in 1926, it seems at first glance to have been a victory for moderation, for Farinacci was more radical on the level of tactics. But Turati had a more radical conception of the ends of fascism. Although he insisted that further fascist violence could only be counterproductive, he was not assuming that the fascist revolution had gone far enough and was essentially over. Nor can we infer from his opposition to the pretensions of the rebellious Farinacci that Turati was acquiescing in mere personal dictatorship under Mussolini. Rather, Turati sought to implement, from within the power base fascism had already won, his vision of a totalitarian corporativist superdemocracy. So the extremist Turati played a major role in the ongoing push for serious institutional change, while Farinacci, despite his tactical extremism, operated largely on a day-to-day level, without a comparable long-term vision.

Again, focus on tactical differences may lead to the assumption that those who deplored the renewed *squadristi* violence of 1924 thought fascism had gone far enough. There was indeed sharp dispute over the legitimacy of further violence in 1924, but there were also differences in ultimate objectives that were more fundamental than such differences over methods. Some who opposed the extremists in 1924 nevertheless had revolutionary objectives for fascism, while many among the extremists sought to achieve goals that were primarily personal rather than ideal. Operating near the personal place-seeking end of the left fascist continuum, such violent fascists were frustrated by the mild outcome of the March on Rome. By resorting again to violence, they hoped to force fascism to go further in the direction of "empty" social revolution, purging the old elites to make way for themselves. This sort of frustration fueled one kind of extremism, but the push toward radical change based on an ideal populist vision constituted another kind of extremism within fascism, even though it was not always associated with radical methods. At the same time, there were radical differences in ends among those calling for moderation and opposing Farinacci's unruliness. For example, we cannot lump Turati, because of his conflict with Farinacci, with Farinacci's other great antagonist, Luigi Federzoni, the former Nationalist and Minister of the Interior in 1925–26. The only way to make sense of Turati and others like him is to develop a set of criteria for differentiating fascist components that is complex enough to transcend differences in tactics and short-term concerns; the populist, petty bourgeois current in fascism must be viewed as a continuum with an ideal pole that cannot be understood in terms of those like Farinacci. Only thus can we recognize that such fascists as Grandi and Bottai and Turati and Panunzio, despite differences in tactics, contributed to a single current for change having a significant measure of continuity and consistency.

The issue of extremism in means and ends leads to the fourth young fascist idealist, Curzio Suckert, who later became a well-known novelist under the name Curzio Malaparte. In considering Suckert, we approach the idealist component in left fascism from yet another angle, for he was an ally of Farinacci during the pivotal period from 1923 to 1925 and at first considered apparently moderate fascists like Giuseppe Bottai to be his enemies. Suckert played a major journalistic role in the struggle to push fascism beyond neotransformist compromise and toward serious institutional innovation during the first few years after the March on Rome. He was willing to support extreme methods, including the dread second wave of *squadristi* violence, to implement his vision of fascist ends, which he derived primarily from neosyndicalism.[65]

Born into a lower-middle-class Tuscan family in 1898, Suckert was attracted to Corridoni's syndicalism while a teenager. He fought and was wounded in the war, which he found an overpowering experience, and became active in fascism in 1921.[66] In his journalistic pieces after the March on Rome, he found an irreconcilable conflict between genuine revolutionary fascism, an expression of the real nation out in the provinces, and the compromising, bourgeois, parliamentary, political fascism centered in Rome.[67] At first glance, Suckert's emphasis on the provinces seems to indicate that the mainspring of his fascism was a desire to preserve traditional local or even rural culture against the inroads of urbanization and modern values. What especially bothered Suckert, however, was the unpopular quality of the Italian liberal state, which, he emphasized, had been imposed from above during the Risorgimento, not created in collaboration with the people in the provinces. The new state, soon centered in Rome, was able to keep the society weak, even in a kind of subjection, and so the people continued to perceive the state as something extraneous to them. Socialism had emerged before the war as the spearhead of a popular movement for revolutionary political change, but Giolitti had managed to domesticate it through his network of transformist compromises. Nevertheless, the political awakening of the people out in the provinces had continued, giving birth to fascism, which Suckert claimed had fallen heir to what was still viable in the socialist tradition. But now, after the March on Rome, fascism too was becoming ensnared in the existing political system, as ambitious fascist politicians began to compromise fascism's guiding purpose, the full-scale populist conquest of the state.[68] So for Suckert the conflict within fascism between the March on Rome and the crisis of 1924–25 pitted the genuine, popular fascism of the provinces, still aiming to replace the liberal state, against the pseudofascism of those being absorbed by the old political system. Obviously, then, "Rome" to Suckert did not mean modern urban civilization, but the old Italian state. And "provincialism" did not mean a defense of traditional patterns, but the chance to overturn them. Nor was Suckert in any sense antiproductivist; syndicalism attracted him partly as a way of ordering and enhancing production.[69]

Although Suckert sometimes juxtaposed syndicalist themes with bizarre and rhetorical notions characteristic of the petty bourgeois litterateur,[70] he was quite serious about neosyndicalism, which seemed to offer fascism the means to create the necessary populist alternative to the liberal state. Writing in Italo Balbo's newspaper *Corriere padano* in

December 1925, Suckert stressed that his vision of a popular conquest of the state, and his important part in pushing fascism in a postliberal direction in practice, had been inspired above all by Sergio Panunzio's ideas.[71] According to Suckert, in fact, Panunzio's conception had given fascism the direction it had lacked even after the March on Rome. In his vision of the purpose of fascism, then, Suckert went far beyond Farinacci, despite their convergence as extremists on the level of tactics in 1924. And even though Suckert and Bottai differed sharply over tactics, they shared a belief that the long-standing Italian political problem could be overcome in a populist way through neosyndicalism. Even through his extreme tactics of 1924–25, Suckert was contributing to the ongoing corporativist thrust in the regime, the same thrust which involved Giuseppe Bottai.

Fascists with similar long-term goals could plausibly differ over tactics and immediate priorities. There were disputes, for example, over how much party interference in the affairs of the economic organizations was necessary, or over how fast it was necessary to go if fascism was to change the old political system and avoid being absorbed by it. In 1924, when much of fascism seemed to have gotten bogged down in politics as usual in Rome, Suckert believed that only renewed extremism in the provinces could save fascism and force it on to serious change. So he became a leading journalistic supporter of a violent second wave, converging with Farinacci and diverging from Bottai. But he was not making a long-term commitment to Farinacci: in the wake of Farinacci's dismissal as party secretary in 1926, Suckert criticized him for the same reasons "moderates" like Bottai did, accusing him of demagoguery and indiscipline, of seeking a kind of petty personal dictatorship in the provinces.[72] Suckert correctly perceived that Farinacci, for all his tactical intransigence, was not the man to lead the implementation of long-term radical fascist goals.

The case of Italo Balbo dramatizes the fragility of the left fascist current. On the continuum Balbo was somewhere between Farinacci and Grandi, his colleague and rival in the new fascism centered in Emilia-Romagna in 1921. Born in 1896, the son of a school teacher, Balbo fought in the war, then was active in the Republican party until he joined the Fascist movement in February 1921. Like so many fascists of his age and background, Balbo was a Mazzini enthusiast, earning his university degree in October 1920 with a thesis on Mazzini's social thought. He publicized Mazzinian ideas, emphasizing especially the antithesis between Mazzini and Marx, in lectures he gave in the Romagna in November, before becoming a fascist.[73] Balbo had also been attracted to syndicalist ideas well before joining fascism. Writing on the death of Michele Bianchi in 1930, he recalled the great impact that

Bianchi and revolutionary syndicalism had had on him as a youth in Ferrara before the war; the fascism of 1922, he insisted, could not be separated from the syndicalism of 1911.[74] Balbo and Panunzio had known each other since 1914, when they were both active in the interventionist *Fascio* in Ferrara.[75] The two remained close enough for Panunzio, who was ten years Balbo's senior, to exert an important political influence on the young student. In 1923, Panunzio even contributed a biographical sketch of Balbo for a series on young Fascist leaders. This rhetorical propaganda piece symbolizes the link between the young veterans and the old syndicalists and manifests especially clearly the deep resentment of the war's detractors which helped to bring fascists like Panunzio and Balbo together. As Panunzio put it, "The fascists came onto the stage of Italian history after the Italians, and because the Italians, had lost their sense of liberty and had fallen into license, into dissolution, had insulted the war veterans and had dared to despise the Victory and its Heroes: the immense, magnificent Victory—unique in the history of the world—of 'all' the Italian people."[76]

Propelled by the same kind of resentment of the Socialists, Balbo led the *squadristi* assault in the province of Ferrara and elsewhere in northern Italy in 1921 and 1922. But he also sought to develop new Fascist labor organizations to replace those being destroyed. At the much-publicized meeting on corporativism in Ferrara in 1932, he stressed that his destructive and constructive activities in 1921 had been two sides of the same objective—which now, eleven years later, was finding its fulfillment in corporativism.[77] In becoming a fascist in 1921, Balbo complained of the lack of ideals in Italian parliamentary politics, and thus he opposed Mussolini's moderate strategy of 1921 in the name of a radical alternative based on the principles of the *Carta del Carnaro*.[78] Still, Balbo's vision of an institutional alternative to liberalism was only rudimentary at first; in a speech in Rome in April 1923, for example, his longing for a hard-working, productive Italy was evident, but he exalted above all the value of the new Fascist militia for engendering a sense of discipline, duty, and sacrifice in the Italian people—for engendering a new military spirit.[79] Nevertheless, Balbo was a capable and energetic young man, and he could have made a major contribution to the struggle for populist institutional change in the Fascist regime. In a sense, he could have gone either way, depending on the effectiveness of the populist current overall. When fascism in practice got bogged down in petty squabbling and infighting in the mid-1920s, Balbo turned away, devoting his energies almost exclusively to technical and administrative matters.[80] He worked effectively to build the Italian Air Force and later to engineer Italian colonization in Libya. So the impatient and ambitious young fascist who had done so much to destroy the institutions of liberal Italy contributed little to the attempts to create populist alternatives. Balbo's case indicates that fascists who were not merely place-seekers from the beginning, but who failed to translate their motivating ideals into a program of thoroughgoing institutional change, could end up settling for the advent of new personnel and for the mere trappings of change, especially if they were given a kind of militarized veneer. Since Balbo was relatively able and intelligent, it was easy for him to see a circulation of elites, bringing people like himself to power, as genuinely revolutionary, and as the key to implementing the barely formed vision of a new order that had led him to fascism in the first place. Looking back on his relationship with Balbo during the 1930s, even the former Nationalist Federzoni could praise the "humanity" of the once violent younger fascist.[81] Balbo had mellowed; he was not such a radical and dangerous fellow after all.

Others of his generation had a more coherent vision, but Balbo's case exemplifies the "instability" of positions along the left fascist continuum. Depending on how the regime developed, those beginning with genuine social ideals could settle for mere place-seeking; place-seekers could settle for a mere cult of the Duce. Commitments near the ideal end were real and effective—and account for much of what we seek to explain about Italian fascism. But at the same time, these ideal commitments could be sporadic—operative sometimes, but not at other times, even in a single individual. And given the problematic side of the background of many of those involved in the petty bourgeois current, these commitments were often fragile as well; under certain circumstances, they could degenerate or dissolve altogether. We will see that the circumstances of the regime, as manipulated by the skillful tactician at the helm, fragmented the ideal current, exploited it, undermined its effectiveness, but never buried it altogether. Leading subordinates like Grandi, Balbo, Farinacci, Turati, Bottai, and Rossoni were in and out of favor, in and out of influence, but the radical corporativist thrust remained until the end, picking up new supporters among young fascists in the 1930s as the energy or influence of some of the earlier supporters waned. The regime survived by leaving things open.

9 / Beyond Liberalism, 1921–1925

To understand why the Fascist regime finally moved in the direction it did, it is essential to grasp the continuity and unity of the period from 1921 to 1925. Through continued pressure, and despite setbacks, the radical fascism that became a major force in 1921 did manage to overcome the more limited, "parliamentary" fascism during these years, and fascism began to move toward a corporative system to replace the liberal parliamentary state. But difficulties of conceptualization, and the complex realities of this tortured period, make it easy to miss the essential element of continuity. We can better understand what was at stake if we focus at the outset on the highly indicative dispute over strategy that gripped fascism between August and November of 1921, threatening to tear the movement apart. At issue was whether fascism had a place in the parliamentary system, or whether it was to be the vehicle for a postliberal, even antipolitical system, replacing parliament altogether. And it was not clear until the end of 1925 that fascism was going to change institutions and move beyond the liberal parliamentary system once and for all.

Having skillfully engineered a place for fascism in the National bloc which Giolitti put together for the elections of May 1921, Mussolini suddenly found himself in the national political mainstream. When the elections produced significant success for the fascists, with thirty-five of them elected to the Chamber, Mussolini began to perceive a unique role for himself within the parliamentary system, as the "supertransformist" who could work with a wide variety of political forces—reformist Socialists as well as fascists, Popolari as well as liberal democrats—and put the country back together after the postwar crisis. The system would still require a political master to balance forces and provide direction, but he would have to be a new man, identified with the war and capable of working with the new political forces that the war had brought forth. Mussolini could claim to be the new helmsman because he was the leader of fascism, the most novel of these new forces. But fascism for Mussolini was still only one component in the situation; it had no exclusive claims—it had no genuinely revolutionary role. Now that Mussolini had a personal foothold in the political system, he was even willing to consider giving up fascism altogether if the movement should impede his personal political maneuvering.[1] He preferred to keep fascism available, but it would have to be a more respectable fascism, more content with a parliamentary role and less prone to rhetoric about revolution.

In his attempt to become the new political arbiter, Mussolini sought to promote a coalition government of fascists, Popolari, and reformist Socialists, in which he himself would remain the mastermind. But this strategy required the cessation of fascist violence in the provinces, so after considerable debate within fascism, he engineered a "Pacification Pact" with the Socialists—signed by the two parties on 2 August 1921. Reflecting Mussolini's conception of fascism, this agreement implied that fascism's extralegal tasks had essentially been completed; fascism could now work with other political forces—including, Mussolini felt, the existing labor movement.[2] For Mussolini, despite his new prospects, still clung to the hopes of 1919 for a political alliance with the workers. One of his most intimate collaborators at the time and a major advocate of the Pacification Pact was Cesare Rossi, who seriously hoped to link fascism to at least part of the existing labor movement, including his old friend De Ambris and the UIL. Fascism could play an ongoing role as a kind of nationalist labor party. The Pacification Pact, then, was a legacy of 1919-style fascism, intended in part to return fascism to its leftist origins.

It is well known that the original fascism of 1919 had a leftist and syndicalist tone and that the influx of new elements in 1920–21 ended up altering the character of fascism permanently and fundamentally.[3] The vaguely syndicalist potential seems to have fallen away as fascism became—apparently—pure right-wing reaction, fueled by petty bourgeois resentments but serving the purposes of the large landowners. By mid-1921, Mussolini and collaborators like Cesare Rossi from the fascism of 1919 felt the reaction had gone far enough and thus engineered the Pacification Pact. But a revolt against the pact and Mussolini's strategy of parliamentary compromise immediately developed, involving new provincial fascists who wanted to complete the task of destroying the existing labor organizations. It is easy to assume that, whatever vague ideals they may have had in their heads, those who opposed Mussolini's strategy were essentially the tools of those right-wing elements, especially the landowners, who wanted the reaction to go all the way.[4] Some of the opposition surely did stem from such reactionary motives. But mixed with this impulse, and hard to distinguish from it in short-term practice, was opposition to compromise within the parliamentary system in the name of a fascist revolution to replace the system. Most fascists disliked Mussolini's preoccupation with conventional parliamentary politics and insisted that if fascism intended to create something new, it should seek power through an insurrectionary march on Rome.[5]

The revolt against the Pacification Pact was led by Dino Grandi, Italo Balbo, and Piero Marsich, who inferred from Mussolini's tactics that he did not believe fascism to have a further revolutionary role. Frustrated by fascism's prosaic parliamentary outcome, they insisted that Italy's crisis required an extraparliamentary solution, a nonsocialist revolution to create entirely new political forms.[6] Now especially these and other young fascists affirmed their commitment to the neosyndicalist principles of De Ambris's *Carta del Carnaro*. Some even contemplated abandoning Mussolini in favor of D'Annunzio; Grandi and Balbo visited D'Annunzio in August 1921, urging him to lead fascism in an insurrectionary march on Rome.[7]

The crisis of fascism during the second half of 1921 seemed to enhance considerably the chance for the D'Annunzian, neosyndicalist alternative to fascism that De Ambris and Olivetti had been working to promote. Here if ever was the opportunity for national syndicalists and radical young war veterans to come together around D'Annunzio instead of Mussolini. But nothing came of it. D'Annunzio was evasive when Grandi and Balbo visited him in August; disillusioned, they began the gradual process of patching things up with Mussolini which would lead to a compromise in November. In December 1921, D'Annunzio refused support for the continuing activities of De Ambris and Olivetti, especially their plans for a new D'Annunzian, national syndicalist publication. In fact, D'Annunzio's perpetual hesitation undermined their efforts throughout 1921 and 1922. He refused to commit himself, because he was seeking to save himself as a unique figure above ordinary parties who could offer himself at a moment of crisis and save the nation.[8]

Meanwhile, in August of 1921, Mussolini wrote in *Il popolo d'Italia* that the provincial fascist opposition to the Pacification Pact left him "more or less indifferent," for fascism, he insisted, was not an end in itself, but only a means to ends of national reconstruction that had largely been achieved.[9] In fact, fascism was beginning to show signs of degeneration, but the Pacification Pact offered the movement a chance to go beyond the sterile class hatred that threatened to suffocate it. Fascism had to make up its mind. If it was to be nothing but reaction, Mussolini claimed to be prepared to wash his hands of it.

Despite his solicitude for the national political situation, however, Mussolini was chiefly concerned with his own immediate prospects. He knew that D'Annunzio's appeal was greater than his own for the young provincial fascists; should fascism move in the direction Grandi advocated, explicitly embracing the principles of the *Carta del Carnaro*, there was a serious danger that Mussolini would end up losing out to D'Annunzio. Yet Mussolini did not want to abandon fascism, his political trump card, so despite his brave talk in *Il popolo d'Italia*, he was willing to give up the Pacification Pact in order to compromise with the dissidents and keep the movement together. At the same time, given the obscurity of D'Annunzio's intentions, the young radicals did not want to cut themselves off from Mussolini. They had concluded that, for better or worse, the chances for their fascist revolution depended on Mussolini, since he seemed to be the only fascist with sufficient national prominence to lead fascism to power. So gradually the dispute was patched up between August and November of 1921, when the Fascist movement held its third national congress at the Augusteo in Rome.[10] There the Pacification Pact was formally renounced, but the Grandi-Marsich group was forced to accept both a more conservative program than it preferred and the official transformation of fascism from a movement into a political party, a change which seemed to blunt its revolutionary thrust.

The leading spokesman for the anti-Mussolinian position was Dino Grandi. From his first days as a fascist in 1920, Grandi saw how heterogeneous fascism was and how some were seeking to exploit it, but he insisted that potentially, there was more to fascism than bourgeois reaction.[11] By the time of the dispute over the Pacification Pact, however, Grandi was growing impatient. Writing in October 1921, he found the electoral alliance with Giolitti and the Pacification Pact to be symptoms of the ongoing disarray in fascism, which seemed to lack doctrinal coherence and clear purposes.[12] Merely to transform fascism into a party, as some were proposing, was no solution. But Grandi insisted that through national syndicalism, fascism could realize its potential, bring to fruition the vague aspirations of the young veterans, and overcome the fundamental Italian political problem. By organizing society into economic groupings, fascism could fashion a new form of state, one which would make possible a more intense kind of mass participation.[13] Throughout the dispute over the Pacification Pact, Grandi contrasted the "national" and antipolitical vision of this program with the emphasis on parliamentary politics of Mussolinian fascism.

Grandi's national syndicalism was not confined to theory, for he and Italo Balbo were especially instrumental in developing a new system of labor organizations, broadly under the aegis of fascism, during 1921. That January, Grandi and Gino Baroncini set up a new Syndical Chamber of Bologna and called on the veteran syndicalist organizer Mario Racheli to direct the organization. Balbo followed suit in June of 1921, establishing a similar organization at Ferrara, which he entrusted to Edmondo Rossoni.[14]

Racheli and Rossoni would have preferred an alliance between fascism and the neosyndicalist UIL to the further development of this system of fascist unions. Along with Panunzio, they worked to win support within the UIL for such an alliance—especially prior to the confederation's fourth national congress, held at Rome in September 1921.[15] But by this time antifascist sentiment was too strong in the UIL, especially among the rank and file, but also among some of the leadership. For example, the General Secretary Guido Galbiati criticized fascism for reactionary violence against the workers in the speech which inaugurated the congress.[16] The UIL's inflexible position sparked some bitter criticism from Sergio Panunzio, who insisted that the confederation must not have understood the principles of Olivetti's *Manifesto dei sindacalisti*, even though the congress had unanimously adopted the document as the program of the UIL.[17] On the other hand, Olivetti defended the UIL, disputing Panunzio's charges.[18] But as it became apparent that there could be no alliance between the UIL and fascism, and as the fascists continued to develop unions of their own, more and more of the UIL's original leaders decided to follow Rossoni and Racheli into fascism.

Throughout 1921 fascist violence was essentially forcing the workers out of the old organizations and into the new ones controlled by fascists. As a result, fascism soon had a substantial trade union movement of its own. Mussolini was by no means responsible for these efforts, which were incompatible with the conciliatory strategy—envisioning accommodation with the existing labor movement—that he had in mind. Grandi opposed the Pacification Pact in part because he feared, quite plausibly, that the new Fascist syndical movement centered in the provinces of Ferrara and Bologna would be undermined if Mussolini's strategy were to succeed.[19] If fascism was to fulfill its long-term populist mission, it seemed, the violent seizure of hegemony over Italian labor had to continue. In pursuing trade union development, Grandi constantly emphasized the long-term political import of the new organizations. Speaking in Bologna in October of 1921, at a national meeting which established a federation of Fascist railroad workers' unions, he portrayed the new syndicates as the building blocks for the antiparliamentary state which fascism had a mission to create.[20] To achieve this political purpose, fascism had to organize producers of all varieties —not only manual labor, but also capitalists, managers, technicians, and the like.

At its national congress at the Augusteo in November, the Fascist movement formally ended the dispute over strategy with a typically ambiguous compromise. It can even be made to appear that both sides lost and that the only winners were the landowners who were exploiting fascism. Since Mussolini was forced to abandon the Pacification Pact and let the reaction continue, the outcome is often portrayed as Mussolini's surrender to the agrarian bloc.[21] At the same time, however, Mussolini was hardly embracing Grandi's national syndicalist conception of fascism; so the outcome was not an unequivocal victory for the dissidents, despite the repudiation of the Pacification Pact. They lost out to Mussolini on several important questions.

Mussolini, in fact, had not done badly. He emerged with his prestige and authority within fascism enhanced; the challenge to his personal ascendancy within the movement had fizzled, and he would have, in some ways at least, more freedom of movement from now on.[22] Moreover, fascism became a party as a result of the November compromise, abandoning its more ambiguous and potentially subversive status as a movement. This made fascism seem more respectable and made it in fact more readily controlled by the leadership. The compromise, then, in some ways facilitated Mussolini's continuing political maneuvering, although now, with the Pacification Pact scrapped, he could no longer hope to find allies on the left.

To be sure, it was Grandi who made the most notable speech to the Congress; soon published under the title "The Origins and the Mission of Fascism," it won him a good deal of applause and helped to publicize his revolutionary conception of fascism.[23] Grandi was not conciliatory on the issue of fascism's ultimate purposes; he roundly condemned the recent political heresy which had threatened to divert fascism from its revolutionary path. But for Mussolini, Grandi's speech about long-term goals was a small price to pay; he himself was now firmly in control of the immediate fortunes of the party, which was really all that mattered. Who could tell, after all, what might happen in the long term? And so, for Renzo De Felice, Grandi's speech at the Rome congress was nothing less than his swan song; the success which Grandi enjoyed was purely personal, not political.[24] In the same way Ferdinando Cordova considers Grandi to have been "defeated" at the Augusteo, while for Adrian Lyttelton, the national revolutionary current would reach its definitive end a bit later, early in 1922, when a follow-up challenge to Mussolini failed to get off the ground, partly because this time Grandi refused to go along.[25] But there were very few swan songs and definitive defeats in Italian fascism. Before accepting such judgments as these, we must look more closely at what Grandi said at the Augusteo and at what happened in the months—and years—that followed.

In his speech Grandi indulged in a good deal of rhetoric, exalting, for example, "the heroic and Mazzinian beauty of sacrifice," but he still was able to rise to a political perspective, placing his fascist national syndicalism in the context of fundamental Italian problems. He linked the fascist revolt back through the Fiume experience and intervention to the deficiencies of the Risorgimento and stressed the continuity between the Mazzinian vision and fascism. Mazzini's idea of a tightly knit people's community had not been realized during the Risorgimento, but the war had been the catalyst for the long-awaited civic revival of Italy.[26] The broader, more idealistic perspective that Italians had gained through the war was a prerequisite for a more meaningful kind of popular political participation, which had to involve a vision of long-term goals, transcending immediate interests and hardships. A genuinely popular political movement like fascism had to have such a great moral end, or myth, to capture the imagination of the people, just as modern "popular" wars were experienced as great moral crusades. In the new order Grandi envisioned, "the people will participate in the political struggle just as they participated in the war."[27] His conception of popular politics, then, pointed toward totalitarian mobilization for great popular political projects, to be accompanied if necessary by military trappings and rhetoric.

This syndrome conforms to a widespread conception of fascist totalitarianism linking popular mobilization, grandiose projects to provide a kind of perpetual dynamism, and ultimately war. But Grandi's case makes clear that this pattern in Italian fascism cannot be explained in the conventional way, in terms of the rulers' need to manipulate the masses in order to keep the regime together—and enhance their own power. These notions came together in Grandi's mind because he was seriously searching for a way to overcome the separation of the people from the political order which seemed to be inherent in the liberal system, especially in Italy. For Grandi and other young fascists, war and "militarized" projects were ways to politicize people more fully, not merely ways to divert energies and keep people in check. To some extent, to be sure, Grandi's emphasis on the value of the war was rhetorical and implausible; to this extent, it cannot be taken at face value but requires deeper interpretation in sociopsychological terms. But Grandi's notion also had some basis in the actual Italian wartime experience, the major impact the war had had on popular political awareness. It is still true, of course, that under certain circumstances fascism as a movement born of war might seek to return to its origins, to war as a source of popular purpose and virtue.

For Grandi, however, dynamism and myth were hardly sufficient in themselves; the key was institutional change. Fascism, he insisted, "has the responsibility first of all of resolving the great problem, before which socialism increasingly manifests its practical impotence: *that of making the masses adhere to the National State.* A solution possible only if fascism, casting aside the old liberal and collectivist conceptions, becomes the basis and instrument of a *national syndicalism*, which considers the individual no longer as a subject or citizen, but as a producer, and recognizes in the syndicate the cell of a new and more vast social function . . . destined to transform . . . the decaying parliamentary state of today."[28] Grandi bitterly attacked the recent involvement in parliamentary politics as a betrayal of fascism's revolutionary mission.[29] It was especially foolish to have gotten mixed up with Giolitti, the incarnation of all that Fascism was to overcome. Despite Giolitti's sinister temptations, however, fascism had not been ruined; mass fascism had remained hostile to parliamentary fascism—and thus the rebellion against Mussolini and his parliamentary strategy. So as the dispute over the Pacification Pact came to an end, Grandi was claiming victory.

Compromise between Mussolini and Grandi was possible because the two leaders were operating on different levels and thus saw the dispute and its outcome from different perspectives; each could believe he had gotten the better of the bargain because the compromise left the situation sufficiently open for each to pursue his own course. It removed the immediate source of conflict without settling the deeper issue over which there could be no compromise—whether fascism was to be parliamentary or revolutionary.

The radicals had forced Mussolini to abandon the immediate strategy he had envisioned, involving compromise with the Left, but not his overall strategy of parliamentary compromise, so Mussolini continued his political maneuvering, unleashing or restricting his newly established party according to short-term tactical considerations. But while the radicals had not converted Mussolini to a revolutionary position, they had achieved a crucial success in sabotaging Mussolini's chances to maneuver on the parliamentary left and to establish ties with the existing labor movement. Since the reaction was to continue, he was more or less stuck on the right. And as far as their goals were concerned, it was not parliamentary maneuvering in general, but accommodation with the established Left that threatened immediate strangulation. By compelling Mussolini to abandon the Pacification Pact, the dissidents had won the opportunity to continue the process they had already started—forcing the workers out of their old unions and into fascist unions. Since Mussolini had to abandon his version of a leftist fascism, they still had the chance to develop their alternative, more grandiose kind of leftist fascism, which seemed to require new syndical organizations and hegemony over the rank and file of the existing left.

Because the more limited and more obviously leftist fascism of 1919 died with the Pacification Pact in 1921, and because Mussolini, as a result, found space for his immediate political maneuvering on the right, the outcome of the crisis of 1921 has usually been understood as the definitive turn to the right of both Mussolini and fascism. For Renzo De Felice, the negative reaction to the Pacification Pact indicates an irreconcilability with socialism which puts fascism in 1921 clearly on the right. Mussolini quickly followed his movement and moved to the right when he realized it would not accept the Pacification Pact.[30] Ernst Nolte portrays Mussolini's abandonment of the Pacification Pact as his moral capitulation to Nationalism, as the end of his unsuccessful struggle to maintain intellectual continuity with his leftist past.[31] Similarly Carlo Vallauri finds it no accident that Grandi and those supporting the new national syndicates opposed the Pacification Pact and struggled to undermine the autonomy of the labor movement.[32] To him the whole pattern is evidence of the hegemony of Nationalism within fascism.

These formulations, with their rigidly dualistic conceptions of left and right, are all seriously misleading. The dissidents ruined whatever chance fascism had to establish links with the existing labor movement, but from their perspective fascism would have far more potential for radical populist innovation if it developed its own syndical movement. They had undermined the possibility of one kind of left fascism in the name of a more sweeping and all-encompassing left fascism. This forced Mussolini to maneuver on the political right for now, but that was incidental as far as fascism's long-term purposes were concerned. The future remained open after the November congress, but it had become more uncertain, potentially more revolutionary, with higher stakes for fascism than Mussolini had ever imagined. The new radical fascism, with its links to the Fascist labor movement, had held its own, manifesting sufficient strength to survive even Mussolini's opposition. For the moment, Mussolini might seem to have regained the initiative, but the process the radicals envisioned was a long one. And they had served notice that they did not intend to settle for compromise within the old political system. Grandi's speech at the Augusteo was not the swan song of radical, populist, neosyndicalist fascism, but its definitive inauguration.

To be sure, the new Fascist program of December 1921 contained virtually nothing of Grandi's national syndicalism, only a vague reference to corporations.[33] However, it had not been a now-or-never situation in 1921; in the aftermath of the November congress, the Fascist unions were not a major factor in the immediate power configuration or in Mussolini's political maneuvering, but Grandi and the others were operating on a different level, concerned with the long-term ends of fascism. So despite the vagueness of the 1921 program, they continued to develop the fascist syndical movement as the institutional basis for a new order and to insist that fascism's ultimate raison d'être was revolutionary.

This revolutionary goal did not require revolutionary tactics—a coup d'état, an insurrectionary March on Rome. So Grandi, more the flexible politician than some of his colleagues, began to accept a moderate, "reformist" tactic in 1922, above all because he saw the need for tactical compromise with Mussolini. The tactical issue led to a split between Grandi and Piero Marsich, who had been more deeply opposed than Grandi to the transformation of fascism into a party in 1921, and who continued to insist that the process of replacing the liberal state could only be initiated by extralegal action. When Mussolini continued to maneuver within the system after the November congress, Marsich concluded that fascism had no revolutionary future and left the movement altogether early in 1922. To the observer preoccupied with tactics and the short-term level, Grandi's agreement with Mussolini, and Marsich's disillusionment, seem to confirm that the radical fascists had been defeated for good in November of 1921.[34] But Grandi emphasized explicitly that his disagreement with Marsich was over tactics and methods, not over the ultimate goals of fascism.[35] There was no reason why fascism could not implement its revolution gradually, from within the old state. So Grandi was not giving up his major political objectives, which remained quite different from Mussolini's and essentially the same as Marsich's.

Ultimately, we can understand the stakes in the Pacification Pact dispute only if we manage to grasp the implications of the objectives of both "syndicalists" like Grandi and the wider groups of lower-middle-class fascists who were making fascism a mass movement. It is essential to recognize the extent to which their objectives converged, giving the new radical fascism a measure of coherence and force. Grandi's neo-syndicalism was not merely a variety of trade unionism concerned with immediate working class interests, and his chances for success did not require that he immediately develop an autonomous power base within the working class.[36] Only if we manage to avoid a preoccupation with short-term class interests and a rigidly dualistic, left-right conception of the political alternatives, can we grasp the broader political purposes underlying Grandi's theoretical position and practical strategy. Those purposes complemented the vaguer ideals of the wider groups of young fascists who also disliked Mussolini's moderate strategy of 1921.

Many observers have recognized that there was more to the new fascism of 1921, even to the violent *squadrismo*, than pure agrarian reaction. For Renzo De Felice, for example, those involved were often threatened middle-class elements who saw fascism as a force for moral renewal in opposition to the capitalists and the workers, both of which seemed to be egotistical forces.[37] These fascists were deeply resentful when Mussolini and lieutenants like Cesare Rossi claimed that fascism had become mere class reaction and terror. But implicitly for De Felice, "this confused and contradictory amalgam" of fascist aspirations could have no positive outcome; those aspirations stemmed more from a psychological-moral crisis than from real political awareness. Elsewhere De Felice discerns in the new fascism a "reactionary anarchism"—"a kind of antipolitical anarchism" viewing politics as the source of all Italian problems—that he finds simply absurd.[38] Apparently, then, this form of fascism had no real potential for political development.

It is certainly valid to characterize this petty bourgeois fascism as antipolitical, and no doubt this impulse was absurd in some ways, for it was both excessive and partly unrealizable. But the antipolitical impulse developed enough coherence to guide the actions of some fascists over the long term; it was possible to try, at least, to create an "antipolitical" order, repudiating not only conventional politics, but also class particularism. This was precisely what Grandi envisioned through the neosyndicalist program that he proposed for fascism. And despite the compromise of November 1921, many fascists continued to dream of replacing the liberal parliamentary system with an order transcending politics and class particularism. Their aspirations were not very coherent, but the potential for a neosyndicalist direction for fascism remained —and remained to be drawn out and shaped. Prospects for a radical fascism did not depend on such matters as the autonomy of the fascist syndicates vis-à-vis the new Fascist party or the enthusiasm with which the workers joined the Fascist unions in 1921 and 1922. To understand the new fascism of 1921, we must grasp the relationships among all the components—petty bourgeois resentments, violent *squadrismo*, fascist trade unionism, the antipolitical impulse, the ideals of the war, and the neosyndicalist idea. All of them had their place in Dino Grandi's conception of fascism.

The possibility that this conception could have led to something other than reaction is obviously hard to grasp, given the aura of inevitability that hindsight casts on events. Certainly, however, a different outcome is theoretically conceivable, and it was possible for contemporaries to envision an alternative that could be pursued in practice. And only practice—over the long term—could indicate how much chance of success there was. Grandi and the others were in many ways naive, but their conception was capable of further implementation in practice, and they went on with it even after November 1921, and even after Grandi himself accepted tactical moderation. Despite temporary setbacks, tactical compromises, and changes in strategy, the radical populist push continued after 1921 and reached a climax only late in 1925. The period must be seen as a whole, for an unbroken chain links the dispute of 1921 to the commitment to institutional change that had been made by late 1925.

Continued pressure during 1922 forced Mussolini to countenance further outbreaks of *squadrismo* although, typically, he managed to manipulate the ongoing threat of fascist violence to further his own political ambitions. But because the struggle for control of the labor movement was still going on, and because an insurrectionary conquest of the state remained a serious possibility, discontents with Mussolini's parliamentary maneuvering and rightward orientation did not prove debilitating.[39] For now, deeper questions about the purpose of power remained in abeyance, but they could not be postponed indefinitely.

Nevertheless, Mussolini and the fascist labor organizers were frequently at odds, and the union leaders could not agree among themselves how "Fascist" and "political" the new organizations should be. Those like Rossoni and Racheli who most feared contamination by the Fascist party, with its focus on parliamentary politics, sought to maximize the autonomy of the new unions. The matter came to a head in January 1922, when representatives of the fascist syndical organizations met at Bologna and formed the National Confederation of Syndical Corporations, to be headquartered in Bologna. The confederation was to be nominally autonomous—the term "Fascist" was omitted from its name—but it was to maintain close links with the Fascist party. The leaders of the member unions had to be party members, although the rank and file were not required to be. The overall compromise was essentially in accord with Grandi's position, though it represented something of a victory for Michele Bianchi and Massimo Rocca, who represented Mussolini and the party at the meeting, and something of a defeat for those like Rossoni and Italo Balbo who had sought greater autonomy for the confederation.[40]

But ambiguity was in a way the essence of Italian fascism, which generally eschewed clear-cut victories and defeats, and which had an uncanny knack for leaving things open despite the appearance of a definitive decision. In this case the loser Rossoni was promptly made head of the new union confederation, a position of considerable power which he held until being forced out in 1928. Meeting in Milan on 10 February 1922, the party directorate and the provisional central committee of the confederation elected Rossoni general secretary and decided to publish a newspaper, *Il lavoro d'Italia*, also under his direction, to serve as the confederation's journalistic organ.[41] *Il lavoro d'Italia* immediately sought to develop a firmer doctrinal basis for fascism's socioeconomic organizations; the long-term direction and purpose of fascism still seemed to be open, even though certain tactical problems had been more or less settled. So Rossoni, seeking a theoretical statement for the first issue of *Il lavoro d'Italia*, turned to Sergio Panunzio.

By this time Panunzio had become much concerned with the tangled relationships—on the level of practice—among socialism, the labor movement, fascism, and postwar Italian renewal. We find him grappling with this set of problems, for example, in a confused but highly indicative article published in July of 1921 in *Cultura sindacale*, a nonfascist journal designed "to educate the workers."[42] After stressing that socialism, despite the excesses of the *biennio rosso*, must be revived and not buried, Panunzio warned that those who sought to create socialism must have the courage to oppose the proletariat for the moment, "in order to restore its sense of limits." He also suggested that fascism could perhaps play a crucial role in the long-term creation of socialism. At some points in the article, Panunzio seems to have expected fascism to promote socialism only indirectly, as the strong conservative bourgeois party necessary to restore the healthy class struggle crucial for proletarian maturation. Other Italian leftists, including Enrico Leone, were beginning to envision the same useful role for fascism.[43] But Panunzio, still in a period of ambiguity while on his way to fascism, also implied that fascism might play a more direct role, that fascism itself might create socialism. He found it essential to warn, however, that fascism must not become an end in itself; it could only be a means—to essentially the same socialist objective which he had always held.

We have seen that Panunzio was bitter over the UIL's repudiation of fascism at its congress of September 1921, which Olivetti had urged him to attend. At issue was not only the question of the immediate relationship between fascism and the UIL, but also the deeper problem of whether nonmanual workers should be included in the neosyndicalist union movement. Panunzio insisted that technical, "intellectual" employees, like those in banking, for example, were indeed "practical and positive" forces with essential parts to play in the neosyndicalist order that Olivetti had outlined in his *Manifesto dei sindacalisti*. The UIL had adopted this *Manifesto* as its program, but it continued to insist on proletarian exclusivism nevertheless, so Panunzio concluded that the congress had not really understood the principles of Olivetti's document: "It is no longer a matter—and this the congress failed to grasp—of *pure* professional Syndicalism—isolated, localistic, partial, negative, prone to indulge in strikes—but of general, integral, organic, reconstructive Syndicalism; not of *a single* class—the workers—but of *all* the working classes—manual and intellectual—of the free proletariat and of the administrative proletariat."[44] Panunzio's verbal gymnastics here are typical and indicate the syndicalists' reluctance to admit the populist or petty bourgeois underpinnings of their position. Syndicalism was for a wide spectrum of the society, not just the workers; lots of socioeconomic sectors had progressive roles to play. But the proletariat proper was by no means to be excluded; the syndicalists genuinely wanted its support and participation. Meanwhile, young fascists like Marsich and Grandi were also insisting on the need to include non-manual, "intellectual," middle-class labor in the organizational network they were developing.[45]

In pondering the UIL's recent congress, Panunzio concluded that this particular confederation ought to disappear, but he was not yet ready to give up on the existing labor movement.[46] He felt that the CGL itself might still have a progressive role, since it seemed to be—and was—moving away from its long-standing relationship with the Socialist party. So the future, as Panunzio saw it in October 1921, depended in part on the direction of the CGL, but it also depended on what happened within fascism—whether fascism evolved toward national syndicalism.

Panunzio expanded his ideas about fascism and the labor movement in March 1922, in his contribution to the first issue of Rossoni's *Il lavoro d'Italia*. His article, in the form of a letter to Rossoni, called on fascism to organize the masses as the basis for a neosyndicalist state.[47] A single, unified "labor" movement had to be created, but the problem, Panunzio recognized clearly, was how to go about this in practice. Viewing the current ambiguous situation in fascism, Panunzio was not at all sure about the value of the Fascist unions and still hoped that fascism could work through sectors of the existing labor movement, especially the CGL. Perhaps the CGL could be brought intact under fascism's nationalist and antipolitical umbrella. But he emphasized that "antinational" organizations would have to be excluded, and Rossoni commented at the conclusion of Panunzio's article that his own newly established National Confederation of Syndical Corporations would now become the center of attraction for all the national elements.[48]

Panunzio wanted to consider working with the CGL because he had doubts about Rossoni's prospects, given the partly reactionary purposes fascism was presently being made to serve. He feared that fascism would simply destroy the old unions and disperse the workers, rather than develop alternative organizations that could be used to integrate the laboring masses into political life. It seemed clear to him that the neosyndicalist potential in fascism might be dissolved altogether by those exploiting fascism's anti-Socialist activity for their own ends. He had no sympathy whatsoever for the purposes behind this reaction: "Only fools and deluded people, only niggardly conservatives and defenders of 'obscure and shady interests' can take delight in and hope to exploit the 'dispersal of the workers.'"[49] In general, Panunzio's concerns in this article manifest his conviction that despite everything—the workers' neutralism and quasi-Bolshevism, the syndicalists' repudiation of Marxism—proletarian involvement was essential for the Italian renewal he had in mind.

Although his conception of fascism's role was still ambiguous, Panunzio was obviously well aware of the gamble involved in joining forces with fascism. But despite the risks, fascism seemed to offer great possibilities if the syndicalists worked to push it, to shape it, to give it direction. Like Panunzio, most of the other syndicalists had also begun moving to fascism, one by one, during 1921, although Olivetti held out until 1924, and De Ambris remained in opposition. It was evident that fascism included many of the idealistic young war veterans. It was also clear that these fascists were quite responsive to neosyndicalist principles, which they had discovered especially in the *Carta del Carnaro*. And they envisioned a radical, antiparliamentary direction for fascism, as the dispute over the Pacification Pact made clear. At the same time, many Fiume veterans, activists at first in De Ambris's organization of exlegionnaires, began passing to fascism in 1921, as the futility of waiting for D'Annunzio to lead the third-way, "national" revolution became clear.[50] They obviously felt that fascism could become something more than pure agrarian reaction. Moreover, fascism's own trade union activity indicated at least the potential for some kind of link between fascism and sectors of the working classes.

The fascists were seeking to force the workers into Fascist organizations by any means necessary, but Fascist union leaders, in 1922 and during the years that followed, did pursue the interests of their members and did not hesitate to criticize the employers for failures of collaboration.[51] During 1922, there was much friction between union leaders and the agrarians, who dragged their feet in respecting agreements they had made with the Fascist unions. Mussolini, attuned to short-term power considerations and still suspicious of the Fascist union movement, forced the labor organizers to ease their pressure on the agrarians to abide by these accords. The resulting frustrations led the Fascist unions to a major strike in the province of Ferrara in May 1922.[52] Indeed, the strike remained a tactical option for several more years; in March 1925, for example, Augusto Turati led the Fascist metalworkers' union of Brescia in a strike which quickly spread to other major industrial centers.[53]

As fascism developed during 1921 and 1922, the syndicalists began to believe that it had the potential to become something other than a narrow reactionary instrument or a limited parliamentary party. The Fascist movement seemed to be the nucleus of the new nonproletarian revolutionary force, linked to the war experience, which the syndicalists' revised doctrine required. To be sure, fascism as a movement and doctrine was still being formed, but the syndicalists themselves could shape it, giving its uncertain radical tendencies a definite national syndicalist direction.[54] In becoming fascists, then, the syndicalists were adopting no new principles; no further theoretical evolution was required. Neither did they place any particular emphasis on the personality of Mussolini as they passed to fascism. The neosyndicalist doctrine had no place for charismatic leadership concepts, nor did Mussolini, with his political maneuvering and tactical concerns, seem to embody the revolutionary potential which the syndicalists saw in fascism. The syndicalists, then, were not making some sort of new intellectual commitment, only a political decision based on their assessment of fascism's potential for radical change.

It was this assessment that Alceste De Ambris did not share, even though he had been a full participant in the syndicalist intellectual evolution from 1917 to 1921. He diverged from his colleagues simply because he did not think fascism could achieve their common goals. De Ambris proved correct in his belief that fascism would never implement the neosyndicalist revolution, but he rejected fascism on the basis of an interpretation that was not entirely accurate. Fascism, he felt in 1921, would merely strengthen the existing political caste led by Giolitti.[55] By September 1922 he shared the view of many Italian leftists that fascism would soon disintegrate because of its internal contradictions, the incompatibility between its revolutionary and reactionary components.[56] Although these internal contradictions were real enough, fascism did not disintegrate but ended up moving much further in the direction of radical change than De Ambris had thought possible in 1921 and 1922. The other syndicalists had greater confidence in the potential of fascism's revolutionary component, but they felt that it could come to fruition only if they worked to shape it. The future was still open.

De Ambris went into exile in France in 1923, never to return to Italy. After the failure of an antifascist general strike in August 1922, he had worked hard to promote the unification of the Italian labor movement, proposing to rebuild from the bottom, through a constituent assembly of labor. As a basis for unity, De Ambris proposed common acceptance of both the "national principle" and the principle of union independence from political parties. He blamed the CGL for the failure of these efforts in a bitter postmortem published in *Sindacalismo*, a weekly which he and his collaborators Rinaldo Rigola and Guido Galbiati put out from January through April 1923.[57] This publication not only called for a constituent assembly of labor, but also claimed title to the legacy of Mazzini, Corridoni, and the *Carta del Carnaro*, seeking to preserve the national syndicalist patrimony from what seemed to be contamination in fascism.

From his exile in France, De Ambris continued to portray fascism as too divided against itself to have any positive prospects, despite the sincerity of some of those involved in it. In a perceptive article in *Mercure de France* in February 1923, he explained to a French audience that fascism did contain a revolutionary component, which had developed largely from the war experience of the junior officers. De Ambris was still bitter over the Socialist party's uncomprehending, mocking attitude toward these young veterans and the war experience. But fascism also contained a component committed to stopping any radical change; if it managed to break out of its present equivocal position, it could not survive. One way or the other, fascism would probably degenerate into a mere reactionary dictatorship.[58]

De Ambris had given up on fascism for good, but fascism had not given up on him. To those involved in the ongoing struggle for a corporative state, De Ambris continued to seem a potential ally. Twice serious attempts were made to enlist his efforts. The first of these endeavors, late in 1923 and early in 1924, even involved Mussolini himself. Seeking to maximize his freedom of maneuver after the March on Rome, Mussolini hoped to diversify his political base by establishing more genuine links with the working class. De Ambris perhaps could provide a kind of bridge, helping fascism win over more of the workers, so Mussolini seriously but indirectly sought to convince him to return.[59] Mussolini's intentions are hard to gauge, but no doubt De Ambris was to have a major post in the regime, perhaps Minister of Labor, or perhaps a position in the Fascist labor movement at the expense of Rossoni, for there was still friction between Rossoni and the leadership in the party. At any rate, De Ambris had a wider vision than Rossoni, and he was not personally tied to the existing Fascist union confederation, so perhaps he could have promoted an understanding between fascism and the CGL.

The fascist most directly involved in this overture to De Ambris was Curzio Suckert, who even visited the veteran syndicalist in Paris seeking to convince him to return. From his national syndicalist perspective, Suckert obviously envisioned De Ambris as an ally in the ongoing struggle within fascism for popular corporativist development. But De Ambris refused to go along, explaining his reasons in a letter to Suckert late in January 1924.[60] Genuine innovation, he said, required syndical autonomy, the repression of unjust violence, and, above all, corporative representation, the only way that fascist antiparliamentarianism could transcend mere demagoguery. At present, too much of the old Italy remained, and De Ambris saw no probability that fascism would return to its radical origins and carry out a real revolution in Italian values and institutions.

De Ambris was one of thirteen anti-Fascist exiles stripped of their Italian citizenship in 1926, but his presence continued to be felt, especially with the debates surrounding the development of the corporative system in the 1930s. The law of 5 February 1934, setting up corporations for the first time, aroused widespread interest abroad, even in the Italian exile community in France. De Ambris felt he should make his opinions known, and his niece suggested that he write a full-length book on corporativism. In his letters to her early in 1934, De Ambris expressed the same old scorn for the liberal parliamentary system and considerable pride in having been the first to offer a design for a corporative state, in the *Carta del Carnaro*.[61] He admitted he lacked solid evidence about fascist corporativism, but he feared that conservative interests within fascism were exploiting the corporativist label, developing a system lacking vitality and purpose. When some of De Ambris's old syndicalists friends within fascism learned of his intention to write a book on corporativism, they let him know that they might be able to use his ideas to influence Mussolini, and thereby to give fascist corporativism a clearly leftist direction. De Ambris apparently took this possibility into account, though the book was certainly not favorable to fascism. *Dopo un ventennio di rivoluzione: il corporativismo* [Corporativism after twenty years of revolution] was completed just before his death in December 1934 and published posthumously in France a few months later; it was not allowed into Italy.

So De Ambris watched from a distance as his long-time colleagues sought through fascism to implement the neosyndicalist vision which he had helped to elaborate. They had an important measure of success;

their continuing efforts assisted the process of self-definition going on within fascism and helped to push the movement into radical change during the period from 1921 to 1925. Especially after the March on Rome, it was hard to avoid the key question—power for what?—and the syndicalists were among the few who had some convincing answers.

Fascism's purpose was still very much up in the air when Mussolini became prime minister in October 1922. During his first year and a half in power, Mussolini seemed to be more concerned with containing the radical energies in his own party than with directing those energies toward radical change. The old elites tolerated Mussolini as the man who could keep order, and this required that he be able to control not only Socialist radicalism, which was no longer much of a threat anyway, but above all fascist radicalism, the revolutionary pretensions—and the violence—of the militants in his own party. Mussolini was generally willing to oblige. When it was tactically expedient, he indulged in some tough talk, including talk about further revolution; and probably he really did vacillate, since the anti-establishment revolutionary in him was not entirely dead. But he had no desire to jeopardize the unique position of power he had managed to achieve. So the March on Rome had brought to power Mussolini the legitimate prime minister, wearing the traditional frock coat and top hat for his weekly consultations with the king, not Mussolini the black-shirted Duce of revolutionary fascism.

As prime minister, Mussolini wanted to persevere—to stay in power indefinitely if possible—but not in order to implement a coherent set of objectives. He certainly did not set out to "coordinate" all elements of the national life, to make them instruments of his purposes, the way Hitler did at the outset of the Nazi regime. Mussolini felt as many Italians did that the pacification of the country had been completed after the dislocations of the war and the *biennio rosso*, and that now Italy could return to normal. With Mussolini as prime minister, there would be some changes, but not revolutionary changes. Government would become more vigorous and efficient; the swollen Italian bureaucracy would be streamlined; there would be more emphasis on authority and law and order. There would be less party squabbling and less of the consequent governmental instability. The trains would run on time. As we saw in the last chapter, Mussolini seems to have seen himself as uniquely qualified to serve as political mediator and unifier. But there was no suggestion that the parliamentary system was to be undermined, that the masses were to be mobilized through a variety of Fascist party organizations, that Italy was soon to be on the way to a monolithic, quasi-totalitarian state.

Mussolini was not seeking to eliminate all the competing political
forces, but to absorb them.

The most radical measure which Mussolini's government sponsored during its first year and a half was the Acerbo electoral law,
which was passed late in 1923. Replacing the proportional representation established in 1919, the new law specified that the party winning a
plurality of the vote—as long as it was at least 25 percent—would gain
two-thirds of the seats in the Chamber of Deputies. At first glance, this
appears a means to make fascism the exclusive master of the country,
but it was intended to eliminate the governmental instability that can
ensue when a multiple party system is combined with proportional
representation. Thus it had considerable support even among liberals.
Mussolini, in his strategy for the elections of April 1924, used the
new law not to give his party absolute power, but to lure a wide
variety of existing political forces under the fascist umbrella through a
broad electoral coalition.

In a perceptive article written just after the elections, the young
liberal Piero Gobetti pointed out that the 1924 elections had been in the
same tradition as the national bloc elections of 1921, except that the
pupil Mussolini had proved more adept than the teacher Giolitti.
Mussolini had become the "super-Giolitti"; his neotransformism was
bringing to nought the aspirations for serious change that Gobetti
admitted could be found in fascism. Gobetti's interpretation of the
outcome of fascism's first eighteen months constituted an implicit
challenge to serious fascists: "The most obvious result of the Ministry's
electoral victory, then, is the defeat of fascism. The March on Rome
has been for nothing."[62]

Given Mussolini's course in power, it is hardly surprising that
there was much frustration among those who expected a radical
change in the Italian political system after the March on Rome. The
syndicalists worried aloud that fascism might settle for a foothold
within the system and not fulfill its revolutionary mission.[63] It seemed
obvious to radical fascists that they had to keep pushing, to emphasize
that the defeat of maximalist Socialism and the advent of Mussolini's
ministry did not mean it was time to return to normal. In an article in
Gerarchia in the aftermath of the March on Rome, the tactically moderate
Dino Grandi emphasized that the real fascist revolution had scarcely
begun and now had to be carried forward—toward the definitive transformation of the Italian state.[64] Giuseppe Bottai, speaking in Rome
early in 1924, cautioned that fascism was presently still cleaning up the
problems left by others; it had not yet begun its original phase, becoming the instrument of a radical democracy.[65]

Writing in December 1923, Sergio Panunzio urged his countrymen "to be the first to give Europe a real, living example of a national state based on syndicates, which is the ultimate end and the primary and essential spirit of fascism."[66] In his numerous speeches and newspaper articles, he sought to indicate the place to start, calling for obligatory syndical membership, juridical recognition of the syndicates and their collective contracts, and a magistracy of labor.[67] The syndical network would gradually become the foundation of the state, the source of all private and public law. It was Panunzio, especially, who injected these proposals into the ongoing discussion among Fascist union leaders and idealists about the role of the Fascist union movement in the process of change that fascism was supposed to be initiating. In May 1924, for example, he spoke at a meeting of the national council of the Fascist union confederation, which included some of his proposals, including the labor magistracy, in its final resolution.[68] As some Fascist union leaders began calling on the government to bring collective labor contracts under the sphere of law, as a preliminary to full juridical recognition of the unions, Panunzio asserted that these measures would necessarily lead to obligatory syndical membership and a neosyndicalist state.[69]

Panunzio's proposals, however, certainly did not win universal acceptance. "Volt" (Vincenzo Fani-Ciotti) disputed Panunzio's arguments from a Nationalist perspective,[70] anticipating the objections that Carlo Costamagna would raise, in a more systematic way, during his important polemic with Panunzio in 1926. Even left-leaning fascists who agreed that the syndical movement had to play the central role in fascism did not always agree with the strategy Panunzio suggested. For example Silvio Galli, writing in Bottai's *Critica fascista*, attacked the coercive features of Panunzio's conception, especially the notion of obligatory syndical membership.[71] Emphasizing syndical autonomy, freedom of association, and the basic right of individuals to determine their own interests, Galli argued that Panunzio's program would merely intensify class hatreds; even the labor magistracy would lead to overcentralization and corruption. Augusto De Marsanich similarly objected to Panunzio's design out of concern for the individual and for spontaneous development in the unions.[72] Although he agreed that fascism should be based on its syndical organizations, De Marsanich feared that the relationship between state and syndicate that Panunzio advocated would invite bureaucratic interference. He even insisted that strikes would continue to be useful. Galli and De Marsanich were more liberal than Panunzio, but Panunzio's more thoroughgoing and totalitarian conception would have greater influence on subsequent development.

Despite much discussion, the institutional harvest of 1923 was hardly encouraging for fascist radicals. Rossoni's attempt to extend his organizational network over the employers through a system of mixed syndicates came to nought in December with the Palazzo Chigi pact, which established that separate organizations for workers and employers would be maintained. There were tentative attempts to develop *gruppi di competenza*, or technical councils, to supplement the parliamentary system, yet even this mild innovation got bogged down in the infighting among tactically moderate fascists like Bottai, extremist provincial leaders like Farinacci, and union leaders like Rossoni.[73] Fascism hardly seemed to be on the way to a postliberal, totalitarian corporativism, but an extraordinary event in 1924 changed the situation dramatically, enabling the disparate energies at work within fascism to fall, temporarily, into more effective alignment. As a result, fascism moved unequivocally beyond liberalism at last.

When Panunzio enthusiastically proclaimed a few years later that "the Fascist state is in essence the syndical and corporative state," he admitted that this happy outcome had required the severe crisis occasioned by the Matteotti murder in 1924, for it was only in this context that fascism had finally managed "to free itself from conservative ties and impediments."[74] And indeed the Matteotti murder and its aftermath constituted the real turning point in the history of the Fascist regime. Giacomo Matteotti was a moderate Socialist deputy and an outspoken antifascist. In June of 1924, not long after he had courageously risen in the Chamber to denounce the fascist violence that accompanied the April election, Matteotti was murdered by fascist thugs. A great public outcry followed, keeping Mussolini's government in serious jeopardy during the rest of 1924. Mussolini seems seriously to have considered resignation at first, but after he weathered the initial shock and uncertainty, he decided to persevere, to play for time. At first his political survival seemed to require a more explicit commitment to moderation, so he took a number of steps to bring fascist extremists under control. Even when the Mazzinian syndicalist Armando Casalini was murdered on a Rome trolley in September, apparently in retaliation for the murder of Matteotti, Mussolini insisted on rigorous discipline and nonviolence. At the same time, however, those discontented with the mild outcome of the fascist revolution saw the crisis as a precious opportunity to force fascism beyond parliamentary compromise and on to a new order. Some, like Curzio Suckert, stood ready to condone further violence; others, like Agostino Lanzillo, insisted that more violence could only be counterproductive. The situation was now so dynamic, however, that the efforts of radical fascists who disagreed over tactics were complementary. All agreed that fascism could—and should—survive only if it finally committed itself to a definite course of radical change and force-fully began to implement it. And now, finally, Mussolini's predicament provided an opening. Since his personal prestige had been severely shaken, he could no longer justify his government on the old basis. If he was to remain in power, fascism would have to prove its credibility as an innovative political force by embarking on a program of institu-tional change.[75]

In this uncertain situation, ideas could have a real impact on events, since there was a vacuum to be filled and the content, or a credible illusion of content, had to come from somewhere. And it was now, with the future of Mussolini's government in doubt, that A. O. Olivetti became an active fascist publicist; he was hardly jumping on a bandwagon. Olivetti had remained skeptical of fascism's revolutionary capacity after the March on Rome, feeling that fascism would settle for power within the parliamentary system: "The so-called fascist revo-lution is up to now nothing more than a parliamentary revolution and represents little more than did the coming of the Left to power in 1876. It was accomplished by Fascist politicians, and the syndical cor-porations have so far remained outside. No government program has yet been developed that could lead one to foresee an integral renewal of Italian life; if such a program were to be developed, we would be the first to applaud the fascist takeover."[76] Olivetti anticipated a struggle within fascism between neosyndicalism and conventional politics, but he was not yet prepared to lend his energies to the former current. But in mid-1924, with fascism in crisis, he began, tentatively at first, to identify himself and his ideas with fascism.[77] While he deplored the Matteotti murder and warned against further violence, Olivetti felt that now fascism could no longer settle for the uncertain compromise of its first twenty months in power.

Since Mussolini realized he needed help, he probably made a personal effort to win over Olivetti, no doubt making certain commit-ments to him. One contemporary report suggested that Olivetti was to replace Rossoni as the head of the Fascist union confederation.[78] There was considerable dissatisfaction with Rossoni's leadership within the movement, and the appointment of Olivetti would have signaled a new, potentially more radical beginning. Rossoni managed to survive, but meanwhile Olivetti became a regular collaborator on *Il popolo d'Italia* and soon was named to the commission to propose institutional changes which was an immediate fruit of the crisis. In his first articles in *Il popolo d'Italia*, he adopted a pseudonym—"Lo spettatore"—which in-dicates that he still had reservations; in any case, the style and con-tent of these articles surely made the identity of this "spectator" clear to contemporaries. Olivetti's first article under this pseudonym, featured on the front page of *Il popolo d'Italia* on 11 July 1924, was prefaced by an editorial note, no doubt by Mussolini's brother Arnaldo, which introduced "Lo spettatore" as "an expert on Italian politics" and "a rigorous student of social and syndical questions." After noting that the author had neglected unnecessarily fascism's achievements of the past two years, the editor stressed that the article contained some profound truths.

Olivetti sought to place the present crisis in historical perspective.[79] Given the bankruptcy of the old ruling class after the war, he claimed, leadership in creating a new Italy should have fallen to the Socialist party, which could have brought together the workers and the young veterans in a broad national democracy. But the Socialists had preferred instead "the puerile satisfaction of trying to show that they had been right with their neutralism," and fascism had fallen heir to their mission. Now, however, fascism was merely drifting and could not long survive unless it took on a more precise commitment—which for Olivetti, of course, could only be the neosyndicalist revolution. It was up to fascism to spearhead "the organic, national transformation of the forms of production, of the system of representation, of the parliament, of the entire life of the country—to minimize the political and to maximize the economic." A few days later, in another featured article in *Il popolo d'Italia*, Olivetti proposed syndical representation as the first concrete step on the way to a postliberal order.[80] He insisted, however, that before anything positive could be accomplished, extremist fascist violence, which simply kept the country in an uproar, had to be eliminated for good.

The other syndicalists took similar positions during the crisis of 1924, calling on fascism to intensify its activities in the face of liberal criticism, to get on with the positive tasks of national syndicalist revolution.[81] Lanzillo condemned the extremists and their "second wave" of violence, but he went on to remind fascists of the mission of their movement: to bridge the gap between the workers and the state, to create a society based on collectivist law.[82] Late in December 1924, as pressure for change was reaching a climax, he wrote to Mussolini advocating modification of the electoral system, to depart from liberal democratic procedures.[83] He stressed that the discontents in the Fascist party which had led to the present crisis—and even to the new wave of violence—were not without foundation. So despite his repudiation of extremist tactics, Lanzillo was trying to push Mussolini to abandon the liberal parliamentary system once and for all. It is worth emphasizing that Lanzillo, who had been the syndicalist closest to Sorel, always stressed that violence was not inherently creative; it was only an instrument, and its value depended on the value of the ideal to be implemented. Late in 1925, he acknowledged that there had been much useless violence in fascism and insisted that now, with fascism solidly established in power, further violence could only be counterproductive.[84] Moreover, Lanzillo considered violence and terrorism to be atomizing forces which could only undermine the mass political education and the social unification that fascism was seeking to promote.

Pressures for fascism to commit itself to thoroughgoing change focused on the meeting of the National Council of the party, which brought together Fascist deputies and local party leaders early in August 1924.[85] And it was indeed at this meeting that fascism finally made its formal break with liberalism. Since Mussolini recognized that fascism had to appear, at least, to have some coherent political proposals to offer if it was to justify its continuance in power, he was open at last to the suggestions of fascists who advocated serious institutional change.

Panunzio played a major part in the council's deliberations; he called for juridical recognition of the syndicates as the first step toward a neosyndicalist state and worked with Curzio Suckert for a resolution with an explicitly revolutionary thrust.[86] Right fascist objections forced a compromise, however, so the outcome of the meeting was by no means an unequivocal victory for left fascist idealists. But the compromise motion offered by Panunzio, Suckert, and the right fascist Carlo Costamagna, and unanimously adopted by the council, did commit fascism to reform the parliamentary system, and this resolution began a process that eventually led to new institutions.[87] Fascism's postliberal commitment was now sufficiently explicit that the right liberal leader Antonio Salandra finally turned against fascism for good, although he did not make his opposition public until later. At last fascism would have to go it alone. The immediate result of the resolution was the appointment, in September, of a Commission of Fifteen to devise institutional changes. Olivetti, Lanzillo, and Rossoni were members, but so were Enrico Corradini and several conservative senators. Suckert complained about the commission's excessively conservative composition; it was becoming clear that the struggle for a radical populist fascism was only beginning.

Mussolini finally announced the beginning of a new regime and accepted responsibility for all that happened in his famous—or infamous—speech to the Chamber of Deputies on 3 January 1925. The chain of circumstances which followed from the murder of Armando Casalini in September led Mussolini finally to cut himself off from the old political system.[88] But even now, the alternative remained open. The Commission of Fifteen had begun its labors in October and was proceeding slowly. At the end of January it was reconstituted, with eighteen members and broader responsibilities. The majority favored a corporativist transformation of the state, but there were thorny questions about the measures to be adopted. There was even sharp disagreement among the three veteran syndicalists on the commission. Nevertheless, Panunzio was gratified that now, after Mussolini's speech of 3 January, fascism was free to develop its own institutions, and he expressed confidence that the commission was designing the kind of neosyndicalist system which he himself had proposed for fascism. The measures presently being discussed, he insisted, were essentially those he had publicized at the National Council meeting of August 1924 and throughout the early period of fascism.[89] Olivetti similarly stressed continuity, portraying the present course as a victory for neosyndicalism, in his speech to the conference on fascist culture held at Bologna in March of 1925.[90] When this speech provoked the socialist labor leader Gino Baldesi to accuse Olivetti of political and intellectual incoherence, Olivetti responded that the corporativist system which the Commission of Eighteen was devising was identical to the regime outlined in the *Carta del Carnaro*.[91]

Meanwhile, in the May 1925 issue of *Gerarchia*, Mussolini himself published an article, entitled "Fascism and Syndicalism," which stressed the value of the Fascist organizations for educating the workers and for bringing them increasingly into public life.[92] He also emphasized that fascism should consider juridical recognition of the syndicates and the institution of a magistracy of labor. So Mussolini helped to focus attention on neosyndicalist themes as the process of constructing a fascist order began, but his formulations were not precise, and they left open the major questions about practice. These were proposals long associated with the syndicalists, and especially with Sergio Panunzio, but they were also associated with Alfredo Rocco. And Rocco had been made Minister of Justice on 6 January, just after Mussolini's decisive speech to the Chamber of Deputies.

Rocco quickly achieved considerable power, for Mussolini was much impressed by his energy and technical competence. Rocco obviously knew what he was doing. And it turned out to be Rocco, and not the Commission of Eighteen, who formulated the law which initiated development toward corporativism. After a good deal of internal squabbling, the commission issued a majority report proposing new provincial professional councils as the basis for a relatively open and pluralistic corporativist system.[93] This program drew criticism from a variety of sectors within fascism, partly because of plausible differences over how to proceed, partly because of personal power considerations. Rossoni, for example, opposed the majority report because he feared the new institutions it envisioned would undermine the power of his own existing institutional structure. In any case, discussion of the commission's blueprint generally concerned methods, not the ends of fascism or the direction in which the regime should begin to move. When in October of 1925 the Fascist Grand Council respectfully buried the commission's specific proposals, opening the way for Rocco's syndical law of April 1926, it was not really a victory of Right over Left, but rather a victory for the more extreme, potentially totalitarian course which such disparate fascists as Rocco, Panunzio, Rossoni, and Farinacci desired, each for reasons of his own. It was a defeat for those like Olivetti, Bottai, and Costamagna, who favored a more flexible and pluralistic approach. Even though its specific proposals did not prevail, the Commission of Eighteen had played an essential role in focusing attention on corporativism during the crucial year when fascism was beginning to choose its own path. From now on, the purpose and the future of fascism would seem to be indissolubly bound up with corporativism, although it was not clear at the end of 1925 what this was to mean in practice.

Rocco's role was uniquely important under these circumstances. He was respectable, yet at the same time he was a radical, willing to implement change in some ways more systematic than the Commission of Eighteen had proposed. Whatever Rocco's own purposes, the essentials of his syndical law were neutral; their meaning depended on subsequent practice. The law had four related but distinguishable elements: first, juridical recognition and discipline of the syndicates; second, juridical discipline of collective labor contracts, which meant that labor contracts had to be made collectively and would be legally binding and enforced by the state; third, prohibition of strikes and lockouts; fourth, a magistracy of labor to impose state justice in labor conflicts.[94] In principle, these measures were by no means incompatible with syndicalist objectives; indeed, they could even constitute the entering wedge for the long-term neosyndicalist transformation of the state. So the struggle over direction would continue, and there was plenty of room for those like Olivetti and Bottai who had favored a more moderate outcome in 1925 to continue to try to influence the practical implementation of corporativism.

In December 1925, during the Chamber debate on Rocco's proposed syndical law, Paolo Orano rose to praise Rocco's bill, which he portrayed as the fulfillment of the Italian syndicalist tradition, the culmination of all the syndicalists' efforts since 1903.[95] Panunzio lauded Orano's speech for its "brilliant and impassioned" demonstration of the historical connection between revolutionary syndicalism and fascist corporativism.[96] Orano and Panunzio were seeking to cast the Rocco law in the best possible light, to arouse expectations, and thereby to influence further development, including practice under the new law. As part of their campaign, the syndicalists could claim considerable credit for all that had happened so far. It was largely because of their efforts that corporativism had become credible as the postliberal alternative that wider groups of fascists had been seeking since 1921—and that the regime itself required in the wake of the crisis of 1924. Throughout this period, the antiliberal proposals of Panunzio, Olivetti, and the others had drawn the fire of such leading liberal spokesmen as Guido De Ruggiero, Luigi Albertini, Umberto Ricci, and Vittorio Emanuele Orlando.[97] Such polemics enabled the syndicalists to show other fascists that they had alternatives to liberalism that the liberals took seriously—and did not like at all.

By December 1925, for better or worse, fascism was on its way to something new, and it seemed to Curzio Suckert a time for taking stock. Suckert had played a major role in the ongoing extremist pressure after the March on Rome. He had remained skeptical even after Mussolini's speech of 3 January; he approved the decisive break with the past which Mussolini promised, yet the first measures of implementation under Minister of the Interior Luigi Federzoni seemed to herald only a conservative police state, not revolutionary corporativism.[98] But writing in Italo Balbo's *Corriere padano* in December 1925, Suckert looked back with satisfaction on all that had happened since the March on Rome and anticipated the fruition of the seeds which now seemed securely planted. It seemed to him to be the triumph of the ideas of Sergio Panunzio. In outlining Panunzio's contribution, Suckert stressed explicitly that ideas had played a crucial role in the recent Italian drama, for fascism, when it assumed power, had been uncertain about how to proceed to reform the state. At first, in fact, many had confused the ultimate purpose of the fascist revolution with a mere seizure of state power. "It is in the context of this indecision and unpreparedness on the part of fascism—both the party and the government —that the work of criticism, of stimulation, and of ideal construction carried out by Sergio Panunzio must be considered."[99] It had been Panunzio who had indicated, in specific, concrete terms, the course that fascism had to follow if it was not to wither away. Suckert stressed that his own intransigent role during the 1924 crisis, and at the pivotal National Council meeting of August 1924, had been inspired by Panunzio's conception of fascism. And now, Suckert insisted, Panunzio's revolutionary blueprint was being implemented; his ideas revealed the true meaning of the Rocco law and the real substance of fascism.

Suckert had particular praise for Panunzio's recent collection *Lo Stato fascista*; Panunzio had first given the title essay as a speech, on

Giuseppe Bottai's invitation, to inaugurate the Roman Center for Fascist Studies in March 1925. Suckert found the categories of this book "definitive and essential for the objective study of the fascist revolution." But not all fascists agreed. In a review of the same book, Carlo Costamagna criticized Panunzio's conception of fascism, sparking a polemic which attracted considerable interest. Although he had not been a Nationalist, Costamagna worked closely with Rocco during this period,[100] and he and Panunzio interpreted in radically different ways the process of change that fascism was now initiating. Their debate raised the most basic questions about the nature of fascism and made quite explicit the fundamental difference between its populist and elitist components. Only now, with fascism finally embarked on an original course, did such sharply focused debate begin to develop.

10 / Participatory Totalitarianism

The polemic between Panunzio and Costamagna, which unfolded in *Rivista internazionale di filosofia del diritto* during 1926, centered on the fundamental relationships between society and state and syndicates and state. The focus of disagreement was not so much specific institutional proposals, but what the new Fascist socioeconomic groupings were for, what problems they were intended to solve. The basic question was whether fascism was revolutionary or whether it was an adjustment in the existing state in light of a new threat. Panunzio had first considered these issues systematically in a lecture at the University of Ferrara in November 1922, and he stressed in his debate with Costamagna that this lecture had established once and for all his conception of the basic relationships among syndicates, society, and state.[1]

In the Ferrara lecture, Panunzio was responding most immediately to the concerns of the noted liberal jurist and former prime minister Vittorio Emanuele Orlando, who was troubled both by the threat which trade unions posed to the sovereignty of the state and by proposals to transform the state by giving the syndicates some form of political power. But in disagreeing with Orlando, Panunzio was also outlining, in abstract terms, a revolutionary conception which responded to the problematic relationship between society and state in Italy. According to Panunzio, the current development of syndical organization outside the state was not a symptom of social dissolution and pathology, but rather a manifestation of health, of energy and renewal in society.[2] This spontaneous development of social organization, which so troubled Nationalists and conservative jurists, Panunzio found to be the key to creating a new, radically popular state based on the organized society. The old liberal state had remained aloof and isolated from the people precisely because it was based only on abstract individuals and not on the concrete, living society, which was now finding expression in economic organizations. With the liberal state exhausted, unable to contain the social content now overflowing it, it was up to the dynamic society to constitute a new state, based on the structured society of economic groupings. Even within the liberal order, Panunzio argued, social organizations tended spontaneously to federate and confederate, thereby creating in embryo the syndical state of the future.

But Costamagna saw that same syndical development as a threat, "a symptom of the liberal disintegration of the state." He denied that the kind of union development Italy had experienced was historically progressive: "the syndicate is a protest; it is not an instrument of creation. It is a symptom of a crisis of the law and of the state, not the source of a new law."[3] Costamagna viewed fascism not as a revolution constituting a new state through social organization, but as a means for the existing state to overcome a social pathology, "a contingent and transitory phase of difficulty for the state." Thus fascism would develop corporations, instruments of control from above, as antidotes to the crisis which spontaneous social-syndical development had caused.

Replying to Costamagna, Panunzio denied that fascism understood the relationship between society and state in such static terms. That relationship was really a dynamic process in which the society, a network of syndical organizations, was reconstructing the state on a new basis. Panunzio sought to pinpoint explicitly the basis of his difference with Costamagna: "The first principle for me is the Society. The State is a form, a way of being of the Society. Sociology is consequently prior to the Theory of the State."[4] Costamagna found this emphasis on the primacy of society distasteful and dangerous; it placed Panunzio in the tradition of contractualism and democracy. For Costamagna, the state was not a form which the dynamic society gave itself; rather it was prior and aloof and ordered society from above.[5] Although he agreed that new corporativist institutions were necessary, he insisted that they were to be organs of the preexisting state, to be used to control the increasingly threatening society.

In contrast, Panunzio proposed to make this traditionally aloof state more concrete and down-to-earth, and thereby more popular, by diffusing state sovereignty and legislative capacity into the organized society. Fascism was making the syndicates state organs not to enable the existing state to control the society, but to transform and broaden the state itself. It was for this reason that Panunzio, in his polemic with Costamagna and throughout his career as a fascist publicist, emphasized so strongly the revolutionary implications of the juridical recognition of the syndicates, which was finally accomplished with the 1926 syndical law. As the economic groupings in society gradually took over public functions, the people would participate more actively in public life, and the state would become increasingly tangible.[6]

While the state for Costamagna and other right fascists was a fixed point of stability vis-à-vis an untrustworthy society, Panunzio insisted that "The state is not a *given*, a mass of stone, that is what it is, and that always will be what it is. The state is not a fact but a process." He was seeking to demythologize the state, to make it accessible to the people: "The state is not simply there, but is made—and is made by us ourselves, with all our efforts, and it is made by revolutions, wars, and the passions and the blood of men."[7] Having matured and organized, Italian society had overflowed the old state form and was now beginning to create a more concrete and popular state based on its organizations. There was, to be sure, an important element of equivocation in Panunzio's conception, for it was not the social organizations that emerged spontaneously as Italian society matured which were now to become the foundation of the new state. Those organizations had been destroyed. We will encounter the practical implications of this basic ambiguity in the syndicalist position in the next two chapters. But it was not illogical to argue that the emergence of trade unions in Italy was fundamentally healthy, despite the excesses and the antinationalism of the *biennio rosso*. Within a different framework, the same capacities that made possible the trade union activity of the *biennio rosso* could make possible a new kind of state. The new Fascist organizations would have to be subject to surveillance—and education—by the new elite in the Fascist party, but Panunzio was offering a framework for understanding from within which it was possible to envision a popular direction for fascist corporativism. He was seeking to influence the process of change which he expected to follow from the juridical recognition of the syndicates. In 1927 he insisted that his conception was essential for getting beyond the mere letter to the meaning and spirit of the syndical law of April 1926.[8] In the same way, as we have seen, Curzio Suckert had stressed in December of 1925 that Panunzio's neosyndicalist conception revealed the true meaning of Rocco's law.

Whatever these other fascists chose to believe, Alfredo Rocco was hardly relying on Panunzio to interpret the purposes behind the 1926 syndical law. In speeches presenting the bill to parliament, and in all his statements as Mussolini's minister of justice, Rocco laid down his conception of fascism in the most unequivocal terms. Generally, in fact, Rocco simply followed the Nationalist blueprint that he had played the major role in devising, but it is useful to consider briefly what he was saying from 1925 to 1927, as Fascist minister of justice, about the meaning of the institutional change that fascism was then initiating.

Some of Rocco's measures were more conservative and authoritarian than totalitarian in thrust; he worked especially to enhance the power of the executive—and with it the monarchy—vis-à-vis the legislature. But while some right fascists emphasized this reactionary side of fascism almost exclusively, Rocco himself had no illusions that a mere "return to the *Statuto*" would be sufficient, for the power of parliament had been only part of the problem. The basic threat to the state's sovereignty was the general tendency toward social particularism, which found expression outside parliament as well as within it. If the Italian state was to survive, it had to move beyond liberal pluralism and dominate the society more directly—through totalitarian coordination of all social activities.[9]

Rocco portrayed the syndical law of April 1926 as a response to the most immediate social threat—and as the key to giving the Fascist state its postliberal form.[10] In presenting his bill to the Chamber of Deputies, he justified state control of the unions by recalling the anarchy that had resulted when the trade union challenge of the *biennio rosso* overwhelmed the weak liberal state. But since, as Rocco put it, "the syndical phenomenon is an insuppressible aspect of modern life," the state had to develop an active relationship with the syndicates, extending its sovereignty over them and taking on new form in the process.[11] When Agostino Lanzillo, in the Chamber discussion of Rocco's bill, worried that the state would impose an excessive, authoritarian kind of control, Rocco replied with characteristic bluntness: "The organization of the syndicates must be a means to discipline the syndicates, not a means to create powerful and uncontrolled organisms capable of dominating the state."[12]

The syndical law also extended the state's sovereignty by outlawing strikes and lockouts and establishing a labor magistracy to adjudicate labor conflicts. Rocco emphasized that he envisioned not merely a system of compulsory arbitration, which would retain the character of compromise between private interests, but the imposition of the state's authority over interests that were no longer to be viewed as private in the liberal sense. While the Italian state in its liberal form had remained agnostic in the face of class conflicts in the economy, it was now taking on a new fascist form, moving toward totalitarianism by becoming involved in more spheres of social activity. Major social phenomena like class organization and economic conflict would no longer be left to develop outside the state's control; social decisions which were made haphazardly through the struggle of particular interests in the liberal system would now be made by the state and imposed through law.[13]

Rocco's purposes were not only defensive. The Fascist state was moving toward totalitarianism partly to coordinate the national life for new purposes. Organization would enable the state to foster the class collaboration essential for success in international economic competition. And more generally, through organization the Fascist state could instill the values necessary to overcome the indiscipline and laziness of centuries and make Italy a great military nation.[14]

Despite these new purposes, Rocco insisted that fascism was restoring sovereignty to the traditional Italian state, not creating a new state. It was possible to adjust the political system in order to make the masses identify more fully with the nation, but it was not possible to create a popular state based on some sort of homogeneous community. While liberalism portrayed society as a collection of equal citizens, fascism grasped "the necessary differences among men, the differences in their value, and the diversity of the functions entrusted to each individual." At the same time, Rocco linked fascism to German juridical theories which held that sovereignty rests not with the people, but with the state, understood as "an organism distinct from the citizens" who constitute the society at any given time. And he insisted explicitly on the rigidly elitist implications of this conception: "If in fact the state is sovereign, if it has in hand an overwhelming power, which dominates and disciplines all the other forces existing in the society, it means that the state carries out its own ends, superior to those of individuals."[15]

Especially given Rocco's powerful position, it was impossible to ignore the place of Nationalism within fascism, and the syndicalists sometimes applauded the Nationalists' contribution to the fascist revolution. Writing just before Rocco's syndical bill became law, Panunzio called for the publication of Rocco's speeches, to make them accessible for the essential work of political education that lay ahead.[16] Throughout the history of the regime, Panunzio portrayed fascism as a synthesis of syndicalism and Nationalism: syndicalism provided the social content and Nationalism the governmental form.[17] This interpretation stemmed in part from tactical political considerations, but the Nationalists and syndicalists did have some perceptions and goals in common.

The two groups were involved in a common departure from the tradition of Italian pessimism that found expression, for example, in Giustino Fortunato's gloomy conclusion to *Dopo la guerra sovvertitrice*. In contrast to Fortunato, they were confident that Italy, after the war, was ready to become a more viable nation. Belief in the value of the war was fundamental to both schools and was the primary bond in the fascist synthesis.[18] At the same time, both the Nationalists and the syndicalists linked Italy's prospects to the evolution of modern industrial capitalism. Fascism for both groups was in part a way of ordering the nation for its essential productive activity, a way of freeing the potentially healthy economic nation from the old liberalism, with its political caste of lawyers and others divorced from modern production. So both envisioned a more substantial role in public affairs for those with capacities derived from experience in the modern industrial world. Both sought to promote economics to a higher place in the hierarchy of the nation's affairs.

Even when it came to institutional alternatives to the liberal order, the Nationalists and syndicalists had important ideas in common. Rocco and Corradini, Panunzio and Olivetti, Grandi and Bottai all saw the twentieth century as the age of social organization based on economic function. Panunzio, writing in 1926, emphasized explicitly that the common denominator between syndicalism and Nationalism—and the essence of fascism—was the principle of social organization, in contrast to liberal individualism.[19] For both Nationalism and syndicalism, social organization—and ultimately a corporative system—could give structure to liberal Italy's atomized society and enable the nation to concentrate its energies. The result would be a better integrated nation and a stronger state, able to exert more extensive and effective authority vis-à-vis the society. More generally, the Nationalists and syndicalists agreed that Italy could overcome her defects only by moving beyond liberal individualism, conventional politics, and the parliamentary system in the direction of totalitarianism. A further area of convergence, having to do with elitism and the process of revolutionary implementation, can best be considered in the next chapter.

Despite these points of agreement, the internal heterogeneity of fascism was so obvious to antifascists that many, like Alceste De Ambris, expected at first that fascism would soon disintegrate. As the years wore on, however, it became clear that fascism had more internal consistency than these skeptics had realized. The syndicalists and Nationalists played major roles in establishing the necessary "ideological" underpinnings, the basis for convergence among the heterogeneous components in fascism. The perceptions and purposes they shared define the basis of the fascist synthesis, the least common denominator that enabled committed fascists with different backgrounds to participate in the same regime. But while it did not disintegrate from within, neither did fascism as a whole ever develop a coherent theoretical framework or practical program. It had enough coherence to hold together and to destroy the liberal parliamentary system, but not enough to implement a meaningful alternative. While the points of agreement between syndicalist and Nationalist ideas define the basis of convergence, their points of contrast define the deeper disagreement in fascism, a conflict between populism and elitism that produced the underlying tension in the Fascist regime. It was partly because fascism was so deeply divided against itself that the Fascist regime never accomplished much. If fascism was to avoid disintegration along the lines De Ambris and others anticipated, it had to maintain a certain ambiguity over the most basic questions—whether, for example, fascist elitism was a temporary means or a permanent end.

We have seen that the syndicalists sometimes emphasized the complementary quality of Nationalism and syndicalism, but they also explicitly attacked the Nationalists' doctrine, denying that it represented the meaning of fascism. Panunzio, for example, criticized Maurizio Maraviglia's inaugural lecture for the 1928–29 academic year at the University of Perugia, especially Maraviglia's insistence that the state was conceptually and historically prior to the nation.[20] Maraviglia's statist position led him to argue that fascism was changing the relationship between society and state not, as many seemed to suppose, by creating a new corporative state out of social organizations, but by organizing a corporative society within the preexisting national state— as a means to control the society. Panunzio grasped the stakes in the argument when he insisted that, on the contrary, the nation was conceptually and historically prior, the necessary substratum of the state. He criticized Rocco's insistence on the primacy of the state for much the same reason.[21] While Rocco had asserted that the fascist concept of the state was not new, that it could be derived from German juridical theories of state sovereignty, Panunzio insisted on the revolutionary quality of the fascist concept and thus of the Fascist state itself. The advent of syndicates made possible a state with a new social basis. In 1925, while portraying fascism as a synthesis of syndicalism and Nationalism, Panunzio warned that the Nationalist notion of the state was excessively abstract, that the idea of the state was empty without the complementary concept of a syndically based society. On another occasion, he insisted that fascism was more profoundly linked to syndicalism than to Nationalism, because fascism, like syndicalism, was radically populist, while Nationalism was restrictive and aristocratic. Panunzio charged repeatedly that the Nationalists were too preoccupied with such secondary problems as the juridical form of executive power and the relationship between executive and legislature; it was the syndicalists who were defining the essential relationship for fascism—between the organized society and the state.[22] And for the syndicalists, in sharp contrast to the Nationalists, the society-nation was always primary, the state always derivative. As Panunzio put it in 1933: "In place of the abstract entity—State—succeeds the real, concrete, psychological-sociological entity—Nation. . . . One should no longer speak of sovereignty of the State, but only of sovereignty of the nation."[23] Younger left fascist idealists like Giuseppe Bottai criticized Nationalism and right fascism for essentially the same reasons.[24]

While right fascists like Rocco and Maraviglia felt that democracy had worked too well, giving the masses too much power, left fascists like Panunzio and Bottai felt that parliamentary democracy had not proven an adequate vehicle of popular sovereignty and mass political participation.[25] An attempt to use socioeconomic organization to reconstruct the Italian state on a more popular basis was the keystone of the program of radical change which they proposed for fascism.

The problem of insufficient popular participation in the political system was the center of a cluster of five interrelated but distinguishable problems that the syndicalists sought to overcome through fascism. The other four were: the deficiencies in Italy's economic development; the problems of the Italian character and self-image; the atomization and lack of community in Italian society; and the weakness of the Italian liberal state, its inability to promote the collective interest. All of them were genuine problems, so there was some objective basis to the discontents which provoked the syndicalists' quest for solutions. But that quest led the syndicalists, through a kind of dialectical overreaction, to move beyond liberalism toward one form of totalitarianism. Although they were responding seriously, and sometimes effectively, to genuine problems, their perspective on these problems was somewhat skewed, and this led them to propose a blueprint for solution that was in some ways excessive, clumsy, and unrealistic. We can best consider the reasons for the excesses in the syndicalist program, and the relevance of the tricky concept "totalitarianism," after we have seen how the syndicalist-fascist program responded to the five basic problems. Since these problems seemed to be very much bound up together, the syndicalists proposed a single revolutionary process designed to overcome all five simultaneously. We cannot fully understand how that process responded to any one problem until we have considered all five, since the solution to each contributed to the solution of the others. Indeed we could consider the five problems in any order.

To begin the process, it seemed necessary to attack two clusters of more specific problems; in each cluster, problems with liberalism in general seemed especially acute in Italy because they had become interwoven with particularly Italian problems that tended to produce the same results. First, there were problems with the political system. The Italian state was aloof, and Italy still suffered from acute political alienation. But this was a problem partly because the liberal parliamentary system in general produced a merely representative democracy, which enabled the masses to participate only sporadically and indirectly, through the suffrage system. Thus, as critics like Mosca and Pareto had shown, the people even in a liberal parliamentary system, with universal suffrage, were easily manipulated by demagogues and political elites. This system, with its abstract relationship between state and atomized individuals, could not overcome—and ultimately only reinforced—the traditional gap between people and state in Italy.

But the Italian liberal state was only half the problem. The second cluster concerned the quality of the social base and the nature of the society's values. Both Italian values and liberal values were too individualistic, with insufficient premium on the social sphere. The Italian people had been too egotistical and undisciplined, too narrow in their concerns, to develop a sense of the collective interest and to participate effectively in politics. Liberalism had only reinforced the uniquely Italian side of the problem by portraying society as a collection of equal citizens, each standing as an individual vis-à-vis the state. Despite the periodic elections, it left too great a distance between the individual and state for the ordinary individual to grasp political issues and to make himself politically effective. Moreover, liberalism placed too much emphasis on the private well-being of individuals and thus did not nurture the social potential that the syndicalists believed to be inherent in man.

But even though the liberal system had proven inadequate, the syndicalists were not prepared to abandon the original democratic aspiration. It was time, however, to try new institutions and new forms of political education.[26] The two-way problem of state and society called for a two-way, simultaneous process of solution: it was necessary to "lower" and enrich the state, and it was necessary to raise the masses, to politicize the individual through new forms of sociopolitical participation.

Each half of this process challenged the values and assumptions of liberalism, and we can best understand what the syndicalists had in mind if we consider the running debate with major liberals that their proposals provoked. Guido De Ruggiero criticized Panunzio's neo-syndicalist proposals just after the March on Rome, insisting that the essential task for the present was not to replace parliament, but to develop a worthier form of political education.[27] Because of inadequate political education, the quality of Italy's ruling class had been poor, and thus the unhealthy patterns of the Italian parliamentary system had developed. Responding to De Ruggiero, Panunzio agreed that political education was the crucial problem, but he turned the tables by asking why parliamentary liberalism had failed so miserably as an educational vehicle.[28] At issue, of course, was a difference in perception over whether the liberal parliamentary system had had its chance in Italy or not. Perhaps the syndicalists were too hasty in assuming that it had. But it was easy—and seemed plausible to others—for Panunzio to argue that since the essential political education had not been accomplished under the old system, with its territorially based suffrage system, it was time to try something else. Panunzio proposed that syndicates, made obligatory and extended throughout the society, could carry out the necessary political education and provide new forms of political participation. Through the expansion of syndicalism, the values of the labor aristocracy which the syndicalists had anticipated before the war would be made universal: "Mazzini's meaning has been revealed by Sorel. Through this ethic of association, which is syndicalism, we are aiming at a new aristocracy, that is, at a universal aristocracy and thus at a new democracy."[29]

Olivetti responded to the criticism of the liberals Luigi Albertini and Umberto Ricci in much the same way. In two rather sarcastic *Corriere della sera* editorials after the National Council meeting of August 1924, Albertini ran through the major syndicalist-fascist themes, questioning their novelty and effectiveness. He concluded that neosyndicalism would produce a narrow, selfish system "in which the day-to-day content would be low-grade bargaining over the division of the common spoils among the corporations strongest at the outset."[30] To give existing economic interests political power would only freeze present economic patterns, excluding new interests and ideas. Albertini stressed the continued viability of the traditional liberal framework, with political parties representing different conceptions of the collective interest competing in parliamentary elections and alternating in power. And true to the conservative side of his liberal heritage, he argued that the liberal system provided the best way for minorities, men of noble character and high ideals, to emerge to lead the disoriented, sluggish society.

In mocking the rhetorical justifications for fascist corporativist proposals, Albertini was clearly fastening upon A. O. Olivetti, who was quick to respond in a series of articles in *Il popolo d'Italia*. Olivetti wrote regularly for the official Fascist newspaper at this point, and his articles in polemic with Albertini were unsigned; he was speaking for fascism as a whole in taking on the distinguished liberal spokesman. After recalling the hostility between Mazzini and the nineteenth-century liberalism that was the source of Albertini's own position, Olivetti insisted that liberalism was now frozen and inappropriate, especially because of the impact of the war on the Italian nation. With dazzling rhetoric, he proclaimed the old liberalism to be "contrary to the violent and fecund expression of life on the part of a people which, in the midst of the travail of its reconstruction, feels all of its will to power, strained to the point of spasm, in a glorious energy of renewal."[31] This blast must have left Albertini shaking his head, but Olivetti's argument that a more active kind of "liberalism" was necessary had considerable force. Politics, said Olivetti, had to be pulled down from the clouds and made accessible to the people; a more constant kind of political education was needed to raise the people to political consciousness and competence. The people were ready now, so it was time to go beyond liberalism to the sort of radical populist politics that Mazzini had had in mind in the first place.

Olivetti found another liberal adversary in Umberto Ricci, a distinguished economist whose criticism of fascist corporativism cost him his professorship at the University of Rome in 1927.[32] Much like De Ruggiero and Albertini, Ricci warned that a neosyndicalist system would yield a stifling *"polipolio,"* a collection of monopolies each protecting its own narrow interests; to give these monopolies political power would undermine the collective interest and threaten the dissolution of the state itself.[33] Responding to Ricci, Olivetti insisted that the particularism initially at the root of economic organization would gradually give way to a new sociopolitical sensibility, thanks to organizational experience and education. Ricci had been wrong to suppose that there could be a genuine neosyndicalist regime "without a syndical consciousness, or rather an 'intersyndical' consciousness among producers." And besides, Olivetti went on, neosyndicalism would be conceivable only in the context of a postliberal " 'organic state' that reflects and encompasses the whole effort of production."[34] For Panunzio and Olivetti, then, neosyndicalism as a form of political education could succeed where the old parliamentary liberalism had failed; and because the liberals failed to grasp the educational significance of syndicalism, many of their criticisms were simply irrelevant.

The syndicalists and the other left fascist idealists were "leftist," and differed radically from right fascists, precisely in their confidence that the masses could—and should—be made politically competent. Despite the political indifference of the masses at present, sociopolitical potential was inherent in man as such, not just in an elite. In the process of education, a moment of elitist manipulation would obviously be necessary, but elitism had only to be a temporary instrument, not a permanent condition of political life. To raise the individual to sociopolitical awareness, it was necessary to structure his life through organization, especially organization based on economic function, but also organizations for leisure-time activities, for women, for youth. In an address to the Chamber of Deputies in 1929, Panunzio called for the whole network of party organizations to be fused with the established educational system, to create a vast, specifically fascist educational apparatus. This was essential since "fascism, confronting the whole man, wants to—and has to—mold and educate him from the earliest age."[35]

Through such organizations, the politically conscious elite could instill new values into wider sectors of society. But in addition, organizational involvement in itself enhanced the sociopolitical sensibility of individuals.[36] In 1938, after thirty-five years as a syndicalist, Panunzio was still arguing that group membership gradually developed the ethical-political capacity inherent in men, enabling the individual to transcend his "initial economic egotism" and to achieve "a unitary political economic-productive consciousness or, as we say today, a corporative consciousness."[37] With this new consciousness, the individual would be able to understand himself and his activity in terms of the collective interest. The syndicalists felt that organizations based on economic function could have the greatest impact, because the individual's job was his most "social" activity, and because it involved him every day. Within these organizations, the people would participate together in making decisions that directly affected them—and that also had broader implications. Gradually, the general, "political" nature of their activities, the impact they would have on the collective, would become clear to the organization's members.

The Fascist economic organizations could serve this pedagogical function, however, only if they themselves had responsibility for a kind of political decision-making. Here we encounter the other side of the overall process of solution which the syndicalists envisioned. Given the gulf between people and state in liberal Italy, it would not be enough merely to instill political values and then rely, as before, on universal suffrage and the parliamentary system. Rather, it was necessary to create a more tangible state by diffusing state attributes into the organizations constituting society. As these organizations became state entities through fascism, they would actually participate in the state's sovereignty by taking on legislative functions. Two stages would be involved. Their representatives would replace the old politicians in a revitalized parliament, but this legislative capacity would also be exercised more directly and immediately, by the syndicates themselves.[38] The new socioeconomic organizations would take over public functions that were presently the preserve of the old bureaucracy, and they would also carry out new public functions, for the state itself was to expand its sovereignty to encompass traditionally private forms of individual and social activity.

The debate between Panunzio and De Ruggiero clarifies these new sources of political capacity—and reveals the basis of the left corporativist departure from liberalism. In his critique of December 1922, De Ruggiero charged that Panunzio's devaluation of liberal parliamentary politics, and his proposal to base political life on economic groupings, manifested the mentality of historical materialism, which had portrayed the political sphere as a mere superstructure, reducible to the economic sphere.[39] Panunzio, it seemed, was merely offering a variation of the socialist criticism of parliamentary government; and the syndicates must have political power because of their importance on the economic level. In opposition to this materialist conception, De Ruggiero held that while politics develops first in a determined way out of economic relationships, it ultimately involves a creative departure—into the realm of freedom.

In criticizing fascism in his masterpiece, *The History of European Liberalism*, De Ruggiero focused more sharply on the syndicalist-fascist conception, although here he did not single out Panunzio by name.[40] In giving economic organizations political roles, he argued, fascism was infecting the state with the particularism of societal interest groups, thereby undermining the state's universal, genuinely political quality. Because they failed to understand the harmonizing role of politics, the fascists were seeking to make the formerly autonomous political sphere simply reproduce the socioeconomic conflicts in society. While an economic grouping was limited to a particularist perspective, a truly political grouping sought—and could to some degree attain—a universal perspective and program, based on a genuine sense of the collective interest. This political perspective could be achieved only by rising above the socioeconomic level of the syndicate, not by eliminating political parties and politicizing economic groupings and economic functions.

Panunzio and the syndicalists interpreted in quite the opposite way the process which De Ruggiero and the liberals condemned: fascism was not degrading the political to the level of economic egotism, but raising the socioeconomic sphere to the political level. Responding to De Ruggiero's critique of 1922, Panunzio insisted that his own conception involved not the triumph of *tecnica*, as De Ruggiero had charged, but the triumph of *politica*.[41] This was true partly because fascism was exposing the individual to a more thoroughgoing kind of political education, but primarily because fascism was expanding political sovereignty over the economy. From the syndicalist perspective, De Ruggiero's conception of politics as a unifying sphere above the particularism of society was hopelessly abstract; the liberal insistence on the separation of political state and economic society was a major source of the present crisis. The liberal state had remained too indifferent to what was going on in society. There was too much that it did not do, too many spheres of life that it did not harmonize—labor conflicts, for example, and the whole sphere of production, the economy itself. So the syndicalists insisted that it was fascism, not liberalism, that embodied the political principle. Just before the March on Rome, Panunzio argued that neosyndicalism was the way to make the political idea concrete—by giving it economic content: "Syndicalism . . . is the negation of the old political conception, the negation of the *parties*, the affirmation of the classes and of their organization in the corporations or syndicates, the rejection of the old, so-called ideological conception of politics, and certainly not, it must be emphasized, the substitution of the economic sphere as such for the political sphere, but rather the *promotion* of the economy to the political level."[42]

It was partly because the political sphere was to expand to encompass more of the socioeconomic sphere that the new economic organizations would have significant public functions to perform. At first they would assume control over such mundane decisions as collective labor contracts and job placement—areas traditionally of concern to the unions. But as the regime evolved and popular political capacities developed, fascist economic organizations would acquire more important kinds of public responsibilities, ultimately to include a form of economic planning.

De Ruggiero's critique did not stop with accusations of materialism. More specifically, he warned that in practice Panunzio's neosyndicalism, with its devaluation of parliament and the properly political side of the state, would only end up enhancing the power of the bureaucracy.[43] This was especially dangerous in the aftermath of the war, when government reliance on decree laws had made the bureaucracy more powerful than ever. Subsequent events justified De Ruggiero's fears: fascism did end up enhancing the power of the bureaucracy, since it undermined parliament but never managed to create a viable corporativist alternative. Nevertheless, De Ruggiero in 1922 had not fully grasped the radically decentralizing quality of the neosyndicalist conception and the antibureaucratic intention behind it.

Responding to De Ruggiero in *Il popolo d'Italia*, Panunzio agreed that the hypertrophy of bureaucracy posed a severe danger, but he insisted that there could be no turning back in the direction of parliament.[44] The parliament's loss of legislative power to the bureaucracy was by no means a temporary aberration caused by the war; as with so much else, the war had merely accelerated an already irreversible process. The only way out, Panunzio insisted, was to make the syndicates the basis of legislative capacity—first by bringing their representatives directly into the parliament. At the very least, this would raise the level of technical competence in the old representative bodies and enable them better to resist further bureaucratic inroads. But this was only a point of departure for more radical change. It would be possible to break the stranglehold of the bureaucracy, making the Italian state less remote, by decentralizing legislative capacity into the occupational groupings comprising society. Those organizations gradually would take over many of the functions of the old centralized administration, thereby enabling the society more and more to govern itself.[45]

In offering these proposals, the syndicalists envisioned a network of varied organizations—new corporations grouping all those involved in a given economic category, as well as the more traditional syndical organizations. When Panunzio responded to De Ruggiero early in 1923, he was not specific about the social groupings that would handle various kinds of legislation. He implied at this point, and stressed more explicitly as the Fascist regime developed, that the new system would require flexibility and pluralism, with a complex network of organizational links, including various levels of intersyndical grouping. The precise configuration of the new order could not yet be discerned, but the purpose of the process was clear: through its network of corporativist organizations, the state could simultaneously expand and decentralize its functions, enabling the people to participate more constantly and directly in public life—and expand their political horizons in the process.[46] So the syndicalist-fascist blueprint required not only raising the masses through fascist education, but also "lowering" and expanding the state, to make the political sphere more tangible and accessible. To overcome the divorce between state and society in liberal Italy, a kind of decentralizing totalitarianism seemed to be required.

It was Panunzio who developed this program most systematically, but for all the syndicalists, the essence of fascism was the new relationship between the state and the economic society that the regime was creating by giving economic groupings political and legislative roles.[47] The corporations' status as state entities meant not that they were mere administrative organs of the state, but that they were the bases of political decision making. As Olivetti put it in 1928, in a speech at the International Center for Fascist Studies at Lausanne: "The corporations are the raw materials for the *self-government* of the nation; indeed, they are the nation itself, making itself state."[48] Luigi Razza called for these entities to absorb the legislative functions of bureaucracy and parliament and to regulate production by setting outputs and prices.[49] For Razza, the economic organizations were the essential political organs of the Fascist regime; they would afford the workers a serious role in decision making—especially in regulating the economy. Through fascist corporativism, the real economic nation would finally be able to govern itself, as economics and politics converged.

This unification of politics and economics was the core of the left fascist conception.[50] Panunzio proclaimed in 1934 that "today the economy and the political sphere are one and the same," while for Luigi Razza: "there is no economy torn away from the political sphere, and to act politically means to dictate the laws and the norms for the economic activity of a collectivity."[51] Fascism, then, was not an economic system but a political idea, an expansion of the political principle over central activities of the economic society which the liberal state had neglected. The Fascist state would discipline production, no longer leaving the economy to operate on its own, without reference to the collective interest. And that state would be composed of the people themselves, organized in their economic groupings; it was they who would do the regulating—and thereby act politically.

This was the direction for change which the syndicalists proposed and which left fascist idealists worked to have implemented in the regime. Giuseppe Bottai spearheaded this effort on the basis of a conception virtually indistinguishable from—and essentially derived from —the syndicalist blueprint we have just discussed. He repeatedly insisted that the Fascist corporative state was a postliberal political order, intended to make possible a more meaningful kind of popular self-government. The key step was to diffuse the political decision-making and power of the old centralized bureaucracy into the economically based groupings in society.[52]

The syndicalists were obviously preoccupied with the economic sphere, even though they insisted that fascism was a political system. They understood fascism as a new political form for the economy, and their second basic purpose was to make Italy more effective economically. Economic backwardness had seemed a major symptom of Italy's decadence, while industrial development had been the foundation for the confidence which marked the syndicalists' departure from pre-industrial radicalism before World War I. Italy's potential to become a more viable nation after the war meant in part that she could develop a healthier economy. Addressing the meeting on fascist culture in Bologna in 1925, Olivetti emphasized that the principle of more intense production was a major presupposition of both syndicalism and fascism.[53]

The syndicalists, sensibly enough, viewed capitalism with ambivalence: it still seemed the most effective means of economic development, but it could not be counted on to unfold automatically in the collective interest. Capitalism fostered a selfish, "materialistic" outlook and a relatively chaotic, unstable economic system. In principle, political action could alleviate these deficiencies, but the links between the political and economic spheres in liberal Italy had only exacerbated the unproductive side of capitalism. As a result, Italian economic development had been chaotic and sporadic. The weak liberal state had left the economic system to operate unchecked, but then had sought political support by offering favors to special interests; the strong Fascist state, on the other hand, would reverse this relationship, extending political control over the economy, the central sphere of social activity.[54] As Rossoni put it in 1929, the best course available in Italy for now was to stimulate to productive uses the capital and property that had long remained "irresponsible and incapable of any beneficial function whatsoever," especially in certain regions.[55] For all the syndicalists, fascism would politicize both economic activity, which would become a public function, and private property and capital, which would lose their absolute private status and become pragmatic instruments in the society's effort to maximize production.[56]

The syndicalist-fascist blueprint sought to combine economic planning with spontaneity, to provide greater coordination of production without the collectivization and bureaucratic control which the syndicalists had always considered to be stifling and inefficient.[57] Planning through a decentralized network of corporations would be much more flexible, and thus more effective, than planning from the top, through the centralized bureaucracy. At the same time, there would still be free competition among economic units. Particular firms and economic sectors were no longer to be left to operate unchecked, pursuing their short-term interests, but neither was the state to operate them directly, undermining individual initiative. Under the aegis of the expanded state, each economic sector would develop the forms of ownership and management which experience indicated to be the most productive. The result would be a mixed economy, with a place for private, state-owned, parastate, and even syndically owned entities.

So the syndicalists proposed to constitute self-governing groups of producers not only to further popular participation in public life, but also to promote ordered productivity in the economy. It was possible to pursue both through a single process, since it would be largely the decentralized political coordination of the economy that would make possible a more intense kind of popular political participation. As the new economic organizations gradually took on political attributes, their major responsibility would be to regulate the economy.[58] Their concerns would be down-to-earth and practical. As Olivetti emphasized to the Commission of Eighteen in 1925, the Fascist corporations would foster a greater use of statistics in the economy and would use statistics themselves as they studied concrete economic problems.[59] Through the use of statistics, and ultimately, through the corporative network itself, decisions about profit rates, or collective labor contracts, or the impact an improvement in working conditions would have on a firm's competitive position, would become less arbitrary and short-sighted, and more rational and "technical." For Panunzio as well, the use of statistics would keynote the factual, hard-headed studies of particular industries and firms that the corporations would carry out in coordinating the nation's economy.[60] The syndicalists saw the corporative order as a means to greater practicality in Italian life, an antidote to the tendencies toward rhetoric and abstract speculation in the culture. They liked to think that this productivism went hand in hand with the participation they were also seeking, but this juxtaposition entailed some significant tensions, which we will consider in concluding this chapter.

The syndicalists also expected to enhance production through the other half of the process—through "corporativist" education. The new values to be inculcated were to be practical, productive values; each individual, whatever his place in the economy, would learn to grasp the social dimensions of his economic role and thus to understand his labor in "political" terms, as a social duty and function.[61] Invoking Sorel's ethic of producers, Panunzio insisted that fascism was transforming the ordinary man, the old economic man, into a producer—a creative, moral individual fit for the new world of industry, which required enthusiasm and self-discipline. Indeed, fascist corporativism was a means of democratizing technocracy, of making universal the values and capacities which all the producers needed to become effective, lucid participants in the politicized economy.[62]

Whatever the practicality of this conception, it is clear that the syndicalists hardly viewed fascism as a means to preserve traditional values. Panunzio insisted that the traditional conception of the nation as a cultural, historical, political, and moral entity was incomplete; the nation was also an economy, in some ways essentially an economy.[63] Fascism for Panunzio was a vehicle for enhancing the role of the economy in the national life, and he could plausibly argue that it was the humanistic liberal tradition, and not fascism, which dismissed the economic sphere as merely material and thus inferior. By implication, it was the old liberals, not he and the fascists, who refused to adjust to "modernity" and the exigencies of industrial production. Again and again, the syndicalists and other left fascists linked fascism to productivism and industrial development.[64] For Giuseppe Bottai, for example, the corporative system was to promote technical progress and economic rationalization in an effort to maximize the economic capacities of the nation.[65]

The syndicalists viewed fascism, then, as a means to overcome traditional values, to make Italian life more practical and productive. Their program for fascism was a response to a third long-term problem —the apparent weaknesses of the Italian character which had pre-occupied them all along.[66] The fascist revolutionary process would complete the work which the Risorgimento had only started, revitalize Italian society, and enable the Italians to get down to serious business.

As they dreamed of a fascist Italy, the syndicalists often manifested in exaggerated form cultural sensitivities that were widespread in Italy. Speaking shortly after the March on Rome, Edmondo Rossoni stated proudly that now, with the advent of fascism, conciseness and punctuality were no longer only American, English, and German traits.[67] A few years later Rossoni insisted: "This is not an era of serenades with guitar and mandolin. It is a dynamic era, not only in the formation of the new *sentiments* of the Italian people, but in all aspects of the life of the nation."[68] But sometimes the syndicalists managed to examine the defects of Italian life more sensitively and systematically. In his *Caratteri della vita italiana*, published in 1927, Alighiero Ciattini sought to trace the relationships among what he considered to be the major Italian vices—superficiality, impracticality, cynicism, egotism, political factiousness, and disrespect for the law. The Italians had only "a superficial, external ability, fit more for *judging* than for *acting*, suitable more for *criticism* than for *creation*, inclined more to abstraction than to concreteness." These tendencies, Ciattini felt, helped to explain "the prevalently individualistic nature of the Italian temperament." At the same time, "in no country is the use and abuse of rhetoric so widespread as in Italy," and this rhetoric often obscured the impracticality of Italian culture. The whole syndrome produced an all-pervading cynicism which contributed, in turn, to the petty indiscipline in Italian society: "Among the peoples of the earth, the Italians are perhaps the least respectful, the least obedient to the laws and to rules in general. This does not change the fact that we have on our backs one of the heaviest and most complicated bureaucratic-juridical apparatuses."[69]

In conclusion, Ciattini called for simplification, for weeding out the outmoded, empty forms of Italian life, for a new realism, practicality, and sincerity.[70] It was up to fascism to lead the way, as Ciattini emphasized in a manifesto also published in 1927:

It is necessary to make Italy young again, to free her from the whole rotten breed of antiquarians, rhetoricians, false mystics, revellers, "culture quacks," aesthetes, from all those who, if they were to prevail, would make our country into one big hotel, or reduce it to a museum, or an academy, or a romantic vacation spot—admired by all the idlers and pseudo-sentimentalists, but lacking in any serious reason for living.

It is necessary to make of Italy—in accord with the Duce's generous effort—a country sober in words and gestures, rich in civil works, serious, disciplined, compact, loving wholesome and humble things. There is the material for this. Our people is sound, when it is not polluted, diverted, and disheartened by the rummaging and false pleading of the so-called intellectual classes operating on the margins of productive life.[71]

Since 1909, Marinetti and the Futurists had expressed much the same sensibility in more extreme terms, but the mixture of hopes and traumas, confidence and despair, realistic criticism and exaggerated cultural insecurity underlying Ciattini's statement had been fundamental to the syndicalists' vision from the beginning. The forms of Italian fascism are simply incomprehensible if we neglect the problems of self-image, the cultural sensitivities, which statements like Ciattini's reveal. It has been argued that fascism exploited such cultural self-doubts,[72] but in fact fascism embodied and manifested them; they were a major source of fascism in the first place.

Fascism was the antidote. For all the left fascist idealists, fascism was changing the very ethos of Italian culture, making Italians more serious and disciplined, more practical and hard-working. Orano declared in 1929 that now, through fascism, the Italians had overcome the moral laxity which had led to the corruption once endemic in Italian political life.[73] The younger fascist Augusto Turati, in his numerous speeches as party head from 1926 to 1930, constantly underscored the "anti-Italian" quality of fascism. His statements were filled with rhetoric and exaggeration reflecting his populist, petty bourgeois background, but their thrust was explicitly productivist, modernizing, and antitraditional. This former soldier and *squadrista* insisted that fascism was by no means to exhaust itself in activism and enthusiasm: "What is needed is a virtue which is rarely Italian, but which is certainly fascist: the virtue of patient perseverance, the virtue of industrious silence . . . a virtue by means of which we can transform ourselves . . . into a marvelous people of builders, of workers, of craftsmen." In another speech Turati called for "a patient effort to overcome ourselves, a continuous discipline of our behavior. . . . We must learn to scorn many of the things that yesterday we loved."[74] The war for Turati had been the catalyst enabling some Italians, at least, to begin the process of changing first themselves, and then their country. After the war, they had soon realized that the lazy, egotistical middle-class way of life no longer suited them; the result had been fascism, which was extending the new ethos into the entire society.[75]

The program the syndicalists proposed for fascism was also intended to solve the fourth long-term problem—the lack of community in liberal society, and especially, again, in atomized Italy. The syndicalists from the beginning had been seeking the basis for a deeper solidarity in their poorly integrated nation. Mazzini's vision of Italian unity had not been realized in the nineteenth century, but it had remained as a goal for those who found inadequate the kind of unity that had developed instead. The basis for a more intense kind of national community, for the left fascists as for Mazzini, was common "politicized" labor, labor understood as a social duty.[76]

Productivism and the new solidarity went hand in hand. Economic modernization, as pursued within the framework of fascist corporativism, was a great common enterprise which would bring everybody together.[77] The new solidarity would become possible in part because the nation, through fascism, was coming to understand itself essentially as an economy, and it was their economy—their economic interdependence—that the Italians most immediately shared. Because of the objective necessities of the productive process, a technical hierarchy in the economy remained necessary, but since this differentiation was essential for efficiency, it was quite consistent with the solidarity of Italian producers, which was based on a common commitment to the nation's goal of maximum production.[78] In the same way, the syndicalists generally conceded that class differences over distribution were an inevitable feature of the modern world, and thus in part the ongoing need for syndicates as well as corporations proper. But the fact of class differences did not preclude the development of a broader solidarity based on common participation in the politicized economy, although the new ethic and discipline obviously had to be extended to everyone, not only to the workers.[79]

The syndicalists hoped to create within the nation the same closely knit, psychologically based unity which they had originally believed to be developing within the workers' organizations. After the war, in fact, Olivetti continually referred to the Italian nation as "the largest syndicate," envisioning a kind of monolithic national solidarity.[80] And Paolo Orano, reviewing a book by Panunzio in 1929, expressed quite explicitly his desire for this sort of solidarity, insisting that, through fascism, "the psychological process toward the pure unity of the people is becoming irresistible in everyone."[81] For Agostino Lanzillo, in the same way, extreme homogeneity was necessary if Italy's extreme social fragmentation was to be overcome; fascism was "to mold into one body and to inspire with a single spirit a heterogeneous plurality, to render mutually comprehensible forces and currents of life that did not interact and that did not understand each other. A grandiose, difficult, rigorous undertaking that can resolve the entire drama of Italian life."[82]

The fifth problem which fascism was to overcome was the weakness of the Italian liberal state—its susceptibility to special interest pressures and its inability to harmonize important areas of social life through law. We have seen that the liberal De Ruggiero criticized neosyndicalism and fascism for degrading the political sphere to the level of economic particularism in society. However, the syndicalists argued that it was before, under the liberal parliamentary system, that economic particularism had undermined the political, that the state had been too weak to protect the collective interest.[83] Here again, a combination of purely Italian and more general liberal problems was responsible.

First was a general problem: because the liberal state had sought to remain aloof from the socioeconomic sphere, too many aspects of socioeconomic life were left to develop on their own, outside the sovereignty of the state. The Italian people had remained so indifferent to the liberal state partly because it had not been involved in areas of vital concern to them.[84] A major example, which the syndicalists cited again and again, was the problem of labor relations under liberalism and the civil law system. Betraying their bourgeois underpinnings, liberal states had developed careful systems of laws governing property relations, but had remained relatively indifferent to labor relations.[85] The individual worker had been left to deal with the individual employer on his own, on terms that were anything but equal. The workers had organized in order to confront the employer collectively, but their syndicates had no legal standing, so the collective labor contracts they won remained outside the law, not enforceable by the liberal state. This argument was not merely speculative: in practice Italian employers had not always lived up to their collective contracts, and the workers could not turn to the state for redress, because the liberal state claimed no sovereignty over this sphere of social activity.[86] It was partly for this reason that the workers could not identify with the state. And this lack of broad social support was a major source of the state's weakness.

In Italy, especially, the economic sphere, left out in theory, crept into the state by the back door. The Italian political elite had yielded to interest group pressures because it was desperate for political support. The people, suspicious of the state from the beginning, found their suspicions confirmed as the political elite, suspicious of the people, made the national state the vehicle for a collection of interest groups. Individual Italians remained skeptical of the civic virtue of their fellow citizens and thus tended—partly in self-defense—to exploit the state and disobey the law. The politically strong used the state for their own narrow interests—and got away with it because of the political apathy and cynicism of the weak. Neither the strong nor the weak had enough confidence in the state to identify with it and to accept the legitimacy of the law. The Italian state had remained too weak even to enforce some of the laws it did make. The syndicalists liked to point to the example of social and labor legislation, which often either was not applied at all or was violated with impunity by employers.[87] Thus Olivetti, calling for a labor magistracy in 1925, emphasized the inadequacy of existing Italian labor legislation, which no one, he said, took very seriously; the state's failure to enforce what laws there were discredited the state in the eyes of the working masses.[88]

Through the process of change which the syndicalists outlined, the Fascist state would cut at several points into this vicious circle of cynicism, corruption, and disobedience. Most basically, since the nation-society was fundamentally an economy, a strong and legitimate state could be constructed only on the basis of the economic organizations in society.[89] More specifically, two kinds of change were necessary for Italy to have a strong state. First, the state would have to enforce the law more vigorously. Panunzio always insisted that the essence of the state in the limited, immediate sense was its enforcement power. While legislative capacity was to be diffused into the organized society, the state proper would become primarily a vehicle—and a much more effective vehicle—for enforcing the laws, including the laws made by the economic groupings out in society.[90] In the same way, Olivetti proposed a special labor police to enforce labor legislation.[91] But the state would also have to extend its sway over the socioeconomic sphere, both to check particularist abuses and to further the interests of ordinary people. It was especially through law that the state could promote the collective interest, so as fascism expanded the "political" sphere, more and more individual and social activities were to be brought within the sphere of law.[92] Syndical membership was to become obligatory, collective labor contracts were to be legally binding, and ultimately the economy itself would be regulated through law. The corporations would actually be making law as they ordered the economy; the stipulation that property and capital be used as instruments of the collective interest would similarly take legal form—and be subject to enforcement by the state.[93]

In extending the state's sovereignty over new areas of social activity, fascism was making the state more tangible and concrete—and thus more comprehensible. The state had to reach out and encompass the people before they could learn that the law should be a collective instrument, before they could become politically competent. The Fascist state was moving in this direction by giving the economic organizations in society legal standing as state entities and by making the creations of those organizations, like collective labor contracts, legally binding and enforceable by the state. As the sphere of law was both expanded and diffused into the organized society, the socioeconomic groupings would make laws governing all the conditions of labor, laws which the strong Fascist state would rigorously enforce.[94] More generally, the syndicalists lauded the Fascist Labor Charter of 1927 for its commitment to give labor the same kind of legal standing and protection that property had long enjoyed.[95] Thus the syndicalists could claim that the Fascist state had transcended class, while practice had proven the liberal state and legal system to be the instruments of bourgeois property-owners.

However, the syndicalists did not deny the political reality and significance of many of the economic interests that had sought to take advantage of the liberal state. While the liberals claimed that politics ought to transcend these interests, the syndicalists insisted that they be expressed openly, through economic organizations having a public character, subject to state sovereignty. This would be a major function of the fascist corporative system, which would enable the economic categories to elaborate and pursue their interests, but within a framework of expanded state sovereignty that would ensure that they be harmonized with the collective interest. This open and coordinated pursuit of economic interests would be healthier, and more productive in its consequences, than the corrupting, surreptitious struggle for political influence that had characterized the liberal regime.[96]

So the syndicalists claimed, in rebuttal of liberal criticism, that fascism was not turning the state over to special interests, but exerting the state's sovereignty over them by making them public and responsible. The political coordination of the economy needed to spur economic growth would strengthen the state vis-à-vis socioeconomic particularism at the same time. The liberal state's weakness with respect to the economic sphere had produced both political corruption and economic disorder; by expanding the state's sovereignty over the economy, bringing the economic interests into the state, fascism was overcoming both.

A major aspect of this expansion of the state's sovereignty was the establishment of a labor magistracy to settle labor disputes without strikes and lockouts. This innovation had been included in De Ambris's *Carta del Carnaro* and had been among the steps which Panunzio had advocated for fascism from the beginning. There was widespread syndicalist support for the proposal both before and after the syndical law of April 1926 finally established a labor magistracy.[97] Normally, the appropriate economic groupings, now become public entities, would interact on their own to resolve conflicts and to work out collective labor contracts, which would, of course, be legally binding and enforceable by the state. But should these organizations reach an impasse, they would have recourse to the labor judges. The liberal state's emptiness was most obvious in its willingness to let conflicting social interests resolve their differences through the classic methods of class self-defense—strikes and lockouts. Major economic decisions were left to be resolved through the anarchy of relative power, with no guarantee that the result would be best for the nation or even fair to the parties involved. The outcome was fortuitous, not political. Moreover, the old methods involved an unnecessary and damaging interruption of production.

Ultimately, then, the entire process of change which the syndicalists proposed for fascism would contribute to the creation of a stronger state. The expansion of the state's sovereignty, the more direct kind of political participation, the new solidarity based on shared productive values—all served to create the social consensus and the sense of political responsibility necessary for the state to become the sphere of the collective interest.[98] Through fascism, the syndicalists believed, the once-vicious circle was beginning to run in the opposite—benign— direction: the state was strong because people identified with it and believed it was theirs; they believed in it because it was strong and effective in ordering socioeconomic life and pursuing the collective interest. Now that the Italians had begun to trust each other and to understand the state, and now that the state was worth believing in, they were beginning to respect and obey the law. According to Augusto Turati, in one of his speeches as party leader in 1926, a "sublime task" of fascism was to teach the Italians the meaning and value of law, to enable them to experience the law as "an active principle embodying their own efforts and energies," and no longer as something rigid and alien.[99] Paolo Orano, discussing a lecture by Panunzio in 1929, made explicit the relationship between the new popular political sensibility and the strength of the new Fascist state: "It is the sublime political sense that increasingly animates the Italians. From this sentiment millions and millions of men unite and subordinate themselves to obey a single Goal and a single Power, which are not even visible and tangible like the small ancient city-state. Sergio Panunzio finds the extraordinary element in the fact that this sentiment is not to be explained by the mechanism of physical coercion by the public power, but, on the contrary, this sentiment determines that coercion and power and makes them possible."[100]

There was no cult of the Duce, no emphasis on common submission to a charismatic leader, in the way either Panunzio or Orano portrayed the subordination of all Italians to the new Fascist state. Rather, as they viewed the situation, people believed in the new state, giving it the strength the old state had lacked, because it was a new kind of state, totalitarian to the core. The sphere of law was expanding; the private sphere was becoming public; individual sensibilities were becoming political; and civic duty and function were replacing the private, individualistic basis of social relationships and law. As Panunzio put it in a particularly unattractive statement: "The law, even that involving hereditary property, is no longer understood—it should be noted well!—as pure private law, but as a civil duty and function; we are all animated instruments in that truly Beethovenian symphony which is the national life."[101]

The concept of "totalitarianism" has come under considerable attack in recent years, and justifiably so, since it has often been misused.[102] We cannot abandon the concept, however, because it is not merely a value-laden conceptual tool developed by cold-war political scientists, but a category which the Italian fascists invented and applied with pride to the novel regime they were trying to create.[103] It was an essential part of the Italian fascist self-image, even though the Italian fascist regime was never totalitarian in fact. But Italian fascism, in practice as well as in theory, was a departure beyond liberalism in the *direction* of totalitarianism. We can make sense of what totalitarianism meant to the fascists, and use the concept effectively ourselves, if we understand it not as a "system," in which components like ideology, mass party, and charismatic leader "function," but simply as a postliberal direction. To move in this direction means to extend the sphere of law, to mobilize the masses in order to "politicize" more and more of the individual's life, and ultimately to eliminate or devalue authentic politics. Only by moving in this direction did it seem possible to left fascist idealists to bring the masses into the state, to unify the nation, to instill productive values, and to create a state strong enough to pursue the collective interest. Our inquiry has indicated that the totalitarian impetus in twentieth-century European politics did not stem only from reactionary impulses, or from pathological desires for power by the leaders, or from pathological cravings for authority and submission by the led.

Nevertheless, while the syndicalists were responding to genuine problems of the Italian liberal order, their totalitarian antidote was a kind of dialectical overreaction: from atomized society to monolithic unity, from insufficient political consensus to the elimination of politics, from political alienation and anarchical individualism to a total identification of the individual with the state, from a relative dearth of productive values to a conception of the nation as an economic entity. The syndicalists dreamed of Italian society as a monolithic productive mechanism, so unified in its common economic activity that conventional politics would be superfluous: "The Nation is, today, with the problem of discipline and authority resolved, a great economic entity."[104] Olivetti, responding in 1925 to criticism by the liberal Mario Borsa, anticipated that a postpolitical mentality would emerge through fascism, with no more political opinion in the strict sense, no more political class, no more political parties.[105] In 1928 Olivetti concluded, a bit prematurely, that "the State is no longer anything but the Nation itself, ordered in its economic activities, which provides itself with self-government."[106] But while liberal politics would wither away, the syndicalists portrayed fascism as the triumph of the political in a more general sense. At the much-discussed meeting on corporativism held at Ferrara in 1932, Panunzio exulted that fascism was overcoming the old economic idea and ushering in a new era dominated by the political idea; fascism was "this profound elevation of the State, of the Political, over all of life."[107] Individuals were learning to understand themselves in terms of a public or social perspective; the formerly private citizen was becoming a public producer. And the sphere of law was expanding over new areas of social life, making the formerly private economic sphere public and political.

But the process was not establishing the basis for a genuine politics, for the syndicalists insisted on a degree of solidarity incompatible with value-based political conflict. The nation, as they understood it, was not so much a polity, with divisive but legitimate differences in social goals, as an economy, in which all participated, in some ways as equals, in the drive to maximize national production. The syndicalists sought through fascism to foster the political awareness that liberal Italy had apparently lacked, but this education merely equipped the individual to work hard for the society and to think in terms of the collective interest as he participated in making collective socioeconomic decisions. Fascism was instilling national-political values, but there was only one legitimate set of these values, valid for everyone. So fascism was not developing individuals capable of autonomous political values, nor was it establishing a meaningful political process for the resolution of the inevitable and legitimate conflicts among those values. As the syndicalists overreacted to the genuine flaws in Italian liberalism, moving toward totalitarianism, they ended up denying the presuppositions for a genuine form of politics.

Insofar as the problems the syndicalists claimed to find were real, and insofar as we take their responses to be plausible, we must judge those problems themselves to be the causes of the syndicalist response, including their contribution to fascism. But we may conclude, first, that the problems were not as serious as the syndicalists believed them to be, or second, that while the problems were that serious, more viable solutions would have been possible from within a liberal parliamentary framework. And insofar as we judge the syndicalists' response, with its totalitarian rejection of politics, to have been an overreaction, and thus an anomaly, we require further explanation. The syndicalists' reaction was unnecessarily extreme, and thus we must identify the personal and contextual admixtures that account for the excesses in their position.

In the first place, it is not unusual for fragmented societies without much political experience to have difficulty finding the consensus to establish the legitimacy of politics. In this sort of context, public authority is more likely to become the vehicle for special interests than it is in politically more mature countries. The prevalence of political particularism and corruption may lead sensitive observers to believe that politics is illegitimate altogether. In confusing political partisanship with corruption, radical critics may come to advocate the replacement of political values by purely technical ones.[108] To the extent that Italy can be understood as simply one modernizing country among others, the left fascist rejection of politics was a function of backwardness— and was not without precedent.

If we view the syndicalists and their fascist constituents as individual personalities, it is clear that they were extremists with a low tolerance for the ambiguities and conflicts of genuine politics. The syndicalists had always hated politics, which they identified with mere factional squabbling. Writing during the Matteotti crisis, Olivetti lamented that, in Italy at least, every movement with ideals that became a parliamentary political party ended up corrupting itself, denying its origins, and finally bogging down in petty factional struggles.[109] He was so intolerant of ambiguity that he inferred from the corruptibility of politics that politics was inherently corrupting and must be eliminated. The individuals who became syndicalists and left fascists had in common personal values and psychological needs, not derived directly from their socioeconomic positions, which led them to seek a degree of solidarity incompatible with genuine politics.

In addition, the syndicalists ended up overreacting to the political problems of liberal Italy partly because they shared some of the traditional lack of confidence in the political capacity of the Italians.[110] Italy could become a more healthy and productive nation, but only if she abandoned any pretense of real politics. Although these unadmitted doubts about Italian political capacities had some basis in fact, Italy's political experience had not been so different from experiences elsewhere that the attempt at democratization from within a liberal framework had to be abandoned. Largely because of cultural self-doubts, the syndicalists underestimated the extent to which the defects they saw in Italian politics could also be found elsewhere—and could be considered tolerable, if not edifying. They saw others as more disciplined, organized, and politically responsible than they were and Italians as even more deficient in these areas than they were in fact. Thus they overreacted to the genuine abuses in Italian liberal politics, gave up what appeared a futile attempt to catch up to countries with healthier liberal systems, and threw out politics altogether.

There was also a "petty bourgeois" component in the syndicalist overreaction, for their thinking betrayed a superficiality, a tendency toward rhetoric and abstraction and exaggeration, which their marginality vis-à-vis the modern industrial economy helps to explain. As we listen to them exalting the tightly knit nation of producers that was emerging, it is hard to forget that they were on the outside looking in. They stood in some awe of industrialists and the whole industrial world, and thus in part they played up the value of technical attributes at the expense of political attributes. Rossoni, for example, lauded the ambitions and capacities of the aggressive industrialist, who compared very favorably, he felt, to a mere politician.[111] At the same time, the syndicalists tended to be giddily optimistic, insisting that Italy was not inferior, but superior, that in finding a postliberal politics appropriate to her, she was pointing the way to a postliberal future for everyone. Desperately wanting to believe in their society and in themselves, but afflicted with unadmitted doubts, the syndicalists succumbed to "petty bourgeois" myths rather than engage in the more difficult, less glamorous task of building the foundations for a more viable kind of politics.

Not surprisingly, this propensity detracted from the force of the syndicalist-fascist program. Despite some realism and ingenuity, the syndicalists were too prone to exaggerated enthusiasm to understand the tensions in their program, to grasp the need for choices, to establish clear priorities. Nevertheless, their paradoxical blueprint, with its decentralizing totalitarianism, was ingenious as well as awkward, for it did respond to a set of mutually reinforcing problems. It was paradoxical partly because of the complex, contradictory quality of the chief enemy, the Italian liberal state, which was at once nonpopular, overcentralized, and weak. Fascist corporativism seemed a way to decentralize, dissolving the bureaucratic power bloc, without reviving the dangers of regionalism. Decentralization through corporativism would ultimately strengthen the still fragile Italian state by involving the formerly passive society in the state's decisions. At the same time, the syndicalists claimed to have found a way to make the state at once more coercive and more popular; the expansion of the sphere of law would go hand in hand with greater popular involvement in the state.

What was increasing was not control of the society by the old, restricted state, but self-regulation by the organized society, which was now taking on state attributes. This would be a participatory totalitarianism. And in combining spontaneity with political discipline and planning in the economic sphere, the syndicalists were proposing a way to overcome a more general modern dilemma at the same time.

Although it required a significant measure of insight for the syndicalists to devise this program, the attempt to confront these problems all at once inevitably led to clumsiness and loss of force; sharp focus on one problem necessarily meant blurred focus on another. The components were hard to fuse, but clearer thinking about the necessary choices and trade-offs would have been possible. The relationships between populism and productivism, between participation and modernization, between community and technocracy are especially problematic. It is not valid to assume that the populist thrust in fascism was inherently antiproductivist and antimodern;[112] the two impulses logically could be, and were in fact, combined in the goals of leftist fascists. But the result could only be an uneasy mixture, given Italy's uneven industrial development. In the Italian context, to seek the fuller participation of the existing people in politicized economic decision making was not the same as to seek more political power for productive sectors in order to speed economic development. The syndicalists merely glossed over this point of tension through the concept of "producer"; it was only the producers in Italy who merited fuller political roles. But insistence on this partly rhetorical category increased the danger that existing economic patterns in Italy would end up being frozen, since the category was applied so indiscriminately to those with roles in the present underdeveloped Italian economy, with all its flaws and weak spots. And in general, when the syndicalists were confronted with frustrations and tensions, they lapsed into exaggerated enthusiasm and rhetoric that kept them from facing up to the dilemmas in their conception. They simply were not as realistic as they might have been, and this damaged their effectiveness in the regime.

Like the Nationalists, then, the syndicalists ended up moving beyond liberalism toward totalitarianism, but the two groups were responding to a different set of problems, on the basis of different values and needs. The syndicalists' totalitarian departure did not stem from a mania for total control over everything, resulting from fear and an extreme psychological need for order. They longed for a tightly knit community of producers with no need for politics, but they genuinely desired autonomy, spontaneity, and real decision-making power for the socioeconomic groupings operating within this rigid framework. In a statement that combines most of the purposes we have discussed in this chapter, Olivetti insisted on the popular sovereignty that had to underlie the new Fascist state—which would be radically totalitarian:

> . . . a merely political system can stand empirically on the basis of force or contingently on the basis of an equilibrium—stable or not—of interests, while the corporative state cannot exist and function without an extensive consensus of the people. . . . A state that wants to be, and every day increasingly becomes, an *ordered and spontaneous society of producers*, implies and demands the consensus and the awareness of the producers themselves regarding their own political-economic position in the new order. In substance such a constitution cannot be artificial, bureaucratic, authoritarian: either it is natural and spontaneous or it does not exist at all. Here there is no place for the counterfeit of politics. Here the integral citizen, called to fulfill his duty as an associate in the economic nation and to exercise his right of joint ownership in the political sovereignty, must express all of himself, with all of his conviction, with all the discipline and with all the virtue of one who wants to rise from bourgeois-socialist anarchy to a higher, solidary form of civilization, within the sacred limits of the nation.[113]

Speaking at the University of Pisa in 1930, the younger fascist Giuseppe Bottai expressed in the most explicit terms the postliberal, populist totalitarianism of the left fascist vision. After insisting that corporativism was the essence of fascism, Bottai sought to explain the relationship between fascism and the great tradition of the French revolution. The revolution had been made in the name of the political aspirations and capacities of man as such; it indicated that the individual was ready to anchor himself in a state of his own. But these ideals had not been realized through the liberal parliamentary system, which perhaps had been the necessary first step—but which had frustrated those ideals at the same time. Liberalism, Bottai argued, had become an atomizing force because it portrayed the juridical order as a system of limits, to defend the individual from the state, rather than as "the form in which the life of the social man is realized, the form in which the individual celebrates his essence as social man." Now it was necessary to fulfill the original promise of the French revolution, to go beyond liberalism and create a deeper, more immediate relationship between individual and state. The individual, said Bottai, "must coincide completely" with the state: "The conclusion and the definitive fulfillment of the principles of 1789 is therefore a state in which *the whole life of the citizen is truly and completely realized, in which the citizen finds and truly composes his moral personality, in which he finds an effective and total ordering of his life.*"[114] Bottai understood fascist corporativism as a means to provide this totalitarian state based on an intensely politicized society. In overcoming the problems which liberalism had left unsolved, fascism was not repudiating, but fully implementing at last the ideas of 1789.

Despite their intolerance of politics, the syndicalists and the other left fascist idealists were genuine populists, while Nationalism was elitist to the core. This was an authentic difference of principle, not merely a difference over which social classes were to replace the exhausted liberal elite. Nor was this merely a difference between "revolution from above" and "revolution from below." Although both the Nationalists and syndicalists were seeking to create a healthier nation and a stronger state, although they agreed on the need to expand the sphere of law and "politics," they differed radically over what made a nation viable and a state strong.

Despite its tensions and weaknesses, the neosyndicalist conception provided an autonomous, populist basis for fascist corporativism and totalitarianism. So the origins of the basic thrust in fascism were more varied than the usual interpretation would have it, and the unfolding of the regime itself was much more complex than it would have been had Nationalism been the only substantial program at work. The program the syndicalists offered was capable of practical development, of influencing the direction of fascism, making it more genuinely populist than right fascists desired. To make the syndicates state entities, even to make collective labor negotiations public functions, could be vehicles of control from above, or ways of giving political attributes directly to the society. Everything depended on how the regime would develop in practice.

11 / Critics and Myth Makers, 1925–1943

During the years of the Fascist regime proper, from 1925 on, the syndicalists continued to publicize their proposals for radical change. They formed part of a wider left fascist current that worked until the fall of the regime in 1943 to give fascism a radical and populist direction, especially through corporativism. That current, needless to say, was not successful: the much-discussed corporative state never amounted to much. Yet, for two basic reasons, their efforts were quite important for the practice of the regime. First, this current was one of the forces that Mussolini sought to balance. Because the syndicalists and their colleagues goaded and criticized, institutions that seemed to provide the foundation for a corporativist alternative to parliamentary liberalism were erected. And second, because they never gave up, because they continued to insist that fascism was on its way to serious change, the syndicalists and other left fascist idealists helped to give the regime a veneer of revolutionary legitimacy that masked, to some extent, its real hollowness. In so doing, they helped the regime to stay together as well as it did; Italians of unquestionable integrity and seriousness continued to hope that fascism would amount to something. The syndicalists, then, ended up myth makers, serving the dictatorship by making it seem to others that fascism was involved in an ongoing process of revolutionary implementation.

We have seen that Mussolini sought to avoid dependence on any particular constituency, to avoid precise commitments, to keep his options open. He did not see himself as a tool of the old elites or of big business, nor could it have satisfied him, psychologically, to preside over a merely conservative, authoritarian regime. The generic radicalism in him was never entirely dead; perhaps, sporadically at least, he was even genuinely interested in the kind of change which left corporativists proposed. But his skepticism invariably got the upper hand. He doubted the new corporativist institutions would work; he did not trust the people who would have to make them work and tried to keep the developing system under tight control. The extent of his compromise with, for example, the traditional bureaucracy no doubt made him uncomfortable, but he lacked the confidence to create a new order in which he could do without it.

Still, Mussolini's fundamental ambivalence made the regime ambiguous and produced an ongoing sense of openness and potential. There continued to be room for lively discussion about corporativism and the purpose of fascism, room even for remarkably explicit criticism of the practice of the regime. It seemed that those willing to keep pushing, to publicize their vision of what fascism was to become, could influence its direction. Given all the ambiguity and uncertainty, in fact, the outcome seemed to depend on how hard and effectively one pushed, on how convincingly one argued, and on how large an audience one was able to reach.

Mussolini himself sought to convince the world that fascism was moving toward corporativism. The neosyndicalist program envisioned gradual change, not the imposition of a fully developed corporative system, and Mussolini invariably counseled patience. When the pressure built up, or when he needed to move leftward to maintain the regime's equilibrium, he talked a good game and let changes take place, changes that seemed to be leading step by step to a meaningful corporativist order. So to those involved, the corporativist push did not seem to be futile; fascism did evolve—just enough to keep alive the hopes of committed left fascists, just enough to maintain the appearance of ongoing innovation and purpose that Mussolini's system required.

It is only because matters never seemed settled that Italian business remained uneasy about fascism until the fall of the regime.[1] For example, the General Confederation of Italian Industry (*Confindustria*) opposed Rocco's syndical law of 1926, especially the magistracy of labor provision, preferring to keep labor relations a private matter. Nor did the business community welcome the launching of the National Council of Corporations in 1930, for businessmen feared that now at last they might begin to lose their autonomy and suffer political coordination. There was considerable friction between wary business organizations and Giuseppe Bottai at the Ministry of Corporations. Clearly, then, the possibility of a more serious outcome to the corporativist experiment was taken seriously at the time—even by those who were by no means sympathetic. One could never be sure of Mussolini, after all. And it was Mussolini's genius to be able to provide the illusion of dynamism necessary to sustain the efforts of committed fascists. It was never as clear to them as it is to us that the changes and new institutions added up to very little, above all because they never knew how little time they had.

In syndicalist statements after 1925, there is a three-way pattern of argument, mixing buoyant affirmation with frustration, doubt, and bitterness. At each stage in the regime's history, the syndicalists insisted that fascism was involved in the necessarily gradual process of implementing the neosyndicalist program. But they always emphasized that the process was far from complete, that the present situation could by no means be taken as fulfillment. And as they stressed this point, notes of criticism crept into their statements. Not only was the revolution only in its initial stages, but there were obstacles within fascism itself that seemed to be undermining the revolution, bogging it down.

The problem was that for the syndicalists to maintain their license to criticize and push, they had to make compromises that served to justify the regime as it was. This was true especially of their glorification of the Duce and his essential role in fascism, although such ritualistic praise had more positive purposes as well.[2] The syndicalists' personal positions depended to some extent on Mussolini's favors. For example, when Olivetti complained of financial difficulties to Mussolini, whom he had known by then for twenty-five years, he was soon made a full professor at Sergio Panunzio's Fascist Faculty of Political Science at the University of Perugia.[3] Olivetti could assume a position at this rank because of a special law waiving certain requirements for appointment to the Perugia faculty. Lanzillo approached Mussolini several times in search of personal favors—in an unsuccessful attempt to launch his own periodical, for example, and in quest of more favorable academic employment.[4] While teaching at Cagliari in Sardinia in 1934, he wrote complaining of "exile" and asked Mussolini for the help of the Ministry of National Education in securing a position then open at the Istituto Superiore di Scienze Economiche e Commerciali at Venice. The ensuing chain of events is unclear, but Lanzillo soon won appointment to the Institute's faculty and ended up its rector on the eve of World War II.

By lauding Mussolini in public, the syndicalists hoped not only to stay on his good side, but also to play up their own kinship with him and thus to influence his policies. They praised him because, as they represented the situation, he was spearheading precisely the revolution they were advocating.[5] Moreover, they glorified the Duce because, for better or for worse, he seemed the best available cutting edge for radical change, especially once the strength of the obstacles to serious innovation had become clear after 1925.[6] If fascism was to have any chance of overcoming the resistance of the old bureaucracy, a powerful position for Mussolini no doubt really was necessary. To place one's hopes on Mussolini was a gamble, but it was not clear there was any alternative.

Glorification of the Duce, then, was not exclusively a compromise enabling the syndicalists to continue prodding, but it was mostly that. And the compromising did not stop there. During the 1930s, Panunzio, especially, sometimes constructed sweeping syntheses having a place for all aspects of Mussolini's haphazard regime. In his *Teoria generale dello Stato fascista*, based on his course at the University of Rome and intended as a textbook of fascism for classroom use, Panunzio devised a precise, legalistic outline of the existing Fascist state, giving the whole chaotic hodgepodge a veneer of logical order and purpose. He talked about the role of the army, for example, and insisted that fascism was, and could only be, monarchical. By 1939 attempts were afoot to interject certain features of German Nazism into Italian fascism, and Panunzio also found a place in his synthesis for anti-Semitism, linking the Jews to Bolshevism and the international counterrevolutionary conspiracy against fascism.[7] Without trying to justify this, the seediest of Panunzio's compromises, we should note that he went out of his way to contrast the Italian fascist and German Nazi positions on race. For fascism, he explained, the nation was ultimately an autonomous historical product, not reducible to race. This meant that Jews, for example, could be assimilated into the Italian nation. In explicitly disavowing the biological racism of the Nazis, Panunzio clearly was taking an antiextremist position in context. And despite these elements of compromise, Panunzio continued until the fall of the regime to devote much the greater part of his efforts to working for a popular corporativist order.

Two significant implications for practice in the syndicalist-fascist blueprint affected the syndicalists' ability to criticize. Despite all their rhetoric about the real nation overcoming the antinational state, the syndicalists recognized that the process of political maturation in society was not complete. The masses, including the socialist workers, were not ready to have the state turned over to them immediately; rather, they were ready to be educated, ready for the process of change that would gradually make them fuller participants in the national life. So the syndicalists and their colleagues always insisted that revolutionary implementation would have to be a gradual process, with the organized society taking on more and more serious public functions as political education and maturation proceeded.[8] Implementation would have to be gradual partly because experiment and trial and error were necessary to determine the most effective set of institutional relationships.[9] The syndicalists claimed that this respect for a sometimes-incalculable reality was one measure of fascism's superiority to the Soviet system, with its reliance on abstract schemas. But their plausible belief in gradual implementation affected their perceptions of the Fascist regime and helped to soften their criticism. Since a full-blown corporative state could not be established all at once, present inadequacies did not necessarily mean that the system could never be made to develop in a meaningful way. Each imperfect measure was only a step in a gradual process, which would overcome the imperfections sooner or later.

Moreover, since the masses still required political education, there was room for some degree of interference with the unions and corporations from the top—by the state and especially by the Fascist party. The syndicalists, in emphasizing the central place of corporativism in fascism, were not seeking to downplay the role of the party. The economic organizations and the party were not rivals, but had complementary roles. As we saw in chapter eight, the party leader Augusto Turati and the corporativist advocate Giuseppe Bottai essentially shared this view. The party in the syndicalist-fascist conception was the elite, the conscious vanguard, with the major responsibility for implementing the revolution; it was up to the party to inspire the new socioeconomic organizations with fascist principles.[10] At a time of frustration in 1933, the union leader Luigi Razza called for more intimate links between the party and these organizations as a way of stimulating the disappointing corporative system.[11]

The fact that the people still had to be raised to political consciousness by the elite meant that, for now at least, the Nationalists and syndicalists had something else in common beyond the perceptions discussed in the preceding chapter. In the short term, the elitist control of the organized society from the top that the Nationalists expected to be permanent partly converged with the mobilization by the new elite that the syndicalists saw as a temporary phase of revolutionary implementation. So some of the patterns of the practice of the regime could satisfy both, but the deeper differences were never far beneath the surface. In a revealing statement in 1927, Panunzio calmly admitted that the current emphasis on authority, centralization, and discipline in fascism was excessive, a dialectical overreaction, but he reassured his readers that any present authoritarianism was by no means the final goal of fascism, but only a phase, "a means for the better education of man to liberty."[12]

Although revolutionary implementation required a phase of elitist manipulation, left fascist idealists understood the fascist elite to be an open one. The party was to universalize its values and raise the whole society to its level, and as it completed this task, a new democracy would emerge. For Olivetti, the party was a new aristocracy, but one completely open to the young generation of fascists as they reached political maturity.[13] He looked forward to the day when the party, having fulfilled its mission and become universal, would no longer be necessary. In the same way, Panunzio pointed out that the Fascist state of 1925 was a party state only because fascism had not yet realized its universal principles; the party was simply the instrument for their realization.[14] Later, as it became increasingly clear that the party was not likely to wither away, Panunzio assigned the party a permanent, but no longer elitist, role. Even after fascist values had been universalized, the party would remain as a kind of populist "church," a source of structure and sociality to the individual's experience, a focus of common feeling in the new totalitarian order.[15] So the party as an organization would still be useful, but totalitarian fulfillment would mean homogeneity, not a permanent cleft between the elite and the masses.

It was questionable, to say the least, whether the Fascist party was fit to raise the rest of the society to a higher level of political consciousness. The Fascist movement had fallen heir to some of the idealism bound up with the war experience, and certainly Augusto Turati, party leader from 1926 to 1930, understood the party's role in the dynamic, revolutionary way that the syndicalist blueprint for fascism required. By the early 1930s, however, it was hard to ignore the fact that this idealism had become considerably diluted. The party was becoming a vehicle for place-seeking and petty squabbling as it lost power in the regime to Mussolini and the old state apparatus, including such collaborators as Arturo Bocchini, the chief of the secret police. Bocchini was an authoritarian bureaucrat, not a totalitarian idealist associated with the party. The decline in vigor and commitment in the party was especially obvious after December 1931, when Achille Starace became party secretary. But already at the beginning of 1931, Olivetti warned that the party, despite its potentially fruitful role, might become a mere oligarchy existing as an end in itself, without its original idealism.[16] He feared especially that the party was not really instilling new values into the economic organizations but undermining their autonomy for narrow, partisan reasons. If the party lost its revolutionary capacity, and especially if it began to compromise the corporativist essence of fascism, it would have to be eliminated altogether. The severe tone of Olivetti's warning leaves no doubt that he found these dangers only too real.

Such criticisms of fascism in practice, however, did not have to wait until 1931, nor was the party the only source of frustration. Fascism did move decisively beyond liberalism beginning in 1925, and sometimes in the corporativist direction which the syndicalists desired. But it continued to be a struggle. There was occasionally dissension among the syndicalists themselves. The first case involved Agostino Lanzillo, who began to fall out with the others as soon as revolutionary implementation began in 1925. Although he favored a neosyndicalist political system, Lanzillo disliked some of the more coercive features of the program which Panunzio and Olivetti advocated, especially the labor magistracy and the attendant elimination of the right to strike. As a member of the Commission of Eighteen, Lanzillo did not favor the majority proposal, which Olivetti had a major hand in shaping. Reporting on the commission's labors while they were still in progress, Olivetti claimed that Lanzillo's opposition stemmed from a rigidly Sorelian, revolutionary syndicalist perspective.[17] Olivetti's son Ezio Maria, praising the commission's contribution to fascist corporativism in a book published in 1927, contended that Lanzillo had by then become completely isolated from the neosyndicalist mainstream.[18] As a member of the commission, Lanzillo had been too "individualistic," too much the classic revolutionary syndicalist for the younger Olivetti's taste.

These accusations were considerably exaggerated, since Lanzillo had played a major part in the syndicalists' evolution away from their original revolutionary orthodoxy. But while he accepted the essentials of the syndicalist-fascist blueprint, and while he considered himself a good fascist, there were some differences of emphasis, and Lanzillo was not as influential as the other syndicalists within fascism after 1926. Of all the syndicalists, Lanzillo had the deepest reservations about Rocco's syndical law of April 1926, which he criticized sharply in the Chamber debate which preceded its passage.[19] His statement expressed very clearly the neosyndicalist vision he shared with the others, but he wondered aloud whether the Fascist economic organizations could ever have the autonomy and spontaneity they needed to reach maturity from within Rocco's framework, especially given Rocco's own coercive purposes. No wonder the Nationalists had been so opposed, though to no avail, when Lanzillo had been named to the original Commission of Fifteen in 1924.[20] The other syndicalists also had misgivings about the Rocco law, but most would be more circumspect and would continue the struggle more covertly. And Lanzillo, despite his doubts and diminished influence, continued to publicize the syndicalist-fascist conception throughout the years of the regime.

The other syndicalist who expressed explicitly his misgivings about the Rocco law was Edmondo Rossoni, who worried that the law could lead to excessive state interference in the functioning of the Fascist unions. In 1926 he warned—rather starkly—that a lasting new regime based on neosyndicalism could not be created with the mentality and the methods of the police, and when ensuing experience seemed to confirm his fears, he called again and again for more freedom for the Fascist economic organizations.[21] He also complained about the unequal treatment for business and labor implied in the syndical law, which did not subject business organizations to the same state regulation as it did the workers' syndicates.[22] Rossoni himself had been seeking to ensure equality of treatment—and to begin the evolution toward a fuller form of corporativism—by forcing the employers into Fascist organizations too. When Italian businessmen fought strenuously—and ultimately successfully—against this attempt at fascist coordination, Rossoni attacked them with surprising openness and bitterness. He insisted repeatedly that fascism's most urgent task was to subject the employers to fascist discipline, for the business mentality had not been transformed the way the labor mentality had; obviously mere party membership and vague formulas about class collaboration and the national interest were not enough. The stakes were clear: "If we hesitate or compromise in disciplining those in the upper levels of production, how will we be able for long to ward off the accusation of having adopted a double standard and of having constituted tame organizations in the service of the employers?"[23]

Once Rocco's bill became law in April of 1926, Rossoni admitted temporary defeat in his efforts to subject businessmen to fascist discipline.[24] Despite a good deal of bitterness, however, he anticipated that sooner or later, given the logic of its revolutionary conception, fascism would bring the employers under the same kind of coordination as the workers. Rossoni's optimism in the wake of defeat was a bit forced, but fascism had a way of conciliating its losers and leaving the future apparently open. And the next corporativist measures did what they were largely designed to do: persuade Rossoni and his colleagues that the game was not over. The Ministry of Corporations was established in July 1926, and Giuseppe Bottai quickly emerged as its leading figure, first as undersecretary from 1926 until 1929, then as minister until July 1932, when he was removed as part of a general reshuffling of the governmental leadership. For now, Rossoni argued, the new ministry would provide a measure of the coordination between business associations and the organizations of workers and technical employees that he had been seeking; it could pave the way for a system of genuine corporations in the future.[25]

Rossoni could point to the new ministry to minimize his defeat, but he was hardly satisfied, and it was partly because of his grumbling that Mussolini thought of promulgating a labor charter. The circumstances surrounding the drafting of the Labor Charter of 1927, and the document itself, epitomize the ambiguous compromise of the Fascist regime, especially with respect to corporativism.[26] Mussolini envisioned

the charter as a way to pacify discontents in the Fascist union movement, and, more broadly, to reassure fascist idealists, although he
wanted a document that would not seriously antagonize business.
Bottai was given the first chance to draft the document; Mussolini even
wrote to him on 3 March 1927 to recommend an article by Olivetti,
published in *Il popolo d'Italia* the day before, which called for a charter
of concrete, practical commitments, without rhetorical generalities.[27]
Mussolini seemed to be serious. The industrialists, of course, favored a
different direction for the charter than left fascists like Bottai and
Rossoni, and when Bottai proved unable to resolve the differences,
Mussolini asked Alfredo Rocco to work out a compromise. But Rocco,
in attempting to define the fascist position on private property, went
too far to the right for Mussolini, who was apparently responsible for
the significant changes in the final draft. Since Mussolini was seeking
to reestablish his flexibility, he did not want to commit himself to a
position so clearly conservative and probusiness as the one Rocco had
outlined. The Grand Council of Fascism approved the final version in
April 1927, along with a resolution calling on the government to begin
immediately to develop a program of legislation to implement its
principles, from state enforcement of collective labor contracts to the
corporative organization of the state.[28]

The document itself was an awkward conglomeration of abstract
and concrete, of radical- and conservative-sounding statements.[29] It
stressed the social responsibility of labor and capital, the significance of
the juridical recognition of the syndicates, the sociopolitical import of
collective labor contracts, and the possibility of coordinating the economy through the economic groupings and the Ministry of Corporations.
While it certainly did not commit fascism to a fully developed corporative state, the Labor Charter did help to reassure serious corporativists
that the fascist revolution was just starting—and that Mussolini was
on their side. In the article which Mussolini recommended to Bottai,
Olivetti had portrayed the charter as a foundation for the more concrete
corporativist measures to follow and had stressed that Mussolini obviously understood the document in the same light.[30] Panunzio, writing
shortly after the charter was promulgated, linked it to the neosyndicalist tradition and found it "saturated with the creative will of Benito
Mussolini."[31] The Labor Charter, and the measures of 1925–27 in
general, were evidence that fascism was revolutionary after all; those
who had seen fascism as merely reinforcing the old order, and who
had laughed at the fascist revolutionaries as the heretics of the movement, were now being proven wrong. In times of frustration later on,
the syndicalists referred back to the Labor Charter, portraying it as the
foundation for ongoing development, as they continued their efforts to

push and shape—and sought to reassure themselves at the same time.[32]

By interpreting the Labor Charter and Mussolini's intentions in this light, the syndicalists were able to maintain or raise expectations and thereby to keep up the pressure. And change did continue, on a piecemeal basis, with every new institution giving the syndicalists the chance to proclaim, once again, that Mussolini was leading fascism in the desired direction. Discussion of corporativist issues remained open and lively, and the syndicalists continued to have no difficulty reaching an audience. They were able to publish explicit criticisms even in the quasi-official organs of the regime, *Il popolo d'Italia* and *Gerarchia*. Olivetti no doubt felt encouraged when Mussolini wrote him a warm personal letter in 1927 to praise Ezio Maria Olivetti's book on fascist corporativism.[33] In his famous article on fascist doctrine, written for the *Enciclopedia Italiana* of 1932 but also published separately in newspapers and as a book, Mussolini enhanced the syndicalists' pedigree by lauding the contributions that Olivetti's *Pagine libere*, Orano's *La lupa*, and Leone's *Divenire sociale* had made to the renewal in Italy that had culminated in fascism.[34] The considerable and quasi-official hagiography that developed around Filippo Corridoni also increased the syndicalists' prestige, for they could plausibly claim to bear the legacy of their late colleague.[35]

Mussolini consistently portrayed the fascist revolution as an ongoing process that was by no means complete. When Olivetti, in February 1928, was preparing a lecture on corporativism to be given at the Center for Fascist Studies at Lausanne the next month, he sent his comments to Mussolini beforehand, hoping to influence him. In his reply, Mussolini referred especially to the reform of the Chamber of Deputies which was about to be implemented, giving the Fascist economic organizations a modest, indirect voice in selecting the deputies. His letter shows how encouraging he could be:

I read with great interest your remarks on the corporations. The truth is as you have indicated: we do not yet have a corporative regime; we are still in the syndical phase. But I would add that the syndical phase is, in my opinion, the necessary entrance way for the truly corporative phase. . . . I remind you of my earlier statement regarding national political representation and the reform solution, which is not definitive, even though it is, in my opinion, notable as a departure and as a mechanism. Still, when we remember that this gigantic task of ordering all the activities of a great nation has been achieved in two years, we must recognize, with some pride, that the fact is without precedent in world history. Let me say, finally, that the improvements that you indicate in the last part of your study should not have to wait long to be implemented.[36]

In his lecture at Lausanne, Olivetti served as an effective propagandist, citing the Labor Charter and recent speeches by Mussolini as evidence that fascism was firmly committed to corporativism. And naturally he went on to emphasize that implementation had to proceed gradually and that fascism was still in its preliminary syndical stage.[37]

Meanwhile, Panunzio had convinced Mussolini that fascism needed an academy of its own—to develop fascist doctrine and to teach fascist principles to those who would administer the new fascist state. The two began to discuss the idea during the summer of 1925, not long after Panunzio had called for the more formal elaboration of fascist doctrine at the meeting on fascist culture in Bologna the previous March.[38] Around the end of the year, Panunzio presented a proposal to Mussolini, and the outcome was the Fascist Faculty of Political Science, attached to the University of Perugia. Legally authorized in 1927, it began to function in March 1928, with Panunzio as its director. To staff the faculty, Panunzio gradually assembled an important group of fascist publicists and scholars, including the syndicalists Orano and Olivetti, the Nationalists Maraviglia and Coppola, the renowned social scientist and one-time syndicalist Robert Michels, and able younger scholars such as Carlo Curcio, Giuseppe Chiarelli, and Vincenzo Zangara. According to Curcio, Panunzio himself held together this heterogeneous faculty and gave it direction. Both Curcio and Panunzio's son, Vito, have stressed how serious Panunzio was about the new institution and the role it could play in the regime.[39] Writing in January 1925, just as fascism seemed to be committing itself to radical change, Panunzio had emphasized the primacy of the party over the Fascist government in revolutionary implementation.[40] Since the government had to be concerned primarily with the day-to-day operation of the state, its perspective was bound to be limited and the scope of its activities circumscribed. Panunzio was implicitly acknowledging that Mussolini's government still rested to an important degree on compromise with the old order. It fell to others to focus on the long-term tasks of education and doctrinal development that were essential if a new order was to be created. Panunzio had a point: if fascism was serious about revolutionary implementation, there were crucial tasks—and powerful roles—outside the sphere of immediate governmental decision making. His faculty was something new and special when it began, and it seemed to have the support of the fascist political leadership. Augusto Turati gave the featured speech, dealing with the complementary roles of party and syndicates, during ceremonies closing the first term in June 1928, and Panunzio presented the members of the faculty to Mussolini at a reception the next month.[41]

In an interview with *Il popolo d'Italia* just before the first session began, Panunzio outlined the double mandate which he felt that he and his colleagues had from Mussolini. On the most immediate level, "this Faculty will be, by the will of the Duce, an organ, even the Seminary, of the Regime," offering a sound fascist education to those preparing for positions in the Fascist state: "The Faculty that is emerging responds to a very serious need of the Regime. Fascism . . . requires that its doctrine and its political, economic, and juridical institutions be the object of rigorous study on the part of young people embarking on administrative, syndical-corporative, diplomatic, and colonial careers."[42] If fascism was to assume full control of the Italian state, it did require a way of training a new bureaucratic elite that would be both technically competent and politically committed. Traditionally, the faculties of law had trained the upper bureaucracy in Italy, but they could hardly be relied upon for the present task, even if those comprising them were nominally fascists. For one thing, their curriculum was too old-fashioned and did not consider sufficiently the modern realities—involving syndical development, for example—that especially concerned fascism.[43] Moreover, when established scholars discussed fascist innovations in such areas as syndical law, they often did so from what seemed to committed fascists to be a dangerously detached point of view. Writing in 1927, Panunzio inveighed against "old entrenched professors and scholars, stuck in the old formulas and the old system, who do not feel and follow our movement, and who observe it, more or less skeptically and distrustfully, from the outside." It was up to committed believers to examine fascist legislation, in an atmosphere of revolutionary enthusiasm; "only they can read the books on fascist syndicalism in order to translate them into action, as opposed to subjecting them to scholarly criticism."[44] Like Panunzio, A. O. Olivetti played a major part in attempts to make Italian higher education more genuinely fascist during the later 1920s.[45]

Through his Fascist faculty, then, Panunzio was seeking both to develop a system of education relevant to the tasks that fascism intended to tackle and to undercut the role of the old, hide-bound university establishment in training civil servants. It was Panunzio's understanding in 1928 that Mussolini would guarantee graduates of the new Fascist faculty at least equal access to government jobs. Finally, in 1932, with new Fascist political faculties established elsewhere as well, he managed to get Mussolini to advise the ministers that, in their hiring, they were no longer to insist on the traditional juridical training. Ultimately, as a result of Panunzio's efforts, graduates of the new political faculties were able to compete equally in most branches of the administration.[46] This was a breach in the armor of the traditional bureaucracy, which constituted one of the major obstacles to serious fascist innovation. At the same time, Panunzio called on the state to provide the student financial aid necessary to insure that these careers were open to talent. For access to such careers to be a function of wealth would be fundamentally antithetical to fascist principles.[47]

To fulfill its educational mission, the faculty offered courses on syndical and corporativist doctrine and law, on the history and doctrine of fascism, on diplomacy and diplomatic history, on the history of economic and political doctrines, and on similar subjects of particular concern for fascism. The courses were passed around from one faculty member to another, although Coppola, for example, continued to specialize in international relations, while Michels focused on the history of economic doctrines, giving ample attention to fascism's Labor Charter and corporative system.[48]

To provide the kind of training Panunzio envisioned, the new faculty would have to assume a broader role as well and work to elaborate and propagate fascist doctrine.[49] If fascism was to be a revolutionary movement worthy of the name, Panunzio insisted, it needed a doctrine of its own, one that could seriously claim to challenge liberalism and communism. Even in 1928, this task still seemed to him to be open, but it could no longer wait, since the regime was beginning to develop specifically fascist institutions. So the new faculty could not simply educate; it also had to determine what needed to be taught. The faculty's teaching would, of course, seek to inspire enthusiasm and faith in the superiority of fascism; Panunzio stressed this point in a memorandum to the faculty in 1930.[50] Still, Panunzio had no illusions that revolutionary fervor—or, for that matter, activism or intuition— afforded a substitute for serious doctrinal development, based on careful study and hard intellectual work. And by doctrine, he insisted that he intended not abstract theories, but concrete principles that could guide the formation and functioning of new Fascist institutions. To influence subsequent practice, it was necessary to study the situation, to define what needed to be done, and to prepare people to do it.

As its major doctrinal endeavor, the faculty sponsored a series of books, the *Collana di studi fascisti*, dealing with the principles and program of fascism. Twelve titles were published in all, including important works by Panunzio, Michels, Curcio, and Chiarelli. They constitute a significant collection, but the series fell short of Panunzio's initial hopes. In a report to Mussolini on the faculty in January 1934, Panunzio found the *Collana* promising, but he admitted that it had scarcely begun to fulfill its objective of establishing and publicizing a definitive fascist doctrine.[51] Nine of the books had already been published by this time, however, so the impetus behind the endeavor was obviously waning, despite Panunzio's predictably optimistic assertion that it was still in its initial stages.

Syndicalists and Nationalists could coexist at Perugia partly because the syndicalists, for reasons of their own, overplayed the prewar convergence of the two movements and even depicted the Nationalists, especially Rocco and Corradini, as convinced syndicalists.[52] No doubt the syndicalists needed, psychologically, to minimize the differences that still separated them from the Nationalists; it was hard to admit how deeply fascism was divided against itself. But they were also seeking to enhance their own influence. If, as the syndicalists claimed, a symbiosis between Nationalism and syndicalism lay at the root of fascism, with Nationalism responsible for the fascist emphasis on state sovereignty, and syndicalism responsible for the fascist conception of the new social content of the state, then it was the syndicalists who were most qualified to influence the most important decisions still to be made, for these concerned the role of the syndicates and corporations. By admitting the great contribution of Nationalism to fascism, and by stressing that they themselves were the source of the syndicalist elements even in Nationalism, the syndicalists could claim a kind of hegemony over the areas of policy development that seemed most important for the future. Panunzio endorsed changes in the form and exercise of executive power which the Nationalists had spearheaded; he was admitting the Nationalists' leadership in matters which preoccupied them but which he considered secondary.[53] Despite the collaboration at Perugia, Panunzio continued to insist that syndicalism, not Nationalism, had made the most significant contribution to fascism, by showing how to unify state and society.[54]

Seeking to present syndicalism as the heart of fascism, the syndicalists adopted another device as well and began to overemphasize the place of Georges Sorel— and sometimes even Henri Bergson—in their tradition. This not only seemed to enhance their intellectual pedigree, but also enabled them to claim a more intimate kinship with Mussolini, whose intellectual debt to these Frenchmen they emphasized at the same time.[55] They were trying to convince the fascist public—and no doubt Mussolini as well—that whatever the necessity of short-term compromises, Mussolini was essentially one of them. But while the syndicalists were willing to manipulate the facts of their own past, they did not play down their subversive backgrounds. They referred frequently to the revolutionary syndicalist tradition, seeking to explain its connection with fascism. Even in 1936, thirty-three years after he had first encountered the work, Panunzio quoted at length from Sorel's *Avenir socialiste des syndicats* in an article in the official review *Gerarchia*, as he sought to recall the Fascist unions to their educational mission.[56]

Meanwhile there continued to be innovations in practice. The syndicalists repeatedly called for a new system of political representation, based on economic organizations, and finally, late in 1927, fascism committed itself to a fundamental reform of the Chamber of Deputies. The ensuing law of May 1928 did not create the kind of procedure the syndicalists had called for, but it seemed a significant step in that direction.[57] The economic organizations in society were not to elect representatives directly, but were to offer a list of candidates, from which the Fascist Grand Council would designate those to be proposed, in a bloc, to the electorate for ratification. At this point even some committed corporativists doubted that full-scale corporative representation would be a good idea, given the present balance of forces in the country, and given the questionable role that Edmondo Rossoni seemed to envision for his union confederation. Because of these misgivings, there was considerable agreement when the Grand Council declared that the Fascist economic organizations were mature enough only for the first step toward full-fledged corporative representation. It was still necessary for the Grand Council itself to make certain that the candidates proposed were committed fascists with a sure national consciousness. But the Grand Council was careful to emphasize that "this does not exclude the possibility that, as the syndical organizations are consolidated and perfected, a typically and exclusively fascist form of national corporative representation could be achieved, after the next legislature has had a trial."[58]

When Olivetti discussed the electoral law in his speech at Lausanne in March 1928, he admitted that the new system was hardly optimal. But for now, he insisted, it was the best that could be expected, for fascism had to "exercise control over syndical electoral participation, which especially at first could . . . commit errors that would affect the entire policy of the regime; and the regime, in assuming the weighty responsibility for a transformation of the system of representation, clearly has the right to be sure that this transformation is achieved in a normal, orderly way and in a way that is consistent with the supreme interests of the nation."[59] Olivetti justified the role of the Fascist Grand Council in the process by stressing, once again, that the Fascist party was "the active elite of the entire fascist nation," but he insisted that the present arrangement was only provisional and that a full-fledged corporative assembly would not be long in coming. The pattern was typical: Olivetti could find enough in the new system to warrant continued efforts to push and shape, but only by justifying present imperfections and by giving present realities a gloss of revolutionary meaning they merited less and less.

There was a place in the syndicalist blueprint for party interference and even for the new Ministry of Corporations to play a key role of coordination, at least until real corporations were instituted. In light of practice, however, the syndicalists developed misgivings about the party, about the Ministry of Corporations, and, surprisingly, even about the Fascist syndical confederation. The rivalries that had developed by the late 1920s among Rossoni's union movement, Turati's party, and Bottai's Ministry of Corporations were a serious source of weakness for left fascism. Some friction was inevitable, given the personal ambitions involved and given the sensitive short-term relationships among the three entities which the theory itself envisioned. The inadequacies of corporative development in practice only intensified hostilities; all three of the leaders, at least, genuinely wanted to move in the same direction, but each blamed the others for present problems.

By 1928 Rossoni was faced with a varied array of adversaries, including not only leaders from business, the party, and the Ministry of Corporations, but also major neosyndicalist publicists like Olivetti and Panunzio and union leaders like Mario Racheli. Even to these old syndicalist colleagues, Rossoni seemed too prone to personal ambition, too concerned with preserving the autonomy of his confederation for its own sake, and too willing to play on old class antagonisms. Panunzio disagreed publicly with Rossoni's negative assessment of the 1926 syndical law, while Olivetti complained that Rossoni's confederation concentrated power excessively and preserved too much traditional class dualism.[60] Thus Olivetti was calling by early 1928 for Rossoni's class-based confederation to be broken down to make way for truly corporativist organization linking all those involved in a given economic sector. Mario Racheli wrote to Olivetti in December 1927, noting that the present labor and employer organizations were organized along traditional class lines and would have to be replaced by organizations based on economic category if a meaningful corporative state was ever to be created.[61]

The controversy over Rossoni and his confederation stemmed in part from personal rivalries, but plausible differences in strategic emphasis were involved as well. Rossoni still hoped to impose the collective interest in the economy by subjecting the employers to fascist discipline, and he genuinely wanted to enhance the role of labor in economic decision making.[62] However, he was also beginning to draw a distinction between the economic and political spheres, one that was incompatible with the syndicalist-fascist program but that did promise to enhance his personal position. Although he favored corporative representation, Rossoni portrayed the political and economic spheres not as a convergent, but as parallel.[63] This meant that Mussolini and his party were to be dominant in the political sphere, with Rossoni and his confederation dominant in the economic sphere. While fascist-style political unity in Italy had already been achieved, Rossoni claimed, a comparable measure of unity in the economic sphere still had to be created, through his organizational network. Seeking to counter charges of untoward personal ambition, Rossoni modestly insisted that the head of the vast confederation of the entire economy could only be Mussolini himself.[64] But such a concentration of power in the economic sphere would have made Rossoni a brilliant second, even a *piccolo Duce*, precisely what his adversaries claimed he was seeking to become. The other neosyndicalists, including union leaders like Razza and Racheli, as well as younger fascists like Turati and Bottai, had a more integral conception of fascism, requiring a symbiotic relationship between the party and the economic organizations, between the political and the economic spheres.

Rossoni's opponents finally prevailed in November of 1928, when he was ousted and his confederation broken up into six smaller syndical groupings based on economic sector.[65] This outcome has generally been judged a defeat for the radical or leftist elements in fascism, because it is assumed that the "leftist" course was to seek to maintain working-class autonomy. Rossoni's large and relatively powerful confederation had served to some extent to protect the immediate economic interests of the workers and to preserve their class consciousness. And certainly businessmen hostile to this confederation helped to bring about its fragmentation, or *sbloccamento*. But if we view the situation in this light, we cannot understand why party and corporativist leaders, as well as many of Rossoni's old syndicalist colleagues, worked for the *sbloccamento* as well. Opposition to Rossoni did not prevent Olivetti and Bottai, for example, from criticizing the narrow class mentality which they found still characteristic of too many employers.[66] As it turned out, of course, the *sbloccamento* was bad for labor and in some ways good for business, but the measure was consistent with the serious corporative evolution that some of Rossoni's opponents were seeking; the radical change they envisioned did not require the preservation of labor's autonomy and class consciousness. So the *sbloccamento* of 1928 was not the end of the national syndicalist current in fascism, any more than was the compromise of 1921, or the Palazzo Chigi Pact of 1923, or the Rocco law of 1926. The import of the change depended on what would happen subsequently, whether meaningful organization of the society by economic sector was to be forthcoming or not. And discussion of what should be done next began immediately in the wake of the *sbloccamento* and led to the institution of the National Council of Corporations in 1930.

For the moment, however, much depended on the functioning of the Ministry of Corporations, which had become Giuseppe Bottai's institutional base almost immediately after it was established in 1926. The new ministry found itself frequently involved in jurisdictional conflicts with the older, traditional ministries, especially the Ministry of National Economy. These representatives of the old bureaucracy took a dim view of genuine corporativism and thus played down the competence of the Ministry of Corporations, seeking to restrict it to syndical matters. At the same time, the new ministry itself turned into another preserve of traditional bureaucratic elements, despite Bottai's committed leadership and despite its allegedly revolutionary import. Thus an institution that was supposed to foster serious innovation became its obstacle, as new forms only masked the absence of real change and the depth of the compromise between fascism and the old elites.[67]

Serious corporativists quickly began to complain of bureaucratic interference with the network of Fascist economic organizations—and would continue to do so until the fall of the regime. Olivetti warned again and again that the Fascist unions had to be more active and dynamic—in negotiations for collective labor contracts, for example—if their members were to believe in them.[68] The party leader Augusto Turati wrote to Mussolini in January 1930 to complain of the complicated bureaucratic apparatus that, he said, was suffocating fascism's network of economic organizations.[69] Turati proposed that major functions of the Ministry of Corporations be taken over by the local representatives of his own Fascist party. Anticipating objections that he was seeking to enhance the position of the party at the expense of other institutions, Turati insisted that he wanted only to reduce the number of bureaucratic place-seekers, to streamline the system, and thereby to enable fascist corporativism to develop in a healthier way.

The rivalry that was developing between Turati's party and Bottai's ministry stemmed from genuine dilemmas and plausible differences in perception, not simply from a self-serving competition for power. Turati and Bottai were both frustrated with the evolution of the corporative system in practice, but Turati blamed interference from the ministry, while Bottai blamed interference from the party. They were both right, for neither the party nor the ministry was the supple, dynamic instrument of revolutionary implementation which the syndicalist-fascist conception required. At the same time, Bottai continued to find a major role for the party, while Turati continued to view corporativism as the key to the new order which the party was trying to create.[70] From the beginning of his tenure as party secretary in 1926, Turati worked to make the party more active and influential on the syndical level, seeking, for example, to develop intersyndical committees as nuclei for subsequent corporations.[71] More generally, he wanted the party to become more active in the political education of the unions. The workers, he was quite willing to admit, did not yet believe in fascism, and this he found a major source of weakness, damaging, for example, the regime's chances of imposing political coordination on business.

Although the syndicalists by the early 1930s had serious misgivings about interference from both the party and the ministry, their conception still specified that the corporative order could not emerge in an entirely spontaneous way. So they sought to distinguish between legitimate and excessive forms of supervision. Olivetti's attempt in 1931 to strike a balance between elitist control from the top and spontaneous development was awkward, to say the least. After stressing the Fascist state's educational role, he cautioned that "the formative process of the corporations cannot be rushed, nor can it be completely external. The state *cannot make* the corporations, just as the midwife does not *make* the newborn child. They must make themselves on their own, but the state must not watch their development passively, because it is not a liberal state, but a corporative state in the making."[72]

The equivocation in Olivetti's statement indicates the unresolved dilemmas of revolutionary practice in the context of fascist Italy. Implementing the syndicalist-fascist conception required that a very fine line be drawn between elitist control and popular spontaneity. The masses were capable of being educated and raised to the level of the elite, but only through participation in living organizations that had serious decisions to make. On the other hand, the organizations could not be allowed freedom and power until the process of education was well advanced. So there was a danger that corporativism would enable the people merely to go through the motions of participation—and leave them in a state of permanent political inferiority. The inadequacies of the two major candidates for revolutionary leadership before 1930—the party and the Ministry of Corporations—complicated this dilemma immeasurably. The syndicalists called incessantly for the Fascist economic organizations to be allowed more spontaneity and more serious functions. But there was also continued equivocation in their statements about the relative importance of state intervention and spontaneity, elite manipulation and the natural pedagogical qualities of organization.

Despite its novelty, the Ministry of Corporations was an entity in the traditional bureaucratic mold. However, the 1926 law which established the ministry had also authorized a National Council of Corporations, to have a modest consultative role, although such an entity had not been set up by 1929. Corporativists now began to call for the National Council to be instituted, with functions far exceeding those envisioned in the 1926 law, as the way to move toward real corporativism in the wake of the Labor Charter of 1927 and the reorganization of the Fascist union movement of 1928.[73] Bottai proposed a corporative council with serious deliberative functions to the Grand Council in April 1929, while the syndicalists, in the subsequent Chamber debate and in the press, played up the revolutionary implications of the proposed institution.[74] When Mussolini keynoted the inaugural meeting of the National Council, on 21 April 1930, he too emphasized its revolutionary significance.[75] His speech naturally drew raves from the syndicalists, who stressed its commitment to continuing corporative development. Mussolini's ingratiating tone reassured them that he had been on their side all along, and the advent of the new institution seemed to indicate that the corporative state would now begin to develop in earnest.[76]

The National Council of Corporations seemed a major step toward real corporativism because it was composed of sections—seven in all—corresponding to the major branches of the economy. The council was to have deliberative and consultative functions, and it could have become a powerful body if this had been Mussolini's desire. But little came of it. Mussolini himself was head of the council, and others from the traditional state apparatus were given important ex officio roles. Lacking initiative and autonomy, the council was unable even to make effective use of the normative powers it had, and had no chance to try to expand them. What political coordination of the economy there was during the early 1930s took place in the traditional way, under the aegis of Mussolini and the appropriate ministries, with the council virtually ignored. Its powerlessness became increasingly obvious; the full body was not convoked at all after actual corporations were organized in 1934.

Livio Ciardi, as president of the Fascist Transport Union Confederation, was still advising patience in 1932, but at the meeting on corporativism held at Ferrara the same year, Panunzio condemned the vacillation of fascism and called for a reaffirmation of the principles of the Labor Charter.[77] And A. O. Olivetti was completely running out of patience. Between mid-1930 and his death in November of 1931, he produced some of the most bitter and remarkably explicit criticisms to appear during the entire fascist period. Serious fascists had to admit, he warned in 1930, that all their efforts and sacrifices—in interventionism, in the struggle against Italian socialism, in accepting fascist discipline—might simply have been in vain.[78] Too many of those calling themselves fascists understood fascism as a mere restoration of order, so it was possible that fascism would end up revolutionary in name only, producing nothing but vague corporativist slogans. A year later, his criticisms becoming ever more shrill, Olivetti declared that the future of fascism depended on the outcome of the present struggle between two conceptions of the fascist corporative system. The first, linked to revolutionary syndicalism, required broad autonomy and serious functions for the fascist socioeconomic organizations. From this perspective, the National Council of Corporations was to be a transitional body, paving the way for concrete corporative organisms, which had to be authentically representative. Olivetti warned, however, that present practice betrayed too much of the second conception, which viewed corporations as administrative organs of the state, to be developed and controlled from above. With chilling prescience, he concluded "that this latter conception is not only counterrevolutionary, but is also completely lacking social and historical meaning; it is an arid and contrived device that inevitably will produce a superbureaucracy and a police state."[79]

This statement reveals not only that Olivetti still believed himself to be an active participant in an ongoing struggle, but also that the struggle was allowed to go on—and with surprising openness. The fact that such a statement could appear in a major Fascist monthly no doubt reassured Olivetti and others that the contest was not hopeless. From our perspective, it seems clear that Mussolini's relative tolerance merely provided a safety valve; to contemporaries, however, it seemed that Mussolini really was not sure, that the outcome could still be influenced, as long as the push continued.

And the push did continue, although the personnel involved changed at the same time. For example, Turati was replaced as party secretary in October 1930 and Olivetti died in November 1931, but now younger fascists like Carlo Curcio, Gherardo Casini, Luigi Fontanelli, and Ugo Spirito joined the struggle for a populist form of corporativism. There continued to be differences in strategy and emphasis, leading committed left fascists to expend valuable energies fighting each other. One of these squabbles has been the source of considerable confusion about the nature of the corporativist Left within fascism. The dispute concerned the proposals for proprietary corporations which the young philosopher Ugo Spirito offered, especially at the Ferrara meeting on corporative studies of May 1932.[80] Spirito wanted corporations that would actually own and operate businesses, not merely provide "political" coordination. A system of proprietary corporations, he felt, would provide the desirable features of collective ownership without undesirable economic centralization. This seemed to him the logical end toward which the regime must move, given the fascist belief in class collaboration in production. By bringing together all the productive elements in a given sector, in fact, the new corporations would render the old class-based syndicates superfluous. Fascism would finally overcome these legacies of past class divisions altogether.

Spirito's position is often portrayed as the extreme left of the fascist spectrum. Certainly, Spirito could see his own stance as radical, but there were plausible reasons for dissent from a left fascist perspective, and Panunzio, Bottai, Razza, and others promptly attacked his proposal. In his remarks to the Ferrara meeting, Panunzio underscored the political and juridical import of fascist corporativism and accused Spirito of falling into economic reductionism. Mario Racheli specifically endorsed Panunzio's criticism. For both, the problems calling for corporativist solutions were primarily political, not economic, and had to do with coordinating economic activities in terms of the public interest.[81] Spirito's focus on a secondary issue—the relative merits of public and private ownership—could only confuse matters. Panunzio warned repeatedly that the political entity, the corporation, and the economic entity, the firm, must not be confused.[82] The corporation's purpose was to order the economic sphere through law, not to carry out economic activity.

More specifically, Panunzio, Bottai, and other left fascists disagreed with Spirito's contention that fully developed corporations could replace syndicates altogether. This point merits special emphasis, because it is sometimes assumed that the trade unionist and corporativist currents in fascism after 1925 were hostile or mutually exclusive.[83] This misunderstanding derives from overemphasis on the extreme positions represented, among the syndicalists, by Rossoni before the *sbloccamento* of 1928 and by Spirito among the corporativists. Most, in fact, like Panunzio, Bottai, Razza, and Luigi Fontanelli, continued to insist that the system required both class-based syndicates and corporations transcending class.[84] These critics of Spirito feared that the workers would be totally submerged if they had no institutional base of their own. For all their emphasis on class harmony and collaboration, these left corporativists continued to view class differences as inevitable and to find class-based organizations essential if the corporations were genuinely to involve the workers.

In addition, Panunzio feared that Spirito's system would produce the kind of bureaucratic uniformity in the economy that the syndicalists had always opposed. While Spirito's blueprint seemed to smack of schematism and rigidity, Panunzio argued for a flexible and mixed economic system, one which did not exclude a direct proprietary role for the workers. Whenever capacities warranted, the syndicates themselves should assume the responsibilities of ownership and management.[85] Panunzio had in mind producers' cooperatives that would grow out of the present unions, developing new firms or taking over existing firms on a case by case basis.

These proposals led Panunzio into disagreement with another of Spirito's left fascist critics, the young journalist Gherardo Casini. Arguing that Panunzio's cooperatives would involve only limited sectors and not change the basic shape of the economy, Casini called for syndical participation in the management of existing firms. Each of the two antagonists argued that his was the really dynamic and revolutionary proposal and that the other's would have only a limited impact in practice.[86] But as both recognized, they agreed on a deeper level, since each of them anticipated an increasingly important economic role for the workers through their syndicates. Only a plausible difference in strategy divided them. The distance separating each of them from Spirito was obviously greater, yet he too was trying to devise a system in which labor would have more real power in the economy. Again, the difference was essentially one of strategy and emphasis. Given the balance of forces at the time, however, it was possible to believe that Spirito's program, by downplaying the role of the class-based syndicates, might prove counterproductive in practice, weakening the role of the workers.[87] Certainly a committed left fascist was not obliged to agree with Spirito, nor was it a defeat for the corporativist Left when Spirito's proposals found little support. His failure was no more decisive for the current as a whole than Rossoni's defeat had been in 1928.[88] As Luigi Razza emphasized in 1933, Spirito's was an extreme position which did not represent the thinking of the left corporativist mainstream.[89]

Meanwhile, the left corporativist current continued to encounter opposition of varying degrees of sophistication from other elements in fascism. Roberto Farinacci felt that corporativism placed too much emphasis on the economic sphere at the expense of "ideal," political factors.[90] He had a point, of course, but he was unable to grasp the relationship between economics and politics at the basis of the left corporativist idea. In an article entitled "A Corporativist Danger?" Gherardo Casini responded directly to objections like Farinacci's, insisting on the political and ethical import of corporativism.[91] More conservative fascists like Carlo Costamagna continued to warn of the dangers of the left corporativist position and to portray the new socioeconomic organizations as tools of subordination and control.[92] Some fascists favored further corporativist innovation for essentially technical purposes. Alberto Benaglia, writing in 1941, called for more active corporations as vehicles for the economic coordination which autarky seemed to require; the corporations would become administrative instruments of a new superministry of autarky and economics.[93] Panunzio was quick to respond, insisting that Benaglia's conception would undermine the legislative role, and thus the revolutionary constitutional import, of the corporations.[94] The left corporativists, of course, did not deny that the party and the Ministry of Corporations had to be involved in the functioning of the corporations during this period of implementation, but they did not envision a structural relationship in which these organizations would be clearly subordinated to the party or the bureaucracy.

Although most left corporativists were not converted to Ugo Spirito's position during all the discussion in 1932, they were as anxious as he was to have actual corporations organized. Luigi Razza declared that the present system was a sham since entities like the National Council were not being given serious things to do; it was time for fascism to institute real corporations and for these promptly to take over major legislative powers.[95] Panunzio's accents were similar when he addressed the Assembly of the National Council of Corporations on 8 November 1933, complaining that the present corporative system was too cumbersome to be accessible to the people. If fascist institutions were not made more popular, he warned, they would prove as ineffective as the abstract institutions of liberalism, "which the people never understood and felt, and which never got the people very excited."[96]

With such frustration increasing, Mussolini committed fascism to organizing real corporations in a speech before the Assembly of the National Council of Corporations on 14 November 1933.[97] Panunzio responded with an enthusiastic article entitled "Diciannove" [1919] in *Il popolo d'Italia*, linking the innovations to come to early fascism and the radical hopes of 1919.[98] Finally a law of 5 February 1934 and a series of follow-up decrees actually established twenty-two corporations.[99] Earlier laws had anticipated the subsequent development of corporations, but the measures of 1934 established entities which had, on paper, considerably more extensive attributes than had been envisioned before. Above all, the new corporations were to have the power to elaborate norms governing production, so once again committed fascists could believe that progress was being made. At the same time, the innovations of 1934 included an attempt to revitalize the existing syndical structure. There was to be greater emphasis on the local union as opposed to the national confederation and more scope for initiatives from below, including elections to enable the rank and file to choose their own leaders.

The measures of 1934 could have constituted a significant departure, but again practice fell far short of promise. The new corporations lacked the autonomy and vitality to exercise the functions they were supposed to have. The suspicious, cynical, pessimistic Duce was unwilling to decentralize decision making; he simply lacked confidence in the new system.[100] In addition, the traditional bureaucracy remained hostile and obstructive. The corporations were constantly subject to interference—sometimes from the Ministry of Corporations, sometimes from the party. Despite the reforms of 1934, leaders and representatives at all levels of the system continued to be imposed and controlled from above. The corporations quickly turned into areas for traditional bureaucratic place-seeking and clientism, and so hardly constituted a revolutionary alternative to the traditional mores of Italian public life.[101]

The deficiencies of the system were evident both to antifascist exiles like Carlo Rosselli and to serious corporativists like Bottai and Panunzio. Writing as the corporations were being established in 1934, Rosselli anticipated that despite all the rhetoric, the whole corporative structure would continue to lack vitality and purpose. He could see that even after eleven years in power, fascism was still groping for an innovation to give it historical justification.[102] But Panunzio, Bottai, Lanzillo, and younger fascists like Gherardo Casini and Luigi Fontanelli were not prepared to give up. Panunzio called for a more serious, active syndical movement in an outspoken article in the official review *Gerarchia* in 1936. Lanzillo sought to take advantage of the League of Nations sanctions accompanying the Ethiopian War to prod the regime. If Italy was to meet the challenge, he said, more genuine mass participation was essential, and this required that the corporative entities become autonomous and authentically representative.[103]

As frustration with the corporations grew, Bottai and others began to focus on reform of the Chamber of Deputies. Preparations for a definitive reform began late in 1936, culminating in the law of 19 January 1939, which established the Chamber of Fasces and Corporations.[104] At the outset, the new Chamber comprised the National Council of Corporations, with 525 members, the National Council of the party, with 139 members, and the Grand Council of Fascism, with 18 members. Members of the Chamber were replaced one by one as they left these other offices; there was no periodic renewal of all or part of the body through elections.

Panunzio had been much involved in the discussions which led to the reform of 1939, and now he greeted the new body with his usual enthusiasm, linking it to the hopes for a radical reform of the Chamber in 1919. He was willing to admit, however, that a "not brief" process of experiments and "successive approximations" had been necessary to reach the present fulfillment. But Panunzio could link the essential features of the new Chamber to the changes in the idea of political participation and sovereignty which he had advocated for years. The

Chamber of Fasces and Corporations was an emanation of the organizations in society, organizations to which the individual belonged—and in which he participated—permanently and continuously. Through membership in these organizations, Panunzio argued, individuals were involved more directly and constantly, and no longer in the indirect, sporadic way which the liberal suffrage system had made possible. He pointed out that elections within the corporate organizations remained essential, but the Chamber itself was to be based on a more direct and immediate identity between the organized society and the governmental body.[105]

The reform of 1939 proved more fruitful than its predecessors. Mussolini and the executive branch remained predominant in legislation, but the new Chamber, through the legislative commissions into which it was divided, was allowed genuinely to collaborate in the drafting of legislation. There was now a serious attempt to overcome the widespread use of decree laws characteristic of Italian governments since before the rise of fascism.[106]

In fact, this revitalization of the Chamber was part of a general radicalization and quickening of activity in what turned out to be the regime's final phase. Some of the underlying contradictions of the regime were now coming to the surface, as Mussolini sought a way out of the impasse through imperialism and the German alliance. This dangerous course raised new doubts about fascism in the monarchical and business circles that had tolerated Mussolini for so long. Partly for this reason, the thrust of the final radical phase was overtly populist and "antibourgeois." It included the semicomic reform of custom as well as some anti-Semitic legislation. Anti-Semitism, of course, had been lacking at the origins of Italian fascism. It is too facile, however, to attribute its sudden appearance in the late 1930s entirely to the influence of Nazi Germany, for it was symptomatic of the degeneration of fascism, as we will see in the next chapter. Still, anti-Semitism went as far as it did only because of official desires to establish cultural foundations for the alliance with Nazi Germany. At the same time, there were some, like Roberto Farinacci, who felt that Italian fascism could be revitalized by aping the apparently more dynamic Nazi movement.

However, this final phase also included commitments and activities which seemed to point toward the fulfillment of long-term left fascist goals. Giuseppe Bottai, who had been replaced as Minister of Corporations shortly after the Ferrara meeting of 1932, returned to favor as Minister of Education in 1936; such vicissitudes were typical and manifest the fluid, uncertain quality of the Fascist regime. His Educational Charter, approved by the Grand Council in February 1939, established that manual labor would become part of the curriculum at all levels, "so that the social and productive consciousness that is characteristic of the corporative system may be developed."[107] Bottai intended to replace "bourgeois" education with a more populist, egalitarian system. At the same time, the Fascist labor movement was becoming more effective. For years, the Fascist unions had not had sufficient political clout to prevent business from violating collective contracts and social legislation. But the movement achieved a considerable success in October of 1939, when firms in the metals and machinery industries were forced to recognize factory labor representatives—one for every two hundred workers.[108] It is impossible to say whether this would have signaled the beginning of a serious change in industrial relations had the war not intervened, and had the regime not collapsed.

Also in 1939, Dino Grandi returned from Great Britain, where he had been ambassador since 1932, to become Minister of Justice. Committed fascists were calling for a "fascist" reform of Italy's public and private legal codes, especially for a change in the legal basis of property. Panunzio and Lanzillo made the usual left fascist points in their contributions to a collection on the fascist conception of private property which the Confederation of Agricultural Workers published in 1939.[109] For years, in fact, Panunzio had been calling with considerable impatience for a radical reform of Italy's legal codes, to eliminate the liberal individualism that informed them and to establish the formal legal standing of norms elaborated by syndicates and corporations. Ultimately, he argued, this required constitutional change, recognizing the juridical pluralism of the Fascist state, with its corporativist basis.[110] As a member of the Commission for the Reform of the Legal Codes from 1937 to 1941, Panunzio sought to maximize the specifically fascist quality of the changes being worked out.[111]

New codes were finally established in 1942. Although most of the novel features were not specifically fascist, there were some significant departures in the direction of corporativism. The initial article of the civil code formally recognized the corporations as sources of law, while subsequent articles specified the particular capacities of the corporations.[112] The articles declaring property ownership to be a social function, subject to corporativist discipline, were especially significant, because they indicated methods of enforcement and seemed to commit fascism to serious implementation in this sensitive area. A private entrepreneur who failed to conform to the principles of the new corporativist order would be removed from control of his enterprise. The Magistracy of Labor would adjudicate such cases. In his contribution to the anthology on property in 1939, Panunzio had advocated such an expanded role for the Magistracy of Labor and recalled his own central role in publicizing the labor magistracy concept during the early years of the regime.[113] In a book also published in 1939, Paolo Orano took much the same tack, stressing the links between fascist corporativism, with its conception of property as a social function, and the *Carta del Carnaro* of 1920.[114]

During its last years, then, fascism appeared to be committing itself more precisely, but these still-tentative steps by no means satisfied serious corporativists, who continued goading and criticizing even during World War II. Writing in *Critica fascista* in 1941, Panunzio went so far as to remind fascists of the value of the second wave of violent *squadrismo* in 1924 and to portray the wartime context as a kind of third wave, an opportunity to accelerate the implementation of fascism.[115] Now was the time to improve the still-imperfect Chamber, to enhance the legislative role of the corporations, to implement the postulates about labor and property in the Labor Charter, and even to begin preparations for an international corporativist order, as a foundation for the kind of international justice the syndicalists had envisioned after World War I. A year later, in the official review *Gerarchia*, Panunzio cited the generally lamented "inertness and dearth of normative activity in the corporations," and called for the corporations to carry out their crucial task of legally binding economic planning.[116] By now Panunzio's son Vito had become a significant fascist publicist in his own right, working closely not only with his father, but also with Giuseppe Bottai. In his wartime writings, Vito Panunzio leveled strikingly explicit and damaging criticisms against the corporative system and reaffirmed the populist principles that were supposed to underlie the new order. He insisted, for example, that genuine elections within the constituent syndical organizations were essential if their unrepresentative quality was to be overcome. And writing in *Critica fascista* in 1943, shortly before the fall of Mussolini, the younger Panunzio warned that Mussolini's regime could win the war only if, at long last, it finally carried out the fascist revolution.[117]

It is impossible to doubt the sincerity of corporativists like these, who kept pushing even as the regime was collapsing around them. We wonder, though, how they were able to keep their faith for so long, in light of so many frustrations over the long term. It is essential to remember, of course, that fifteen or twenty years is not a long time to implement a revolutionary program, especially one that, for plausible reasons, called for experiment, pragmatism, and gradual change. And considerable change in institutions had indeed taken place—and presumably more could be made to follow. At the same time, it is only natural that these fascists tended to accentuate the positive, especially since they had already devoted so much to the fascist cause and were now identified with the movement, for better or for worse. But obviously there were serious flaws in their perception of fascism's prospects, and thus we sense that a more intangible kind of psychological mechanism must have been operative for these publicists to have remained available, explaining and justifying Mussolini's regime until its very bitter end. They desperately needed to believe it was all leading somewhere, that it all had not been for nothing, because their own self-image as Italians depended so heavily on the outcome.

Fascism was understood as an antidote to traditional defects in the Italian character, but the effort of self-overcoming was difficult. Thus myths developed, providing psychological compensation as well as the confidence necessary for fascists to believe that Italy really could be made more healthy and dynamic, despite her sociocultural flaws. The talk about the Roman Empire during the Fascist regime shored up confidence by providing images of what Italians working in common could accomplish. Despite its orientation toward the past, the fascist cult of Rome does not manifest a desire to escape from "modernity" and return to a happier era. Committed fascists looked to Rome, however, not as a preindustrial utopia, but as an example— one which reassured them about Italian capacities and gave them the confidence for nation-building, modernizing, and constructing a post-liberal order. If "modernity" as it is usually understood had been bothering them, we could expect to find a different kind of past orientation, emphasizing preindustrial, preurban, peasant values. The past-oriented myths of the German Nazis were much closer to this syndrome and did stem from an inability to handle aspects of "modernity"; those in Italian fascism, however, were not analogous in origin or function.[118]

This is not to say that the myth of Rome was rational or comprehensible on its own terms. It obviously stemmed in part from precisely the rhetorical propensities in some sectors of Italian society that fascism was supposed to overcome. Ultimately, it hindered realism and effectiveness and contributed to the regime's overall hollowness. And this was true primarily because the Roman empire myth got bound up with fascist corporativism, thanks to our myth-making publicists. It was not enough that Italy had had an imperial and civilizing vocation in the past; nor was it enough for her now simply to catch up, to develop a mature liberal parliamentary system. Rome provided an image not merely of viability but of leadership. And now Italy again had an imperial mission—to offer something new and superior to others through her colossal corporativist achievements.

At the very outset of the regime, committed fascists began to describe their aims in grandiose terms, as the solution to a crisis in the liberal system in general. The stakes for Italy were high; the challenge was exhilarating. She could confront her own problems effectively only by leapfrogging over those like Great Britain with mature liberal systems and leading the advanced world beyond liberalism altogether. The world badly needed a third way between outmoded liberalism and misguided communism. Writing early in 1923, just a few months after the March on Rome, Panunzio was already claiming that while England and France were too smug and traditional to develop new political principles, "Italy, and only Italy, can give Europe the first example of a new organic, solid, and realistic political-national constitution on a syndical basis."[119] A few months later, Panunzio proudly announced that now England would have much to learn from Italy and her fascist national syndicalism. And he concluded: "It was not for nothing that Spaventa called Italy *la Nazione 'Mattiniera'* of Europe."[120]

This was not the only time that Panunzio would invoke the name of Bertrando Spaventa (1817–1883), who had taught the history of philosophy at the Unversity of Naples after the Risorgimento, devising an interpretive schema which enabled him substantially to overestimate Italian contributions.[121] In his lecture "The Sentiment of the State," given at the University of Rome in 1928, Panunzio told his audience: "We must highlight the superiority and the greatness of the reality and of the doctrine of the Fascist state, a product of the Italian spirit, which with Fascism, resumes the function of *nazione 'mattiniera,'* to use Spaventa's phrase, the initiator and anticipator in the world of nations, a function that was lost during the long centuries of servitude and foreign imitation."[122] Panunzio's use of Spaventa symbolizes the persistence of traumas about national worth among educated Italians. Like Spaventa, Panunzio desperately needed to believe that Italy had something uniquely hers, with roots in Italian traditions, but sufficiently relevant to present problems to be worthy of export.

Italy's task was not merely to catch up with others, but to work out her own political forms, based on her own traditions. According to Olivetti, the liberal parliamentary system which Italy had imported in the nineteenth century was not consistent with the talents of the Italian people; there was thus nothing surprising about its failure to take root. It was useless for Italy to try to catch up because, as Olivetti put it, "the English suit does not fit us."[123] Fortunately, however, Italy had talents and traditions of her own. Sometimes the syndicalists cited the role of the guilds in the medieval Italian communes or the structure of early modern Venice in an effort to convince themselves that corporativist democracy was specifically Italian.[124] As history, this was all a bit fanciful, to say the least, but myths of an Italian corporativist tradition helped provide the confidence necessary to build something new. Here again, use of the Italian past does not reveal some sort of rejection of modernity or defense of traditional values; the syndicalists invariably —and correctly—stressed the novelty of corporativism and the modernity of the problems to which it was supposed to provide solutions.[125] They fell into contradiction, insisting that corporativist forms were both purely modern and traditionally Italian, in order to convince themselves that Italy was especially qualified to offer a nonliberal and noncommunist solution to a set of genuine modern problems. It was not absurd, of course, for Italians to seek the bases of cultural self-confidence in traditions that were uniquely theirs, but these preoccupations were dangerous, for they could easily reinforce the old provincialism and lead to unrealistic myth making.

The left fascist cult of Mazzini was more plausible. Mazzini was continually invoked as a prophet who had rejected both liberal individualism and Marxist socialism and devised an alternative based on duty and association. Again and again, Olivetti portrayed fascist corporativism as the practical fulfillment of Mazzini's ideas and concluded that now, thanks to fascism, Italy was at last worthy of the mission of leadership which Mazzini had assigned to her.[126] Like Mazzini, Olivetti envisioned a kind of Italian primacy resting not on military conquest, but on the value of the new forms of civilization she had to offer.

The syndicalists repeatedly indulged in this kind of argument, linking Mazzinian ideas, fascist achievements, and Italy's "imperial" mission to lead civilization to a higher stage.[127] For Rossoni, fascism was nothing less than "the great revolution of the twentieth century: a revolution which in its subsequent development will be nourished by the immortal spirit of the Italian people, which has returned once again to the vanguard of history, to impose its direction on the future of civilization."[128] Panunzio pointed with pride to the interest which the sociopolitical innovations of fascist Italy were attracting abroad; it meant a great deal to him to have Italy again setting the pace.[129] After Hitler came to power, Panunzio often made deprecating remarks about Nazism, which lacked, he said, the social content of fascism, the commitment to corporativism. Nazi Germany was merely reactionary—and thus no challenge to Italy's position of leadership.[130]

The syndicalists were occasionally willing to admit some admiration for certain of the Soviet regime's achievements—in economic planning, for example—and to acknowledge some parallels in the practice of Soviet Russia and fascist Italy.[131] But generally, they claimed, the Soviet experience only confirmed what they had said all along about the authoritarian and bureaucratic implications of collectivist socialism. Fascism was superior because it was a synthesis, overcoming the economic anarchy and social exploitation of liberal capitalism, but fostering decentralization, spontaneity, and popular self-government at the same time. While Soviet communism produced a dull uniformity, fascism would order the economy without undermining flexibility and initiative.[132]

During the 1930s, such myths of fascist Italy's mission were an essential part of the fascist self-image, providing compensation for all the frustration and criticism. In the statements of committed fascists, we find these grandiose claims uneasily mixed with criticisms of present inadequacies and with practical proposals for making the corporative system work. The contradictions of this pattern betray the fundamental ambiguity of left fascism, which was a serious attempt to solve a set of complex modern problems, but which also embodied the rhetorical traditions of Italy's "intellectual petty bourgeoisie." Despite the seriousness of their quest for solutions, the left fascists were prone to revert to rhetoric when they suffered frustration and failure. As they sought to overcome the hated part of their society and themselves, and as they criticized the performance of the Fascist regime, they projected a reassuring myth of the leadership role that Italy was now playing through fascism. The greater the frustration, the more grandiose their claims became. Inevitably, these soothing fictions distorted their perceptions, keeping them from gauging realistically the Fascist regime's prospects for success. They so desperately wanted fascism to work and Italy to count that they could never admit, even to themselves, that they were on a treadmill. By clinging to rhetorical myths, they helped to blind others as well to fascism's real prospects for success—and thereby helped Mussolini's hollow regime to persevere.

When Mussolini's wars came, these publicists stood ready to portray them in the best possible light, discussing imperial conquest in terms of Italy's corporativist mission.[133] For Vito Panunzio, writing in 1940, the war could break down barriers to a new order both at home and abroad.[134] If fascism had not yet realized its revolutionary corporativist program, the plutocracies with whom she was presently at war were largely to blame. And the war would enable Italy to conquer other peoples to corporativism. The same year, Sergio Panunzio portrayed the war as a crusade by fascist Italy to create the kind of just international order which the last war had failed to achieve.[135] Under the cover of such rhetoric, of course, the two Panunzios were seeking to arouse expectations and thereby to force fascism finally to realize its radical program. They no doubt believed it was true when they insisted that here at last was the chance. But this meant, once again, that they ended up providing a veneer of idealism for a shoddy enterprise—one, in this case, that soon led fascism and Italy to ruin.

There is cruel irony in the fact that fascism, which was supposed to enable Italy to lead, ended up bringing her more ridicule and discredit than anything else in modern times. But the whole tragic experience dissolved some of the long-standing cultural traumas that made fascism possible—though not necessary—and created a cultural framework enabling Italians to respond to modern problems in a more genuinely creative way.

12 / Italian Fascism in European History

If we ask what fascism was, we are asking several questions at once—questions that simply cannot be answered in the same breath. Above all, we must distinguish the purposes that made fascism possible from the realities of the regime, from what it all added up to when the end came in 1943. There was incongruity between intentions and effects, yet interpretation of the place of fascism in history must have room for both. As a regime, fascism ended up regimenting the working class, undercutting the possibility of popular participation in decision making, and enhancing the power of the traditional bureaucracy within the state. But these effects were evidence of the failure of some of the most important objectives that made fascism possible—not of their success. Some of the fundamental features of the regime were accidental, for the regime was not a "system," but an improvisation based on capricious personal dictatorship. Committed fascists kept pushing, but it is hardly surprising that the existing elites in business and the bureaucracy also sought to make the most of fascism. They succeeded as well as they did largely because of the weaknesses and divisions among the genuinely fascist components. All the components, fascist and nonfascist alike, looked to Mussolini, for the logic of the situation made him the key to the practice of the regime. Thus it is crucial to understand Mussolini, what made him as he was, the phenomenology of his being as he was. His activism, his cynicism, his opportunism were symptomatic of certain problematic features of modern culture, and so Mussolini has his own place in modern European history.[1]

Questions about how this dictatorial regime worked and what it did are essential, but additional questions must also be asked if our concern is fascism's place in history. Impulses that never found fulfillment in practice made the regime possible in the first place and had some effect on its overall shape. And whatever their outcome in practice, these impulses are historically significant, because they help to reveal the frustrations and aspirations at work in the experience of Italians—and Europeans—in the twentieth century. The traumas and hopes that gave rise to the totalitarian corporativist thrust in fascism were real and operative, whether fascism ended up a totalitarian corporativist regime or not.

Even when we move beyond effects to intentions, however, no single answer will do, for the creators of Italian fascism had different, even conflicting, values and objectives. The difference between populist and elitist currents was the most fundamental. Still, both kinds of fascism emerged in Italy partly because of her relative backwardness and political immaturity. Among more or less liberal nations, Italy was an extreme case, with problems close to the surface. Thus emerged the basic right and left fascist perspectives: the masses seemed to pose a threat everywhere—but especially in Italy; the masses were left out of the liberal parliamentary system everywhere—but especially in Italy. Moreover, both of the major components in fascism aimed at modernization and nation building. In seeking to promote national solidarity and a strong state, fascists of both left and right were trying to build a cohesive modern nation out of a fragmented society. Because of objective economic difficulties, and because she was poorly integrated as a nation, Italy would have to adopt new, totalitarian methods of mass mobilization if she was to catch up. The more advanced countries of western Europe did not face the same problems.

If we could make sense of Italian fascism solely in terms of backwardness and modernization, then the phenomenon would not be central to the modern European experience, and we could best consider fascist Italy as a nationalist-socialist developmental dictatorship— much like those that have emerged in the third world in the wake of decolonization.[2] Despite her relative backwardness, however, Italy had experienced many of the same problems with parliamentary liberalism and industrial capitalism that afflicted more advanced countries. Through its elitist current, Italian fascism has a place in the conservative, antidemocratic tradition of Europe as a whole. In Italian fascism that tradition was evolving, as its exponents began to devise new methods in response to the rise of the masses during the first decades of the twentieth century. The populist current, however, was a response to a different set of problems and links Italian fascism to the long-term processes of European history in an altogether different way.

It is widely assumed that fascism as a mass movement, in both

Italy and Germany, was an attempt to find traditionalist or backward-looking solutions to problems of modernization and modernity. Fascism, it seems, attracted people from the lower middle class who were losing out as modernization proceeded.[3] Much of German Nazism was indeed a kind of revolt against modernity, although the motives of committed Nazis often cannot be understood in terms of the standard socioeconomic categories. In addition to the familiar petty bourgeois traumas, "modernity" raises less tangible problems of individuation and identity, freedom and powerlessness, problems which afflict certain personalities or psychological types more than others. The Himmlers and Eichmanns and Hösses in Nazism were indeed "losers" in the wake of modernization, but they revolted against aspects of modern life because of personal, psychological weaknesses, not because of membership in declining socioeconomic groups.[4] At the same time, responses to problematic features of modernity may well take "alienated" and irrational forms if the problems are inherently insoluble—insoluble, at least, within the modern framework. Those responsible for the most troubling features of Nazism simply did not understand the relationship between the essential structures of modern life and their own existential problems. The Jews were to blame; the Jews were the agents of the troubling features of modernity; problems could be overcome by eliminating the Jews. Unable to conceive of genuine solutions, these Nazis operated in terms of a fictional view of reality, which included archaic myths and images as well as biological racism and anti-Semitism.

Although left fascism and Nazism obviously had some major enemies in common—especially liberal individualism and Marxism—their concerns were fundamentally different; left fascism was not involved with modernity in the same way as Nazism. As we already noted briefly, left fascism sought to promote modernization. Moreover, left fascism sought to respond to modern problems in a comparatively rational and forward-looking way.

Italy was relatively backward as an economy and poorly integrated as a nation—far behind Germany in both respects. Despite its superficialities and petty ambitions, left fascism responded to these features of the Italian context with a program that was modernizing and nation-building in intention. The left fascists' shrill nationalism, and their unusually intense traumas about national worth, manifested the threatened "petty bourgeois" mentality in some respects, but these concerns led them to favor modernization, not to cling to tradition. They longed to be part of a more modern, productive—and respected—nation, and they saw fascism as the vehicle for the desired change. Left fascism, then, was not a revolt against modernity, but an awkward, often superficial attempt to make Italy more modern and productive on the part of people who were in many ways ill-equipped for the task. They did not have much concrete experience of the modern industrial world.

Here it is useful to return to the thesis of Luigi Salvatorelli, the first to portray fascism as an expression of petty bourgeois losers. Another early critic of fascism, Giovanni Ansaldo, raised some telling objections to Salvatorelli's thesis in 1922 and 1923, pointing out that the petty bourgeois elements which formed the core of fascism were very much taken with modern industrialism, but in a superficial and rhetorical way.[5] These fascists emphasized change, dynamism, and the future and dreamed of the great productive Italy that fascism would create. In response to Ansaldo's critique, Salvatorelli began to back off, explaining that he had intended to link fascism to the superficial, rhetorical mentality characteristic of the Italian preindustrial bourgeoisie; the fascist cult of speed, dynamism, and modernity that Ansaldo cited was merely a new manifestation of the same propensity.[6] Indeed, Salvatorelli went on, it was symptomatic of the relative backwardness of Italy's middle classes that here even interest in industrial modernization tended to assume an artificial and rhetorical character. But Salvatorelli was giving up most of his original argument: he was offering a useful explanation of the rhetorical forms of fascism, but if petty bourgeois fascists were not opposed to modern industrial society, if they were not clinging to traditional preindustrial values, then his original explanation of their motives in creating fascism had no value.

In contrast to Nazism, populist fascism in Italy was not notable for the diatribes against department stores and chain stores indicative of the standard petty bourgeois concerns. Sometimes the fascists indulged in rhetorical attacks on the financial plutocracy, and Salvatorelli cited them as confirmation of his thesis; but given the questionable, highly speculative role which large financial groups had played in Italy's industrial development, it was possible for Italians favoring industrial development to deplore the machinations of big finance capital. In the same vein, early fascist support of free trade has been portrayed as a manifestation of the concerns of static middle-class consumers.[7] But since protectionism had so often interfered with healthy industrial growth in Italy, Italians could support free trade out of a desire for more viable economic development.

These two examples indicate how easy it is simply to find what we expect to find when we consider fascist statements about the economy. If we prejudge the fascists on the basis of a priori assumptions about the traumas of the petty bourgeoisie, then we can use virtually anything they said to explain their concerns away. Insofar as they objected to any of the features of Italian industrial capitalism, they can be taken as losers unable to adjust to modernity. On the other hand, insofar as they favored large-scale industrial development in Italy and insisted on the progressive role which capitalists could play, we assume they must have swallowed the Nationalist line.[8] And this can be explained only because of their susceptibility to irrational nationalist appeals, since surely the declining petty bourgeoisie could not have embraced modern industrial development for any other reason. In fact, of course, the performance of Italy's capitalist economy had been contradictory, and there is a good deal of ambivalence and confusion in left fascist statements about the economy. Since ambivalence about Italian capitalism was plausible on its own terms, however, the ambivalence in fascism does not necessarily manifest the incoherence of those being left out as modernization proceeds. To promote healthier industrial development in Italy, it was necessary to attack some aspects of Italian economic life and to favor others. It was necessary simultaneously to foster and to control the development of Italian capitalism. The left fascists understood economic matters only superficially, and they were not sure how to make the necessary distinctions in practice, but they wanted to distinguish between "producers" and "parasites," to get more productive elements into politics, to overcome the old unproductive patterns of Italian life, and to involve the whole society in the great task of economic modernization. To be sure, the Nazis ended up enhancing the modernization of Germany, despite their rhetoric against department stores. But this was only an unintended by-product of their quest for the means to implement their utopian, antimodern vision.[9] The Nazis were not modernizers, not even superficial and rhetorical modernizers, the way the left fascists were.

It was partly because of Italy's relative backwardness that liberalism and capitalism seemed so problematic to critical Italians. Liberal individualism appeared to be a problem partly because Italy was especially atomized. The liberal state seemed weak, and the parliamentary system seemed an inadequate vehicle for popular participation, partly because of the political expedients which Italy's youth as a nation made necessary. Certainly Italy had never had a mature liberal system, and the creators of fascism were unwilling to allow liberalism a full-fledged trial. Partly because of cultural sensitivities that were themselves symptomatic of Italy's relative backwardness, they refused to settle for the prosaic task of catching up with others by working to improve Italy's liberal parliamentary system; they insisted instead that Italy required something new, a postliberal antidote to the problems of the modern bourgeois order. There was much empty rhetoric to such leadership pretensions, but many of Italy's problems also afflicted more advanced countries. Left fascism, as a response to these difficulties, has a place in the supranational history of Europe, in the ongoing quest for solutions to the problems of modern liberalism and capitalism.

During the nineteenth century, a tradition developed on the left involving those who believed that the problems of liberalism and capitalism could be overcome only if the bourgeois order itself were transcended. Some grew disillusioned with the system only as its postulates found practical realization—with the advent of universal suffrage, for example. Georges Sorel was one of those who became so frustrated with democratic government in practice that he was drawn into the radical current; experience seemed to have proven by 1898 that it had been utopian to believe that elected representatives of the people would provide good and popular government.[10] The results of universal suffrage and parliamentary government were so disillusioning that something altogether different seemed necessary. Leftist critics tended to agree that the bourgeois order, with its narrow individualism, undermined or failed to foster the nobler, social capacities in man. But there were many questions about the basis of the problems afflicting the advanced liberal capitalist countries of the West—and about what was required to overcome them.

By the 1890s, Marxism had established a kind of hegemony, if not an absolute supremacy, within the tradition of radical opposition to the bourgeois order in Europe. In achieving this dominant position, Marxism had apparently relegated its rivals—the doctrines of such other opponents of liberalism as Sismondi, Proudhon, and Mazzini—to the junk heap of history. These figures, Marxists claimed, were essentially spokesmen for the petty bourgeoisie, a class which had no progressive role to play. It fell to the industrial proletariat to become the universal class, capable of leading society beyond the liberal and capitalist order.

But during the 1890s, of course, serious strains became evident in the Marxist tradition. The revisionist Bernstein recognized, among other things, that the petty bourgeoisie was not disappearing, being sucked into the proletariat. In fact, a new lower middle class of technicians and white-collar workers was emerging as capitalism became more complex. Socialists, he said, must not forget this class, which could play a progressive role as long as the socialists themselves provided imaginative leadership. In Bernstein's conception, objective class basis was giving way to subjective consciousness, for socialism ultimately depended on the ethical capacity which pertains to man as such. At about the same time, Sorel showed that Marxism lacked an adequate theory of the psychological development of the proletariat and insisted that the workers could claim to lead, and to create socialism, only if they had undergone a process of psychological maturation, acquiring a socialist consciousness. Lenin went a step further, arguing that experience had proven that the workers, left to themselves, could develop only a limited, trade union consciousness.[11] Socialist revolution required something more universal—a political consciousness involving a synthetic view of the whole. It was the attribute of an elite definable only in terms of its consciousness, not socioeconomic class. In other words, political consciousness was autonomous; it did not depend on one's place in the socioeconomic structure. And from a Leninist perspective, the essence of the revolution is to impart political values; economic changes are secondary and, in important respects, dependent upon prior changes in consciousness.

At the same time, the Marxist tradition was being attacked from the outside, as such thinkers as Durkheim, Pareto, and Léon Duguit, certainly "bourgeois" themselves, but still critical of central aspects of the bourgeois order, developed some of their ideas in intellectual confrontation with Marxism. Obviously Durkheim, for example, was no revolutionary, but he perceived problems with liberalism and capitalism that could not be overcome merely through continued evolution in the present direction, through existing institutions. Something new was required.

Marxism had a major impact in Italy during the 1890s, when it began to establish the foundations that would enable it to become an ongoing force in Italian culture and politics. But partly because of Italy's backward lags, elements from her strong Mazzinian and anarchist traditions remained close to the surface in some segments of her radical tradition. The strains in Marxism afforded these "backward" forms of radicalism an opportunity to reassert themselves, in modified form, and to claim that they had something progressive to offer after all. Francesco Saverio Merlino was the pivotal figure in this development. A Neapolitan lawyer who started as an anarchist, Merlino has recently been portrayed as a petty bourgeois degeneration in Italian socialism.[12] From a Marxist perspective, this characterization is apt. But it was partly because of his links to pre-Marxist radical traditions, and partly because his perspective was "petty bourgeois," that Merlino was able to play a major role in the revision of Marxism, anticipating Bernstein and inspiring Sorel. In the person of Merlino, those whom Marx had relegated to the dustbin of history—including the Proudhons and Mazzinis on the intellectual level, the preindustrial middle classes on the mass level—were beginning to fight back, claiming to have more to say than the Marxists and workers about how to solve modern problems. It was happening in Italy because this was a country that rested on the borderline between backwardness and modernity. Merlino's emphasis on the people, as opposed to the proletariat, was both premodern, a legacy of Italian preindustrial radicalism, and "postmodern," responding to the impasse into which the Marxist overemphasis on the proletariat was leading the radical tradition in Europe in general. At issue, in fact, were not merely abstract intellectual satisfactions. The problems of the bourgeois order in Europe called for a response in practice, and the value of Marxism was becoming ever more questionable.

Those problems were especially close to the surface in Italy, where they helped to produce a crisis in the aftermath of World War I. And it was symptomatic of the disarray afflicting the Marxist tradition in general that the Italian Socialists and workers were not able to put forth a credible claim to leadership. Their perspective did not enable them to offer a convincing analysis of the problems causing the crisis or to propose convincing solutions. For now, at least, the proletariat did not seem to merit the great historical role which Marxism had assigned to it. In addition, Marxist categories seemed to be of limited value since in Italy, as in twentieth-century European experience in general, political and cultural problems were increasingly coming to seem autonomous —and even primary.[13] This perception, in fact, has been bound up with the overall breakdown of classical Marxism in the twentieth century. If the focus of the revolution against the bourgeois order was to be political and cultural rather than socioeconomic, then surely a group defined in terms of its political and cultural consciousness, and not its objective place in the socioeconomic structure, could claim to spearhead it. An influential critic of Marxism, Vilfredo Pareto, found consciousness or values to be the defining attributes of both the decadent elites responsible for social problems and the revolutionary elites which could claim to solve them. Moreover, given the intractability of nationality and national differences, and given the importance of longstanding national problems, a revolutionary program had to be sensitive to the special needs of the particular nation.

The trouble with Marxism, then, was not that it was linked to the cause of labor, and not that it envisioned changing the world by making transcendent values practical and actual, to use Ernst Nolte's categories.[14] The basis of the assault upon Marxist socialism in practice in Italy need have been neither of these. The problem, rather, was simply that Marxism seemed inadequate as a practical guide to overcoming the problems of the bourgeois order in Italy.

If capitalism did not appear to be heading toward collapse, and if the proletariat was capable of developing only a trade union consciousness, was there no hope of transcending the bourgeois order? Lenin, almost in spite of himself, had already indicated the direction in which the radical tradition must move by emphasizing political consciousness. Later on, Antonio Gramsci proved that the Marxist tradition could be renewed from within, as he worked out his sensitive blueprint largely in response to the inadequacies of the Socialist posture during Italy's postwar crisis. For Gramsci, the proletarian revolutionary program must respond to long-standing Italian political and cultural problems distinguishable from problems bound up with the capitalist economy. And the proletariat develops its right to rule—establishes its hegemony—through a cultural process which does not depend on the unfolding of capitalism. Gramsci's accents, like Lenin's, were on changes in consciousness, culture, and politics, not on changes in the economic sphere. Since those seeking to restore the Marxist tradition to viability have tried to overcome precisely the deficiencies which its critics had indicated, the Marxist and anti-Marxist variants in the radical tradition have moved in parallel directions in the twentieth century.

The Marxist tradition, then, was certainly not dead, but in Italy in 1920 it was possible to doubt that the Socialists and the proletariat were fit to lead. Yet the problems called for solution. And now others stepped forward, individuals with the kind of "petty bourgeois" populist perspective which Marx felt would become ever more outmoded; they indulged in a measure of revenge on Marx's followers and the class which he had expected to lead, but they also claimed that they themselves could spearhead the solution to the problems with the bourgeois order now coming to a head in Italy. The syndicalists constituted their intellectual vanguard. Though heir to certain anarchist and populist perspectives, the syndicalists still had participated in the vogue of Marxism in Italy and had made a serious effort to work within the Marxist tradition. Isolated and alienated, they had been eager for the leadership which the emerging industrial proletariat would apparently be able to offer, sooner or later. But gradually they had encountered the tensions and questions afflicting the Marxist tradition in Europe. As Marxist categories began to seem inappropriate, they set out on their own, drawing on Marx's critics and enemies, developing a new blueprint, and finally encountering a new constituency. They became part of the postwar "petty bourgeois" revolt in Italy, giving it the measure of consistency and direction that it had. In part, then, the left fascist revolt was a challenge to the dominant position in the tradition of leftist opposition to the bourgeois order which Marxism had managed to achieve. In its quest for alternative solutions, and in its quest for its own roots, the left fascist current resurrected a number of Marx's apparently vanquished rivals—populist, "petty bourgeois," antiliberal leftists from the nineteenth century like Mazzini, Proudhon, and Sismondi. It also drew sustenance from participants in the revision of Marxism like Merlino, Sorel, and Bernstein, and even from critical "bourgeois" thinkers like Pareto, Durkheim, and Léon Duguit. The result was a new synthesis, left fascism, intended as a third way, a more appropriate response to the problems of liberalism and capitalism than communism could offer.

As spokesmen for this current, the syndicalists sought explicitly to establish its place in the tradition of the anti-Marxist Left in Europe. Again and again, Panunzio claimed that fascism was implementing what remained of the socialist tradition after the revision of Marxism, the war, and the anomalies of the Bolshevik revolution. According to Panunzio, in fact, Mussolini's speech of 14 November 1933, announcing the organization of corporations, finally brought to a close the long crisis in the socialist tradition that had begun in the 1890s.[15] For Olivetti, in the same way, fascism was to carry out the social revolution that all the socialist schools had proven unable to bring to fruition.[16] Lanzillo, writing in 1918, proclaimed that the war had shattered the old socialism, but as a fascist, he portrayed socialism as a tendency inherent in modern society—one which could best come to fruition within the fascist context.[17] Younger fascists like Grandi, Suckert, and Bottai similarly portrayed the historical significance of fascism in terms of the inadequacies and failures of socialism.[18]

Panunzio praised Sorel, Bernstein, and Merlino for perceiving the excesses of Marxism and for helping to refurbish the tradition of radical opposition to the bourgeois order in Europe.[19] With its exclusivist pretensions, Marxism had become rigid and dogmatic, but the radical tradition did not have to be a Marxist monopoly. Olivetti played up the anti-Marxist implications of Sorel's ideas, while Panunzio singled out his fellow Italian Merlino for special credit: "Whoever today reads Merlino's writings finds that many of the criticisms and objections of fascism against Marxist scientific socialism are to be found in our fellow Italian writer even earlier than in Bernstein and Sorel."[20]

We have already discussed the left fascist cult of Mazzini, but the syndicalists also linked fascism to other nineteenth-century enemies of Marx. Olivetti placed fascism in the tradition of Proudhonian socialism, which he contrasted with the allegedly centralizing, authoritarian, and bureaucratic variety of "German" Marxism.[21] Panunzio claimed that fascism embodied the legacy of Jean Sismonde de Sismondi, whom Marx and Engels had dismissed in the *Communist Manifesto* as the head of petty bourgeois socialism.[22] Panunzio took special note of Sismondi's fate at the hands of Marx, but the "petty bourgeois" charge did not perturb him, for history, he claimed, had proven Sismondi right and Marx wrong. Indeed, those like Sismondi and Proudhon had been the real revolutionaries, while Marx could only be called a conservative, since he had welcomed the full development of capitalism, with all its excesses, and since he had envisioned the ongoing primacy of the economic sphere. Panunzio cited the Soviet experience as evidence that Marxism accepts and fosters the tyranny of the economic over the political. As a critique of Marxism, this was all quite shallow and misdirected, yet it was typical and manifested the measure of superficiality in the syndicalists' overall position. Even Panunzio was not capable of a more serious and sustained critique of the great historical adversary. Marx simply did not envision the permanent subjection of the state to the economic society that Panunzio described. On the contrary, the Marxist revolution was to make possible the *Aufhebung* of the state, which means the end of the separation between state and society, the triumph of the universal-political over the particularism of the economy-society.[23]

But still it was possible for a radical critic of the bourgeois order to deny the relationship between economics and politics that Marxism postulated. At issue for Panunzio was not the ultimate intention of Marxism, but the immediate relevance of the Marxist strategy. While Marx certainly did not envision the permanent subjection of mankind to the material-economic sphere, he did insist that the leap into "political" freedom could result only in a determined, dialectical way; an economic-material process would produce an economically defined class capable of a revolution which would reverse the previous relationship between economics and politics. Panunzio portrayed Sismondi as revolutionary and Marx as conservative because he denied that this dialectical process was necessary to reverse—in a revolutionary way—the relationship between politics and economics characteristic of liberalism. The essential problem was political; the process of radical change would be essentially political as well. It was possible to transcend the bourgeois order, even overcoming some of the central problems of capitalism, by attacking the legal, political, and ethical systems in society, but without abolishing private property.

In exalting such non-Marxists as Merlino, Proudhon, and Sismondi, Panunzio and his colleagues were concerned in part about the bias toward monolithic state socialism which they claimed to find in the Marxist conception. For Marx, the tendency toward concentration inherent in capitalism would indeed reach its culmination in the collectivization of the socialist order during its initial stage; the proletariat would use its new monopoly of political power "to centralize all instruments of production in the hands of the state."[24] In Marxist theory, of course, this was only to be a transitional stage—toward the communist fulfillment which Marx never sought to delineate precisely. But

Panunzio could plausibly have his doubts since, as George Lichtheim put it, Marx failed to face up to "all the implications of the problem of social control in a planned economy."[25] So Panunzio recommended Merlino's critique of collectivism as a useful rejoinder to Marxism.[26] In the work Panunzio resurrected, Merlino had found a dangerous authoritarian tendency inherent in collectivist socialism and had advocated a more pluralistic, decentralized kind of socialist economy, with room for competition, price, and supply and demand. A rigidly collectivist system, with economic decisions imposed by bureaucratic planners from above, was bound to damage both economic productivity and human freedom.

The syndicalists had accented socioeconomic pluralism from the beginning, envisioning postliberal society as a network of partly autonomous productive groupings. In fact, Italian syndicalism was obviously part of a Franco-Italian tradition, linking those like Proudhon and Durkheim, Merlino and Sorel, Duguit and Panunzio, who shared certain misgivings about both the bourgeois order and the Marxist tradition. Proudhon placed greater emphasis on pluralism, conflict, and bargaining than Marx did, and Durkheim saw society in analogous terms, accenting the role of social subgroups in the developent of political authority.[27] Panunzio turned to Durkheim again and again throughout his career, ultimately linking the theories of the great French sociologist to fascist corporativism.[28] To be sure, Durkheim was a liberal republican, not a fascist, but the problems in the bourgeois order that bothered him also troubled the left fascists, and some of his proposals for solution paralleled those of fascism. For Durkheim, as for Panunzio, the combination of societal individualism, relatively anarchical capitalism, and liberal parliamentary politics lay at the root of the major problems of modern society. And Durkheim found corporativism to be the best way of overcoming this set of patterns. Through a network of occupational groupings, it would be possible to socialize individual behavior and, at the same time, to regulate the economy, limiting the egotism of the present capitalist system.[29] Like Proudhon, Durkheim considered the economic sphere to be too complex to be ordered by a centralized, bureaucratic system.[30] It would be much more effective to let the appropriate corporative groupings coordinate each sector on the basis of its particular conditions. In addition, Durkheim suggested that occupational groupings should ultimately replace geographical groupings as the basis of political life. In general, these corporations would be public entities, carrying out public functions.

Durkheim's ideas had considerable influence on his contemporary, the solidarist jurist Léon Duguit, from whom Panunzio obviously learned a good deal.[31] Panunzio's first book, published in 1906, had been a critique of the solidarist—or juridical socialist—school, which included such figures as Anton Menger in Austria and Giuseppe Salvioli and Enrico Cimbali in Italy, as well as Duguit in France.[32] Writing in the full flush of revolutionary syndicalism, the twenty-year-old Panunzio was so preoccupied with the difference in methods which separated the syndicalists from these very bourgeois law professors that he failed to appreciate how much he could learn from them, given the conception of the basis of social problems that was already taking shape in his mind. The juridical socialists all considered it possible to overcome the excesses of liberal individualism and to foster solidarity in society by expanding the sphere of law and by breaking down the distinction between public and private law. Léon Duguit found the emergence of new forms of binding social obligation out in society—the rules of professional associations, for example, or agreements arrived at through collective bargaining—to be carrying society spontaneously beyond the old liberalism in significant respects.[33] The increasing role of groups outside the state in imposing obligations upon individuals tended to blur the traditional distinction between public and private law. The dualism between state and individual characteristic of liberalism was breaking down as the network of groups comprising society assumed more and more power vis-à-vis both state and individual. No longer could the state as a distinguishable entity claim a monopoly of legislative capacity; no longer could individuals claim an absolute, "anarchical" right over their own property. These new forms of social law, Duguit felt, would make possible social solidarity without the authoritarian and centralizing tendencies of collectivist socialism. A kind of pluralistic socialism was possible now, as a result of political and juridical changes which did not require a revolutionary change in the organization of the means of production. At the same time, Duguit envisioned more effective forms of economic and political integration through a network of syndicates encompassing all classes.[34]

The problems that bothered all these non-Marxist critics of liberalism, from Proudhon and Mazzini to Durkheim and Duguit, were very much involved in the crisis of liberal Italy, so Italians seeking a non-Marxist way of moving beyond the present system could learn from them. The syndicalist tradition synthesized these sources, thus providing young Italians seeking radical change with a program that enabled them, in turn, to offer a plausible claim to leadership. Had it implemented the corporativist revolution, left fascism would have brought to fruition a major strand in the tradition of anti-Marxist criticism of liberalism and capitalism. Despite its ambiguities, the program was capable of a more meaningful kind of implementation than its proponents managed to achieve in the Fascist regime.

It was not merely socioeconomic dislocation, or the new irrationalism, or some sort of nihilistic activism, that gave rise to the left fascist revolt, but genuine, still open problems with liberalism and capitalism. How is it possible, for example, simultaneously to strengthen the state against particularism and to foster autonomous social energies? If revolution against capitalism is neither possible nor desirable, how can the anarchical and antisocial aspects of the capitalist system be checked? How can economic planning be combined with broadly based participation, as opposed to stifling and elitist bureaucratization? What is to be the relationship between political and economic power, between political and economic decision making? How can legitimate interest groups express their interests without corrupting the political process? Can political parties and parliamentary systems satisfactorily educate the people for—and involve them in—public life? Is the territorially based suffrage system the best foundation for popular participation? Is it possible simultaneously to foster such broad-based participation and to minimize the premium on pure politics—understood as an empty game based on petty personal ambitions—which seems to be bound up with universal suffrage and the parliamentary system? Does popular involvement necessarily produce a tendency toward mediocrity, or can it be made compatible with quality and expertise? The subsequent history of western Europe was to make clear that these are genuine dilemmas, which raise questions about central aspects of the modern liberal-capitalist order. In Germany and elsewhere, for example, parliament as an institution has gradually lost power to political parties and to bureaucratic experts, leading to concern about the quality of popular involvement in the modern parliamentary system. In postwar France, the problems of combining technocracy and participation, planning and decentralization, modernization and consensus, have been very much at issue, and sensitive critics have pondered the need for a new kind of institutional layer between the individual and the state.[35] Left fascism emerged in Italy partly because of such universal modern problems as these; the left fascist program sought to respond to them by combining economic planning, decentralization, and participation, and by deemphasizing pure electoral politics.

The antipolitical thrust was fundamental. Liberal politics has not been wholly edifying anywhere, but historical circumstances made some of its worst features stand out sharply in Italy. To the left fascists, the political sphere was a parasitical encrustation stifling a healthy society and impeding effective decision making. Political life seemed inevitably divorced from the real needs of the country. With its emphasis on election and representation, in fact, liberal politics seemed to foster the petty ambitions of those directly involved and to leave ordinary people politically incompetent. The whole system meant untoward power for mere politicians. So these fascists sought to promote direct and continuous participation in public life, at the expense of election and representation. This seemed possible largely because it was necessary for the state to take on more functions, for more decisions to be made collectively, as society became more complex. Through fascist corporativism, it seemed possible to expand the state and to foster societal initiative and a more direct kind of participation at the same time. Not all of those involved in the left fascist revolt grasped the corporativist program, but disgust with the liberal political system bound them all together—from Panunzio and Bottai to the young *squadristi* of 1921, with their "absurd" antipolitical "anarchism."

The left fascist program was intended to respond to central problems of the mature bourgeois order in Europe, problems which seemed to be capable of immediate solution from within the present capitalist framework. Marxism, on the other hand, by placing these problems in faulty perspective, seemed to impede their solution. The fundamental deficiencies in the "bourgeois" legal system, for example, could be overcome without abolishing private property. It was possible to solve some of the central social problems even though conflicting interests among classes would remain, given the persistence of the capitalist economy. These class conflicts were significant, but not decisive. Like the other problems inherent in capitalism, they could be handled within the new political and legal framework. But that new framework could not be created through an accumulation of reforms; antiliberal revolution was required.

In a book on counterrevolution, a major American historian has proclaimed ours to be "the era of the communist revolution." And those who oppose this particular revolution are either counterrevolutionaries, conservatives, or reactionaries.[36] But surely the era can better be understood in terms of the failure of the communist revolution, in terms of the bankruptcy of the old Marxist blueprint for radical change, in the advanced countries of the West. In Italy, that revolution failed after World War I not because fascism as a reaction defeated it, for fascism, historians are fond of emphasizing, merely "gave the *coup de grâce* to the revolution after its failure."[37] And fascism emerged not only to wreak vengeance on a failed adversary, but also to replace that adversary, once it had become clear that the dominant revolutionary tradition was at an impasse. Left fascism was not a cause, but a symptom, of the disarray and breakdown of the old Marxism. To portray twentieth-century reality in dualistic terms, with communist revolution and defense of the status quo as the only alternatives, impedes both historical understanding and the ongoing quest for more useful critical categories.

Left fascism, then, has a different place in European history than German Nazism. It was not so much personal-existential problems of identity and freedom that bothered the left fascists, but a different set of modern problems, more tangible, more sociopolitical, and, in principle, more capable of solution through concrete institutional changes. The left fascists understood what they disliked about modern life better than the Nazis did, and thus in part they were able to propose a more plausible, rational, forward-looking blueprint for change.

Through neosyndicalism, left fascism developed a nationalist, antiparliamentary, totalitarian corporativism on its own. This current was not subservient to Nationalism; nor were fascists like Roberto Farinacci its typical representatives. Focus on those like Farinacci leads us to underestimate the coherence of the populist current, the chance it had to create a different kind of fascist regime.[38] Our study has shown that left fascism, taken as a whole, envisioned something far more sweeping than a mere take-over of the old state by the Fascist party, and certainly it was not defeated when Farinacci was forced out as party Secretary in 1926.

But left fascism did fail, and its failure was no accident. Capacity for the vision necessary for genuine leadership varied considerably among those involved; the left fascists were not all Farinaccis, but the Farinaccis were there too. So despite the important measure of force it managed to achieve, left fascism as a whole suffered from serious weaknesses, which stemmed in important respects from characteristics of its "petty bourgeois" social base. Ultimately, problems on three levels undermined this current's political effectiveness. First, there were tensions, unanswered questions, and elements of superficiality even in the most coherent expressions of the left fascist program. This was true in part because those involved were trying to solve so many problems at once, but their rhetorical propensities, their shrill insistence on fascist Italy's mission, helped to prevent the left fascists from confronting their dilemmas directly. Second, the left fascist current was too heterogeneous, too divided against itself, to be successful. Some remained stuck on the level of resentment and place-seeking and did not fully grasp the left fascist program in its coherent form. As a result, they did not lend their energies to the struggle for its implementation. Some of those who did share in the long-term left fascist vision ultimately proved willing to settle for places in the regime, for Mussolini's superficial dynamism, for the mere trappings of change, once the obstacles to serious implementation of the program became clear. And third, the left fascists proved unable to overcome the split with the working class, and thus they failed to develop as much political force within the regime—and with Mussolini—as they might have. They were caught in a vicious circle that made it almost impossible for them to overcome the hostility or apathy of labor. Left fascists from Turati to Panunzio seriously desired to win over the workers, and perhaps the more genuinely populist policy they sought for fascism would have made this possible. But partly because they lacked working-class support, they did not have the power to force the regime to move in this direction.

The case of Paolo Orano manifests the fragility of left fascism— even in its intellectual manifestations. Orano had always been more eclectic and rhetorical than Panunzio or Olivetti, but he had contributed to the syndicalist evolution toward fascism and he continued to dream of rapid industrial modernization. During the years of the regime, however, as fascism bogged down and as Orano himself achieved the status of a major personage, his thinking lost much of its substance. He remained committed to the basic goals that had motivated his political behavior all along, but the superficial, rhetorical tendencies always present in his thinking now got the upper hand. The desire for national solidarity began to take the form of an exaggerated concern with the achievement of Italy's past, rather than a quest for serious institutional change.[39] Orano lamented, for example, that Italian scientific achievements were not sufficiently appreciated abroad, especially in France, and called on the Fascist regime to promote an international congress where each nation could present the case for its own precedence in scientific discoveries. An international tribunal of experts would sift the evidence and apportion the glory. Orano portrayed Italy's Catholic tradition as a sort of spontaneous popular expression and stressed its value as a source of common purpose among contemporary Italians. The Catholic conception of life which he deemed especially Italian had spontaneously come to the fore in fascism. Even now, Orano was talking about the lucid productivism and solidarity in labor that he had always wanted, but in emphasizing Catholic tradition rather than corporativist institutional change, he was making less and less contribution to bringing those ideals to fruition in practice.

Nevertheless, Orano continued in the same direction, finally producing his much-discussed anti-Semitic tract, *Gli ebrei in Italia*, in 1937.[40] His anti-Semitism was comparatively mild—and was strictly cultural-historical, as opposed to biological and racist. Giovanni Preziosi and those around his review *La vita italiana* promptly criticized Orano for being too soft on the Jews and argued for a more genuinely racist conception. While Preziosi considered Jews to be inherently antinational, Orano simply questioned the patriotism of the existing Jewish community in Italy and exhorted Italian Jews to renounce their claim to special cultural identity within the nation. From a totalitarian perspective, it is perfectly plausible—and not specifically racist—to insist on a measure of sociocultural homogeneity incompatible with any kind of special ethnic identity. But under the circumstances, with all the obstacles to revolutionary implementation confronting serious fascists, to focus on the alleged lack of national integration of the Italian Jewish community could only be diversionary and counterproductive. In a situation of difficulty, Orano lapsed into "petty bourgeois" superficialities and became a mere conservator of certain Italian traditions, turning away from the serious problems that he and his colleagues had originally claimed to be able to solve.

Only if the forms of the degeneration of left fascism are kept in mind is it possible to confront the controversial problem of continuity between the liberal and Fascist regimes in Italy. Those who stress continuity point out that fascism left the monarchy and the old power structure largely intact and conclude that fascist Italy was nothing but the previous regime without the artificial façade of liberalism.[41] Certainly right fascism, though more dynamic and confident, embodied part of the tradition of conservative opposition to the compromises of Depretis and Giolitti. In fascism, the pessimistic elitism which had bound together the old political class was becoming explicit and brutal, with all pretence of liberalism, all hope for evolution in a liberal direction, dropping out altogether.

It is not as easy to assess the continuity in left fascism, which sought to overcome the basic weaknesses of liberal Italy, but ended up reproducing some of them in extreme form. The continuity for which the leftist current was responsible was largely a measure of its own inadequacy and failure. Its members helped to undermine parliament, but the corporativist alternative some of them worked to build was never very strong, so the tendencies toward bureaucratic decision making characteristic of liberal Italy only got worse. At the same time, as the thrust toward institutional change bogged down, left fascism itself tended to degenerate, with traditional Italian rhetoric and place-seeking coming to the fore and setting the tone. The most problematic area of continuity, however, is in the common lack of genuine political life in the liberal and fascist periods. In a famous passage written in November 1922, Piero Gobetti raised this troubling issue, portraying fascism as an accurate reflection of a nation "which renounces the political struggle out of laziness."[42] At first glance, it seems that an ongoing incapacity for real politics produced the peculiar political patterns of both the liberal and fascist periods. The matter is not so simple, however, for left fascism was not only "subpolitical," but also "postpolitical"; the left fascists rejected liberal politics not just because they were too immature or lazy for it, but, at least in part, because they grasped its problematic features and sought to go beyond it. From a liberal perspective, left fascism was an overreaction, but overreaction and continuity have quite different historical meanings, even if they produce conditions with some features in common. The wellsprings of the antipolitical impulse simply were different for fascists like Olivetti than they were for liberals like Depretis. Of course, the fascist regime failed to implement the corporativist alternative to liberal politics, so fascism in practice was not so much postpolitical as "nonpolitical." And Mussolini's nonpolitical regime had some features in common with "subpolitical" regimes of Depretis and Giolitti. But this does not mean that fascism arose in the first place as an attempt to keep things the same. Ultimately much in Italy remained the same under fascism, but only as the result of a complex process, in which reasonably serious attempts at change got buried.

Mussolini, seeking to enhance his own position, exploited both the strengths and the weaknesses of left fascism. He used its serious ideals to give his haphazard regime the appearance of purpose and historical justification. At the same time, he fostered personal rivalries, played on petty ambitions, and thus defused the left fascist current. His methods of personal dictatorship encouraged the weaknesses of his movement, not its strengths. In a sense, then, Mussolini ended up a supertransformist in the tradition of Depretis and Giolitti, bringing new elements into the system, but taking advantage of their weaknesses to fragment them and buy them off. Insofar as Mussolini's system brought transformism up to date, expanding the political base but still leaving the monarchy and the old elites in place, Mussolini himself was the major source of continuity. To the extent that this is all fascism amounted to, Mussolini justified the hopes of those who acquiesced as he assumed power.

Still, Mussolini himself was a new man, one of the outsiders seeking political access after the war, and a man who genuinely resented the old political system. Thus he was quite a departure from Depretis and Giolitti and, despite his pessimism, quite a risk. For most of his regime, the egocentric but cynical leader was content to balance, accumulating personal power and prestige. But increasingly, Mussolini vacillated between the giddy self-confidence that the cult of the Duce reinforced and a gloomy sense of the impasse that he was caught up in. Without something extraordinary, he felt, his regime was in danger of wearing out, of running down; at the very least, it would not survive him.[43] So the needs of the personal dictatorship gave the regime a momentum of its own, and, given the near impasse on the domestic scene, it is not surprising that Mussolini was led to devote his restless energies increasingly to foreign policy.

With his conquest of Ethiopia in 1935–36, and with his defiance of the League of Nations, Mussolini's personal prestige reached a peak, but the old elites, as well as many fascists of both left and right, had serious misgivings about his subsequent policy. The more coherent left fascists like Bottai, Grandi, Lanzillo, and Panunzio disliked the alliance with Nazi Germany and resisted the drift toward war, but for Farinacci and others, racism, imperialist war, and the link with Nazism seemed ways of revitalizing fascism. With the latter as his allies, Mussolini sought to maintain his momentum, turning against the old elites who seemed to have trapped him. One result was the radicalization of the final phase, including the antibourgeois campaign—and the anti-Semitism. But the major thrust was toward war—a war of conquest, but also a war of vengeance against the intractable old Italy. Ultimately a dangerous possibility inherent in fascism from the beginning came to the fore, as Mussolini, sensing himself at an impasse, sought to return fascism to its origins, to war as revolution. The noble tragedy of Italy's World War I became the tragic farce of Italy's World War II. And now the whole system quickly began to unravel, for the one thing that Mussolini's hollow regime had not done—and could not have done—was to prepare the Italian people to fight a major war on the side of Nazi Germany.

Notes

Chapter 1 / Ideas, Ideologies, and the Problem of Italian Fascism

1. Benedetto Croce, "L'obiezione control la 'Storia dei propri tempi'" pp. 36–38; Costanzo Casucci, "Fascismo e storia," pp. 427–31; Delio Cantimori, *Conversando di storia*, pp. 134–35; Renzo De Felice, *Fascism*, pp. 25–26, 37. This last item is a translation of De Felice's controversial interview with Michael A. Ledeen, published as *Intervista sul fascismo* in 1976. De Felice's call for a less polemical and more truly historical approach to fascism provoked a spirited discussion, as reported by Michael A. Ledeen in "Renzo De Felice and the Controversy over Italian Fascism." For an excellent introduction to the literature on Italian fascism, see Adrian Lyttelton, "Italian Fascism."

2. Franco Gaeta, *Nazionalismo italiano*, pp. 203–4; Roberto Vivarelli, *Il dopoguerra in Italia e l'avvento del facismo*, 1: chap. 3. On Rocco, see Paolo Ungari, *Alfredo Rocco e l'ideologia giuridica del fascismo*.

3. Claudio Giovannini portrays the central role of the petty bourgeoisie as an established fact in his useful historiographical article "Alle origini del fascismo," p. 894. H. Stuart Hughes comes to much the same conclusion in discussing the critique of fascism in *The Sea Change*, pp. 130–32.

4. See especially Adriano Tilgher, "Piccoli borghesi al bivio," from *Tempo*, 7 Dec. 1919, in *La crisi mondiale e saggi critici di marxismo e socialismo*, pp. 175–85; and the unsigned article by Antonio Gramsci and Palmiro Togliatti from *L'ordine nuovo*, 6–13 Dec. 1919, in Antonio Gramsci, *L'ordine nuovo 1919–1920*, p. 61.

5. Luigi Salvatorelli, *Nazionalfascismo*, p. 16.

6. Ibid., pp. 18–19.

7. Ibid., p. 26.

8. Renzo De Felice, *Mussolini il fascista*, 1:117–24; Renzo De Felice, *Le interpretazioni del fascismo*, pp. 157–60. It should be noted that De Felice begins to move away from the Salvatorellian interpretation in his recent *Fascism*, pp. 46–49; fascism now appears as the expression of an emerging, more modern petty bourgeoisie, not a sector in socioeconomic decline.

9. Giovannini, "Alle origini del fascismo," pp. 902–4.

10. Major examples include Enzo Santarelli, *Storia del movimento e del regime fascista*, 1:218–24; Alessandro Roveri, *Le origini del fascismo a Ferrara*, pp. 56–58, 110n., 134–36; Gaeta, *Nazionalismo*, pp. 23–26; Vivarelli, *Il dopoguerra*, 1:253–59, 266, 278–80, 329n., 498–500.

11. Vivarelli, *Il dopoguerra*, 1:266–67, 276.

12. Edward R. Tannenbaum, *The Fascist Experience*, p. 4.

13. De Felice, *Mussolini il fascista*, 1:46, 116–19, 158–59.

14. This is Adrian Lyttelton's view in *The Seizure of Power*, p. 50.

15. Ibid., pp. 50, 56; Salvatorelli, *Nazionalfascismo*, pp. 16–23.

16. Santarelli, *Storia del movimento*, 1:220–22.

327

17. De Felice, *Mussolini il fascista*, 1:46, 116–19; De Felice, *Le interpretazioni*, pp. 160–61.

18. Lyttelton, *The Seizure of Power*, p. 334.

19. Ibid., p. 74.

20. Ibid., p. 46.

21. Vivarelli, *Il dopoguerra*, 1:235–37, 257–58, 272–76.

22. De Felice, *Mussolini il fascista*, 1:17–18, 116–18; De Felice, *Le interpretazioni*, pp. 160–61.

23. For example, see the evaluation of Augusto Turati's role in De Felice, *Mussolini il fascista*, 2:176.

24. Mussolini is portrayed as a syndicalist in Renzo De Felice, *Mussolini il rivoluzionario*, p. xxv; and in A. James Gregor, *The Ideology of Fascism*, especially chap. 3.

25. See, for example, Carlo Vallauri, "Il programma economico nazionalista e la genesi del corporativismo fascista," pp. 622–24.

26. On the centrality of corporativism, see Camillo Pellizzi, *Una rivoluzione mancata*, pp. 55–57, 64. Pellizzi's emphasis is especially significant, since he himself was involved in a variety of fascist cultural enterprises, not all of them specifically corporativist.

27. Giovanni Spadolini, *Lotta sociale in Italia*, pp. 186–87. For two more recent examples, see Alberto Aquarone, *L'organizzazione dello Stato totalitario*, pp. 112–13; and De Felice, *Mussolini il rivoluzionario*, pp. 515–16. Aquarone deems syndicalism and Nationalism to be the major sources of fascist corporativism, while De Felice shows that Mussolini drew heavily from Panunzio and the syndicalist review *Il rinnovamento* as he sought to reorient himself during the pivotal years 1918–19.

28. Curzio Suckert, "La conquista dello Stato nella concezione organica di Sergio Panunzio," p. 1. On the liberal side, Vittorio Emanuele Orlando, for example, expressed admiration in dissent for Panunzio's ideas in "Lo 'stato sindacale' e le condizioni attuali della scienza di diritto pubblico," p. 8.

29. L[ouis] Rosenstock-Franck, *L'économie corporative fasciste en doctrine et en fait*, p. 10; Marcel Prélot, *L'Empire fasciste*, pp. 72–83; Herbert L. Matthews, *The Fruits of Fascism*, pp. 151–53.

30. We find mention of Panunzio's importance in, for example, Norberto Bobbio, "La cultura e il fascismo," p. 234; Aquarone, *L'organizzazione dello Stato*, p. 272; and Lyttelton, *The Seizure of Power*, p. 205. Roberto Vivarelli ignores Panunzio in *Il dopoguerra*, 1, even though his interpretation rests on the meaning of national syndicalist ideas. See especially chap. 3.

31. For a brief biographical sketch, see Leonardo Paloscia, *La concezione sindacalista di Sergio Panunzio*, pp. 46–48.

32. Panunzio recalls his conversion to socialism in his "Prefazione" to Luigi Viesti, *Stato e diritto fascista*, p. 10.

33. Sergio Panunzio, *Il sentimento dello Stato*, pp. 13–127.

34. Sergio Panunzio, *Lo Stato fascista*.

35. "La morte improvvisa di A. O. Olivetti," *Il popolo d'Italia*, 18 Nov. 1931, p. 3.

36. Archivio Centrale dello Stato, Ministero dell'Interno, Direzione generale della pubblica sicurezza, Casellario politico centrale, Fascicolo individuale, Olivetti Angelo Oliviero, Cenno biografico, 15 Sept. 1894 and Cenno biografico, 10 May 1906. Antonio Graziadei recalls Olivetti's role at the university in *Memorie di trent'anni*, p. 35.

37. Mario Racheli, "Angelo Oliviero Olivetti," p. 9.

38. See, for example, Sorel's letters to Mario Missiroli, dated 30 May and 23 Sept. 1910, in Georges Sorel, *Lettere a un amico d'Italia*, pp. 73, 81.

39. Newspaper accounts of the murder include considerable biographical information about Casalini. See *Il popolo d'Italia*, 13 Sept. 1920, pp. 1–2; and *Corriere della sera*, 13 Sept. 1920, pp. 1–2.

40. Alceo Riosa, "Sindacalismo riformista e sindacalismo rivoluzionario," p. 109.

41. Carlo Curcio, "Sindacalisti e nazionalisti a Perugia fra il 1928 e il 1933," p. 22.

42. For some helpful observations about these tricky relationships in the context of the problem of European fascism, see Barbara Miller Lane, "Nazi Ideology," pp. 3–30; Eberhard Jäckel, *Hitler's Weltanschauung*, pp. 21–22, 67, 72–74, 119; Alan Cassels,

"Janus," pp. 166–67; Zeev Sternhell, "Fascist Ideology," pp. 317–19; Juan J. Linz, "Some Notes toward a Comparative Study of Fascism in Sociological Historical Perspective," pp. 13–14; and Eugen Weber, "Revolution? Counterrevolution? What Revolution?" p. 444.

43. George Lichtheim, *The Concept of Ideology and Other Essays*, p. 3. See also John Plamenatz, *Ideology*, for a valuable discussion of the uses and abuses of the concept.

44. See Lane, "Nazi Ideology," p. 29, for some perceptive observations about this source of confusion.

45. For an excellent English-language treatment of Gentile's thought, see H. S. Harris, *The Social Philosophy of Giovanni Gentile*. The most lucid statement of Gentile's fascism is his *Origini e dottrina del fascismo*. See also the anthology of earlier speeches and articles, *Che cosa è il fascismo*.

46. Augusto Del Noce, "Per una definizione storica del fascismo," pp. 36–43; Augusto Del Noce, "Idee per l'interpretazione del fascismo," pp. 370–83; Gregor, *The Ideology of Fascism*, chaps. 3–5.

47. Roland Sarti, in his commentary in his anthology, *The Ax Within*, p. 102. Edward Tannenbaum's conception of syndicalism is similarly limited in "The Goals of Italian Fascism," pp. 1192–95. See also S. J. Woolf, "Italy," pp. 48–49, where the syndicalists are portrayed as relatively isolated and unimportant, since fascism never enjoyed much working-class support.

48. Gaetano Salvemini, *Dal patto di Londra alla pace di Roma*, pp. xxx–xxxi. On the overrepresentation of southerners among the intellectual petty bourgeoisie, see Gaetano Salvemini, "La piccola borghesia intellettuale nel Mezzogiorno d'Italia," from *La voce*, 16 March 1911, in *Opere, 4: Il Mezzogiorno e la democrazia italiana*, 2:481–93.

49. Gaetano Arfé, *Storia del socialismo italiano*, pp. 120–21. For other examples of this line of interpretation, see Enzo Santarelli, *La revisione del marxismo in Italia*, pp. 13, 124; Giuseppe Ludovico Goisis, "Sorel e i soreliani italiani," pp. 621–24; Giuseppe Mammarella, *Riformisti e rivoluzionari nel Partito Socialista Italiano*, pp. 183–84.

50. Gaetano Arfé, "Le origini del movimento giovanile socialista," pt. 2, pp. 25–26.

51. Umberto Ricci, *Dal protezionismo al sindacalismo*, pp. 115–16, 163n.–164n. See A. O. Olivetti, *Il sindacalismo come filosofia e come politica*, pp. 9–10, 13–15, for the passages that elicited Ricci's sarcasm.

52. See, for example, Agostino Lanzillo, *La disfatta del socialismo*, pp. 278–80.

53. For example, much of A. O. Olivetti's *Storia critica dell'utopia comunista*, 1, falls under this category.

54. For a few examples, see ibid., pp. 105–39; A. O. Olivetti, "Ascensione," *Il lavoro d'Italia*, 25 April 1928, p. 1; Sergio Panunzio, "La fine di un regno," p. 344.

55. See George Mosse, "Fascism and the Intellectuals," pp. 205–25, for a useful introduction to this problem.

Chapter 2 / The Politics of Pessimism

1. The "parenthesis" thesis is identified with Benedetto Croce, the "revelation" thesis with Giustino Fortunato, Carlo Rosselli, Piero Gobetti, and others. For an introduction to the vast literature on this subject, see Renzo De Felice, *Le interpretazioni del fascismo*, especially pp. 29–30, 173–77, 202–5. De Felice stresses that the parenthesis-revelation axis of debate was transcended during the years after the war, but it is still true that a variation of the "revelation" thesis, stressing continuity, is widely propounded today. See Claudio Giovannini, "Alle origini del fascismo," pp. 890–920. Two recent essays that provide valuable introductions, from contrasting points of view, to the problems of liberal Italy are Alberto Aquarone's relatively favorable "Alla ricerca dell'Italia liberale," in his *Alla ricerca dell'Italia liberale*, pp. 275–344; and Roberto Vivarelli's more critical "Italia liberale e fascismo," pp. 669–703. For a more strictly bibliographical essay, see Leo Valiani, "La storia d'Italia dal 1870 al 1915," pp. 35–130.

2. Francesco De Sanctis, "L'uomo del Guicciardini," p. 23.

3. Ibid., p. 25.

4. Giustino Fortunato, "Dopo la guerra sovvertitrice," in *Pagine e ricordi parlamentari*, 2:67–68. This piece was originally published separately by Laterza (Bari) in 1921.

5. Ibid., p. 68.

6. Ibid., p. 81.

7. Guido De Ruggiero, *The History of European Liberalism*, pp. 340–42.

8. For some significant examples of these themes, see Alberto Caracciolo, *Stato e società civile*, pp. 12, 14, 112, 126–27; Aquarone, *Alla ricerca*, pp. 315, 320, 341; Ernesto Ragionieri, *Politica e amministrazione nella storia dell'Italia unita*, pp. 123–24; Giuliano Procacci, "Appunti in tema di crisi dello Stato liberale e di origini del fascismo," p. 224; and Roland Sarti, *Fascism and the Industrial Leadership in Italy*, pp. 141–42.

9. Aquarone, *Alla ricerca*, p. 299n.

10. Edward R. Tannenbaum, *The Fascist Experience*, pp. 14–15.

11. Gabriel A. Almond and Sidney Verba, *The Civic Culture*, pp. 402–3.

12. Ibid., p. 228.

13. Luciano Gallino, "L'evoluzione della struttura di classe in Italia," p. 124; Joseph LaPalombara, "Italy: Fragmentation, Isolation, Alienation," pp. 282, 286, 298.

14. Joseph LaPalombara, "Integrazione sociale e partecipazione politica," pp. 62–66. The passage quoted is on p. 62.

15. Piero Pieri, "Fascismo e resistenza," p. 576.

16. On the decision for centralization, see especially Denis Mack Smith, *Victor Emanuel, Cavour, and the Risorgimento*, pp. 252–74.

17. Aquarone, *Alla ricerca*, pp. 292, 320; Ragionieri, *Politica e amministrazione*, p. 121.

18. Giampiero Carocci, *Agostino Depretis e la politica interna italiana dal 1876 al 1887*, pp. 26, 33–36.

19. Ibid., pp. 72, 125, 128; Vivarelli, "Italia liberale," pp. 685–86.

20. Carocci, *Agostino Depretis*, pp. 91, 125, 128. For a perceptive contemporary analysis, see Pasquale Turiello, *Governo e governati in Italia*, pp. 319–30, 341.

21. Carocci, *Agostino Depretis*, pp. 89–90, 176–77, 349, 601.

22. Fernando Manzotti, "I partiti politici italiani dal 1861 al 1918," p. 152.

23. Bruno Caizzi, *Storia dell'industria italiana*, p. 317; Rosario Romeo, *Breve storia della grande industria in Italia*, p. 58; Carocci, *Agostino Depretis*, pp. 341–42.

24. Carocci, *Agostino Depretis*, pp. 90, 149; Paolo Farneti, *Sistema politico e società civile*, p. 185.

25. Carocci, *Agostino Depretis*, p. 633.

26. See ibid., pp. 76, 216, 262–63, 267, 271, 622–23, for some observations about the significance of this aspect of transformism.

27. For example, see Salvatore La Francesca, *La politica economica italiana dal 1900 al 1913*, p. 11, on the relationship between transformism and the lack of a coherent economic policy in liberal Italy.

28. Caracciolo, *Stato e società civile*, pp. 113–16.

29. Ibid., pp. 92–93.

30. R[ichard] A. Webster, *Industrial Imperialism in Italy*, pp. 52–53.

31. Caizzi, *Storia dell'industria*, pp. 340–41.

32. Renato Zangheri, "Dualismo economico e formazione dell'Italia moderna," p. 293; Vivarelli, "Italia liberale," p. 693.

33. Alexander Gerschenkron, "Notes on the Rate of Industrial Growth in Italy, 1881–1913," in *Economic Backwardness in Historical Perspective*, pp. 79–83; Carocci, *Agostino Depretis*, p. 406; Romeo, *Breve storia*, pp. 56–57; Caizzi, *Storia dell'industria*, pp. 314–16, 344–46.

34. Farneti, *Sistema politico*, p. 164.

35. Marco Minghetti, *I partiti politici e la ingerenza loro nella giustizia e nell'amministrazione*. See especially pp. 95, 145–46, 224–25, 245–48.

36. Some of the best writings of Mosca and Pareto on the ills of parliamentary government, especially in Italy, are available in English. See Gaetano Mosca, *The Ruling Class*, chap. 10, and particularly pp. 259–60, 265–66; and Vilfredo Pareto, "The Parliamentary Regime in Italy," especially pp. 678–710.

37. Pareto, "The Parliamentary Regime," pp. 709–10.

38. Vilfredo Pareto, "L'Etatisme en Italie," from *Bibliothèque Universelle et Revue Suisse*, March-April 1897, in *The Ruling Class in Italy before 1900*, pp. 140–43.

39. Mario Delle Piane, *Gaetano Mosca*, pp. 90–95.

40. Caracciolo, *Stato e società civile*, pp. 137–38.

41. Giosuè Carducci, "Per la morte di Giuseppe Garibaldi," in *Edizione nazionale delle opere di Giosuè Carducci*, 7:449.

42. Caizzi, *Storia dell'industria*, pp. 347–48.

43. Ibid., pp. 358–59; Romeo, *Breve storia*, pp. 62–64, 68–72.

44. Gerschenkron, "Notes," in *Economic Backwardness*, p. 88; Luciano Cafagna, "La formazione di una 'base industriale' fra il 1896 e il 1914," pp. 150–53; Caizzi, *Storia dell'industria*, p. 371.

45. Caizzi, *Storia dell'industria*, pp. 387–91.

46. Ibid., p. 371; Cafagna, "La formazione," p. 152.

47. Benedeto Croce, *A History of Italy*, pp. 150, 156.

48. Rodolfo De Mattei, *Dal "trasformismo" al socialismo*, pp. 83–96.

49. Sidney Sonnino [Un deputato], "Torniamo allo Statuto," pp. 9–28.

50. A classic treatment in English is A. William Salomone, *Italy in the Giolittian Era*. Though highly favorable to Giolitti, Salomone conveys a good sense of both sides of the question. Roberto Vivarelli is quite critical in "Italia liberale," pp. 694–703, but he admits Giolitti's basically good intentions. See also Franco De Felice, "L'età giolittiana," p. 115, on the historiographical significance of evaluation of the Giolittian era.

51. Giampiero Carocci, *Giolitti e l'età giolittiana*, pp. 68–69.

52. Ibid., p. 98; Vivarelli, "Italia liberale," pp. 702–3; Aquarone, *Alla ricerca*, p. 311.

53. De Felice, "L'età giolittiana," pp. 159–71; Carocci, *Giolitti*, pp. 21, 69–70.

54. See especially the retrospective analysis by Gaetano Salvemini, the most persistent critic of electoral abuses in the South under Giolitti, "Fu l'Italia prefascista una democrazia?" from *Il ponte*, 1952, in *Opere, 4: Il mezzogiorno e la democrazia italiana*, 1:540–67.

55. Farneti, *Sistema politico*, pp. 183, 189–90; Carocci, *Giolitti*, pp. 91–92; Vivarelli, "Italia liberale," pp. 700–703.

56. Carocci, *Giolitti*, pp. 35, 43–45.

57. Ibid., p. 72; Caizzi, *Storia dell'industria*, pp. 375–80, 404–5; Romeo, *Breve storia*, pp. 78–79, 83; Webster, *Industrial Imperialism*, pp. 67–75.

58. Gerschenkron, "Notes," in *Economic Backwardness*, pp. 78, 81.

59. Ibid., pp. 86, 88; Sarti, *Fascism and the Industrial Leadership*, pp. 7–8.

60. Francesco Saverio Nitti, *Il partito radicale e la nuova democrazia industriale*, passim.

61. See Giuseppe Are, *Economia e politica nell'Italia liberale*, pp. 79–102, on the insights and errors of free traders during the Giolittian era.

62. Carocci, *Giolitti*, pp. 50, 72.

63. De Felice, "L'età giolittiana," p. 165.

64. Carocci, *Giolitti*, pp. 99–100.

65. See Manzotti, "I partiti politici," pp. 184–87, on Giolitti's continuity with earlier traditions. See also Vivarelli, "Italia liberale," pp. 700–703, and Carocci, *Giolitti*, p. 20, for effective remarks on the limits of Giolitti's strategy.

66. Gaetano Mosca, "Il concetto moderno della libertà politica," from *Corriere della sera*, 8 Aug. 1911, in *Il tramonto dello Stato liberale*, pp. 149–55; Luigi Albertini, *Venti anni di vita politica*, pt. 1: *L'esperienza democratica italian dal 1898 al 1914*, 1:150–51, and 2:66.

67. Luigi Einaudi, *Cronache economiche e politiche di un trentennio*, 3:220.

68. Enrico Corradini, "Per coloro che risorgono," pp. 441–43. See also Salvatore Saladino, "Italy," pp. 231–35.

69. Vilfredo Pareto and Giuseppe Prezzolini, "La borghesia può risorgere?" pp. 467–71.

70. See especially Giuseppe Prezzolini, "L'aristocrazia dei briganti," pp. 455–60. Here Prezzolini credits Pareto and Mosca with having provided the intellectual underpinnings of the movement around *Il regno*.

71. See, for example, Giovanni Papini, "La vita non è sacra," pp. 205–8; and Giovanni Papini, "Amiamo la guerra!" pp. 329–31.

72. Emilio Gentile, *"La voce" e l'età giolittiana*, pp. 14–15.

73. Franco Gaeta, *Nazionalismo italiano*, pp. 24–27; Webster, *Industrial Imperialism*, passim.

74. Norberto Bobbio, "Profilo ideologico del novecento," p. 144.

75. See especially Enrico Corradini, "Nazionalismo e sindacalismo," *La lupa* 1, no. 1 (16 Oct. 1910): 2; and Francesco Coppola, *La crisi italiana*, p. 7.

76. Gaeta, *Nazionalismo*, pp. 118–25; Paolo Ungari, *Alfredo Rocco*, p. 24.

Chapter 3 / The Origins of an Antipolitical Vision

1. Dora Marucco, *Arturo Labriola e il sindacalismo rivoluzionario in Italia*, p. 146. The most detailed study of the early period of revolutionary syndicalism in Italy is Alceo Riosa's recent *Il sindacalismo rivoluzionario in Italia*; see especially pp. 15–145 on the protosyndicalist reaction against reformism of 1902–04.

2. Giuseppe Mammarella, *Riformisti e rivoluzionari nel Partito Socialista Italiano*, pp. 103, 149–51.

3. See, for example, Paolo Spriano, *Storia di Torino operaia e socialista*, pp. 99–101, on Labriola's impact on the workers and Socialists of Turin in 1903.

4. For a good summary of this presyndicalist revolutionary position, see Walter Mocchi, "Il nostro ordine del giorno al congresso Lombardo di Brescia," *Avanguardia socialista*, 21 Feb. 1904, p. 1. See also Alceo Riosa, "Alcuni elementi dell'ideologia sindacalista rivoluzionaria in Italia all'indomani dello sciopero generale del 1904," pp. 86–87, 95, on the ongoing ambiguity in the syndicalist position even in 1904.

5. Giuliano Procacci, *La lotta di classe in Italia agli inizi del secolo XX*, pp. 373–74.

6. On the general strike of 1904, see ibid., chap. 5; and Riosa, *Sindacalismo rivoluzionario*, pp. 145–72.

7. Georges Sorel, preface to the 1905 edition of "Avenir socialiste des syndicats," in *Matériaux d'une théorie du prolétariat*, pp. 74–75.

8. Mammarella, *Riformisti e rivoluzionari*, pp. 51, 79, 95, 100, 188, 197, 207–8. See also p. 77 for a statement by Turati that well expresses the reformist position.

9. Christopher Seton-Watson, *Italy from Liberalism to Fascism*, p. 301.

10. Gaetano Arfé, *Storia del socialismo italiano*, pp. 112, 164, 167; Mammarella, *Riformisti e rivoluzionari*, p. 109.

11. Salvemini's writings on the Giolittian system and on prewar socialism have been collected in his *Opere, 4: Il mezzogiorno e la democrazia italiana*, 2 vols.

12. For examples of this line of argument, see Marucco, *Arturo Labriola*, pp. 130–35, and Giuseppe Ludovico Goisis, "Sorel e i soreliani italiani," pp. 620, 623–24.

13. Antonio Gramsci, "The Southern Question," in *The Modern Prince and other Writings*, pp. 37–38. For the Italian original, see Antonio Gramsci, *La questione meridionale*, pp. 22–23. For some examples of the reliance on Gramsci's interpretation by major authorities, see Marucco, *Arturo Labriola*, p. 134; Enzo Santarelli, *La revisione del marxismo in Italia*, p. 109; and Renzo De Felice, *Sindacalismo rivoluzionario e fiumanesimo nel carteggio De Ambris-D'Annunzio*, p. 16. Raffaele Colapietra comments critically on Gramsci's interpretation in *Napoli tra dopoguerra e fascismo*, p. 38n.

14. Marucco, *Arturo Labriola*, p. 156.

15. See Giuseppe Are, *Economia e politica nell'Italia liberale*, pp. 63–79, for a valuable discussion of some aspects of reformist confidence.

16. Arturo Labriola, *Spiegazioni a me stesso*, pp. 18–19; Gaetano Arfe, "Arturo Labriola e il riformismo," p. 222; Antonio Papa, "Arturo Labriola," p. 672.

17. Papa, "Arturo Labriola," pp. 673–74; Arfé, "Arturo Labriola," p. 223; Marucco, *Arturo Labriola*, pp. 39–40; 44; Arturo Labriola, "I nuovi orizzonti della critica socialista," p. 213.

18. Arturo Labriola, "La crisi della teoria socialista," pp. 1153–55, 1160–62.

19. Labriola, *Spiegazioni*, p. 118.

20. Filippo Corridoni, "Dopo la sconfitta sindacalista a Milano: Verità necessarie," *L'internazionale*, 6 April 1912, p. 2.

21. Franco Pedone, *Il Partito Socialista Italiano nei suoi congressi*, 1:164–65; Mammarella, *Riformisti e rivoluzionari*, pp. 137–38.

22. See, for example, Sergio Panunzio, "Dove sta il socialismo?" *Il divenire sociale* 2, no. 19 (1 Oct. 1906):301; and Sergio Panunzio, "Socialismo—progresso—civiltà," pt. 2, *Il divernire sociale* 2, no. 7 (1 April 1906):109.

23. The syndicalists would always accept the revisionist critique of Marx's economic predictions. For examples, see Arturo Labriola, *Contro G. Plekanoff e per il sindacalismo*, p. 91; Sergio Panunzio, "Il momento critico del socialismo," *Pagine libere* 2, nos. 4–5 (28 Feb. 1908):209–10; Arturo Labriola, *Marx nell'economia e come teorico del socialismo*, pp. 233–40; Enrico Leone, *Il sindacalismo*, pp. 134–35, 157.

24. Labriola, "I nuovi orizzonti della critica socialista," pp. 212–13.

25. Labriola, *Marx nell'economia*, p. 240.

26. Arturo Labriola, *Decadenza della civiltà*, p. 206n.; Labriola, *Spiegazioni*, pp. 82–84; Arfé, "Arturo Labriola," p. 224; Marucco, *Arturo Labriola*, pp. 87–95.

27. Vilfredo Pareto, *Les systèmes socialistes*, 1:62–64, 74–75; and 2:432–39, 451–54, 460–64. See also Vilfredo Pareto, *The Rise and Fall of the Elites*, pp. 77, 82–83.

28. Sergio Panunzio, for example, cites Pareto's analysis with approval in *Il socialismo giuridico*, p. 241n.

29. Vilfredo Pareto, "Socialismo legalitario e socialismo rivoluzionario," p. 108. Sergio Panunzio quotes from this article in *Il socialismo giuridico*, p. 133.

30. Marucco, *Arturo Labriola*, pp. 98, 105; Labriola, *Spiegazioni*, pp. 87–88. See also Arfé, "Arturo Labriola," p. 225, on Labriola's period in France.

31. Georges Sorel, "Mes Raisons du syndicalisme," from *Il divenire sociale*, 1 March–16 May 1910, in *Matériaux*, pp. 252–53; see also Georges Goriely, *Le Pluralisme dramatique de Georges Sorel*, p. 116. For a detailed examination of Sorel's relationship with Merlino and other Italian intellectuals during the formative period of revolutionary syndicalism, see Gian Biagio Furiozzi, *Sorel e l'Italia*, pp. 50–235.

32. Georges Sorel, "Pro e contro il socialismo," pp. 854–88; Georges Sorel, "Préface."

33. G[eorges] Sorel, "Dommatismo e pratica," pp. 217–18.

34. Ibid., pp. 211–18; G[eorges] Sorel, "La crisi del socialismo scientifico," pp. 134–38; Sorel, "Préface," pp. xxi, xxvi, xxix, xlii.

35. Georges Sorel, "Avenir socialiste des syndicats," in *Matériaux*, p. 127.

36. Sorel, "Préface," pp. xl, xlv.

37. Sorel, "Mes Raisons du syndicalisme," in *Matériaux*, pp. 252–53; Paul de Roussiers, *The Labor Question in Britain*, especially pp. 367–74.

38. Sorel, "Avenir socialiste des syndicats," in *Matériaux*, p. 104; see also pp. 106–7, 128–29.

39. Sorel, "La crisi del socialismo scientifico," p. 138.

40. Mammarella, *Riformisti e rivoluzionari*, pp. 111–13, 117, 128; Papa, "Arturo Labriola," p. 676.

41. Vittorio Frosini, *Breve storia della critica al marxismo in Italia*, pp. 23–33; Ernesto Ragionieri, *Socialdemocrazia tedesca e socialisti italiani*, pp. 261–80; Aldo Venturini, "Saverio Merlino," p. 8.

42. See especially [Francesco] Saverio Merlino, *Collettivismo, lotta di classe e . . . ministero!*, passim.

43. [Francesco] Saverio Merlino, *L'utopia collettivista*, pp. 28, 37–52, 127–28.

44. Georges Sorel, "Les Théories de M. Durkheim," pp. 1–26, 148–80.

45. Sorel, "Avenir socialiste des syndicats," in *Matériaux*, pp. 127–29. Sorel was responding to Emile Durkheim, *Suicide*, especially pp. 373–74, 378–80. See also Goriely, *Le Pluralisme dramatique*, p. 187; and Steven Lukes, *Emile Durkheim*, p. 326n., on Sorel's response to Durkheim.

46. Emile Durkheim, review of *Formes et essence du socialisme*, by [Francesco] Saverio Merlino, pp. 433–39. The quoted passage is on p. 437.

47. Durkheim, *Suicide*, pp. 378–84; Emile Durkheim, "Preface to the Second Edition: Some Notes on Occupational Groups," *The Division of Labor in Society*, pp. 1–31.

48. For example, Sergio Panunzio, *L'economia mista*, pp. 29n., 71.

49. On Merlino, see especially Arturo Labriola, "Obbietto e limiti del programma minimo (Nota sommaria)," *Critica sociale* 10, no. 16 (16 Aug. 1900):251. Though admitting the value of Merlino's doctrinal objectives, Labriola had been more critical in his earlier review, "Pro e control il socialismo," *Critica sociale*, 1 May 1897, pp. 213–15.

50. Arturo Labriola, "I nuovi orizzonti della critica socialista," pp. 241–43, 265–66.

51. Sergio Panunzio, "La politica socialista delle camere di lavoro," *Avanguardia socialista*, 22 Nov. 1903, p. 2.

52. See A. O. Olivetti, "Presentazione," p. 3, for perhaps the best statement of what the proletariat meant to the syndicalists. For another example, see Antonio Renda, "Il congressso socialista," *Pagina libere* 4, nos. 20–21 (15 Oct.–1 Nov. 1910):490.

53. A. O. Olivetti, "I sindacalisti e la 'élite,'" orig. pub. 1 July 1909, now in *Cinque anni di sindacalismo e di lotta proletaria in Italia*, pp. 267–68.

54. Leone, *Il sindacalismo*, pp. 81, 90; Enrico Leone et al., "Il socialisti rivoluzionari al Partito Socialista Italiano," *Il divenire sociale* 2, no. 16 (16 Aug. 1906):241; Sergio Panunzio, "Punti di dissenso: Socialismo legalitario e socialismo rivoluzionario," *Avanguardia socialista*, 3 Jan. 1904, p. 2, and 10 Jan. 1904, p. 1; Sergio Panunzio, *Sindacalismo e medio evo*, p. 59; Labriola, *Marx nell'economia*, pp. 201, 212, 247; Alceste De Ambris, *L'azione diretta*, p. 26.

55. Arturo Labriola, "I limiti del sindacalismo rivoluzionario" (lecture delivered 28 May 1910), in *Economia, socialismo, sindacalismo*, p. 100.

56. A. O. Olivetti, *Problemi del socialismo contemporaneo*, pp. 277–78; Arturo Labriola, "Bilancio di riforme (per il discorso dell'On. Turati)," *Avanguardia socialista*, 2 Aug. 1903; Labrioloa, *Contro G. Lekanoff*, p. 109; Enrico Leone, "Partito e organizzazioni economiche," *Il divenire sociale* 2, no. 18 (16 Sept. 1906):274–75.

57. Arturo Labriola, *Riforme e revoluzione sociale*, p. 195; Arturo Labriola, "Alla vigilia del congresso di Firenze," *Pagine libere* 2, nos. 16–17 (1 Sept. 1908):907; Tommaso Sorricchio, "Crisi socialista e crisi sindacalista," *Il divenire sociale* 4, nos. 4–5 (1 March 1910):41–42.

58. See Marucco, *Arturo Labriola*, p. 60, on the syndicalists' lack of an effective strategic alternative.

59. Stanley Payne, *The Spanish Revolution*, p. 35; Peter N. Stearns, *Revolutionary Syndicalism and French Labor*; F. F. Ridley, *Revolutionary Syndicalism in France*.

60. Olivetti, *Problemi del socialismo*, pp. 280, 291–93; Panunzio, "La politica socialista delle camere del lavoro," p. 2; Arturo Labriola, "La prima conferenza Labriola sul 'sindacalismo,'" *Avanguardia socialista*, 18 Nov. 1905, pp. 1–2.

61. The syndicalists consistently admitted the utility of parliamentary action. For example, see De Ambris, *L'azione diretta*, p. 25; Labriola, *Contro G. Plekanoff*, pp. 106, 109; Sergio Panunzio, "Il problema della rappresentanza politica dei sindacati," *Il divenire sociale* 3, no. 12 (16 June 1907):187; and A. O. Olivetti, "L'iniziative sindacalista," orig. pub. 15 Sept. 1908, now in *Cinque anni di sindacalismo*, p. 188.

62. Panunzio, "Socialismo—progresso—civiltà," pt. 2, p. 108.

63. Sergio Panunzio, *La persistenza del diritto*, p. 163. Durkheim and Tarde were intellectual antagonists whose conceptions of the relationship between individual and society differed, but Panunzio's concerns were so immediate and, in a sense, superficial that he could use both to buttress his argument. See Lukes, *Emile Durkheim*, pp. 302–13, on the dispute between Durkheim and Tarde.

64. See, for example, Leone, "Partito e organizzazioni economiche," p. 274; Arturo Labriola, "L'azione politica del partito socialista" (address to the Socialist Party's National Congress of 1906), in *Economia, socialismo, sindacalismo*, p. 186; Alighiero Ciattini, "Democrazia e sindacalismo," *Pagine libere* 3, no. 11 (1 June 1909):639; Arturo Labriola, "L'azione diretta nella concezione del sindacalismo," *Avanguardia socialista*, 11 Feb. 1905, p. 1; Alfonso De Pietri-Tonelli, "Il socialismo giuridico," *Lotta di classe* 1, no. 3 (19 Jan. 1907):2.

65. For example, Giuseppe Santonastaso, *Pensiero politico e azione sociale*, pp. 288–89. See also Riosa, *Sindacalismo rivoluzionario*, pp. 187–202, on Leone's brand of syndicalism.

66. Enrico Leone, "Le coalizioni operaie e il liberismo," pp. 233–35.

67. Ibid.; Enrico Leone, *La revisione del marxismo*, pp. 55–56, 160–61; Enrico Leone,

"L' 'atto di accusa' control lo sciopero di Parma: Glossa lineare ad un articolo di L. Bissolati," *Il divenire sociale* 4, no. 17 (1 Sept. 1908):284. See also Rodolfo Mondolfo's perceptive discussion of Leone's position, originally published in 1912 and now in his *Umanismo di Marx*, pp. 104–5, 105n.

68. Leone, *Il sindacalismo*, p. 162.

69. Enrico Leone, *Indirizzo sindacale e politica*.

70. Sergio Panunzio, for example, uses Leone's categories in "Socialismo—liberismo—anarchismo," pt. 1, pp. 46–47, and pt. 2, pp. 63–64.

71. Labriola, *Marx nell'economia*, p. 217; Panunzio, "Il momento critico del socialismo," p. 227.

72. Franz Weiss, "La base morale dell'organizzazione socialista del lavoro," pt. 3, p. 94.

73. Franz Weiss, "La base morale," pt. 1, p. 54.

74. Leone, "Le coalizioni operaie," p. 235.

75. Weiss, "La base morale," pt. 3, p. 93; Panunzio, *Il socialismo giuridico*, pp. 240–43; A. O. Olivetti [Ausonio Semita], "Violenza," *Avanguardia socialista*, 20 Jan. 1906, p. 1; A. O. Olivetti, review of *Il socialismo giuridico* by Sergio Panunzio, *Pagine libere* 1, no. 3 (15 Jan. 1907):211.

76. Labriola, *Contro G. Plekanoff*, p. 119; Labriola, "I limiti del sindacalismo rivoluzionario," p. 106; Paolo Orano, "Perchè il sindacalismo non è popolare in Italia," *Il divenire sociale* 3, no. 15 (1 Aug. 1907);226; Weiss, "La base morale," pt. 1, p. 55.

77. Alighiero Ciattini, "Sciopero generale e partiti politici," *Pagine libere* 3, no. 1 (1 Jan. 1909):12–13; Panunzio, *Il socialismo giuridico*, p. 243; Sergio Panunzio, "Lotta di classe el solidarietà umana," *Avanguardia socialista*, 1 May 1904, p. 2.

78. Olivetti, *Problemi del socialismo*, pp. 41–44; Panunzio, *La persistenza del diritto*, pp. 12–14; Alfredo Polledro, "Dal congresso di Bologna alla palingenesi sindacalista," *Pagine libere* 3, no. 14 (15 July 1909):87.

79. Antonio Graziadei, *Socialismo e sindacalismo*, p. 72.

80. Arturo Labriola, "Tirando le somme," *Avanguardia socialista*, 24 Sept. 1904, p. 2; De Ambris, *L'azione diretta*, p. 18; A. O. Olivetti, "Anima nuova: A proposito dello sciopero di Parma," orig. pub. June 1908, now in *Cinque anni di sindacalismo*, pp. 151–53; Agostino Lanzillo, "Lo sciopero di Parma e l'ultimo tradimento rei riformisti," *Il divenire sociale* 4, no. 14 (16 July 1908):251; Paolo Orano, "Gli insegnamenti di uno sciopero," *Lotta di classe* 1, no. 15 (13 April 1907):1.

81. See, for example, Alceste De Ambris, "'L'esperimento sindacalista,'" *L'internazionale*, 16 Aug. 1913, pp. 1–2.

82. See especially the pamphlet by A. O. Olivetti, *Azione diretta e mediazione*. Arturo Labriola had high praise for this work in *Economia, socialismo, sindacalismo*, p. 90.

83. Panunzio, *La persistenza del diritto*, p. 199; A. O. Olivetti, "Per chiudere una polemica," orig. pub. 1 Aug. 1909, now in *Cinque anni di sindacalismo*, pp. 277–325.

84. Panunzio, "Socialismo—liberismo—anarchismo," pt. 3, p. 73; Paolo Mantica, "Nessuna libertà contro l'ordine pubblico?" *L'internazionale*, 18 April 1914, p. 1.

85. Panunzio, "Socialismo—liberismo—anarchismo," pt. 3, p. 74.

86. Ibid., p. 73; Arturo Labriola, *Sindacalismo e riformismo*, p. 24; Olivetti, *Problemi del socialismo*, pp. 40, 45. See also Riosa, *Sindacalismo rivoluzionario*, pp. 209–12, on the distinction between syndicalism and anarchism in Italy.

87. Panunzio, *La persistenza del diritto*, pp. 269–70, 279–82; Panunzio, *Il socialismo giuridico*, pp. 208–12, 233; De Pietri-Tonelli, "Il socialismo giuridico," p. 2.

88. Panunzio, *La persistenza del diritto*, p. 259; Panunzio, *Il socialismo giuridico*, pp. 233, 240.

89. Arturo Labriola, "Per la teoria dello sciopero generale," in *Economia, socialismo, sindacalismo*, pp. 89–90; Panunzio, *La persistenza del diritto*, p. 199; Panunzio, *Sindacalismo e medio evo*, p. 82; A. O. Olivetti, "Socialismo e movimento operaio," pt. 2, *Lotta di classe* 1, no. 7 (16 Feb. 1907):1–2.

90. Richard A. Webster, "From Insurrection to Intervention: The Italian Crisis of 1914," *Italian Quarterly* 5–6, nos. 20–21 (Winter 1961–Spring 1962):32–36. The anarchist Armando Borghi stresses the differences between anarchism and syndicalism in Italy in *Mezzo secolo di anarchia*, pp. 91–92.

91. Labriola, "L'azione politica del partito socialista," p. 182; Sergio Panunzio, "Socialisti ed anarchici," *Avanguardia socialista*, 23 July 1904, p. 2, and 30 July 1904, p. 1; Olivetti, "Socialismo e movimento operaio," pt. 2, p. 1; De Ambris, *L'azione diretta*, pp. 16–17.

92. Agostino Lanzillo, "Gli anarchici e noi," *Il divenire sociale* 6, nos. 8–9 (1 May 1910):103–4.

93. Tommaso Sorricchio, "Storia e sindacalismo," *Pagine libere* 5, no. 20 (15 Oct. 1911):369.

94. Olivetti, *Problemi del socialismo*, pp. 54–56; Arturo Labriola, "Per la teoria dello sciopero generale," in *Economia, socialismo, sindacalismo*, pp. 85–87; Alceste De Ambris, "L'azione pratica," *L'internazionale*, 25 Jan. 1913, p. 1.

95. See, for example, Paolo Mantica, "Per intenderci (di alcuni atteggiamenti pratici del sindacalismo italiano)," *Il divenire sociale* 1, no. 9 (1 May 1905):142. Mantica was responding to Turati's criticisms in light of the failure of a recent syndicalist railroad strike; see Filippo Turati, "Mentre si è in tempo ancora . . . ," *Critica sociale* 15, no. 8 (16 April 1905):113–15. In 1914, the syndicalists were still accenting patience and the need for continued proletarian maturation. For example, see [Alceste De Ambris], "1915," *L'internazionale*, 7 March 1914, p. 1.

96. For the syndicalist interpretation of the 1904 general strike, see especially Arturo Labriola, "Dopo lo sciopero generale," *Avanguardia socialista*, 7 Oct. 1904, p. 2; and Arturo Labriola, *Storia di dieci anni*, p. 252.

97. Quoted in Biagio Riguzzi, *Sindacalismo e riformismo nel Parmese*, p. 129. See also the quotation on p. 128.

98. For example, see Alceste De Ambris, "La natura e i fini dello sciopero parmense," *L'internazionale*, 13 June 1908, p. 1.

99. Luigi Lotti, *La settimana rossa*, pp. vii, 256–60; Orietta Lupo, "I sindacalisti rivolusionari nel 1914," *Rivista storica del socialismo* 10, no. 32, pp. 70–71, 78. See also Edward R. Tannenbaum, *The Fascista Experience*, p. 20.

100. Lotti, *La settimana rossa*, pp. vii, 119–26, 146, 221–28, 236, 258.

101. Ibid., pp. 256–60; Lupo, "I sindacalisti," pp. 70–71, 78.

102. Agostino Lanzillo, "Per determinare la nostra via verso la 'meta immediata': La nuova ubriacatura," *L'internazionale*, 11 July 1914, p. 2.

103. Alceste De Ambris, "La meta immediata," *L'internazionale*, 4 July 1914, p. 3. For De Ambris's basic strategic position, see especially *L'azione diretta*.

104. Paolo Spriano, for example, refers to "quell'irrazionale che sta alla base della teoria anarcho-sindacalista" in *Storia di Torino*, p. 209. For examples of the widespread tendency to overemphasize syndicalist involvement with the avant-garde circles around Prezzolini, Papini, and Marinetti, see Paola Maria Arcari, *Le elaborzaioni della dottrina politica nazionale fra l'unità e l'intervento*, 1:501; Enzo Santarelli, "Prefazione," p. 21; and Zeev Sternhell, "Fascist Ideology," pp. 330–36.

105. Giuseppe Prezzolini, *La teoria sindacalista*.

106. Sergio Panunzio, "Ancora . . . sul duello e contro il futurismo: a F. T. Marinetti," *Pagine libere* 4, nos. 14–15 (15 July–1 Aug. 1910): 103–111; see especially p. 105.

107. Sergio Panunzio, "Preludio di rivoluzione," *Gazzettino rosa* (Ferrara), 27 Nov. 1914, p. 2.

108. Olivetti, "Presentazione," pp. 1–4; A. O. Olivetti, "Intorno ad un nuovo misticismo," *Pagine libere* 1, no. 7 (15 Mar. 1907):46–72; A. O. Olivetti, "Ancora del neomisticismo," *Pagine libere* 1, nos. 17–18 (15 Aug.–1 Sept. 1907):234–37.

109. Sergio Panunzio, "Per la revisione del socialismo," pt. 5 (30 July–30 Sept. 1918), p. 88.

110. See for example, Hubert Lagardelle, *Le Socialisme ouvrier*, pp. 283–92.

111. For examples of this emphasis on lucidity, see Sergio Panunzio, "Socialismo, sindacalismo e sociologia," pt. 1, *Pagine libere* 1, no. 3 (15 Jan. 1907):180; Paolo Orano, "Il secondo congresso sindacalista italiana: Il principio è salvo," *La lupa* 1, no. 10 (18 Dec. 1910):1; Sergio Panunzio, "Psicologia dello sciopero," *Avanguardia socialista*, 14 Jan. 1905, p. 3; Olivetti, *Problemi del socialismo*, p. 193.

112. For example, see Paolo Orano, "La teoria sindacalista," *Pagine libere* 3, nos. 8–9 (15 April–1 May 1909):430–31.

113. Georges Sorel, *Reflections on Violence*, p. 129.

114. Ibid., p. 229.

115. Ibid., p. 148. Several major students of Italian syndicalism have noted the limits of Sorel's influence; see Riosa, *Sindacalismo rivoluzionario*, pp. 212–17; Marucco, *Arturo Labriola*, p. 15; Santarelli, "Prefazione," p. 24; Papa, "Arturo Labriola," p. 678. See also A. O. Olivetti, "Polemichette," *Pagine libere* 3, no. 17 (1 Sept. 1909):277. For a remarkably non-Sorelian interpretation of Sorel's mature position, see Enrico Leone's "Prefazione" to Sorel's *Lo sciopero generale e la violenza*, and early version of *Reflections on Violence*.

116. Panunzio, "Psicologia dello sciopero," p. 3.

117. Labriola, *Marx nell'economia*, p. 228.

118. Labriola, *Spiegazioni*, pp. 141–43.

119. Sorel, *Reflections on Violence*, p. 126.

120. For examples of the place of violence in syndicalist thinking, see Arturo Labriola, "L'economico e l'extra-economico," pt. 2, *Pagine libere* 3, no. 6 (15 March 1909):310; De Ambris, *L'azione diretta*, p. 27; Ciattini, "Democrazia e sindacalismo," p. 639.

121. Panunzio, *Sindacalismo e medio evo*, pp. 72–73; Labriola, *Storia di dieci anni*, p. 318; Panunzio, "Socialismo—progresso—civiltà," pt. 2, p. 109.

122. Gregor, *The Ideology of Fascism*, pp. 110–11.

123. For example, see Labriola, *Riforme e rivoluzione sociale*, p. 205; and Panunzio, *Il socialismo giuridico*, p. 83.

124. Labriola, *Riforme e rivoluzione sociale*, p. 239; Olivetti, *Problemi del socialismo*, pp. 147, 184; Panunzio, "La politica socialista delle camere del laboro," p. 2.

125. A. O. Olivetti, note in reply to J. Novicow, "È l'elettorato politico una funzione sociale od un diritto?" *Pagine libere* 4, no. 10 (15 May 1910):620.

126. Leone, *Il sindacalismo*, p. 154; Panunzio, *La persistenza del diritto*, p. 192.

127. Labriola, *Riforme e rivoluzione sociale*, p. 27; Orano, "La teoria sindacalista," p. 431; Panunzio, "La politica socialista delle camere di lavoro," p. 2; Alfonso De Pietri-Tonelli, "Per un elogio da non meritare," *Avanguardia socialista*, 5 Aug. 1905, p. 1; Panunzio, "Il momento critico del socialismo," p. 226.

128. For two of many examples, see Cesare Spellanzon, "L'ora presente," *Il divenire sociale* 1, no. 16 (16 Aug. 1905):245–46; and A. O. Olivetti, note in reply to V. M. Fovel, "Dopo il terzo congresso radicale," *Pagine libere* 1, no. 14 (1 July 1907):19.

129. Olivetti, "Presentazione," p. 2.

130. Sergio Panunzio, "Degenerazione," *Avanguardia socialista*, 21 Oct. 1905, p. 2; A. O. Olivetti [Ausonio Semita], "La rivolta dei tondi di cuoio," *Pagine libere* 2, no. 23 (1 Dec. 1908):1403; Paolo Orano, "La 'curée' avvocatesca," from *Pagine libere*, 15 Dec. 1908, in *Discordie: Studi e polemiche*, pp. 159–76. For some other examples, see Leone et al., "I socialiste rivoluzionari al Partito Socialista Italiano," p. 241; Arturo Labriola, "Gli eccidi proletari e la decomposizione del Partito Socialista Italiano," *Pagine libere* 2, no. 8 (31 May 1908):450; and Paolo Orano, "Più che il colera," *Pagine libere* 5, no. 18 (15 Sept. 1911):243.

131. Alighiero Ciattini, "La rinascita dell'idealismo," *Pagine libere* 3, no. 23 (1 Dec. 1909):652–53. For another example of this sort of emphasis, see Panunzio, *Il socialismo giuridico*, pp. 208–9.

Chapter 4 / The Corruption of the Proletariat

1. Benedetto Croce, "Introduzione," to Georges Sorel, *Considerazioni sulla violenza*, pp. 41–42. Croce's introduction, dated 1907, was originally published in the first Italian edition (Bari, 1909).

2. Benedetto Croce, "La morte del socialismo," pp. 501–2.

3. Georges Sorel to Benedetto Croce, 15 Feb. 1911, in *La critica* 26, no. 5 (20 Sept. 1928):345.

4. Georges Sorel to Mario Missiroli, 1 Nov. 1910, in Georges Sorel, *Lettere a un amico d'Italia*, p. 85.

5. Georges Sorel to Benedetto Croce, 25 Jan. 1911 and 19 Feb. 1911, in *La critica* 26, no. 5 (20 Sept. 1928):345, 347.

6. See Giuseppe Mammarella, *Riformisti e rivoluzionari nel Partito Socialista Italiano*, pp. 181–82, on the impact of the unfavorable outcome of this strike. For the syndicalist position in the subsequent debate over the responsibility for the strike's failure, see Paolo Mantica, "Per intenderci (di alcuni atteggiamenti pratici del sindacalismo italiano)," *Il divenire sociale* 1, no. 9 (1 May 1905):141–43. For the reformist position, see the editorial by Filippo Turati, "Mentre si è in tempo ancora . . . ," *Critica sociale* 15, no. 8 (16 April 1905):113–15. Chapters 5–7 of Alceo Riosa's *Il sindacalismo rivoluzionario in Italia* provide a detailed account of syndicalist activities and debates during 1905–7.

7. Mammarella, *Riformisti e rivoluzionari*, pp. 215, 228.

8. Luigi Lotti, *La settimana rossa*, p. 16.

9. Franco Pedone, *Il Partito Socialista Italiano nei suoi congressi*, 2:107–110.

10. Thomas Ronald Sykes, "The Practice of Revolutionary Syndicalism in Italy 1905–1910," pp. 193–95, 358–59.

11. Ibid., pp. 306–8. The best study of the Parma strike is Thomas R. Sykes, "Revolutionary Syndicalism in the Italian Labor Movement." For a negative assessment of both the Parma strike and the revolutionary syndicalist strategy in general, see Biagio Riguzzi, *Sindacalismo e riformismo nel parmese*, pp. 110–45. Luigi Preti takes a similar tack, accusing De Ambris of arrogance and adventurism at the expense of the workers, in *Le lotte agrarie nella valle padana*, pp. 292–98.

12. These are government figures. See Sykes, "The Practice of Revolutionary Syndicalism," p. 330.

13. Ibid., pp. 245–346, 378–97.

14. Adolfo Pepe, *Storia della CGdL dalla guerra di Libia all'intervento*, p. 64; Lotti, *La settimana rossa*, pp. 20–23.

15. See especially Alceste De Ambris, "Verso il 'Partito del lavoro' e la scissura del proletariato," *L'internazionale*, 11 May 1912, p. 3; Alceste De Ambris, "La 'confederazione del lavoro' vuole la scissura del proletariato," *L'internazionale*, 18 May 1912, p. 1; Alceste De Ambris, "Sempre in tema di unità: Il matrimonio di Pulcinella," *L'internazionale*, 24 Aug. 1912, p. 1.

16. Filippo Corridoni, "Dopo la sconfitta sindacalista a Milano: Verità necessarie," *L'internazionale*, 6 April 1912, p. 3.

17. For a good example of the renewed confidence, see Alceste De Ambris, "La nuova fede," *L'internazionale*, 23 Nov. 1912, p. 1.

18. Lotti, *La settimana rossa*, p. 26; Christopher Seton-Watson, *Italy from Liberalism to Fascism*, pp. 299–300.

19. Paolo Spriano, *Storia di Torino operaia e socialista*, pp. 208–9, 215–20.

20. Piero Bolchini, "Milano 1915," pp. 272–73.

21. Tullio Masotti, "Il problema essenziale," *L'internazionale*, 13 Dec. 1913, p. 5.

22. Lotti, *La settimana rossa*, pp. 30–31.

23. See especially Arturo Labriola, "Sindacalisti e partito socialista in Italia," *Il divenire sociale* 2, no. 12 (16 June 1906):180; A. O. Olivetti, "Il congresso della dedizione," orig. pub. 1 June 1909, now in *Cinque anni di sindacalismo*, p. 262; Alceste De Ambris, "Quel che potrà essere il 'partito del lavoro,'" *L'internazionale*, 25 May 1912, p. 1.

24. Tommasco Sorricchio, reply to A. O. Olivetti, *Pagine libere* 3, no. 15 (1 Aug. 1909):135–36.

25. For some typical examples, see Paolo Orano, "Perchè il sindacalismo non è popolare in Italia," *Il divenire sociale* 3, no. 15 (1 Aug. 1907):226; Enrico Leone, "Per un secondo convegno sindacalista," *Il divenire sociale* 6, nos. 8–9 (1 May 1910):100; Filippo Corridoni, *Sindacalismo e repubblica*, pp. 37–38; Alfonso De Pietri-Tonelli, "Di una 'scienza della politica,'" *Pagine libere* 5, no. 8 (15 April 1911):475.

26. Enrico Loncao, "Dobbiamo costituire il partito sindacalista?" *Pagine libere* 4, no. 17, (1 Sept. 1910):280.

27. For examples of this pattern of argument, see Paolo Orano, "Rinascita sindacale," *Pagine libere* 4, no. 5 (1 March 1910):259; Alighiero Ciattini, "La rinascita dell'idealismo," *Pagine libere* 3, no. 23 (1 Dec. 1909):649; A. O. Olivetti, "Il blocco dei bloc-

chi," orig. pub. 15 April 1911, now in *Cinque anni di sindacalismo*, p. 339; Agostino Lanzillo, "La confederazione industriale in Italia," *Il divenire sociale* 6, no. 12 (16 June 1910):175–76.

28. Dora Marucco, *Arturo Labriola e il sindacalismo rivoluzionario in Italia*, pp. 187, 190–91.

29. Ibid., pp. 156, 189–91.

30. Arturo Labriola, *Storia di dieci anni*, pp. 240–41, 245, 326.

31. Ibid., pp. 198, 230, 233, 237, 269, 304–7, 327–8.

32. Ibid., pp. 321–22.

33. Ibid., pp. 198–99, 306. See also Marucco, *Arturo Labriola*, pp. 213, 220.

34. *L'internazionale*, 13 Sept. 1913, p. 2. The item is unsigned and untitled.

35. Georges Sorel to Mario Missiroli, 23 Nov. 1913, in Sorel, *Lettere a un amico d'Italia*, p. 111.

36. Labriola, *Storia di dieci anni*, pp. 103, 190–95, 313.

37. Arturo Labriola, *La conflagrazione europea e il socialismo*, pp. 193–99.

38. Arturo Labriola, *La dittatura della borghesia e la decadenza della società capitalistica*, passim.

39. Corridoni, *Sindacalismo e repubblica*, pp. 15, 53.

40. Ibid., pp. 21, 24, 27–29, 35, 66.

41. Ibid., p. 35.

42. Ibid., pp. 21, 27–29, 35–36, 49, 70–71.

43. Ibid., pp. 29–30, 74, 76, 85.

44. Ibid., pp. 36–38, 45–46, 49, 62.

45. Paolo Mantica, "Il momento buono per i sindacati," p. 582. See also Paolo Mantica, "La 'morta gora,'" *Pagine libere* 4, no. 9 (1 May 1910):546–49.

46. Mantica, "La 'morta gora,'" pp. 549–50.

47. Paolo Mantica, "Sinecurismo e Stato," *La lupa* 2, no. 15 (22 Jan. 1911):1–2.

48. Alfonso De Pietri-Tonelli, "Il sindacalismo come problema della libertà operaia," *Pagine libere* 3, nos. 8–9 (15 April–1 May 1909):449. See also A. O. Olivetti [Ausonio Semita], "Sapore politico e battaglie operaie," *Pagine libere* 5, no. 15 (1 Aug. 1911):135.

49. Paolo Mantica, "Mentre si attua il suffragio universale," p. 1. Mantica had warned in 1911 that universal suffrage would not improve the parliamentary system; see Mantica, "Il momento buono per i sindacati," p. 583.

50. Mantica, "Mentre si attua il suffragio universale," p. 1.

51. See especially Paolo Mantica, "Noi e gli altri," *L'internazionale*, 26 July 1913, p. 1.

52. Alfredo Polledro, "Partito sindacalista o partito rivoluzionario?" *Il divenire sociale* 6, no. 15 (1 Aug. 1910):217–19.

53. Sergio Panunzio, "Per il partito rivoluzionario," *Pagine libere* 4, nos. 18–19 (15 Sept.–1 Oct. 1910):361–62; Giulio Barni, "Per la sincerità!: Sindacati, sindacalismo e sindacalisti," *Pagine libere* 5, no. 2 (15 Jan. 1911):70.

54. For example, see Tommaso Sorricchio, "Deviazioni del sindacalismo," *Pagine libere* 5, no. 8 (15 April 1911):466–68; and Enrico Leone, "Rivoluzione del tricchi-tracco?" *Il divenire sociale* 4, nos. 19–20 (1–16 Oct. 1908):311–13.

55. Franz Weiss, "Il congresso di Modena," *Il divenire sociale* 4, nos. 19–20 (1–16 Oct. 1908):316, 318.

56. Leone, "Per un secondo convegno sindacalista," p. 100.

57. For examples of this internal quarreling, see Arturo Labriola, "Il riformismo alla riscossa (il convegno di Firenze e lo sciopero generale)," *Pagine libere* 1, no. 22 (1 Nov. 1907):518–19; Arturo Labriola, *Contro G. Plekanoff e per il sindacalismo*, p. 143n; and Franz Weiss, "L'ombra di Blanqui ed il sindacalismo," *Il divenire sociale* 4, no. 13 (1 July 1908):230.

58. Maria Rygier, a one-time syndicalist who was now turning to anarchism, described the rancor and futility of the first Bologna congress in *Il sindacalismo alla sbarra*. On p. 27, Rygier accepts Labriola's assessment of Leone as fundamentally conservative. See also Armando Borghi, *Mezzo secolo di anarchia*, p. 108, on the embarrassment which Rygier's pamphlet caused the syndicalists. For another bitter postmortem, see Spiritus Asper [pseud.], "Il congresso degli spostati," *Pagine libere* 4, no. 24 (15 Dec. 1910):682–83.

59. Giorgio Pini and Duilio Susmel, *Mussolini*, 1:83.

60. Renzo De Felice, *Mussolini il rivoluzionario*, pp. 40–41, 162.

61. See especially the review of the Italian translation of Sorel's book which Mussolini wrote for *Il popolo* (Trent), 25 June 1909, now in *Opera omnia di Benito Mussolini*, 2:163–68. See also Mussolini's discussion of Giuseppe Prezzolini's *La Teoria sindacalista*, from *Il popolo* (Trent), 27 May 1909, in *Opera omnia*, 2:123–28.

62. Benito Mussolini, "Fine stagione," from *La lotta di classe*, 17 Dec. 1910, in *Opera omnia*, 3:289–92.

63. See especially Gregor, *The Ideology of Fascism*, chap. 3, on the nature of Mussolini's revisionist socialism.

64. Alceste De Ambris, "L'azione diretta," *L'internazionale*, 1 Feb. 1913, p. 4.

65. See especially Alceste De Ambris, "Dopo la vittoria dei rivoluzionari in seno al Partito socialista," *L'internazionale*, 13 July 1912, p. 1; Alceste De Ambris, "Noi e il Partito Socialista: In guardia contro le illusioni!" *L'internazionale*, 27 July 1912, pp. 1–2; Alceste De Ambris, "Una questione ardente: Partito e sindacato," *L'internazionale*, 14 June 1913, p. 2; and Alceste De Ambris, "Spunti e appunti: Lettera confidenziale a Giuseppe De Falco," *L'internazionale*, 13 Sept. 1913, p. 2.

66. De Ambris, "Noi e il Partito Socialista," pp. 1–2.

67. See De Felice, *Mussolini il rivoluzionario*, pp. 162–74, on the complex relationship between Mussolini and syndicalism in 1913. See also Lotti, *La settimana rossa*, p. 34.

68. De Ambris, "Una questione ardente," p. 2.

69. For example, see Tullio Masotti, "La nuova crisi socialista," *L'internazionale*, 19 July 1913, p. 1; and Mantica, "Noi e gli altri," p. 1. See also De Felice, *Mussolini il rivoluzionario*, p. 174, on the context of this polemic.

70. Leonardo Paloscia, *La concezione sindacalista di Sergio Panunzio*, p. 26.

71. Alceste De Ambris, "Dopo la bufera," *L'internazionale*, 20 June 1914, p. 1; Alceste De Ambris, "La meta immediata," *L'internazionale*, 4 July 1914, p. 3; Alceste De Ambris, "Ancora in tema di 'unità,'" *L'internazionale*, 1 Aug. 1914, p. 1; Alceste De Ambris, "Il discorso di Alceste De Ambris," *L'internazionale*, 5 Dec. 1914, p. 1; Alceste De Ambris, "Programma d'azione," *L'internazionale*, 30 Jan. 1915, p. 1.

72. De Ambris, "Dopo la bufera," p. 1.

73. Agostino Lanzillo, "Per determinare la nostra via verso la 'meta immediata': La nuova ubriacatura," *L'internazionale*, 11 July 1914, p. 2.

74. Ibid.

75. De Ambris, "La meta immediata," p. 3.

76. Sergio Panunzio, "La guerra," *Avanguardia socialista*, 6 Aug. 1904, p. 2. For a more explicit exploration of this relationship between war and progress, see Cesare Spellanzon, "La politica internazionale del socialismo," *Il divenire sociale* 1, no. 23 (1 Dec. 1905):368–69.

77. Sergio Panunzio, "Il momento critico del socialismo," *Pagine libere* 2, nos. 4–5 (28 Feb. 1908):224; Arturo Labriola, "Intorno all'herveismo (antimilitarismo e antipatriottismo)," *Pagine libere* 1, no. 20 (1 Oct. 1907):389–99. See also Marucco, *Arturo Labriola*, pp. 193–94, on the importance of this article in Labriola's evolution.

78. Calcante [pseud.], "L'Italia e la rivoluzione: A proposito del libro di F. S. Nitti," *Pagine libere* 1, no. 3 (15 Jan. 1907):169.

79. Arturo Labriola, "La prima impresa collettiva della nuova Italia," p. 49. A. O. Olivetti's accents were similar; see especially "L'altra campana," p. 117.

80. Paolo Maltese, *La terra promessa*, p. 128.

81. Enrico Leone, *Espansionismo e colonie*.

82. Alceste De Ambris, "Contro il brigantaggio coloniale e per l'interesse del proletariato," *Pagine libere* 5, no. 20 (15 Oct. 1911):337–45; Tommaso Sorricchio, "Il sindacalismo e l'impresa tripolina," *Pagine libere* 5, nos. 23–24 (1–15 Dec. 1911):559–62; Alfredo Polledro, "Tripoli e triboli," *Pagine libere* 5, no. 22 (15 Nov. 1911):456–57; Giulio Barni, "Tripoli e il sindacalismo," *Pagine libere* 5, nos. 23–24 (1–15 Dec. 1911):487. The articles by Polledro, Barni, and De Ambris are also in Giulio Barni et al., *Pro e contro la guerra di Tripoli*.

83. Barni, "Tripoli e il sindacalismo," p. 487.

84. See especially Paolo Mazzoldi, "I pericoli d'un conflitto internazionale e l'atteggiamenti dei socialisti," *Avanguardia socialista*, 22 July 1905, p. 2; and Paolo Mazzoldi, "I benefici della Triplice," *Avanguardia socialista*, 29 July 1905, pp. 1–2.

Chapter 5 / Socialist Society and the Italian Nation

1. For a historiographical discussion of the complex problem of Italian intervention, see Leo Valiani, "Le origini della guerra del 1914 e dell'intervento italiano nelle ricerche e nelle publicazioni dell'ultimo ventennio," pp. 584–613. See also Brunello Vigezzi, *Da Giolitti a Salandra*, pp. 53–200, for two sensitive essays on the problem.

2. Alceste De Ambris, "I sindacalisti e la guerra," *L'internazionale*, 22 Aug. 1914, pp. 1–2.

3. Renzo De Felice, *Sindacalismo rivoluzionario e fiumanesimo nel carteggio De Ambris-D'Annunzio*, p. 40.

4. Brunello Vigezzi, *L'Italia di fronte alla prima guerra mondiale*, 1:387–92, 860–64.

5. A. O. Olivetti et al., "Ai lavoratori d'Italia," *Pagine libere* 6, no. 1 (10 Oct. 1914):36–39. The manifesto has been reproduced as an appendix to Renzo De Felice, *Mussolini il rivoluzionario*, pp. 679–81.

6. Alceste De Ambris, "Chiaramenti," *L'internazionale*, 5 Sept. 1914, p. 1; Agostino Lanzillo, "I paladini della Germania," *Il popolo d'Italia*, 2 Jan. 1915, p. 1. For other examples of this line of argument, see Sergio Panunzio, "Il socialismo e la guerra," *Utopia* 2, nos. 11–12 (15 Aug.–1 Sept. 1914):323–35; A. O. Olivetti, "Europa 1914," *Pagine libere* 6, no. 1 (10 Oct. 1914):5–12; Edmondo Rossoni, "La guerra . . . vista dall'America," *L'internazionale*, 17 Oct. 1914, p. 1; and the statements by Filippo Corridoni, Livio Ciardi, and Edmondo Rossoni in response to a survey by *Pagine libere*, under the title "Inchiesta su la guerra europea: Risposte all'inchiesta" in *Pagine libere* 6, no. 1 (10 Oct. 1914):13–19, for Rossoni and Ciardi, and 6, no. 4 (30 Nov. 1914):29–30, for Corridoni.

7. A. O. Olivetti, "Ricominciando . . . ," *Pagine libere* 6, no. 1 (10 Oct. 1914):3.

8. Edmondo Rossoni, *Le idee delle ricostruzione*, p. 10.

9. Alceste De Ambris, *Gli italiani all'estero*. For another example, see Alberto Argentieri, "Il problema dell'emigrazione italiana: Per un movimento concorde tra le organizzazioni operaie italo-americane," *Pagine libere* 5, no. 18 (15 Sept. 1911):263–69. Argentieri was a syndicalist organizer operating in the United States.

10. Paolo Orano, "Le illusioni di Gompers," *Pagine libere* 3, no. 19 (1 Oct. 1909):388.

11. A. O. Olivetti, "Carezze austriache," orig. pub. 1 Dec. 1908, now in *Cinque anni di sindacalismo*, p. 204.

12. Arturo Labriola, *La guerra di Tripoli e l'opinione socialista*, pp. 19–20.

13. Arturo Labriola, *La conflagrazione europea e il socialismo*, p. 47. See pp. 42–47, 55, 60, for the argument summarized in this paragraph.

14. Labriola, *La guerra di Tripoli*, p. 120.

15. Agostino Lanzillo, "Il fallimento del socialismo," *Pagine libere* 6, no. 3 (15 Nov. 1914):3. For another example, see A. O. Olivetti, "Il vaso di Pandora: Il nuovo manifesto del Partito Socialista," *Pagine libere* 6, no. 2 (30 Oct. 1914):2–3.

16. Arturo Labriola, "Intorno all'herveismo (antimilitarismo e antipatriotismo)," *Pagine libere* 1, no. 20 (1 Oct. 1907):398; Labriola, *La guerra di Tripoli*, pp. 20–25.

17. A. O. Olivetti, untitled editorial, *Pagine libere*, 10 Jan. 1915, p. 4; Labriola, *La conflagrazione europea*, p. 85.

18. Filippo Corridoni, letter of 12 Sept. 1915, in Alceste De Ambris, *Filippo Corridoni*, pp. 38–41. See especially pp. 40–41.

19. Agostino Lanzillo, "La guerra di redenzione," *Il popolo d'Italia*, 10 Feb. 1915, p. 1.

20. See, for example, Agostino Lanzillo, "La 'nostra' guerra," *Il popolo d'Italia*, 21 Jan. 1915, p. 1.

21. G. D. H. Cole, *A History of Socialist Thought*, 3: *The Second International 1889–1914*, pt. 2, pp. 551–57. See also Alfred G. Meyer, *Leninism*, p. 147.

22. Labriola, "Intorno all'herveismo," p. 391; Olivetti, "Il vaso di Pandora," pp. 2–3; Olivetti, "Polemichette," *Pagine libere* 3, no. 7 (1 Sept. 1909):277; Paolo Mazzoldi, "Socialismo e patriottismo," *Avanguardia socialista*, 17 June 1905, p. 1; Lanzillo, "La 'nostra' guerra," p. 1.

23. Labriola, *La conflagrazione europea*, p. 192.

24. Lanzillo, "La 'nostra' guerra," p. 1.

25. Sergio Panunzio, "Principio e diritto di nazionalità," orig. pub. 1920, now in *Popolo Nazione Stato*, p. 49.

26. Vigezzi, *L'Italia di fronte alla prima guerra mondiale*, 1:868–69. Vigezzi's remarks are suggestive, but it was not contradictory for the syndicalists simultaneously to stress indeterminacy and the need for action to dominate events.

27. De Ambris, "I sindacalisti e la guerra," pp. 1–2.

28. Sergio Panunzio, "Guerra e socialismo," *Avanti!*, 12 Sept. 1914, p. 2.

29. Vigezzi, *L'Italia di fronte alla prima guerra mondiale*, 1:395–97.

30. Pietro Bolchini, "Milano 1915," p. 275.

31. De Felice, *Mussolini il rivoluzionario*, pp. 234–60.

32. Sergio Panunzio, "Un ministro fortunato," *Gazzettino rosa* (Ferrara), 6 Dec. 1914, pp. 2–3.

33. Bolchini, "Milano 1915," p. 287; De Ambris, *Filippo Corridoni*, p. 29.

34. Nello Quilici, "Storia del fascismo ferrarese," pp. 195–98, 206–7.

35. Alceste De Ambris, "Il discorso di Alceste De Ambris," *L'internazionale*, 5 Dec. 1914, p. 1.

36. Filippo Corridoni, in *Avanguardia*, 5 Dec. 1914; quoted in De Felice, *Mussolini il rivoluzionario*, p. 293.

37. De Ambris, "Il discorso," p. 1; Panunzio, "Guerra e socialismo," p. 2; Paolo Mantica, "Questioni di chiarire: Patria e sindacalismo rivoluzionario," *L'internazionale*, 21 Nov. 1914, p. 1.

38. For example, see Sergio Panunzio, "Preludio di rivoluzione," *Gazzettino rosa* (Ferrara), 27 Nov. 1914, p. 2.

39. Filippo Corridoni, letter of 12 Sept. 1915, in De Ambris, *Filippo Corridoni*, pp. 40–41.

40. Alceste De Ambris, "Visioni di sangue (note ed impressione d'un volontario di guerra)," *Il popolo d'Italia*, 27 Nov. 1915, p. 2.

41. See "La grande adunata interventista," *Il popolo d'Italia*, 25 Jan. 1915, pp. 1–2, for an extensive report on Olivetti's speech.

42. Alceste De Ambris, "Programma d'azione," *L'internazionale*, 30 Jan. 1915, p. 1; Alceste De Ambris, "Il trionfo di filiste," *L'internazionale*, 24 Oct. 1914, p. 1.

43. Sergio Panunzio, "La monarchia nazionale," *Il popolo d'Italia*, 24 June 1915, p. 3.

44. Ottavio Dinale, "La Camera di Giolitti," *Il popolo d'Italia*, 13 Dec. 1916, p. 1. See also Ottavio Dinale [Jean Jacques], "La guerra al regno della guerra," *Il popolo d'Italia*, 11 March 1917, p. 3.

45. Georges Sorel, *Lettere a un amico d'Italia*, pp. 141–142.

46. For some of the many variations on this theme, see Norberto Bobbio, "Profilo ideologico del novecento," pp. 148, 152–53; Enzo Santarelli, *La revisione del marxismo in Italia*, p. 112; Nino Valeri, *Da Giolitti a Mussolini*, p. 28; Adrian Lyttelton, *The Seizure of Power*, p. 368.

47. Ernst Nolte, *Three Faces of Fascism*, p. 184.

48. Enrico Corradini, "Sindacalismo, nazionalismo, imperialismo," lecture of Dec. 1909, in *Discorsi politici*, pp. 54–60, 68–69.

49. Enrico Corradini, "Nazionalismo e socialismo," lecture of Jan. 1914, in *Discorsi politici*, p. 218.

50. See ibid., pp. 211–29, for a good summary of the proletarian nation argument. See also Enrico Corradini, *L'ora di Tripoli*, pp. 1–34; and Corradini, "Sindacalismo, nazionalismo, imperialismo," in *Discorsi politici*, pp. 60–61. For an example of subsequent use of the argument by a different Nationalist, see Alfredo Rocco, "Manifesto," *Politica* 1, no. 1 (15 Dec. 1918): 10–11, 16.

51. Corradini, *L'ora di Tripoli*, pp. 21–25.

52. Enrico Corradini, "Nazionalismo e sindacalismo," *La lupa* 1, no. 1 (16 Oct. 1910):2.

53. Paolo Orano, editorial response to ibid., p. 2. See also Paola Maria Arcari, *Le elaborazioni della dottrina politica nazionale fra l'unità e l'intervento*, pp. 669–70, 680, for some

useful observations about the differences between Nationalism and syndicalism at the time of *La lupa*.

54. Labriola, *La guerra di Tripoli*, pp. 127–29.

55. Paolo Orano, "L'agguato del ciompo," *Il popolo d'Italia*, 23 March 1919, p. 1. For additional examples of this line of argument, see the untitled editorial in *L'Italia nostra*, 1 May 1918; A. O. Olivetti, "Nazione e classe," *L'Italia nostra*, 1 May 1918; Alceste De Ambris, "Il nostro 'nazionalismo,'" *Il sindacato operaio*, 15 Oct. 1921, p. 1; and A. O. Olivetti, "Ripresa," *Pagine libere* 7, no. 1 (15 Feb. 1920):1–4.

56. Sergio Panunzio, "Il massimo problema politico di domani: la scuola," p. 446. See also Agostino Lanzillo, *Le rivoluzioni del dopoguerra*, p. 230; and A. O. Olivetti, "Sindacalismo e repubblica federativa," *Pagine libere* 8, no. 11 (Nov. 1921):392–93.

57. "Nazionalismo," *La patria del popolo* 1, no. 1 (12 Oct. 1922):1.

58. For example, see Sergio Panunzio, "Gli scopi politici ed economici," *Il popolo d'Italia*, 24 Jan. 1917, p. 3; and Paolo Mantica, "Patriottismo popolare ed internazionalismo," *Il popolo d'Italia*, 10 May 1917, p. 3. See also Arcari, *Le elaborazioni della dottrina politica nazionale*, pp. 669–70.

59. Sergio Panunzio, "Una forza," from *Giornale del mattino* (Bologna), 28 April 1918, in *Stato nazionale e sindacati*, p. 34. The ellipses are in the original.

60. Rocco, "Manifesto," pp. 9, 12. For another example of this mode of argument, see Enrico Corradini, *La marcia dei produttori*, pp. 187–89, 194.

61. Corradini, *L'ora di Tripoli*, pp. 11–12.

62. Corradini, "Nazionalismo e socialismo," p. 226.

63. Francesco Coppola, *La crisi italiana*, pp. 5–6.

64. Francesco Coppola, *La rivoluzione fascista e la politica mondiale*, p. 22.

65. Rocco, "Manifesto," pp. 1–4. The quoted passage is on p. 1.

66. Sergio Panunzio, "Engels, Mazzini, il prof. Levi e altre cose," pp. 111–12. See also De Ambris, "Il discorso," p. 1; and A. O. Olivetti, "Parole chiare," *Pagine libere* 6, no. 4 (30 Nov. 1914):1.

67. See Labriola's contribution to Arturo Salucci's collection, *Il nazionalismo giudicato da letterati, artisti, scienziati, uomini politici e giornalisti italiani*, p. 112.

68. Alceste De Ambris, "Libertà e federazione: Una questione d'opportunità," *Il popolo d'Italia*, 24 July 1917, p. 3; Alceste De Ambris, "Politica e fini di guerra," *Il popolo d'Italia*, 8 July 1917, p. 1; Alceste De Ambris, "Libertà e federazione," *Il popolo d'Italia*, 10 July 1917, p. 3.

69. Sergio Panunzio, "L'idealista," *Il popolo d'Italia*, 31 July 1915, p. 3.

70. Sergio Panunzio, *Il concetto della guerra giusta*, pp. 54, 66, 77, 82.

71. Ibid., pp. 50, 61, 75–76, 88.

72. Ibid., p. 54.

73. Ibid., p. 79. See also p. 77.

74. Ibid., pp. 18, 33–34, 81–83, 90.

75. Panunzio, "Gli scopi politici ed economici," p. 3. For some socialist statements on the progressive side of colonialism, see *Karl Marx on Colonialism and Modernization*, pp. 43, 88–89; and Eduard Bernstein, *Evolutionary Socialism*, pp. 178–79.

76. Sergio Panunzio, *Introduzione alla società delle nazioni*, p. 44.

77. Sergio Panunzio, "La questione internazionale," *Il popolo d'Italia*, 26 Jan. 1917, p. 3; see also Sergio Panunzio, "Gli scopi della guerra," *Il popolo d'Italia*, 20 Jan. 1917, p. 3.

78. Sergio Panunzio, *La lega delle nazioni*. See also "Un concorso della Società per la pace," *Corriere della sera*, 16 June 1919, p. 3.

79. Sergio Panunzio, "Nazionalità e umanità nella scuola," pp. 866–70; Panunzio, *Introduzione alla società delle nazioni*, pp. 56–57, 61.

80. Panunzio, *Introduzione alla società delle nazioni*, pp. 44, 53–55, 60–63.

81. Panunzio, *La lega delle nazioni*, p. 62.

82. The fullest statement, besides Panunzio's, is Antonio Renda, *I valori della guerra*, especially pp. 30–32; see also Paolo Orano's laudatory introduction, "Antonio Renda." For other examples, see Alceste De Ambris, "La società delle nazioni," *Il rinnovamento* 1, no. 7 (31 July 1918):12–20; Agostino Lanzillo, "Bassa marea," *Il popolo d'Italia*, 4 Nov. 1919, p. 3; Edmondo Rossoni, "Le ambasciate del lavoro," *Cultura sindacale* 1, no. 1 (30

Dec. 1920):2–3; A. O. Olivetti, "Un discorso dell'Avv. Olivetti sui rapporti internazionali," *Il sindacato operaio*, 1 Oct. 1921, p. 3; Dinale, "La guerra al regno della guerra," p. 3.

83. Alceste De Ambris, "Per la nostra emigrazione: Un grande problema italiano e proletario," *Il rinnovamento* 1, no. 8 (31 Aug. 1918):132, 136.

84. Panunzio, *Introduzione alla società delle nazioni*, pp. 41–42.

85. Alceste De Ambris, "Rapporti internazionali," *Il sindacato operaio*, 3 Sept. 1921, pp. 1–2.

86. Ibid.; Olivetti, "Un discorso," p. 3; Sergio Panunzio, *Che cos'è il fascismo*, p. 56.

87. De Ambris, "Rapporti internazionali," pp. 1–2; Sergio Panunzio, "I compiti del sindacalismo e le finalità immediate delle organizzazioni politiche e sindacali," p. 1.

88. De Ambris, "Rapporti internazionali," pp. 1–2.

89. A. O. Olivetti [Lo spettatore], "Il problema della popolazione: Le soluzioni," *Il popolo d'Italia*, 2 Sept. 1924, p. 3. See also A. O. Olivetti, "Relazione al convegno di cultura fascista di Bologna," pp. 6–7, March 1925, in the Olivetti papers, Rome.

90. A. O. Olivetti, "Nuove situazioni nella politica europea: L'imperialismo americano e le sue incognite," *La stirpe* 6, no. 10 (Oct. 1928):583. See also A. O. Olivetti [Lo spettatore], "Il massimo problema," *Il popolo d'Italia*, 6 Aug. 1924, p. 3; and A. O. Olivetti [Lo spettatore], "Le ore storiche," p. 1.

91. A. O. Olivetti, "Gli elementi costituivi della rivoluzione fascista," *La stirpe* 7, no. 10 (Oct. 1929):520; Olivetti, "Nuove situazioni nella politica europea," p. 585.

92. A. O. Olivetti, "La ricchezza delle nazioni," *Il lavoro fascista*, 28 Aug. 1931, p. 7.

93. Sergio Panunzio, "La S. d. N.: Capolavoro sbagliato," *Critica fascista* 14, no. 3 (1 Dec. 1935):35–37. The quoted passage is on p. 37.

94. Panunzio, "Gli scopi politici ed economici," p. 3; Panunzio, "La questione internazionale," p. 3.

Chapter 6 / The Postwar Crisis and the Nationalist Response

1. Piero Melograni, *Storia politica della grande guerra*, pp. 389, 404, 467–69. For a sensitive contemporary perspective, see the interview with Leonida Bissolati in Olindo Malagodi, *Conversazioni della guerra*, 1:196. The interview took place on 13 Nov. 1917.

2. Melograni, *Storia politica della grande guerra*, p. 468.

3. Giovanni Gentile, "Esame di coscienza," orig. pub. 15 Dec. 1917, now in *Guerra e fede*, pp. 62–63.

4. Giovanni Gentile, "Natale," orig. pub. 25 Dec. 1917, now in *Guerra e fede*, pp. 67–68.

5. Roberto Vivarelli, *Il dopoguerra in Italia e l'avvento del fascismo*, 1:20–22, 28–33.

6. Melograni, *Storia politica della grande guerra*, pp. 548–53.

7. Ibid., pp. 14–15, 92–93; Giuliano Procacci, "Appunti in tema di crisi dello Stato liberale e di origini del fascismo," pp. 235–36.

8. Bruno Caizzi, *Storia dell'industria italiana*, pp. 412–14.

9. Alberto Caracciolo, "La grande industria nella prima guerra mondiale," pp. 211–13; Caizzi, *Storia dell'industria*, pp. 425–27, 431–32, 443–49; Rosario Romeo, *Breve storia della grande industria in Italia*, pp. 128–31.

10. Caracciolo, "La grande industria," pp. 198–219; Caizzi, *Storia dell'industria*, pp. 314–453.

11. Procacci, "Appunti in tema di crisi," pp. 231–35; Vivarelli, *Il dopoguerra*, 1:253–54.

12. Melograni, *Storia politica della grande guerra*, pp. 71, 88–90, 102–5, 325, 359, 365.

13. Ibid., p. 99; Procacci, "Appunti in tema di crisi," p. 236.

14. Vivarelli, *Il dopoguerra*, 1:28n–29n; Melograni, *Storia politica della grande guerra*, pp. 558–59; Gaetano Salvemini, *The Origins of Fascism in Italy*, p. 181.

15. Vivarelli, *Il dopoguerra*, 1:32–33.

16. Ibid., pp. 50, 405.

17. Ibid., pp. 426, 430–35, 457–58, 516–18.

18. Costanzo Casucci, "Fascismo e storia," pp. 449–54.

19. Vivarelli, *Il dopoguerra*, 1:53.

20. Adolfo Omodeo, "Educazione politica," from *L'educazione nazionale*, 29 Feb., 15

May, and 30 May 1920, in *Libertà e storia*, pp. 18–30. See also Alessandro Galante Garrone, "Introduzione," pp. xxi–xxv.

21. Guido De Ruggiero, "Il problema dell'autorità," from *Il paese*, 8 Dec. 1921, in *Scritti politici*, pp. 421–22.

22. Gaetano Arfé, *Storia del socialismo italiano*, pp. 219–20; Melograni, *Storia politica della grande guerra*, pp. 266–77.

23. Melograni, *Storia politica della grande guerra*, pp. 113–14, 325–27, 357–69; Vivarelli, *Il dopoguerra*, 1:397–98.

24. Vivarelli, *Il dopoguerra*, 1:69–74, 314, 322–25.

25. Idomeneo Barbadoro, *Storia del sindacalismo italiano dalla nascita al fascismo*, 2:351; Christopher Seton-Watson, *Italy from Liberalism to Fascism*, p. 520; Paolo Spriano, *L'occupazione delle fabbriche*, p. 39.

26. Vivarelli, *Il dopoguerra*, 1:318–19, 323.

27. Massimo Roccs, *Come il fascismo divenne una dittatura*, pp. 66–73; Seton-Watson, *Italy*, pp. 512, 515.

28. Pietro Nenni, *Il diciannovismo*, especially pp. 59, 66. Nenni's book was originally published as *Storia di quattro anni* in 1946. It was supposed to have been published in 1926, but it was confiscated by the Fascist authorities.

29. For a few examples, see Vivarelli, *Il dopoguerra*, 1:54–55, 59, 83–84, 323, 442–43; Salvemini, *The Origins of Fascism*, pp. 164–68, 181; Antonio Gramsci, *Passato e presente*, pp. 53–54; Renzo de Felice, *Mussolini il riovoluzionario*, chap. 11; Enzo Santarelli, *Storia del movimento e del regime fascista*, 1:221, 223n.; Leo Valiani, "Il problema politico della nazione italiana," pp. 7–10.

30. Casucci, "Fascismo e storia," pp. 444–47.

31. Adrian Lyttelton, *The Seizure of Power*, pp. 202–4.

32. See, for example, Luigi Federzoni's explicit and forceful treatment of these problems in a speech delivered in Rome on 11 March 1917, published as *L'Italia di domani*, especially pp. 11–13.

33. Alfredo Rocco, untitled comment, in Pier Ludovico Occhini, ed., *Il Nazionalismo italiano e i problemi del lavoro e della scuola*, pp. 39–40.

34. For example, see Carlo Vallauri, "Il programma economico nazionalista e la genesi del corporativismo fascista," pp. 612–36; Vivarelli, *Il dopoguerra*, 1:99–100, 235, 238–39.

35. Alfredo Rocco, *La trasformazione dello Stato*, p. 14.

36. Francesco Coppola, *La rivoluzione fascista e la politica mondiale*, p. 20.

37. Alfredo Rocco, "Manifesto," *Politica*, 1, no. 1 (15 Dec. 1918):11.

38. Ibid., pp. 6–11; Enrico Corradini, *Il regime della borghesia produttiva*, pp. 20–21.

39. Corradini, *Il regime della borghesia*, pp. 36–37.

40. Ibid., p. 30; Enrico Corradini, "Politica ed economia della nazione e delle classi," lecture delivered 17 Dec. 1916, in *Discorsi politici*, pp. 379, 384–90; Enrico Corradini, *La marcia dei produttori*, pp. 45–54; Enrico Corradini, "Diritti e doveri nazionali dei produttori," lecture delivered 28 July 1918, in *Discorsi politici*, pp. 353–54.

41. Corradini, *Il regime della borghesia*, especially pp. 31, 52.

42. Luigi Federzoni, "Prepararsi alla crisi del dopo guerra," lecture delivered 11 March 1917, in *Presagi alla nazione*, pp. 91–93.

43. Corradini, *Il regime della borghesia*, pp. 45–46, 50.

44. Ibid., pp. 34, 46–47.

45. Vallauri, "Il programma economico nazionalista," pp. 615–17; Paolo Ungari, *Alfredo Rocco e l'ideologia giuridica del fascismo*, p. 27.

46. Franco Gaeta, *Nazionalismo italiano*, pp. 157–64; Vivarelli, *Il dopoguerra*, 1:256; Occhini, ed., *Il Nazionalismo italiano*, pp. 181–204.

47. Enrico Corradini, "La politica economica-sociale del Nazionalismo," and Alfredo Rocco's untitled comment, in Occhini, ed., *Il Nazionalismo italiano*, pp. 31–46. See also Rocco, "Manifesto," p. 16; and Alfredo Rocco, "Il momento economico e sociale," from *Politica*, 24 April 1919, in *Scritti e discorsi politici*, 2:590–91.

48. Rocco, untitled comment, in Occhini, ed., *Il Nazionalismo italiano*, p. 43.

49. Ibid., p. 98.

50. Ibid., pp. 40–41. See also pp. 43–44.
51. Federzoni, *Presagi alla nazione*, pp. 335–36.
52. Alfredo Rocco, "Fallimento," from *L'idea nazionale*, 1 Feb. 1920, in *Scritti*, 2:625.
53. Alfredo Rocco, "Crisi dello Stato e sindacati," inaugural lecture, University of Padua, 15 Nov. 1920, in *Scritti*, 2:631, 639.
54. Ibid., p. 645.
55. Ibid., pp. 640–41.
56. Ibid., pp. 642–43; Rocco, "Il momento economico e sociale," in *Scritti*, 2:591.
57. See especially Gaetano Mosca, "Il pericolo dello Stato moderno," from *Corriere della sera*, 27 May 1909, in *Il tramonto dello Stato liberale*, pp. 210–17; and Santi Romano, "Lo Stato moderno e la sua crisi," pp. 97–114. See also Ungari, *Alfredo Rocco*, pp. 35–39, on the importance of Santi Romano's statement.
58. Gaetano Mosca, *The Ruling Class*, pp. 480–82. See also Mario Delle Piane, *Gaetano Mosca*, pp. 319–20, 345, on the ambiguities of Mosca's conservative liberalism during the postwar crisis. For other examples, see Oreste Ranelletti, "I sindacati e lo Stato," pp. 257–79; and Umberto Ricci, *Dal protezionismo al sindacalismo*, pp. 107–79.
59. Gaetano Mosca, *Partiti e sindacati nella crisi del regime parlamentare*, pp. 313–15, 321–323; both statements date from 1925. See also Vittorio Ambrosini, *La battaglia per lo Stato sindacale*, pp. 71–81, for an interview with Mosca on the subject.
60. Giustino Fortunato, "Dopo la guerra sovvertitrice," in *Pagine e ricordi parlamentari*, 2:70–71, 82–83.
61. Ibid., p. 83.
62. Ibid., pp. 79–82, 87–93.
63. Ibid., p. 85.
64. Ibid., pp. 82, 87.
65. Ungari, *Alfredo Rocco*, pp. 49–52; Ranelletti, "I sindacati e lo Stato," pp. 257–79; Rocco, "Crisi dello Stato e sindacati," in *Scritti*, pp. 631–45.
66. See, for example, Corradini's effective point about Italy's disadvantaged position in *Discorsi politici*, pp. 221–22.
67. See Alberto Aquarone's perceptive observations about this sensitive issue in *Alla ricerca dell'Italia liberale*, pp. 321–28, and especially p. 323.
68. Enrico Corradini, "Sindacalismo, nazionalismo, imperialismo," lecture of Dec. 1909, in *Discorsi politici*, p. 69.
69. Rocco, "Manifesto," pp. 9–11.

Chapter 7 / The Neosyndicalist Program, 1917–1921

1. Paolo Orano, *L'Italia e gli altri alla conferenza della pace*, pp. 22, 93. See also pp. 34, 72–73.
2. See especially Alceste De Ambris, "La tempesta che viene," p. 133.
3. A. O. Olivetti, "Il manifesto dei sindacalisti," p. 154; Agostino Lanzillo, *La dittatura del proletariato*, p. 29.
4. A. O. Olivetti, *Bolscevismo, comunismo, e sindacalismo*, pp. 63–70; Lanzillo, *La dittatura del proletariato*, pp. 52–57; Sergio Panunzio, "Un programma d'azione," p. 85; De Ambris, "La tempesta che viene," p. 134.
5. De Ambris, "La tempesta che viene," p. 135.
6. For example, see the May Day Manifesto of the *Unione Italiana del Lavoro*, "Primo Maggio 1919," *Il rinnovamento* 2, no. 4 (1 May 1919):194.
7. A. O. Olivetti, "Ripresa," *Pagine libere* 7, no. 1 (15 Feb. 1920):2.
8. Paolo Orano, "Il controllo operaio," *Pagine libere* 7, nos. 20–21 (10 Nov. 1920):473–76.
9. Agostino Lanzillo, *Le rivoluzioni del dopoguerra*, pp. 141–42.
10. Sergio Panunzio, "Socialismo in ritardo," *Pagine libere* 8, nos. 8–9 (Aug.–Sept. 1921):293–94.
11. Agostino Lanzillo, "Il proletariato e la sua morale," *Il popolo d'Italia*, 27 March 1918, p. 3. Lanzillo was following the economist Giuseppe Prato in making this case against the workers; see Paolo Spriano, *Storia di Torino operaia e socialista*, pp. 382–85.

12. Sergio Panunzio, "Una forza," from *Giornale del mattino* (Bologna), 28 April 1918, in *Stato nazionale e sindacati*, pp. 35–36.

13. Alceste De Ambris, "I limiti dell'espropriazione necessaria," *Battaglie dell'Unione Italiana del Lavoro*, 31 May 1919, p. 1.

14. Alceste De Ambris, "I rimedi eroici," *Il rinnovamento* 2, no. 4 (1 May 1919):195–96.

15. "Dal programma di *Cultura sindacale*," *Cultura sindacale* 2, no. 1 (22 Jan. 1921):12.

16. Lanzillo, *La dittatura del proletariato*, pp. 69–70; Alceste De Ambris, "Per la realtà rivoluzionaria," *Il sindacato operaio*, 2 July 1921, p. 2; A. O. Olivetti, "De profundis," *Pagine libere* 7, nos. 14–15 (20 Aug. 1920):328.

17. Filippo Corridoni, quoted in *Battaglie dell'Unione Italiana del Lavoro*, 24 May 1919, p. 3.

18. A. O. Olivetti, "La rivolta delle classi intellettuali," *Pagine libere* 7, no. 19 (15 Oct. 1920):446.

19. A. O. Olivetti, "Il supercapitale," *Pagine libere* 7, nos. 12–13 (31 July 1920):288. See also A. O. Olivetti, "Nel regno di Mammone," *Pagine libere* 7, nos. 2–3 (15 March 1920):34.

20. A. O. Olivetti, "La danza macabra del capitalismo bancario," *Pagine libere* 7, no. 4 (31 March 1920):98–100. See also Sergio Panunzio, "I compiti del sindacalismo e le finalità immediate delle organizzazioni politiche e sindacali," p. 1, for an explicit endorsement of Olivetti's analysis.

21. Agostino Lanzillo, *La disfatta del socialismo*, pp. 61–64; Lanzillo, *La dittatura del proletariato*, pp. 21–23, 63–64, 76; Lanzillo, *Le rivoluzioni*, p. 209.

22. Panunzio, "I compiti del sindacalismo," p. 1.

23. Adrian Lyttelton, for example, portrays Lanzillo in this light in *The Seizure of Power*, pp. 50 (see n. 37), 55, 203–4.

24. Alighiero Ciattini, *Lo Stato e i suoi fini sociali*, pp. 4–14.

25. A. O. Olivetti, "Rinnovare!" *Pagine libere* 8, no. 7 (July 1921):237–38. For another example, see Ottavio Dinale [Jean-Jacques], "L'uova e la gallina," *Pagine libere* 8, no. 3 (25 March 1921):113.

26. A. O. Olivetti, "Problemi urgenti: La delinquenza," *Pagine libere* 7, nos. 7–8 (31 May 1920):157–58.

27. Olivetti, "Rinnovare!" p. 237. See also p. 235.

28. Ciattini, *Lo Stato*, p. 113.

29. Lanzillo, *La disfatta del socialismo*, pp. 277–78.

30. Sergio Panunzio, "Dalla guerra alla pace," *Il popolo d'Italia*, 30 Dec. 1916, p. 1; Sergio Panunzio, "Engels, Mazzini, il prof. Levi e altre cose," pp. 110–13.

31. Leonardo Paloscia, *La concezione sindacalista di Sergio Panunzio*, pp. 24–26; Sergio Panunzio, "Il lato teorico e il lato pratico del socialismo," *Utopia* 2, nos. 7–8 (15–31 May 1914):201.

32. Sergio Panunzio, "Per la revisione del socialismo," pt. 2 (20 July–31 Aug. 1917), pp. 101–2.

33. Panunzio, "Per la revisione del socialismo," pt. 6 (1–31 March 1919), pp. 54–57. The quotation is from p. 56. See also Panunzio, "Per la revisione del socialismo," pt. 5 (30 July–30 Sept. 1918), p. 89.

34. Panunzio, "Per la revisione del socialismo," pt. 1 (1–20 July 1917), p. 85; and pt. 3 (10 Oct.–20 Nov. 1917), p. 140.

35. [Francesco] Saverio Merlino, *Pro e contro il socialismo*, p. 316. See also pp. 16, 27–28, 320–22.

36. [Francesco] Saverio Merlino, *Collettivismo, lotta di classe e . . . ministro!*, p. 38; Merlino, *Pro e contro*, p. 53.

37. Panunzio, "Engels, Mazzini," p. 110–13.

38. Merlino, *Pro e contro*, pp. 367, 370.

39. For example, see Lanzillo, *La disfatta del socialismo*, pp. 205, 259; and Sergio Panunzio, "Il sindacalismo nazionale," from *Il lavoro d'Italia*, 12 May 1923, in *Stato nazionale e sindacati*, p. 116.

40. Vilfredo Pareto, *The Mind and Society*, 3:1293.

41. Vilfredo Pareto, *Trasformazioni della democrazia*, pp. 61–62. See also Olivetti, "Ripresa," pp. 1–4.

42. Lanzillo, *La disfatta del socialismo*, pp. 171–75, 194–96.

43. Ibid., p. 258.

44. Alceste De Ambris, "Sempre e più che mai sindacalisti: Intermezzo polemico," *Il rinnovamento* 2, no. 6 (15 July 1919):306–7.

45. Alceste De Ambris, "Il fallimento della rivoluzione," *Il sindacato operaio*, 21 Sept. 1921, p. 4.

46. A. O. Olivetti, "Nel libirinto," *Pagine libere* 9, nos. 5–6 (May–June 1922):164–65.

47. For example, see A. O. Olivetti, "La Réforme du parlement et la problème de la représentation," p. 115.

48. Massimo Rocca, "L'errore di Sorel," *Gerarchia* 1, no. 7 (25 July 1922):368–70.

49. Panunzio, "Il sindacalismo nazionale," in *Stato nazionale e sindacati*, p. 116.

50. Sergio Panunzio, "Studiamo Mazzini," *Il popolo d'Italia*, 6 Jan. 1917, p. 3; and 8 Jan. 1917, p. 3.

51. A. O. Olivetti, "Sindacalismo e mazzinianismo," *Pagine libere* 9, no. 4 (April 1922):126; Olivetti, "Il manifesto dei sindacalisti," p. 157; A. O. Olivetti, "La contemporaneità di G. Mazzini," *Il sindacata operaio*, 10 March 1922, p. 1.

52. *La patria del popolo* 1, no. 1 (12 Oct. 1922):1.

53. Armando Casalini, "Il pensiero di Mazzini ed il sindacalismo," *Cultura sindacale* 1, no. 1 (30 Dec. 1920):13–15; Armando Casalini, "Democrazia e sindacalismo," *Cultura sindacale* 2, no. 1 (22 Jan. 1921):11–12.

54. Olivetti, "Rinnovare!" p. 239; A. O. Olivetti, "La fiaba del 'governo forte' ed altre piacevolezze," *Pagine libere* 8, no. 12 (Dec. 1921):420.

55. Panunzio, "Una forza," in *Stato nazionale e sindacati*, pp. 32–34.

56. For example, see Olivetti, "La rivolta delle classi intellettuali," p. 445; and Olivetti, *Bolscevismo, comunismo e sindacalismo*, p. 119.

57. Sergio Panunzio to Benito Mussolini, orig. pub. in *Il popolo d'Italia*, 9 Nov. 1919, now in Sergio Panunzio, *Riforma costituzionale*, p. 108.

58. Sergio Panunzio, "Il sindacalismo, il socialismo, e la crisi attuale," p. 4.

59. Sergio Panunzio, "Nazionalità e umanità nella scuola," pp. 871–72.

60. Ibid., pp. 872–76.

61. Luigi Federzoni, "Prepararsi alla crisi del dopo guerra," lecture delivered 11 March 1917, in *Presagi alla nazione*, pp. 94–95.

62. Panunzio, "Nazionalità e umanità nella scuola," p. 875.

63. Ibid., pp. 876–77.

64. Ciattini, *Lo Stato*, pp. 81–84. The quoted passage is on p. 82.

65. Agostino Lanzillo, "Contro l'elezionismo democratico," *Il popolo d'Italia*, 21 May 1919, p. 1.

66. Sergio Panunzio, "La rappresentanza di classe," pp. 398–413. For other examples, see Livio Ciardi, "La politica del lavoro," *L'Italia nostra*, 24 Aug. 1918; and Mario Racheli, "Il parlamento del lavoro," *Cultura sindacale* 2, no. 5 (17 July 1921):6–7.

67. Olivetti, "Il manifesto dei sindacalisti," pp. 143–60.

68. Armando Casalini, "La repubblica dei sindacati," *Il sindacato operaio*, 28 May 1921, p. 2.

69. Sergio Panunzio, *La lega delle nazioni*, pp. 50, 61.

70. Panunzio, "Il sindacalismo, il socialismo, e la crisi attuale," p. 4.

71. See, for example, Olivetti, "Il manifesto dei sindacalisti," pp. 158–59; and Panunzio, "Un programma d'azione," pp. 85–86.

72. Dinale, "L'uova e la gallina," pp. 113–14.

73. Alighiero Ciattini, "Tutto da rifare," *L'Italia nostra*, 18 May 1918, p. 1.

74. Ciattini, *Lo Stato*, pp. 132–33.

75. Olivetti, "La contemporaneità di G. Mazzini," p. 1; Olivetti, "Ripresa," p. 2; Paolo Orano, "D'Annunzio è con noi," *Pagine libere* 7, no. 18 (25 Sept. 1920):409; Armando Casalini, "Partiti e classi," *Cultura sindacale* 2, no. 4 (30 April 1921):4; Panunzio, "Un programma d'azione," p. 88.

76. Olivetti, *Bolscevismo, communismo e sindacalismo*, p. 45.

77. Olivetti, "Il supercapitale," p. 287. See also Alceste De Ambris, "I sovraprofti di guerra," *Il rinnovamento* 1, no. 4 (1918):225.

78. Panunzio, "Un programma d'azione," pp. 86–87.

79. Renzo De Felice, *Sindacalismo rivoluzionario e fiumanesimo nel carteggio De Ambris-D'Annunzio*, pp. 49–50.

80. For example, see [Secondo] Nosengo, "Forza bruta e forza morale," *L'Italia nostra*, 7 Dec. 1918; "Il problema educativo," *Cultura sindacale* 2, no. 2 (20 Feb. 1921):1–2; Sergio Panunzio, "Lettera di uno non candidato," *Il popolo d'Italia*, 9 Nov. 1919, p. 3.

81. A. O. Olivetti, "Ricordiamo l'eroe rivoluzionario Filippo Corridoni," *La patria del popolo* 1, no. 2 (2 Nov. 1922):2. For other examples of the Corridoni cult, see "Filippo Corridoni: L'uomo e l'idea immortale," *L'Italia nostra*, 26 Oct. 1918; Cesare Rossi, "I nuovi aspetti di una vecchia battaglia (nell'anniversario della morte di Filippo Corridoni)," *Il rinnovamento* 1, no . 11 (30 Nov. 1918):398–401; and the portrait of Corridoni on the front page of the first issue of *La gioventù sindacalista*, 11 April 1920.

82. " 'Il rinnovamento': In cammino!" *Il popolo d'Italia*, 15 Feb. 1918, p. 3.

83. Renzo De Felice, *Mussolini il rivoluzionario*, pp. 418–20, 515–16. See also Emilio Gentile, *Le origini dell'ideologia fascista*, pp. 80–90, for a sensitive discussion of the relationship between Mussolini and the syndicalists in the immediate postwar period.

84. De Felice, *Mussolini il rivoluzionario*, p. 405n. See also Panunzio, *Stato nazionale e sindacati*, p. 28n., on the discussions between Panunzio and Mussolini in Ferrara early in 1916.

85. Giorgio Pini and Duilio Susmel, *Mussolini*, 1:306.

86. See Benito Mussolini's two "Divagazioni" from *Il popolo d'Italia*, 18 Aug. 1918 and 8 Sept. 1918, in *Opera omnia*, 11:270, 343–44.

87. De Felice, *Sindacalismo rivoluzionario e fiumanesimo*, pp. 58–61.

88. Ibid., pp. 63–66; De Felice, *Mussolini il rivoluzionario*, p. 522; Renzo De Felice, "Gli esordi del corporativismo in alcune lettere di Alceste De Ambris," p. 306. See also Michael A. Ledeen, *The First Duce*, pp. 139–43, 161–94, on the role of De Ambris at Fiume.

89. For the versions of both De Ambris and D'Annunzio, see Renzo De Felice, ed., *La Carta del Carnaro nei testi di Alceste De Ambris e di Gabriele d'Annunzio*. See also De Felice's introduction to this edition, pp. 7–31; and Umberto Foscanelli, *Gabriele D'Annunzio e l'ora sociale*, pp. 138–44, 151–52. Other syndicalists enthusiastically endorsed the Carta del Carnaro; for example, see Orano, "D'Annunzio è con noi," p. 411.

90. De Ambris, "Per la realtà rivoluzionaria," p. 2; Alceste De Ambris, "Il nostro 'nazionalismo,' " *Il sindacato operaio*, 15 Oct. 1921, p. 1; Alceste De Ambris, "Il 'Manifesto dei sindacalisti' e la costituzione fiumana," *Il sindacato operaio*, 25 Aug. 1921, pp. 2–3.

91. La Reggenza Italiana del Carnaro, *Disegno di un nuovo ordinamento dello Stato libero di Fiume*, especially pp. 133, 136–39, 145.

92. De Felice, *Sindacalismo rivoluzionario e fiumanesimo*, pp. 66–69.

93. De Ambris's two drafts and Mussolini's comments are published as an appendix in De Felice, *Mussolini il rivoluzionario*, pp. 749–61.

94. De Felice, *Mussolini il rivoluzionario*, pp. 634–62, especially pp. 634–35. See also De Felice, *Sindacalismo rivoluzionario e fiumanesimo*, pp. 107–9.

Chapter 8 / The Varieties of Italian Fascism

1. Roberto Vivarelli, "Benito Mussolini dal socialismo al fascismo," p. 449.

2. Renzo De Felice, *Mussolini il fascista*, 1:20, 163–65, 474–75, 537.

3. Ibid., p. 467; Renzo De Felice, *Mussolini il fascista*, 2:359–60.

4. De Felice, *Mussolini il fascista*, 1:475.

5. Renzo De Felice, *Mussolini il Duce*, 1:177. It seems to me, however, that De Felice goes too far here in portraying Mussolini as a committed corporativist. This is not consistent with the image of Mussolini that emerges from the previous volumes of De Felice's biography.

6. Ferdinando Cordova, "Le origini dei sindacati fascisti," pp. 931–32, 937.

7. Ibid., pp. 929, 950–52, 952n.; Renzo De Felice, *Mussolini il rivoluzionario*, pp. 515–16; Edoardo Malusardi, *Elementi di storia del sindacalismo fascista*, p. 27.

8. De Felice, *Mussolini il rivoluzionario*, pp. 571–98; Cordova, "Le origini dei sindacati fascisti," pp. 952–62.

9. Cordova, "Le origini dei sindacati fascisti," pp. 954–55, 959–60.

10. De Felice, *Mussolini il rivoluzionario*, pp. 634–62.

11. See, for example, Edmondo Rossoni, "Fascismo e movimento sindacale," *Cultura sindacale* 2, no. 4 (30 April 1921):2; Ottavio Dinale, "Reliquati di guerra: Il fascismo," *Pagine libere* 7, no. 23 (15 Dec. 1920):548; and Agostino Lanzillo, *Le rivoluzioni del dopoguerra*, p. xvii.

12. Dinale, "Reliquati di guerra," p. 549.

13. Agostino Lanzillo, "Azione e programmi nel fascismo," *Il popolo d'Italia*, 12 June 1921, p. 3.

14. De Felice, *Mussolini il fascista*, 1:66; Renzo De Felice, *Sindacalismo rivoluzionario e fiumanesimo nel carteggio De Ambris-D'Annunzio*, pp. 118–19.

15. A. O. Olivetti, "Rinnovare!" *Pagine libere* 8, no. 7 (July 1921):235; Alceste De Ambris, "Il programma del 'Partito fascista' nel discorso Mussolini," *Il sindacato operaio*, 18 Nov. 1921, p. 2; "Mussolini e il sindacalismo," *La patria del popolo* 1, no. 1 (12 Oct. 1922):1.

16. For a detailed examination of these activities, see Ferdinando Cordova, *Arditi e legionari dannunziani*, pp. 113–86.

17. See Pier Ludovico Occhini, ed., *Il Nazionalismo italiano e i problemi del lavoro e della scuola*, pp. 88–91, for Federzoni's discussion. See also Franco Gaeta, *Nazionalismo italiano*, p. 162.

18. Luigi Federzoni, *Presagi alla nazione*, pp. 215–20 (lecture delivered 3 Feb. 1921). See also Luigi Federzoni, *Italia di ieri per la storia di domani*, p. 79.

19. Federzoni, *Presagi alla nazione*, pp. 243–44 (lecture delivered 10 May 1921).

20. Ibid., pp. 333–34 (lecture delivered 8 Oct. 1922).

21. Bruna Uva, *La nascita dello Stato corporativo e sindacale fascista*, pp. 44–45; Ferdinando Cordova, *Le origini dei sindacati fascisti*, p. 418.

22. Federzoni, *Italia di ieri*, p. 105.

23. Balbino Giuliano, *L'esperienza politica dell'Italia*, pp. 179–86. The quoted passage is on p. 185. See also Federzoni, *Presagi alla nazione*, p. 243 (lecture delivered 10 May 1921); and Francesco Coppola, *La rivoluzione fascista e la politica mondiale*, pp. 12, 34.

24. See especially De Felice, *Mussolini il fascista*, 1:116–17.

25. Adrian Lyttelton, *The Seizure of Power*, p. 67; Giorgio Spini, "Toscana e fascismo," pp. 5–6. For some particularly perceptive remarks about the need for a flexible approach to the problem of the social composition of Italian fascism, see Juan J. Linz, "Some Notes toward a Comparative Study of Fascism in Sociological Historical Perspective," pp. 33–47, 56, 60–68. See also the profascist account by Gioacchino Volpe, *Storia del movimento fascista*, pp. 46–47, on the need to supplement the petty bourgeois category.

26. Wolfgang Sauer, "National Socialism," pp. 419–22; Edward R. Tannenbaum, *The Fascist Experience*, p. 50.

27. Adolfo Omodeo, *Momenti della vita di guerra*, pp. 142–43, 143n.

28. Alessandro Galante Garrone, "Introduzione," pp. xxxvii–xxxviii.

29. For example, this is the implication of Lyttelton, *The Seizure of Power*, p. 56.

30. See, for example, Guido De Ruggiero, *The History of European Liberalism*, p. 440.

31. Piero Gobetti, *La rivoluzione liberale*, pp. 12–13, 33–37; Norberto Bobbio, *Italia civile*, pp. 39, 43.

32. Farinacci has found few defenders among historians and memorialists. For some useful—and typically negative—remarks, see Cesare Rossi, *Personaggi di ieri e di oggi*, p. 318.

33. De Felice, *Mussolini il fascista*, 2:56n.; Roland Sarti, *The Ax Within*, pp. 117–18.

34. See, for example, Roberto Farinacci, "L'inaugurazione dell'anno giuridico," *La vita italiana* 41, no. 1 (Jan. 1933):3–4.

35. For example, see Lyttelton, *The Seizure of Power*, pp. 55, 65, 73–74, 164, 170, 306, 391.

36. Federzoni, *Italia di ieri*, pp. 150–65.

37. Quoted in De Felice, *Sindacalismo rivoluzionario e fiumanesimo*, p. 98n. The letter is dated Aug. 30, 1920. On the impact of the *Carta del Carnaro*, see also Malusardi, *Elementi*

di storia, pp. 31–37, 41; Pietro Capoferri, *Venti anni col fascismo e con i sindacati*, pp. 32–33; De Felice, *Mussolini il fascista*, 1:47, 147; Piero Marsich, "Salvare il fascismo," *L'assalto*, 29 Oct. 1921, p. 1.

38. "Il fascismo di fronte allo stato," *Audacia*, 29 Jan. 1921, p. 1. See also Malusardi, *Elementi di storia*, p. 41.

39. Gabriele Invernizzi, "Dino Grandi dal fez alla feluca," p. 15.

40. Dino Grandi, "Filosofia della rivoluzione," from *Il resto del carlino*, 28 May 1920, in *Giovani*, p. 205.

41. Invernizzi, "Dino Grandi," pp. 9–10, 13–18; Domenico Bartoli, "Dino Grandi," *Corriere della sera*, 1 Oct. 1965, p. 3.

42. Nello Quilici, "Storia del fascismo ferrarese," p. 212; Dino Grandi, "Le origini e la missione del fascismo," p. 49; Invernizzi, "Dino Grandi," p. 13.

43. Dino Grandi, "L'elezione di Ferrara," from *L'azione*, 18 April 1914, in *Giovani*, pp. 19–20.

44. Dino Grandi, "Il mito sindacalista," from *La libertà economica*, 31 July 1920, in *Giovani*, p. 220.

45. Dino Grandi, "Lettera a un socialista," from *Il resto del carlino*, 11 Sept. 1920, in *Giovani*, pp. 223–26; Dino Grandi, "Vecchi e giovani," from *La libertà economica*, 15 Oct. 1919, in *Giovani*, pp. 134–35; Dino Grandi, "Liberismo e socialisti," from *La libertà economica*, 30 Sept. 1919, in *Giovani*, p. 118.

46. Grandi, "Le origini e la missione del fascismo," pp. 58, 65–67.

47. Dino Grandi, "La guerra non risolverà nulla," from *L'azione*, 6 Dec. 1914, in *Giovani*, pp. 39–42.

48. Dino Grandi, "La coscienza nazionale," from *La libertà economica*, 29 Aug. 1919, in *Giovani*, p. 96; Dino Grandi, "Vincenzo Gioberti e il pericolo slavo," from *La libertà economica*, 10 March 1920, in *Giovani*, p. 161.

49. Grandi, "Lettera a un socialista," in *Giovani*, p. 224.

50. Dino Grandi, "Società delle nazioni—ultima menzogna," from *La libertà economica*, 10 Jan. 1920, in *Giovani*, p. 152.

51. Ibid., pp. 149–53.

52. Sabino Cassese, "Un programmatore degli anni trenta," p. 406. For a reasonably sympathetic account of Bottai's career from an antifascist perspective, see Giordano Bruno Guerri, *Giuseppe Bottai, un fascista critico*.

53. Giuseppe Bottai, *Vent'anni e un giorno*, p. 9.

54. Giuseppe Bottai, *Il fascismo e l'Italia nuova*, pp. 28, 31–33, 68–69.

55. Giuseppe Bottai, *Scritti*, p. 49 (from *Critica fascista*, 15 June 1923).

56. Bottai, *Scritti*, pp. 54–55 (lecture delivered 27 March 1924).

57. Bottai, *Scritti*, pp. 121, 126 (lecture delivered 20 July 1928).

58. See Rossi, *Personaggi*, pp. 318, 322, 325, for some effective observations on the contrast in character between Turati and Farinacci. See also Harry Fornari, *Mussolini's Gadfly*, p. 144.

59. Giorgio Chiurco, *Storia della rivoluzione fascista*, 4:232–33; Guido Nozzoli, *I ras del regime*, pp. 50–65; Rossi, *Personaggi*, p. 326.

60. Lyttelton, *The Seizure of Power*, p. 75.

61. Augusto Turati, *Il Partito e i suoi compiti*, pp. 9–10, 165–83; Augusto Turati, *Ragioni ideali di vita fascista*, pp. 77, 108; Augusto Turati, "Il Partito e i sindacati," pp. 10–13. See also Rossi, *Personaggi*, pp. 324, 327; Enzo Santarelli, *Storia del movimento e del regime fascista*, 1:426–29; and De Felice, *Mussolini il fascista*, 2:192–200, for some indications of Turati's seriousness of purpose. This seriousness emerges from the accounts of Santarelli and De Felice, even though neither of them places Turati's purposes in clear perspective.

62. Bottai, *Scritti*, pp. 59–60 (orig. pub. 25 Feb. 1925); Tannenbaum, *The Fascist Experience*, p. 64. See also Camillo Pellizzi, *Una rivoluzione mancata*, p. 55; and Guerri, *Giuseppe Bottai*, p. 102. Pellizzi portrays Turati and Bottai as major forces in the struggle for serious change from 1924 until 1932, in contrast to those willing to serve merely as lieutenants of the dictator, while Guerri stresses the mutual esteem that united the two fascist leaders.

63. See, for example, De Felice, *Mussolini il fascista*, 2:331n.; Edward Tannenbaum, "The Goals of Italian Fascism," pp. 1192–95; and Sarti, *The Ax Within*, p. 102.

64. De Felice, *Mussolini il fascista*, 2:270–71, 328–29, 329n., 332–33.

65. See, for example, Curzio Suckert, "La conquista dello Stato nella concezione organica di Sergio Panunzio," p. 1; and Curzio Suckert, "Il sindacalismo è forza espansionistica," *L'impero*, 11 April 1923, p. 1.

66. A. J. DeGrand, "Curzio Malaparte," pp. 74–75.

67. See especially Suckert's unsigned piece "Fascismo storico e fascismo politico (Farinacci e Rocca)," in his periodical *La conquista dello Stato* 1, no. 1 (10 July 1924):4.

68. Ibid.; Curzio Suckert, "Il problema fondamentale," *La conquista dello Stato* 1, no. 1 (10 July 1924):1.

69. Suckert, "Il sindacalismo è forza espansionistica," p. 1.

70. See especially Curzio Suckert, "L'Europa vivente: Teoria storica del sindacalismo nazionale," orig. pub. 1923, now in Curzio Malaparte (Suckert's adopted name), *L'Europa vivente e altri saggi politici*.

71. Suckert, "La conquista dello Stato," p. 1.

72. Fornari, *Mussolini's Gadfly*, p. 137.

73. De Felice, *Mussolini il fascista*, 1:15; Sergio Panunzio, *Italo Balbo*, pp. 8, 32.

74. Italo Balbo, "Michele Bianchi," *Gerarchia* (1930), pp. 89–91.

75. Panunzio, *Italo Balbo*, p. 5.

76. Ibid., p. 41; see also Italo Balbo, *Diario 1922*, p. 29.

77. Italo Balbo, untitled comment, Ministero delle corporazioni, *Atti del secondo convegno di studi sindacali e corporativi*, 3:19–20.

78. Balbo, *Diario 1922*, p. 6.

79. Italo Balbo, *Lavoro e milizia per la nuova Italia*, pp. 18–20, 37–44.

80. De Felice, *Mussolini il fascista*, 2:69.

81. Federzoni, *Italia di ieri*, pp. 150–65.

Chapter 9 / Beyond Liberalism, 1921–1925

1. Renzo De Felice, *Mussolini il fascista*, 1:20, 46. See also Massimo Rocca, *Come il fascismo divenne una dittatura*, pp. 82, 97, 104.

2. De Felice, *Mussolini il fascista*, 1:145, 169. For the text of the Pacification Pact and other information, see *Dai fasci al Partito Nazionale Fascista*. 1:155–62.

3. See De Felice, *Mussolini il fascista*, 1:116–17, for one major example. See also Charles S. Maier, *Recasting Bourgeois Europe*, pp. 305–22.

4. See Adrian Lyttelton, *The Seizure of Power*, chap. 3, especially pp. 73–74, for an example of the prevailing perspective on the crisis of 1921.

5. De Felice, *Mussolini il fascista*, 1:166.

6. Ibid., pp. 147, 158–59; Dino Grandi, "Verso il congresso," *L'assalto*, 22 Oct. 1921, p. 1; Piero Marsich, "Salvare il fascismo," *L'assalto*, 29 Oct. 1921, p. 1.

7. De Felice, *Mussolini il fascista*, 1:151 and 151n.

8. Renzo De Felice, *Sindacalismo rivoluzionario e fiumanesimo nel carteggio De Ambris-D'Annunzio*, pp. 129–39.

9. Benito Mussolini, "La culla e il resto," from *Il popolo d'Italia*, 7 Aug. 1921, in *Opera omnia*, 17:90–91.

10. De Felice, *Mussolini il fascista*, 1:46–48, 153–56, 166–67, 172–73. For a summary of the deliberations of the congress, see *Dai fasci al Partito*, 1:163–83.

11. Dino Grandi, "Lettera a un socialista," from *Il resto del carlino*, 19 Sept. 1920, in *Giovani*, pp. 226–27.

12. Grandi, "Verso il congresso," p. 1.

13. Ibid.; Dino Grandi, "Le origini e la missione del fascismo," p. 70; Dino Grandi, "Per intenderci," *Il popolo d'Italia*, 2 Feb. 1922, p. 3; Dino Grandi, "Il mito e la realtà (alla vigilia del consiglio nazionale fascista)," *Il popolo d'Italia*, 2 April 1922, p. 1.

14. Edoardo Malusardi, *Elementi di storia del sindacalismo fascista*, p. 42; Ferdinando Cordova, "Le origini dei sindacati fascisti," p. 984.

15. Sergio Panunzio, "Ipotesi ed eventi," *La stirpe* 1, no. 1 (Dec. 1923):20.

16. Cordova, "Le origini dei sindacati fascisti," pp. 984n.–85n.

17. Sergio Panunzio, "I compiti del sindacalismo e le finalità immediate delle organizzazioni politiche e sindacali," p. 1.

18. A. O. Olivetti, "Risposta di A. O. Olivetti a Sergio Panunzio: Sui compiti del sindacalismo," *Il sindacato operaio*, 22 Oct. 1921, p. 2.

19. De Felice, *Mussolini il fascista*, 1:147.

20. Cordova, "Le origini dei sindacati fascisti," pp. 981–83.

21. See for example Lyttelton, *The Seizure of Power*, p. 70.

22. De Felice, *Mussolini il fascista*, 1:190.

23. Grandi, "Le origini e la missione del fascismo," pp. 51–71; De Felice, *Mussolini il fascista*, 1:186–88.

24. De Felice, *Mussolini il fascista*, 1:186–88.

25. Cordova, "Le origini dei sindacati fascisti," p. 987; Lyttelton, *The Seizure of Power*, p. 75.

26. Grandi, "Le origini e la missione del fascismo," pp. 53–54, 63.

27. Ibid., p. 69.

28. Ibid., p. 70.

29. Ibid., pp. 56, 59–60.

30. De Felice, *Mussolini il fascista*, 1:123, 160.

31. Ernst Nolte, *Three Faces of Fascism*, pp. 202–8.

32. Carlo Vallauri, "Il programma economico nazionalista e la genesi del corporativismo fascista," p. 626.

33. De Felice, *Mussolini il fascista*, 1:191.

34. See especially ibid., pp. 183, 192, 201. De Felice overemphasizes the depth of Grandi's convergence with Mussolini, implying that Grandi changed his mind about tactics because he recognized that his own revolutionary conception of fascism had no chance of success.

35. Grandi, "Il mito e la realtà," p. 1.

36. De Felice, *Mussolini il fascista*, 1:17, 186–87, provides an example of what seems to me to be an excessively narrow interpretation of Grandi's syndicalism.

37. Ibid., pp. 116–19, 158–59.

38. Ibid., pp. 46, 116.

39. Ibid., pp. 216, 248–49, 256, 263.

40. Cordova, "Le origini dei sindacati fascisti," pp. 987–92.

41. Ibid., pp. 992–93.

42. Sergio Panunzio, "Il sindacalismo, il socialismo e la crisi attuale," pp. 3–5.

43. Enrico Leone, "Fascismo, democrazia, sindacalismo: Una lettera di Enrico Leone," *Rassegna sindacale* 1, no. 1 (Oct. 1924):1–3.

44. Panunzio, "I compiti del sindacalismo," p. 1. See also Sergio Panunzio, "Il sindacalismo," p. 360.

45. *Dai fasci al Partito*, 1:146; Cordova, "Le origini dei sindacati fascisti," pp. 981–82.

46. Panunzio, "I compiti del sindacalismo," p. 1.

47. Sergio Panunzio, "Il sindacalismo nazionale," from *Il lavoro d'Italia*, 30 March 1922, in *Stato nazionale e sindacati*, p. 108.

48. See Rossoni's unsigned editorial comment appended to Panunzio's article, ibid., p. 113.

49. Panunzio, "Il sindacalismo nazionale," in *Stato nazionale e sindacati*, p. 107.

50. Umberto Foscanelli, *D'Annunzio e il fascismo*, p. 66; De Felice, *Sindacalismo rivoluzionario e fiumanesimo*, pp. 120–21.

51. See, for example, Luigi Razza, "L'opera delle corporazioni fasciste," *Il popolo d'Italia*, 15 July 1924, p. 5. See also De Felice, *Mussolini il fascista*, 2:91; Roland Sarti, *Fascism and the Industrial Leadership in Italy*, pp. 30–31; Edward R. Tannenbaum, *The Fascist Experience*, p. 107; and Paul Corner, *Fascism in Ferrara*, pp. 144–47, 165–66.

52. Cordova, "Le origini dei sindacati fascisti," pp. 999–1001.

53. Malusardi, *Elementi di storia*, p. 89; Bruno Uva, *La nascita dello Stato corporativo e sindacale fascista*, pp. 92–122.

54. Agostino Lanzillo, "Esame dei nuovi compiti," *Il popolo d'Italia*, 10 Nov. 1922, p.

4; A. O. Olivetti, "Dottrina e prassi dello Stato corporativo," p. 68; A. O. Olivetti, *Lineamenti del nuovo Stato italiano*, p. 12.

55. De Felice, *Sindacalismo rivoluzionario e fiumanesimo*, pp. 122–23.

56. Alceste De Ambris, "Il fascismo al bivio," p. 341.

57. Alceste De Ambris, "Sei mesi dopo: Punto e a capo. La veridica ed eziandio lacrimevole istoria della mancata unità sindacale," *Sindacalismo*, 17 March 1923, pp. 1–2.

58. Alceste De Ambris, "L'Evolution du Fascisme," pp. 5–6, 18–19, 25–26.

59. Renzo De Felice, "Gli esordi del corporativismo in alcune lettere di Alceste De Ambris," pp. 306–7; De Felice, *Sindacalismo rivoluzionario e fiumanesimo*, p. 141. Cesare Rossi, in *Personaggi di ieri e di oggi*, p. 393, suggests that untoward promises of personal advantage were made.

60. De Felice, "Gli esordi del corporativismo," pp. 307–9; De Felice, *Sindacalismo rivoluzionario e fiumanesimo*, pp. 141–45.

61. See De Felice, "Gli esordi del corporativismo," pp. 304–20, for De Ambris's letters and a valuable introduction by De Felice. See also De Felice, *Sindacalismo rivoluzionario e fiumanesimo*, pp. 149–52.

62. P[iero] G[obetti], "Dopo le elezioni," p. 174. See also Maier, *Recasting Bourgeois Europe*, pp. 422–40, on the uncertainty about the future of fascism in the wake of the 1924 elections.

63. See, for example, Lanzillo, "Esame dei nuovi compiti," p. 4; and Edmondo Rossoni, "Restare nella nuova storia," *La stirpe* 2, no. 7 (July 1924):532.

64. Dino Grandi, "Primo atto," *Gerarchia* 1, no. 11 (Nov.–Dec. 1922):603–4.

65. Giuseppe Bottai, *Scritti*, pp. 52–54 (lecture delivered 27 March 1924).

66. Panunzio, *Stato nazionale e sindacati*, p. 11.

67. See especially Sergio Panunzio's three articles: "Per lo Stato forte," from *Giornale di Roma*, 13 May 1923; "La disciplina dei sindacati," from *Giornale di Roma*, 28 June 1923; and "Il carattere essenziale del fascismo," from *Il popolo d'Italia*, 28 June 1923; all in ibid., pp. 164–67, 176–77, 190–91.

68. Carlo Vallauri, *Le radici del corporativismo*, p. 75; Sergio Panunzio, "Prime osservazioni giuridiche sul concetto di proprietà nel regime fascista," p. 116n.

69. Sergio Panunzio, "La questione sindacale," from *Gazzetta di Puglia*, 22 July 1923, in *Stato nazionale e sindacati*, pp. 179, 185–86; Ferdinando Cordova, *Le origini dei sindacati fascisti*, p. 214.

70. Cordova, *Le origini dei sindacati*, pp. 252–53.

71. Silvio Galli, "Contrasto decisivo," *Critica fascista* 1, no. 3 (15 July 1923):52–54.

72. Augusto De Marsanich, "L'individuo, i sindacati e lo Stato (Risposta a Sergio Panunzio)," *Critica fascista* 1, no. 7 (15 Sept. 1923):131–33.

73. See Cordova, *Le origini dei sindacati*, chap. 2, for a detailed examination of these relationships within fascism during 1923.

74. Panunzio, "Il sindacalismo," pp. 351–52; see also Olivetti, "Dottrina e prassi dello Stato corporativo," p. 90.

75. Lyttelton, *The Seizure of Power*, p. 252.

76. [A. O. Olivetti], "Tempi nuovi?" *La patria del popolo* 1, no. 3 (20 Nov. 1922):1. See also Olivetti's unsigned and untitled editorial in *La patria del popolo* 1, no. 2 (2 Nov. 1922):1.

77. Olivetti had contributed an abstract, theoretical article, entitled "Sindacalismo integrale," to Rossoni's *La stirpe* in April of 1924 (2, no. 4:277–79), but he did not seek to portray fascism as the vehicle for his own neosyndicalist program.

78. Lyttelton, *The Seizure of Power*, p. 311.

79. A. O. Olivetti, "Le ore storiche," p. 1.

80. A. O. Olivetti [Lo spettatore], "Parlamento e nazione," *Il popolo d'Italia*, 20 July 1924, p. 1.

81. Paolo Orano, "Sull'Aventino," *Il popolo d'Italia*, 25 July 1924, p. 2; Sergio Panunzio, "La meta del fascismo," from *Il popolo d'Italia*, 28 June 1924, and "'Indietro non si turna!'" lecture delivered 30 June 1924, both in *Rivoluzione e costituzione*, pp. 7–17.

82. Agostino Lanzillo, "La crisi fascista (la strada maestra)," *Critica fascista*, 2, no. 15 (1 Aug. 1924):559–60.

83. De Felice, *Mussolini il fascista*, 1:700n.

84. Agostino Lanzillo, "Violenza e violenza," pp. 131–38.

85. See, for example, Razza, "L'opera delle corporazioni fasciste," p. 5. On the importance of this meeting, see Lyttelton, *The Seizure of Power*, pp. 252–54. See also Attilio Tamaro, *Venti anni di storia*, 1:460–65, for a summary of its deliberations.

86. Sergio Panunzio, "Per la riforma della costituzione," speech to the National Council of the Fascist party, Rome, 4 Aug. 1924, in *Rivoluzione e costituzione*, pp. 18–20.

87. Panunzio, *Rivoluzione e costituzione*, p. 21; Curzio Suckert, "La conquista dello Stato nella concezione organica di Sergio Panunzio," p. 1; Tamaro, *Venti anni*, 1:464; Lyttelton, *The Seizure of Power*, pp. 253–54.

88. De Felice, *Mussolini il fascista*, 1:676.

89. Sergio Panunzio, "La vera chiarificazione," from *Il popolo d'Italia*, 20 Jan. 1925, and "La riforma costituzionale," from *Il resto del carlino*, 9 June 1925, both in *Rivoluzione e costituzione*, pp. 24, 31.

90. A. O. Olivetti, "Relazione al convegno di cultura fascista di Bologna," in the Olivetti papers, Rome.

91. A. O. Olivetti, "Nella Tombuctù socialista," *Il popolo d'Italia*, 3 May 1925, p. 2. Gino Baldesi attacked Olivetti first in "Nella Bisanzio sindacale," *La giustizia*, 29 April 1925; he continued the polemic in "Risposta a Bisanzio . . . ," *La giustizia*, 9 May 1925, and "Chiusura di polemica: Chiaramenti a Bisanzio," *La giustizia*, 22 May 1925.

92. Benito Mussolini, "Fascismo e sindacalismo," from *Gerarchia*, May 1925, in *Opera omnia*, 21:325–36. See also Uva, *La nascita dello Stato corporativo*, p. 55, on the place of this article in the discussions of 1925.

93. Cordova, *Le origini dei sindacati*, pp. 389–96, 417–34; Uva, *La nascita dello Stato corporativo*, pp. 30–79; Lyttelton, *The Seizure of Power*, p. 321.

94. Charles F. Delzell provides an English translation of the text of the syndical law in his collection, *Mediterranean Fascism*, pp. 111–20. See also Cordova, *Le origini dei sindacati*, pp. 434–42.

95. Paolo Orano, *Dal sindacalismo rivoluzionario allo Stato sindacalista*, pp. 5–6, 13–14.

96. Panunzio, "Il sindacalismo," p. 352.

97. See, for example, Guido De Ruggiero, "Il trionfo della tecnica," from *Il resto del carlino*, 19 Dec. 1922, in *Scritti politici*, pp. 595–600; and Vittorio Emanuele Orlando, "Lo 'Stato sindacale' e le condizioni attuali della scienza di diritto pubblico," pp. 4–18.

98. De Felice, *Mussolini il fascista*, 1:724.

99. Suckert, "La conquista dello Stato," p. 1.

100. Celestino Arena, "Scrittori fascisti: Carlo Costamagna," *Bibliografia fascista*, Sept. 1928, pp. 5–7; De Felice, *Mussolini il fascista*, 2:276n.

Chapter 10 / Participatory Totalitarianism

1. Sergio Panunzio, "Ancora sulle relazioni fra Stato e sindacati," p. 280.

2. Sergio Panunzio, "Stato e sindacati," p. 6. See also pp. 7–14.

3. Carlo Costamagna, review of *Lo Stato fascista*, by Sergio Panunzio, in *Rivista internazionale di filosofia del diritto* 6, no. 1 (Jan.–March 1926): 167–68.

4. Panunzio, "Ancora sulle relazioni fra Stato e sindacati," p. 275.

5. Carlo Costamagna, "Stato corporativo," pp. 414, 419–20.

6. See especially Sergio Panunzio, *Il riconoscimento rivoluzionario dei sindacati*, pp. 8–11, on the significance of the juridical recognition of the syndicates. See also Sergio Panunzio, "Il diritto sindacale e corporativo," p. 273.

7. Panunzio, *Il riconoscimento*, pp. 7, 9.

8. Ibid., p. 13.

9. Alfredo Rocco, *La trasformazione dello Stato*, pp. 23–25, 28–29.

10. For his three parliamentary speeches in support of this bill, see Alfredo Rocco, *Scritti*, 3:957–1006. See also Rocco, *La trasformazione*, p. 21.

11. Rocco, *Scritti*, 3:961; Rocco, *La trasformazione*, pp. 22–23, 30.

12. Rocco, *Scritti*, 3:991.

13. Ibid., pp. 972–78; Rocco, *La trasformazione*, pp. 21–22.

14. Rocco, *Scritti*, 3:963, 983–85; Rocco, *La trasformazione*, pp. 20–21.

15. Rocco, *La trasformazione*, pp. 16–19, 22–23.

16. Sergio Panunzio, "Le leggi fasciste," from *Il telegrafo*, 11 March 1926, in *Rivoluzione e costituzione*, p. 54.

17. See, for example, Sergio Panunzio, "Il sindacalismo nazionale," from *Il lavoro d'Italia*, 30 March 1922, in *Stato nazionale e sindacati*, p. 118; Sergio Panunzio, "Idee sul fascismo," *Critica fascista* 3, no. 6 (15 March 1925):108; Sergio Panunzio, "Principio di organizzazione," from *Il resto del carlino*, 21 Dec. 1926, in *Rivoluzione e costituzione*, pp. 63–67; and Sergio Panunzio, *Teoria generale dello Stato fascista*, pp. 17–18.

18. For the Nationalist conception of the value of the war, see especially Luigi Federzoni, *Presagi alla nazione*, pp. 89, 167–68.

19. Panunzio, "Principio di organizzazione," in *Rivoluzione e costituzione*, p. 65. See also Sergio Panunzio, *Alfredo Rocco*, pp. 5, 15–16.

20. Maurizio Maraviglia, "Nazione e Stato nel regime fascista," in *Alle basi del regime*, pp. 5–8, 11–13. See also Maraviglia's "La nuova rappresentanza politica," also in *Alle basi del regime*, p. 60. For Panunzio's attack, see his *Popolo Nazione Stato*, pp. 16–17.

21. Panunzio, *Il sentimento dello Stato*, pp. 145–49. Panunzio focused especially on Rocco, *La trasformazione*, pp. 18–19.

22. Panunzio, "Idee sul fascismo," p. 108; Panunzio, *Teoria generale*, pp. 18–19; Panunzio, "La riforma costituzionale," from *Il resto del carlino*, 9 June 1925, in *Rivoluzione e costituzione*, pp. 28–30.

23. Panunzio, *Popolo Nazione Stato*, p. 31.

24. Sabino Cassese, "Un programmatore degli anni trenta," p. 411; Giuseppe Bottai, *Scritti*, pp. 52–54.

25. For an especially forceful statement on each side of the question, see Maraviglia, "Nazione e Stato," in *Alle basi del regime*, p. 13; and Agostino Lanzillo, "Violenza e violenza," p. 131.

26. For examples of this cluster of themes, see A. O. Olivetti, "Dottrina e prassi dello Stato corporativo," p. 68; A. O. Olivetti [Lo spettatore], "Parlamento e nazione," *Il popolo d'Italia*, 20 July 1924, p. 1; Lanzillo, "Violenza e violenza," p. 131; Edmondo Rossoni, "Per il congresso delle corporazioni e per una politica nazionale del lavoro," *La stirpe* 2, no. 11 (Nov. 1924):886; Massimo Rocca, "La ricostruzione morale della nazione," lecture delivered Feb. 1, 1924, in *Idee sul fascismo*, pp. 145–46.

27. Guido De Ruggiero, "Il trionfo della tecnica," from *Il resto del carlino*, 19 Dec. 1922, in *Scritti politici*, pp. 599–600.

28. Panunzio, *Stato nazionale e sindacati*, pp. 143–47.

29. Panunzio, "Idee sul fascismo," p. 113.

30. [Luigi Albertini], "Stato liberale e Stato organico fascista," *Corriere della sera*, 16 Aug. 1924, p. 1. See also [Luigi Albertini], "I nuovi organi dello Stato: corporazioni e consigli tecnici," *Corriere della sera*, 15 Aug. 1924, p. 1.

31. [A. O. Olivetti], "Le trombe di Gerico," *Il popolo d'Italia*, 3 Oct. 1924, p. 1. See also [A. O. Olivetti], "Contributo allo studio della Commissione dei Quindici: Per il nuovo ordine della nuova Italia," *Il popolo d'Italia*, 21 Aug. 1924, p. 3; and [A. O. Olivetti], "La seconda ai Corinti," *Il popolo d'Italia*, 30 Aug. 1924, p. 1.

32. Charles F. Delzell, *Mussolini's Enemies*, p. 92n.

33. Umberto Ricci, *Dal protezionismo al sindacalismo*, pp. 107–16, 167–78.

34. A. O. Olivetti, "Il polipolio," *Il popolo d'Italia*, 11 June 1925, p. 2.

35. Sergio Panunzio, *Lo Stato educativo*, p. 11; see also pp. 4–8, 23. In addition, see Sergio Panunzio, "La donna nel fascismo," *Critica fascista* 6, no. 13 (1 July 1928):247–48.

36. Sergio Panunzio, "Scheda e tessera," from *Il popolo d'Italia*, 14 Jan. 1928, in *Rivoluzione e costituzione*, p. 128; A. O. Olivetti, "A proposito di economia corporativo," *La stirpe* 9, no. 5 (May 1931):195; Sergio Panunzio, *Lo Stato fascista*, p. 114; Rocca, "La ricostruzione morale," in *Idee*, p. 159.

37. Sergio Panunzio, "L'essenza etico-educativa del sindacalismo fascista," *Civiltà fascista* 5, no. 11 (Nov. 1938):1029–32. For another example, see A. O. Olivetti, "La realtà corporativa intesa come 'passione storica,'" *Il lavoro fascista*, 12 Aug. 1931, p. 2.

38. For example, see Olivetti, "Parlamento e nazione," p. 1; and Sergio Panunzio,

"Per la camera di domani," from *Echi e commenti*, 15 Oct. 1927, in *Rivoluzione e costituzione*, pp. 101–5.

39. De Ruggiero, "Il trionfo della tecnica," in *Scritti*, pp. 596–97.

40. Guido De Ruggiero, *The History of European Liberalism*, pp. 382–86, 426–27.

41. Panunzio, *Stato nazionale e sindacati*, p. 147.

42. Sergio Panunzio, "La politica dei sindacati," from *Giornale di Roma*, 16 Sept. 1922, in *Stato nazionale e sindacati*, p. 158.

43. De Ruggiero, "Il trionfo della tecnica," in *Scritti*, p. 599.

44. Sergio Panunzio, "Sulla 'riforma dello Stato,'" *Il popolo d'Italia*, 18 Feb. 1923, p. 1.

45. This was a major syndicalist-fascist theme. See, for example, A. O. Olivetti, "La Carta del Lavoro," *Il popolo d'Italia*, 2 March 1927, p. 1; Sergio Panunzio, *L'economia mista*, pp. 170–73; Sergio Panunzio, "Per l'ordinamento delle corporazioni," *Gerarchia*, Sept. 1942, p. 352.

46. Panunzio, "Scheda e tessera," in *Rivoluzione e costituzione*, pp. 126–27; Panunzio, *L'economia mista*, p. 244.

47. For a few examples, see A. O. Olivetti, "Le leggi della rivoluzione: Prolusione di A. O. Olivetti alla Facoltà Fascista di Scienze Politiche di Perugia," *Il primato*, 1–15 Jan. 1931, pp. 3–5; A. O. Olivetti, "Rivoluzione fascista e realtà sindacale," *La stirpe* 6, no. 11 (Nov. 1928):646; Agostino Lanzillo, *Lo Stato nel processo economico*, p. 102; Agostino Lanzillo, Address to the Chamber of Deputies, 5 Dec. 1925, pp. 4849–50; Paolo Orano, "Rivoluzione e legge: La corporazione fascista," *La stirpe* 4, no. 3 (March 1926):133; Alighiero Ciattini, *Politica nazionale*, p. 46; Edmondo Rossoni, "La rivoluzione e il suo contrario," *La stirpe* 4, no. 7 (July 1926):339.

48. A. O. Olivetti, "La Réforme du parlement et le problème de la représentation," p. 101. See also Olivetti, "Le leggi della rivoluzione," p. 5.

49. Luigi Razza, *La corporazione nello Stato fascista*, especially pp. 13–14, 20, 26, 31, 44; Luigi Razza, "La dottrina corporativa," pp. 97–107.

50. See Giuseppe Bottai, *Il Consiglio nazionale delle corporazioni*, pp. 109–14, for an especially forceful statement of this theme. See also Panunzio, *L'economia mista*, pp. 87–88; Olivetti, "La Réforme du parlement et le problème de la représentation," pp. 100–104; Edmondo Rossoni, "Nel nostro secolo rivoluzionario: Il fascismo di fronte al comunismo e al sistema capitalistica," *La stirpe* 9, no. 12 (Dec. 1931):532; Panunzio, *Il sentimento dello Stato*, p. 139.

51. Panunzio, *L'economia mista*, p. 42; Razza, *La corporazione*, p. 31.

52. For example, see Giuseppe Bottai, *Il cammino delle corporazioni*, especially pp. 22, 27–32, 95–97.

53. A. O. Olivetti, "Relazione al convegno di cultura fascista di Bologna," p. 6, in the Olivetti papers, Rome. For another example, see Olivetti, "Il polipolio," p. 2.

54. Panunzio, *Lo Stato fascista*, pp. 158–59; Panunzio, *Il sentimento dello Stato*, pp. 247–50; A. O. Olivetti, "Diritti e doveri della produzione," *Il popolo d'Italia*, 19 Oct. 1929, p. 1; Orano, "Rivoluzione e legge," p. 132.

55. Edmondo Rossoni, "La nuova economia: Soluzione corporativa nello Stato fascista," *La stirpe* 7, no. 1 (Jan. 1929):1–2.

56. A. O. Olivetti, "Il nuovo Stato italiano," *Il popolo d'Italia*, 3 Nov. 1929, p. 1; Paolo Orano, "Bonifica integrale," *Il lavoro d'Italia*, 15 Aug. 1928, p. 1; Ciattini, *Politica nazionale*, p. 37; Razza, "La dottrina corporativa," pp. 101–7; Sergio Panunzio, "La fine di un regno," p. 343.

57. Olivetti, "Il polipolio," p. 2; A. O. Olivetti, "Le corporazioni nel presente," *Il popolo d'Italia*, 1 Oct. 1924, p. 2; A. O. Olivetti, "Individuo, Stato, associazione," *Il lavoro fascista*, 28 June 1929, p. 1; Panunzio, "La fine di un regno," p. 343; Panunzio, *L'economia mista*, p. 87; Lanzillo, *Lo Stato nel processo economico*, pp. 205, 224–25.

58. Razza, *La corporazione*, pp. 13–44; Lanzillo, *Lo Stato nel processo economico*, pp. 206, 224–25.

59. A. O. Olivetti, "Rapporti tra sindacati giuridicamente riconosciuti e corporazioni," report to the Commission of Eighteen, 7 July 1925, pp. 2–4, in the Olivetti papers, Rome.

60. Panunzio, *L'economia mista*, pp. 95–96, 100.

61. See, for example, Edmondo Rossoni, "Volontà e capacità nelle organizzazioni dei produttori," *La stirpe* 7, no. 11 (Nov. 1929):578; and Agostino Lanzillo, "La proprietà privata e la corporazione," pp. 334–37.

62. Panunzio, *L'economia mista*, pp. 189–90, 226; Sergio Panunzio, "Sindacalismo integrale," *Gerarchia* 15 (Aug. 1936):671–72. See also Georges Sorel, *Reflections on Violence*, chap. 7.

63. Panunzio, *Popolo Nazione Stato*, pp. 20–21.

64. For examples, see Olivetti, "Diritti e doveri della produzione," p. 1; Orano, "Rivoluzione e legge," p. 133; Augusto Turati, *Il Partito e i suoi compiti*, pp. 117, 160; and Curzio Suckert, "Il sindacalismo è forza espansionistica," *L'impero*, 11 April 1923, p. 1.

65. Bottai, *Il cammino delle corporazioni*, pp. 80–93.

66. For examples of this conviction that Italy was plagued by special weaknesses—weaknesses that fascism was overcoming—see Paolo Orano, "Sull' Aventino," *Il popolo d'Italia*, 25 July 1924, p. 2; A. O. Olivetti, "La ricchezza delle nazioni," *Il lavoro fascista*, 28 Aug. 1931, p. 7; Panunzio, "La politica dei sindacati," in *Stato nazionale e sindacati*, p. 162; and Ciattini, *Politica nazionale*, p. 43.

67. Edmondo Rossoni, *Le idee della ricostruzione*, p. 39.

68. Edmondo Rossoni, "Discutere il sindacalismo," *Il lavoro d'Italia*, 24 April 1926, p. 1. See also Paolo Orano, "Roberto Michels," p. 13.

69. Alighiero Ciattini, *Caratteri della vita italiana*, pp. 6–7, 14–15.

70. Ibid., pp. 16, 48–49.

71. Alighiero Ciattini, *Postulati fascisti*, pp. 11–12.

72. Edward R. Tannenbaum, *The Fascist Experience*, pp. 14, 218.

73. Paolo Orano, "L'integrazione dello Stato," p. 1.

74. Augusto Turati, *Ragioni ideali di vita fascista*, pp. 18, 97.

75. Ibid., pp. 180–82.

76. Panunzio, *Il sentimento dello Stato*, p. 93; A. O. Olivetti, "Mazzini e lo Stato corporativo," *Il lavoro fascista*, 15 May 1930, p. 3.

77. Orano, "Rivoluzione e legge," p. 133; Olivetti, "Il polipolio," p. 2; Olivetti, "Le leggi della rivoluzione," p. 5; Razza, "La dottrina corporativa," p. 108; Agostino Lanzillo, "Economia, corporazione e punti sugl'i," *Critica fascista* 6, no. 11 (1 June 1928):209.

78. A. O. Olivetti, "Il futuro delle corporazioni," *Il popolo d'Italia*, 2 Oct. 1924, p. 3; Edmondo Rossoni, "La corporazione fascista," *La stirpe* 1, no. 1 (Dec. 1923):11.

79. Paolo Orano, *Il fascismo*, 1:7; A. O. Olivetti, "Una crisi di dissolvimento," *Critica fascista* 7, no. 18 (15 Sept. 1929):365; Panunzio, *L'economia mista*, p. 137; Edmondo Rossoni, "Il sindacalismo fascista e la collaborazione economica," *La stirpe* 2, no. 5 (May 1924):355–58; Giuseppe Bottai, *Scritti*, p. 107 (lecture delivered 15 Jan. 1928).

80. For example, see A. O. Olivetti, "Ripresa," *Pagine libere* 7, no. 1 (15 Feb. 1920):2.

81. Orano, "L'integrazione dello Stato," p. 1.

82. Lanzillo, "Violenza e violenza," p. 131.

83. Olivetti, "Dottrina e prassi dello Stato corporativo," p. 68; Paolo Orano, "Lo Stato sindacalista," *La Stirpe* 3, no. 2 (Nov. 1925):761–63; Alighiero Ciattini, "Lo Stato su nuovi basi," *Critica fascista* 2, no. 1 (1 Jan. 1924):278.

84. Panunzio, *Il sentimento dello Stato*, pp. 106–7; Bottai, *Il onsiglio*, pp. 109–12; Razza, "La dottrina corporativa," p. 96; A. O. Olivetti, "Legislazione e Magistratura del lavoro," *Il popolo d'Italia*, 5 Aug. 1925, p. 2.

85. Sergio Panunzio, "La disciplina dei sindacati," from *Giornale di Roma*, 28 June 1923, in *Stato nazionale e sindacati*, p. 176; Ottavio Dinale, "L'imperativo categorico della vita," *La stirpe* 4, no. 3 (March 1926):138; Luigi Viesti, "Fascismo e diritto," *La stirpe* 4, nos. 11–12 (Nov.–Dec. 1926):600–601.

86. Adrian Lyttelton's account in *The Seizure of Power*, pp. 311, 329, 331, indicates that this was a genuine problem in the early Fascist period, before the regime began claiming to solve the problem by giving juridical status to the syndicates and their collective contracts.

87. For example, see Bruno Caizzi, *Storia dell'industria italiana*, p. 352. See also Joseph LaPalombara, "Integrazione sociale e partecipazione politica," p. 66, for evidence that this was still a problem in the new liberal system after 1945.

88. A. O. Olivetti, "Legislazione e Magistratura del lavoro," p. 2.

89. Panunzio, *Lo Stato fascista*, pp. 92, 102; A. O. Olivetti, "Verso la rappresentanza degli interessi," *Gerarchia* 4 (1925):161; Edmondo Rossoni, "Dalla rivolta politica al nuovo ordine corporativo," *La stirpe* 5, no. 3 (March 1927):130; Armando Casalini, "La rivoluzione nello Stato," *La stirpe* 2, no. 8 (Aug. 1924):615.

90. Panunzio, "La riforma costituzionale," in *Rivoluzione e costituzione*, pp. 31–32; Panunzio, *Il sentimento dello Stato*, pp. 110–11; Panunzio, "Il diritto sindacale e corporativo," pp. 249–50.

91. Olivetti, "Legislazione e Magistratura del lavoro," p. 2.

92. Ibid.; Bottai, *Scritti*, pp. 81–83 (from *Il diritto del lavoro*, 1 Jan. 1927).

93. Panunzio, *L'economia mista*, p. 158; Sergio Panunzio, "Prime osservazioni giuridiche sul concetto di proprietà nel regime fascista," pp. 109–23; Lanzillo, "La proprietà privata e la corporazione," pp. 333–44; Bottai, *Scritti*, pp. 106–7 (lecture delivered 15 Jan. 1928).

94. Lanzillo, Address to the Chamber of Deputies, 5 Dec. 1925, p. 4850; Viesti, "Fascismo e diritto," pp. 600–602; Panunzio, *L'economia mista*, p. 16.

95. For example, see Razza, "La dottrina corporativa," p. 96; and Edmondo Rossoni, "Appunti per la Carta del lavoro," *La stirpe* 5, no. 1 (Jan. 1927):1–2.

96. Olivetti, "Parlamento e nazione," p. 1.

97. Paolo Orano, *Dal sindacalismo rivoluzionario allo Stato sindacalista*, pp. 5, 13–14, 25–27; Panunzio, *Lo Stato fascista*, pp. 139–42; Olivetti, "Legislazione e Magistratura del lavoro," p. 2; Livio Ciardi, "La sostanza e la forma," *La stirpe* 2, no. 1 (Jan. 1924):13–14; Agostino Lanzillo, *Origine e contenuto dell'economia corporativa*, p. 101.

98. Panunzio, *Il sentimento dello Stato*, especially pp. 101, 105; A. O. Olivetti, "Nella Tombuctù socialista," *Il popolo d'Italia*, 3 May 1925, p. 2; Ciattini, "Lo Stato su nuovi basi," pp. 278–79; Edmondo Rossoni, "Restare nella nuova storia," *La stirpe* 2, no. 7 (July 1924):532.

99. Turati, *Ragioni ideali di vita fascista*, pp. 20–21.

100. Orano, "L'integrazione dello Stato," p. 1. See Panunzio, *Il sentimento dello Stato*, p. 105, for the passage which Orano was echoing in this quotation.

101. Sergio Panunzio, *Che cos'è il fascismo*, p. 16.

102. For two major critical analyses of the concept, see Benjamin R. Barber, "Conceptual Foundations of Totalitarianism," pp. 3–52; and Arno J. Mayer, *Dynamics of Counterrevolution in Europe*, pp. 9–34. On the other hand, Leonard Schapiro offers a qualified defense of the concept in his *Totalitarianism*, and Zeev Sternhell finds totalitarianism to be the essence of fascism in his recent essay, "Fascist Ideology," p. 356.

103. For a few examples, see Panunzio, *Il sentimento dello Stato*, pp. 239–40; Ciattini, *Politica nazionale*, p. 42; Rossoni, "Dalla rivolta politica al nuovo ordine corporativo," pp. 129–30; Olivetti, "Legislazione e Magistratura del lavoro," p. 2; Olivetti, "La Réforme du parlement et le problème de la représentation," p. 124; Bottai, *Il Consiglio*, pp. 109–14.

104. Ciattini, *Postulati fascisti*, p. 5.

105. A. O. Olivetti, "Polemica inutile," *Il popolo d'Italia*, 25 Feb. 1925, p. 2.

106. A. O. Olivetti, *Le corporazioni e la loro formazione naturale*, p. 7.

107. Sergio Panunzio, speech of 6 May 1932, in Ministero delle Corporazioni, *Atti del secondo convegno di studi sindacali e corporativi*, 3:129.

108. For a discussion of this problem in modernizing countries in general, see Samuel P. Huntington, *Political Order in Changing Societies*, pp. 62–63, 71.

109. Olivetti, "Parlamento e nazione," p. 1.

110. This lack of confidence is implicit in the whole syndicalist conception. For an unusually explicit manifestation, see ibid.

111. Edmondo Rossoni, "Il sindacalismo nella rivoluzione fascista," p. 367.

112. For example, see Tannenbaum, *The Fascist Experience*, pp. 80, 219.

113. Olivetti, "Dottrina e prassi dello Stato corporativo," p. 68.

114. Giuseppe Bottai, "Corporativismo e principi dell'ottantanove," inaugural lecture, University of Pisa, 10 Nov. 1930, in *Scritti*, pp. 175–77.

Chapter 11 / Critics and Myth Makers, 1925–1943

1. See especially Roland Sarti, *Fascism and the Industrial Leadership in Italy*, passim, and pp. 72–74, 135, in particular. See also Sabino Cassese, "Un programmatore degli anni trenta," pp. 415, 418; and Felice Guarneri, *Battaglie economiche tra le due grandi guerre*, 1:278–88.

2. For some typical examples, see A. O. Olivetti, "Le leggi della rivoluzione: Prolusione di A. O. Olivetti alla Facoltà Fascista di Scienze Politiche di Perugia," *Il primato*, 1–15 Jan. 1931, p. 5; Sergio Panunzio, *Il concetto di dittatura rivoluzionaria*, pp. 9–10; Sergio Panunzio, "Il Consiglio nazionale delle corporazioni (prime osservazioni giuridiche)," pt. 2, *Lo stato* 1, no. 4 (July–Aug. 1930):387–88; Alighiero Ciattini, *Politica nazionale*, pp. 24–29; Luigi Razza, *La corporazione nello Stato fascista*, p. 24.

3. Carlo Curcio, "Sindacalisti e nazionalisti a Perugia fra il 1928 e il 1933," p. 23.

4. Agostino Lanzillo to Benito Mussolini, 5 May 1926 and 2 July 1934, in Archivio Centrale dello Stato, Segreteria particolare del Duce, Carteggio riservato, 1922–1943, Busta 83, Fascicolo W/R, "Lanzillo, Agostino."

5. For example, see Sergio Panunzio, *Il riconoscimento rivoluzionario dei sindacati*, pp. 11–13; Razza, *La corporazione*, p. 24; Edmondo Rossoni, "La rivoluzione e il suo contrario," *La stirpe* 4, no. 7 (July 1926):339.

6. See Luigi Razza, "La dottrina corporativa," pp. 104–5, for a reasonably explicit statement of this belief.

7. Sergio Panunzio, *Teoria generale dello Stato fascista*, pp. ix, 31–32, 50, 73. See also Alberto Aquarone, *L'organizzazione dello Stato totalitario*, p. 309n., for some observations about the unreality of Panunzio's conception of the party in his *Teoria generale*.

8. Sergio Panunzio, "Riforma politica in atto," from *Il popolo d'Italia*, 27 Jan. 1927, in *Rivoluzione e costituzione*, pp. 71–72; A. O. Olivetti, "Crepuscolo corporativo," *Il lavoro d'Italia*, 8 Nov. 1928, p. 2; A. O. Olivetti, "La Réforme du parlement et le problème de la représentation," pp. 125–27; Edmondo Rossoni, "Dalla rivolta politica al nuovo ordine corporativo," *La stirpe* 5, no. 3 (March 1927):129–30; Giuseppe Bottai, *Scritti*, pp. 106–7 (lecture delivered 15 Jan. 1928).

9. Panunzio, "Riforma politica in atto," in *Rivoluzione e costituzione*, pp. 71–72; Sergio Panunzio, *L'economia mista*, p. 46; Bottai, *Scritti*, pp. 106–7 (lecture delivered 15 Jan. 1928).

10. A. O. Olivetti, "Il Partito," *Università fascista* 2, no. 1 (Dec. 1930–Jan. 1931):34–35; Paolo Orano, "L'integrazione dello Stato," p. 1; Sergio Panunzio, "Le leggi fasciste," from *Il telegrafo*, 11 March 1926, in *Rivoluzione e costituzione*, pp. 50–54; Sergio Panunzio, *Il sentimento dello Stato*, p. 232; Sergio Panunzio, "Il Partito," from *Università fascista*, July 1930, in *Rivoluzione e costituzione*, pp. 180–81; Antonio Renda, "Quel che manca allo Stato sindacale," *L'ordine fascista* 5, no. 6 (June–July 1926):9.

11. Razza, *La corporazione*, p. 21.

12. Sergio Panunzio, "La politica di Sismondi," p. 10.

13. Olivetti, "Il Partito," p. 36.

14. Sergio Panunzio, "Idee sul fascismo," *Critica fascista* 3, no. 6 (15 March 1925):113.

15. Panunzio, *Il sentimento dello Stato*, pp. 227–40.

16. Olivetti, "Il Partito," pp. 33–36, especially p. 34.

17. [A. O. Olivetti], "La verità su la Commissione dei Diciotto," *Il popolo d'Italia*, 28 June 1925, p. 2.

18. Ezio Maria Olivetti, *Sindacalismo nazionale*, p. 130.

19. Agostino Lanzillo, Address to the Chamber of Deputies, 5 Dec. 1925, pp. 4849–55.

20. Renzo De Felice, *Mussolini il fascista*, 1:670n.

21. Rossoni, "La rivoluzione e il suo contrario," p. 339.

22. Edmondo Rossoni, "Le leggi della rivoluzione: Il sindacalismo nello Stato," *La stirpe* 4, no. 6 (June 1926):274–75. See also Edmondo Rossoni, "Il sistema fascista dell'organizzazione," *La stirpe* 4, no. 2 (Feb. 1926):66.

23. Edmondo Rossoni, "Il sistema fascista dell'organizzazione: Principio e metodo unitario," *La stirpe* 4, no. 3 (March 1926):129–31. See also Edmondo Rossoni,

"L'educazione sindacale delle classi e la valorizzazione economica della nazione," *La stirpe* 5, no. 7 (July 1927):387.

24. Edmondo Rossoni, "La corporazione integrale," *Il lavoro d'Italia*, 5 May 1926, p. 1: Rossoni, "Le leggi della rivoluzione," p. 274.

25. Edmondo Rossoni, "L'ordine economico della corporazione," *La stirpe* 4, nos. 4–5 (April–May 1926):193.

26. On the coming of the Labor Charter, see De Felice, *Mussolini il fascista*, 2:286–96; and Adrian Lyttelton, *The Seizure of Power*, pp. 330–31.

27. De Felice, *Mussolini il fascista*, 2:290n.; A. O. Olivetti, "La Carta del Lavoro," *Il popolo d'Italia*, 2 March 1927, p. 1.

28. De Felice, *Mussolini il fascista*, 2:292n., 293–96.

29. The "Carta del Lavoro" is included as an appendix to Aquarone, *L'organizzazione dello Stato*, pp. 477–81. Charles F. Delzell provides an English translation in *Mediterranean Fascism*, pp. 120–26.

30. Olivetti, "La Carta del Lavoro," p. 1.

31. Sergio Panunzio, "Il sindacalismo fascista," *Bibliografia fascista* 2, no. 6 (June 1927):1.

32. For examples, see Sergio Panunzio, speech of 6 May 1932, in Ministero delle Corporazioni, *Atti del secondo convegno di studi sindacali e corporativi*, 3:130–31; Agostino Lanzillo, "La proprietà privata e la corporazione," p. 322; and Olivetti, "Le leggi della rivoluzione," p. 5.

33. Benito Mussolini to A. O. Olivetti, 22 Nov. 1927, in *Opera omnia*, 23:301. The book in question was E. M. Olivetti, *Sindacalismo nazionale*, cited above.

34. Benito Mussolini, "La dottrina del fascismo," in *Opera omnia*, 34:122. For an English translation of Mussolini's article, see Delzell, ed., *Mediterranean Fascism*, pp. 91–106; the relevant passage is on pp. 96–97.

35. For examples of the cult of Corridoni in the Fascist regime, see Vito Rastelli, *Filippo Corridoni*; and Ivon De Begnac, *L'arcangelo sindacalista*. For examples of the syndicalists' attempts to portray Corridoni as a precursor of fascism, see Edmondo Rossoni, "Ricordando Corridoni," *La stirpe* 8, no. 12 (Dec. 1930):510–12; and Tullio Masotti, "Il 'Dopolavoro' dei gassisti milanesi: Una mirabile impresa di operai," *La stirpe* 6, no. 6 (June 1928):365–67.

36. Benito Mussolini to A. O. Olivetti, 22 Feb. 1928, in *Opera omnia*, 23:304–5.

37. Olivetti, "La Réforme du parlement et le problème de la représentation," especially p. 125.

38. [Sergio Panunzio], *La Facoltà Fascista nei primi sei anni di vita*, pp. 11–12; Panunzio, *Teoria generale*, p. viii; Curcio, "Sindacalisti e nazionalisti," p. 24; Emilio R. Papa, *Storia di due manifesti*, p. 55.

39. Curcio, "Sindacalisti e nazionalisti," p. 24. Vito Panunzio emphasized this point in conversations with the author, Rome, July 1973.

40. Sergio Panunzio, "La vera chiarificazione," from *Il popolo d'Italia*, 20 Jan. 1925, in *Rivoluzione e costituzione*, pp. 24–25.

41. Panunzio, *La Facoltà Fascista nei primi sei anni*, p. 32. Turati's speech was published as "Il Partito e i sindacati."

42. See the interview with Panunzio, entitled "La Facoltà Fascista di Scienze Politiche alla R. Università di Perugia," in *Il popolo d'Italia*, 3 March 1928, p. 3. See also Sergio Panunzio, "Prefazione," to Sergio Panunzio et al., *Dottrina e politica fascista*, pp. vii–viii.

43. Panunzio, *La Facoltà Fascista nei primi sei anni*, pp. 128–29; Sergio Panunzio, "L'insegnamento politico in Italia e le facoltà di scienze politiche," pp. 475–90; Curcio, "Sindacalisti e nazionalisti," p. 20.

44. Panunzio, "Il sindacalismo fascista," p. 2.

45. De Felice, *Mussolini il fascista*, 2:343n.

46. Panunzio, *La Facoltà Fascista nei primi sei anni*, pp. 128–29; Curcio, "Sindacalisti e nazionalisti," p. 20.

47. Panunzio, "L'insegnamento politico," p. 490.

48. For information on the faculty and curriculum, see Panunzio, *La Facolta Fascista*

nei primi sei anni, pp. 60–100. See also Paolo Orano, "Roberto Michels," pp. 7–14, on Michels's role at Perugia.

49. Panunzio, "La Facoltà Fascista di Scienze Politiche," p. 3.

50. Panunzio, *La Facoltà Fascista nei primi sei anni*, p. 50.

51. Ibid., p. 104.

52. See, for example, Sergio Panunzio, "Il sindacalismo," pp. 355–58; Sergio Panunzio, "Origini e sviluppi storici del sindacalismo fascista," pp. 46–48; and A. O. Olivetti, "Rivoluzione fascista e realtà sindacale," *La stirpe* 6, no. 11 (Nov. 1928):644.

53. Sergio Panunzio, "Logica costituzionale," *Il popolo d'Italia*, 28 Aug. 1929, p. 1; Sergio Panunzio, "Il Comitato Corporativo Centrale," from *Il popolo d'Italia*, 11 Nov. 1931, in *Rivoluzione e costituzione*, p. 245. For an example of Panunzio's insistence that this area was secondary, see Sergio Panunzio, "La riforma costituzionale," from *Il resto del carlino*, 9 June 1925, in *Rivoluzione e costituzione*, pp. 28–29.

54. Panunzio, *Teoria generale*, pp. 18–19; Sergio Panunzio, *Popolo Nazione Stato*, pp. 16–17.

55. For examples of these themes, see A. O. Olivetti, "L'antimarxismo di Giorgio Sorel," *La stirpe* 8, no. 1 (Jan. 1930):7–11; A. O. Olivetti, "Alcune pagine non conosciute di Michele Bianchi," *La stirpe* 9, no. 9 (Sept. 1931):388; Agostino Lanzillo, *Lo Stato nel processo economico*, p. 103; Sergio Panunzio, *Riforma costituzionale*, p. 17; Panunzio, "Il sindacalismo," p. 356.

56. Sergio Panunzio, "Sindacalismo integrale," *Gerarchia* 15 (Aug. 1936):669–70; see also pp. 666–67. For other examples, see Rossoni, "La rivoluzione e il suo contrario," pp. 337–39; A. O. Olivetti, "Le corporazioni come volontà e come rappresentazione," pp. 145–46; and Sergio Panunzio, "I sistemi del sindacalismo," *La stirpe* 8, nos. 8–9 (Aug.–Sept. 1930):395–96.

57. On the electoral reform of 1928, see Aquarone, *L'organizzazione dello Stato*, pp. 149–59; and De Felice, *Mussolini il fascista*, 2:314–26.

58. Declaration of the Grand Council of Fascism, 10 Nov. 1927, in *Opera omnia di Benito Mussolini*, 23:62–63.

59. Olivetti, "La Réforme du parlement et le problème de la représentation," p. 122.

60. De Felice, *Mussolini il fascista*, 2:270–71; Panunzio, "Il sindacalismo," p. 363. Panunzio was responding especially to Rossoni's "La corporazione integrale," cited above.

61. Mario Racheli to A. O. Olivetti, 19 Dec. 1927, quoted in De Felice, *Mussolini il fascista*, 2:329n.

62. See, for example, Rossoni, "Dalla rivolta politica al nuovo ordine corporativo," pp. 129–34; and Edmondo Rossoni, "Il contratto legale di lavoro," *La stirpe* 5, no. 4 (April 1924):194–95.

63. Rossoni, "Dalla rivolta politica al nuovo ordine corporativo," p. 129; Rossoni, "Ricordando Corridoni," p. 511; Edmondo Rossoni, "Riflessioni sulla rivoluzione fascista: La corporazione come idea," *La stirpe* 9, no. 3 (March 1931):99.

64. Edmondo Rossoni, "Il sistema fascista dell'organizzazione," *La stirpe* 4, no. 2 (Feb. 1926):66.

65. On the syndical reorganization of 1928, see De Felice, *Mussolini il fascista*, 2:326–41; Aquarone, *L'organizzazione dello Stato*, pp. 144–47; and Sarti, *Fascism and the Industrial Leadership*, pp. 88–89.

66. A. O. Olivetti, *Sindacalismo e fascismo*, p. 21; A. O. Olivetti, "Dal sindacalismo rivoluzionario alla corporazione," *Il lavoro d'Italia*, 14 Aug. 1928, p. 1; Bottai, *Scritti*, p. 107 (lecture delivered 15 Jan. 1928).

67. Aquarone, *L'organizzazione dello Stato*, pp. 75, 136–37; Cassese, "Un programmatore," pp. 414–15.

68. For example, see A. O. Olivetti, *Lineamenti del nuovo Stato italiano*, p. 77; and Olivetti, "Dal sindacalismo rivoluzionario alla corporazione," p. 1. For an example by another syndicalist, see Rossoni, "Riflessioni sulla rivoluzione fascista," p. 99.

69. Augusto Turati to Benito Mussolini, 1 Jan. 1930, published as an appendix to Aquarone, *L'organizzazione dello Stato*, pp. 350–52.

70. See Bottai, *Scritti*, p. 60 (orig. pub. 25 Feb. 1925), for Bottai's conception of the

symbiotic relationship between party and syndicates. See also Edward R. Tannenbaum, *The Fascist Experience*, p. 64.

71. Enzo Santarelli, *Storia del movimento e del regime fascista*, 1:427; De Felice, *Mussolini il fascista*, 2:176, 196–97, 281.

72. A. O. Olivetti, "A proposito di economia corporativa," *La stirpe* 9, no. 5 (May 1931):195–96. For another example, see Edmondo Rossoni, "Soluzione fascista del sindacalismo," *La stirpe* 8, no. 6 (June 1930):283.

73. See Aquarone, *L'organizzazione dello Stato*, pp. 188–94; and Santarelli, *Storia del movimento*, 1:27–31, on the advent and operation of the National Council of Corporations.

74. For example, see Panunzio, "Logica costituzionale," p. 1; and Razza, "La dottrina corporativa," pp. 97–107.

75. Benito Mussolini, "Per il Consiglio Nazionale delle Corporazioni," speech of 21 April 1930, in *Opera omnia*, 24:214–19.

76. See, for example, Edmondo Rossoni, "Il sindacalismo e l'economia eroica del fascismo," *La stirpe* 8, no. 5 (May 1930):225; and Panunzio, *Il concetto di dittatura rivoluzionaria*, p. 8. See also Giordano Bruno Guerri, *Giuseppe Bottai, un fascista critico*, pp. 111, 128, on Bottai's continuing optimism, not only in 1930, but also in the wake of frustrations later on.

77. Livio Ciardi, "I trasporti e l'ordinamento corporativo," *Archivio di studi corporativi*, 1932, p. 382; Panunzio, speech of 6 May 1932, in Ministero delle Corporazioni, *Atti del secondo convegno di studi sindacali e corporativi*, 3:131.

78. A. O. Olivetti, "Problema di fede," *Il lavoro fascista*, 6 June 1930, p. 1.

79. Olivetti, "Le corporazioni come volontà e come rappresentazione," pp. 145–46.

80. Ugo Spirito, "Individuo e Stato nella concezione corporativo," pp. 84–93. See also Camillo Pellizzi, *Una rivoluzione mancata*, pp. 76–91; Antimo Negri, *Dal corporativismo comunista all'umanesimo scientifico*, pp. 51–91; and Gianpasquale Santomassimo, "Ugo Spirito e il corporativismo," p. 87–113.

81. Panunzio, speech of 6 May 1932, and Mario Racheli, untitled comment, in Ministero delle Corporazioni, *Atti del secondo convegno di studi sindacali e corporativi*, 3:131–35, 136–38. Antonio Gramsci, in his prison notebooks, criticized Spirito's conception for much the same reasons that Panunzio did; see Antonio Gramsci, *Passato e presente*, pp. 75–82. On the other hand, Gramsci also had some very critical things to say about Panunzio's antipolitical conception at about the same time; see Antonio Gramsci, *Note sul Machiavelli, sulla politica e sullo Stato moderno*, pp. 138–40.

82. For example, see Sergio Panunzio, "Sindacati, corporazioni, aziende, cooperative," *Critica fascista* 12, no. 18 (15 Sept. 1934):357; and Panunzio, *L'economia mista*, pp. 79–81.

83. For example, see Roland Sarti, "Fascist Modernization in Italy," p. 1041.

84. Panunzio, *L'economia mista*, pp. 6, 137; Panunzio, "Sindacalismo integrale," pp. 666–67; Razza, *La corporazione*, pp. 31–32; Luigi Fontanelli, *Logica della corporazione e relative polemiche*, p. 18 (originally a speech to the assembly of the National Council of Corporations, 19 Jan. 1933); Bottai, *Scritti*, pp. 183–90, especially pp. 188–89 (from his statement to the Ferrara meeting, May 1932); Giuseppe Bottai, *Il cammino delle corporazioni*, pp. 61–63; Aquarone, *L'organizzazione dello Stato*, pp. 201, 201n.–202n. See also Lanzillo, *Lo Stato nel processo economico*, p. 206, on the ongoing reality of class differences in a corporativist regime.

85. Panunzio, *L'economia mista*, pp. 11, 141–42, 164–65; Panunzio, "Sindacati, corporazioni, aziende, cooperative," p. 358.

86. G[herardo] C[asini], "Sindacato-cooperativa o sindacato nell'azienda?" *Critica fascista* 12, no. 18 (15 Sept. 1934):359–60. For Panunzio's response to Casini, see Sergio Panunzio, "Sindacati e cooperative," *Critica fascista* 13, no. 10 (15 March 1935):195; and Panunzio, "Sindacalismo integrale," pp. 670–71.

87. Aquarone makes this point in *L'organizzazione dello Stato*, p. 201n.

88. See Santarelli, *Storia del movimento*, 2:60, for an example of the widespread belief that Spirito's failure meant the definitive defeat of left corporativism.

89. Razza, *La corporazione*, p. 44.

90. Roberto Farinacci, "L'inaugurazione dell'anno giuridico," *La vita italiana* 41, no. 1 (Jan. 1933):4.

91. Gherardo Casini, "Un pericolo corporativo?" *Critica fascista* 13, no. 7 (1 Feb. 1935):125–27.

92. Carlo Costamagna, "Il principio corporativo dello Stato fascista," pp. 82–89.

93. Alberto Benaglia, "Quel che fanno e che non fanno le corporazioni," pp. 71–74.

94. Sergio Panunzio, "Sviluppi corporativi necessari," *Il diritto del lavoro*, May 1941, pp. 117–22; Sergio Panunzio, "Per l'ordinamento delle corporazioni," *Gerarchia*, Sept. 1942, pp. 346–48.

95. Razza, *La corporazione*, pp. 11, 20–21, 26, 38–40, 47, 55.

96. Panunzio, *Riforma costituzionale*, p. 25. See also G. Lowell Field, *The Syndical and Corporative Institutions of Italian Fascism*, pp. 162–76, on the debate in the National Council of Corporations which preceded the establishment of the corporations themselves. For a sensitive leftist discussion of the role of the depression in damaging the credibility of the Fascist unions, thereby stimulating the quest for new institutions, see Camillo Gibelli, "I sindacati fascisti a Genova negli anni della grande crisi (1929–1933)," pp. 303–55.

97. Mussolini, *Opera omnia*, 26:86–96.

98. Sergio Panunzio, "Diciannove," from *Il popolo d'Italia*, 28 Nov. 1933, in *L'economia mista*, pp. 35–39.

99. See Aquarone, *L'organizzazione dello Stato*, pp. 203–7, for a discussion of these innovations. Charles F. Delzell includes a translation of the text of the law in his *Mediterranean Fascism*, pp. 126–28.

100. See Aquarone's suggestive remarks on this point in *L'organizzazione dello Stato*, pp. 220–21. More generally, see Renzo De Felice's penetrating analysis of Mussolini's position in the 1930s in *Mussolini il Duce*, 1:172–81. This is one of the most effective passages in De Felice's monumental work.

101. See Aquarone, *L'organizzazione dello Stato*, pp. 210–34, for a good summary of the deficiencies of the entire syndical-corporative system in practice. See also Field, *The Syndical and Corporative Institutions*, pp. 194–203, for an interesting contemporary view of the corporations in operation.

102. Carlo Rosselli, "La realtà dello Stato corporativo: Corporazione e rivoluzione," pp. 213–24. See also the classic critique by Gaetano Salvemini, *Under the Axe of Fascism*, as well as H. Stuart Hughes, *The Sea Change*, pp. 82–100, 125–33, on the significance of Salvemini's role in unmasking fascist corporativism.

103. Panunzio, "Sindacalismo integrale," p. 666; Agostino Lanzillo, "Ciò che è provvisorio e ciò che sarà definitivo," *La vita italiana* 24 (Feb. 1936):157–58. For another example, see Bottai, *Il cammino*, pp. 31–32.

104. Aquarone, *L'organizzazione dello Stato*, pp. 215–16, 271–81. See Delzell, ed., *Mediterranean Fascism*, pp. 129–32, for a text of the law.

105. Sergio Panunzio, *La Camera dei fasci e delle corporazioni*, pp. 7, 28–30. For Panunzio's earlier proposals for a reform of the Chamber, see Sergio Panunzio, "Contributo all'esame dei problemi relativi alla istituzione della Camera dei fasci e delle corporazioni," pp. 175–228.

106. Aquarone, *L'organizzazione dello Stato*, pp. 277–79.

107. See Delzell's collection, *Mediterranean Fascism*, pp. 148–55, for an English translation of Bottai's "Carta della Scuola"; the quoted passage is on pp. 149–50. See also Cassese, "Un programmatore," pp. 431–32.

108. Aquarone, *L'organizzazione dello Stato*, pp. 230–34.

109. Franco Angelini et al., *La concezione fascista della proprietà privata*. Panunzio's piece is "Prime osservazioni giuridiche sul concetto di proprietà nel regime fascista," pp. 109–23; Lanzillo's is "La proprietà privata e la corporazione," pp. 309–44.

110. Sergio Panunzio, "Il problema dei codici e i limiti della codificazione," *Lo Stato* 7, no. 12 (Dec. 1936):644–45, 651–59. See also Panunzio, *Riforma costituzionale*, pp. 34, 46.

111. Leonardo Paloscia, *La concezione sindacalista di Sergio Panunzio*, p. 48.

112. Aquarone, *L'organizzazione dello Stato*, p. 288n.

113. Panunzio, "Prime osservazioni giuridiche sul concetto di proprietà nel regime fascista," p. 116.

114. Orano, *Il fascismo*, 1:270–71.

115. Sergio Panunzio, "La terza ondata," *Critica fascista* 20, no. 1 (1 Nov. 1941):2–4.

116. Panunzio, "Per l'ordinamento delle corporazioni," pp. 350–52.

117. Vito Panunzio, *Fedeltà al sindacato e alla corporazione*, pp. 9–10; Vito Panunzio, "Necessità di un estremismo sindacale e corporativo," *Critica fascista* 21, no. 13 (1 May 1943):162–63.

118. In an otherwise excellent article, Henry Ashby Turner, Jr., tries to draw such inappropriate analogies, though only in a hypothetical way; see his "Fascism and Modernization," pp. 547–59, especially pp. 555–59. Writing in response to Turner, A. James Gregor portrays the Fascist appeal to ancient glories as a means of mobilizing energies for development; see his "Fascism and Modernization: Some Addenda," pp. 370–84, especially pp. 378–79.

119. Sergio Panunzio, "Sulla 'riforma dello Stato,' " *Il popolo d'Italia*, 18 Feb. 1923, p. 1.

120. Sergio Panunzio, *Stato nazionale e sindacati*, p. 123 (orig. pub. 12 May 1923).

121. See Bertrando Spaventa, *La filosofia italiana nelle sue relazioni con la filosofia europea*, which contains the lectures Spaventa delivered at the university during 1861–62, including his famous inaugural lecture, "Della nazionalità nella filosofia."

122. Panunzio, *Il sentimento dello Stato*, p. 25.

123. A. O. Olivetti [Lo spettatore], "Parlamento e nazione," *Il popolo d'Italia*, 20 July 1924, p. 1. See also A. O. Olivetti, "La realtà corporativa intesa come 'passione storica,' " *Il lavoro fascista*, 12 Aug. 1931, p. 2.

124. For example, see Olivetti, "Parlamento e nazione," p. 1; and Panunzio, "Sindacalismo integrale," pp. 664–66.

125. For some examples, see A. O. Olivetti, "Le corporazioni del passato," *Il popolo d'Italia*, 24 Sept. 1924, p. 3; A. O. Olivetti, "La verità su la nuova economia," *Il popolo d'Italia*, 14 April 1931, p. 1; Sergio Panunzio, "Il diritto sindacale e corporativo," p. 268; Panunzio, *Il sentimento dello Stato*, p. 167; and Panunzio, "Sindacalismo integrale," pp. 664–66.

126. A. O. Olivetti, "Mazzini e lo Stato corporativo," *Il lavoro fascista*, 15 May 1930, p. 3; A. O. Olivetti, "Verso l'economia corporativa," *Il lavoro fascista*, 31 May 1929, p. 1; Olivetti, "A proposito di economia corporativa," p. 195. See also Panunzio, *Stato nazionale e sindacati*, p. 147; and Sergio Panunzio, "Il sindacalismo e la crisi del socialismo," *Augustea* 1, no. 1 (21 Dec. 1925):4.

127. For examples of this cluster of themes, see Panunzio, *Il sentimento dello Stato*, pp. 69–70, 76; Agostino Lanzillo, "Anti-sindacalismo dei sovieti," *La stirpe*, April 1933, pp. 193–98; Paolo Orano, "In tema di cultura: Si domanda la sospensiva," *Bibliografia fascista* 2, no. 1 (31 Jan. 1927):1–2; Alighiero Ciattini, *Caratteri della vita italiana*, pp. 21–24; Olivetti, "La Réforme du parlement et le problème de la représentation," pp. 96–100; Edmondo Rossoni, "Insegnamenti per l'estero della rivoluzione fascista," *La stirpe* 5, no. 10 (Oct. 1927):577–79.

128. Edmondo Rossoni, "Appunti per la Carta del lavoro," *La stirpe* 5, no. 1 (Jan. 1927):1.

129. Panunzio, *L'economia mista*, p. 43; Panunzio, speech of 6 May 1932, in Ministero delle corporazioni, *Atti del secondo convegno di studi sindacali e corporativi*, 3:135–36.

130. See especially Panunzio, *L'economia mista*, pp. 10, 14, 42, 163. See also Carlo Curcio's response to "La nuova inchiesta di *Pagine libere*: Fascismo e fascismi a confronto," p. 86, for some further indications of Panunzio's hostility to Nazism.

131. For example, see Lanzillo, "Antisindacalismo dei sovieti," p. 194; and Panunzio, "La fine di un regno," pp. 342–43.

132. For examples of this pattern of argument, see Lanzillo, "Antisindacalismo dei sovieti," pp. 193–98; Panunzio, *L'economia mista*, pp. 14, 46; A. O. Olivetti, "Le corporazioni nel presente," *Il popolo d'Italia*, 1 Oct. 1924, p. 2; A. O. Olivetti, "Individuo, Stato, associazione," *Il lavoro fascista*, 28 June 1929, p. 1.

133. For examples regarding the Ethiopian War, see Bottai, *Il cammino*, p. 98; and Panunzio, "La S. d. N.: Capolavoro sbagliato," *Critica fascista* 14, no. 3 (1 Dec. 1935):37.

134. Vito Panunzio, "Nuova Europa: Punti fermi per il nuovo ordine," *Critica fascista* 18, no. 24 (15 Oct. 1940):396–98.

135. Sergio Panunzio, "L'impero italiano del lavoro," *Gerarchia* 19, no. 9 (Sept. 1940):462–63. See also Panunzio, "Sviluppi corporativi necessari," p. 122.

Chapter 12 / Italian Fascism in European History

1. See especially Augusto Del Noce, "Per una definizione storica del fascismo," pp. 27–43. Here Del Noce seeks to place some of Renzo De Felice's ideas about Mussolini's character and outlook into wider historical perspective.

2. A. James Gregor is a tireless advocate of this interpretation. See especially "Fascism and Modernization," pp. 370–84; and *The Fascist Persuasion in Radical Politics*. See also Ludovico Garruccio, *L'industrializzazione tra nazionalismo e rivoluzione*, pp. 103–6, 135–41, on the modernizing thrust of Italian fascism.

3. See, for example, Wolfgang Sauer's influential "National Socialism," especially pp. 417–22.

4. For some examples of this syndrome, see Joachim Fest, *The Face of the Third Reich*, passim; and Hannah Arendt, *Eichmann in Jerusalem*, pp. 21–55.

5. See the two articles by Giovanni Ansaldo, "Ceti medi e operai," pp. 345–62; and "La piccola borghesia," pp. 417–22.

6. Luigi Salvatorelli, "Risposta ai critici di nazionalfascismo," pp. 425–27.

7. Adrian Lyttelton, *The Seizure of Power*, p. 204.

8. This is the implication of Roberto Vivarelli's interpretation in *Il dopoguerra in Italia e l'avvento del fascismo*, 1:235–39, 253–59, 266, 272–74, 329n, 498–500.

9. Henry Ashby Turner, Jr., "Fascism and Modernization," pp. 552–58. Turner forcefully argues a point which is often forgotten in studies of Nazism—that it is possible for people whose basic concerns are antimodern to use modern means.

10. G[eorges] Sorel, "La crisi del socialismo scientifico," p. 134.

11. V[ladimir] I[llich] Lenin, "What is to be done?" in *Essential Works of Lenin*, pp. 74–75; Alfred G. Meyer, *Leninism*, p. 31; Sheldon S. Wolin, *Politics and Vision*, pp. 421–22.

12. Giacomo Marramao, *Marxismo e revisionismo in Italia*, pp. 8–10.

13. Wolin, *Politics and Vision*, pp. 421–22; Martin Jay, *The Dialectical Imagination*, pp. 53–54; Judith N. Shklar, *After Utopia*, p. 263; George Lichtheim, *Marxism*, p. 396.

14. Ernst Nolte, *Three Faces of Fascism*, passim, especially pp. 20–21, 429–46.

15. Sergio Panunzio, *L'economia mista*, pp. 44–45. See also Sergio Panunzio, *Che cos'è il fascismo*, p. 61; Sergio Panunzio, "Il sindacalismo e la crisi del socialismo," *Augustea* 1, no. 1 (21 Dec. 1925):4; Sergio Panunzio, "Il sindacalismo," p. 353; Sergio Panunzio, "I sistemi del sindacalismo," *La stirpe* 8, nos. 8–9 (Aug.–Sept. 1930):395.

16. A. O. Olivetti, "Dal sindacalismo rivoluzionario alla corporazione," *Il lavoro d'Italia*, 14 Aug. 1928, p. 1.

17. Agostino Lanzillo, *La disfatta del socialismo*, pp. 130–32; Agostino Lanzillo, "La lettera degli organizzatori," p. 1.

18. See, for example, Curzio Suckert, "Il problema fondamentale," *La conquista dello Stato* 1, no. 1 (10 July 1924):1; Dino Grandi, "Le origini e la missione del fascismo," p. 70.

19. Panunzio, "Il sindacalismo e la crisi del socialismo," p. 4; Panunzio, "Il sindacalismo," p. 353; Panunzio, *L'economia mista*, pp. 29n., 71; Sergio Panunzio, *Riforma costituzionale*, p. 22.

20. A. O. Olivetti, "L'antimarxismo di Giorgio Sorel," *La stirpe* 8, no. 1 (Jan. 1930):7–11; Panunzio, *L'economia mista*, p. 71.

21. A. O. Olivetti, "Relazione al convegno di cultura fascista di Bologna," pp. 3–4, in the Olivetti papers, Rome; A. O. Olivetti, "La Réforme du parlement et le problème de la représentation," pp. 95–100.

22. Sergio Panunzio, "La politica di Sismondi," especially pp. 6–9; Karl Marx and Friedrich Engels, "Manifesto of the Communist Party," in *Basic Writings on Politics and Philosophy*, pp. 31–32.

23. Shlomo Avineri, *The Social and Political Thought of Karl Marx*, pp. 202–9.

24. Anthony Giddens, *Capitalism and Modern Social Theory*, pp. 60–61; Marx and Engels, "Manifesto," in *Basic Writings*, p. 28.

25. Lichtheim, *Marxism*, p. 392.

26. Panunzio, *L'economia mista*, p. 29n.; Panunzio, *Riforma costituzionale*, p. 22; [Francesco] Saverio Merlino, *L'utopia collettivista*, pp. 37–52, 128–29.

27. Alan Ritter, *The Political Thought of Pierre-Joseph Proudhon*, pp. 151–55; J. E. S. Hayward, "Solidarist Syndicalism," pt. 1, pp. 28–32.

28. For some examples, see Sergio Panunzio, *La persistenza del diritto*, p. 163; Sergio Panunzio, *Stato nazionale e sindacati*, pp. 50–52 (from *Il rinnovamento*, 15 Aug. 1919) and p. 119 (from *Il lavoro d'Italia*, 12 May 1923); and Sergio Panunzio, *Teoria generale dello Stato fascista*, p. 23.

29. Durkheim first advocated a form of corporativism in *Suicide*, especially pp. 373–74, 378–80; he developed these ideas more fully in "Some Notes on Occupational Groups," the preface to the second (1902) edition of *The Division of Labor in Society*, pp. 1–31. See also Emile Durkheim, *Socialism*, pp. 245–46.

30. Hayward, "Solidarist Syndicalism," pt. 1, p. 32.

31. Matthew H. Elbow, *French Corporative Theory*, p. 116; Hayward, "Solidarist Syndicalism," pt. 2, pp. 190–91. For examples of Panunzio's use of Duguit, see Sergio Panunzio, *La lega delle nazioni*, p. 20; Panunzio, *Stato nazionale e sindacati*, p. 95; and Sergio Panunzio, "Prefazione," to Luigi Viesti, *Stato e diritto fascista*, p. 12.

32. Sergio Panunzio, *Il socialismo giuridico*. Among the most important of the works which Panunzio considered were Anton Menger, *Lo Stato socialista*; G[iuseppe] Salvioli, *I difetti sociali delle leggi vigenti di fronte al proletariato e il diritto nuovo*; Enrico Cimbali, *La nuova fase del diritto civile nei rapporti economici e sociali*; and Cesare Vivante, "La penetrazione del socialismo nel diritto privato," pp. 345–51.

33. Hayward, "Solidarist Syndicalism," pt. 2, pp. 186–87; Léon Duguit, *L'Etat, le droit objectif et la loi positive*, pp. 612–18.

34. Léon Duguit, *Le Droit social, le droit individuel et la transformation de l'Etat*, p. 104.

35. For a few indications of these problems and concerns, see Alfred Grosser, *Germany in our Time*, pp. 124, 134; John Ardagh, *The New French Revolution*, p. 22; Philip M. Williams and Martin Harrison, *Politics and Society in de Gaulle's Republic*, pp. 431–43; Stanley Hoffmann, *Decline or Renewal?* pp. 443–86; André Gorz, *Strategy for Labor*; and Jean-Jacques Servan-Schreiber, *The Radical Alternative*.

36. Arno J. Mayer, *Dynamics of Counterrevolution in Europe*, pp. 1, 69. For an especially perceptive critique of Mayer's schema, see Eugen Weber, "Revolution? Counterrevolution? What Revolution?" pp. 443–51, 460.

37. Nolte, *Three Faces of Fascism*, p. 196.

38. For example, see Renzo De Felice, *Mussolini il fascista*, 2:66–68.

39. Paolo Orano, *L'educazione fascista*, pp. 24–29, 56–62, 78.

40. On the discussion which Orano's book stimulated, see Renzo De Felice, *Storia degli ebrei italiani sotto il fascismo*, pp. 211–17; and Luigi Preti, *Impero fascista africani ed ebrei*, pp. 108–13, 224–32.

41. See especially Claudio Giovannini, "Alle origini del fascismo," pp. 909–11. Giovannini both articulates this view and provides a useful summary of the historiography upon which it is based.

42. Piero Gobetti, *La rivoluzione liberale*, p. 179.

43. De Felice, *Mussolini il fascista*, 2:359, 363–67.

Bibliography

Since this book is concerned with "public" ideas, I have relied primarily on published sources. However, I also used the private papers of A. O. Olivetti and Ottavio Dinale in Rome and documents from the following collections in the Archivo Centrale dello Stato: Ministero dell'interno, direzione generale della pubblica sicurrezza, casellario politico centrale; Mostra della rivoluzione fascista; Segreteria particolare del Duce, Carteggio riservato, 1922–43.

It is not feasible to list every useful article in the various socialist, syndicalist, and fascist periodicals that I consulted more or less systematically. Thus, I have included only the most significant of these articles in the bibliography proper. The paragraphs below provide a brief discussion of the periodicals themselves. They are indispensable sources for the problems considered in this work.

For the presyndicalist period in Italian socialism, see especially Filippo Turati's review *Critica sociale* (Milan), founded in 1891, Francesco Saverio Merlino's short-lived but highly significant revisionist review *Rivista critica del socialismo* (Rome), which appeared during 1899, and the Socialist party's national newspaper, *Avanti!*, founded in 1896. Arturo Labriola's newspaper *Avanguardia socialista* (Milan, 1902–6) was the first revolutionary syndicalist publication, although Enrico Leone's *Il divenire sociale* (Rome, 1905–10) and A. O. Olivetti's *Pagine libere* (Lugano; Milan), founded in 1906, were more important for the doctrinal development of Italian syndicalism. *Lotta di classe* (Milan) was an ill-fated syndicalist newspaper published from January to May 1907. Paolo Orano's short-lived but influential review *La lupa* (Rome) appeared in 1910–11, as some of the syndicalists were beginning to consider new ideas. Still more eclectic was Ottavio Dinale's *La demolizione* (Milan), published during 1910. The major organ of the revolutionary syndicalist labor movement after the demise of *Avanguardia socialista* was *L'internazionale* (Parma), founded late in 1907. The Italian syndicalists also contributed periodically to the major organ of the "New School" in France, Hubert Lagardelle's *Le Mouvement Socialiste* (Paris), which appeared from 1899 to 1914.

Mussolini's newspaper *Il popolo d'Italia*, which began to appear in November 1914, is essential both for the period of theoretical transition and for the

369

fascist period. Mussolini's theoretical review *Utopia* (Milan, 1913–14) is significant for the theoretical reappraisal that preceded the dispute over intervention. Sergio Panunzio contributed frequently to the local interventionist paper *Gazzettino rosa* (Ferrara) during 1914–15. The journalistic focus for the elaboration of the neosyndicalist program after 1917 was Alceste De Ambris's *Il rinnovamento* (Milan, 1918–19). Also important were Edmondo Rossoni's review *Cultura sindacale* (1920–21) and the journalistic organs of the syndicalist labor movement, *L'Italia nostra* (1918), *Battaglie dell'Unione Italiana del Lavoro* (1919), and *Il sindacato operaio* (1920–22). See also *La gioventù sindacalista* (Parma, 1920–21), the organ of the national organization of syndicalist youth. In addition to his highly important postwar series of *Pagine libere* (1920–22), A. O. Olivetti edited *La patria del popolo* (Milan), another neosyndicalist and non-fascist periodical, for a few months during 1922 and 1923. Other heterodox socialist publications important in the discussions of this twilight period were *Sindacalismo* (Milan), edited by Rinaldo Rigola, Alceste De Ambris, and Guido Galbiati from January to April 1923; *Rassegna sindacale* (Milan, 1924–25); and the reformist newspaper *La giustizia*. The major review of the Italian Nationalist Association after the war was *Politica*, which began publication in December 1918 and remained a major focus for right fascist ideas, especially in foreign affairs, during the Fascist regime.

For the fascist period, the more or less official publications were *Il popolo d'Italia* and Mussolini's monthly review *Gerarchia* (1922–43). The Fascist union movement's newspaper was *Il lavoro d'Italia*, founded under Edmondo Rossoni's direction in March 1922; it became *Il lavoro fascista* in the wake of Rossoni's ouster and the syndical reorganization of 1928. The monthly magazine of the Fascist trade union movement was *La stirpe*, initiated in December 1923. *L'idea sindacalista* (Milan) was the journalistic organ of a movement which A. O. Olivetti spearheaded in opposition to Edmondo Rossoni and the existing Fascist union hierarchy in 1924 and 1925. Good examples of the local newspapers which constituted the journalistic focus for the new provincial fascism of 1920–21 are *L'assalto* (Bologna), founded in November 1920, and *L'audacia* (Verona), founded in January 1921. Curzio Suckert began his own organ of intransigent fascism, *La conquista dello Stato*, in July 1924. I also consulted Italo Balbo's *Corriere padano* (Ferrara), which began publication in 1925, and *L'impero*, edited by the former futurists Mario Carli and Emilio Settimelli beginning in March 1923.

A remarkable variety of political and cultural reviews emerged under the fascist umbrella, each with somewhat different accents. Surely the most significant, and the most important for this study, was Giuseppe Bottai's *Critica fascista* (1923–43). *Il diritto del lavoro*, the organ of the Ministry of Corporations, also began publication under Bottai's aegis, in January 1927. In addition, Bottai was in charge of the *Archivio di studi corporativi* issued by the school for corporative studies at the University of Pisa beginning in 1930. Panunzio and some of his younger followers contributed important pieces to *Rivista internazionale di filosofia del diritto*, which began publication in 1921 and which was less explicitly fascist. Other reviews especially concerned with corporative and juridical matters were *Nuovi studi di diritto, economia e politica* (Rome, 1927–35), the organ of the circle around Ugo Spirito; *Nuovi problemi di politica, storia ed economia* (Ferrara, 1930–40), edited by Nello Quilici and Giulio Colamarino; and *Lo Stato* (Rome, 1930–43), a more conservative, or right fascist, organ, edited by Carlo Costamagna and Ettore Rosbach. The subjects of this study also contributed to *Bibliografia fascista* (Rome, 1926–35); *L'ordine fascista* (1925–36); Ottavio Dinale's *Augustea*, initiated in December 1925; Vincenzo Zangara's *Il primato*; *Universalità fascista* (founded as *Università fascista* in 1929, published as *Universalità fascista* from 1931 until March 1940); *Civiltà fascista*, which superseded *Educazione fascista* in 1934, and became the organ of the Istituto nazionale di cultura fascista in Rome; and *La vita italiana* (Rome), founded well before the fascist period, in 1913, by Giovanni Preziosi.

Books and Articles

Abrate, Mario, et al. *Il problema storico del fascismo*. Florence: Vallecchi, 1970.

[Albertini, Luigi]. "I nuovi organi dello Stato: Corporazioni e consigli tecnici." *Corriere della sera*, 15 Aug. 1924, p. 1.

———. "Stato liberale e Stato organico fascista." *Corriere della sera*, 16 Aug. 1925, p. 1.

Albertini, Luigi. *Venti anni di vita politica*. Pt. 1, *L'esperienza democratica italiana dal 1898 al 1914*. 2 vols. Bologna: Nicola Zanichelli, 1950.

Almond, Gabriel A., and Verba, Sidney. *The Civic Culture: Political Attitudes and Democracy in Five Nations*. Princeton: Princeton University Press, 1963.

Ambrosini, Gaspare. *Sindacati, consigli tecnici e parlamento politico*. Rome: Anonima Romana Editoriale, 1925.

Ambrosini, Vittorio. *La battaglia per lo Stato sindacale*. Rome: Anonima Romana Editoriale, 1925.

Andreu, Pierre. *Notre Maître, M. Sorel*. Paris: Bernard Grasset, 1953.

Angelini, Franco, et al. *La concezione fascista della proprietà privata*. [Rome]: Confederazione Fascista dei Lavoratori dell'Agricoltura, [1939].

Ansaldo, Giovanni. "Ceti medi e operai." From *La rivoluzione liberale*, 19 Oct. 1922. In *Antologia della "Rivoluzione liberale."* Edited by Nino Valeri. Turin: Francesco De Silva, 1948.

———. "La piccola borghesia." From *Il lavoro* (Genoa), 3 June 1923. In *Antologia della "Rivoluzione liberale."* Edited by Nino Valeri. Turin: Francesco De Silva, 1948.

Aquarone, Alberto. *Alla ricerca dell'Italia liberale*. Naples: Guida, 1972.

———. "Aspirazioni tecnocratiche del primo fascismo." *Nord e sud* 11, no. 52 (April 1964):109–28.

———. *L'organizzazione dello Stato totalitario*. Turin: Giulio Einaudi, 1965.

———. "La politica sindacale del fascismo." *Il nuovo osservatore*, Dec. 1965, pp. 874–88.

Arbizzani, Luigi. "L'avvento del fascismo nel Bolognese 1920–1922." *Movimento operaio e socialista* 10, no. 2 (April–June 1964):83–102; 10, nos. 3–4 (July–Dec. 1964):253–76.

Arcari, Paola Maria. *Le elaborazioni della dottrina politica nazionale fra l'unità e l'intervento (1870–1914)*. 3 vols. Florence: Marzocco, 1934–39.

Ardagh, John. *The New French Revolution*. New York: Harper and Row (Colophon), 1969.

Are, Giuseppe. *Economia e politica nell'Italia liberale (1890–1915)*. Bologna: Il Mulino, 1974.

Arena, Celestino, et al. *La camera dei fasci e delle corporazioni*. Florence: G. C. Sansoni, 1937.

Arendt, Hannah. *Eichmann in Jerusalem: A Report on the Banality of Evil*. Rev. ed. New York: Viking (Compass), 1965.

————. *The Origins of Totalitarianism*. 2nd ed. Cleveland: World Publishing Co. (Meridian), 1958.

Arfé, Gaetano. "Arturo Labriola e il riformismo." In *Ricerche storiche ed economiche in memoria di Corrado Barbagallo*, 3:219–51. Edited by Luigi De Rosa. Naples: Edizioni Scientifiche Italiane, 1970.

————. "Le origini del movimento giovanile socialista." 3 pts. *Mondo operaio* 10, no. 4 (April 1957); 10, no. 5 (May 1957); 10, no. 6 (June 1957).

————. *Storia del socialismo italiano (1892–1926)*. 2nd ed. rev. Turin: Giulio Einaudi, 1965.

————, et al. *Socialismo e socialisti dal risorgimento al fascismo*. Bari: De Donato, 1974.

Asor Rosa, Alberto. *Scrittori e popolo: Il populismo nella letteratura italiana contemporanea*. 4th ed. Rome: Samonà e Savelli, 1972.

Avineri, Shlomo. *The Social and Political Thought of Karl Marx*. Cambridge: Cambridge University Press, 1968.

Balbo, Italo. *Diario 1922*. Milan: A. Mondadori, 1932.

————. *Lavoro e milizia per la nuova Italia*. Rome: Giorgio Berlutti, [1923].

Balestrazzi, Umberto. "Lo sciopero parmense del 1908 nel ricordo e nelle considerazioni di un vecchio sindacalista." *Movimento operaio e socialista* 11, nos. 1–2 (Jan.–June 1965):129–44.

Banfield, Edward C. *The Moral Basis of a Backward Society*. New York: The Free Press, 1958.

Barbadoro, Idomeneo. *Storia del sindacalismo italiano dalla nascita al fascismo*. 2 vols. Florence: La Nuova Italia, 1973.

Barber, Benjamin R. "Conceptual Foundations of Totalitarianism." In *Totalitarianism in Perspective: Three Views*, by Carl J. Friedrich, Michael Curtis, and Benjamin R. Barber. New York: Praeger, 1969.

Barbieri, Alfredo. "Per il quarentennio dell'attività politica, scientifica e letteraria di Paolo Orano." In *Regia Università degli Studi di Perugia*. Rome: Mediterranea, 1937.

Barni, Giulio, et al. *Pro e contro la guerra di Tripoli: Discussioni nel campo rivoluzionario*. Naples: Società Editrice Partenopea, 1912.

Bartoli, Domenico. "Dino Grandi." *Corriere della sera*, 1 Oct. 1965, p. 3.

Basso, Lelio, et al. *Fascismo e antifascismo (1918–1948): Lezioni e testimonianze*. 2 vols. Milan: Feltrinelli, 1962.

Benaglia, Alberto. "Quel che fanno e che non fanno le corporazioni." *Politica sociale*, 15 Jan. 1941, pp. 71–74.

Bernstein, Eduard. *Evolutionary Socialism: A Criticism and Affirmation*. Translated by Edith C. Harvey. New York: Schocken, 1961.

Bertrand, Charles Lloyd. "Revolutionary Syndicalism in Italy, 1912–1922." Ph.D. dissertation, University of Wisconsin, 1969.

Bianchi, Michele. *I discorsi, gli scritti*. Rome: Libreria del Littorio, 1931.

Bibes, Geneviève. "Le Fascisme italien: État des travaux depuis 1945." *Revue Française de Science Politique* 18, no. 6 (Dec. 1968):1191–245.

Bobbio, Norberto, "La cultura e il fascismo." In *Fascismo e società italiana*. Edited by Guido Quazza. Turin: Giulio Einaudi, 1973.

———. *Italia civile*. Manduria: Lacaita, 1964.

———. "Profilo ideologico del novecento." In *Storia della letteratura italiana*, 9: *Il novecento*, pp. 119–228. Edited by Emilio Cecchi and Natalino Sapegno. Milan: Garzanti, 1969.

———. *Saggi sulla scienza politica in Italia*. Bari: Laterza, 1971.

Bolchini, Piero. "Milano 1915: Il socialismo e la guerra." *Movimento operaio e socialista* 16, no. 4 (Oct.–Dec. 1970):261–91.

Bonghi, Ruggero. "Una questione grossa: La decadenza del regime parlamentare." *Nuova antologia*, 1 June 1884, pp. 482–97.

Borghi, Armando. *Mezzo secolo di anarchia (1898–1945)*. Naples: Edizioni Scientifiche Italiane, 1954.

Bottai, Giuseppe. *Il cammino delle corporazioni*. Florence: Casa Editrice Poligrafica Universitaria del Dott. Carlo Cya, 1935.

———. *Il consiglio nazionale delle corporazioni*. Milan: A. Mondadori, 1933.

———. *Esperienza corporativa (1929–1934)*. Florence: Vallecchi, 1934; 2nd ed., rev., 1935.

———. *Il fascismo e l'Italia nuova*. Rome: Giorgio Berlutti, ca. 1923.

———. *L'ordinamento corporativo dello Stato*. Rome: Edizioni del *Diritto del Lavoro*, 1927.

———. *Scritti*. Edited by Roberto Bartolozzi and Riccardo Del Giudice. Bologna: Cappelli, 1965.

———. *Vent'anni e un giorno*. Milan: Garzanti, 1949.

———. "Verso il corporativismo democratico o verso una democrazia corporativa?" *Il diritto del lavoro* 26, nos. 3–4 (March–April 1952):121–42.

Bowen, Ralph H. *German Theories of the Corporative State with Special Reference to the Period 1870–1919*. New York: McGraw-Hill, 1947.

Bracher, Kárl Dietrich. *The German Dictatorship: The Origins, Structure, and Effects of National Socialism*. Translated by Jean Steinberg. New York: Praeger, 1970.

———. "Problems of Parliamentary Democracy in Europe." In *A New Europe?* Edited by Stephen A. Graubard. Boston: Beacon, 1967.

Buchheim, Hans. *Totalitarian Rule: Its Nature and Characteristics*. Translated by Ruth Hein. Middletown, Conn.: Wesleyan University Press, 1968.

Cafagna, Luciano. "La formazione di una 'base industriale' fra il 1896 e il 1914." In *La formazione dell'Italia industriale: Discussioni e ricerche*. Edited by Alberto Caracciolo. Bari: Laterza, 1969.

Caizzi, Bruno. *Storia dell'industria italiana dal XVIII secolo ai nostri giorni*. Turin: Unione Tipografico-Editrice Torinese, 1965.

Canaletti Gaudenti, Alberto, and De Simone, Saverio, eds. *Verso il corporativismo democratico*. Bari: Francesco Cacucci, 1951.

Cancogni, Manlio. *Storia del squadrismo*. Milan: Longanesi, 1959.

Cannistraro, Philip V. "Mussolini's Cultural Revolution: Fascist or Nationalist?" *Journal of Contemporary History* 7, nos. 3–4 (July–Oct. 1972):115–39.

Cantagalli, Roberto. *Storia del fascismo fiorentino 1919/1925*. Florence: Vallecchi, 1972.

Cantimori, Delio. *Conversando di storia*. Bari: Laterza, 1967.

Capoferri, Pietro. *Venti anni col fascismo e con i sindacati*. Milan: Gastaldi, 1957.

Carracciolo, Alberto. "La grande industria nella prima guerra mondiale." In *La formazione dell'Italia industriale: Discussioni e ricerche*. Edited by Alberto Caracciolo. Bari: Laterza, 1969.

――――. *Stato e società civile: Problemi dell'unificazione italiana*. 2nd ed., rev. Turin: Giulio Einaudi, 1968.

――――, ed. *La formazione dell'Italia industriale: Discussioni e ricerche*. Bari: Laterza, 1969.

Carducci, Giosuè. *Edizione nazionale delle opere di Giosuè Carducci*. 30 vols. Bologna: Nicola Zanichelli, 1941–58.

Carocci, Giampiero. *Agostino Depretis e la politica interna italiana dal 1876 al 1887*. Turin: Giulio Einaudi, 1956.

――――. *Giolitti e l'età giolittiana*. Turin: Giulio Einaudi, 1961.

Carsten, Francis L. "Interpretations of Fascism." In *Fascism, A Reader's Guide: Analyses, Interpretations, Bibliography*. Edited by Walter Laqueur. Berkeley: University of California Press, 1976.

Cassels, Alan. *Fascism*. New York: Thomas Y. Crowell, 1975.

――――. "Janus: The Two Faces of Fascism." *The Canadian Historical Association Historical Papers*, 1969, pp. 166–84.

Cassese, Sabino. "Un programmatore degli anni trenta: Giuseppe Bottai." *Politica del diritto*, 1970, no. 3, pp. 404–47.

Casucci, Costanzo. "Fascismo e storia." In *Il fascismo: Antologia di scritti critici*. Edited by Costanzo Casucci. Bologna: Il Mulino, 1961.

――――, ed. *Il fascismo: Antologia di scritti critici*. Bologna: Il Mulino, 1961.

Chabod, Federico. *Storia della politica estera italiana dal 1870 al 1896*. 2 vols. Bari: Laterza, 1965.

Chiarelli, Giuseppe. "Il sentimento dello Stato." *Rassegna bibliografica delle scienze giuridiche sociali e politiche* 5, no. 2 (April–June 1930):201–34.

Chiesa, Giovan Battista. "Il 'patto col diavolo' di Alfredo Rocco." *La rivista trimestrale* 4, nos. 13–14 (March–June 1965).

Chiurco, Giorgio. *Storia della rivoluzione fascista*. 5 vols. Florence: Vallecchi, 1929.

Ciattini, Alighiero. *Caratteri della vita italiana*. Rome: Tipografia Rilievografia Coppitelli e Palazzotti, 1927.

――――. *Politica nazionale*. Rome: Berlutti, ca. 1926.

――――. *Postulati fascisti*. Rome: Il Nuovo Stato, 1927.

――――. *Problemi di politica e di cultura*. Bergamo: Edizione di *Pagine libere*, 1920.

――――. *Lo Stato e i suoi fini sociali*, Città di Castello: Il Solco, 1921.

Cimbali, Enrico. *La nuova fase del diritto civile nei rapporti economici e sociali (con proposte di riforma della legislazione civile vigente)*. Turin: Unione Tipografico-Editrice, 1885.

Colapietra, Raffaele. *Napoli tra dopoguerra e fascismo*. Milan: Feltrinelli, 1962.

Cole, G. D. H. *A History of Socialist Thought*. Vol. 3, *The Second International, 1889–1914*. 2 pts. London: Macmillan, 1956.

Coppola, Francesco. *La crisi italiana, MCMXIV–MCMXV*. Rome: L'Italiana, 1916.

———. *La rivoluzione fascista e la politica mondiale*. Rome: Edizioni di *Politica*, ca. 1923.

Cordova, Ferdinando. *Arditi e legionari dannunziani*. Padua: Marsilio, 1969.

———. "Le origini dei sindacati fascisti." *Storia contemporanea* 1, no. 4 (Dec. 1970):925–1009.

———. *Le origini dei sindacati fascisti, 1918–1926*. Bari: Laterza, 1974.

Corner, Paul. *Fascism in Ferrara, 1915–1925*. London: Oxford University Press, 1975.

Corradini, Enrico. *Diario postbellico*. Rome: Alberto Stock, 1924.

———. *Discorsi politici (1902–1923)*. Florence: Vallecchi, [1923].

———. *La marcia dei produttori*. Rome: L'Italiana, 1916.

———. *L'ora di Tripoli*. Milan: Fratelli Treves, 1911.

———. "Per coloro che risorgono." From *Il regno*, 29 Nov. 1903. In *La cultura italiana del '900 attraverso le riviste*, 1: *"Leonardo," "Hermes," "Il regno."* Edited by Delia Frigessi. Turin: Giulio Einaudi, 1960.

———. "La politica economica-sociale del Nazionalismo." In *Il Nazionalismo italiano e i problemi del lavoro e della scuola: Atti del secondo convegno Nazionalista di Roma*. Edited by Pier Ludovico Occhini. Rome: L'Italiana, 1919.

———. *Il regime della borghesia produttiva*. Rome: L'Italiana, 1918.

———. *La rinascita nazionale*. Edited by Goffredo Bellonci. Florence: Felice Le Monnier, 1929.

Corridoni, Filippo. *Le forme di lotta e di solidarietà*. Parma: Tipografia Camerale, 1912.

———. *Sindacalismo e repubblica*. Parma: La Commerciale, 1921.

Costamagna, Carlo. "Il principio corporativo dello Stato fascista." In *Le corporazioni fasciste*. Edited by Luigi Lojacono. Milan: Ulrico Hoepli, 1935.

———. "Stato corporativo (A proposito del neo sindacalismo di stato)." *Rivista internazionale di filosofia del diritto* 6, no. 3 (July–Sept. 1926):414–23.

Croce, Benedetto. *Historical Materialism and the Economics of Karl Marx*. Translated by C. M. Meredith. London: George Allen and Unwin, 1914.

———. *A History of Italy, 1871–1915*. Translated by Cecilia M. Ady. Oxford: Clarendon Press, 1929; reprint ed., New York: Russell and Russell, 1963.

———. "Introduzione" to *Considerazioni sulla violenza*, by Georges Sorel. Bari: Laterza, 1970; from 1st Italian ed., 1909.

———. "La morte del socialismo." *La voce* 3, no. 6 (9 Feb. 1911):501–2.

———. "L'obiezione contro la 'Storia dei propri tempi.'" *Quaderni della critica* 6, no. 16 (March 1950):32–38.

La cultura italiana del '900 attraverso le riviste. Turin: Giulio Einaudi.

Vol. 1: *"Leonardo," "Hermes," "Il regno."* Edited by Delia Frigessi. 1960.

Vol. 2: *"La voce" (1908–1914)*. Edited by Angelo Romanò. 1960.

Vol. 4: *"Lacerba," "La voce" (1914–1916)*. Edited by Gianni Scalia. 1961.

Cunsolo, Ronald S. "Libya, Italian Nationalism, and the Revolt against Giolitti." *Journal of Modern History* 37, no. 2 (June 1965):186–207.

Curcio, Carlo. "Contenuto sociale ed universale del corporativismo." In *Le corporazioni fasciste*. Edited by Luigi Lojacono. Milan: Ulrico Hoepli, 1935.

―――. Response to "La nuova inchiesta di *Pagine libere*: Fascismo e fascismi a confronto." *Pagine libere*, N.S. 22, no. 29 (April–Sept. 1968):83–93.

―――. "Il sentimento dello Stato fascista." *La stampa*, 19 Aug. 1929, p. 3.

―――. "Sindacalisti e nazionalisti a Perugia fra il 1928 e il 1933." *Pagine libere*, N.S. 1, no. 16 (Dec. 1956):19–26.

Dahrendorf, Ralf. *Society and Democracy in Germany*. Garden City, N.Y.: Doubleday (Anchor), 1969.

Dai fasci al Partito Nazionale Fascista. 2 vols. Rome: Casa Editrice dei "Panorami di Realizzazioni del Fascismo," ca. 1942.

De Ambris, Alceste. *L'azione diretta: Pagine di propaganda elementare sindacalista*. 4th ed. Parma: Camera del Lavoro, 1912.

―――. "Gli esordi del corporativismo in alcune lettere di Alceste De Ambris." Edited by Renzo De Felice. *La cultura* 2, no. 3 (May 1964):304–20.

―――. "L'Evolution du fascisme." *Mercure de France*, série moderne 162 (15 Feb. 1923):5–27.

―――. "Il fascismo al bivio." From *La riscossa dei legionari fiumani*, 12 Sept. 1922. Appendix to *Sindacalismo rivoluzionario e fiumanesimo nel carteggio De Ambris-D'Annunzio*, by Renzo De Felice. Brescia: Morcelliana, 1966.

―――. *Filippo Corridoni*, Piacenza: Porta, 1922.

―――. *Gli italiani al estero: L'Argentina e l'emigrazione italiana*. N.p., 1911.

―――. "La tempesta che viene." *Il rinnovamento* 2, no. 3 (15 April 1919):129–36.

―――. *L'unità operaia e i tradimenti confederali*. Parma: L'internazionale, 1913.

De Begnac, Ivon. *L'arcangelo sindacalista (Filippo Corridoni)*. Milan: A. Mondadori, 1943.

De Felice, Franco. "L'età giolittiana." *Studi storici* 10, no. 1 (Jan.–March 1969):114–90.

De Felice, Renzo. "Gli esordi del corporativismo in alcune lettere di Alceste De Ambris." *La cultura* 2, no. 3 (May 1964):304–20.

―――. *Fascism: An Informal Introduction to Its Theory and Practice: An Interview with Michael A. Ledeen*. New Brunswick, N.J.: Transaction Books, 1976.

―――. "Le Fascisme italien et les classes moyennes." In *Fassismus a Evropa. Fascism and Europe: An International Symposium*, 2:186–202. Prague: Czechoslovak Academy of Sciences, Institute of History, 1970.

―――. *Le interpretazioni del fascismo*. Bari: Laterza, 1969.

―――. *Mussolini il Duce*. Vol. 1, *Gli anni del consenso, 1929–1936*. Turin: Giulio Einaudi, 1974.

―――. *Mussolini il fascista*. 2 vols. Vol. 1, *La conquista del potere, 1921–1925*. Vol. 2, *L'organizzazione dello Stato fascista, 1925–1929*. Turin: Giulio Einaudi, 1966–68.

―――. *Mussolini il rivoluzionario, 1883–1920*. Turin: Giulio Einaudi, 1965.

―――. "Le origini del fascismo." In *Nuove questioni di storia contemporanea*, 1:719–98. By Franco Valsecchi et al. Milan: Marzorati, 1968.

―――. *Sindacalismo rivoluzionario e fiumanesimo nel carteggio De Ambris-D'Annunzio (1919–1922)*. Brescia: Morcelliana, 1966.

―――. *Storia degli ebrei italiani sotto il fascismo*. 3rd ed. Turin: Giulio Einaudi, 1972.

———, ed. *La Carta del Carnaro nei testi di Alceste De Ambris e di Gabriele D'Annunzio*. Bologna: Il Mulino, 1973.

———. *Il fascismo e i partiti politici italiani: Testimonianze del 1921–1923*. Bologna: Cappelli, 1966.

DeGrand, A. J. "Curzio Malaparte: The Illusion of the Fascist Revolution." *Journal of Contemporary History* 7, nos. 1–2 (Jan.–April 1972):73–89.

Della Torre, Odoardo. *Il concetto sindacalista dello Stato: Studio filosofico-giuridico*. Florence: Vallecchi, 1925.

Delle Piane, Mario. *Gaetano Mosca: Classe politica e liberalismo*. Naples: Edizioni Scientifiche Italiane, 1952.

Del Noce, Augusto. "Idee per l'interpretazione del fascismo." In *Il fascismo: Antologia di scritti critici*. Edited by Costanzo Casucci. Bologna: Il Mulino, 1961.

———. "Per una definizione storica del fascismo." In *Il problema storico del fascismo*, by Mario Abrate et al. Florence: Vallecchi, 1970.

———. *Il problema dell'ateismo: Il concetto di ateismo e la storia della filosofia come problema*. Bologna: Il Mulino, 1964.

Delzell, Charles F. *Mussolini's Enemies: The Italian Anti-Fascist Resistance*. Princeton: Princeton University Press, 1961.

———, ed. *Mediterranean Fascism, 1919–1945*. New York: Harper and Row, 1970.

De Martino, Francesco, et al. *Il movimento operaio e socialista: Bilancio storiografico e problemi storici*. Milan: Edizioni del Gallo, 1965.

De Mattei, Rodolfo. *Dal "trasformismo" al socialismo*. Florence: G. C. Sansoni, 1941.

De Pietri-Tonelli, Alfonso. *Economia e politica: Scritti vari*. Padua: CEDAM (Casa Editrice Dott. A. Milani), 1963.

———. "Sindacalismo rivoluzionario e illusioni riformistiche (Per gli operai)." *La lotta proletaria* 1, no. 8 (19 Aug. 1905):2.

De Ruggiero, Guido. *The History of European Liberalism*. Translated by R. G. Collingwood. Boston: Beacon, 1959.

———. *Scritti politici 1912–1926*. Edited by Renzo De Felice. Bologna: Cappelli, 1963.

De Sanctis, Francesco. "L'uomo del Guicciardini." in *Saggi critici* 3:1–25. Bari: Laterza, 1969.

Dinale, Ottavio. *Critica e psicologia socialista*. Mirandola: Tipografia cooperativa, 1906.

———. *Quarant'anni di colloqui con lui*. Milan: Ciarrocca, 1953.

Di Palma, Giuseppe. *Apathy and Participation: Mass Politics in Western Societies*. New York: The Free Press, 1970.

Dolléans, Edouard. *Histoire du mouvement ouvrier*. Vol. 2, *1871–1920*. 6th ed. Paris: Armand Colin, 1967.

Dorso, Guido. *Dittatura, classe politica, e classe dirigente: Saggi editi ed inediti*. Turin: Einaudi, 1949.

Duguit, Léon. *Le Droit social, le droit individuel et la transformation de l'Etat*. Paris: Félix Alcan, 1908.

———. *L'Etat, le droit objectif et la loi positive*. Paris: Albert Fontemoing, 1901.

Durkheim, Emile. Review of *Formes et essence du socialisme*, by [Francesco]

Saverio Merlino. *Revue Philosophique de la France et de l'Etranger* 48 (Oct. 1899):433–39.

―――. *The Division of Labor in Society*. Translated by George Simpson. New York: The Free Press, 1964.

―――. *Socialism*. Edited by Alvin Gouldner; translated by Charlotte Sattler. New York: Collier, 1962.

―――. *Suicide: A Study in Sociology*. Translated by John A. Spaulding and George Simpson. New York: The Free Press, 1966.

Einaudi, Luigi, *La condotta economica e gli effetti sociali della guerra italiana*. Bari: Laterza, 1933.

―――. *Cronache economiche e politiche di un trentennio (1893–1925)*. 8 vols. Turin: Giulio Einaudi, 1959–65.

―――. "Trincee economiche e corporativismo." *La riforma sociale* 44, no. 6 (Nov.–Dec. 1933):633–56.

Elbow, Matthew H. *French Corporative Theory, 1789–1948: A Chapter in the History of Ideas*. New York: Columbia University Press, 1953.

Farinacci, Roberto. *Andante mosso 1924–1925*. Milan: A. Mondadori, 1929.

―――. *Un periodo aureo del Partito Nazionale Fascista*. Edited by Renzo Bacchetta. Foligno: Franco Campitelli, 1927.

Farneti, Paolo. *Sistema politico e società civile: Saggi di teoria e ricerca politica*. Turin: Giappichelli, 1971.

Favilli, Paolo. "Economia e politica del sindacalismo rivoluzionario. Due riviste di teoria e socialismo scientifico: 'Pagine libere' e 'Divenire sociale.'" *Studi storici* 16, no. 1 (Jan.–March 1975):205–30.

Federzoni, Luigi. *L'Italia di domani*. Rome: L'Italiana, 1917.

―――. *Italia di ieri per la storia di domani*. Milan: Arnaldo Mondadori, 1967.

―――. *Paradossi di ieri*. Milan: A. Mondadori, 1926.

―――. *Presagi alla nazione: Discorsi politici*. Milan: Imperia, 1924.

Ferrero, Guglielmo. *La democrazia in Italia: Studi e precisioni*. Milan: Edizioni della *Rassegna Internazionale*, 1925.

Fest, Joachim C. *The Face of the Third Reich: Portraits of the Nazi Leadership*. Translated by Michael Bullock. New York: Pantheon, 1970.

Field, G. Lowell. *The Syndical and Corporative Institutions of Italian Fascism*. New York: Columbia University Press, 1938.

Fontanelli, Luigi. *Logica della corporazione e relative polemiche*. 7th ed. Rome: Unione Editrice Sindacale Italiana, 1941; orig. pub. ca. 1934.

Fornari, Harry. *Mussolini's Gadfly: Roberto Farinacci*. Nashville: Vanderbilt University Press, 1971.

Fortunato, Giustino. *Pagine e ricordi parlamentari*. Vol. 1: Florence: Vallecchi, [1926]. Vol. 2: Florence: Vallecchi, 1927; 2nd ed., enlarged, Rome: Collezione Meridionale Editrice, 1947.

Foscanelli, Umberto. *D'Annunzio e il fascismo*. Milan: Casa Editrice Italiana, [1923].

―――. *Gabriele D'Annunzio e l'ora sociale*. Milan: Carnaro, 1952.

Friedrich, Carl J.; Curtis Michael; and Barber, Benjamin R. *Totalitarianism in Perspective: Three Views*. New York: Praeger, 1969.

Frosini, Vittorio. *Breve storia della critica al marxismo in Italia*. Catania: Bonanno, 1965.

Furiozzi, Gian Biagio. *Sorel e l'Italia*. Messina and Florence: G. D'Anna, 1975.

Gaeta, Franco. *Nazionalismo italiano*. Naples: Edizioni Scientifiche Italiane, 1965.

_____, ed. *La stampa nazionalista*. Bologna: Cappelli, 1965.

Galante Garrone, Alessandro. "Introduzione" to *Momenti della vita di guerra: Dai diari e dalle lettere dei caduti, 1915–1918*, by Adolfo Omodeo. Turin: Giulio Einaudi, 1968.

Galli, Giorgio, and Prandi, Alfonso. *Patterns of Political Participation in Italy*. New Haven: Yale University Press, 1970.

Gallino, Luciano. "L'evoluzione della struttura di classe in Italia." *Quaderni di sociologia*, April–June 1970, pp. 115–54.

Garin, Eugenio. *La cultura italiana tra '800 e '900*. Bari: Laterza, 1962.

Garruccio, Ludovico. *L'industrializzazione tra nazionalismo e rivoluzione: Le ideologie politiche dei paesi in via di sviluppo*. Bologna: Il Mulino, 1969.

Gattamorta, Giordano. *Luigi Razza: L'uomo–l'opera*. Rome: Efficienza, [1935].

Gay, Peter. *The Dilemma of Democratic Socialism: Eduard Bernstein's Challenge to Marx*. New York: Collier, 1962.

Gentile, Emilio. *Le origini dell'ideologia fascista (1918–1925)*. Rome and Bari: Laterza, 1975.

_____. *"La voce" e l'età giolittiana*. Milan: Pan, 1972.

Gentile, Giovanni. *Che cosa è il fascismo: Discorsi e polemiche*. Florence: Vallecchi, 1925.

_____. *Guerra e fede*. Naples: Riccardo Ricciardi, 1919.

_____. *Origini e dottrina del fascismo*. Rome: Libreria del Littorio, 1929.

Germani, Gino. *Autoritarismo, fascismo e classi sociali*. Bologna: Il Mulino, 1975.

_____. "Fascism and Class." In *The Nature of Fascism*. Edited by S[tuart] J. Woolf. New York: Random House (Vintage), 1969.

Germano, Michele. *Per lo sfollamento parlamentare*. Bari: Laterza, 1899.

Germino, Dante. "Italian Fascism in the History of Political Thought." *Midwest Journal of Political Science* 8, no. 2 (May 1964):109–26.

_____. *The Italian Fascist Party in Power: A Study in Totalitarian Rule*. Minneapolis: University of Minnesota Press, 1959.

Gerschenkron, Alexander. *Economic Backwardness in Historical Perspective*. Cambridge: Harvard University Press, 1962.

Giacalone-Monaco, Tommaso. "Pareto e A. de Pietri-Tonelli." *Giornale degli economisti e annali di economia*. N. S. 23, nos. 9–10 (Sept.–Oct. 1963):687–94.

Giampaoli, Mario. *1919*. Rome: Libreria del Littorio, 1928.

Gibelli, Camillo. "I sindacati fascisti a Genova negli anni della grande crisi (1929–1933)." *Movimento operaio e socialista* 19, no. 4 (Oct.–Dec. 1973):303–55.

Giddens, Anthony. *Capitalism and Modern Social Theory: An Analysis of the Writings of Marx, Durkheim and Max Weber*. London: Cambridge University Press, 1971.

_____. *The Class Structures of the Advanced Societies*. London: Hutchinson, 1973.

Giolitti, Giovanni. *Memorie della mia vita*. 2 vols. Milan: Fratelli Treves, 1922.

Giovannini, Claudio. "Alle origini del fascismo: Il ritorno dell'interpretazione radicale." *Il mulino* 21, no. 223 (Sept.–Oct. 1972):890–920.

Giuliano, Balbino. *L'esperienza politica dell'Italia*. Florence: Vallecchi, 1924.

Giulietti, G[iuseppe]. *Pax mundi: La Federazione Marinara nella bufera fascista e so-*

luzione della questione sociale con sindacati produttori come la "Garibaldi." Naples: Rispoli, 1944.

Gobetti, Piero. "Dopo le elezioni." From *La rivoluzione liberale*, 15 April 1924. In *Antologia della "rivoluzione liberale."* Edited by Nino Valeri. Turin: Francesco De Silva, 1948.

———. *La rivoluzione liberale: Saggio sulla lotta politica in Italia.* Turin: Giulio Einaudi, 1966; orig. pub. 1924.

Goetz-Girey, Robert. *La Pensée syndicale française: Militants et théoriciens.* Paris: Libraire Armand Colin, 1948.

Goisis, Giuseppe Ludovico. "Sorel e i soreliani italiani." *Il mulino* 22, no. 228 (July–Aug. 1973):615–26.

Gorgolini Pietro. *Il fascismo nella vita italiana.* 6th ed., rev. Turin: G. B. Paravia, 1926.

Goriely, Georges. *Le Pluralisme dramatique de Georges Sorel.* Paris: M. Riviere, 1962.

Gorz, André. *Strategy for Labor: A Radical Proposal.* Translated by Martin A. Nicolaus and Victoria Ortiz. Boston: Beacon, 1967.

Gradilone, Alfredo. *Bibliografia sindacale corporativa (1923–1940).* Rome: Istituto Nazionale di Cultura Fascista, 1942.

Gramsci, Antonio. *Gli intellettuali e l'organizzazione della cultura.* Turin: Giulio Einaudi, 1949.

———. *The Modern Prince and Other Writings.* Translated by Louis Marks. New York: International, 1957.

———. *Note sul Machiavelli, sulla politica e sullo stato moderno.* Turin: Giulio Einaudi, 1966.

———. *L'ordine nuovo 1919–1920.* Turin: Giulio Einaudi, 1954.

———. *Passato e presente.* Turin: Giulio Einaudi, 1966.

———. *La questione meridionale.* Rome: Rinascita, 1951.

Grandi, Dino. *Giovani.* Bologna: Nicola Zanichelli, 1941.

———. "Le origini e la missione del fascismo." In *Il fascismo*, by Adolfo Zerboglio and Dino Grandi. Bologna: Licinio Cappelli, 1922.

Graziadei, Antonio. *Memorie di trent'anni (1890–1920).* Rome: Rinascita, 1950.

———. *Socialismo e sindacalismo.* Rome: Mongini, 1909.

Gregor, A. James. "Fascism and Modernization: Some Addenda." *World Politics* 26, no. 3 (April 1974):370–84.

———. *The Fascist Persuasion in Radical Politics.* Princeton: Princeton University Press, 1974.

———. *The Ideology of Fascism: The Rationale of Totalitarianism.* New York: The Free Press, 1969.

———. *Interpretations of Fascism.* Morristown, N.J.: General Learning Press, 1974.

———. "On Understanding Fascism: A Review of Some Contemporary Literature." *American Political Science Review* 67, no. 4 (Dec. 1973):1332–47.

Grosser, Alfred. *Germany in Our Time: A Political History of the Post-War Years.* New York: Praeger, 1971.

Guarneri, Felice. *Battaglie economiche tra le due grandi guerre.* 2 vols. Milan: Garzanti, 1953.

Guerri, Giordano Bruno. *Giuseppe Bottai, un fascista critico: Ideologia e azione del gerarca che avrebbe voluto portare l'intelligenza nel fascismo e il fascismo alla liberalizzazione*. Milan: Feltrinelli, 1976.

Halpern, Ben. "'Myth' and 'Ideology' in Modern Usage." *History and Theory* 1, no. 2 (1961):129–49.

Harris, H. S. *The Social Philosophy of Giovanni Gentile*. Urbana: University of Illinois Press, 1960; Illini Books, 1966.

Hayward, J. E. S. "Solidarist Syndicalism: Durkheim and Duguit." 2 pts. *Sociological Review* N.S. 8, no. 1 (July 1960):17–36; 8, no. 2 (Dec. 1960):185–202.

Hoffmann, Stanley. *Decline or Renewal? France since the 1930's*. New York: Viking, 1974.

Horowitz, Daniel L. *The Italian Labor Movement*. Cambridge: Harvard University Press, 1963.

Horowitz, Irving Louis. *Radicalism and the Revolt against Reason: The Social Theories of Georges Sorel*. New ed. Carbondale: Southern Illinois University Press, 1968.

Howard, Dick, and Klare, Karl E., eds. *The Unknown Dimension: European Marxism since Lenin*. New York: Basic Books, 1972.

Hughes, H[enry] Stuart. *The Sea Change: The Migration of Social Thought, 1930–1965*. New York: Harper and Row, 1975; reprint ed., McGraw-Hill, 1977.

Humphrey, Richard. *Georges Sorel, Prophet without Honor: A Study in Anti-Intellectualism*. Cambridge: Harvard University Press, 1951.

Huntington, Samuel P. *Political Order in Changing Societies*. New Haven: Yale University Press, 1968.

Invernizzi, Gabriele. "Dino Grandi dal fez alla feluca." *Historia* 11, no. 120 (Nov. 1967):4–33.

Isnenghi, Mario. *Il mito della grande guerra*. Bari: Laterza, 1970.

————, and Lanaro, Silvio. "Fascismo esorcizzato: Cinque schede sulla 'rivolta piccolo-borghese.'" *Belfagor* 25, no. 2 (31 March 1970):219–29.

Jacobitti, Edmund E. "Labriola, Croce, and Italian Marxism (1895–1910)." *Journal of the History of Ideas* 36, no. 2 (April–June 1975):297–318.

Jäckel, Eberhard. *Hitler's Weltanschauung: A Blueprint for Power*. Translated by Herbert Arnold. Middletown, Conn.: Wesleyan University Press, 1972.

Jay, Martin. *The Dialectical Imagination: A History of the Frankfurt School and the Institute for Social Research*. Boston: Little, Brown and Co., 1973.

Jocteau, Gian Carlo. "Lo Stato fascista e le origini della magistratura del lavoro." *Politica del diritto* 4, nos. 2–3 (1973):163–221.

Julliard, Jacques. *Fernand Pelloutier et les origines du syndicalisme d'action directe*. Paris: Seuil, 1971.

Labriola, Antonio. *Saggi sul materialismo storico*. Edited by Valentino Gerratana and Augusto Guerra. Rome: Riuniti, 1964.

Labriola, Arturo. *Il capitalismo: Lineamenti storici*. Turin: Fratelli Bocca, 1910.

————. *La conflagrazione europea e il socialismo*. Rome: Athenaeum, 1915.

————. *Contro G. Plekanoff e per il sindacalismo*. Pescara: Casa Editrice Abruzzese, 1909.

————. "La crisi della teoria socialista." *La riforma sociale*, 2nd ser. 5, no. 8 (1898):1150–62.

————. *Decadenza della civiltà (limiti)*. Rome: Faro, 1947.

————. *La dittatura della borghesia e la decadenza della società capitalistica*. Naples: Alberto Morano, 1924.

————. *Le due politiche: Fascismo e riformismo*. Naples: A. Morano, 1924.

————. *Economia, socialismo, sindacalismo*. Naples: Società Editrice Partenopea, ca. 1911.

————. *La guerra di Tripoli e l'opinione socialista*. Naples: S. Morano, 1912.

————. "Lettere di Arturo Labriola a Ernesto Cesare Longobardi." Edited by Enzo Santarelli. *Rivista storica del socialismo* 5, no. 17 (Sept.–Dec. 1962).

————. *Marx nell'economia e come teorico del socialismo*. Lugano: Edizioni di *Pagine libere*, 1908.

————. *Ministero e socialismo: Risposta a Filippo Turati*. Florence: G. Nerbini, 1901.

————. "I nuovi orizzonti della critica socialista." 3 pts. *Rivista popolare di politica, lettere e scienze sociali* 8, no. 8 (30 April 1902):209–14; 8, no. 9 (15 May 1902):239–43; 8, no. 10 (30 May 1902):264–67.

————. "La prima impresa collettiva della nuova Italia." In *Pro e contro la guerra di Tripoli: Discussioni nel campo rivoluzionario*, by Giulio Barni et al. Naples: Società Editrice Partenopea, 1912.

————. *Riforme e rivoluzione sociale*. Milan: Società Editoriale Milanese, 1904; 2nd ed., Lugano: Società Editrice *Avanguardia*, 1906.

————. *Sindacalismo e riformismo*. Florence: G. Nerbini, 1905.

————. *Il socialismo contemporaneo*. Naples: Alberto Morano, 1922.

————. *Spiegazioni a me stesso: Note personali e colturali*. Naples: Rispoli, 1945.

————. *Storia di dieci anni: 1899–1909*. Milan: Casa Editrice *Il viandante*, 1910.

La Ferla, Giuseppe. "Georges Sorel e Vilfredo Pareto: due spiriti inattuali." *Nuova antologia*, July 1963, pp. 303–12.

La Francesca, Salvatore. *La politica economica italiana dal 1900 al 1913*. Rome: Edizioni dell'Ateneo, 1971.

Lagardelle, Hubert. *Le Socialisme ouvrier*. Paris: V. Giard et E. Brière, 1911.

————, ed. *Syndicalisme et socialisme*. Paris: Marcel Rivière, 1908.

Lane, Barbara Miller. "Nazi Ideology: Some Unfinished Business." *Central European History* 7, no. 1 (March 1974):3–30.

Lanzillo, Agostino. Address to the Chamber of Deputies, 5 Dec. 1925. In *Atti parlamentari, Camera*, Legislatura 27, Sessione 1924–25, *Discussioni*, vol. 5, pp. 4849–55.

————. "Colloquio con Giorgio Sorel." *La voce* 1, no. 52 (9 Dec. 1909):220–21.

————. *La disfatta del socialismo: Critica della guerra e del socialismo*. 2nd ed., rev. Florence: Libreria della Voce, 1918.

————. *La dittatura del proletariato*. Milan: Corbaccio, 1919.

————. *Giorgio Sorel*. Rome: Libreria Editrice Romana, 1910.

————. "La lettera degli organizzatori: Sintomi." *La Provincia di Como*, 5 Feb. 1927, p. 1.

————. *Le Mouvement ouvrier en Italie*. Translated by S. Piroddi. Paris: Marcel Riviere, n.d.

————. "L'ora di Sorel." *La rivoluzione liberale* 1, no. 37 (14 Dec. 1922):141.

————. *Origine e contenuto dell'economia corporativa*. Padua: CEDAM (Casa Editrice Dott. A. Milani), 1937.

―――. "La proprietà privata e la corporazione." In *La concezione fascista della proprietà privata*, by Franco Angelini et al. [Rome]: Confederazione Fascista dei Lavoratori dell'Agricultura, [1939].

―――. *Relazione del Rettore Prof. Agostino Lanzillo sull'anno accademico 1937–38: R. Istituto Superiore di Economia e Commercio, Venezia.* Venice: Ca' Foscari, 1939.

―――. *Le rivoluzioni del dopoguerra: Critiche e diagnosi*, Città di Castello: Il Solco, 1922.

―――. *Lo Stato e la crisi monetaria e sociale postbellica.* Milan: Fratelli Treves, 1920.

―――. *Lo Stato nel processo economico.* Padua: CEDAM (Casa Editrice Dott. A. Milani), 1936.

―――. "Violenza e violenza." *L'ordine fascista* 4 (Oct.–Dec. 1925):131–38.

LaPalombara, Joseph. "Integrazione sociale e partecipazione politica." In "La partecipazione politica e i partiti in Italia." *Tempi moderni*, 1962, no. 8, pp. 62–66.

―――. *Interest Groups in Italian Politics.* Princeton: Princeton University Press, 1964.

―――. "Italy: Fragmentation, Isolation, Alienation." In *Political Culture and Political Development.* Edited by Lucian W. Pye and Sidney Verba. Princeton: Princeton University Press, 1965.

Laqueur, Walter, ed. *Fascism, A Reader's Guide: Analyses, Interpretations, Bibliography.* Berkeley: University of California Press, 1976.

―――, and Mosse, George L., eds. *International Fascism, 1920–1945.* New York: Harper and Row, 1966.

Lasswell, Harold D., and Lerner, Daniel, eds. *World Revolutionary Elites: Studies in Coercive Ideological Movements.* Cambridge: M.I.T. Press, 1966.

Ledeen, Michael A. *The First Duce: D'Annunzio at Fiume.* Baltimore: Johns Hopkins University Press, 1977.

―――. "Renzo De Felice and the Controversy over Italian Fascism." *Journal of Contemporary History* 11, no. 4 (Oct. 1976):269–83.

―――. *Universal Fascism: The Theory and Practice of the Fascist International, 1928–1936.* New York: Howard Fertig, 1972.

Leff, Gordon. *History and Social Theory.* Garden City, N.Y.: Doubleday (Anchor), 1971.

Lenin, V[ladimir] I[llich]. *Essential Works of Lenin.* Edited by Henry M. Christman. New York: Bantam, 1966.

Lenski, Gerhard. *Power and Privilege: A Theory of Social Stratification.* New York: McGraw-Hill, 1966.

Leone, Enrico. *Anti-Bergson.* Naples: Casa Editrice "La luce del pensiero," 1923.

―――. "Le coalizioni operaie e il liberismo." *Critica sociale* 10, no. 15 (1 Aug. 1900):231–35.

―――. *L'economia edonistica.* Rome: Biblioteca del *Divenire sociale*, 1910.

―――. *L'economia sociale in rapporto al socialismo (volgarizzamento).* Genoa: Libreria Moderna, 1903.

―――. *Espansionismo e colonie.* Rome: Tipografia Editrice Nazionale, 1911.

―――. *Indirizzo sindacale e politica.* Bologna: Sindacato Ferrovieri Italiani, 1921.

―――. *Il neo-marxismo: Sorel e Marx.* Bologna: Sindacato Ferrovieri, 1923.

―――. "Prefazione" to *Lo sciopero generale e la violenza*, by Georges Sorel. Rome: Biblioteca del *Divenire sociale*, 1906.

————. *La revisione del marxismo*. Rome: Biblioteca del *Divenire sociale*, 1909.

————. *Il sindacalismo*. 2nd ed., rev. Milan: Remo Sandron, ca. 1910.

Lichtheim, George. *The Concept of Ideology and Other Essays*. New York: Random House, 1967.

————. *Marxism: An Historical and Critical Study*. New York: Frederick A. Praeger, 1961.

Linz, Juan J. "Some Notes toward a Comparative Study of Fascism in Sociological Historical Perspective." In *Fascism, A Reader's Guide: Analyses, Interpretations, Bibliography*. Edited by Walter Laqueur. Berkeley: University of California Press, 1976.

Lojacono, Luigi, ed. *Le corporazioni fasciste*. Milan: Ulrico Hoepli, 1935.

Lotti, Luigi. *La settimana rossa*. Florence: Felice Le Monnier, 1965.

Lowi, Theodore J. *The End of Liberalism: Ideology, Policy and the Crisis of Public Authority*. New York: W. W. Norton, 1969.

Lukes, Steven. *Emile Durkheim, His Life and Work: A Historical and Critical Study*. London: Allen Lane, Penguin Press, 1973.

————. *Individualism*. New York: Harper and Row, 1973.

Lupo, Orietta. "I sindacalisti rivoluzionari nel 1914." *Rivista storica del socialismo* 10, no. 32:43–82.

Lyttelton, Adrian. "Fascism in Italy: The Second Wave." In *International Fascism: 1920–1945*. Edited by Walter Laqueur and George L. Mosse. New York: Harper and Row, 1966.

————. "Italian Fascism." In *Fascism, A Reader's Guide: Analyses, Interpretations, Bibliography*. Edited by Walter Laqueur. Berkeley: University of California Press, 1976.

————. *The Seizure of Power: Fascism in Italy, 1919–1929*. New York: Charles Scribner's Sons, 1973.

————, ed. *Italian Fascisms from Pareto to Gentile*. New York: Harper and Row, 1975.

Mack Smith, Denis. *Victor Emanuel, Cavour, and the Risorgimento*. London: Oxford University Press, 1971.

Maier, Charles S. *Recasting Bourgeois Europe: Stabilization in France, Germany, and Italy in the Decade after World War I*. Princeton: Princeton University Press, 1975.

————. "Some Recent Studies of Fascism." *Journal of Modern History* 48, no. 3 (Sept. 1976):506–21.

Malagodi, Olindo. *Conversazioni della guerra, 1914–1919*. 2 vols. Edited by Brunello Vigezzi. Milan and Naples: Riccardo Ricciardi, 1960.

Malaparte, Curzio. *L'Europa vivente e altri saggi politici (1921–1931)*. Edited by Enrico Falqui. Florence: Vallecchi, 1961.

Malgeri, Francesco. *La guerra libica (1911–1912)*. Rome: Edizioni di Storia e Letteratura, 1970.

Maltese, Paolo. *La terra promessa: La guerra italo-turca e la conquista della Libia 1911–1912*. Milan: Sugar, 1968.

Malusardi, Edoardo. *Elementi di storia el sindacalismo fascista*. 3rd ed. Lanciano: R. Carabba, 1938.

Mammarella, Giuseppe. *Riformisti e rivoluzionari nel Partito Socialista Italiano, 1900–1912*. Padua: Marsilio, 1968.

Mangoni, Luisa. *L'interventismo della cultura: Intellettuali e riviste del fascismo*. Bari: Laterza, 1974.

Mantica, Paolo. "Il fascismo in Italia." Edited by Alceo Riosa. *Historica* 23, no. 2 (June 1970):66–84.

———. "Mentre si attua il suffragio universale." *L'internazionale*, 4 Oct. 1913, p. 1.

———. "Il momento buono per i sindacati." *Pagine libere* 5, no. 10 (15 May 1911):581–83.

———. "Patriottismo, socialismo e dopo guerra (considerazioni d'attualità)." *Vie nuove* 1, no. 4 (20 May 1917):55–56.

Manzotti, Fernando. "I partiti politici italiani dal 1861 al 1918." In *Nuove questioni di storia del Risorgimento e dell'unità d'Italia*, 2:147–208. By Piero Pieri et al. Milan: Marzorati, 1961.

Maranini, Giuseppe. *Storia del potere in Italia (1848–1967)*. Florence: Vallecchi, 1967.

Maraviglia, Maurizio. *Alle basi del regime*. Rome: Libreria del Littorio, 1929.

Marchetti, Luciana, ed., *La Confederazione Generale del Lavoro negli atti, nei documenti, nei congressi: 1906–1926*. Milan: Edizioni *Avanti!*, 1962.

Marramao, Giacomo. *Marxismo e revisionismo in Italia dalla "Critica sociale" al dibattito sul leninismo*. Bari: De Donato, 1971.

Marucco, Dora. *Arturo Labriola e il sindacalismo rivoluzionario in Italia*. Turin: Fondazione Einaudi, 1970.

Marx, Karl. *Karl Marx on Colonialism and Modernization*. Edited by Shlomo Avineri. Garden City, N.Y.: Doubleday, 1968.

———, and Engels, Friedrich. *Basic Writings on Politics and Philosophy*. Edited by Lewis S. Feuer. Garden City, N.Y.: Doubleday (Anchor), 1959.

Masotti, Tullio. *Corridoni*. 3rd ed. Milan: Casa Editrice Carnaro, 1935.

Matthews, Herbert L. *The Fruits of Fascism*. New York: Harcourt, Brace and Co., 1943.

Mayer, Arno J. *Dynamics of Counterrevolution in Europe, 1870–1956: An Analytic Framework*. New York: Harper and Row, 1971.

———. "The Lower Middle Class as Historical Problem." *Journal of Modern History* 47, no. 3 (Sept. 1975):409–36.

Mazzoldi, Paolo. "Il valore morale del sindacalismo." *La voce* 1, no. 3 (3 Jan. 1909):10.

Meisel, James H. *The Genesis of Georges Sorel*. Ann Arbor: George Wahr, 1951.

Melis, Renato, ed. *Sindacalisti italiani*. Rome: Giovanni Volpe, 1964.

Melograni, Piero. "The Cult of the Duce in Mussolini's Italy." *Journal of Contemporary History* 11, no. 4 (Oct. 1976):221–37.

———. *Storia politica della grande guerra, 1915–1918*. Bari: Laterza, 1969.

Menger, Anton. *Il diritto civile e il proletariato: Studio critico sul progetto di un codice civile per l'impero germanico*. Translator anon. Turin: Fratelli Bocca, 1894.

———. *Lo Stato socialista*. Translated by Oda Lerda Olberg. Turin: Fratelli Bocca, 1905.

Merlino, [Francesco] Saverio. *Collettivismo, lotta di classe e . . . ministero! (Controreplica a F. Turati)*. Florence: G. Nerbini, 1901.

Merlino, Francesco Saverio [Xavier Merlino]. *L'Italie telle qu'elle est*. Paris: Nouvelle Librairie Parisienne (Albert Savine), 1890.

Merlino, [Francesco] Saverio. *Pro e control il socialismo: Esposizione critica dei principii e dei sistemi socialisti*. Milan: Fratelli Treves, 1897.

————. *Il socialismo senza Marx: Studi e polemiche per una revisione della dottrina socialista (1897–1930)*. Edited by Aldo Venturini. Bologna: Massimiliano Boni, 1974.

————. *L'utopia collettivista e la crisi del "socialismo scientifico."* Milan: Fratelli Treves, 1898.

Meyer, Alfred G. *Leninism*. New York: Frederick A. Praeger, 1962.

Michels, Robert. *Political Parties: A Sociological Study of the Oligarchical Tendencies of Modern Democracy*. Translated by Eden and Cedar Paul. New York: The Free Press, 1966.

————. *Storia critica del movimento socialista italiano: Dagli inizi fino al 1911*. Florence: La Voce, 1926.

Milward, Alan S. "Fascism and the Economy." In *Fascism, A Reader's Guide: Analyses, Interpretations, Bibliography*. Edited by Walter Laqueur. Berkeley: University of California Press, 1976.

Minghetti, Marco. *I partiti politici e la ingerenza loro nella giustizia e nell'amministrazione*. Bologna: Nicola Zanichelli, 1881.

Ministero delle Corporazioni. *Atti del primo convegno di studi sindacali e corporativi: Roma, 2–3 maggio 1930*. 2 vols. Rome: Edizioni del *Diritto del Lavoro*, 1930.

————. *Atti del secondo convegno di studi sindacali e corporativi: Ferrara, 5–8 maggio 1932*. 3 vols. Rome: Tipografia del Senato, 1932.

Missiroli, Mario. *Il fascismo e il colpo di Stato dell'ottobre 1922*. Bologna: Cappelli, 1966.

Molinelli, Raffaele. *Per una storia del nazionalismo italiano*. Urbino: Argalía, 1966.

Mondolfo, Rodolfo. *Umanismo di Marx*. Edited by Norberto Bobbio. Turin: Giulio Einaudi, 1968.

Moore, Barrington, Jr. *Social Origins of Dictatorship and Democracy: Lord and Peasant in the Making of the Modern World*. Boston: Beacon Press, 1967.

Mori, Giorgio. *Studi di storia dell'industria*. Rome: Riuniti, 1967.

Mosca, Gaetano. *Partiti e sindacati nella crisi del regime parlamentare*. Bari: Laterza, 1949.

————. *The Ruling Class*. Translated by Hannah D. Kahn. New York: McGraw-Hill, 1939.

————. *Il tramonto dello Stato liberale*. Edited by Antonio Lombardo. Catania: Bonanno, 1971.

Mosse, George L. "Fascism and the Intellectuals." In *The Nature of Fascism*. Edited by S[tuart] J. Woolf. New York: Random House (Vintage), 1969.

————. "Introduction: The Genesis of Fascism." In *International Fascism 1920–1945*. Edited by Walter Laqueur and George L. Mosse. New York: Harper and Row, 1966.

Mussolini, Benito. *Opera omnia di Benito Mussolini*. Edited by Edoardo and Duilio Susmel. 35 vols. Florence: La Fenice, 1951–62.

Negri, Antimo. *Dal corporativismo comunista all'umanesimo scientifico (Itinerario teoretico di Ugo Spirito)*. Manduria: Lacaita, 1964.

Nenni, Pietro. *Il diciannovismo (1919–1922)*. 3rd ed. of *Storia di quattro anni*. Milan: Edizioni *Avanti!*, 1962.

Neufeld, Maurice F. *Italy, School for Awakening Countries: The Italian Labor Movement in its Political, Social, and Economic Setting from 1800 to 1960*. Ithaca: New York State School of Industrial and Labor Relations, Cornell University, 1961.

Nitti, Francesco Saverio. *Il partito radicale e la nuova democrazia industriale: Prime linee di un programma del partito radicale*. Turin and Rome: Società Tipografico-Editrice Nazionale, 1907.

Nolte, Ernst. *Three Faces of Fascism: Action Française, Italian Fascism, National Socialism*. Translated by Leila Vennewitz. New York: Holt, Rinehart and Winston, 1966.

Nozzoli, Guido. *I ras del regime: Gli uomini che disfecero gli italiani*. Milan: Bompiani, 1972.

Nye, Robert A. "Two Paths to a Psychology of Social Action: Gustave Le Bon and Georges Sorel." *Journal of Modern History* 45, no. 3 (Sept. 1973):411–38.

Occhini, Pier Ludovico, ed. *Il Nazionalismo italiano e i problemi del lavoro e della scuola: Atti del Secondo Convegno Nazionalista di Roma*. Rome: L'Italiana, 1919.

Olivetti, A[ngelo] O[liviero]. "L'altra campana." In *Pro e contro la guerra di Tripoli: Discussioni nel campo rivoluzionario*, by Giulio Barni et al. Naples: Società Editrice Partenopea, 1912.

———. *Azione diretta e mediazione*. Naples: Società Editrice Partenopea, 1914 (orig. pub. ca. 1908).

———. *Bolscevismo, comunismo e sindacalismo*. Milan: Casa Editrice *Rivista nazionale*, 1919.

———. *Cinque anni di sindacalismo e di lotta proletaria in Italia*. Naples: Società Editrice Partenopea, 1914.

———. *Commercio e corporativismo: Saggi raccolti a cura della Confederazione Nazionale Fascista del Commercio*. Rome: Carlo Colombo, 1934.

———. "Le corporazioni come volontà e come rappresentazione." *La stirpe* 9, no. 4 (April 1931):145–46.

———. *Le corporazioni e la loro formazione naturale*. Rome: Edizioni del *Diritto del lavoro*, 1928.

———. "Dottrina e prassi dello Stato corporativo." *Critica fascista* 5, no. 4 (15 Feb. 1927):68–69; and 5, no. 5 (1 March 1927):89–90.

———. *Lineamenti del nuovo stato italiano*. Rome: Libreria del Littorio, 1930.

———. "Il manifesto dei sindacalisti." *Pagine libere* 8, nos. 4–5 (April–May 1921):143–60.

———. [Lo spettatore]. "Le ore storiche." *Il popolo d'Italia*, 11 July 1924, p. 1.

———. *Il pensiero del secolo che muore*. Bologna: Libreria Fratelli Treves di L. Beltrami, 1899.

———. "Presentazione." *Pagine libere* 1, no. 1 (15 Dec. 1906):1–4.

———. "Il problema della folla." *Nuova antologia*, 16 Sept. 1903, pp. 281–91.

———. *Problemi del socialismo contemporaneo*. Lugano: Società Editrice *Avanguardia*, 1906.

———. *Questioni contemporanee*. Naples: Società Editrice Partenopea, 1913.

———. "La Réforme du parlement et le problème de la représentation." Centre International d'etudes sur le Fascisme. *Annuaire* 1 (1928):91–127.

———. *Il sindacalismo come filosofia e come politica: Lineamenti di sintesi universale*. Milan: Alpes, 1924.

———. *Sindacalismo e fascismo*. Milan: Ravagnati, 1928.

———. *Storia critica dell'utopia comunistica*. Vol. 1. Rome: Libreria del Littorio, 1930. (No further volumes published.)

Olivetti, Ezio Maria. *Sindacalismo nazionale*. Milan: Monanni, 1927.

Omodeo, Adolfo. *Libertà e storia: Scritti e discorsi politici*. Turin: Giulio Einaudi, 1960.

———. *Momenti della vita di guerra: Dai diari e dalle lettere dei caduti 1915–1918*. New ed. Turin: Giulio Einaudi, 1968.

Orano, Paolo. *Ad Metalla: I lavoratori della morte*. Pescara: Casa Editrice Abruzzese, 1909.

———. "Antonio Renda." In *I valori della guerra*, by Antonio Renda. Milan: Fratelli Treves, 1917.

———. *Dal sindacalismo rivoluzionario allo Stato sindacalista*. Rome: Tipografia della Camera dei Deputati, 1925.

———. *Discordie: Studi e polemiche*. Lanciano: R. Carabba, 1915.

———. *Gli ebrei in Italia*. Rome: Pinciana, 1937.

———. *L'educazione fascista*. Rome: Pinciana, 1933.

———. "La Facoltà fascista di scienze politiche." In *Regia Università degli Studi di Perugia*. Rome: Mediterranea, 1937.

———. *Il fascismo*. 2 vols. Vol. 1, *La vigilia sindacalista dello Stato corporativo*. Vol. 2, *Rivoluzione delle camicie nere: Lo Stato totalitario*. Rome: Pinciana, 1939–40.

———. "L'integrazione dello Stato." *La nazione* (Florence), 27 July 1929, p. 1.

———. *L'Italia e gli altri alla conferenza della pace*. Bologna: Nicola Zanichelli, 1919.

———. *Lode al mio tempo: 1895–1925*. Bologna: Casa Editrice Apollo, 1926.

———. *Mussolini di fronte della storia*. Rome: Pinciana, 1941.

———. *Nel solco della guerra*. Milan: Fratelli Treves, 1915.

———. *Psicologia sociale*. Bari: Laterza, 1902.

———. *La rinascita dell'anima*. Rome: Presso La Fionda, 1922 (orig. pub. 1913).

———. "Roberto Michels: L'amico, il maestro, il camerata." In *Studi in memoria di Roberto Michels*. Regia Università degli Studi di Perugia, *Annali della Facoltà di giurisprudenza*, 49 (1937):7–14. Padua: CEDAM (Casa Editrice Dottor A. Milani), 1937.

Organski, A. F. K. "Fascism and Modernization." In *The Nature of Fascism*. Edited by S[tuart] J. Woolf. New York: Random House (Vintage), 1969.

———. *The Stages of Political Development*. New York: Alfred A. Knopf, 1965.

Orlando, Vittorio Emanuele. "Recenti indirizzi circa i rapporti fra diritto e Stato (Ordinamento giuridico—regola di diritto—istituzione)." *Rivista di diritto pubblico e della pubblica amministrazione in Italia*, 1926, pp. 273–307.

———. "Lo Stato e la realtà." Republished as "Sul concetto di Stato" in *Diritto pubblico generale: Scritti varii (1881–1940)*. Milan: A. Giuffrè, 1940.

———. "Lo 'stato sindacale' e le condizioni attuali della scienza di diritto pubblico." *Rivista di diritto pubblico e della pubblica amministrazione in Italia*, ser. 2, 16 (Jan. 1924):4–18.

Paladin, Livio. "Il problema della rappresentanza nello Stato fascista." *Jus: Rivista di scienze giuridiche* (Milan), 1968, nos. 1–2, pp. 46–88.

Paloscia, Leonardo. *La concezione sindacalista di Sergio Panunzio*. Rome: Casa Editrice Gismondi, 1949.

Panunzio, Sergio. *Alfredo Rocco*. Rome: I quaderni di *Lo Stato*, ca. 1936.

————. "Ancora sulle relazioni fra Stato e sindacati (Il neosindacalismo di Stato." *Rivista internazionale di filosofia del diritto* 6, no. 2 (April–June 1926):272–83.

————. *La camera dei fasci e delle corporazioni*. Rome: Collana di studi della Confederazione Fascista dei Commercianti, 1939.

————. *Che cos'è il fascismo*. Milan: Alpes, 1924.

————. "I compiti del sindacalismo e le finalità immediate delle organizzazioni politiche e sindacali (Nostra intervista col prof. Sergio Panunzio)." *Il giornale del popolo* (Rome), 2 Oct. 1921, p. 1.

————. *Il concetto della guerra giusta*. Campobasso: Giov. Colitti e Figlio, 1917.

————. *Il concetto di dittatura rivoluzionaria*. [Forlì, 1930.]

————. "Consenso e apatia." In *Annuario della Università degli Studi di Ferrara: anno scolastico 1923–1924*. Ferrara: Industrie Grafiche Italiane, 1924.

————. "Contributo all'esame dei problemi relativi alla istituzione della camera dei fasci e delle corporazioni." In *La camera dei fasci e delle corporazioni*, by Celestino Arena et al. Florence: G. C. Sansoni, 1937.

————. *Il diritto e l'autorità: Contributo alla concezione filosofica del diritto*. Turin: Unione Tipografico-Editrice Torinese, 1912.

————. *Diritto, forza e violenza: Lineamenti di una teoria della violenza*. Bologna: Licinio Cappelli, 1921.

————. "Il diritto sindacale e corporativo (programma—concetto—metodo)." Inaugural lecture, course on syndical and corporative law, State University of Perugia, Fascist Faculty of Political Science, 12 April 1928. In *Dottrina e politica fascista*, by Sergio Panunzio et al. Perugia and Venice: La Nuova Italia, 1930.

————. *L'economia mista: Dal sindacalismo giuridico al sindacalismo economico*. Milan: Ulrico Hoepli, 1936.

————. "Engels, Mazzini, il prof. Levi e altre cose." *Rivista popolare di politica, lettere e scienze sociali* 24, no. 6 (31 March 1918):110–13.

————. *La Facoltà Fascista nei primi sei anni di vita. Relazione del Commissario del Governo Prof. Sergio Panunzio al DUCE del Fascismo e CAPO del GOVERNO*. Regia Università di Perugia. Perugia: Tipografia della Rivoluzione Fascista G. Donnini, 1935.

————. "La fine di un regno." *Critica fascista* 9, no. 18 (15 Sept. 1931):342–44.

————. "Forma e sostanza." *Il resto del carlino* (Bologna), 7 Dec. 1922, p. 1.

————. "L'insegnamento politico in Italia e le facoltà di scienze politiche." *Nuova antologia*, 16 June 1932, pp. 475–90.

————. *Introduzione alla società delle nazioni*. Ferrara: A. Taddei e Figli, 1920.

————. *Italo Balbo*. Milan: Imperia, 1923.

————. *La lega delle nazioni*. Ferrara: A. Taddei e Figli, 1920.

————. "Il massimo problema politico di domani: la scuola." *La coltura popolare*, 2nd ser. 7, no. 7 (July 1917):445–55.

————. "Nazionalità e umanità nella scuola." *La coltura popolare*, Oct. 1918, pp. 866–78.

————. "Origini e sviluppi storici del sindacalismo fascista." In *Le corporazioni fasciste*. Edited by Luigi Lojacono. Milan: Ulrico Hoepli, 1935.

————. "Per la revisione del socialismo." 7 pts. *Vie nuove* 1, no. 6 (1–20 July

1917):83–86; 1, nos. 7–8 (20 July–31 Aug. 1917):100–103; 1, nos. 10–12 (10 Oct.– 20 Nov. 1917):139–42; 1, nos. 13–14 (10–30 Dec. 1917):170–173; 2, nos. 23–27 (30 July–30 Sept. 1918):87–90; 3, nos. 38–39 (1–31 March 1919):54–57; 3, no. 10 (1–15 April 1919):63–64.

———. *La persistenza del diritto*. Pescara: Casa Editrice Abruzzese, 1910.

———. "La politica di Sismondi." *Rivista internazionale di filosofia del diritto* 7, no. 1 (Jan.–Feb. 1927):1–22.

———. *Popolo Nazione Stato (esame giuridico)*. Florence: La Nuova Italia, 1933.

———. "Prefazione" to *Dottrina e politica fascista*, by Sergio Panunzio et al. Perugia and Venice: La Nuova Italia, 1930.

———. "Prefazione" to *Stato e diritto fascista*, by Luigi Viesti. Perugia and Venice: La Nuova Italia, 1929.

———. "Prime osservazioni giuridiche sul concetto di proprietà nel regime fascista." In *La concezione fascista della proprietà privata*, by Franco Angelini et al. [Rome]: Confederazione Fascista dei Lavoratori dell'Agricoltura, [1939].

———. "Un programma d'azione." *Il rinnovamento* 2, no. 2 (15 March 1919):83–89.

———. "La rappresentanza di classe." *Il rinnovamento* 2, no. 7 (15 Aug. 1919):398–413.

———. *Il riconoscimento rivoluzionario dei sindacati*. Rome: Edizioni del *Diritto del lavoro*, 1927.

———. *Riforma costituzionale: Le Corporazioni; il Consiglio delle Corporazioni; il Senato*. Florence: La Nuova Italia, 1934.

———. *Rivoluzione e costituzione (Problemi costituzionali della rivoluzione)*. Milan: Fratelli Treves, 1933.

———. *Il sentimento dello Stato*. Rome: Libreria del Littorio, [1929].

———. "Il sindacalismo." In *La civiltà fascista illustrata nella dottrina e nelle opere*. Edited by Giuseppe Luigi Pomba. Turin: Unione Tipografico-Editrice Torinese, 1928.

———. *Sindacalismo e medio evo (politica contemporanea)*. Naples: Società Editrice Partenopea, ca. 1910.

———. "Il sindacalismo, il socialismo, e la crisi attuale." *Cultura sindacale* 2, no. 5 (17 July 1921):3–5.

———. *Il socialismo giuridico (esposizione–critica)*. Genoa: Libreria Moderna, 1906.

———. *Il socialismo, la filosofia del diritto e lo Stato*. Città di Castello: Il Solco, 1922.

———. "Socialismo—liberismo—anarchismo." *Il divenire sociale* 2, no. 3 (1 Feb. 1906); 2, no. 4 (16 Feb. 1906); 2, no. 5 (1 March 1906).

———. *Lo Stato di diritto*. Città di Castello: Il Solco, n.d.

———. "Stato e sindacati." *Rivista internazionale di filosofia del diritto* 3, no. 1 (Jan.–March 1923):1–20. (Originally a lecture at the University of Ferrara, 16 Nov. 1922.)

———. *Lo Stato educativo*. Address to the Chamber of Deputies, 27 May 1929. Rome: Tipografia della Camera dei Deputati, 1929.

———. *Lo Stato fascista*. Bologna: L. Cappelli, 1925.

———. *Stato nazionale e sindacati*. Milan: Imperia, 1924.

_____. *Teoria generale dello Stato fascista*. 2nd ed. Padua: CEDAM (Casa Editrice Dott. A. Milani), 1939.

_____. "Wilson, Rousseau e Kant." *Rivista popolare di politica, lettere e scienze sociali*, 15–31 Jan. 1919, pp. 25–26.

_____, et al. Regia Università di Perugia, Facoltà fascista di scienze politiche. *Dottrina e politica fascista*. Perugia and Venice: La Nuova Italia, 1930.

Panunzio, Vito. *Fedeltà al sindacato e alla corporazione*. Rome: L'Economia Italiana, 1942.

_____. "Mezzo secolo di tradizione: 1906–1956." *Pagine libere*, N.S. 1, no. 16 (Dec. 1956):1–4.

Papa, Antonio. "Arturo Labriola." *Belfagor* 20, no. 6 (30 Nov. 1965):671–92.

Papa, Emilio R. *Storia di due manifesti: Il fascismo e la cultura italian*. Milan: Feltrinelli, 1958.

Papini, Giovanni. "Amiamo la guerra!" From *Lacerba*, 1 Oct. 1914. In *La cultura italiana del '900 attraverso le riviste*, 4: "*Lacerba*," "*La voce*" *(1914–1916)*. Edited by Gianni Scalia. Turin: Giulio Einaudi, 1961.

_____. "La vita non è sacra." From *Lacerba*, 15 Oct. 1913. In *La cultura italiana del '900 attraverso le riviste*, 4: "Lacerba," "La voce" (1914—1916). Edited by Gianni Scalia. Turin: Giulio Einaudi, 1961.

Pareto, Vilfredo. *The Mind and Society: A Treatise on General Sociology*. Translated by Andrew Bongiorno and Arthur Livingston. 4 Vols. in 2. New York: Dover, 1963.

_____. "The Parliamentary Regime in Italy." *Political Science Quarterly* 8, no. 4 (Dec. 1893):677–721.

_____. *The Rise and Fall of the Elites: An Application of Theoretical Sociology*. Translated by Hans L. Zetterberg. Totowa, N.J.: The Bedminster Press, 1968.

_____. *The Ruling Class in Italy before 1900*. New York: Howard Fertig, 1974.

_____. "Socialismo legalitario e socialismo rivoluzionario." *Il divenire sociale* 1, no. 7 (1 April 1905).

_____. *Les Systèmes socialistes*. 2 vols. 2nd ed. Paris: Marcel Giard, 1926.

_____. *Trasformazioni della democrazia*. Bologna: Cappelli, 1964.

_____, and Prezzolini, Giuseppe. "La borghesia può risorgere?" From *Il regno*, 10 Jan. 1904. In *La cultura italiana del '900 attraverso le riviste*, 1: "Leonardo," "Hermes," "Il regno." Edited by Delia Frigessi. Turin: Giulio Einaudi, 1960.

Paris, Robert. *Les Origines du fascisme*. Paris: Flammarion, 1968.

"La partecipazione politica e i partiti in Italia." *Tempi moderni* (1962), no. 8, pp. 61–88; no. 9, pp. 29–76; no. 10, pp. 73–143.

Payne, Stanley G. *Falange: A History of Spanish Fascism*. Stanford: Stanford University Press, 1961.

_____. *The Spanish Revolution*. New York: W. W. Norton, 1970.

Pedone, Franco. *Il Partito Socialista Italiano nei suoi congressi*. 2 vols. Milan: Edizioni *Avanti!*, 1959, 1961.

Pellizzi, Camillo. *Fascismo–Aristocrazia*. Milan: Alpes, 1925.

_____. *Problemi e realtà del fascismo*. Florence: Vallecchi, 1924.

_____. *Una rivoluzione mancata*. Milan: Longanesi, 1949.

Pelloutier, Fernand. *Histoire des bourses du travail: Origine–institutions–avenir*. Paris: Schleicher Frères, 1902.

Pepe, Adolfo. *Storia della CGdL dalla fondazione alla guerra di Libia 1905–1911.* Bari: Laterza, 1972.

———. *Storia della CGdL dalla guerra di Libia all'intervento 1911–1915.* Bari: Laterza, 1971.

I periodici di Milano: Bibliografia e storia. 2 vols. Milan: Feltrinelli, 1956, 1961.

Perozzi, Silvio. *Critica politica.* Bologna: Biblioteca di *Politica* presso Nicola Zanichelli, 1922.

Pieri, Piero. "Fascismo e resistenza." *Itinerari*, 4 (1956):571–602.

Pighetti, Guido. *Sindacalismo fascista.* Milan: Imperia, 1924.

Pini, Giorgio, and Susmel, Duilio. *Mussolini: L'uomo e l'opera.* 4 vols. Florence: La Fenice, 1953–55.

Plamenatz, John. *Ideology.* New York: Praeger, 1970.

Pomba, Giuseppe Luigi, ed. *La civiltà fascista illustrata nella dottrina e nelle opere.* Turin: Unione Tipografico-Editrice Torinese, 1928.

Pozzi, G. B. *La prima occupazione operaia della fabbrica in Italia nelle battaglie di Dalmine.* Bergamo: Società Tipografica Editrice Bergamesca, 1921.

Prélot, Marcel. *L'Empire fasciste: Les origines, les tendances et les institutions de la dictature et du corporatisme italiens.* Paris: Recueil Sirey, 1936.

Preti, Luigi. *Impero fascista africani ed ebrei.* Milan: U. Mursia, 1968.

———. *Le lotte agrarie nella valle padana.* Turin: Giulio Einaudi, 1955.

Prezzolini, Giuseppe. "L'aristocrazia dei briganti." From *Il regno*, 13 Dec. 1903. In *La cultura italiana del '900 attraverso le riviste*, 1: *"Leonardo," "Hermes," "Il regno."* Edited by Delia Frigessi. Turin: Giulio Einaudi, 1960.

———. *La teoria sindacalista.* Naples: Francesco Perrella, 1909.

Procacci, Giovanna. "Italy: From Interventionism to Fascism, 1917–1919." *Journal of Contemporary History* 3, no. 4 (Oct. 1968):153–76.

Procacci, Giuliano. "Appunti in tema di crisi dello Stato liberale e di origini del fascismo." *Studi storici* 6, no. 2 (April–June 1965):221–37.

———. *La lotta di classe in Italia agli inizi del secolo XX.* Rome: Riuniti, 1970.

Quazza, Guido, ed. *Fascismo e società italiana.* Turin: Giulio Einaudi, 1973.

Quilici, Nello. "Storia del fascismo ferrarese: L'intervento." *Rivista di Ferrara* 13, no. 5 (May 1935):194–208.

Racheli, Mario. "Angelo Oliviero Olivetti." In *Commercio e corporativismo*, by A. O. Olivetti. Rome: Carlo Colombo, 1934.

———. "I commercianti e le corporazioni." In *Le corporazioni fasciste.* Edited by Luigi Lojacono. Milan: Ulrico Hoepli, 1935.

Ragionieri, Ernesto. *Politica e amministrazione nella storia dell'Italia unita.* Bari: Laterza, 1967.

———. *Socialdemocrazia tedesca e socialisti italiani, 1875–1895: L'influenza del socialdemocrazia tedesca sulla formazione del Partito Socialista Italiano.* Milan: Feltrinelli, 1961.

Ranelletti, Oreste. "I sindacati e lo Stato." *Politica* 2, no. 3 (1920):257–79.

Rastelli, Vito. *Filippo Corridoni: La figura storica e la dottrina politica.* Rome: Edizioni "Conquiste d'Impero," 1940.

Razza, Luigi. *La corporazione nello Stato fascista.* Rome: Quaderni della Rivista *La Terra*, 1933.

———. "La dottrina corporativa." Address to the Chamber of Deputies, 1929.

In *Luigi Razza: L'uomo–l'opera*, by Giordano Gattamorta. Rome: Efficienza, [1935].

La Reggenza Italiana del Carnaro. *Disegno di un nuovo ordinamento dello Stato libero di Fiume*. In *D'Annunzio e il fascismo*, by Umberto Foscanelli. Milan: Casa Editrice Italiana, [1923].

Renda, Antonio. *Stato e classi*. Milan: Alpes, 1925.

———. *I valori della guerra*. Milan: Fratelli Treves, 1917.

Ricci, Umberto. *Dal protezionismo al sindacalismo*. Bari: Laterza, 1926.

Ridley, F. F. *Revolutionary Syndicalism in France: The Direct Action of Its Time*. Cambridge: Cambridge University Press, 1970.

Rigola, Rinaldo. *Storia del movimento operaio italiano*. Milan: Domus, 1947.

Riguzzi, Biagio. *Sindacalismo e riformismo nel parmese*. Bari: Laterza, 1931.

Riosa, Alceo. "Alcuni elementi dell'ideologia sindacalista rivoluzionaria in Italia all'indomani dello sciopero generale del 1904." In *Socialismo e socialisti dal risorgimento al fascismo*, by Gaetano Arfé et al. Bari: De Donato, 1974.

———. "Ottavio Dinale e le lotte agrarie nel modenese (1901–1906)." *Nuova rivista storica* 53, no. 5–6 (1969):677–705.

———. "Paolo Mantica: Il fascismo in Italia." *Historica* (Reggio Calabria) 23, no. 2 (June 1970):59–84.

———. "Sindacalismo riformista e sindacalismo rivoluzionario." *Il cannocchiale*, 1966, nos. 1–3.

———. *Il sindacalismo rivoluzionario in Italia e la lotta politica nel Partito socialista dell'età giolittiana*. Bari: De Donato, 1976.

Ritter, Alan. *The Political Thought of Pierre-Joseph Proudhon*. Princeton: Princeton University Press, 1969.

Rocca, Massimo. *Come il fascismo divenne una dittatura: Storia interna del fascismo dal 1914 al 1925*. Milan: Edizioni Librarie Italiane, 1952.

———. [Libero Tancredi]. *Dieci anni di nazionalismo fra i sovversivi d'Italia, 1905–1915*. Milan: Casa Editrice Rinascimento, 1918.

———. *Le Fascisme et l'antifascisme en Italie*. Paris: Librairie Felix Alcan, 1930.

———. *Idee sul fascismo*. Florence: La Voce, 1924.

———. *Il primo fascismo*. Rome: Giovanni Volpe, 1964.

———. "Vitalità del sindacalismo." *Pagine libere*, N.S. 1, no. 16 (Dec. 1956):13–18.

Rocco, Alfredo. Untitled comment. In *Il Nazionalismo italiano e i problemi del lavoro e della scuola: Atti del secondo convegno Nazionalista di Roma*. Edited by Pier Ludovico Occhini. Rome: L'Italiana, 1919.

———. *Scritti e discorsi politici*. 3 vols. Vol. 1, *La lotta nazionale della vigilia e durante la guerra (1913–1918)*. Vol. 2, *La lotta contro la reazione antinazionale (1919–1924)*. Vol. 3, *La formazione dello Stato fascista (1925–1934)*. Milan: A. Giuffrè, 1938.

———. *La trasformazione dello Stato: Dallo Stato liberale allo Stato fascista*. Rome: La Voce, 1927.

Rogger, Hans, and Weber, Eugen, eds. *The European Right: A Historical Profile*. Berkeley: University of California Press, 1966.

Romano, Santi. "Oltre lo Stato." *Rivista di diritto pubblico e della pubblica amministrazione in Italia*, 1918, no. 1, pp. 1–13.

————. "Lo Stato moderno e la sua crisi." *Rivista di diritto pubblico e della pubblica amministrazione in Italia* 2, no. 1 (1910):97–114.

Romeo, Rosario. *Breve storia della grande industria in Italia*. 3rd ed., rev. Bologna: Cappelli, 1967.

Rosenstock-Franck, L[ouis]. *L'Economie corporative fasciste en doctrine et en fait: Ses origines historiques et son évolution*. Paris: Librairie Universitaire J. Gamber, 1934.

Rosselli, Carlo. "La realtà dello Stato corporativo: Corporazione e rivoluzione." From *Quaderni di giustizia e libertà*, Feb. 1934. In *Il fascismo: Antologia di scritti critici*. Edited by Costanzo Casucci. Bologna: Il Mulino, 1961.

Rossi, Cesare. *Personaggi di ieri e di oggi*. Milan: Ceschina, 1960.

Rossoni, Edmondo. *Le idee della ricostruzione: Discorsi sul sindacalismo fascista*. Florence: R. Bemporad, 1923.

————. "Il sindacalismo nella rivoluzione fascista." In *La civilta fascista illustrata nella dottrina e nelle opere*. Edited by Giuseppe Luigi Pomba. Turin: Unione Tipografico-Editrice Torinese, 1928.

Roth, Jack J. "The Roots of Italian Fascism: Sorel and Sorelismo." *Journal of Modern History* 39, no. 1 (March 1967):30–45.

Rousiers, Paul de. *The Labor Question in Britain*. Translated by F. L. D. Herbertson, London: Macmillan, 1896.

Roveri, Alessandro. *Dal sindacalismo rivoluzionario al fascismo: Capitalismo agrario e socialismo nel Ferrarese (1870–1920)*. Florence: La Nuova Italia, 1972.

————. *Le origini del fascismo a Ferrara, 1918–1921*. Milan: Feltrinelli, 1974.

Rutkoff, Peter M. "The *Ligue des Patriotes*: The Nature of the Radical Right and the Dreyfus Affair." *French Historical Studies* 8, no. 4 (Fall 1974):585–603.

Rygier, Maria, *Il sindacalismo alla sbarra: Riflessioni d'una ex-sindacalista sul congresso omonimo di Bologna*. Bologna: La Scuola Moderna, 1911.

Sacco, Italo Maria. *I tre sindacalismi: La restaurazione sociale sulla base delle classi organizzate*. Vicenza: Società Anonima Tipografica, 1919.

Sacerdoti, Pietro. *L'associazione sindacale nel diritto italiano*. Rome: Edizioni del Diritto del lavoro, 1928.

Saladino, Salvatore. "Italy." In *The European Right: A Historical Profile*. Edited by Hans Rogger and Eugen Weber. Berkeley: University of California Press, 1966.

Salomone, A. William. *Italy in the Giolittian Era: Italian Democracy in the Making, 1900–1914*. New ed. Philadelphia: University of Pennsylvania Press, 1960.

Salucci, Arturo, ed. *Il nazionalismo giudicato da letterati, artisti, scienziati, uomini politici e giornalisti italiani*. Genoa: Libreria Editrice Moderna, 1913.

Salvadori, Massimo. *Il mito del buon governo: La questione meridionale da Cavour a Gramsci*. Turin: Giulio Einaudi, 1960.

Salvatorelli, Luigi. *Irrealtà nazionalista*. Milan: Corbaccio, 1925.

————. *Miti e storia*. Turin: Giulio Einaudi, 1964.

————. *Nazionalfascismo*. Turin: Piero Gobetti, 1923.

————. "Riposta ai critici di nazionalfascismo." From *La rivoluzione liberale*, 13 Nov. 1923. In *Antologia della "Rivoluzione liberale."* Edited by Nino Valeri. Turin: Francesco De Silva, 1948.

————, and Mira, Giovanni. *Storia d'Italia nel periodo fascista*. Turin: Giulio Einaudi, 1964.

Salvemini, Gaetano. *Dal patto di Londra alla pace di Roma*. Turin: Piero Gobetti, 1925.

————. *Opere, 4: Il mezzogiorno e la democrazia italiana*. Pt. 1, *Il ministro della mala vita e altri scritti sull'Italia giolittiana*. Edited by Elio Apih. Pt. 2, *Movimento socialista e questione meridionale*. Edited by Gaetano Arfé. Milan: Feltrinelli, 1962–63.

————. *Opere, 9: Carteggi*. Pt. 1, *1895–1911*. Edited by Elvira Gencarelli. Milan: Feltrinelli, 1968.

————. *The Origins of Fascism in Italy*. Edited by Roberto Vivarelli. New York: Harper and Row, 1973.

————. *Under the Axe of Fascism*. New York: Viking, 1936.

Salvioli, G[iuseppe]. *I difetti sociali delle leggi vigenti di fronte al proletariato e il diritto nuovo*. Palermo: Alberto Reber, 1906.

Santarelli, Enzo. *Origini del fascismo (1911–1919)*. Urbino: Argalia, 1963.

————. "Prefazione" to *Considerazioni sulla violenza*, by Georges Sorel. Bari: Laterza, 1970.

————. *La revisione del marxismo in Italia: Studi di critica storica*. Milan: Feltrinelli, 1964.

————. *Storia del movimento e del regime fascista*. 2 vols. Rome: Riuniti, 1967.

————, ed. "Lettere di Arturo Labriola a Ernesto Cesare Longobardi." *Rivista storica del socialismo* 5, no. 17 (Sept.–Dec. 1962).

Santomassimo, Gianpasquale. "Il fascismo degli anni trenta."*Studi storici* 16, no. 1 (1975):102–25.

————. "Ugo Spirito e il corporativismo." *Studi storici* 14, no. 1 (Jan.–March 1973):61–113.

Santonastaso, Giuseppe. *Pensiero politico e azione sociale*. Naples: Morano, 1967.

Sapelli, Giulio. "Sindacati fascisti, grande industria e classe operaia a Torino (1929–1934)." *Rivista di storia contemporanea*, Jan. 1973, pp. 40–64.

Sarti, Roland, *Fascism and the Industrial Leadership in Italy, 1919–1940: A Study in the Expansion of Private Power under Fascism*. Berkeley: University of California Press, 1971.

————. "Fascist Modernization in Italy: Traditional or Revolutionary?" *American Historical Review* 75, no. 4 (April 1970):1029–45.

————, ed. *The Ax Within: Italian Fascism in Action*. New York: Franklin Watts (New Viewpoints), 1974.

Sauer, Wolfgang. "National Socialism: Totalitarianism or Fascism?" *American Historical Review* 73, no. 2 (Dec. 1967):404–24.

Schapiro, Leonard. *Totalitarianism*. New York: Praeger, 1972.

Segrè, Claudio. "Italo Balbo and the Colonization of Libya." *Journal of Contemporary History* 7, nos. 3–4 (July–Oct. 1972):141–55.

Servan-Schreiber, Jean-Jacques. *The Radical Alternative*. New York: Dell (Delta), 1972.

Seton-Watson, Christopher. *Italy from Liberalism to Fascism, 1870–1925*. London: Methuen, 1967.

Settembrini, Domenico. "Mussolini and the Legacy of Revolutionary Social-ism." *Journal of Contemporary History* 11, no. 4 (Oct. 1976):239–68.

Shklar, Judith N. *After Utopia: The Decline of Political Faith*. Princeton: Princeton University Press, 1957; reprint ed., 1969.

Signoretti, Alfredo. *Come diventai fascista*. Rome: Giovanni Volpe, 1967.

Sonnino, Sidney [Un deputato]. "Torniamo allo statuto." *Nuova antologia*, 1 Jan 1897, pp. 9–28.

Sorel, Georges. "La crisi del socialismo scientifico." *Critica sociale* 8, no. 9 (1 May 1898):134–38.

––––––. *"Da Proudhon a Lenin" e "L'Europa sotto la tormenta."* Rome: Edizioni di Storia e Letteratura, 1973.

––––––. "The Decomposition of Marxism." Translated by Irving Louis Horo-witz. In *Radicalism and the Revolt against Reason: The Social Theories of Georges Sorel*, by Irving Louis Horowitz. Carbondale: Southern Illinois University Press, 1968.

––––––. "Dommatismo e pratica." *Rivista critica del socialismo* 1, no. 3 (1 March 1899):211–18.

––––––. *The Illusions of Progress*. Translated by John Stanley and Charlotte Stan-ley. Berkeley: University of California Press, 1969.

––––––. *Insegnamenti sociali della economia contemporanea: Degenerazione capitalista e degenerazione socialista*. Palermo: Remo Sandron, 1907.

––––––. *Lettere a un amico d'Italia*. Bologna: Cappelli, 1963.

––––––. "Lettere di Georges Sorel a B. Croce." *La critica* 25, no. 1 (20 Jan. 1927)– 28, no. 3 (20 May 1930).

––––––. *Matériaux d'une théorie du prolétariat*. Paris: Marcel Rivière, 1919.

––––––. "Préface" to *Formes et essence du socialisme*, by [Francesco] Saverio Mer-lino. Paris: V. Giard et E. Brière, 1898.

––––––. "Pro e control il socialismo." *Le Devenir Social*, Oct. 1897, pp. 854–88.

––––––. *Reflections on Violence*. Translated by T. E. Hulme and J. Roth. London: Collier-Macmillan, 1961.

––––––. *Saggi di critica del marxismo*. Palermo: Remo Sandron, 1903.

––––––. "Les théories de M. Durkheim." *Le Devenir Social* 1 (1895):1–26, 148–80.

Soucy, Robert. *Fascism in France: The Case of Maurice Barrès*. Berkeley: University of California Press, 1972.

Spadolini, Giovanni. *Lotta sociale in Italia*. Florence: Vallecchi, 1948.

Spaventa, Bertrando. *La filosofia italiana nelle sue relazioni con la filosofia europea*. 3rd ed. Edited by Giovanni Gentile. Bari: Laterza, 1926.

Spini, Giorgio. "Toscana e fascismo." In *La Toscana nel regime fascista (1922–1939)*, by Giorgio Spini et al., 1:3–15. Florence: Leo S. Olschki, 1971.

––––––, et al. *La Toscana nel regime fascista (1922–1939)*. 2 vols. Florence: Leo S. Olschki, 1971.

Spirito, Ugo. *Capitalismo e corporativismo*. Florence: G. C. Sansoni, 1933.

––––––. "Individuo e Stato nella concezione corporativa." *Nuovi studi di diritto, economia e politica* 5, no. 2 (1932):84–93.

––––––. "Interpretazioni del corporativismo (Scritti di Giuseppe Bottai)." *Il di-ritto del lavoro*, July–Oct. 1965, pp. 280–83.

Spriano, Paolo. *L'occupazione delle fabbriche: Settembre 1920*. Turin: Giulio Einaudi, 1964.

———. *Storia di Torino operaia e socialista: Da De Amicis a Gramsci*. Turin: Giulio Einaudi, 1972.

Stearns, Peter N. *Revolutionary Syndicalism and French Labor: A Cause without Rebels*. New Brunswick: Rutgers University Press, 1971.

Sternhell, Zeev. "Fascist Ideology." In *Fascism, A Reader's Guide: Analyses, Interpretations, Bibliography*. Edited by Walter Laqueur. Berkeley: University of California Press, 1976.

Strappini, Lucia; Micocci, Claudia; and Abruzzese, Alberto. *La classe dei colti: Intellettuali e società nel primo novecento italiano*. Bari: Laterza, 1970.

Suckert, Curzio. "La conquista dello Stato nella concezione organica di Sergio Panunzio." *Corriere padano*, 16 Dec. 1925, p. 1.

See also Malaparte, Curzio, Suckert's adopted name.

Sykes, Thomas Ronald. "The Practice of Revolutionary Syndicalism in Italy 1905–1910." Ph.D. dissertation, Columbia University, 1973.

———. "Revolutionary Syndicalism in the Italian Labor Movement: The Agrarian Strikes of 1907–08 in the Province of Parma." *International Review of Social History* 21 (1976):186–211.

Taeye-Henen, Monique de. *Le Nationalisme d'Enrico Corradini et les origines du fascisme dans la revue florentine "Il regno" (1903–1906)*. Paris: Marcel Didier, 1973.

Tamaro, Attilio. *Venti anni di storia, 1922–1943*. 3 vols. Rome: Editrice Tiber, 1953–54.

Tannenbaum, Edward R. *The Fascist Experience: Italian Society and Culture 1922–1945*. New York: Basic Books, 1972.

———. "The Goals of Italian Fascism." *The American Historical Review* 74, no. 4 (April 1969):1183–1204.

Tasca, Angelo. *Nascita e avvento del fascismo: L'Italia dal 1918 al 1922*. Florence: La Nuova Italia, 1950.

Tilgher, Adriano. *La crisi mondiale e saggi critici di marxismo e socialismo*. Bologna: Nicola Zanichelli, 1921.

Todisco, Antonio. *Le origini del nazionalismo imperialista in Italia*. Rome: Giorgio Berlutti, n.d.

Togliatti, Palmiro. *Lectures on Fascism*. New York: International, 1976.

Tranfaglia, Nicola. *Dallo stato liberale al regime fascista: Problemi e ricerche*. Milan: Feltrinelli, 1973.

Turati, Augusto. "Il partito e i sindacati." Address of 17 June 1928 to the State University of Perugia, Fascist Faculty of Politica Science. In *Dottrina e politica fascista*, by Sergio Panunzio et al. Perugia and Venice: La Nuova Italia, 1930.

———. *Il partito e i suoi compiti*. Rome: Libreria del Littorio, 1928.

———. *Ragioni ideali di vita fascista*. Rome: Libreria del Littorio, ca. 1927.

———. *Una rivoluzione e un capo*. Rome: Libreria del Littorio, [1927].

Turiello, Pasquale. *Governo e governati in Italia*. 2nd ed., rev. Bologna: Nicola Zanichelli, 1889.

Turner, Henry Ashby, Jr. "Fascism and Modernization." *World Politics* 24, no. 4 (July 1972):547–64.

————, ed. *Reappraisals of Fascism*. New York: Franklin Watts (New Viewpoints), 1975.

Ulam, Adam B. *The Unfinished Revolution: An Essay on the Sources of Influence of Marxism and Communism*. New York: Random House (Vintage), 1960.

Ungari, Paolo. *Alfredo Rocco e l'ideologia giuridica del fascismo*. Brescia: Morcelliana, 1963.

Uva, Bruno. "Le idee corporative in Italia (dalla restaurazione al 1922)." *Storia e politica* 4, no. 4 (Oct.–Dec. 1965):603–68.

————. *La nascita dello Stato corporativo e sindacale fascista*. Assisi and Rome: Beniamino Carucci, ca. 1974.

————. "Vita e morte del sindacalismo rivoluzionario italiano." *Storia e politica* 2, no. 3 (July–Sept. 1963):403–27.

Valeri, Nino. *Da Giolitti a Mussolini: Momenti della crisi del liberalismo*. Milan: Il Saggiatore, 1967.

————. *D'Annunzio davanti al fascismo*. Florence: Felice Le Monnier, 1963.

————. *Giovanni Giolitti*. Turin: Unione Tipografico-Editrice Torinese, 1972.

————, ed. *Antologia della "Rivoluzione liberale."* Turin: Francesco De Silva, 1948.

————. *La lotta politica in Italia dall'unità al 1925: Idee e documenti*. 2nd ed., rev. Florence: Felice Le Monnier, 1958.

————. *Storia d'Italia*. Vol. 4, *Da Cavour alla fine della prima guerra mondiale*. Turin: Unione Tipografico-Editrice Torinese, 1960.

Valiani, Leo. "Le origini della guerra del 1914 e dell'intervento italiano nelle ricerche e nelle pubblicazioni dell'ultimo ventennio." *Rivista storica italiana* 78, no. 3 (1966):584–613.

————. "Il Partito Socialista Italiano dal 1900 al 1918." *Rivista storica italiana* 75, no. 2 (1963):269–326.

————. *Il Partito Socialista Italiano nel periodo della neutralità 1914–1915*. Milan: Feltrinelli, 1963.

————. "Il problema politico della nazione italiana." In *Dieci anni dopo (1945–1955): Saggi sulla vita democratica italiana*, by Achille Battaglia et al. Bari: Laterza, 1955.

————. *Questioni di storia el socialismo*. Turin: Giulio Einaudi, 1958.

————. "La storia del fascismo nella problematica della storia contemporanea e nella biografia di Mussolini." *Rivista storica italiana* 79, no. 2 (1967):459–81.

————. "La storia d'Italia dal 1870 al 1915: Contributi storiografici dell'ultimo ventennio." *Annali della Fondazione Luigi Einaudi* 1 (1967):35–130. Turin: Fondazione Luigi Einaudi, 1968.

Vallauri, Carlo. "Il programma economico nazionalista e la genesi del corporativismo fascista." *Storia e politica* 7, no. 4 (Oct.–Dec. 1968):612–36.

————. *Le radici del corporativismo*. Rome: Mario Bulzoni, 1971.

Valsecchi, Franco, et al. *Nuove questioni di storia contemporanea*. 2 vols. Milan: Marzorati, 1968.

Venturini, Aldo. "Saverio Merlino (Profilo bio-bibliografico)." In *Il socialismo senza Marx. Scritti dal 1897 al 1930*, by Francesco Saverio Merlino. Bologna: Massimiliano Boni, 1974.

Viesti, Luigi. Review of *La persistenza del diritto*, by Sergio Panunzio. *Rivista italiana di sociologia* 15 (Jan.–Feb. 1911):133–40.

————. *Stato e diritto fascista*. Perugia and Venice: La Nuova Italia, 1929.

Vigezzi, Brunello. *Da Giolitti a Salandra*. Florence: Vallecchi, 1969.

————. *L'Italia di fronte alla prima guerra mondiale*. Vol. 1, *L'Italia neutrale*. Milan: Riccardo Ricciardi, 1966.

Villari, Rosario. "La polemica antiriformista di Arturo Labriola." *Cronache meridionali* 6, nos. 7–8 (July–Aug. 1959).

Vita-Finzi, Paolo. *Le delusioni della libertà*. Florence: Vallecchi, 1961.

Vivante, Cesare. "La penetrazione del socialismo nel diritto privato." *Critica sociale* 12, no. 22 (16 Nov. 1902):345–51.

Vivarelli, Roberto. "Benito Mussolini dal socialismo al fascismo." *Rivista storica italiana* 79, no. 2 (1967):438–58.

————. *Il dopoguerra in Italia e l'avvento del fascismo (1918–1922)*. Vol. 1, *Dalla fine della guerra all'impresa di Fiume*. Naples: Istituto Italiano per gli Studi Storici, 1967.

————. "Introduzione." In *Scritti politici*, by Georges Sorel. Turin: Unione Tipografico–Editrice Torinese, 1963.

————. "Italia liberale e fascismo: Considerazioni su di una recente storia d'Italia." *Rivista storica italiana* 82, no. 3 (Sept. 1970):669–703.

Volpe, Gioacchino. *Italia in cammino: L'ultimo cinquantennio*. 3rd ed. Milan: Fratelli Treves, 1931.

————. *Storia del movimento fascista*. Milan: Istituto per gli studi di politica internazionale, 1939.

Weber, Eugen. "Revolution? Counterrevolution? What Revolution?" In *Fascism, A Reader's Guide: Analyses, Interpretations, Bibliography*. Edited by Walter Laqueur. Berkeley: University of California Press, 1976.

————. *Varieties of Fascism: Doctrines of Revolution in the Twentieth Century*. Princeton: Van Nostrand, 1964.

Webster, Richard A. "Autarchy, Expansion, and the Underlying Continuity of the Italian State." *Italian Quarterly* 8 (Winter 1964):3–27.

————. "From Insurrection to Intervention: The Italian Crisis of 1914." *Italian Quarterly* 5–6, nos. 20–21 (Winter 1961–Spring 1962):27–50.

————. *Industrial Imperialism in Italy, 1908–1915*. Berkeley: University of California Press, 1975.

Weiss, Franz. "La base morale dell'organizzazione socialista del lavoro." *Il divenire sociale* 4, nos. 3–4 (1–16 Feb. 1908):52–56; 4, no. 5 (1 March 1908):69–73; 4, no. 6 (16 March 1908):88–95.

Welk, William G. *Fascist Economic Policy*. Cambridge: Harvard University Press, 1938.

Williams, Philip M., and Harrison, Martin. *Politics and Society in de Gaulle's Republic*. Garden City, N.Y.: Doubleday (Anchor), 1973.

Wolin, Sheldon S. *Politics and Vision: Continuity and Innovation in Western Political Thought*. Boston: Little, Brown and Co., 1960.

Wolff, Robert Paul. *The Poverty of Liberalism*. Boston: Beacon, 1968.

Woolf, S[tuart] J. "Italy." In *European Fascism*. Edited by S[tuart] J. Woolf. New York: Random House (Vintage), 1968.

————. "Risorgimento e fascismo: Il senso della continuità nella storiografia italiana." *Belfagor* 20, no. 1 (31 Jan. 1965):71–91.

————, ed. *European Fascism*. New York: Random House (Vintage), 1968.

————. *The Nature of Fascism*. New York: Random House (Vintage), 1969.

Zangara, Vincenzo. *Rivoluzione sindacale: Lo Stato corporativo*. Rome: Libreria del Littorio, 1927.

Zangheri, Renato. "Dualismo economico e formazione dell'Italia moderna." In *La formazione dell'Italia industriale: Discussioni e ricerche*. Edited by Alberto Caracciolo. Bari: Laterza, 1969.

Zangrandi, Ruggero. *Il lungo viaggio attraverso il fascismo: Contributo alla storia di una generazione*. Milan: Feltrinelli, 1962.

Index

A

Albertini, Luigi, 45, 106; critique of neosyndicalism, 240, 251, 252
Almond, Gabriel, 28
Anarchism, 21, 37, 61–62, 72–75, 77–78, 87, 101, 113, 313, 315, 335 (n. 90). *See also* Radical tradition, preindustrial
Ansaldo, Giovanni, 310
Anti-Semitism, 277, 299, 309, 323–24, 326
Aquarone, Alberto, 27–28
Arfé, Gaetano, 21
Argentieri, Alberto, 341 (n. 9)
Audacia, 200
Avanguardia socialista, 16, 49, 56, 60, 64, 90

B

Balbo, Italo, 114, 168, 199, 209, 215, 217, 224, 240; place in fascism, 210–12
Baldesi, Gino, 238
Barni, Giulio, 16, 104
Baroncini, Gino, 217
Battaglie dell'Unione Italiana del Lavoro, 159
Bauer, Otto, 111
Benaglia, Alberto, 296–97
Bergson, Henri, 60, 76, 77, 287
Bernstein, Eduard, 62, 124, 312, 313, 316
Bianchi, Michele, 15, 210–11, 224
Biennio rosso, 137–38, 146, 148, 189, 245; syndicalist response to, 155–58, 242–44
Bissolati, Leonida, 71, 97, 106, 137, 344 (n. 1)
Bocchini, Arturo, 279
Bonomi, Ivanoe, 135, 162
Borghi, Armando, 74, 113, 335 (n. 90)
Borsa, Mario, 268
Bottai, Giuseppe, 13, 212, 232, 233, 234, 239, 241, 247, 249, 257, 259–60, 272–73, 275, 278, 281, 282, 289, 290, 290–91, 293, 295, 298, 299, 301, 316, 321, 326, 351 (n. 62), 363 (n. 76); place in populist fascism,

198, 200, 203–4, 205, 206–8, 210; and fascist educational charter, 299–300
Brasillach, Robert, 23
Business class, Italian: relationship with fascism, 4, 275, 282, 289–90, 299, 300, 307; relative weakness of, 33, 35–36, 43–44. *See also* Industrialization, Italian

C

Cantimori, Delio, 4
Caracciolo, Alberto, 35
Carducci, Giosuè, 37–38
Carta del Carnaro, 166, 179–81, 206, 229, 230, 265; influence on fascism, 11, 199–200, 205, 211, 215, 216, 227, 238, 301
Casalini, Armando, 15, 168, 174, 234
Casini, Gherardo, 294, 296, 298
Casucci, Costanzo, 4, 138
Cavour, Camillo di, 29–30
Chamber of Fasces and Corporations, 298–99, 301
Chambers of Labor, 39, 84; of Milan, 50, 84, 86–87; of Parma, 84, 85–86
Chiarelli, Giuseppe, 284, 286
Ciardi, Livio, 15, 107, 206, 293
Ciarlantini, Franco, 15
Ciattini, Alighiero, 15, 81, 175; on crisis of liberalism, 160–61, 172–73; on Italian cultural deficiencies, 260–61
Cimbali, Enrico, 319
Colajanni, Napoleone, 58
Collana di studi fascisti, 286
Commission of Fifteen; Commission of Eighteen, 13, 14, 190, 235, 237–39, 258, 280
Confédération Général du Travail, 66
Coppola, Francesco, 121, 141, 189, 190, 284, 286
Cordova, Ferdinando, 218
Corporativism, 11, 19; in interpretation of

401

F

Facta, Luigi, 135
Fani-Ciotti, Vincenzo [Volt], 233
Farinacci, Roberto, 190, 199, 205, 206, 212, 234, 239, 296, 299, 322, 326, 350 (n. 32); place in populist fascism, 197–98, 207–8, 210
Fascio rivoluzionario d'azione internazionalista; Fasci di azione rivoluzionaria, 107, 114, 201, 211
Fascism, Italian: and European radical tradition, 63, 312–22; components within, 188–89, 191–99, 205–12; convergence and divergence of components within, 246–49, 271–73, 308; failure of, 297–98, 322–26; and "modernity," 302–6, 308–12, 320–22. *See also* Corporativism; Fascist labor movement; Fascist movement; Fascist party; Populist fascism; Right fascism
Fascist Faculty of Political Science (at the University of Perugia), 16, 276, 284–87
Fascist labor movement, 20, 238, 282, 291–92, 294–96, 297, 300, 364 (n. 96); and populist fascism, 196–97, 198, 205, 206–7, 211, 217–18, 220–25, 226–28, 229–30, 233, 235; reorganization of 1928, 206–7, 289–90, 293. *See also* Corporativism; Populist fascism
Fascist movement, 135, 177, 178–79, 180–81, 187–88, 279; as antilabor reaction, 187, 188, 193, 196–97, 214–15, 216, 217, 218, 223, 227, 314, 315, 321. *See also* Fascist party; Populist fascism
Fascist party: conceptions of, 198, 278–79, 284, 288–89, 290, 298, 322; and corporativism, 198, 205–6, 207, 244, 278–79, 291–92, 297, 298; national congress of 1921, 216, 218–21; and Fascist labor movement, 224, 229–30; National Council meeting of August 1924, 237, 238, 240, 251. *See also* Fascist movement; Fascist regime; Populist fascism
Fascist regime: role of myth in, 18, 274, 276–77, 288, 301–5; relationship to liberal Italy, 25–26, 324–26, 329 (n. 1); essential characteristics of, 184, 279, 291, 307, 322–26; openness and fluidity in, 184, 275, 281–82, 283, 286, 294, 299; tensions and contradictions in, 185, 247–48, 273, 299, 326; fascist criticism of, 274–75, 276, 283, 290–94, 297–301, 305; reform of Chamber of Deputies (1928), 283, 287–88; establishment of corporations (1934), 297–98; reform of legal codes (1942), 300–301. *See also* Corporativism; Fascism; Mussolini, Benito

Fédération des Bourses du Travail, 66
Federazione nazionale dei legionari fiumani, 188
Federzoni, Luigi, 143, 147, 171–72, 189–90, 199, 208, 212, 240
Ferri, Enrico, 49, 50, 52, 56, 84
Fiume regency and movement, 166, 179–81, 186–87, 188, 199–200, 215, 219, 227
Fontanelli, Luigi, 294, 295, 298
Fortunato, Giustino, 27, 129, 329 (n. 1); on postwar crisis, 148–50, 246
Futurism, 46, 75, 106, 261

G

Galante Garrone, Alessandro, 195
Galbiati, Guido, 217, 229
Galli, Silvio, 233
Gallino, Luciano, 28
General Confederation of Labor (Confederazione generale del lavoro), 51, 84, 85, 86–88, 138, 185, 186, 226–27, 229, 230
Gentile, Giovanni: and fascist ideology, 11, 19; on Italian experience of World War I, 129–30
Gerarchia, 166, 283, 287, 298
Giolitti, Giovanni, 49–50, 52, 64, 65, 90–91, 106, 129, 133, 135, 136, 146, 148, 182, 186–87, 199, 209, 213, 216, 220, 228, 232, 324, 325; political system of, 40–45
Giuliano, Balbino, 191
Giulietti, Giuseppe, 179
Giuriati, Giovanni, 179
Gobetti, Piero, 195, 232, 324, 329 (n. 1)
Gramsci, Antonio, 57, 196, 315, 363 (n. 81); interpretation of syndicalism, 53–54, 199
Grand Council of Fascism, 239, 282, 288, 293, 298
Grandi, Dino, 7, 168, 204, 210, 212, 226, 232, 247, 300, 316, 326, 353 (n. 34); place in populist fascism, 198, 199, 200–203, 205, 208; and neosyndicalism, 201–3, 216–24; and Nationalism, 202–3; on international relations, 202–3; opposition to parliamentary fascism, 215–24; and fascist labor movement, 217–18
Graziadei, Antonio, 71, 97
Gruppi di compentenza, 234

H

Hamon, Augustin, 60
Hervé, Gustave, 103
Hitler, Adolf, 182, 231, 304
Humanité nouvelle, 60

I

Idea nazionale, L', 47
Ideas: in interpretation of fascism, 8–10,

The Author

David D. Roberts is associate professor of history at the Eastman School of Music, University of Rochester.

The Book

Typeface: Stempel V-I-P Palatino
Design and composition: The University of North Carolina Press
Paper: Sixty-pound Olde Style by S. D. Warren Company
Binding cloth: Roxite B 53567 Linen by The Holliston Mills, Incorporated
Printer and binder: Vail-Ballou Press, Incorporated

Published by The University of North Carolina Press